Canvas for Cruisers
The Complete Guide

Canvas For Cruisers
The Complete Guide

Written and illustrated by Julie Gifford

Questions and suggestions are welcome. Please contact:
Julie Gifford
svfreeradical@gmail.com

Orders:
www.canvasforcruisers.com

Acknowledgements

I would like to acknowledge the two hardest-working individuals I have ever met. I thought I knew how to sew, but without the patience and skill of Ursula Winet who was my canvas sewing 'fem-tor', and Ernst Looser who is always right-on in his methods and instruction, this book would have been much harder to write.

Heartfelt thanks to my editor and friend Pam Page-Wood, who carefully read and corrected the manuscript, a very tedious job indeed.

And especially, I would like to acknowledge my sailing partner, technical computer geek, and canvas design engineer – my husband Ed Kettyle, without his assistance and enthusiastic support, this book would have been impossible.

Contents

Introduction

This is a practical guide. I have had the sewing bug ever since I made my first drawstring bag in 7th Grade, and felt the sense of accomplishment that comes from creating things using fabrics.

Many years later, working in a professional loft made me realize that there are certain practical techniques and principles that can make a project look professional, and make it last much longer by applying certain sewing and design methods. I have not seen a book that really gets into these details and reasons why. That is why I wrote this book.

Because I have lived full time on a cruising boat since 1999 and have sailed around the world, I am used to doing repair work and new projects in many countries under less than ideal conditions. Where appropriate I have discussed what materials are practical from a live-aboard point of view. And I have put in my personal recommendations for what works for full time liveaboard conditions in tropical countries for durability, cleaning ability and convenience.

If you have never sewn a stitch then you should start with simple non-fitted projects such as carry bags to get used to the techniques. Starting with a complicated project like a dodger just invites trouble and gets you discouraged.

There are definite benefits of doing it yourself in cases where a custom design is highly engineered and you want it exactly the way you want it. On the other hand what may sound good may not be possible in terms of construction, strength and durability.

This book describes basic techniques and designs – based on sound construction principles. What you do with these principles is only limited by your imagination. Look around at other boats then adapt these ideas for your own particular case. Boat owners are usually more than willing to tell you how much they love this or that, and give you ideas for how to design something better. Remember, sewing is often about style, and there are usually many ways to accomplish the same thing.

Second Edition

In the new and expanded second edition, I have added more detailed instructions for the Big Four exterior projects – Dodger, Bimini, Centerpiece, Enclosure. A Lifesling replacement bag, and more information on new materials available. As things are changing all the time, this information is as recent as I can gather, but understand that the internet is your friend and it is a good source of up to date information as well as new ideas.

Happy sewing!

Terminology

Throughout this book, I have tried to be consistent in the use of certain sewing terms.

<u>Pin it down</u> or Pin it Out – means lay the fabric out on a table or the floor, and stretch it out flat. Anchor it down by driving scratch awls through the fabric into the surface, one at each end.
(More about scratch awls in the Section 1 - Materials and Tools).

<u>Brand Names</u> – Sunbrella brand name is used interchangeably with acrylic canvas material only because it seems to be the most commonly found. Seamstick brand is used interchangeably with any 2-faced sticky tape specially made for fabric work. All other brand names are trademarks of their respective companies and only are mentioned as representatives of the type of fabric, and not meant to endorse any particular brand over another.

<u>Seam allowances</u> are ½" unless stated otherwise.

<u>Hems</u> are either 1" or 2".

Canvas for Cruisers

Section 1
Materials & Tools

Fabric Rolls

Canvas for Cruisers

Fabrics

The term 'canvas' is used to broadly define all the fabrics associated with a boat – from the sails, to the external fabric Biminis and awnings, covers, cushions and all the other miscellaneous pouches, containers, bags and organizers that are found on boats.

Most fabrics used in the construction of boat projects are synthetic fibers, designed for strength, durability, colourfastness and resistance to various environmental influences.

The most common materials in use are Acrylics (such as Sunbrella®), Vinyls (and vinyl meshes), Nylon (cloth and webbings), and Dacron™, which is actually a brand name for a polyester material commonly used for sails. All have different strengths and weaknesses, and are suited for different applications as described in this section.

Included in this section are some hints on care and cleaning. For further details you should go to the Internet or to the manufacturer for information on general cleaning and stain removal. Sometimes the recommendations change as cleaning products change.

Overall, however, you can't go far wrong by rinsing off canvas or vinyl as often as you can with fresh water – synthetic fabrics grow mold on the dirt, not on the fabric. So, keeping it dirt, dust-and-salt free goes a long way to making it last longer. Also as a general principle, when cleaning, don't rub the heck out of the fabric with brushes or abrasive cleaners – be gentle!

Fabric is measured by common terms and it is useful to look up the specifications especially if comparison shopping on line. Aside from fabric content, the most useful are:
Weight – measured in ounces per square yard. It will give you an idea of how heavy the fabric will be – Sunbrella is 9.25 oz per sq yd.

Abrasion Resistance – measured in double rubs by a machine designed to chafe the fabric through to destruction.
UV resistance – measured in the number of hours of sunlight before colour or strength degrades.

Acrylics

Acrylic is by far the most common fabric used for exterior canvas work. Sunbrella is one of the popular brand names of acrylic. It is available just about everywhere in the world in a wide variety of colour choices and is easy to sew.
Material – Solution-dyed acrylic. This means that the dye is incorporated into the fiber, not added on later.
Properties – Provides up to 98% shade factor depending on how dark the colour is. It is water-resistant NOT waterproof. The new product Sunbrella Rain is indeed waterproof.
Strengths – Colourfast, resistant to mildew if it is kept clean, resistant to UV, environmental chemicals and weather. It does not shrink or stretch under normal conditions but it can shrink if it is washed/dried at high temperatures. Use lukewarm water and never machine dry it. Acrylic 'breathes' which means that condensation does not build up under a cover or inside a bag made of acrylic.
Weaknesses – Acrylics have poor resistance to chafe so be sure to place chafe protection patches at the critical areas. It tends to stretch and bag when wet and needs to be re-waterproofed annually after 3-5 years.
It is not resistant to chafe at all, or particularly resistant to tearing, so you have to reinforce it in these stress areas. This means it might not have a good track record for making trailerable boat covers which are subject to high winds, chafe and flapping unless carefully designed and constructed.
Life Expectancy – can be made to last 10 years with proper care.
Width – available in 46" and 60"
Use for – dodgers, awnings, Biminis, dinghy covers, sail covers, sail sacrificial strips, cushions, bags, equipment covers. Just about anything!

Canvas for Cruisers

<u>Cleaning Information</u> – Mold grows on the dirt, not on the fabric, so rinse it regularly (monthly) with fresh water to keep it clean. Remember, the more you scrub, the more you remove the waterproofing. After a vigorous cleaning, re-waterproof the fabric.

<u>Sewing Tips</u> – It is possible to sew acrylic canvas with a decent home sewing machine and many have done it. Exterior projects won't last as long, of course, due to the smaller size of thread and will have to be restitched more often. If your home or industrial sewing machine can handle Tenara™ or Profilen™ brand thread then you will not have to restitch. Ever!

Use staples or seamstick to hold the seam together before stitching (See Section 2 - Seams). Pins are hard to use on heavy fabric and tend to distort it. Regular seamstick does not stick very well to Sunbrella, so press very hard and roll down hard to make the seamstick stick. Or use the seamstick designed especially for acrylics.

The selvedges (edges) are not true woven-in selvedges. They are hot-knifed at the factory. Therefore, they will fray eventually. Keep this in mind if you think you can use the selvedge as a hem edge.

The fabric is not forgiving of mistakes. The stitching holes will show if you rip out a seam.

Be careful of the edges after you have hot-knifed them – they can cut you.

Alternatives to Sunbrella:

Sunbrella has dominated the market so much that it is often used synonymously with acrylic canvas. There is good reason for this, but you should be aware that there are alternatives. The internet is useful for researching, as things are changing all the time.

Lined Acrylics

Sunbrella Plus® is Sunbrella with a urethane coating on one side. It is more water resistant than regular Sunbrella, but it is still not totally permanently waterproof. It does not 'breathe' as well as plain Sunbrella and can build up mold on the underside as a result, and it is not available in all colours.

It is heavier than plain Sunbrella, and is best used for dodgers & Biminis where you need a little more water-resistance.

<u>Cleaning information</u> – don't try removing mold with chlorine bleach or you will damage the urethane coating.

<u>Sewing tips</u>- arrange it so that the coated side is on the underside of the dodger/bimini.

Sea Mark™ is Acrylic with a marine-grade vinyl lining. This fabric has all the benefits of Sunbrella (except breathability), but because it is bonded to vinyl, it is totally waterproof. It can be made to match all the other Sunbrella canvas on your boat. But, it shrinks fast in the tropics, delaminates if it flaps, and light colors are prone to condensation forming on the underside, creating mold. Use it for dodgers & biminis

<u>Sewing tips</u>- Position the vinyl coated side as the underside of the bimini/dodger.

Acrylic canvas alternatives:

Outdura – buys its solution-dyed acrylic fiber from the same supplier as Sunbrella, so it has all the same properties as Sunbrella, same UV resistance etc, it is 9.5 oz (also available in 8 oz). It's big claim is that it is woven tighter to reduce bagging and sagging tendency. And it's a couple of bucks a yard cheaper.

Recacril – is 100% solution dyed acrylic, like Sunbrella, 9 oz and very tightly woven to give 90% UV protection. They advertise zero shrink and zero stretch. It is treated with a special process where both top and bottom surfaces are permanently coated to ensure the lasting quality of the fabric – such as resistance to dirt buildup and resistant to a wide variety of atmospheric agents. This "shop friendly" fabric won't bunch up, and it will lay flat for cutting and overlapping. And a full line of solids and stripes. Being an acrylic though, it needs to be reinforced for chafe, and it will need to be re-waterproofed eventually. Lots of colours and cheaper than Sunbrella.

Uses – everyday canvas, mooring covers

Solution-dyed Polyesters

Topnotch – Solution-dyed (colorfast) Polyester with a 'rich' appearance, it is close in price and a good alternative to Sunbrella and looks almost identical to it. It is heavier though 11.5 oz. – tough and long lasting. Stronger and more abrasion-resistant than acrylics, it is a little stretchy although the manufacturer advertises 'dimensionally stable – won't sag or stretch', and doesn't tear. It doesn't like the hot knife, though, (gums it up) and frays badly when cut with scissors.
Uses – everyday canvas, travel covers, mooring covers (small boats)

Olefin is a synthetic fiber made from polypropylene or polyethylene. It is durable and attractive, almost as UV resistant as Sunbrella. It is easy to sew, but scratchy to the touch. Brands include **Richloom Solarium, or Sunproof.**

Top Gun – heavy (11.5 oz) and slippery so it's not as easy to sew as Sunbrella, being prone to puckered seams. But it doesn't stretch (stretches less than 1%), doesn't bag or shrink – this is called 'dimensionally stable' in the trade. It is resistant to punctures chafe, tears, mildew, UV and atmospheric chemicals. Made from Polyester which itself is not as UV resistant as acrylic – it is coated with a polymeric coating on both sides so the colour is the same on both sides – this coating is designed to resist hardening, cracking or peeling. Highly resistant to water yet supposedly 'breathes'. It looks new for a long time. It is better in terms of water repellent and resistant, but it is strongly recommended that tight fitting storage covers should be vented to allow excess moisture to escape. It is abrasive – so not a good choice for boat covers for painted boats unless lined with a soft fabric like which is used in high-end car storage covers, such as Evolution. It is not as easy to clean as Sunbrella and you might have to pre-soak it. If you wash it with detergents, you need to re-waterproof it.
The colour is reported not as colourfast as solution-dyed acrylics like Sunbrella.
There is a lighter version called **Top Gun 9** or **Mustang**.

Something between acrylic & polyester

WeatherMax80 – Solution-dyed polymer yarn Less expensive and lighter than Sunbrella (8 oz vs. Sunbrella's 9.25 oz), Very tough, strong, and very water resistant. Will last 8+ years if kept clean. Doesn't shrink or expand, stretch or sag but it tends to pucker when sewing. Seamstick bleeds through eventually, so you'll need to use staples instead. 60" wide, 17 colors
Uses – everyday canvas, mooring covers (bigger boats)

Vinyls

Vinyls are typically easy to clean and are resistant to environmental insults. The heavier weight vinyls are extremely useful for making patches for areas of your project that are subject to chafe. Most vinyl fabrics are made of nylon or polyester yarns, coated on one or both sides with vinyl. Nylon is stronger than polyester, and the heavier the weight of the fabric the stronger and more chafe-resistant it is.

Vinyl Coated Nylon

Examples are the brand names Shelterite® or Coverlight®.
Properties – Strong and flexible, waterproof
Strengths – Resists tears and abrasion.
Weaknesses – If this actually is a weakness, a large cover made of Shelterite is tremendously heavy. Also, vinyls do not 'breathe', so condensation can build up inside a cover or bag.
Life Expectancy – 8 years or more
Width – 61 ¼"
Use for – chafe and strength patches (e.g. reinforcing for grommets, bag handles, awning patches). It can also be used for canopies, industrial covers and tarps, keeping in mind the weight factor.
Cleaning Information – do not use abrasives or solvents.

Canvas for Cruisers

<u>Sewing Tips</u> – Look closely - one side of the fabric is smoother because it has the thicker layer of vinyl. This is the *right* side.

All vinyls are very unforgiving of sewing mistakes. When you rip out the stitches, the holes will show. Instead of stitching, vinyl fabric can be glued together with HH-66 Vinyl Cement.

Vinyl-coated Polyesters

Fabrics in this category include Weblon®, Stamoid®, Top Gun™, Odyssey™ and Aqualon®. Polyester is not very resistant to UV, but it is very strong and does not stretch very much. Therefore it is used as a core fiber and coated with vinyl.

<u>Properties</u> – Strong and light. It folds up small, is low-stretch and waterproof.

<u>Strengths</u> – Easy to clean, resists dirt, colourfast. Excellent resistance to UV, mildew, and bird crap.

<u>Weaknesses</u> – won't tolerate chafe or flogging in the wind. Protect 'chafe' areas with patches, and reinforce areas subject to strain. Don't place the fabric on a rough surface like a concrete dock and walk on it – you will hurt the finish.

<u>Life Expectancy</u> – with proper care, it can last 10 years.

<u>Use for</u> – Awnings, Dodgers, Biminis, Equipment Covers, Storage covers, Sunshades.

<u>Cleaning Information</u> – Don't fold up and put away wet – although it is mildew resistant, eventually mildew will grow on the dirt. Do not use abrasive cleaners, solvents or gasoline – you will ruin the finish. Use dish soap and water, and rinse well.

<u>Sewing Tips</u> – When turning up a hem, always seamstick the hem first – don't try to freehand it, it's too slippery.

Other Vinyls

Upholstery Vinyls

These fabrics have soft vinyl coatings on backing fabrics and are most often used for powerboat seats, cockpit cushions and other exterior seating such as center console dinghy seats. Brand names include Naugahyde® and Nautolex®.

<u>Material</u> – Knit-back vinyl or fuzzy-back vinyl.

<u>Properties</u> – The knit-back reduces stretching.

<u>Strengths</u> – easy to clean, waterproof, resistant to UV.

<u>Weaknesses</u> – Nautolex can crack if folded or in cold weather, Naugahyde is resistant to cold. Neither breathe, so are susceptible to mildew on the inside.

<u>Life Expectancy</u> – up to 8 years if kept clean. The sun will bake in dirt and cause the fabric to go hard and crack.

<u>Width</u> – Both are 54" wide.

<u>Use for</u> – Interior & exterior upholstery, fuzzy-back is great for table covers.

<u>Cleaning Information</u> – Abrasives will very quickly ruin the protective finish and it won't be waterproof any more. Rinse often and use mild dish soap and never scouring powders.

<u>Sewing Information</u> – Like all vinyls, upholstery vinyls are very unforgiving of mistakes. Holes will show if you rip out seams. Don't sew over and over the same holes – it will weaken the fabric.

Quilted Vinyl is a fabric with a vinyl front, soft padding and a thin vinyl backing, all pressed together into 'corrugates' (Fig 1-1). It is a fully waterproof version of traditional Roll-and-tuck where you sew the quilted channels in.

<u>Sewing Tips</u> – The quilting tends to pull the fabric in. Really stretch it out when stapling, sewing, measuring and cutting.

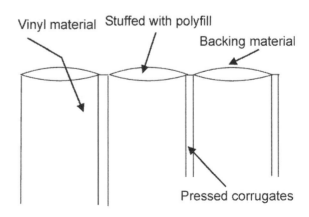

Fig 1-1 Nautolex Quilted vinyl fabric

Ultra Leather is polyurethane-coated-rayon
And is a beautiful although rather expensive
alternative to vinyl. It is very durable, cleanable and
certainly will add beauty and elegance to any yacht's
interior. It's cousin UltraSuede is equally as
awesome, tough and cleanable. If you can afford it
and only want to ever do the job once, maybe these
products are for you.

Vinyl Meshes

Brand names include Phifertex®, Textilene®,
Awntex®, Phifertex Plus®.
Material – Vinyl-coated polyester yarn
Properties – 70% to 90% shade protection
Strengths - stays flexible at all temperatures, flame
retardant, resists UV and mildew. Gives shade
without trapping heat or stopping air flow. The
tighter weaves are more dimensionally stable, and
provide more sun protection.
Width – 54" 12-15 oz/sq yd
Use for – Cushion bottoms, sheet bags, shade
curtains. My personal opinion is that the open-
weave mesh is really too rough to be comfortable to
sit on – sort of like sitting on a screen door. If you
want a vinyl mesh for the cockpit cushions, try a
tighter weave like Awntex or Phifertex Plus.
Sewing Tips – Mesh fabrics – There is no *right* or
wrong sides to these mesh fabrics.
Don't use seamstick on any mesh fabric –
eventually it bleeds right through and makes a dirty
sticky mess.

Cushion Underlining

This is a polyester mesh with a matte vinyl coating.
It is light, inexpensive, easily cleaned and durable
and does not stretch very much.
It can save you money on an upholstery project
because you can make the cushion bottoms of this
material and not have to use a possibly more
expensive upholstery fabric for the bottoms. It is
not really rugged enough for outdoor use, however,
and is best suited for interior upholstery.
It should last the life of the cushions.

Width – 54" 6 oz/yd
Sewing Tips – because it does not stretch as much
as a vinyl like Nautolex, it pulls the cushion in
nicely.

The underlining bottom may be just barely visible in
places such as at the front of the cushion. To hide
the underlining, sew a 1" or 2" strip of the
upholstery fabric to the edge of the cushion bottom
before assembling the cushion as shown in Fig 1-2.
(See also Section 6 – Cushions).
Don't use seamstick on meshes, it will bleed
through.

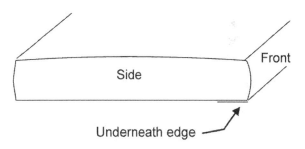

Fig 1-2 Stitch a strip of upholstery fabric
to the underside to hide the bottom
mesh fabric from being seen.

Clear Vinyls (Window Material)

Window materials are usually clear vinyls, although
you can use thin polycarbonate, too. Polycarbonate
is wonderfully clear and non-wavy, but it cannot be
folded and unless specially treated, and does not last
long unprotected in the sun.
Plastics are constantly being improved, so it's best
to do some internet research. A new UV coating on
Lexan called MR10 promises abrasion resistance
and UV protection.

Clear vinyls can be bought by the sheet (called
press-polished vinyls) or off a roll.

The most well-known sheet vinyl is Strataglass™. It
is a polymer-coated press polished vinyl. The

polymer coating seals and makes the vinyl more scratch-resistant, and keeps the vinyl supple. It resists atmospheric chemicals, blocks 70% of UVA and 100% of UVB. It has excellent clarity and longevity – with a life expectancy of 12+ years. But it is quite expensive compared to roll stock.

Width is 54" x 111" sheets, 40 mil or 30 mil thick.

Strataglass is very particular in its care and cleaning. See instructions on their website. Don't use paper towels, or any cleaning products unless recommended by the manufacturer. Don't allow any window vinyl to come into contact with silicone or sunscreen – it will turn the vinyl cloudy.

Window vinyl – is extruded clear PVC, and comes on rolls like many other canvas fabrics – so it is called "Roll Goods" sometimes. It comes 20 mil or 30 mil thick. 20 mil is not as clear as the 30 mil, but rolls up smaller. 30 mil is not as easily rolled, but lasts longer. Use 30 mil for most dodger windows – some applications where the dodger is rolled up small and zipped into a cover will be better with 20 mil.

It is very prone to scratching, so handle it carefully. Use a grease pencil to mark – permanent marker will never come out so you won't be able to fix mistakes. In fact, permanent marker can transfer from your pattern material onto the clear vinyl, so be very careful not to place the marker-side-down onto the clear vinyl.

To clean – hose off any salt crystals – don't rub them off – the salt crystals will scratch the vinyl. Then wash with mild soap and water. Don't use paper towels because they will put tiny scratches in the surface. Use a commercial vinyl window cleaner for best results and nothing containing ammonia.

Sewing Tips – Because window vinyl is so prone to scratching, cut it out on a smooth, clean surface, or better yet, cover the surface with a piece of fabric like a bed sheet. Don't drag the vinyl along the cutting or sewing surface, place it down carefully. Put a bed sheet or something under it and all

around the sewing machine. (Careful you don't sew the bed sheet to the vinyl!) Better yet – cut out a shape of paper about an inch smaller all around than the vinyl you are working with – tape it with small pieces of masking tape to both sides of the clear vinyl and remove when you're all done sewing.

Window vinyl is very prone to picking up marks from permanent marker – such as the marks you make on plastic pattern material when patterning a dodger. If you are quick, you can remove permanent marker with a commercial vinyl cleaner. Use only a grease pencil to mark window vinyl – never permanent marker.

Use a long stitch on the sewing machine to reduce the number of perforations which can weaken the material.

Patterning plastic – You can buy special patterning material, or use clear polyethylene drop sheets – the kind used for painting houses, or TyVek which you can get at the hardware store. It is cleaner to use than newspaper.

Mylar film – 7 mil thick is a good material to use for more permanent patterns, or for patterns that you need to make many copies of – such as corner patches for awnings. Mark it up with permanent marker. Be careful of the edges – they are very sharp. You can also use thin cardboard but the edges get fuzzy after a lot of use.

Sailcloth

Dacron® is actually a brand name but is almost synonymous with sailcloth. It comes in several weights – 9-10 oz being the best for reinforcing patches - and some colours.

Material - polyester
Properties – does not stretch much, does not absorb water
Strengths – very strong, resists many chemicals
Weaknesses – rots in the sun, not chafe-resistant, does not 'breathe'

Cleaning Information – hose off as frequently as possible with fresh water. Wash very gently with a mild detergent and rinse well.

Uses - reinforcing patches for strength. Not a good choice for an awning because it is not all that great for UV resistance, and it can be noisy in the wind.

Sewing Tips – cut with a hot knife.

When patching sails, it is imperative that you match up the grain of the patch with that of the sail, and use the same weight of cloth.

Spinnaker Cloth

Material – rip stop nylon is nylon fabric with an added extra basket weave through it to give it extra strength and to stop it, well, ripping.

Properties – very light and strong, stretches.

Strengths - Strong and resists chafe

Weaknesses – not resistant to UV, stretches when wet, shrinks in the sun

Cleaning Information - never use bleach on nylon

Uses – sail bags, light awnings (these will be noisy in the wind), and bags.

Sewing Tips – reinforce corners and strain areas. This material is very slippery to sew – use seamstick or staples to control it.

Nylon Flag Cloth – is 4 oz nylon. It is fairly strong but not particularly UV resistant, so if you leave your flag up all the time it will not last long.

Insignia – this is Dacron with an adhesive back. It comes in rolls of various widths – 2" through 8" or so, or by the yard in 54" width. If you want to have some on hand for sail repair, keep in mind that the 54" width is very hard to store neatly, the roll stuff is better. Insignia is very lightweight Dacron – like spinnaker material – so don't expect it to repair a big structural rip all on its own.

Leather

Leather used in canvas work is usually split cowhide. It is stretchy, easily machine-sewn and shrinks a little when wet. It breaks down in the sun,

however, and needs to be replaced periodically. Use it for chafe protection like the forward edges of dodgers but if you want better resistance to UV, use vinyl such as Shelterite for this instead.

Sewing Tips – Making seams in leather is not practical because it is usually too thick. Instead, just butt the 2 raw edges together and machine zigzag or hand stitch them together (see Fig 1-3). To hand stitch leather, sometimes it can be easier to 'pre-punch' holes in the leather using your sewing machine. Use the largest machine needle you have and use no thread in the sewing machine. This will also make your hand stitches nice and even.

Making slits in leather – Mark the slit, punch tiny holes with a small punch at each end of the mark, then cut a slit in between the holes (Fig 1-4). The holes at the ends help keeps the slit from tearing.

Fig 1-3 Place edges of leather together and stitch zig zag across the join.

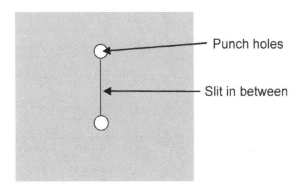

Fig 1-4 To make a slit in leather, punch two holes, and cut in between.

Canvas for Cruisers

Foam

If you start to research foam you will quickly discover how incredibly complicated and diverse the materials used in foam manufacturing are. In your research, pay attention to ILD (firmness) and density (quality), as this is how all foams are measured.

Density is the weight of 1 cubic foot of foam, and it's usually in the neighbourhood of 1.8 to 3.2 lbs. Density is more a measure of quality than what the foam actually feels like when you sit on it – as density goes up, so does the price. Cushions that get a lot of wear like settee seats and mattresses need close to 3LB dense foam because then they will do better under repeated pressure. Less dense foam can be used for seat backs and mattress toppers

ILD (Indentation Load Deflection) is a measurement of how firm the foam feels when you sit or lie on it. A 50 square inch surface is pressed into the foam to compress it 25% of its thickness eg. 4" foam compressed to 3". The weight required to do this is the foam's ILD.

Closed Cell foam is dense, relatively hard and it shrinks. But it floats and does not absorb water. Use it for floatation gear and cushions if you can stand it – it gets pretty hard after awhile sitting on it. I have had good luck with gluing 1" regular interior foam on top of the closed cell to provide a layer of soft padding. Then cover it with exterior-grade upholstery vinyl or waterproof Sunbrella Rain on the top, and vinyl mesh fabric on the bottom. The mesh on the bottom allows the foam to gas out which it will do over time as it shrinks
Made this way, the cushions can take an occasional light rain. Sealing the seams with vinyl cement will make them virtually waterproof, otherwise in a heavy or prolonged rain, water can eventually wick in through the unsealed seams.

Open Cell foam is softer, feels 'crunchy' when you sit on it, and water drains right through. It is light, and it sinks fast if it flies overboard! To prevent this, secure the cushion to the boat with lanyards or other attachment.
To ensure the cushion does not 'bottom out' and to make it float (at least long enough so you can grab it), you can glue ½" closed cell foam to the underside. Punch holes in the closed cell foam before gluing it on to allow the foam to drain.

Most open cell foams are not very UV resistant, so cover them with Sunbrella or other equivalent UV resistant fabric, and store them indoors if you can.

Interior Foam comes in many densities and thicknesses. The best foam is made from latex but if you can't afford this, buy the best quality (usually this means the most expensive) foam that you can afford. Especially for foam that you will be sitting on or sleeping on regularly. If you buy poor quality foam, your hard work will be all to waste when the cushion bottoms out and loses its shape. See Section 6 – Cushions for much more information about working with foam.

For Seat cushions – Dacron-wrapped (Polyester batting) Polyurethane foam, medium to extra firm would be a good place to start when thinking about making new cushions. For average-firm cushions (ILD 24 to 30), Firm seat cushions (ILD 30 to 36). , Density rating should be 2.5 or higher for durability. Settee cushions should be 4 to 6 inches thick. Back cushions or arms – use Dacron-wrapped Polyurethane ILD 10 to 23, Arm rests ILD 33. A density rating of 1.2 to 1.5 for the arms or backs should be enough. Arms and backs can be 1 to 3 inches thick, wrapped in Dacron batting or left as is.

Polyester Batting is used to wrap interior cushions so as to fill up the corners and give them a softer look. This is the same batting that is used in quilting and is available in most fabric shops. Use spray adhesive to stick it to the foam.

Notions

Basting Tape

Once you discover basting tape (seamstick is one of the brand names), you will wonder how you ever managed before! Seamstick is double-faced sticky tape that comes in rolls of various widths. The most common widths to keep on hand are the ¼" for zippers, the ¾" for joining large panels and 3/8" or ½" for everything else. 3M makes a more expensive seamstick that has no plastic carrier strip for the adhesive – it is just pure goo. And there is a super-sticky version that sticks better to acrylic canvas than the regular stuff.

Seamstick does not stretch – in fact, it tends to pucker the fabric it lays on, so apply the seamstick loosely. The easiest way to do this is to stretch the fabric out slightly using scratch awls (which will be described later) before applying the seamstick.

Stitching through the seamstick can help seams to be more waterproof. It can make the sewing machine needle sticky, however, especially as the needle gets hot from friction. Periodically stop and clean the needle with rubbing alcohol and a cotton swab to clean things up periodically. But normally you will apply the seamstick to the seam allowances, and you will not be stitching through the goo.

Seamstick adhesive can bleed out with time and heat. If you apply it too close to the raw edge of the fabric or zipper edge (especially on vinyl), it will show eventually and look dirty and awful. So apply it about 2mm in from the edges.

To store it, keep it wrapped up tightly in a zip lock bag. It will go all sticky if kept in a really hot place, and it will not stick very well in the cold. In the tropics, I keep mine in a zip lock bag, buried in the fridge on the boat, and bring it out to warm it up before using it.

When sewing vinyls, you can use a smaller size of seamstick (say, ¼" instead of the ½" for joining seams), because the seamstick sticks VERY well to vinyl. Keep this in mind – if you make a mistake, it is really hard to get the seamstick adhesive off vinyl fabric.

Seamstick also sticks very well to leather, so is useful when adding the chafe strip along the front edges of biminis and dodgers.

You can use ¼" seamstick on hard surfaces like outboard covers or steel dodger frames to hold patterning plastic in place. Don't leave it on too long though! And make sure when using seamstick in this way, that you use the kind that has a plastic carrier strip (you can tell by taking off the paper and stretching the tape – there is a tough plastic film).

Cleaning information – seamstick glue is really hard to remove. Try Acetone or Mineral Spirits, (check that it doesn't harm the fabric first!) which will soften the adhesive to a horrible goop, then scrape it off as best as you can. Also, if you can find it, "Goo Gone" works pretty well.

Webbing

Webbing comes in several materials, widths and colours.

Polypropylene webbing is the weakest – it is not UV resistant at all, so don't use it for outdoor projects.

Canvas for Cruisers

It is inexpensive, and it floats. Use it for interior reinforcing, and bag handles.

Polyester webbing (Dacron) is the best for use in sunlight.
Nylon webbing shrinks with age but is good for outdoor projects. There are various weights – regular, heavyweight and tubular. Use the heavyweight (commonly bright blue in colour) for jacklines, tethers and straps that people are going to hang on. Nylon is not particularly UV resistant, so make sure you store those jacklines inside when not in use.

Spectra webbing does not stretch or absorb water, it is light and extremely strong (breaking strength around 7000 lbs), very resistant to chafe, (also very expensive) and resistant to UV.

Tubular webbing, white with a distinctive dotted line along its center is made of polyester. It shrinks less than nylon, so is preferred for awnings for its strength and 'less stretch' properties.

Binding

Centerfold binding – is actually flat, but is woven so that it folds easily down the center. The acrylic centerfold binding is 7/8" wide and is sold in a wide variety of colours. You can use it to encase raw edges – on covers, dodgers, biminis, bags – to protect the edges and add a decorative finish.

Double fold binding – comes in ¾" or 1" wide, made of acrylic and is a tape with both edges already folded under. It is great for binding edges. (See Section 2 – Binding Edges)

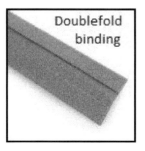

Double fold binding is cut on the bias so that it curves around corners easily. You can make your own by cutting fabric in strips along its bias, fold the edges under and iron with a very cool iron. (If using acrylic canvas, use a very cool or even a cold iron). It's a real fiddly job to do.

<u>Vinyl Binding</u> comes in single or double fold, a couple of different widths. It is strong and resists mildew, but don't use cheap vinyl binding for exterior projects – it will crack over time and look terrible. Use Stamoid binding for exteriors.

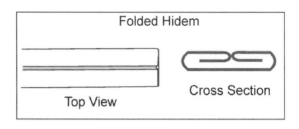

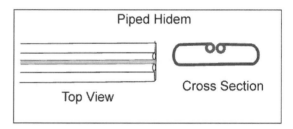

Fig 1-5 Specialty pre-made bindings

Piping and welting

For making up your own piping, you can buy a special cord made of hard foam – this is nice because it does not mildew or rot, it is easy to work with and inexpensive to buy.

Premade vinyl piping is also available. If you are planning to use it for exterior projects, check the UV resistance of the material.

There are a couple of specialty pipings available – "Hidem" is a vinyl binding that is already folded along its edges. The folds can be plain or with a piped edge (Fig 1-5). It is useful in areas where the fabric joins a hard edge. Apply the piping trim by opening up the folds and stapling or tacking it down in between the folded edges.

Boltrope or 'Keder' is used in conjunction with awning track to make a secure attachment for cushions, dodgers and sunshades to the boat. (See Section 2 – Piping)

Zippers

There are several different sizes of zippers. The most common are - #5 (teeth are 3/16" wide when closed), and #10 (5/16" teeth). The #5 size is usually used for cushions, and the #10 for biminis and dodgers and other exterior canvas. Sometimes you will see #8 but because it is not as common, so it could be harder to find replacement heads.

Zipper teeth are usually separate little pieces of plastic, but also available is the 'coil' type. Coil zippers are supposed to be stronger, and curve around corners easier. The plastic coil part is sewn to the tape part of the zipper – and this is the area that fails when exposed to the sun.

Zippers are made as 'continuous' or 'jacket' types. Continuous means you buy the zipper tape by the yard, cut it to length and put on the heads as required. Use continuous zips for openings that don't need to separate completely – like bags and cushions.
Jacket zips open and separate, well, just like a jacket. They have a fitting at the bottom where the 2 sides hook together and are able to be separated entirely. Use these for things like biminis, dodgers and removable shade curtains.

Jacket zips come in standard lengths – 24" through 96" in one foot increments, and also 120" and 180" and others. If you need a different length than the standard length, just buy the next size longer, and cut and finish to the length required. (See Section 2 – Zippers). There is a way to make your own pseudo-jacket zipper in custom lengths – this is also covered in Section 2 Zippers.

Jacket zips are commonly the #10 size, but are also available in #5.

Zip heads are available with a single or double pull slider – double pull meaning they can be opened from one side or the other. Do not use zippers with metal heads if you are sailing in saltwater. Even for interior projects. The salt air corrodes them terribly. If you do have metal heads that are all stuck shut, soak them in vinegar to help work them free. And then take them off and replace them with plastic heads.

Zip heads are also Locking or Non-locking. Locking means you can push the head in the 'down' position, and a little metal tooth comes out inside the head and stops the head from moving. This little metal tooth can cause all kinds of sticking problems from corrosion just like metal heads. If you don't really need it to lock in place, consider using the non-locking which doesn't have the little metal tooth.

The most common zipper in place by far are YKK. They die in the sun pretty quickly – about 2-3 years in the tropics. Black lasts longer than white. Try to sew the zipper so that the teeth are protected from the sun by a flap of fabric.

Also available are Lenzip – UV stabilized Delrin, water resistant and guaranteed for life. And Sunbrella Sunzip if you can find them UV resistant and with Sunbrella tape. Both these are more expensive than YKK.

Zippers can leak water – some of the newer zippers like YKK Aquaguard promise a practically waterproof seal, and other products promise UV resistant and resistance to mold and dirt.

Canvas for Cruisers

Velcro

This is the brand name for the most common form of hook-and-loop fastenings. Velcro is one of those words that is used interchangeably for hook-and-loop, just like Sunbrella is used interchangeably for acrylic canvas.

Velcro is a very useful fastener, and here are a couple of things to know.

Nylon Velcro rots in the sun very quickly. Black lasts longer than white. It also shrinks a lot over the course of time. So, when stitching Velcro on, try to avoid stretching it. In fact, you should pin out the fabric and really stretch it out, so that when you seamstick on the Velcro, it fits more 'loosely' on to the fabric. If the Velcro is going to be anywhere near the sun, make sure you cover it with flaps, or you will be replacing it often.

Velcro is also available made from polyester instead of nylon. It lasts much longer in the sun, and does not shrink very much. I am not sure if studies have been done, but I feel that the polyester does not stick to itself as strongly as the nylon does.

Velcro with a sticky back is useful for outboard motor covers, as you will see in Section 4 – Covers.

A type of hook and loop fastener is available in semi-rigid plastic form, called VelStick. It is great for attaching to hard surfaces, such as cushion backs to the back of your settee, or around the inside of your hatches for attaching mosquito screens.

Rope and cord

Small leech line is useful to have on hand for projects that need a thin cord (e.g. hatch covers) Solid braid polyester cord is commonly used for drawstrings and tie-downs. The table below describes the most common sizes available.
For making your own boltropes and piping, nylon is not a good choice – it shrinks with age – use polypro instead.

Shock Cord or Bungee Cord is the stretchy elastic used in canvas work. Common sizes are 1/8", 3/16", ¼" and 5/16" diameters, depending on the strength needed. It does not last very long in the sun so needs replacing periodically.

To cut shock cord, wrap a little piece of insignia sticky-back tape around the area to be cut. Heat up the hot knife and cut it fast (cuts it faster and stinks a lot less).

To join shock cord, align the two ends next to each other as shown in Fig 1-6. Place a shock cord clamp (also known as hog rings) around the join. Use special shock cord pliers (or ordinary pliers – it's just not as easy) to squeeze the clamp shut. Put on another clamp over the join, with the opening facing in the opposite direction to the one you just squeezed shut. Use the pliers to squeeze this one shut.

Once the shock cord clamps are squeezed on, they re practically impossible to remove. It is easiest to just cut the shock cord.

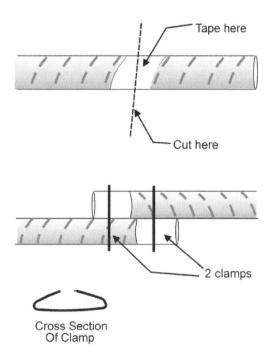

Fig 1-6 Cutting and Joining Shock Cord

Hardware

Grommets

Grommets and the tools used for their installation are referred to either by size or by diameter. See the table below.

Spur Grommets – have little sharp points all around on one half of the grommet and are the best type for canvas work because they attach strongly to the fabric. These spurs lock onto the edge of the other half of the grommet. It can get expensive to have all the set tools and hole punches for all the various sizes, but the most common sizes used in canvas work are #0 and #1.

Eyelet Grommets – or plain rim washer grommets are used for light-duty areas that do not have a lot of stress such as for ventilation holes. They have their own set of die sets but use the same hole punches as the spur grommets.

Grommet Sizes:

Size	Size "
0	1/4
1	5/16
2	3/8
3	7/16
4	½
5	5/8

To install grommets you need a rubber mat (or other surface like hardwood – not metal or it will dull the hole punch), a hammer, a hole punch cutting tool and a matching setting tool with pedestal as shown in Fig 1-8.

Place the rubber mat on a really solid surface. Use a flat faced (rawhide is best) hammer to bang a hole in the fabric with the hole cutting tool. If you have a hard time cutting the hole, move the rubber mat to a more solid, less springy surface like concrete or stone, not wood.

Now take the setting tool. Place the pedestal on a solid surface. Set the male part of the grommet onto the pedestal. Force the hole you just made in the fabric over the grommet's shaft. Place the spur ring on top, spurs down, and wham it hard with a hammer – a heavy rounded hammer with a nylon head as shown in the diagram is a good tool to have if you are doing a lot of grommets.

An eyelet grommet doesn't need nearly the same 'wham' as does a spur grommet.

It is important to know that a spur grommet must be installed in the proper thickness of fabric layers. If the layers of fabric are too thick, the little spurs will not be able to cut through the fabric and grab onto the other half of the grommet. If the fabric is too thin, the spurs will cut a big hole into the fabric and it will rip right out. In that case, add a reinforcing layer of fabric to add thickness.

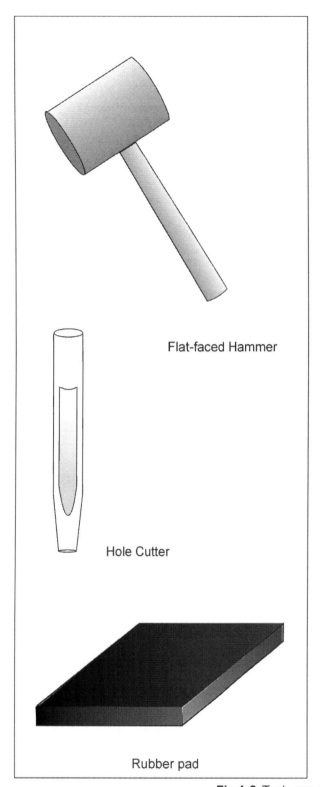

Flat-faced Hammer

Hole Cutter

Rubber pad

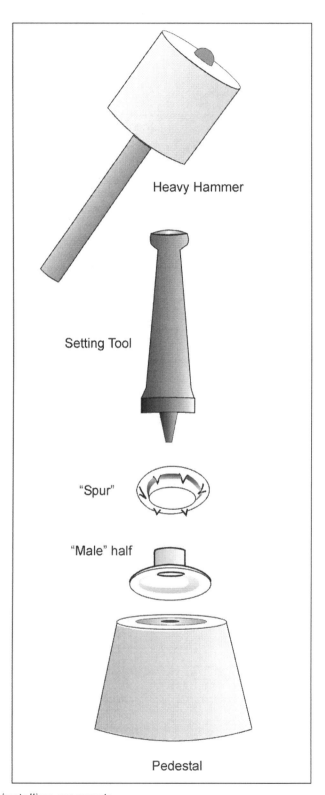

Heavy Hammer

Setting Tool

"Spur"

"Male" half

Pedestal

Fig 1-8 Tools used for installing grommets

To remove spur grommets, turn the grommet 'upside down' (the side with the spurs on top) so that you can see the little retaining ring formed by the male part of the grommet. At several points along the inside of this retaining ring, bang at the edge, towards the grommet hole, with the point of a flat screwdriver (Fig 1-9). Use a screwdriver that you don't care much about. This breaks the ring's seal and lets you separate the two sides.

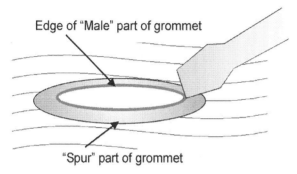

Fig 1-9 Removing a Spur Grommet

To remove eyelet grommets (which are much weaker), just bend the edge up and pull it away from the fabric – use pliers if necessary (Fig 1-10).

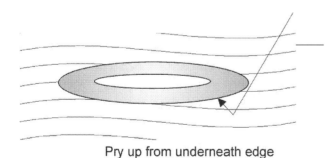

Pry up from underneath edge

Fig 1-10 Removing an Eyelet Grommet

Snaps

Snaps are good general purpose fasteners – stainless steel will corrode far less for outdoor applications than nickel plated brass. You can get regular snaps, or a special 'one way' snap that only opens when pulled in one direction. This is useful but not necessary for dodgers or something that you don't want to come off accidentally. These one-way snaps use a special setting tool, different than the ordinary snap setting tool.

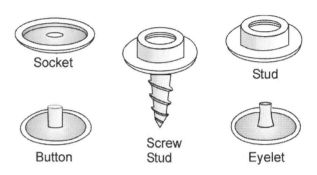

Fig 1-11 Snap Components

To remove snaps, use a pair of side cutters. Insert the jaws of the side cutters between the socket (or stud) and the fabric, and squeeze underneath to pop it off (Fig 1-12).

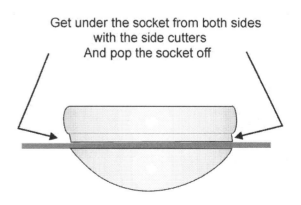

Get under the socket from both sides with the side cutters And pop the socket off

Fig 1-12 Removing a snap

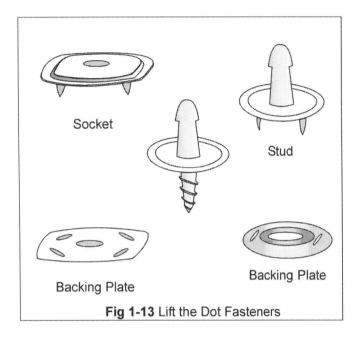

Fig 1-13 Lift the Dot Fasteners

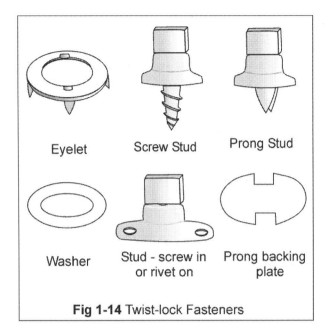

Fig 1-14 Twist-lock Fasteners

Lift the Dot™ Fasteners

Lift the dot fasteners are designed to open when lifted from one side only, making them quite secure against accidental opening. They are most often used to attach dodgers and enclosures to the side of the boat. No special setting tool is required to install them – just make slits with a jackknife (you can heat it up with a flame to seal fabrics like Sunbrella) and use pliers, a hammer and screwdriver or something to bend the little hooks around. The studs are available with a screw for use in attaching to hard surfaces.

Tenax™ & Menax™ Fasteners

These fasteners are not commonly seen in North America but are seen in Europe. They are quite expensive. The Tenax fasteners are metal, and the Menax are plastic. They consist of 4 pieces like a snap fastener – one pair of fittings for one side and one for the other. They operate like a lift-the-dot but are even more secure. Special tools are required to install them.

Twist-lock Fasteners

Also called turn buttons or Commonsense™ fasteners, these consist of an eyelet, through which a stud is pushed, and turned, to secure the attachment. It is a good fastener to use if the connection will be subject to strain.

A special cutting tool is recommended for cutting the oval holes although I have used a grommet hole punch for this. Just punch twice to make an oval hole.

The stud portion of the assembly is available in three styles. A base with screws, prongs for use with a backing plate, or with 2 holes in the base. The studs with 2 holes in the base can be screwed onto a hard surface, or you can use the eyelet portion of a snap fastener to secure the stud to fabric, or you can rivet them onto a backing plate, or you can even sew them on.

Usually these fasteners are made of nickel-plated brass, but there is another brand called Permalock® made of UV resistant plastic – these are long-lasting and don't corrode.

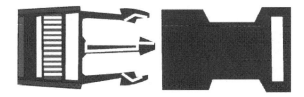

Fig 1-15 Side Release Buckle

Fig 1-16 Ladderlock Buckle

Fig 1-17 Plastic hook and eye

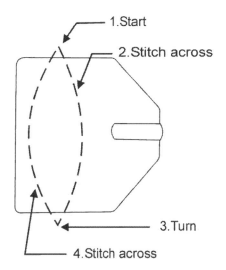

Fig 1-18 Stitching on a plastic hook

Buckles

Side Release buckles are used to make adjustable or fixed-length opening straps with webbing. Section 3 – Buckle Straps – will show how to make them. The buckles are made of nylon or plastic and most used in canvas work are 1" or 2" wide. Black lasts longer in the sun than white.

Ladderlock buckles have serrated teeth and are used to make adjustable webbing straps. They are available in different widths but ½" or 1" will do most jobs. They come in white or black.
(See Section 3 - Rollups for how to use them).

Cam buckles look like a seat belt buckle. They have a hinged top with serrated teeth, which locks the webbing in place. You just feed the end of the webbing through the buckle, pull it to the desired position and push down on the top. To release, pull up the top just like a seatbelt. They can be used to attach cushions – see Section 6 – Cushions – Fastening Methods

Hooks

Sew-on plastic hooks can be used for sail covers to close the bottom hem. They have a flat flange which you sew to the fabric.

To attach, start stitching into the fabric, just off the edge of the hook's flange (Fig 1-18). Stitch in a curve (this prevents the hook from having a weak straight-edge of perforations) to the other side. Without breaking the thread, leave the needle in the 'down' position and turn the work. Then stitch back to the other side in a curve, back to where you started. Stitch over the first line of stitching again for strength – trying to hit the same holes, to limit the number of perforations.
Sew the matching plastic eye to the other side of the sail cover, or hook the hook part into a shock cord (see Section 5 – Mainsail Cover).

Fig 1-19 Wire sail hook

<u>Wire sail hooks</u> are made of stainless, and are sewn to one side of the thing to be closed (like a sail cover). On the other side you can hook to a cord, grommet or shock cord.

Barrel Locks

Barrel Locks are cylindrical shaped fittings through which you thread a cord to make a self-locking drawstring. Cord locks are similar but are shaped differently.

Either way, squeeze the barrel lock, thread the cord through the hole and release. Squeezing on the barrel lock then allows you to pull up the drawstring, and when you release the barrel lock, the spring in it keeps tension on the cord to keep it closed.

Depending on the design of the barrel lock, the second line or cord is sometimes tough to get in. The easiest way is to set the barrel lock down on a table on its end. Push it straight down (easier than squeezing), and force the other line in. It can also help to use a scratch awl to push it through and/or use a hot knife to melt and taper the end of the cord to a sharp point.

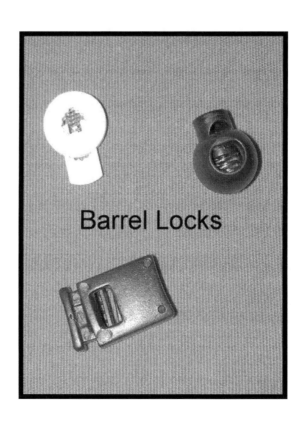

Barrel Locks

Fig 1-20 Lacing Knob

Lacing Knobs

Lacing knobs are plastic and from the side, look like little mushrooms. There is a hole down the center, so you can attach them with a screw drilled into the boat or other hard surface.

These knobs are used to hold a loop (usually a small shock cord) down. These loops are attached to the dodger or side curtains or whatever it is that needs holding down (Fig 1-21).

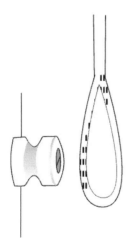

Fig 1-21 Lacing knob installed, and bungee loop

Tools

General Sewing tools

The following list of tools is pretty extensive. Not all are absolutely required but they sure make your sewing go easier. Most are inexpensive, small in size and room to store them can probably be found on the average cruising boat.

A large flat wooden surface – This is only a dream if you live on a boat like I do. Sometimes to mark and cut out a large project, you just have to pack up your fabric, go ashore and find a big floor or clean dock somewhere. But for smaller projects, I have made do with a thin piece of plywood which stores under a bunk and fits over the mattress when I need to cut out something.

Scratch awls – These are about 4" long and look like pointed screwdrivers. Use them to hold fabric down onto a wooden surface and to stretch it out before applying seamstick. Use them to hold pieces together when making a duplicate. Stab into the seam allowance, (particularly important on vinyls) so as not to make holes in the fabric. You can pound the points through the fabric and into the wood with a sharp rap with the heel of your hand but you can hurt yourself doing this. Better to use a mallet!

Fig 1-22 Scratch Awl

Mushroom Pins – are used like scratch awls. They are very sharp and only make a little hole in the fabric. They are not as strong as scratch awls. Keep them well oiled, in a zip lock bag because they rust like crazy. You can get aluminum push pins too, but they are harder on your fingers.

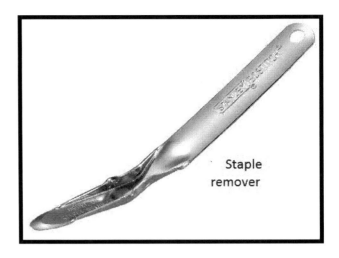

Staple remover

Fig 1-23 Mushroom Pin and Pushpin

Stapler – this is a great substitute for pins. It's quick, holds the fabric nice and flat and accurately in place. An ordinary desktop office stapler is usually too weak – you should really get the heavier duty 'pliers type' which is readily available in office supply stores. Staple into the seam allowance so the holes won't show, and make sure you remove <u>all</u> the staples after sewing. If you miss any, they will rust terribly.

Staple Remover – the fastest and easiest type to use is a flat tool that is shaped like a little spatula, as opposed to the standard office 'jaw type' staple remover.

This little tool also works great as a 'pusher' to help the fabric get under the sewing machine foot. You can use it as a 'press' to make a crease nice and sharp – just zip the edge of the tool along the fold. And you can use it as a press to stick the Seamstick on nice and hard, again, just zip the edge of the tool along the Seamstick..

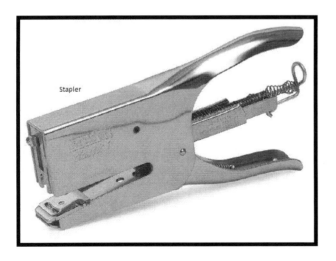

Stapler

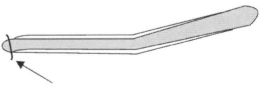

Wedge end under staple and push forward.

Fig 1- 25 Spatula-type Staple Remover

Fig 1-26 Seam Ripper

Seam Ripper – for those mistakes you hate to make. Get a nice sharp one with a large enough handle, and a little ball on the short bottom hook to help prevent cutting the fabric. If it gets dull, just throw it away and get a new one – it's a total waste of time to struggle with a dull ripper.

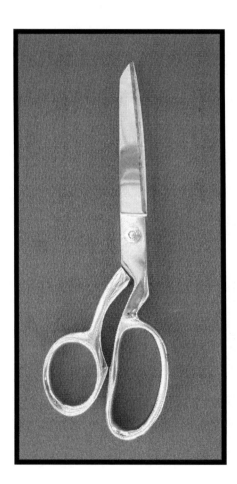

Scissors of course. Get good ones, and never use them for cutting paper or cardboard.

Exacto Knife – used carefully, an exacto knife makes a great seam ripper. Let's say you are removing an old zipper so that you can replace it with a new one. Use the seam ripper to get things started, then get comfortable. Sit on the bimini or whatever it is, hold the zipper tape with one hand and hold the bimini down with your foot – stretching open the seam to be ripped out. Take the exacto knife and carefully peck at the threads. Angle the blade towards the thing you don't care about (in this case the zipper), just in case your hand slips. You don't want to cut your nice bimini! Works great. Then make sure you pick off all the old thread bits. That's the fiddly part.

Hot Knife – if you can afford one and you are doing a lot of canvas work, a hot knife is the ultimate cutting tool.

A hot knife is used for cutting synthetic woven fabrics like acrylic canvas or Dacron, and finishing the edges at the same time. For cutting natural cotton, the hot knife will only burn the edges, and it will melt upholstery vinyl, so don't use it on these fabrics. Use scissors for these.

When using the hot knife, go fast enough so that the edge doesn't burn and go all crunchy and black. (This is less of a problem if you are cutting on a flat metal surface but I don't know of anyone who has a metal floor!) I keep a thin piece of plain, unpainted plywood under a bunk as a portable cutting table. Take off the hot tip once in awhile and clean off the corrosion with fine sandpaper. Don't tighten it back on with a screwdriver – finger tight only, or you will ruin the hot knife.

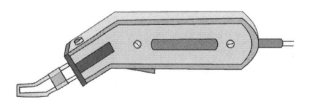

Fig 1-27 Hot knife

Canvas for Cruisers

The smoke and fumes that come off the stuff you are cutting are pretty vile. I suspect they are toxic and carcinogenic although I doubt if any studies have been done on this. Best not to inhale these fumes, and work in a well-ventilated area. Also, be careful of the hot-knifed edge of Sunbrella – it is sharp and will cut you.

Fig 1-28 Seam Roller

Seam Roller – this is a great tool for sticking down seamstick and sticking seams together. It is a hard rubber roller with a handle. They are not easy to find, but you can go to a local home decorating store and buy a wallpaper seam roller as a substitute.

Other general sewing tools – Other tools to have on hand include hand sewing needles (heavy needles for canvas work). A sewing awl or 'speedy stitcher' is very useful for tough hand-sewing jobs.

Measuring Tools – An ordinary 12 ft and a 50 ft measuring tape is useful to have on hand. For marking up fabric, use aluminum yardsticks 1" and 2" wide if you can get them. These standard widths make it easy to mark hem allowances.
A 24" aluminum carpenter's L-square makes it fast & easy to measure and make things square.
A compass is invaluable for making circles, a big one if you can find it. Failing this, I have outlined in Section 2 another way to draw a large circle.

For marking – use ordinary standard HB pencils, white pencils for dark colours, and grease pencils for clear vinyl. Soft, white erasers are useful for erasing pencil marks.

Disposable lighters are good for burning off little thread ends.

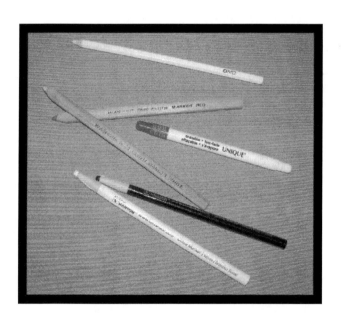

Special Tools

Electric Knife - For cutting foam, an ordinary household electric knife like the kind used for carving a turkey works great. I have used a serrated bread knife in a pinch, with some success. I have even seen a machete used very accurately for cutting foam, but I think it takes practice!

Staple Gun - You will need a staple gun if you are working on upholstery that attaches to a wooden backing. Maybe even an electric one if you do a lot of that kind of work.
Stainless steel staples are the best for boats because they don't rust. Headliners sometimes use backer boards like thin plywood so you will need ¼" stainless steel staples for this.

For installing snaps, you can get an inexpensive tool set which allows you to bang the snaps in with a hammer (Fig 1-29).

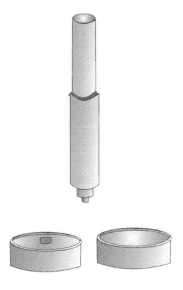

Fig 1-29 Snap Installation tool

If you do a lot of snaps though, it is worth it to get the "press-n-snap" tool which works like a vice grip (see photo). This is an expensive tool but makes it quick and easy to install snaps. It can also do certain spur and rolled rim grommets. You need to get various die sets to allow you do all these fittings.

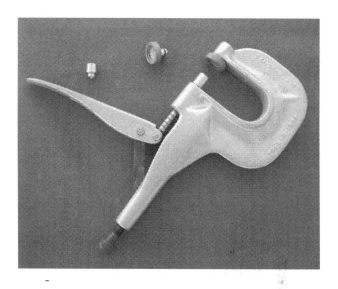

Quick Fit Snap Tool – is a little handful of parts which cost a lot of money so it's hard to justify it. However, it does make your cover or whatever fit like a glove. It comes with a few snap sockets which have a pin welded onto them. You snap the pin part onto the existing studs on the boat. Now you take the cover and stretch it over the pins, poking the pins through the cover where required. This allows you to reposition the cover as many times as you need to get a perfect fit. Mark where the holes are, take the cover off and install the snap buttons. There are little covers for the pins to keep the cover in place on the pins, and a little tool used to pop the pins off after.

Canvas for Cruisers

The Sewing Machine

Finally we get to the most important tool!

It is difficult to find a sewing machine that can do both home sewing and canvas work. A heavy industrial machine is designed to sew heavy fabrics using heavy thread and has a strong motor to drive the needle through the fabric.

A good industrial machine has a 'walking foot' which means that not only the lower feed dogs work to pull the fabric through, but also the upper foot moves the fabric along. The walking foot can be pretty rough on light home-sewing type fabrics.

The machine can have a short arm or a long arm. The long arm refers to the fact that there is a big space under the arm of the machine, so you can sew seams far away from the edges of big projects because you have more room to stuff or roll the excess fabric underneath the arm. Really heavy duty industrial machines tend to be permanent fixtures, although portables can be found too.

Standard Industrial machine motors are noisy and tend to be hard to control in terms of speed. Often they take off at full speed and are hard to control. A Servo-Motor is an electronic controlled motor which allows much greater control. It is virtually noiseless and energy efficient, as it only uses power when the machine is actually sewing.

A home sewing machine usually can handle some canvas work and upholstery, but it can be hard on the machine. There is much discussion on types of machines on line, so have a look and decide what your budget and space allows.

Clean the machine often, especially take all the bobbin assembly apart and clean it – it's a fiddly job and most people avoid it. Keep it well-oiled and it will last a long time.

Thread and Needles

Thread can make or break your sewing day. Store it in a zip lock bag to keep it fresh Even though it is tempting, it is best to not use old, dried up stuff that somebody gave you. However, if all you have is old, dried up thread, try soaking it in a jar of silicone overnight to restore its softness.

Threads come in different weights, materials and colours. Use larger sizes of thread for heavier fabrics.

The minimum size to use for any kind of canvas work is size 92. Size 138 is better (if the machine can handle it). Life expectancy for 92 is only 2-3 years if exposed totally to the tropical sun.

Bonded polyester thread is the most commonly used and if it is described as UV (eg V-92) that means it has also been treated to withstand UV better than just standard bonded polyester.

It is usually 'antiwick' (check for this) which means

that when it gets wet, it will tend to fill in the holes made by the sewing machine needle and make your project leak less along the seams (note I said 'less').

Of the polyester threads, black thread lasts longest, followed by white. Coloured thread looks nice but will fade to white in about 6 months in the sun..

Nylon thread will leak at the seams and degrade faster than polyester, but is very strong. Cotton will totally disintegrate in the sun very quickly.

PTFE threads like Tenara, Profilen, SolarFix, Coats HeliosP, brand threads will last forever but can be tricky and frustrating to sew with. Most are very expensive but certainly worth it when sewing projects like dinghy chaps or stackpacks which are a bear to restitch. These threads are size 92 or 138 and can be much more slippery than polyesters creating sewing issues.

If the machine is not creating a stitch or is getting all tangled up on the bobbin side, switch to a smaller needle.

Sometimes you have to increase the upper tension a lot, and check the lower tension too. Put the loaded bobbin into the bobbin case, thread it, and then hold the loaded case up by its thread. It should not unroll unless you shake it a little.

You can try turning the needle a little from its normal position, and experiment with the top tension knob and possibly the bobbin tension. Some of these threads clog up the tension plates and other thread guides in the machine, particularly the bobbin. Check for this and keep the machine clean.

Be sure to backstitch well, these threads tend to unravel.

Needles -

As far as needles go – if your machine starts to sew badly, the first thing to try is to change the needle. A tiny little burr on the tip or a slight bend in the needle can really affect the machine's sewing ability. Keep lots of needles on hand.

Thread and Needle Guide

Fabric Weight	Needle	Thread Size	Tensile Strength
< 1 ½ oz	#12 or #14	30	4.7 lb
< 3 oz	#14 or #16	46	7.4 lb
Up to 6 oz	#16 or #18	69	10.9 lb
Up to 10 oz	#18 or #20	92	14.5 lb
> 10 oz	#20 or #22	138	22.6 lb

Thread Durability
1 – excellent 2 – good 3 - fair   4 – poor

Resistance to:	Cotton	Nylon	Polyester
Chafe	4	1	1
Breakage	3	1	1
Heat	2	2	2
Mildew	4	1	1
Acid	4	3	1
Alkali	4	2	3
Stretch	4	1	1
UV	4	2	2
Flexibility	4	1	2

If your needle bangs on something like a pin or zipper or something there is a good possibility it now has a burr. If the needle jams the machine totally as you are sewing along at great speed, your timing could be affected so you will have to consult your manual.

An industrial machine has round needle tops, unlike a home sewing machine which has one flat side. So you have to feel for the ridge along the edge of the needle and place that in the correct position for your machine (usually to the left as you are sitting in front of the machine)

Canvas for Cruisers

Basic Sewing Techniques

All the canvas sewing projects described in this book can be accomplished by using a straight stitch. Zigzag is usually described as stronger but there are no scientific tests on the subject. It will though, allow for stretch, spread the load where a straight stitch can create a weaker 'channel' of perforations, and certainly is easier to rip out than straight stitch.

In the case of sail repair a 'triple stitch' zigzag spreads the load more evenly and is really essential for a good, strong, professional repair.

Fig 1-31 Triple stitch zig zag

To finish raw edges of canvas work, the best looking and most durable way is to use a hot knife to cut out the pieces of fabric. If you don't have a hot knife, you can use a flat-felled seam to seal the raw edges inside the seam allowances (see Section 2 - Seams).

One of the most important considerations before you sew too far is to make sure that the thread tension is good. This means that the loop formed between the upper thread and the bobbin thread occurs in the center of the fabric. If you can see a loop at the upper surface of the fabric, this means that the upper tension is too tight or that the lower tension in the bobbin is too loose. A loop seen on the underside means the upper tension is too loose or the bobbin is too tight. Adjust the bobbin tension only after you have tried everything with the upper tension. Trial and error on a scrap piece of fabric is the best way to get it right.

Some machines are particular about starting a seam – they make an ugly knot underneath. This could be because there is not enough 'pull' on the thread upon start-off or because the loose thread at the start gets all tangled up underneath.

To alleviate this, pull the top and bottom threads together, off to the right-hand side (or '2 o'clock' position) and hold them in place with slight tension until the machine starts stitching.

Start and stop all seams with a few backstitches to prevent the seam unraveling. If you are working with PTFE thread you will probably have to backstitch a couple of times because the thread is so slippery.

If the fabric seems to be puckering along the seams, it could be that either:

> the stitch length is too short.
> the needle is too large.
> both tensions are too tight

You can also try stretching the fabric in front and behind the needle as you sew to reduce this tendency. Grab the fabric with one hand in front of the needle, and a section behind the needle. Stretch it as the machine sews along. Be careful to stretch the fabric evenly between your hands and not interfere with the sewing. Let the machine feed itself - if the needle breaks, you are pulling too hard. As far as stitch length goes, make it about 3/16" – a too-short stitch increases puckering and weakens the fabric.

If you are working on a very long piece, add 2% or so to the length of the fabric when you are cutting out to allow for shrinkage, then adjust hems or other marks after sewing and you know what kind of shrinkage you are dealing with. It is much easier to trim off than to add on later!

One cause of uneven-looking seams could be that the sewing machine is pulling the top and bottom pieces of fabric under the foot at an uneven rate. One of the pieces lags behind. This problem is much less with a walking foot.

You can eliminate one piece lagging behind the other is to either seamstick or staple the pieces together before sewing.

Or, if you don't want to do this and wish to 'freehand' it, make 'hatch' marks (described in more detail later in this book), matching them up as you sew, and hold the material into an 'S' curve as shown in Fig 1-32.

This makes it so that the 'underneath' piece is stretched out and allows the top piece to feed through. Also holding the fabric this way helps to keep the fabric from slipping against each other because you are using the twist in the fabric to hold it firmly in place. You are not having to rely just on the strength of your hands to hold the layers tight against each other.

It may also work for you to try to push the top layer forward with your flat right hand as you sew along, helping it to not 'lag' behind. Or you can try holding the bottom layer back with your left hand. You have to develop your own technique.

Turning a Corner

When you are sewing along and need to turn a corner, simply stop sewing at the exact point for the turn (hand cranking if necessary to get to the exact spot), hand crank the needle into the 'down' position, and pick up the presser foot. Adjust the project as required, put the presser foot back down and continue sewing.

This also is necessary when working on big projects and you need to muscle the project back into position. Sometimes it is tough to adjust the project as you are sewing along – it makes for wavy and crooked seams.

***Right* and *Wrong* Sides –**

In this book I refer often to *right* side and *wrong* side of the fabric. The *right* side is the side of the fabric that will be seen in the finished project.

Some fabrics – especially acrylics – don't have a visible *right* and *wrong* side. You may have to remember, or mark which side is which so that you position the pieces and place the seam allowances and hems on the correct sides.

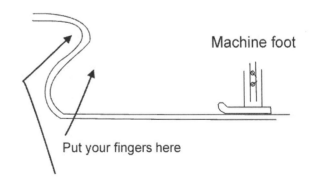

Machine foot

Put your fingers here

Put your thumb here

Fig 1-32 Pick the fabric layers up and make a twist in it - in front of the machine's foot.

Canvas for Cruisers

Section 2
Techniques

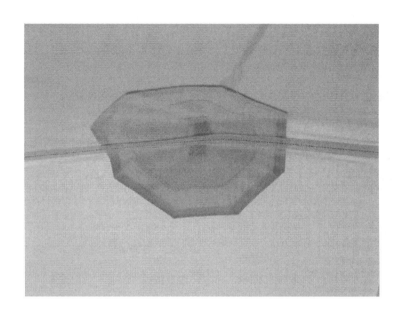

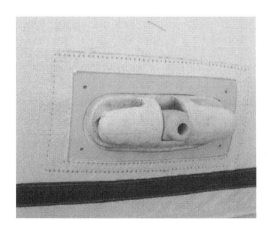

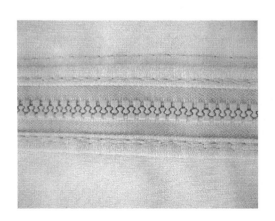

Canvas for Cruisers

Seams and Tension

"Pinning Out" the fabric:

The trickiest part of sewing seams is to get the two pieces of fabric to have the same tension at the seam line. In other words, the seam lays nice and flat and one side or the other is not puckered. This is a technique that takes practice.

To pin out a Lapped Seam:
Cut out the pieces of fabric and lay one piece flat on the floor (*right* side down). Drive a scratch awl into one corner, within the seam allowance. Go to the other end of the fabric. Pull the fabric against the scratch awl so that you get a slight stretch on the fabric, and then drive a scratch awl into that corner to hold it in place. Now apply the seamstick just inside of the raw edge. Seamstick tends to pucker fabric, so it is important to apply the seamstick to stretched fabric. (If you are applying seamstick to nylon webbing, really stretch out the webbing before applying the seamstick).

Remove the scratch awl from one corner. Place the other piece of fabric to be joined on top (just like you were going to pin the fabric together with straight pins, only you aren't going to pin it). Match up the corners and bang in the scratch awl again. Go to the other corner. Remove this scratch awl. Take the corner of one of the panels of fabric in one hand, and the other panel in the other hand. Pull slightly to 'feel' the equal tension between the two panels. When you have an even tension, drive the scratch awl into the fabric to hold it down at this end. Now, with both ends pinned down; you can crawl over and pull off the seamstick paper, all at once. Make sure the edges are overlapped nice and straight and even. Press down with your fingers to stick the pieces of fabric together. Then roll the seam down hard to stick it securely in place (especially on Sunbrella).
In this book, when I say 'pin it out' this is what I mean.

This technique of getting an even tension works equally well on zippers.

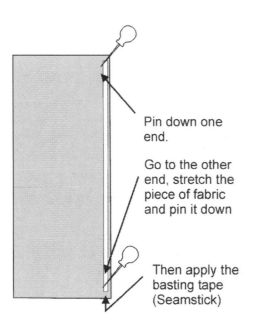

Pin down one end.

Go to the other end, stretch the piece of fabric and pin it down

Then apply the basting tape (Seamstick)

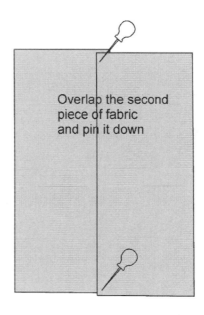

Overlap the second piece of fabric and pin it down

Then go to this end. Remove the scratch awl. Hold one piece of fabric in each hand. Stretch slightly to achieve equal tension. Pin this end down.

Types of Seams

A seam is a line of stitching that joins two pieces of fabric together. The seam allowance is the amount of fabric between the stitching line and the raw edge. In this book, assume a ½" seam allowance unless otherwise specified.

Lapped Seam (Fig 2-1) – this seam is used to join large panels of fabric to make awnings, biminis and other large projects, or when a simple join is all that is required. This seam can be prone to leaking depending on the thread and the fabric.

To make a lapped seam:
Simply overlap the edges of the fabric by ½" or ¾", getting the tension even by 'pinning out' as described above. Stitch 2 rows – one row close to each selvedge or hot-knifed edge.
This seam will not work if the raw edges are cut with scissors and the fabric is subject to fraying.

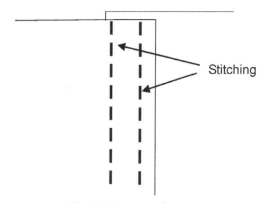

Fig 2-1 Lapped Seam

Topstitched Seam – Also called a Semi-Flat-Felled Seam, this is a little more waterproof, but still not as good as the flat-felled seam described next.

Step 1 – Place the two pieces of fabric *right* sides together. Stitch a seam ½" from the raw edge (Fig 2-2). If cutting with scissors and the fabric is subject to fraying, finish the raw edges by zig zagging or serging.

Step 2 – Open out flat. Fold both the seam allowances over to one side. Topstitch (sew a row of stitches parallel to the first row) to catch in the seam allowance (Fig 2-3).

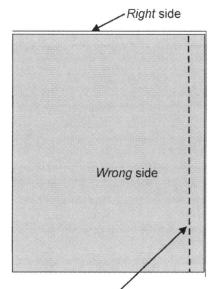

Right side

Wrong side

Fig 2-2 - Stitch *right* sides together.

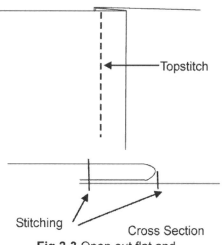

Topstitch

Stitching

Cross Section

Fig 2-3 Open out flat and topstitch

Flat-felled Seam - This seam is strong, quite waterproof, and looks good from both *right* and *wrong* sides.

Step 1 – On the *right* side of one of the pieces of fabric to be joined, stick a line of seamstick close to the raw edge. Place the fabric *right* sides together, so that the raw edges are offset by 1/2". (Fig 2-4)

Step 2 – Apply seamstick to the *right* side of the offset edge. Fold the ½" offset edge up and over and stick down. (Fig 2-5).

Step 3 – Now flip the top piece back over so it lies flat. Stitch one seam, close to one of the folded edges Flip the project over and stitch close to the folded edge on the other side. (Fig 2-6).

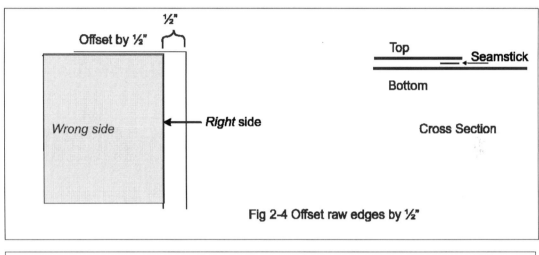

Fig 2-4 Offset raw edges by ½"

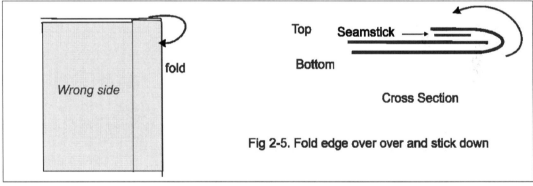

Fig 2-5. Fold edge over over and stick down

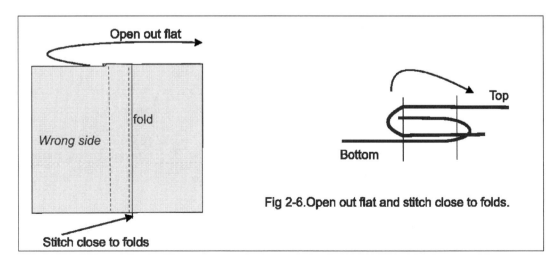

Fig 2-6.Open out flat and stitch close to folds.

37

Topstitching

Topstitching adds strength to a seam, and makes things look nicer and more finished.
Usually you use the machine's foot as a guide (Fig 2-7), or you can topstitch close to the fold.

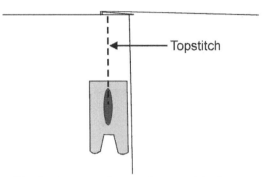

Fig 2-7 Line up the sewing machine's foot along the fold line and make a row of stitches

Fig 2-8 Stretch the seam open with both hands as you topstitch

Wrong - top piece is folded slightly over the bottom piece

Tips:

1. For seams that will be topstitched, cut the seam allowance a little larger than the normal ½". This will help ensure you catch in the seam allowance when doing the topstitching.

2. Always topstitch with the fabric facing *right* side up. This way you can see that you are making a nice straight line parallel to the fold.

3. As you stitch along, really spread the seam open so that the cushion cover or whatever you are working on doesn't get smaller! (Fig 2-8)

4. Try to start and stop the stitching in an unobtrusive place.

5. For cushions, always topstitch onto the cushion's top panel, not the side panels (Fig 2-9).

6. When topstitching projects that will be outdoors exposed to the elements, consider which way water will drain. Fold the seam allowances toward the top as shown in Fig 2-10 so that water doesn't soak into the seam.

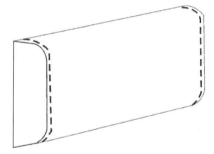

Fig 2-9 Topstitch on the cushion front, not the side panels.

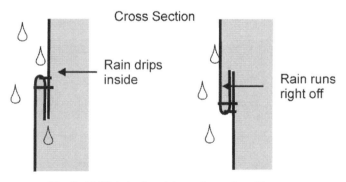

Fig 2-10 Think about how the rain will run off and fold the seam allowance so the rain won't run inside.

Zippers

Canvas work involves the installation of various types and sizes of zippers. Whether you are using continuous zipper chain, or jacket type zippers, you will need to put on the zipper slider head or change the one that came with the jacket zipper. The head can be put on from either side – the large opening or the small. It's a little easier to put it on using the large openings in the head part.

Separate the two sides of the zipper tape to expose about an inch or so of the teeth.
(Fig 2-11). Then insert the ends of the zipper teeth into the large openings of the head. Get both ends in there at the same time so they are lined up nice and even, and then pull the head by its puller up the length of the zip. It's a bit fiddly, but you get used to it.

If you are putting the zip head on using its small opening, the zipper must be fully closed. Position the small opening of the zip head against the zipper teeth and push it on, forcing the teeth to separate.

Sewing on Zippers

Step 1 – Prepare the fabric – Pin out the fabric as described in the beginning of this Section. Stretch it out slightly and apply ½" seamstick to the seam allowance of raw edges where the zip is to go. Turn the edge under and stick it down (Fig 2-12).

Step 2 – Finish the zipper ends if necessary – see below (Zipper Ends), and put on the head. Lay the zipper out flat. Stab mushroom pins or scratch awls into each end of the zip and stretch it out reasonably taut. (See Fig 2-13).

Step 3 –
Apply ¼" seamstick to both of the zipper tapes. (Fig 2-13) Remove the pins or awls.

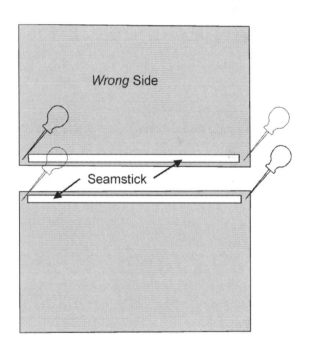

Fig 2-12 Stretch out fabric and apply

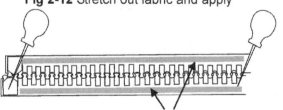

Fig 2-13 Pin zipper out and apply seamstick to both sides.

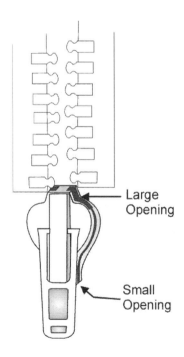

Fig 2-11

Step 4 - Peel a little paper from one end of the seamstick and stick the zipper down to the required spot. Pin this end down with a scratch awl.
Peel a little paper from the other end and stick it down to its required spot. Pin this end in place, stretching the zipper across the required space. Now peel off all the rest of the paper. Stick the zipper down with your fingers nice and straight and even. Then roll down hard with the seam roller. The teeth can be exposed or covered by the fold of the fabric.

Step 5 – Stitch two rows if the zipper will be subject to strain, such as a dodger or bimini. Otherwise just one row is necessary for things like upholstery and shade curtains.

Note - If you are working with vinyl or mesh, you can get away with not having to turn the edges under, because they won't fray like canvas.

Zipper Ends

Zipper ends or stops are used when changing the length of a zip when you want to prevent the head from sliding right off the end.
You can buy commercially made stops, but it is just as easy to make them yourself:

Vinyl end stops

Step 1 – (Fig 2-14) Cut out small rectangles of vinyl – Shelterite or other all-purpose vinyl, about 1 ¾" by ½". Stick ½" seamstick to one side of it. You will need 2 pieces for each zipper. If you are making a bunch, cut out ½' strips, stick on the seamstick and then cut into 1 ¾" lengths.

1 3/4"   ½"

Fig 2-14

Step 2 – Without peeling off the paper, fold the little piece in half, and trim the corners as shown in Fig 2-15.

Step 3 – Take the zipper, and with a pencil, mark the exact length it needs to be. (Not to state the obvious, but make sure you shorten a jacket zipper at the loose ends, not at the end that has the connection fitting!)
If you haven't done so already, put on the zip head. Stick the little vinyl piece over the teeth so that the fold goes between the teeth, and the edge of the vinyl piece is at the marked line (Fig 2-16).
Cut the zipper off at the marked line. With a hot knife, singe the raw edge of the zip to give it a nice finish.

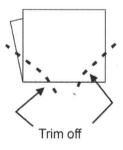

Trim off

Fig 2-15

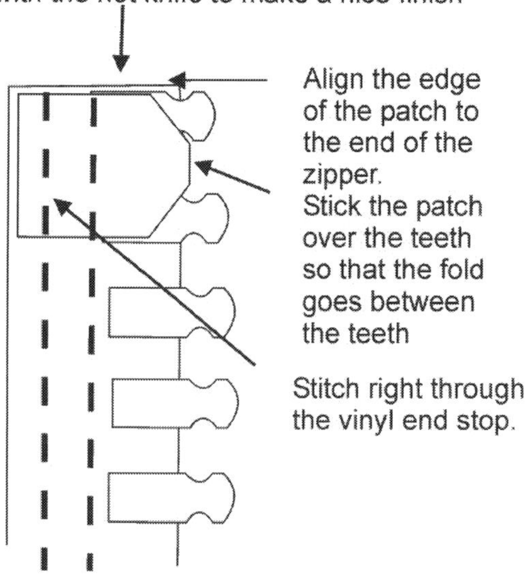

Singe this end of the zipper tape with the hot knife to make a nice finish

Align the edge of the patch to the end of the zipper.
Stick the patch over the teeth so that the fold goes between the teeth

Stitch right through the vinyl end stop.

Fig 2-16 Zipper end

Top Patch – This technique can be used to provide a good looking finish for the ends of a continuous zip. In this example, we are working on a mesh back (shade) curtain which is split up the center. It will open from a hemmed bottom edge upwards to a patch which will keep the top edges together (Fig 2-17).

Step 1 – On the *wrong* side of the fabric, mark the centerline with a pencil.

Step 2 – Cut a length of continuous zip about an inch longer than you need it. Finish one end of the zipper with little vinyl ends as described earlier. (Fig 2-16).

Step 3 – On the *wrong* side of the fabric, place the closed zip along the centerline. Place the end of the zip with the vinyl end stops at the bottom edge (hem). Leave the inch extra hanging out the top edge.
Stitch the zip in place – either stick it down with seamstick (if using fabric or vinyl) or make hatch marks and stitch freehand (if using mesh fabric).

Hatch marks is a technique of making tiny pencil marks on adjoining pieces so that when the project is being sewn you can match up the pieces.

Step 4 – Carefully slit an opening along the center, between the two rows of stitches with a seam ripper
Step 5 – Optional – finish the raw edges of the opening – see Zipper Edge Finishes next.

Step 6 – Split open the zipper where it is hanging out at the top edge and put on the head using its large openings. (That little extra length hanging out the end makes it easier to put on the head.) Once the head is on, trim off this excess length of zipper.

Step 7 – Cut out a piece of vinyl for the end patch. It can be any shape – usually square or triangle. Cut out another one a little larger. (Fig 2-18 & 2-19)

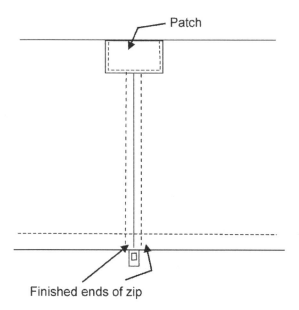

Fig 2-17 Top Patch

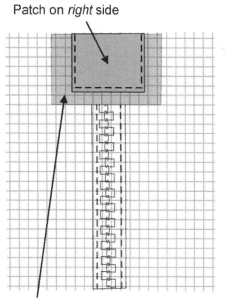

Fig 2-18 Details of top patch

41

Step 8 – Seamstick the smaller patch onto the *right* side. Flip the project over. Apply seamstick to the *wrong* side of the fabric within the patch which is on the other side. Stick the larger patch down so that it completely covers the area of the patch on the other side.

With *right* side up, topstitch all around the edges of the patch. Flip the piece over and trim off the excess fabric on the patch on the *wrong* side, close to the stitching line (Fig 2-19).

If you want to make an opening like this in canvas, you will have to finish the edges after slitting the zipper opening or the canvas will fray.

To finish the edges, you can bind them – see Zipper Edge Finishes next. Or a better way is to cut two separate panels of fabric, and install a zipper as outlined above ('Sewing on Zippers') Zip the two pieces together and then apply an end patch as in Steps 7 & 8 above.

Making a Separating Zipper

There can be times when you need a separating zipper that is longer than standard sizes – such as for an on-boom sail cover. Or if your project requires many zippers it can be cheaper to make your own.

This is not as pretty as a factory made jacket zipper or as easy to use, but it will function just fine. A factory-made jacket zipper has a box on one side – to replace this you will make a vinyl stop to keep the head from coming off.
On the other side, the factory-made jacket zipper has a plastic end which fits into the box – you will replace this with nothing. Instead, you will be inserting the first zipper tooth into the zipper head to get the zipper started.

This can be done for zippers with teeth, or coil type zippers, and also for #10 or #5.

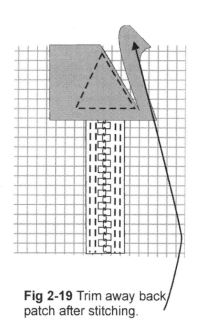

Fig 2-19 Trim away back patch after stitching.

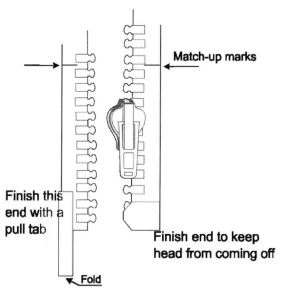

Fig 2-19a Making a Jacket Zipper
Finish one end with a zipper stop, and the other end with a tab.

Step 1 – Cut a length of continuous zipper a couple of inches longer than you need.

Step 2 – Separate one end of the zipper a few inches - enough to put on the head onto one side of the zipper tape. Put the head on so that the big openings are away from the cut end of the zipper (see Fig 2-19a)

Step 3 – Finish off the zipper tape with the head on it, using a vinyl end stop. You could instead, use ½" webbing folded over the end teeth, or you can melt the teeth together with a hot knife.

Step 4 – Finish off the other end of the zipper tape with a piece of ½" webbing, folded over the fabric part of the tape and not covering the teeth. This is used as a pull tab for something to grab on to when you go to push in the first tooth to get the zipper started.

Step 5 – Install the zipper onto the project just like you would a jacket zipper as described earlier in this section "Sewing on Zippers" Make sure you stitch through the little webbing piece and the zipper end stops, so they don't fall off.

Step 6 – To use the zipper, you take the end with the long webbing pull tab, and fit the first tooth into the zipper head, using the pull tab to help get it in there.
If it is critical that the teeth match up exactly, make a couple of match up marks on the zipper tape as shown in Fig 2-19a. Then before you zip too far, you can make sure the match up marks match.

Zipper Edge Finishes

The edge of the fabric where it meets the zipper can be left raw, if you are using vinyl or mesh and you're not concerned with looks (eg cushion bottom).

Raw edges on mesh sometimes can get caught in the zipper head so you can bind the edge to avoid this and make it look nice. The raw edge is not such an issue if it's a cushion bottom and you don't really use the zipper that much.

In the case with canvas the edge should be folded for it to be strong and look good. Use the 'original' technique as first described in this section (pg 39)

Bound Edge – A bound edge looks especially nice on a mesh edge

Step 1 – Install the zipper as outlined in - Top Patch Steps 1 through 4.

Step 2 – Separate the 2 sides completely. With the zipper side on top (that is, *wrong* side up), fold back the zipper teeth out of the way. Stitch double fold vinyl binding all along the raw edge of the mesh. Don't use seamstick, just hold the binding in place and stitch.

Step 3 – Continue with Steps 6 through 8 in the above instructions on Top Patch.

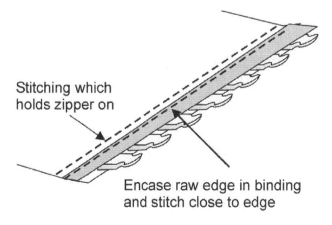

Stitching which holds zipper on

Encase raw edge in binding and stitch close to edge

Fig 2-20 Binding a zip edge

Turned-In Edge – This edge finish will leave the zipper teeth exposed. It looks nice on fairly lightweight vinyl but don't be surprised if it looks a little puckered.

Step 1 – Stick the (closed) zip onto the *wrong* side of the fabric as usual. Stitch very close to the edge of the zipper tape (Fig 2-21).

Step 2 – Turn the work *right* side up. Open up the center by making a nice straight slit between the two rows of stitching with the seam ripper.

Step 3 – Still working with the *right* side of the fabric on top, fold the raw edge under. Make the fold nice and straight, and make sure it clears the zipper teeth. If you used seamstick to stick the zipper down, the seamstick will help hold the edge folded in place.

Topstitch close to this fold (Fig 2-22).

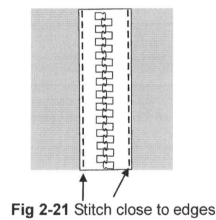

Fig 2-21 Stitch close to edges

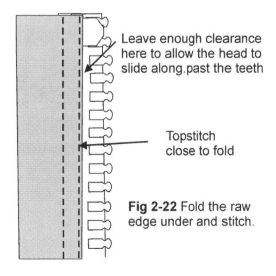

Leave enough clearance here to allow the head to slide along.past the teeth

Topstitch close to fold

Fig 2-22 Fold the raw edge under and stitch.

Zipper on a Curve – Sometimes you have to install a zipper on a curved edge, for example, a dodger with an opening roll-up window in the shape of a smile. The secret is to stitch the Outside curve first.

Step 1 – Apply seamstick to both zipper tapes (Fig 2-13).

Usually it is easiest to separate the 2 zipper halves before trying to place the zipper onto the fabric or vinyl. Mark a curved line onto the fabric or vinyl the shape you need. Place the teeth of the one zipper tape along the marked line so that the zip's tape is along the OUTSIDE of the curve. Gradually remove the seamstick paper on the zipper and stick on the outside curve. Stretch out the fabric tape part of the zip slightly. The teeth of the zipper will tend to crunch in together a little. This is OK as long as it is not <u>really</u> crunched in. Stitch this half on.

If the teeth of the zipper crunch in together too much, the zipper won't work properly. You should use a coil-type zipper for tighter curves.

Step 2 - Put the head of the zipper on, and zip the 2 halves back together. Remove the paper of the zip half going on the inside curve – a little at a time. Gather the zip nice and even with your fingers as you stick it down – and then roll down flat with a seam roller.

Step 3 – Stitch the inside curve.

See Section 5 Dodger for more information on finishing the edges of the 'smile'

Fig 2-23 Zipper on a Curve

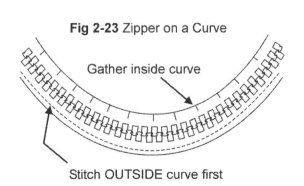

Gather inside curve

Stitch OUTSIDE curve first

Zipper on the Underside of a Cushion Bottom

Most cushions use a #5 size zipper for a closure, so that the foam can be stuffed inside. (I say most because I have used Velcro too). Zippers are often installed in the side bands of the cushion; if the zipper goes around one side plus part of one or two <u>other</u> sides of the cushion, it gets much easier to stuff it.

It is very easy to put the zipper in the bottom, although it can be harder to stuff especially if you are using very dense foam.

Quite often undersides of cushions are made of some kind of vinyl mesh fabric, to allow water to drain away, to reduce cost and to allow the foam inside to breathe.

Position the zipper along any straight-grain of the mesh. A zipper can also be placed along the diagonal of a mesh bottom, but only if the bottom is made of a tight-weave mesh. If you try to sew in a zip on a diagonal to the grain using a more open weave mesh, it will go all distorted and look horrible – the mesh is just too loose.

The following instructions are for the installation of the zipper – for much more information on actually making cushions, refer to Section 6.

<u>Step 1</u> – Cut out the cushion bottom piece and lay it down flat. Mark a pencil line on the *wrong* side of the fabric, where the zipper is going to go. (Fig 2-24) Place the line near the center and make it as long as reasonably possible. This will make it easier to stuff the foam inside.

Depending on the job, and the fabric, you can stitch the end of the zipper right into the seam allowance, or cut the zipper off short of the seam allowance if you think it will make too much of a bump in the seam (Fig 2-25).

<u>Step 2</u> – Place the closed #5 size zipper with its teeth centered over the line you have marked. Mark some hatch marks to help you line things up evenly. If the fabric is mesh, stitch 'freehand' (i.e. do not stick down with seamstick). Stitch as follows (See Fig 2-26):

Start a couple of inches from one end, no backstitch required. Line up the sewing machine foot with the edge of the teeth for a nice straight line. Stitch down to about two inches from the other end, and stop.

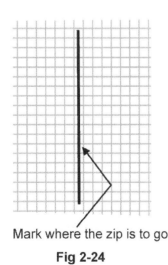

Mark where the zip is to go

Fig 2-24

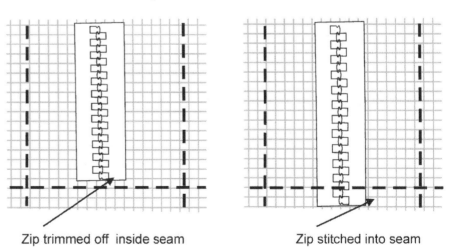

Zip trimmed off inside seam   Zip stitched into seam

Fig 2-25 Trim off the zip short of the seam allowance if you think it will make too much of a bump if it is stitched into the seam.

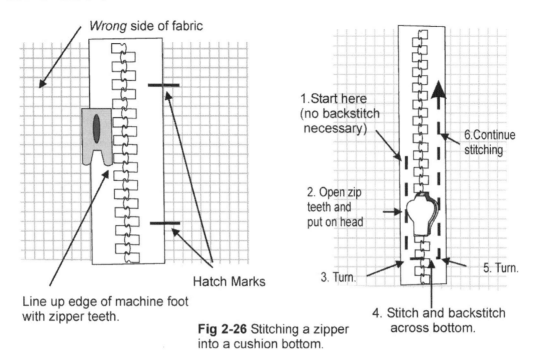

Fig 2-26 Stitching a zipper into a cushion bottom.

Leaving the needle in the fabric, open up the end of the zip a little and put on the head, inserting the teeth into the head's big openings and ensuring the head is face down (i.e. with the zipper pull tab facing the fabric). Slide the head up past the sewing machine's foot. The zipper teeth at the end of the zipper should be closed again after this is done. Now continue stitching to the end. Stitch across the end over the teeth (carefully so you don't break the needle), and up the length along the other side. Stop short of the other end as before. If you are going to have 2 zip heads, put another head on at this end – from the head's big openings as before.

Stitch across the end and back along the couple of inches on the other side. Slide the head(s) up or down, working them around the sewing machine's foot to allow the machine's foot to get by as you sew. If this is difficult, then leave the needle in the 'down' position and raise the foot so you can push the head past.

Overlap a few stitches where you first started, to anchor the thread.

Step 3 – Flip the fabric piece over, so it is *right* side up. Cut a slit carefully down the center between the rows of stitches with a seam ripper, to make the opening. (Fig 2-27) Don't slit the mesh all the way across from one end of the cushion bottom to the other. The little uncut sections at the ends will serve to keep the zip head on. You can leave the raw edges of the mesh raw because, being on the underside of the cushion, they will not be seen.

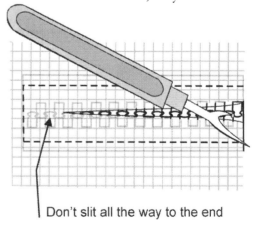

Don't slit all the way to the end

Fig 2-27 Slit open

Double Zipper – this technique is used when you make 2-part seat cushions – the type that has a piece of foam for the seat, and a separate piece for the backrest. Like on a lawn chair or patio chair. These cushions are connected together but capable of being folded in half for storage.

Step 1 – Cut out two pieces of fabric the full size of the seat plus the back (don't forget to add the seam allowances). Cut one of these pieces in 2 – one section for the seat and one section for the backrest (Fig 2-28). Use the cut-in-two piece of fabric as a pattern to cut out 1" or 2" thick foam.

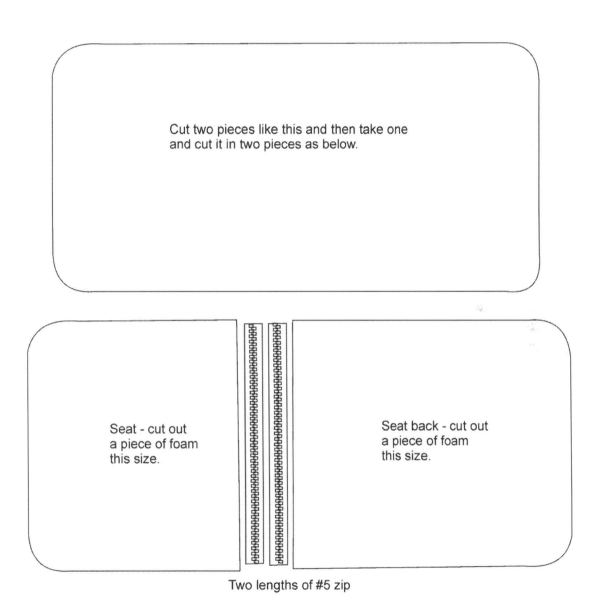

Cut two pieces like this and then take one and cut it in two pieces as below.

Seat - cut out a piece of foam this size.

Seat back - cut out a piece of foam this size.

Two lengths of #5 zip

Fig 2-28 Pieces for the double zip seat

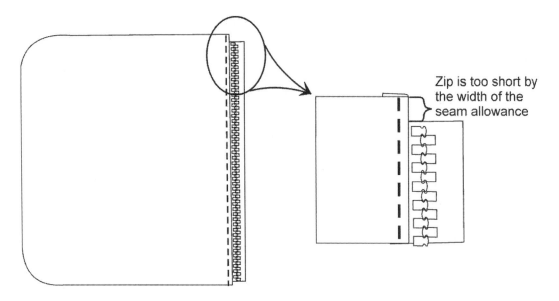

Fig 2-29 Turn the straight edges under and stitch one side of the zip tape so the teeth are exposed.

Step 2 – Cut 2 lengths of continuous #5 zip. The length to cut is the width of the cushion, minus the seam allowances at each end. (E.g. if you use ½" seam allowances, cut the zip 1" too short for the width of the cushion.)

Step 3 – Working with the piece of fabric you cut into 2 halves, apply ½" seamstick to the *wrong* side of the straight edges of both halves and turn under by ½".

Apply seamstick to one of the tapes of each zip. Don't put seamstick on the other half of the zipper tapes yet.

Stick and stitch one side of one of the closed zips to the folded edge of the seat, and the other zip to the folded edge of the seat back. Make sure the teeth are exposed as shown in Fig 2-29.

Step 4 – Overlap the remaining two (unstitched) tapes over each other and seamstick them together. Don't stitch them together yet (see Fig 2-30) Put on the zipper heads.

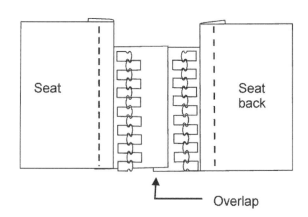

Fig 2-30 Overlap the two Zippers

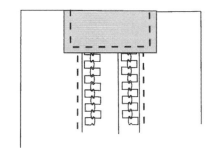

Fig 2-31 Patch of vinyl sewn over the ends

Step 5 – Cut out 2 rectangles of vinyl and stitch one piece across each end to keep the zip heads on (Fig 2-31).

Step 6 – With *right* sides together, sew the zipper assembly piece to the still-intact front piece all around the outside edges (Fig 2-32). Leave one of the zips open so you can turn it *right* side out later.

Step 7 – Carefully turn *right* side out – remember, you still have the 2 zips just stuck together with seamstick. Lay out the project nice and flat. Stitch down the center where you stuck the 2 zips together through all thicknesses (Fig 2-33).

Step 8 – Stuff with the foam.

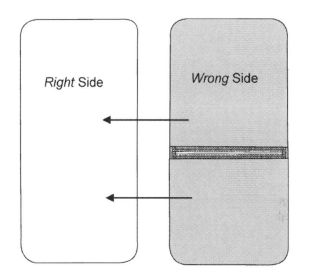

Fig 2-32 Place the two pieces *right* sides together. Stitch all around the outside edge

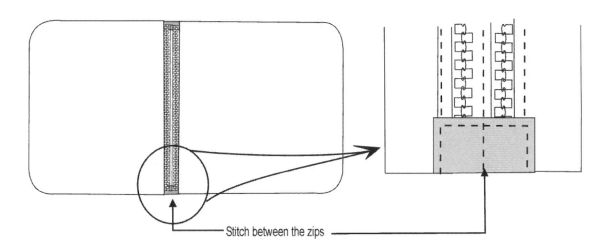

Stitch between the zips

Fig 2-33

Piping

Piping is used to strengthen edges, firm up the shape and make them more attractive. The piping can be of the same colour or contrasting colour to the main fabric. Some people love it, and others hate it, saying it is uncomfortable to sit on, and collects dirt.

To make piping:

Step 1 – Cut 2" strips of fabric.

If you are making a lot of piping, try to find a 2" wide yardstick. Then it is easy to mark out long 2" wide strips. Make them as long as possible. If you are making cushions for example, try to arrange the cushion pieces when you are cutting them out so that you are left with a long strip along one side of the fabric. This you can use for the piping.

NOTE – Fabric piping should really be cut on the bias, but this can take a lot of extra fabric. But if you want perfect piping, cut it on the bias.

If you are working with Sunbrella, you can cut it along the lengthwise grain and it will be OK, but not perfect as it would be if you cut on the bias. Don't cut it along the fabric's width because it will be hard to get the finished piping to curve around corners and curves without making little wrinkles in the piping fabric.

Step 2 – Hold the strips *right* sides together (which doesn't matter for Sunbrella) at 90 degrees to each other. Stitch across the diagonal and trim off the excess seam allowance to ½" (Fig 2-34).

Use a short stitch length or stitch it twice – this ensures that the piping welting inside does not show through the finished piping at the seam.

Crease the seam allowance open and staple it if necessary to keep it open.

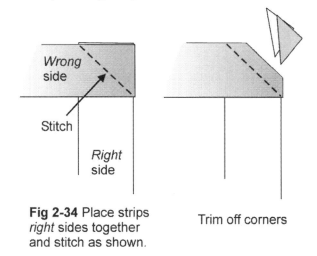

Fig 2-34 Place strips *right* sides together and stitch as shown.

Trim off corners

Step 3 – Fold the strip in half along its length, *wrong* sides together, with the piping inside like a hot dog in a bun. Hold it shut, and stitch a comfortable ½" in from the raw edge (Fig 2-35). This row of stitches just serves to hold the piping inside the fabric.

Fig 2-35 Fold the 2" strip in half with the piping welting inside and stitch ½"away from the raw edge.

Step 4 – If you have a piping foot for your machine, place the groove of the foot over the piping cord, otherwise, use a zipper foot. Stitch close to the piping welting so that the welting is snug inside. (Fig 2-36) Careful, though. If you stitch it too tight, this stitching will show when you go to attach it to the cushion. If you stitch it too loose, you will have trouble getting the piping to be nice and tight around sharp corners. It takes a bit of practice.

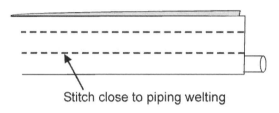

Stitch close to piping welting

Fig 2-36

Step 5 – Trim off the excess fabric along the first line of stitches (Fig 2-37), which should leave a ½" seam allowance. For Sunbrella, use a hot knife.

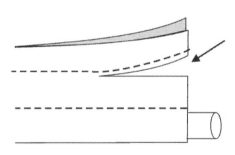

Fig 2-37

If you think this is too many steps, you can cut out and join 1 ¼" wide strips. Fold it in half lengthwise, hold and sew close to the piping all in one step. This, however, is fiddly, hard to do accurately and murder on your hands. Better to use the two step method described above.

Attaching piping:

Stitching piping to fabric is not as simple as it looks. This is another technique that takes a bit of practice.

Step 1 – Staple the made-up piping to the *right* side of the cushion top or bottom, matching the raw edges. Clip curves & corners (for Sunbrella use a hot knife). See Fig 2-38.

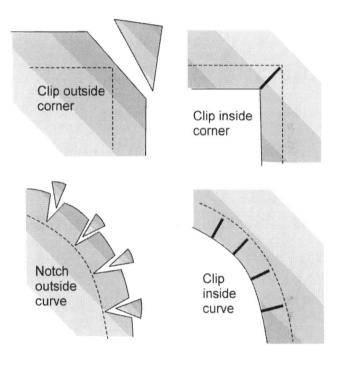

Clip outside corner

Clip inside corner

Notch outside curve

Clip inside curve

Fig 2-38 Trimming corners and curves.

When stapling, keep in mind that you will have to remove all those staples when you are finished sewing. Before you start to staple, think about which way to face the staples so that you can get at them to remove them, and not have them hidden inside seam allowances. The natural tendency is to have the cushion panel underneath and lay the piping on top – then staple. However, this will leave the flat part of the staple (the side you grab to pull it out) buried inside the seam allowance. Then you will have to dig around to make sure you remove them all. Think about it. In this case, hold the stapler upside down to staple the piping on (Fig 2-39).

Step 2 – Staple on the other layer of fabric, sandwiching the piping in between.

Step 3 – Stitch close to the piping welting. (Fig 2-39). The idea is to cover up the row of

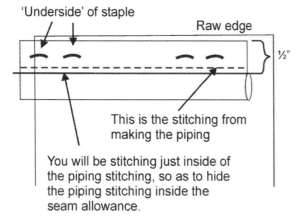

'Underside' of staple

Raw edge

½"

This is the stitching from making the piping

You will be stitching just inside of the piping stitching, so as to hide the piping stitching inside the seam allowance.

Fig 2-39

stitches on the piping, so stitch the welting in nice and tight.

When you are finished stitching, stretch the seam open from the *right* side and check to see how tight the piping is stitched in – you should not be able to see any stitching showing through from the piping. If you need to get the piping tighter to cover up any parts where the piping stitches show, flip the piece over, and stitch those sections again.

Hints – With Sunbrella, especially around corners and tight curves, you will get less puckers in the piping and a much easier job if the piping's welting is already stitched fairly tight before you even start attaching it to the cushion piece.

When using vinyl, which is stretchy, you will get less of a wavy look if you stretch the piping piece slightly more than the cushion piece.

If you don't want to do all the stapling, stitch it freehand – but hold the assembly with the cushion piece on top, and the piping underneath. On machines without a walking foot, this allows the machine to feed the piping through better.

Joining Piping

To join the ends of piping to each other, such as when you are installing piping all around a cushion, there are a couple of ways to do this.

Start stitching the piping a couple of inches from the beginning of the piping. When you come all the way around the cushion and back to where you started, stop stitching a couple of inches short of the join.
Cut the piping off – but leave an inch or so spare.

Lap the ends over each other and mark where the piping has to join together .

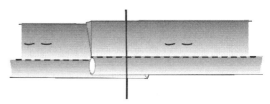

Overlap the two piping pieces. Mark where they will have to join, about 1" from each end.

Take out a couple of inches of stitches in each of the ends of the piping and open out the fabric strips.
Place the fabric ends *right* sides together and staple to hold in place.

Staple the raw edges together and stitch along the marked line.

Holding the piping cord ends out of the way, stitch the piping fabric ends together, using small stitches. Yes, it is a fiddly job.

Trim the seam to ½"

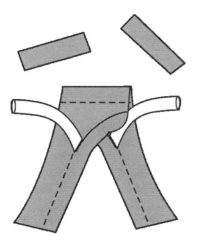

Trim seam allowances to 1/2"

Open out the seam. Cut off the piping cord so that it is ½" short on each side. This way there won't be a bump where the fabric's seam allowance covers the piping cord.

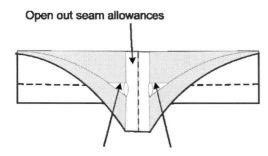

Open out seam allowances

Cut off piping cord just short of the seam allowance, and tuck back inside the fabric strip.

Re-assemble the piping by tucking the cord back inside the fabric strip.

Joining Piping – non-sewn method

Joining the piping by stitching the ends together is definitely the neatest way to do the job. But if this is just too fiddly for you to stand, you can simply lap or fold the end over as follows:

If the fabric is vinyl:

Start stitching the piping a couple of inches from the beginning of the piping. Once you are around to where you started, stop a few inches from the end. Remove the piping stitching a couple of inches so you can get at the cording inside.

Lap the piping ends over each other so you can tell where the piping cord meets. Cut the piping cord so the two ends meet.

Now, cut the vinyl end about ½" too long. Since the raw end won't fray, you can simply wrap this ½" vinyl end around the other layer of piping and keep on stitching.

This doesn't look as good as the stitched method described earlier but might be good enough.

About 1/2"

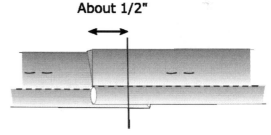

Trim the piping cord so the ends meet.

Wrap the 1/2" around and continue stitching

Canvas for Cruisers

If the fabric is woven

The lap-over method described previously for vinyl won't really work because the fabric will fray over time and look awful.

So when you are stitching on the piping, stop about 3" from the end.
Unpick the stitching from the piping and trim the piping cord so the ends meet.

Make a fold in the fabric part of the piping – this fold should be at a 45 degree angle if you are working with Sunbrella or upholstery fabric to reduce bulkiness. It can be 90 degrees for lightweight materials.

Now just overlap the folded edge onto the other piping piece and continue sewing.

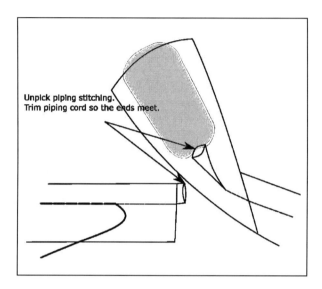

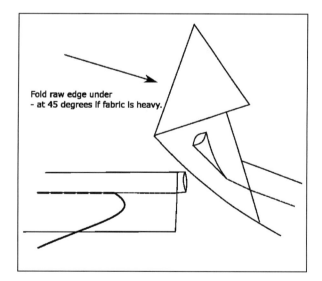

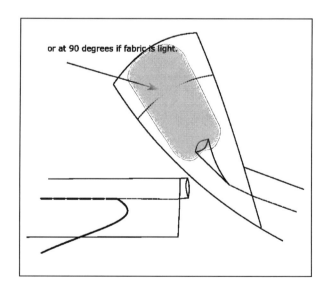

To make piping 'disappear' into a seam:

1. Disappearing into a corner:

This is commonly seen on a 2-piece seat cushion set or V-berth mattress, where there is piping all around except where they meet (Fig 2-40).

Staple the piping onto the fabric as described above, extending the end of the piping out past the seam allowance to the end of the fabric as shown in Fig 2-41.

Force the piping cord out of the casing and trim it off about ¼" short of the seam allowance where the corner will be.

Stitch like a normal 90 degree corner – that is, stitch along one seam to within ½" of the end.

Leave the needle in the 'down' position, raise the foot and pivot the fabric 90 degrees. Stitch along the next seam.

Because the cord is a little too short, it is easier to stitch because you don't have to stitch through the cord. Also there won't be a hard edge poking through the fabric.

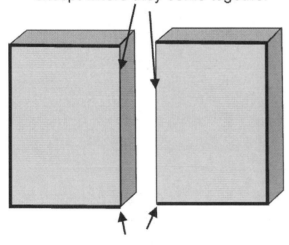

Cushions have piping all around except where they come together

Piping has to 'disappear' into these corners

Fig 2-40

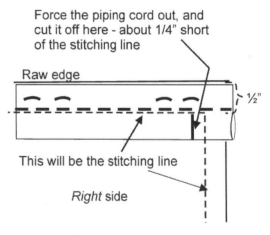

Force the piping cord out, and cut it off here - about 1/4" short of the stitching line

Raw edge

½"

This will be the stitching line

Right side

Fig 2-41 Disappearing into a Corner

2. <u>Disappearing on a straightaway</u>.

You would use this technique if say, you have piping showing on the front of the cushion but don't need to have it go all the way around to the back or side where you can't see it.

Staple the piping onto the fabric. Curve the end of the piping so that it curves off the edge of the fabric at the place you want it to disappear. See Fig 2-42.

Force the piping cord out of its casing and trim it off to just short of the seam allowance. This way you won't have to stitch through the piping cord. Sew the seam as usual.

Piping on a curve:

Installing piping along a curved piece of fabric is a little tricky – you need to get the tension right as follows:

<u>Inside curve</u> – On an inside curve, the piping should be a little taut, or it will go all wavy when you turn the piece *right* side out. So when you are stapling on the piping, just stretch it ever so slightly so it's nice and taut.

<u>Outside curve</u> – Similarly, on an outside curve, leave the piping a little loose, to allow for the extra length required on an outside curve. If you make the piping too taut, the piping will pull the fabric in too much and it will look all puckery.

This is actually easier said than done. One way to make it a little easier is to match up the raw edge of the piping to the raw edge of the fabric and hold it there. Then sort of stretch and pivot the piping cord down onto the fabric away from the raw edge. (Fig 2-43) Staple in place.

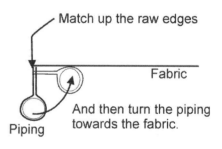

Fig 2-43 Piping on a Curve

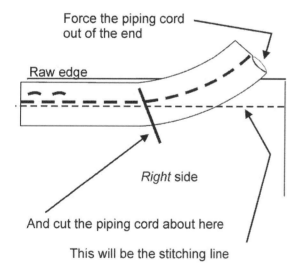

Fig 2-42 Disappearing into a straightaway

Another way is to use mushroom pins or scratch awls – staple the one end – (piping to fabric). Pin it to the table to hold it down. Go to the other end and position the piping onto the fabric. Stretch either the piping or the fabric depending on which side you want the most tension on, then staple this end. Now you can go along and staple in between.

Parallel rows of Piping:

If you are putting piping on both the top and bottom edges of a box cushion, you need to carefully match the tension between the 2 lines of piping. You also need to make sure that the two lines of piping are parallel and straight. The easiest way to do this is to staple the two lines of piping to the long side panel strip – not to the top and bottom pieces. Then staple on the top and the bottom. (More on this in Section 6 - Cushions)

Lay the side panel strip out nice and flat. Staple the piping to the *right* side of each edge of the side panel (Fig 2-44) with raw edges matching and the cord of the piping facing towards the center of the side panel. Measure carefully to make sure the 2 lines of piping are parallel and straight.

Keep the tension even so that, after stapling and stitching, the side panel still lays out nice and flat and straight, and does not curve one way or the other.

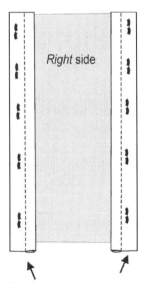

Fig 2-44 Staple the piping along both edges.
The piece should still lay straight and flat after you're finished stapling

Boltrope

Boltrope is a rope (usually plastic) encased in a tape of fabric which enables you to sew the rope to the fabric. It is a good way to make a strong attachment of fabric or cushions to a hard surface. This method of attachment can be used for cockpit cushions, shade curtains, windshields and hanging bags & pouches.

Fold the raw edge of the fabric under ½".

Cut the boltrope 1" – 1 ½" longer than required. See Fig 2-45.

Place the fold of the fabric about 1/8" away from the 'rope' of the boltrope, to allow clearance for the track. Center the fabric along the boltrope to leave the excess ½" or ¾" of boltrope hanging out at each end. This makes it easier to feed the piece into the track, and prevents the edges tearing from overstraining these points.

Stitch the boltrope on with 2 rows of stitches, backstitching well at each end, where it takes the strain most.

Install the track on to the surface and then slide the boltrope piece into the track.

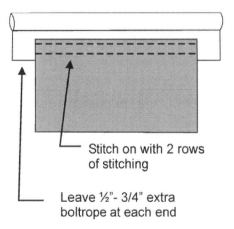

Stitch on with 2 rows of stitching

Leave ½"- 3/4" extra boltrope at each end

Fig 2-45

Hems & Casings:

This section gives details on the different types of hems, when to use them and how to stitch them.

Single Hem

A single hem (when the fabric is folded up just once) is typically used when the edge has been cut with a hot knife, and therefore will not fray. A single hem is also used on vinyls or heavy fabrics where a double hem would be too thick

For a single hem (e.g. 1") cut the fabric 1" longer than the actual finished size to allow for the hem allowance.

For a 1" single hem, mark a light pencil line 2" away from the raw edge. The fastest and easiest way is to use a 2" wide yardstick. Making 'hatch marks' as shown in Fig 2-46 helps you to fold the hem straight up from the bottom, and to stitch the hem so there is no 'roping' (twisting) as shown in Fig 2-48.
Make a single fold up to the pencil line and stitch. If you don't trust yourself to avoid 'roping', seamstick the hem in place and then stitch.

This hem is usually not wide enough for grommets or twist lock fasteners – use a 2" double hem for these. It is also not really strong enough for snaps without reinforcing. In this case, insert a length of

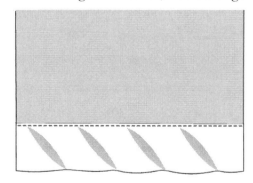

Fig 2-48 Roping - a hem which has twisted during sewing and now is puckered and won't lay flat.

1" webbing inside the hem so that it is hidden from view, then stitch 2 rows – one at the raw edge and one at the foldline, to catch in both sides of the webbing.

If you don't have a hot knife, then you will need to add an extra ½" to allow you to turn the raw edge under. In all the instructions in this book, I am assuming you are cutting out Sunbrella with a hot knife.

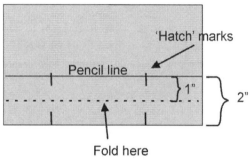

Fig 2-46 1" Single Hem. Mark a line 2" up from the bottom. Fold up to this line and stitch, matching up the hatch marks.

Double Hem

A double hem (when the fabric is folded up and up again) adds strength, weight and structure to the hem. It is usually necessary to use a double hem in order to get enough thickness to allow grommets to get a good 'bite'.

For a double hem (e.g. a 1" double hem) cut the fabric 2" longer. For a 2" double hem, cut the fabric 4" longer.

For a 1" double hem, mark a line 2" from the raw edge. For a 2" double hem, mark a line 4" from the raw edge. (Fig 2-47)

Fold and crease the fabric up to the pencil line. Fold up again along the pencil line and stitch.

Always put a double hem in mesh fabrics if there are going to be grommets in the hem or in the corners. This gives the grommet something to bite into and makes it stronger.

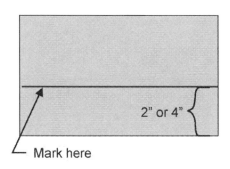

— Mark here

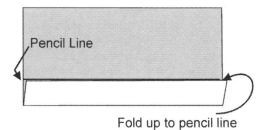

Fold up to pencil line

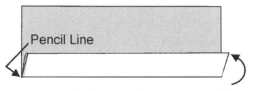

Fold up again along pencil line

Fig 2-47 Double Hem. Mark a pencil line, fold up to the line, fold up again, and stitch.

<u>Stitching hints:</u>

The biggest problem when stitching hems is that the fabric will try to stretch and twist and cause 'roping' (Fig 2-48)

This can be prevented by one of the following:

Seamstick the hem in place prior to stitching – recommended for vinyl.

Staple the hem before stitching. This is marginally OK for Sunbrella but do not staple vinyl because the staples leave holes in the fabric.

Mark hatch marks prior to folding the hem up as shown in Fig 2-46. Line up the hatch marks as you stitch freehand (i.e. no seamstick or staples)

When stitching freehand, it is important how you hold the fabric as it feeds through the machine. Grasp the fabric 'fore' and 'aft' of the sewing machine's foot. Stretch it out as you sew. Hold the 'fore' end (the part closest to you) in your right hand between your thumb and 4 fingers with your thumb on the bottom. Now rotate your hand so that your thumb comes up and your baby finger rests on the sewing table. This twists the fabric up 90 degrees to the sewing table. (see Fig 1-32). Holding the fabric this way makes the bottom layer stretch and the top layer gather very slightly, preventing the 'roping' problem.

When hemming Sunbrella, really stretch the fabric as you sew. It takes practice, since you have to stretch the fabric 'fore' and 'aft' but not interfere with how the machine feeds the fabric through. If the machine is breaking or bending needles, you are probably pulling the fabric through faster than the machine can handle it.

Corner Hems:

<u>Outside Corner</u>:

It is necessary to alleviate the thickness of the many layers of material when you come to the outside corners, especially in a double hem.

As you are sewing along, when you come close to the corner, unfold the hem and trim off as shown in Fig 2-49. Then fold the hem back up again

Stitch the corner as shown in Fig 2-50:
1. Stitch along the hem, folding the trimmed corner over. Remember to match up the hatch marks and stretch out the fabric to avoid 'roping'.
2. At the edge, leave the needle in the down position, and turn the fabric.
3. Stitch to the opposite edge here, where you will turn the piece again.
4. Continue to stitch along the hem.

You will be sewing in this direction

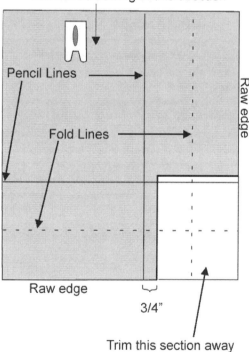

Fig 2-49 Double Hem Outside Corner
Trim off the corner section exactly as shown - just inside of the pencil line on the one side, and 3/4" outside of the line on the next side.

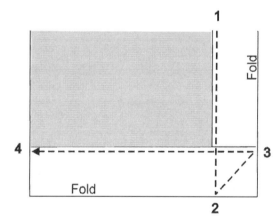

Fig 2-50 Stitching a double hem corner.
1. Start here
2. Stitch to here. Turn.
3. Stitch to here. Turn.
4 Continue stitching the hem.

Now topstitch all around the outside edge as shown in Fig 2-51. It is not as critical for this row of stitches to stretch it out as you sew.

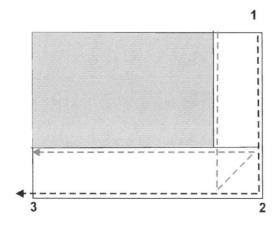

Fig 2-51 Stitching a double hem corner.
1. Start here
2. Turn
3. Continue stitching along edge.

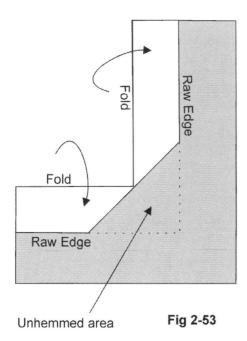

Unhemmed area   **Fig 2-53**

Inside Corner

When hemming an inside corner, it is necessary to clip the fabric to the fold line (Fig 2-52). Once you turn the hem you will see that there is a 'blank spot' section where there is no hem (Fig 2-53).

Step 1 - To cover this area and reinforce it, cut a square patch of vinyl to generously cover the hemmed area as shown in Fig 2-54. Stick the patch over the corner area with seamstick or staple in place.

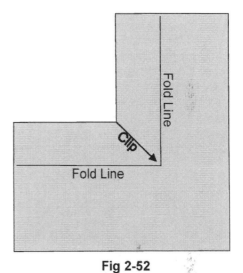

Fig 2-52

Fig 2-54 Cut a piece of vinyl to generously cover the corner area.

Step 2 – Stitch & topstitch the hem. Stitch right through the vinyl as if it were part of the hem. (It is, after all)

Step 3 – Trim off the excess vinyl so you end up with an L-shaped patch which reinforces the corner (Fig 2-55).

Note – use vinyl even if the project is made of Sunbrella – it is stronger and since it is inside the hem, it shouldn't be visible anyway.

Curved Hems:

Outside Curve

Sunbrella, and most heavy canvas and upholstery fabrics are very hard to gather into a curve. To avoid a bunch of gathers in the hem, cut out the fabric's raw edge as a series of straight lines (6" or so). See Fig 2-56

This way, when you fold up the hem, you can make a series of nice, evenly-spaced folded pleats to take in the excess, instead of trying to gather it in.

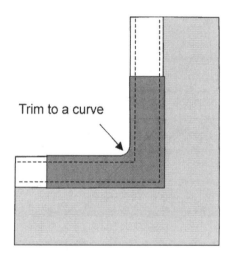

Trim to a curve

Fig 2-55 Trim away the excess vinyl, making the corner into a curve for added strength.

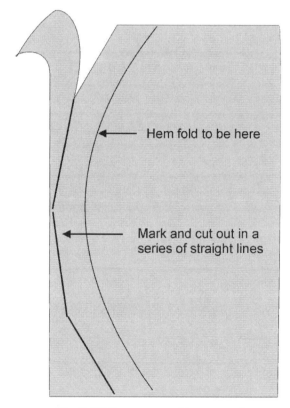

Hem fold to be here

Mark and cut out in a series of straight lines

Fig 2-56 For a curved hem, mark the cutting line in straight line sections.

<u>Inside Curve</u>

To make a hem on an inside curve you would have to clip into the hem area and so will spoil the hem. Instead, make a 'false hem' as described below.

False Hem or Facing

A false hem is used when there isn't enough fabric to make a 'real' hem, or when you have to make a hem on an inside curve. It is also useful for when you have made a mistake (oops), or for a complex-shaped hem like a curve or several angles.

Step 1 – Cut a piece of fabric to match the shape of the hem. The width to cut the hem piece is the width of the hem (say, 1") plus ½" seam allowances on both sides. (Fig 2-57)

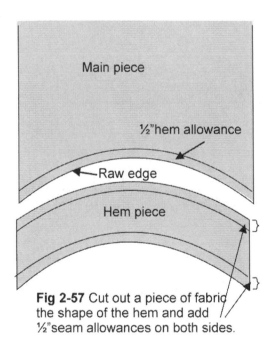

Fig 2-57 Cut out a piece of fabric the shape of the hem and add ½"seam allowances on both sides.

Step 2 – With *right* sides together, stitch the hem piece to the main piece along the lower edge ½" away from the raw edges. (Fig 2-58).

Step 3 – Clip the curve and turn *wrong*-sides-together. Now it looks more like a real hem.

Step 4 – Turn the top edge under ½" and stitch. Topstitch along the lower edge. (Fig 2-59)

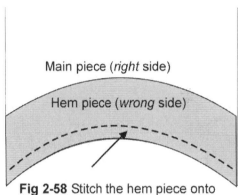

Fig 2-58 Stitch the hem piece onto the main piece.

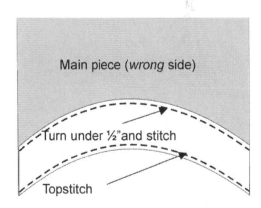

Fig 2-59 Turn the top edge under and stitch the hem like normal. Topstitch close to lower edge.

Canvas for Cruisers

If the single hem is just a small area, you can use a simpler method than the false hem.

Notch the hem allowance, and turn the hem allowance under by ½". (Fig 2-60).

Then just seamstick an oversized curved-shaped piece of vinyl over the notched area to hide it. Stitch the vinyl piece in with the hem.
(Fig 2-61). Trim off the excess.

This works well on wheel covers where you need a bit of reinforcing at the hub

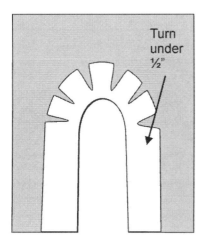

Fig 2-60 Turn raw edge under ½" notching the curve.,

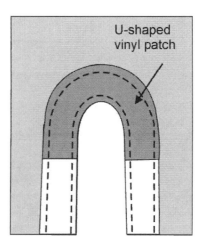

Fig 2-61

Webbing Hem:

Webbing can be used to make a very strong hem.

Step 1 – Cut a piece of nylon or other webbing the required length. Overlap it by about 1/4" along the *right* side of the fabric's edge as shown in Fig 2-62.

Step 2 – Stitch close to the edge of the webbing.

Step 3 – Turn the webbing under, to the *wrong* side of the fabric, so that you can't see the webbing from the *right* side. Stitch like a normal hem and then topstitch along the lower edge as shown in Fig 2-63 & 2-64.

Webbing Hem on a Curve:

Outside Curve:
Step 1 – Overlap the webbing by about ¼" onto the *right* side of the fabric (Fig 2-65).

Step 2 – Stitch close to the edge of the webbing.

Step 3 – Turn the webbing under to the *wrong* side of the fabric. The webbing will want to pucker. Apply seamstick to the webbing if necessary, gathering it evenly to fit, and stitch like a normal hem (Fig 2-66). Topstitch along the lower edge.

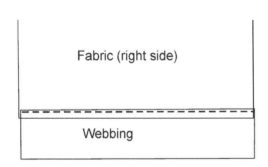

Fig 2-62 Overlap webbing along the *right* side of the fabric's edge and stitch.

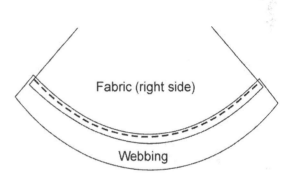

Fig 2-65 Overlap webbing over raw edge of fabric and stitch close to webbing edge.

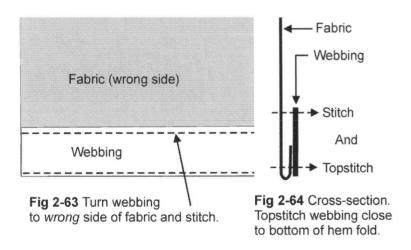

Fig 2-63 Turn webbing to *wrong* side of fabric and stitch.

Fig 2-64 Cross-section. Topstitch webbing close to bottom of hem fold.

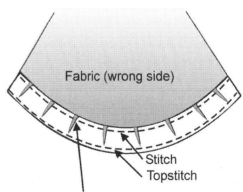

Fig 2-66 Gather the webbing evenly. Stitch and topstitch.

65

Canvas for Cruisers

Inside Curve:

The trick to applying webbing to the hem of an inside curve is to stitch the longest edge first:

Step 1 – Apply seamstick to the *wrong* side of the fabric all along the edge to be hemmed. Pull off the paper then notch the curve. Fold the raw edge under ½" and stick it down. Apply another row of seamstick over the notched seam allowance but do not remove the paper yet. (Fig 2-67)

Step 2 – Apply seamstick to the webbing, along but not too close to one of the edges. Do not remove the paper yet.

Orient the webbing with its seamstick side down and the seamstick farthest from the lower edge. Line up the bottom edge of the webbing to the folded edge of the fabric.
Remove the seamstick paper from the webbing a bit at a time and stick the webbing down
Stitch close to the top edge of the webbing as shown in Fig 2-68. This way, you are stitching the outside curve first.

Step 3 – Now remove the seamstick paper from the folded edge of the fabric.
Gather the webbing evenly and stick it down along the inside edge (Fig 2-69).
Stitch.

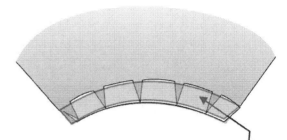

Fig 2-67 Turn the raw edge under ½" and then apply another row of seamstick to the seam allowance.

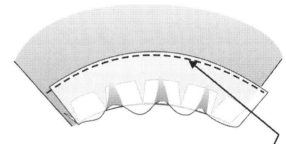

Fig 2-68 Line up the lower edge of the webbing along the folded edge of the fabric. Stick and stitch the upper edge first.

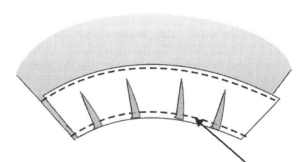

Fig 2-69 Now gather the webbing evenly, and stitch lower edge.

Where a line exits a hem or casing

(e.g. shock cord or drawstring):
In all cases where a line or elastic is to be inserted into a hem, stitch the cord right into the hem. In other words, don't try to fish the cord through the casing after you have done the sewing.
See Fig 2-70.

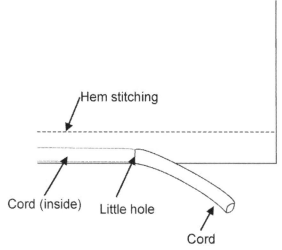

Fold the cord up inside the hem and cut a little hole for the cord to exit. Stitch the hem.

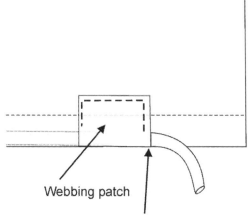

Stitch a webbing patch over the hem fold where the cord exits the hem.

Fig 2-70 Where a cord exits a hem

Step 1 – Mark the fold line for the hem or casing.

Step 2 – Lay out the shock cord or line along the hem fold line and fold up the hem, encasing the cord inside.
Cut or hot knife a little hole at the fold of the hem where the cord needs to exit. Insert the cord through the hole.

Step 3 –Stitch the hem.

Step 4 – Fold a rectangular piece of nylon webbing in half and cover over the fold where the cord comes through, to take the strain and cover the little hole. The area of most strain is 'forward' of the hole as marked in the diagram. Make sure this area is well-covered by the webbing.

Stitch the webbing along 3 sides being careful not to catch in the cord (see Fig 2-70).

Hemming Meshes

When measuring straight lines and square or rectangular pieces of mesh fabrics, and when marking for the hem, don't try to use a square or a ruler. Draw a line along the grain. It may not look straight to you but that could be because of how the fabric was stored. It will revert to its square shape, though don't worry. Hemming meshes along the grain is way easier and looks best. So just cut it exactly along the grain.

Don't use seamstick on meshes – the glue will bleed through eventually and get very dirty. Instead, fold up the hem, lining up the grain and freehand stitch. Stapling can help a bit. Hold and stretch the fabric as you sew, keeping the grain lined up to prevent 'roping

Patches & Reinforcements

All canvas things – from the smallest pouch to the largest awning are subject to stress, strain and chafe. You need to understand where these stresses are likely to be and how to protect your project.

The two reasons for reinforcing are to protect against tearing and to protect against chafing.

Size of patch:

As a general rule, the patch should be about 2" larger all around, than the area you're trying to protect (see Fig 2-71).

On an area with a 'long' stress point, such as a bag handle, it is important to extend the patch 2" beyond the end of the stress point (in this case, the handle end). This is because the direction of 'pull' extends the stress along the fabric grain to well beyond the end of the stress point itself. (Fig 2-72)

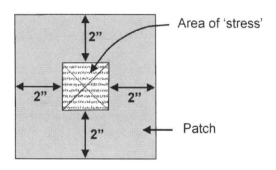

Fig 2-71 The patch should be about 2" bigger all around than the area it is to protect.

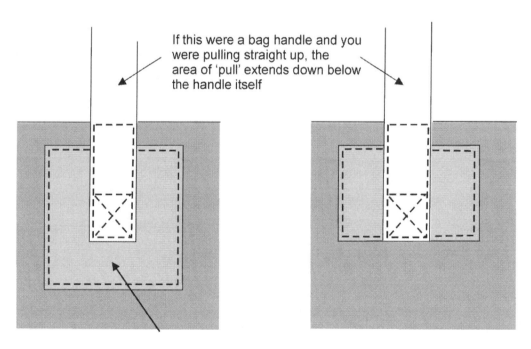

If this were a bag handle and you were pulling straight up, the area of 'pull' extends down below the handle itself

Correct - the patch extends below the end of the handle.

Fig 2-72

Incorrect - the patch is not protecting the area of 'pull'

Shape of patch:

A patch can be square, rectangular, triangular, hexagonal or curved. Straight sides are easier and faster to sew than curves and circles. (Fig 2-73)

Examples of areas to reinforce:
Where bag handles join to the fabric.
Where fasteners or grommets are to be inserted.
Corners of awnings.
Areas where the fabric comes into contact with other fabric or hardware on the boat.

Two-sided vinyl patch

When making a vinyl patch which covers both the *right* and *wrong* sides of the fabric, cut the patch for the *right* side to the desired size. Cut the patch for the *wrong* side oversize.

This way, you can stitch on the pair of patches from the *right* side, through all thicknesses. Then, flip the project over and trim away the excess of the patch on the *wrong* side, close to the stitching.
(See Fig 2-74)

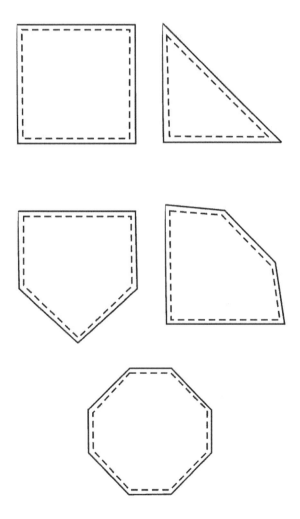

Fig 2-73 Patch shapes
Straight sides are easier
to sew than curves

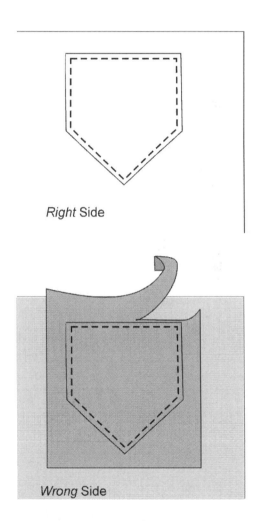

Right Side

Wrong Side

Fig 2-74 Two-sided Vinyl Patch.
Stick patches to both sides of fabric and stitch through all layers.
Then trim off excess from the *wrong* side.

Multi-Layer Patch

The following is how to make a really strong patch with the minimum of thickness – e.g. for an awning corner patch: (Fig 2-75)

Step 1 – Cut the corner patch out of whatever the awning is made of e.g. Sunbrella.
Cut out a piece of Dacron sail cloth the same general shape but smaller (see Fig 2-75). This way, the Dacron will not be caught in the corner seam (eliminating bulk) but it will be big enough to be caught in with the final topstitching.

Step 3 – Stick the Dacron to the *wrong* side of the Sunbrella patch. Seamstick and turn under only the outside edges of the Sunbrella patch ½".

Step 4 – Stick the assembled patch to the corner of the awning. Line up the corner raw edges of the patch to the corner <u>fold</u> lines of the awning so you don't have too many layers of fabric when you turn things under. Then when you finish the edges of the awning this will also serve to finish the raw edges of the patch. Stitch close to the 'turned under' edge of the patch, and stitch along the edge of the Dacron.

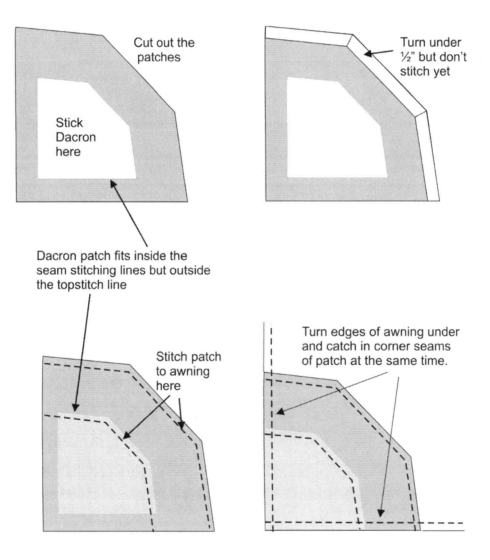

Fig 2-75 Multilayer patch. Dacron patch is cut smaller so as to fit inside the seam allowances to reduce bulk.

Squared off Patch

Step 1 – Cut the patch 1 ½ " wider and longer than the desired finished size.

Step 2 – Stick ½" seamstick all around the outside, just barely inside the raw edges, in one continuous strip, by folding the seamstick at the corners. (This is not absolutely necessary, but makes it less fiddly to remove the paper later). See Fig 2-76.

Step 3 – Peel off the seamstick paper. Miter the corners of the patch with a hot knife. But instead of cutting straight across the corner, make a slight angle as shown in Fig 2-77. This will help eliminate overlap when you turn the edges under.

Step 4 – Turn the edges in on all 4 sides, crease down and roll down hard. Make the sides nice and straight, parallel and make sure the corners are sharp and square.

Step 5 – Stick another line of ½" seamstick about 1/8" inside the folded edge, again, in one continuous strip. If you stick the seamstick too close to the folded edge, the glue might eventually bleed out and make a dirty line all around your nice patch.

Step 6 – Stick the patch onto the project and roll it down hard. Topstitch it on, close to the folded edge of the patch.

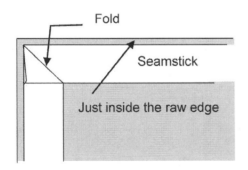

Fold

Seamstick

Just inside the raw edge

Fig 2-76 Squared-off patch.
Apply seamstick just inside
the raw edge, folding at corners.

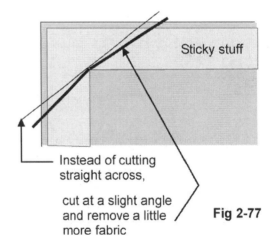

Sticky stuff

Instead of cutting
straight across,

cut at a slight angle
and remove a little
more fabric

Fig 2-77

Canvas for Cruisers

Reinforcing a hole:

This technique is used when you must have a hole in a piece of fabric (e.g. Sunbrella) for something to poke through.

Step 1 – Cut out an octagon of vinyl, 2" bigger all around than the size of the hole. (An octagon, with its straight sides is easier to stitch than a circle.)

Step 2 – Apply seamstick to the edges of the right side of the octagon and stick it down onto the *wrong* side of the fabric. Center the octagon over the area where you are going to make the hole. Stitch the patch onto the fabric, close to the edges of the vinyl. (Fig 2-78)

Step 3 – Flip the project over to the *right* side. On the fabric, mark out the outline of the hole's finished size – in an octagon shape. Mark another smaller octagon ½" inside the one you just drew. This is the cutting line.

Step 4 – Cut out (with scissors) the hole along the line of the small octagon.(Fig 2-79) Make sure you cut only the fabric NOT the vinyl patch. Clip all the corners to the line of the larger octagon (preferably with a hot knife, being careful not to touch the vinyl patch).

Step 5 – Turn all the little clipped edges under by ½". Stitch them down, using small stitch length, close to the fold. (Fig 2-80)

Step 6 – Now, trim away the vinyl to make the hole. (Fig 2-81) Leave a narrow 'margin' of vinyl all around the hole. Cut the corners of the octagon slightly rounded – this makes the corners stronger, and the vinyl will take the strain and chafe, not the fabric.

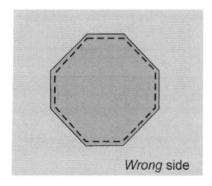

Fig 2-78 Stitch a vinyl patch to the *wrong* side of the fabric, covering the area of the hole.

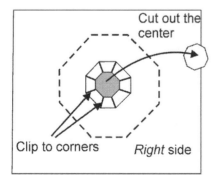

Fig 2-79 Remove the fabric from the center section and clip all the corners.

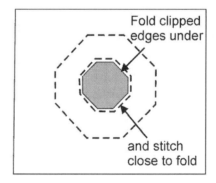

Fig 2-80 Fold the raw edges under and stitch close to the fold.

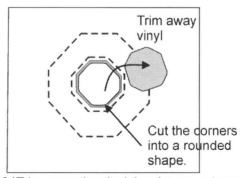

Fig 2-81 Trim away the vinyl, leaving an octagonal hole.

Binding Edges

Binding the edge of fabric is an alternative to hemming. This means that you do not add hem allowance when cutting out your fabric – just cut along the 'finished size' line. The binding will cover this raw edge.

A contrasting colour can be used to add style to your project.

Keep in mind, that bound edges exposed to the sun, say like on a dodger/bimini will have to be restitched (unless you are using Tenara thread). This adds labour to the restitch.

Binding can be made of the same fabric as the project, or you can use vinyl or even webbing. Vinyl and fabric bindings are also available ready-made, with the edges already folded under.

In any case, the trick is to catch in both layers of the binding material when you stitch it so that there is only a single line of stitching. The following instructions tell how.

Vinyl-bound edge

Step 1 – Cut the vinyl strip a little more than twice the desired finished width of the binding.

For example, if you want a 1" bound edge, cut a strip of vinyl about 2 ½" wide.

Step 2 – Apply seamstick to the binding's *wrong* side, 1/8" from one of the edges. Also apply seamstick to the *right* side of the fabric, 1/8" from its raw edge. (Fig 2-82)

Step 3 - Remove the paper from the seamstick on the binding piece only. Pin out the fabric and carefully stick the binding to the *right* side of the fabric along the desired stitching line. Roll it down well. (Fig 2-83).

Now take the paper off the seamstick which is on the fabric. Flatten everything down, carefully stick it down and roll it down well.

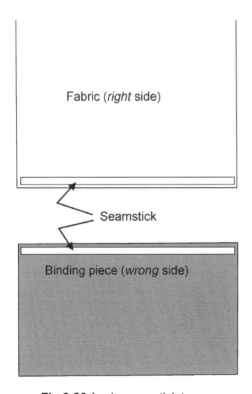

Fabric (*right* side)

Seamstick

Binding piece (*wrong* side)

Fig 2-82 Apply seamstick to edges of binding and fabric.

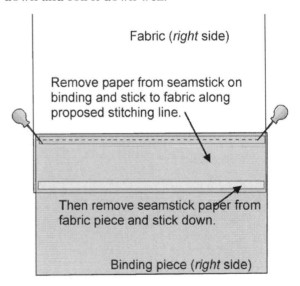

Fabric (*right* side)

Remove paper from seamstick on binding and stick to fabric along proposed stitching line.

Then remove seamstick paper from fabric piece and stick down.

Binding piece (*right* side)

Fig 2-83 Stick *wrong* side of binding to *right* side of fabric, along the line you will be stitching.

Canvas for Cruisers

Step 4 – Flip the project over, *right* side down. Pin it out. Apply 2 rows of seamstick to the fabric – one close to the raw edge, and one just inside of the desired stitching line. (Fig 2-84)

Remove the paper from the seamstick closest to the raw edge of the fabric. Fold the binding up, tight to the fabric's raw edge and stick it down nice & even.

Step 5 – Remove the paper from the seamstick closest to the desired stitching line. Smooth the binding on, again nice & even.

Step 6 – Flip the project over and stitch with the *right* side facing up. Stitch close to the binding's edge.

Step 7 – Flip the project over to the *wrong* side and trim off the excess binding close to the line of stitching. (see Fig 2-85)

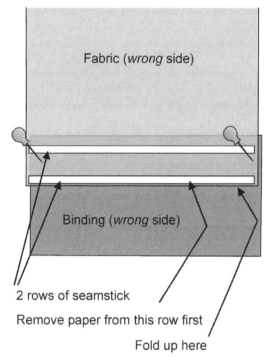

2 rows of seamstick

Remove paper from this row first

Fold up here

Fig 2-84 Apply seamstick to *wrong* side of fabric. Remove lower seamstick paper. Fold binding up along the raw edge of the fabric and stick down.

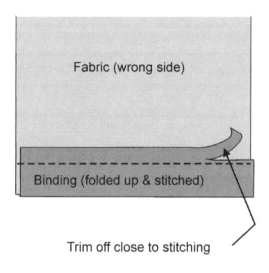

Trim off close to stitching

Fig 2-85 Stitch the binding on, and then trim off the excess from the *wrong* side.

Centerfold and Double fold binding

To attach pre-made binding to the edge of fabric, sandwich the fabric inside the binding, hold the folded binding in place over the raw edge and freehand stitch.

With luck, and practice, you will catch in both sides (Fig 2-86).

If you just can't seem to do this, don't worry, there's another way. Stitch one side of the opened binding to the *wrong* side of the fabric, lining up the fold of the binding along the raw edge of the fabric.

Then flip the project over. Fold the binding over to the *right* side and topstitch the binding neatly along the edge. This way, you will see 2 rows of stitching on the *wrong* side, but only 1 row on the *right* side (Fig 2-87).

If you do a lot of binding, it is worth it to get a special binding attachment for your sewing machine.

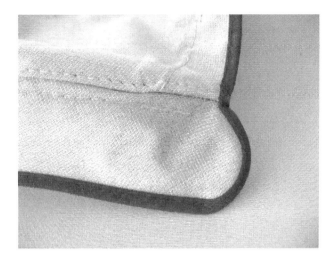

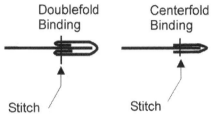

Doublefold Binding   Centerfold Binding

Stitch   Stitch

Fig 2-86 Encase the edge of the fabric in the binding, catching in both sides of the binding in the one row of stitches.

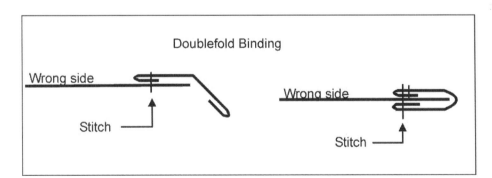

Fig 2-87 Stitch one side of the binding to the *wrong* side of the fabric. Then fold the binding to the *right* side and stitch close to the edge of the binding.

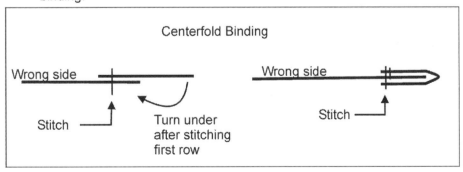

Canvas for Cruisers

Centerfold binding has a natural curve to it. Lay it flat out on a table and you can see it.

When stitching centerfold binding, even along straight-aways, place the inside curve on top, the outside curve underneath and stitch both sides all in one go if you can.

You may have to do curved edges in two steps as described above, until you get practiced.

To Make Bias Binding

Try to buy double-fold binding already made up. If you can't get it, or you can't find the colour you need, you can make flat binding as described below, and fold in the edges, pressing with an iron. It is a very tedious job. Also, be careful when ironing Sunbrella – it can't take very much heat at all.

For yardage requirements, see Appendix i.

Take a length of fabric and fold the ends to the inside as shown in Fig 2-89.

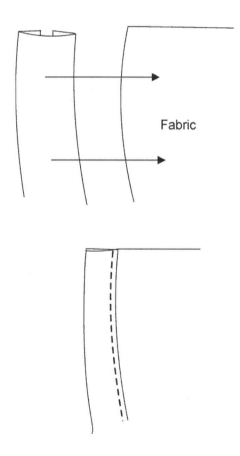

Fig 2-88 Double fold binding on a curve. Notice how the binding tends to curve. Match the direction of curve to the curve of the fabric edge.

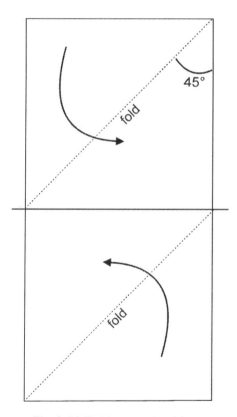

Fig 2-89 Fold a length of fabric.

Then mark the strips perpendicular to the folds and cut out the strips. See Fig 2-90.

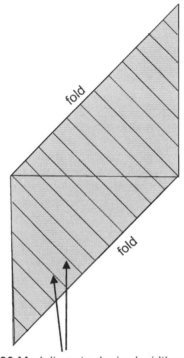

Fig 2-90 Mark lines to desired width and cut out into strips

Join the strips like piping strips – that is, hold the pieces at 90 degrees and stitch, making a diagonal seam. Trim the excess fabric to a ½" seam allowance.

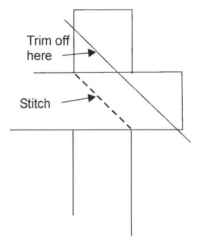

Fig 2-91 To join strips, line up strips perpendicular to each other and stitch at a 45 degree angle from corner to corner.

Drawing A Circle

When making a circle, you need to know what diameter (width) or circumference (distance around) the circle needs to be. To draw a circle, first calculate the radius using the formula:

Radius = (Circumference ÷ 3.14) then divide this result by 2

Or

Radius = Diameter divided by 2.

Take a piece of loosely-woven cord a bit longer than the radius measurement. Tie a loop in one end and using a pin or scratch awl, stick it into the center of the fabric. (Don't do this to vinyl unless you don't mind having a hole. Hold it in place instead)

Push a sharp pencil through the cord at the required radius length away from the pin. Trace the circle, keeping the line taut and the pencil vertical.

Draw a second circle ½" larger all around for the seam allowance.

Marking a Curve

To mark a curve, take a batten, a length of awning track or other long flexible object. Lay it flat out on the fabric, anchoring it at each end by scratch awls. See Fig 2-92.

Curve the batten, holding it in place as required by scratch awls.

Mark the curve onto the fabric along the batten.

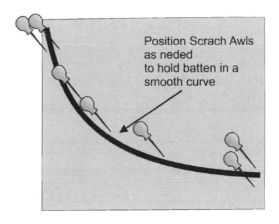

Position Scrach Awls as neded to hold batten in a smooth curve

Fig 2-92 Place scratch awls on both sides of batten at each end. Then place scratch awls along the batten to form a curve.

Making Patterns:

The best material for making patterns is a patterning plastic made especially for this purpose. It is strong but pliable and does not stretch. As a substitute, you can use the clear or milky-clear plastic drop cloth such as you find at hardware stores in the painting supplies section.

To get the plastic to stick to the boat, use seamstick. Place the seamstick along the outside perimeters, support bars or other, to hold the pattern firmly in place. Seamstick can stick too well to plastic (acrylic, Plexiglas) and to hot metal frames. Then it is very hard to remove. So to avoid that, stick down some tape like automotive painters tape, then put the seamstick on top of that.

Use a thick permanent marker to mark outlines, note any right angles, fastening points and tolerances (i.e. can be no longer/shorter or bigger/smaller than something on the boat).

Make sure you mark which is the *right* side of the pattern so that you know which way to lay out the plastic onto the fabric – otherwise you may get a mirror image!

Don't assume things are symmetrical – boats are notoriously uneven. Measure and mark carefully and take your time.

Use clamps to attach the plastic onto bars or edges. Especially on windy days.

After marking up the plastic on the boat, remove it and take it to a flat place. Spread out the plastic nice & flat; correct the lines and angles with a straight edge, smooth out the curves with a batten or other flexible stick.

Then lay out the plastic face down, onto the *wrong* side of the fabric. (This assumes you have made the marks on the *right* side of the plastic).

Pin it all out nice and flat with scratch awls, and using a dull pencil, rub the permanent marker marks onto the fabric. In the case of straight lines & curves, just make a series of dashes and when you remove the plastic you can then join the dashed line with a pencil into a straight line or a curve.

Some vinyls do not transfer marks that easily, so you might have to work the pencil or grease pencil under the plastic and mark it that way.

If you are making a pattern for clear vinyl windows such as for a dodger, note that permanent marker will make a permanent stain on clear window vinyl. Do not lay the pattern plastic marker-side-down onto the window vinyl. Instead, lay the pattern marker-side-down on a flat surface, and then place the window vinyl on top of the pattern. Mark the outlines onto the window vinyl with a grease pencil.

Permanent marker will also make a permanent mark on the *right* side of upholstery vinyl, so be careful.

There is much more detailed information for patterning in each of the projects described later in this book.

Canvas for Cruisers

Fabric layout Considerations:

Sunbrella has a nap – especially dark colours. This means it looks a slightly different shade depending on whether it is viewed across the grain or with the grain. Keep this in mind when laying out sets of cushions or bimini/dodger panels. Especially if it is for a U-shaped settee.

Check how the fabric stretches across and with the grain. Some upholstery vinyls stretch more one way than the other. Lay out the pattern with adjacent seams in the same direction to prevent uneven stretching and make the stitching easier.

If you are making box cushions with piping, lay out the cushion tops and bottoms so that you have a long continuous strip along the edge to make the cushion sides and the piping. Remember that Sunbrella piping must be laid out along the length of the fabric (not crosswise).

There is no 'grain' in leather, so you can cut out pieces in any direction.

Some vinyl meshes are much stronger in one direction that the other. Look at the weave closely. If you see 2 threads running one way and only 1 the other that means the mesh is much stronger along the grain with the 2 threads. This can be important depending on the project you are doing. Consider what direction the strength needs to be.

Meshes should be measured and cut along the grain. Don't try to square things up with a yardstick or measuring square. Even though it looks crooked, it will, over time, straighten itself out.

To mark meshes, hold the pencil at an angle to the fabric and 'drag' it lightly along the grain as shown in Fig 2-93.

To cut a nice straight edge on a heavy-gauge window vinyl such as Strataglass, use a ruler and an exacto knife. Score through the vinyl with the exacto knife along the straight edge ruler, and then it will tear easily along the straight line.

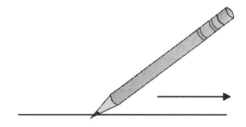

Fig 2-93 To mark mesh, drag a sharp pencil along the grain.

Section 3

Components

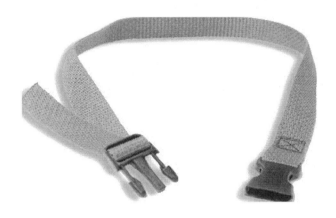

Canvas for Cruisers

There are certain components which are used over and over again in canvas work. In order to save space and repetition in this book, I am covering these components here in detail. Later, when you come to the instructions for the various projects, you can come back here and read the details on how to make these components.

Buckle Strap

The side release buckle is used to make a strap which opens. The strap can be one single piece of webbing with the buckle halves at each end, or it can be two separate pieces of webbing which is then used to join two pieces of fabric together, for example on a sail cover (Fig 3-1).

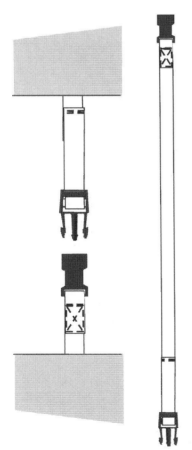

Fig 3-1 Side Release Buckles can be used to make a single strap, or to join two pieces of fabric.

Step 1 – With a hot knife, cut nylon webbing to length. For the 'female' webbing piece, allow an extra 2" in length for looping over. For the webbing piece that will go on the 'male' part of the buckle, you must allow 1" for a little hem in the end of the webbing, and add whatever length you need if you want the strap's length to be adjustable.

Step 2 – 'Female' side - Loop the webbing through the 'female' end of the buckle's crosspiece. Make a box-stitch to hold it strongly in place (Fig 3-2).

Note – when making a box stitch, always stitch at least 3 rows at the 'front' end, for strength. This is the end that takes a lot of strain.

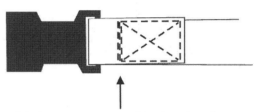

Stitch extra strong at this 'front' end

Fig 3-2 Loop webbing through the slot and stitch with box stitch.

Step 3 – 'Male' side - Have a good look at the 'male' end of the buckle. You will see that there is a row of serrated teeth on one side of the center crossbar. (See Fig 3-3)

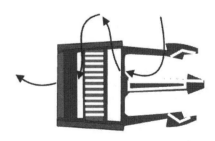

Fig 3-3 Loop webbing from underneath the buckle so that the webbing rests on the serrated teeth.

Face this side of the buckle toward you. Loop the end of the webbing up through the slot closest to the prongs, then down through the slot furthest away from the prongs. This allows the teeth to grab the webbing, and makes it so that you can adjust the length of the strap.

Turn the raw end of the webbing under and under again. (Fig 3-4) Stitch straight across the end a couple of times to hold it well. This makes a little hump so that the webbing cannot pull back through the buckle's slots.

Rollups

Rollups are used to allow vinyl windows or fabric side shades to be rolled up out of the way.

To fasten the roll ups, you can use Ladderlock buckles, Velcro or snaps.

The material you use for the roll ups themselves can be webbing, fabric or clear vinyl depending on the project and your preference.

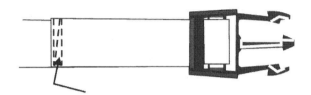

Fig 3-4 Turn the raw edge of the webbing under and stitch.

Ladderlock buckle rollups on webbing straps

Step 1 – Cut ½" webbing (or whatever the width of your buckle) with a hot knife as shown in Fig 3-5. For side shades, the usual length to cut is 16" long.

45°   90°

Fig 3-5 Cut lengths of ½"webbing.

Step 2 – Have a look at the Ladderlock buckle. You will see that there are 'teeth' on a crossbar on the one side. On this same side, the knobbie at the end is smooth, not indented. (See Fig 3-6) If you flip it over to the other side, you will see the indent.

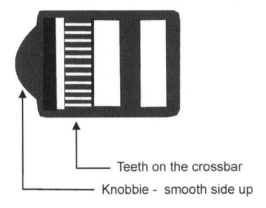

—— Teeth on the crossbar
—— Knobbie - smooth side up

Fig 3-6 Ladderlock buckle detail

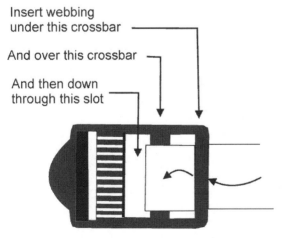

Insert webbing under this crossbar ——
And over this crossbar ——
And then down through this slot ——

Fig 3-7 Feed webbing up and over the center crossbar.

OK, got it oriented the right way? Now, with the buckle's teeth facing towards you, loop the webbing from underneath, up and over the center crossbar and feed it back through to the underside of the buckle as shown in Fig 3-7.

The overlap underneath should be 1" at the most (Fig 3-8).

Step 3 – Stitch the folded area down. A simple z-stitch back and forth will do – no need for a fancy box stitch here. (Fig 3-9)

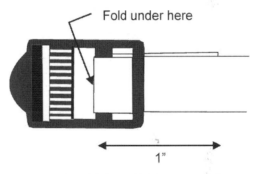

Fold under here

1"

Fig 3-8 Fold the webbing so you have about an inch of overlap.

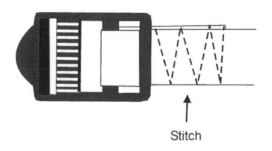

Stitch

Fig 3-9 Stitch the webbing

Step 4 – Position the strap over the top edge of the side curtain. Insert the strap between the zip and the fabric as shown in Fig 3-10. (If the zip is already in, unpick it a bit.) Make sure the buckle is to the inside (to keep it out of the sun).
Fold the tail of the strap down, keeping it tight against the fabric edge – or the zip head will not clear the fold (Fig 3-11)

Step 5 – Stitch in place along the same stitching line as the zip.

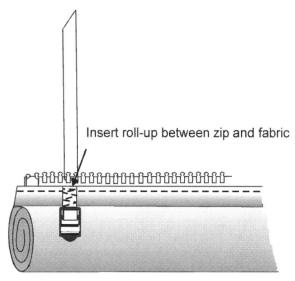

Insert roll-up between zip and fabric

Fig 3-10

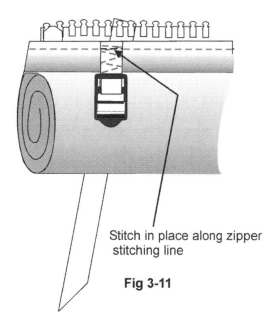

Stitch in place along zipper stitching line

Fig 3-11

Snap roll-ups on clear vinyl straps

Make clear vinyl straps for rollups for clear windows. Use heavy 40 mil vinyl – regular 30 mil clear window vinyl is not really strong enough.

Step 1 – Roll up the window, and measure how long the strap needs to be (Fig 3-12).

Step 2 – Cut out a strip of vinyl about ¾" wide.

Step 3 – Round off one end and put on a snap button and socket (Fig 3-13).

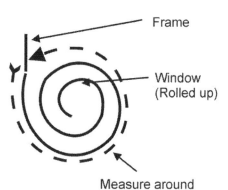

Frame

Window
(Rolled up)

Measure around

Fig 3-12 Side view of rolled-up window. Measure around the rolled up window to find out how long your roll-up strap needs to be.

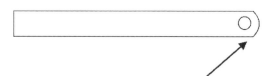

Fig 3-13 Round off one end and install snap button

Step 4 – Position the strap on the window's frame (the outside) with the button's socket facing the inside, as shown in Fig 3-14.

Attach the strap to the frame with a stud/eyelet as shown in Fig 3-15. Don't hammer on the stud/eyelet too tight – the strap needs to be able to rotate.

Step 5 – Rotate the strap 90 degrees as shown in Fig 3-15, and install another stud/eyelet on the frame to hold it aside.

Step 6 – Attach a second strap to the opposite end of the side curtain, the same way. Install an eyelet/stud on the first strap if it reaches, or to the side curtain, to hold the second one up and out of the way. This way, the straps are not hanging and flapping when the window is in its 'down' position (Fig 3-16).

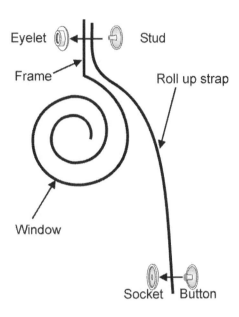

Fig 3-14 Attach the rollup strap to the outside of the rolled-up window using an eyelet/stud.

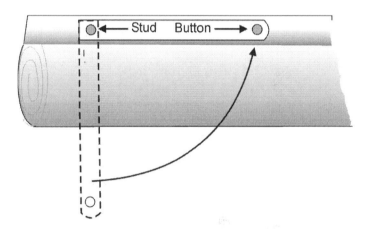

Fig 3-15 Rotate the strap 90 degrees so it lies along the top of the rolled-up window. Install a stud/eyelet so that you can snap the strap up out of the way while not in use.

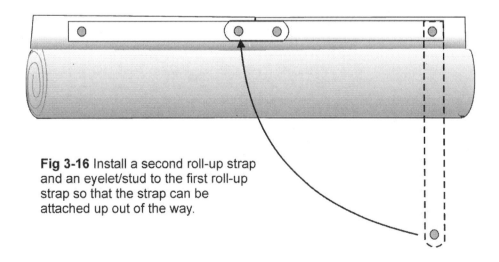

Fig 3-16 Install a second roll-up strap and an eyelet/stud to the first roll-up strap so that the strap can be attached up out of the way.

Canvas for Cruisers

<u>Velcro rollups</u>

If you don't want the bother of fiddling with buckles, or the corrosion problems of snaps, you can use Velcro for roll ups.

Step 1 – Roll up the window or side curtain, and measure how long piece A and piece B need to be (see Fig 3-17)

Step 2 – Cut strips of fabric the width of the Velcro plus ½" turn-in allowance. The fabric will help protect the Velcro from the sun and add strength. Stick & stitch the Velcro to the fabric strips, turning the fabric strips edges under.

Step 3 - If you want to be able to fold up the strips when the window or side curtain is in the 'down' position to prevent flapping and make it look neater, then stitch a little square of matching hooks or loops (whatever the case may be) to the top of each strap so you can loop it up and stick it to itself (Fig 3-18).

Step 4 – Stitch the straps onto the frame of the window or to the top edge of the side curtain. Position the 'loops' so that they face the inside on the inside of the window. Place the 'hooks' also facing to the inside, but on the outside of the window. Check that they will match up when you roll the side curtain up.

Velcro rollups are quick and easy to use, and are my personal favourite.

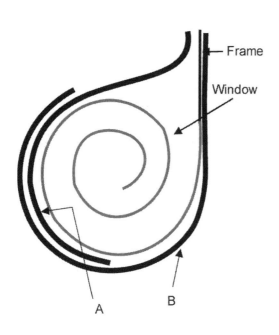

Fig 3-17 Velcro rollups. One piece with the hooks is on the outside, and a separate piece with the loops is on the inside.

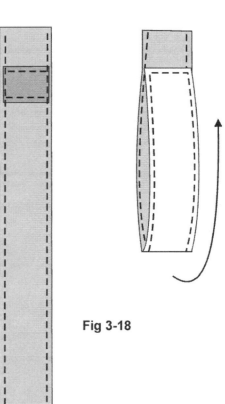

Fig 3-18

Lettering – Sewing on Names or Numbers

Let's say you want to put the boat's name or some numbers on something like a Sunbrella sail cover, weather cloths or a dinghy cover. You can stitch the lettering on from the outside, or from the inside, as follows:

Method 1 – Stitching from the Outside

This method places vinyl lettering on acrylic canvas. Do not use this method for placing vinyl letters onto vinyl – use Method 3

Step 1 – Draw the letters in the required size and font, on plain white paper.

Step 2 – Using carbon paper, transfer the letter outlines onto a piece of vinyl such as Shelterite. Place the entire name on one piece of vinyl, spaced exactly as you want them to appear on the finished item.

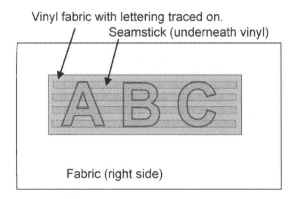

Vinyl fabric with lettering traced on.
Seamstick (underneath vinyl)

Fabric (right side)

Fig 3-19 Trace the lettering onto a piece of vinyl material. Stick it onto the *right* side of the fabric using rows of seamstick.

Step 3 – Stick the entire piece of vinyl to the *right* side of the project with rows of seamstick as shown in Fig 3-19.

Step 4 – Stitch carefully and neatly around all the letters, using a small stitch, just inside the marked lines (Fig 3-20).

Step 5 – Carefully cut away the background vinyl, removing any excess seamstick from the Sunbrella.

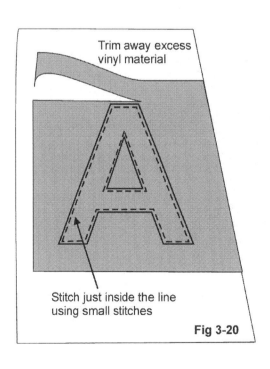

Trim away excess vinyl material

Stitch just inside the line using small stitches

Fig 3-20

89

Canvas for Cruisers

Method 2 – Stitching from the inside.

If you don't want to mark up the vinyl with carbon paper, you can stitch the letters on from the inside of the project.

Step 1 – Trace out the letters on paper, and make a mirror image of them. This is easy if you can use a computer to print out the letters. Otherwise it helps to tape the paper face-down to a window and trace the outline on the opposite side of the paper.

Step 2 – Lay out the paper on the *wrong* side of the project fabric (not the vinyl material), making sure they are in reverse order and mirror-image. Mark the outlines. (Fig 3-21)

Step 3 – Stick a piece of vinyl *right* side up onto the *right* side of the project with rows of seamstick. Make sure the area of the lettering is all covered.

Step 4 – Stitch all around the marked outlines from the *wrong* side of the project.

Step 5 – Flip the project over to the *right* side and carefully cut away the excess vinyl around the letters (Fig 3-22).

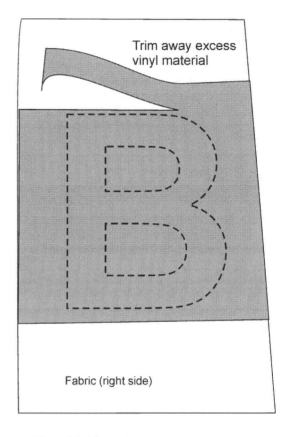

Fig 3-22 After stitching the letter outlines from the *wrong* side of the project, flip it over to the *right* side and trim away the excess vinyl fabric.

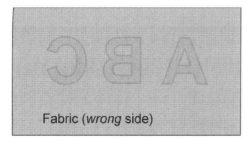

Fig 3-21 Trace the lettering onto the wrong side of the fabric. Seamstick a piece of vinyl to the *right* side of the fabric so as to cover the lettering area.

Method 3 – Vinyl lettering on vinyl projects.

When stitching vinyl letters onto a vinyl project, you will not be able to use the above methods because the seamstick will not come off. Instead:

Step 1 - Mark the letters face up, and in order onto the *right* side of the project.

Step 2 - Seamstick the vinyl piece for the lettering to the *wrong* side of the project, making sure to cover the proposed area of the lettering.

Step 3 - Stitch all around the letters, on the outside of the marked lines.

Step 4 - Cut away the project's fabric inside of the stitched lines, revealing the different colour letters from the piece underneath. You can use vinyl adhesive to permanently hold down the corners and loose edges on the inside.

Other materials

If you are placing lettering on sails, the best material to use is Insignia. It is a sticky back Dacron that comes in several colours. You can make your own logos from this material, and you can also buy pre-cut numbers to save you the trouble.

Insignia sticks well to Dacron, but not so well to Sunbrella. If you use Insignia on anything other than Dacron, you should stitch the edges to make sure it stays down.

Sunbrella can be used to make logos and letters It needs to be cut out with a hot knife though, or the edges will fray. So any logos need to be simple and able to be cut out with the hot knife.

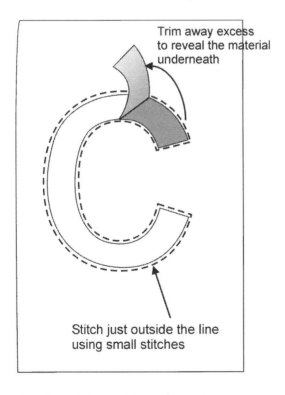

Trim away excess to reveal the material underneath

Stitch just outside the line using small stitches

Fig 3-23 Stitch outside of the lines, then trim away inside of the lines to reveal the contrasting colour underneath.

Simple Open-Bottom Cover (Drop cover)

Whether round or square, the most important consideration in a drop cover is that the cover is wide enough to easily slip over the object to be covered.

Step 1 – Cut out the 'lid' to the size suitable for the object. The fit should be a little loose, so make the lid a little too big. Don't forget to add ½" seam allowances all around.

Step 2 – Measure how long the 'skirt' should be. Allow ½" at the top for seam allowance, and enough to make a single or double hem. Mark the line for the hem.

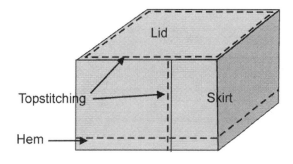

Fig 3-24 The basic features of drop cover are a lid and a skirt, topstitched all around and hemmed.

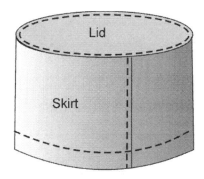

Fig 3-25 To cover a round object, just make the lid round.

Measure how wide the skirt should be. To do this, measure the length of all 4 sides of the lid's <u>raw edges</u>. Not the length along the seam lines. If the cover is round, measure all around the outside <u>raw edge</u> of the lid. For a square or rectangular cover, add at least 1" for each corner, because you will be making little pleats to add some fullness to the skirt.

Whether square or round, also add 1" to the width of skirt for the seam allowances for the side seam. Finally, add a couple of inches for good measure. It is better if the skirt it too wide because you can cut off the excess later if you need to.

Step 3 – With *right* sides together, and the lid on top, start stitching the skirt to the lid freehand (no staples, pins or seamstick).
Start a couple of inches in from the side of the skirt, so you have room to make the seam join in the skirt later. Position the skirt so the side seam will be on a side, not in a corner (Fig 3-26).

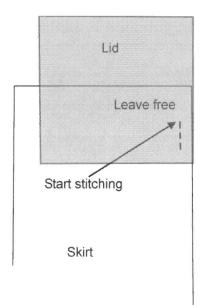

Fig 3-26 Hold the lid on top of the skirt, *right* sides together. Start stitching the skirt to the lid, starting a couple of inches in from the end of the skirt.

If you are making a square cover, when you get to a corner, don't clip the skirt fabric or the lid fabric. Instead, make little pleats at the corners to add fullness to the skirt as shown in Fig 3-27.

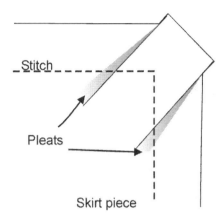

Fig 3-27 When you come to a corner, make small pleats to take in the excess and provide fullness to the skirt.

Step 4 – When you are almost finished stitching the skirt to the lid it will become clear where the side seam of the skirt needs to be. At this point, stop sewing and break off the thread.

Step 5 – Stitch the side seam of the skirt, *right* sides together. Trim seam allowance to ½". Topstitch (optional)

Step 6 – Stitch on the rest of the skirt to the lid.

Step 7 – Stitch the hem.

Step 8 – Topstitch where the lid meets the skirt (optional).Place the topstitching on the lid, so water will drain off.

If the lid is very small, it will be hard to get up in there with the machine to topstitch it. In this case, when it comes time to stitch the side seam of the side skirt, stitch only a couple of inches of the seam at the lid end. Stitch on the rest of the lid. Topstitch the entire lid and an inch of side seam. Backstitch and break off the thread. Now stitch the rest of the side seam and topstitch it.

Nipping Off

For a really narrow cover where a 'lid' is impractical (such as a flagpole cover), you can achieve close to the same look of a lid by 'nipping off' the end:

Step 1 - Fold the fabric in half along its length, *right* sides together. Stitch across the top and down the side as shown, leaving the bottom open (Fig 3-28).

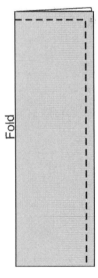

Fig 3-28 Fold a piece of fabric in half and stitch across one end and along the length.

Canvas for Cruisers

Step 2 – Turn the piece so that the seam allowance faces up and is in the center as shown in Fig 3-29. Crease down along both sides as shown.

Step 3 – The top end of the piece will form itself naturally into 2 pointed 'ears'. Stitch across the ends of these ears as shown in Fig 3-30 and trim off the points.

When you turn the piece *right* side out now, the top of the lid will be squared off nicely.

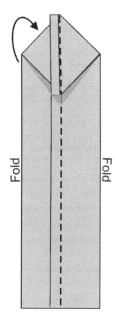

Fig 3-29 Fold so the seam allowance is in the middle and crease along both sides. Crease the top end down.

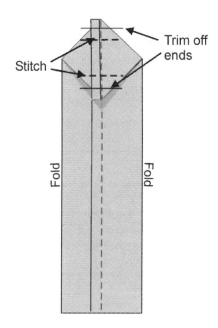

Fig 3-30 Stitch across the points and trim off the ends.

Batten Pocket

A batten pocket is used to hold a batten, stick or even a piece of PVC pipe, which spreads and tensions the fabric.

The batten pocket consists of a long strip of fabric, whose long sides are turned under ½" and topstitched down, to hold the batten. Each short end of the strip is finished differently – the 'pocket end' and the 'tensioning end'.

Step 1 – If it is a flat batten, measure the width of the batten, plus a little – to allow for the thickness of the batten, and so as to allow easy insertion but not to be sloppy.
If it is a round batten, lay it flat on a table, and measure from the table, up and over the batten to the table on the other side, and use this measurement (plus a little for easy insertion), for the width.

Add ½" seam allowances to each side. Cut a long strip of fabric to this width.
The length of the strip should be about 2" longer than the length of the batten.

Step 2 – Apply a line of ¼" seamstick to both long edges, on the *wrong* side of the strip, close to the ½" seam allowance fold line as shown in Fig 3-32. Don't use ½" seamstick – it is a little too wide and may leave some sticky residue inside the batten pocket later, making it difficult to insert the batten. Leave the paper on the seamstick for now and set this fabric strip aside.

Step 3 – We will start with the 'tensioning end' of the batten pocket.
Cut a piece of 1" nylon webbing 11" long.
Cut a piece of 1" Velcro loops 7" long.
Cut a piece of #4 cord about 15" long.

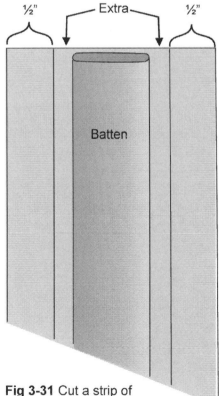

Fig 3-31 Cut a strip of fabric a little wider than the batten, and add ½"seam allowance to both sides.

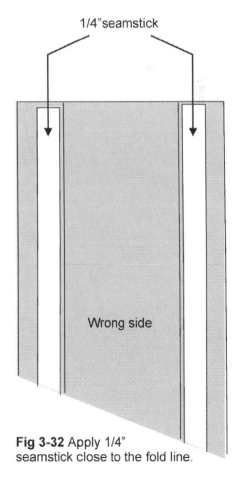

Fig 3-32 Apply 1/4" seamstick close to the fold line.

95

Stitch the cord to the webbing as shown in Fig 3-33, so that it hangs off to one side, about 1" from the end of the webbing. Stitch it well because it will get pulled hard.

Place the piece of Velcro loops on the webbing (you can seamstick it in place if you wish). Turn the end of the webbing over 1" so that the cord and the raw end of the Velcro are hidden inside as shown in Fig 3-34.

Sew the Velcro loops onto the webbing, along the sides only, not across the end.

Cut out a vinyl (e.g. Shelterite) reinforcing patch, a couple of inches wider than the batten pocket. Approx. size assuming a 5/8" flat batten is shown in Fig 3-35 but if the project is a different size, just adjust the size of the patch so it looks about right.

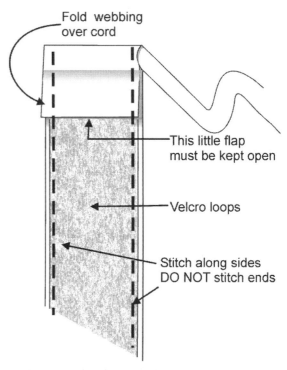

Fig 3-34 Fold the webbing down over the cord and stitch the Velcro to the webbing along the sides only.

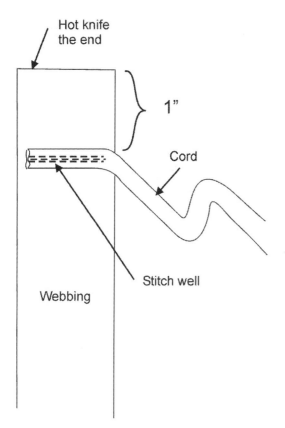

Fig 3-33 Stitch the cord securely to the webbing about 1" in from the end.

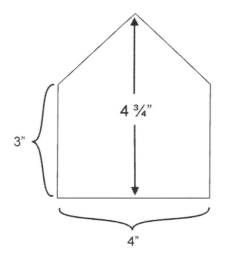

Fig 3-35 Cut out a patch of vinyl material roughly like this.

Position the Velcro-cord-webbing assembly on the patch as shown in Fig 3-36 with the Velcro side down. Stitch it on with a box stitch. Stitch extra strong where shown, as this area will take the strain.

Now stitch the vinyl patch assembly to the *wrong* side of the project at the area where the end of the batten pocket will be, leaving the webbing hanging free.

Step 4 – Now go back to the long fabric strip.

Stitch a ½" single hem at one end of the batten pocket strip. Remove a little of the paper from the seamstick if you have to, but leave the rest of the paper on for now.

Cut out a 7" length of 1" Velcro hooks.
Stick and stitch the Velcro hooks to the center of the *wrong* side of the fabric strip as shown in Fig 3-37. (You can stitch across the ends of this piece)

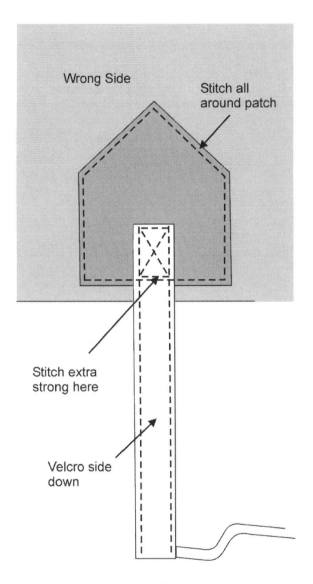

Fig 3-36 Stitch the webbing to the patch and then stitch the patch to the fabric where the batten will end, leaving the webbing part hanging free.

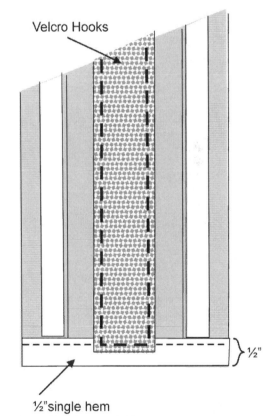

Fig 3-37 Stitch a ½"single hem into one end of the fabric strip, then stick and stitch a 7" strip of Velcro hooks along the center of the fabric strip.

97

Step 5 – Now move to the other end of the batten pocket strip. This will be the 'pocket end'.

Cut a piece of vinyl such as Shelterite 4" long and wide enough to fit within the seam allowances of the batten strip as shown in Fig 3-38.

Seamstick the vinyl down onto the *wrong* side of the batten strip. Stitch only the inside raw edge, and inside of the fold line (about 1 3/4" in from the end) as shown.

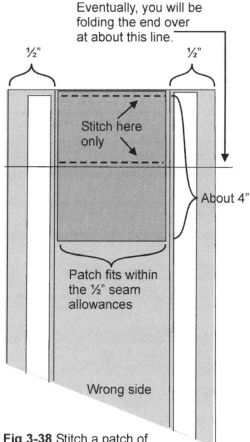

Eventually, you will be folding the end over at about this line.

½"   ½"

Stitch here only

About 4"

Patch fits within the ½" seam allowances

Wrong side

Fig 3-38 Stitch a patch of vinyl material to the *wrong* side, within the side seam allowances. Stitch only where indicated to hold it in place.

Step 6 – Remove the paper from the ¼" seamstick. Fold the seam allowances inside by ½" along the entire length of the pocket. Roll down hard (Fig 3-39).

On the pocket end (the end with the vinyl), fold the end over along the fold line (about 2" in from the end), using seamstick to help it hold, and roll it down hard (Fig 3-40).

Now, apply another line of ¼" seamstick along inside of the entire length of the batten pocket strip, on the seam allowance, and close to the folded edge of the seam allowance. Again, don't use ½" seamstick here (Fig 3-40).

Place the pocket assembly *wrong* side down, onto the project, along where the batten pocket is to be. Place the tensioning end (the end with the Velcro) over the patch as shown in Fig 3-41.

It is important to leave a little 'air' in the pocket (a little hump) so the batten has room to be in there as shown in the cross-section Fig 3-42. Otherwise you will get an ugly hump in the *right* side of the project. If it's a round batten, obviously the 'hump' has to be much bigger.

Step 7 – To insert the batten:

Cut a length of batten a little too long. Better to cut it too long and trim it later!

Insert the batten from the Velcro/cord end (tensioning end). Push it snug into the reinforced pocket at the other end.

Use a short length of small batten or a large flat screwdriver to push the Velcro tail up inside the pocket. The tail end of the cord will hang outside.

To remove the batten, push the screwdriver up inside to separate the Velcro from itself. Leave the screwdriver in there and pull on the cord to open up the pocket.

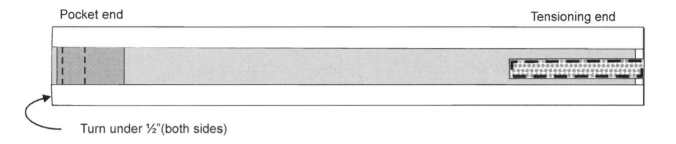

Pocket end   Tensioning end

Turn under ½"(both sides)

Fig 3-39 Remove the seamstick paper and turn the raw edges under ½"

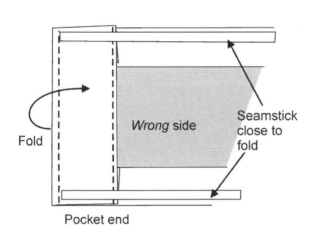

Fig 3-40 Fold the pocket end under about 2" so the line of stitching shows as above. Then apply 1/4" seamstick all along the sides of the fabric strip.

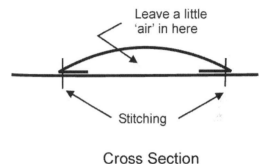

Cross Section

Fig 3-42 When placing the fabric strip down, make sure you leave a little 'hump' to allow for the thickness of the batten.

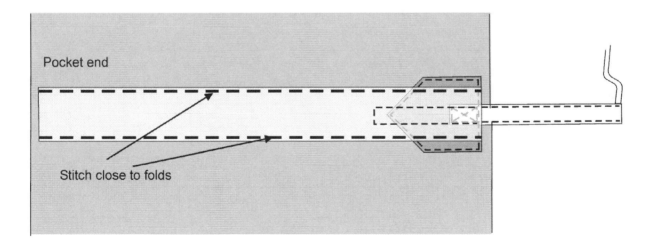

Fig 3-41 Position the fabric strip along where the batten pocket is to be, placing the tensioning end over the vinyl patch as shown.

Canvas for Cruisers

Section 4
Covers

Canvas for Cruisers

One thing is for sure – salt spray, weather and harsh sun will make your pretty boat look tired and dull eventually. Most cruisers end up covering everything in sight on their boats – even those of us who don't like the look of covers.

Covers certainly make sense when you go to lay up the boat for the winter, or to fly home during hurricane season. Covers are also great at hiding things that 'teefs' like to steal from your boat (like a portable generator). When the cover gets really old and crappy looking and blends in with all the other stuff on the deck, it can actually camouflage your 'stuff' from the guy eyeballing your boat as he paddles by.

Acrylic canvas is the ideal fabric for covers – it is water resistant, 'breathes', is very resistant to UV and it comes in lots of great colours.

Vinyl can be used for covers too if you need something totally waterproof. Just make sure to put some ventilation in somewhere to prevent the growth of mold underneath.

This section is written with the simplest projects first, progressing to the most complicated.

Shroud/Turnbuckle Cover

This simple cover is made to protect the lower ends of the shrouds from weather and to protect ankles from getting scratched on the cotter pins.

It is just a piece of leather or tough vinyl, like Shelterite, with Velcro sewn along the long edges so that it wraps around the problem area.

A Leech line is threaded through punched holes at the top, to tie it tight to the shroud.

Measure the height of the cover – enough to cover the area desired, and measure how wide the piece of material needs to be in order to circle the turnbuckle and allow for 1" overlap.

Stitch 1" Velcro loops along one long edge. Flip the piece over and stitch Velcro hooks along the other long edge.

Punch several holes along the top in order to thread some leech line through.
Wrap the cover over the turnbuckle, close using the Velcro and secure tightly at the top with the leech line.

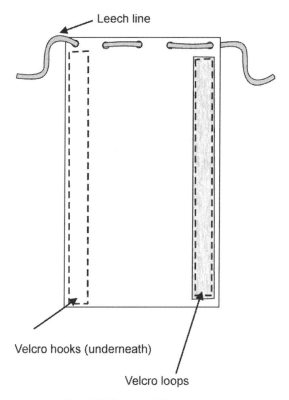

Leech line

Velcro hooks (underneath)

Velcro loops

Fig 4-1 Turnbuckle cover.

Fender Cover

Fender covers are useful if you have nice new fenders that you want to keep that way, or if they are old and ugly and you want them to look better on your boat. They eliminate the squeaking noise when tied alongside a dock or another boat.

A great fabric to use for fender covers is a product called Boat Blanket – a fuzzy, extremely tough fabric that is also kind to your boat's topsides. The fuzziness of the fabric allows Velcro hooks to stick to it directly. No loops needed unless you are using something other than Boat Blanket.
The fabric will pick up dirt and salt. That will scratch and grind into your topsides. So if you find yourself alongside a dirty, greasy industrial dock, clean your covers when you notice them getting dirty.

Step 1 – Measure the height of the fender, and the circumference as shown in Fig 4-2.

Step 2 – Add about 3" to the circumference measurement, and at least 5" to the height. Cut out a piece of fabric to this measurement.

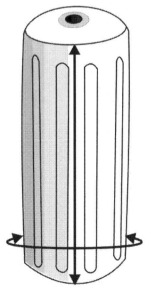

Fig 4-2 Measure the height of the fender, and the circumference.

Step 3 – Lay a length of leech line along the top of the cover – leaving about 8" free at each end. Fold up the hem with the leech line inside and stitch a ½" single hem. (Fig 4-3)
Repeat for the cover's bottom edge.

Step 4 – Stitch a piece of Velcro hooks along the *wrong* side of the fender cover, along the cover's side (Fig 4-3).
Wrap the cover snugly around the fender and secure top and bottom with the leech line drawstring.

Boat Blanket is very thick and fuzzy. If you don't like the look or bulkiness of gathering the top and bottom, make a simple round Lid (see Section 3 – Drop Cover) and gather just the lower hem. Make a hole (Section 2 Reinforcing a Hole) to allow the line to go through

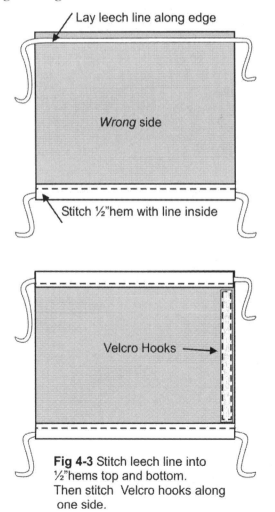

Lay leech line along edge

Wrong side

Stitch ½"hem with line inside

Velcro Hooks

Fig 4-3 Stitch leech line into ½"hems top and bottom. Then stitch Velcro hooks along one side.

Canvas for Cruisers

Life raft Cover

A life raft cover is a square drop cover with a bungee around the bottom. The cover must be designed so that it can be taken off in a hurry. In fact, you should really take the cover off each time you sail.

Certainly, when you store the boat, it makes no sense to let the sun bake your expensive life raft to smithereens while you're away.

Step 1 – Measure the life raft canister – length, width and height. Mark out a rectangle of Sunbrella based on the required length and width. From this rectangle, measure out all around the height of the life raft canister. This is the hem line. You can add ½" or so to allow the cover to extend slightly under the life raft's edge, if that will suit how the raft is attached to the boat.

Mark a third rectangle 1" further out (see Fig 4-4).

Step 2 – Fold each corner diagonally - from the marked inner rectangle's corner to the outside corner. (Fig 4-5) Stitch from the inner corner to the raw edge, on an angle so that the cover will fit loosely. Trim off the excess.

Step 3 – Turn up a 1" single hem, enclosing a length of bungee inside. If you have cut out the Sunbrella with a hot knife, there is no need to turn the raw edge under ½". Try on the cover inside out. Tighten up the bungee to fit, and adjust the location of the corners if necessary. Take the cover off, and topstitch the corner seams.

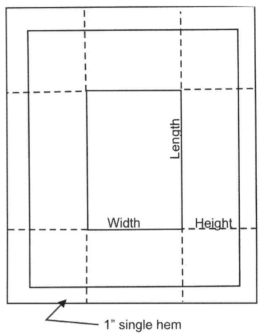

Fig 4-4 Mark out the measurements on a piece of Sunbrella.

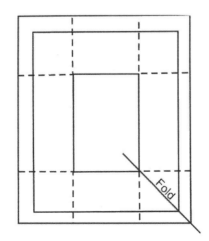

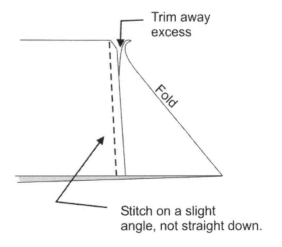

Fig 4-5 Fold the corners diagonally, and stitch down to the hem lines.

Compass Cover

A binnacle compass cover can be a simple 'lid' with a flat top, (See Components – Drop Cover) or it can have a tapered top as shown here.

Step 1 – Measure the circumference of the 'body' of the compass and its height. Also measure the height of the 'dome' part (Fig 4-6)

Step 2 – Cut out a piece of Sunbrella. The width is the circumference measurement, plus 1" for the side seam allowances, plus about 2" to make the fit a bit loose. The height is the measured height (from the bottom of the base to the top of the dome) plus ½" seam allowance plus 1" for the hem as shown in Fig 4-6.

Step 3 – Mark the fabric as in Fig 4-7. Mark ½" in from each end, and the top edge for seam allowances. Divide the remaining length into 8 equal sections. Mark a line 1" up from the bottom for the hem line.

Mark 4 'roofs', each 90 degrees at the top, and the height of the 'dome' measurement if possible. If this is not possible, it is more important to make sure the angles at the tops are 90 degrees and adjust the height of the dome a little

Step 4 – Fold the rectangle in half *right* sides together, and stitch the side seam (Fig 4-7).

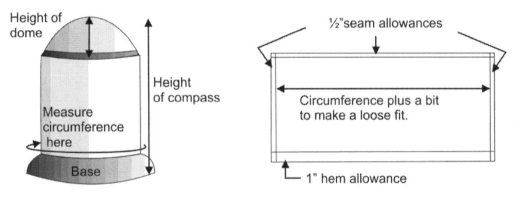

Fig 4-6 Measure up the compass. Cut out fabric to your measurements, and add seam and hem allowances.

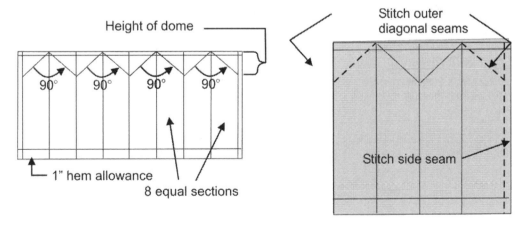

Fig 4-7 Mark up the piece of fabric as above. Fold the piece in half. Stitch the side seam. Then stitch the two outer diagonal seams.

Canvas for Cruisers

Step 5 – Leaving the piece folded in half, nip in the corners by stitching the diagonal seams at the outermost sides as shown in Fig 4-7. Trim the excess off to a ½" seam allowance.

Step 6 – Now open the piece out and re-fold so that the side seam is at the center as in Fig 4-8. Stitch the other 2 outermost diagonal seams as shown. Again, trim off the excess to a ½" seam allowance.
The result is a squared-off roof-like hat with a point in the center where all 4 seams meet.

Step 7 – Try on the compass cover and adjust the mark for its hem if necessary. Turn up the hem and stitch. It will probably be impossible to topstitch the little cover.

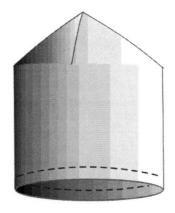

Fig 4-9 The result is a little squared-off hat for your compass.

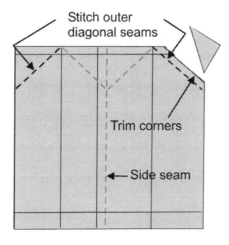

Fig 4-8 Re-fold the work so the side seam is at the center, and stitch the two outermost diagonal seams.

Winch Covers

1. Winch 'cozy'

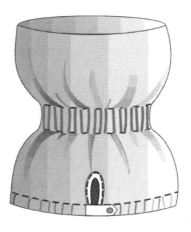

Fig 4-10 A winch 'cozy' is just a little drop cover with an elastic waist and an elasticized opening at the bottom.

A winch 'cozy' is a little more tolerant to variations in fit (in other words, your ability to measure and sew accurately!) than a Tailored cover as described later on. So you can practice with the Winch Cozy.

The winch cozy is basically a cylinder with a lid, elastic at the 'waist' and at the hem, and an optional closure to pull it tight and allow a line to exit.
You can even fancy it up with piping around the lid.

As far as choice of fabric, keep in mind that if the winch is touched all the time, the lid will get all grubby if it is made out of a light coloured fabric. You should choose a dark colour, or make the lid out of vinyl if you want clean-looking covers.

Step 1 – Take the following measurements as shown in Fig 4-11:
a. The diameter of the top
b. The circumference of the base
c. The height of the winch
d. The height of the 'waist' from the base.

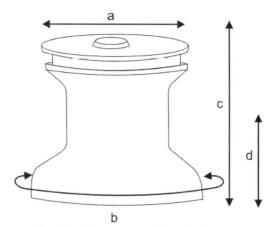

Fig 4-11 Measure up the winch.

Step 2 – Cut out a circle of fabric for the 'lid' (See Section 2 – Drawing a Circle) using the circumference measured. Add ½" seam allowance.

Step 3 – Optional – If you are adding piping, notch the piping's seam allowance as shown in Fig 4-12. Staple piping around the lid along the stitching line. Place the prongs of the staples on the piping side – so that it is easier to remove them later.

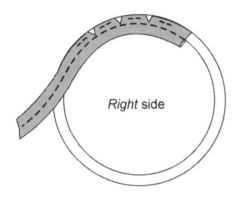

Right side

Fig 4-12 Optional - Staple piping to the *right* side, along the seam line.

Step 4 – Cut out the skirt. Note that it is not a rectangle, but rather a slight arc. See Fig 4-13.

The measurement at the base is a little wider than the actual measured circumference of the winch base, so that the finished cozy will be a little gathered at the base.

The measurement at the top is the same length as the circumference of the lid at the <u>raw edge</u> of the lid. Add a couple of inches– this excess will be trimmed off after you stitch on the lid.

Height –add about 1 ½" to the winch height. This will allow for it to shrink in when the elastic pulls it in at the waist. Also add about 1" for a single hem. Finally add ½" seam allowance at the top.

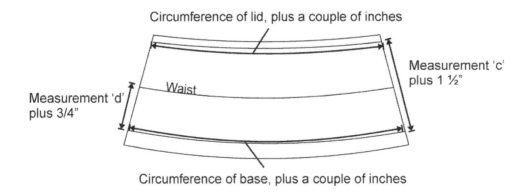

Circumference of lid, plus a couple of inches

Measurement 'c' plus 1 ½"

Waist

Measurement 'd' plus 3/4"

Circumference of base, plus a couple of inches

Fig 4-13 Mark out a piece of fabric for the skirt part.

Mark the hem fold line 1" up from the bottom, and the 'waist' line ¾" higher than the measured height from the winch.

Step 5 – Cut a piece of flat elastic the desired length for the winch base – so that it will stretch and keep the cozy secure onto the winch. Add an extra 1" to the length of the elastic for seam allowances.

See Fig 4-14. Staple the elastic to the bottom edge of the skirt at each end. Stretch the skirt so that the elastic lays flat.

Stitch down one edge of the elastic close to the raw edge of the skirt. This takes some practice to get the tension even. It can help to make hatch marks at the halfway and quarter points on the elastic and the skirt, to get the tension even.

Then stitch the opposite edge of the elastic, again stretching out the skirt and elastic.

Now turn the hem up, with the elastic enclosed inside it. Stretch the skirt out, and stitch and topstitch the hem.

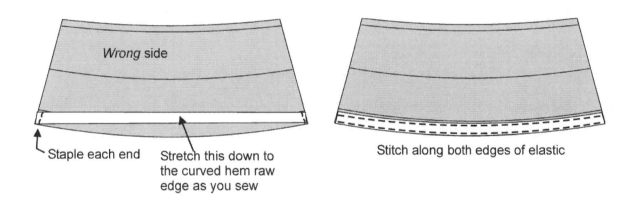

Fig 4-14 Stitching the elastic into the hem. Staple elastic to each end and stitch elastic to fabric, stretching the elastic evenly as you sew.

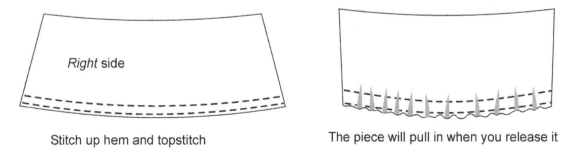

Then turn up the hem, stretching the elastic so the fabric stays smooth, and stitch.

Canvas for Cruisers

Step 6 – Optional Opening for a line.

If you need to make an opening for a line to exit (e.g. for a jib sheet), cut a slit long enough to fit the line, vertically up from the hem, with a hot knife. Make the top end of the slit into a rounded shape. This makes it easier to stitch on the binding.

Open out the slit straight, and bind this edge with 1" nylon webbing or centerfold binding as shown in Fig 4-15.

With a hot knife, cut out a short webbing tab, and install a snap button to the end. Stitch this to one side of the slit. Install a snap socket to the other side of the slit to allow you to close it off.

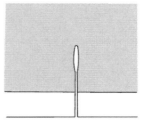

Cut a vertical slit up from the hem, and round off the top edge of the slit.

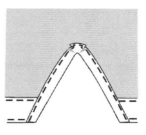

Bind the raw edge.

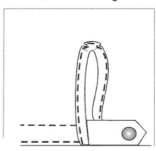

Add a webbing tab so the skirt can be closed around the winch base.

Fig 4-15 Making an opening for a line to exit.

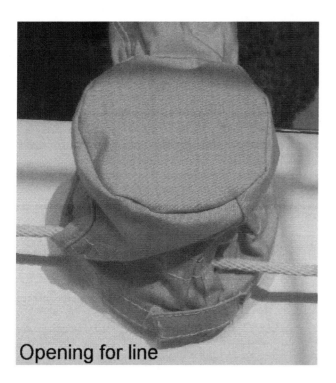

Opening for line

Step 7 – Cut a piece of flat elastic the desired length for the waist – so that it pulls in but is not too tight. The purpose of having elastic at the waist is to help keep the cover from flying off in the wind. So it must be loose enough so you can get it over the top of the winch but tight enough to keep the cover on.

Add 1" to the length of the elastic for the seam allowances.

Staple the elastic to the skirt at each end as shown in Fig 4-16. Stretch the skirt so that the elastic lays flat. Stitch down both edges of the elastic. Keep the tension even and keep the elastic lined up along the marked 'waist' line. It can help to make hatch marks at the halfway and quarter points on elastic and skirt, to get the tension even.

Step 8 – Now stitch the skirt to the lid (See Section 3 – Drop Cover). Remember to start stitching the skirt a couple of inches back from the side, and stitch the side seam only after the lid is almost completely stitched on.

2. Windlass cozy

A cozy for the windlass uses the same construction as a Winch cozy. But you should line the lid with vinyl and make one or 2 cutouts for the chain to come through.

Measure the height and distance apart of these chain openings according to the particular windlass.

Bind the edges of the chain cutouts with Shelterite strips (for chafe protection).

Because of the salty environment, close the cutout openings with webbing tabs and stainless snaps or plastic twist lock fasteners.

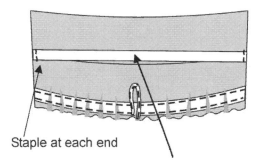

Staple at each end

Stretch this down to the curved waist line as you sew

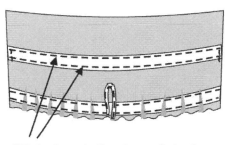

Stitch along both edges of elastic

Fig 4-16 Stitching the elastic at the waist.

3. Tailored Winch Cover

This cover is a cylinder within a cylinder. The short, inner cylinder has an elastic hem for gripping the 'waist' of the winch. The outside cylinder extends down to the base of the winch. (Fig 4-17).

You can add piping around the lid if you wish.

The hem can be finished with binding, or simply turn it up 3/4".

If you need to have an opening for a line to come out, follow the instructions for the Winch Cozy above for creating a bound opening.

Elasticized inner skirt

Fig 4-17 Tailored winch cover

Step 1 – Measure the diameter of the top of the winch, the circumference of the base (the fit should be just a little loose so the skirt hangs nice) and the height from top to base. (See Fig 4-11).

Step 2 – Cut out a circle of fabric, the diameter of the winch top (See Section 2 – Drawing a Circle). Add ½" all around for seam allowances.

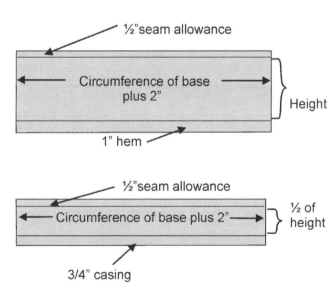

Fig 4-18 Cut out the rectangular pieces

See Fig 4-18. Cut out a rectangle. The width is equal to the circumference of the base plus 2".

The height is equal to the height of the winch plus ½" seam allowance to attach the lid, plus 1" if you are making a hem.

Mark and cut out another rectangle the same width, and half as high. Add a ½" seam allowance at the top, and add ¾" for an elastic casing at the bottom.

Step 3 – If you are putting on piping, staple the piping to the lid. (see Fig 4-12)

With *right* sides together, start stitching the large rectangle onto the lid (Fig 4-19). Begin the stitching a couple of inches in from the side of the rectangle – this will allow you to do the side seam later on.

After 3" or so, start stitching on the small rectangle, *right* side down. (Fig 4-20) Again, start stitching a couple of inches in from this rectangle too, so you can do the side seam later on.

Staggering the start of the seams of these 2 rectangles ensures that the side seams of the skirts will not be in the same place and create a lot of bulk.
Freehand stitch (i.e. just hold them together, don't staple) the rectangles to the circle

As you get close to finishing stitching each of the rectangles on, stop stitching, and stitch each of the side seams.

Step 4 – Turn under a ¾" casing on the smaller rectangle, inserting a shock cord. Tension the shock cord so that it will hold the winch cover on, but not so much that it is a struggle to put it on over the top of the winch.

Tie off the shock cord or connect it with clamps (hog rings). While you have the winch cover on, check the length of the hem so that the skirt hangs nicely and stops just short of touching the boat.

Step 5 – Hem or bind the 'skirt's' lower edge.

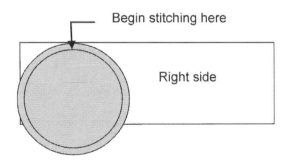

Fig 4-19 Start stitching the larger rectangle onto the lid.

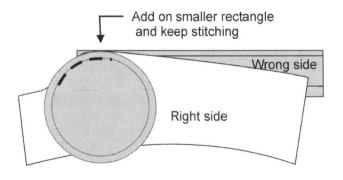

Fig 4-20 After a few inches, start stitching on the smaller rectangle.

115

Canvas for Cruisers

Flagpole Cover or Tiller Cover

This long, skinny little cover is used to cover the flagpole after the flag has been rolled up around it. It can also be adapted as a cover for a tiller or even a beach umbrella.

Step 1 – Measure the length required for the cover, and loosely measure the circumference of the pole with the flag rolled up on it.

Step 2 – Mark a rectangle out on the fabric using these measurements. (Fig 4-21) Add ½" seam allowance along the long sides and one short side, and add hem allowance on the other short side – 2" if it is a large flagpole, or 1" if it is small-ish.

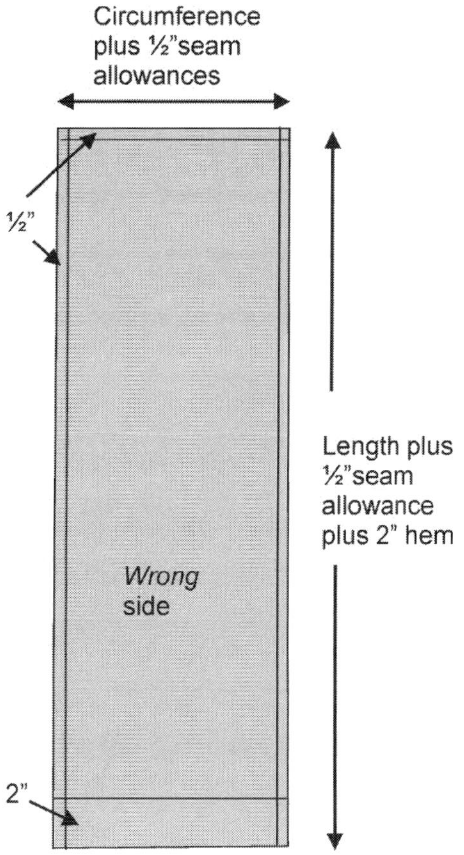

Step 3 – Mark a line from a point 7" up from the hem end, to a point 1 ½" from the lower corner as shown in Fig 4-22.

Fold *wrong* sides together along this line and stitch ½" away from the fold (Fig 4-23).
No need to trim off the excess.

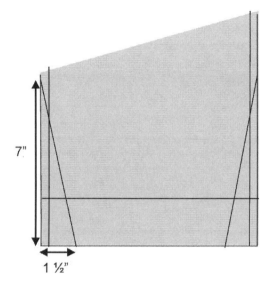

Fig 4-22 Mark angled lines at the bottom edge.

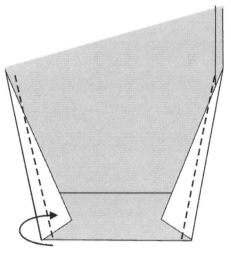

Fig 4-23 Turn under and stitch ½" from fold

Circumference plus ½"seam allowances

½"

Length plus ½"seam allowance plus 2" hem

Wrong side

2"

Fig 4-21 Cut out a rectangle of fabric.

Step 4 – With *right* sides together, fold the piece of fabric in half lengthwise. Stitch across the top and along the long side (Fig 4-24).

Step 5 – 'Nip' the end – Re-fold the work so that the seam is in the center as shown in Fig 4-25.

Use the circumference measurement to mark where the stitching lines have to be to get the right measurement. The result will be a squared-off end which is the same size as the circumference measurement (Fig 4-26).

Stitch across the ends where you marked them, and trim off the excess to ½" seam allowances.

Step 6 – Turn the cover *right* side out.

Step 7 – Hem. Lay a length of small leech line along the hem.
Fold up the hem with the leech line inside, along the marked line, making a 1" or 2" single hem.

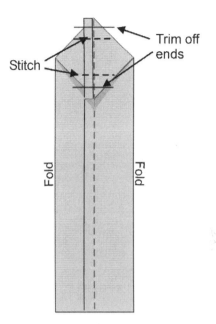

Stitch

Trim off ends

Fold   Fold

Fig 4-25 Re-fold so that the seam is in the center. Stitch across the ends.

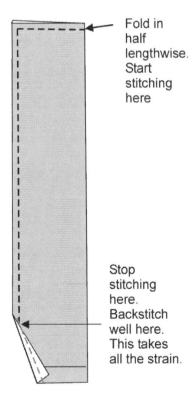

Fold in half lengthwise. Start stitching here

Stop stitching here. Backstitch well here. This takes all the strain.

Fig 4-24 Fold in half lengthwise, and stitch along the end and side.

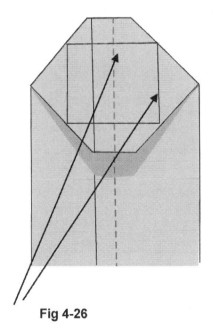

Fig 4-26

This square is the same size as your circumference measurement

Trim the leech line to length so that about 6" sticks out each end. Melt and taper these ends to a point with a hot knife. Stitch the hem, leaving the line extending out each end.

Add a barrel lock closure to the drawstring. For more information on barrel locks, see Section 1 – Hardware.

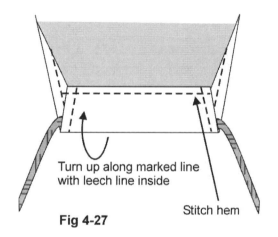

Turn up along marked line with leech line inside

Stitch hem

Fig 4-27

Mast Boot

A Mast Boot is a little cover that goes around the base of the mast.

If it needs to keep out water, make it out of Stamoid or other vinyl, and make it fit really tight to the mast by securing it with a couple of big hose clamps – top and bottom.

If it is to be merely decorative, acrylic canvas works fine.

Step 1 – Measure the distance around the mast where the top of the cover will be (circumference of the mast) (T), and around the base where it flares out (B).

Measure the height the cover will have to be to reach from the mast to the deck (H). See Fig 4-28. For a waterproof mast boot, make sure you allow enough in the height measurement for the hose clamps to bite onto.

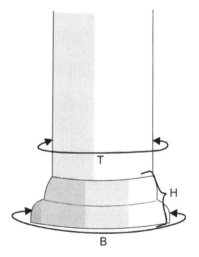

Fig 4-28 Measure the base of the mast.

Step 2 – Draw an arc on the fabric using a scratch awl, a pencil and a piece of string. (See Techniques – Marking a Circle)

How long to make the string? Use the following calculation:

First calculate the diameter of the mast where the top edge of the cover will be:
t = T measurement divided by 3.1416

and at the base of the cover
b = B divided by 3.1416

Refer to Fig 4-29.
Calculate L1:

L1 = (H x b) divided by (b – t)
Mark a curve using your L1 measurement as shown in Fig 4 29

How long to make this curve? The length of the curve is the B measurement, plus a couple of inches for overlap.

Move the pencil up the string, away from the first arc, by the height measurement (H) and mark out another curve. (Fig 4-29). The length of this curve is the T measurement, again with the same allowance for overlap.

Step 3 – If you are using Sunbrella, add ½" seam allowance at the top and bottom for a hem. Cut out the fabric.

Step 4 – Stitch Velcro hooks to one side at one end, and loops to the opposite side at the other end. (Fig 4-30)

Step 5 – Wrap the cover around the mast and secure it tight with Velcro, and circular hose clamps if desired.

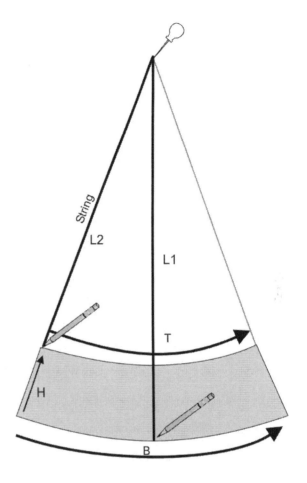

Fig 4-29 Use a string and a scratch awl to mark 2 arcs on a piece of fabric. The distance between the arcs is the height measurement (H)

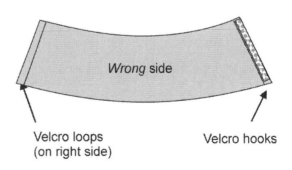

Fig 4-30 Stitch Velcro hooks to one end and loops to the other end.

Canvas for Cruisers

Decorative Mast Boot (Mast 'cozy')

Use Sunbrella or other fabric. This mast boot is just meant to cover any ugliness or hose clamps at the base of the mast and not necessarily keep out any water.

Step 1 – Measure the circumference of the mast and the base where it flares out. Measure how high the cover will have to be to cover the area you want. (see Fig 4-28)

Step 2 – Cut out a rectangle of Sunbrella or other fabric. (Fig 4-31) Decide if you want the mast cozy to be fairly flat and tailored, or gathered and puffy.

If you want the flat and tailored look, cut the length of the rectangle to the measurement of the base of the mast, plus 2" for overlap.

If you want the puffy look, add 3 or 4 more inches to the length.

The height of the rectangle is the required height plus 2" – for a 1" single hem at the top and at the bottom.

Step 3 – Make a couple of little darts along the top edge to help take in the excess. Space them evenly. To make a dart, fold the fabric *right* sides together and stitch from the raw edge, tapering out to the point at the fold as shown in Fig 4-32.

Step 4 – Hot knife 2 small slits in each end, just inside of the hem fold line and seam lines as shown in Fig 4-33. This is for a leech line to come through.

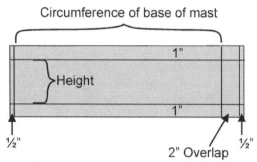

Fig 4-31 Cut out a rectangle of acrylic canvas

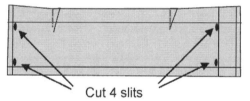

Cut 4 slits

Fig 4-33 Cut 4 slits big enough for a leech line, just inside of the lines as shown.

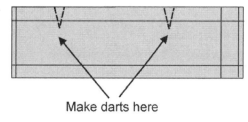

Make darts here

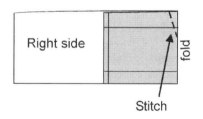

Fig 4-32 Make a couple of darts in the top edge - just fold along the desired line and stitch as shown.

Finish the short ends as follows.

Work with the "overlap" end first – that is, the end with the 2" allowance. On the *wrong* side stitch a length of centerfold binding over the slits as shown in Fig 4-34.
Break the stitching and leave a little unstitched space on the 'inboard' side of each slit.

Now work with the other end. (Fig 4-34) Turn the edge under ½", toward the *wrong* side. Line up

one edge of the binding to the folded edge. Stitch the binding on the *wrong* side, again breaking the stitching at the 'inboard' side of each slit.

Step 5 – Turn the raw edge of the "overlap" end under by ½" and stitch it down (Fig 4-35).
Cut 2 pieces of leech line about 8" longer than the length of the rectangle. Lay one piece along each of the hem folds and thread the ends under the binding and through the small slits. (Fig 4-35).

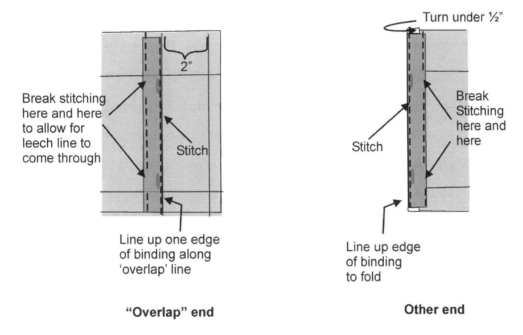

"Overlap" end   **Other end**

Fig 4-34 Stitch centerfold binding to the *wrong* side of both ends

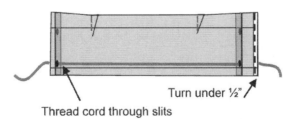

Fig 4-35 Turn the raw edge under ½"and stitch down.
Insert a piece of leech line along each hem fold
pushing the ends through the slits through to the outside.

Stitch the 1" single hems both top and bottom with the cord inside (Fig 4-36).

Step 6 – Stitch Velcro hooks to the *wrong* side of the 'overlap end, and loops to the *right* side of the other end – 2" Velcro is best. See Fig 4-37

Step 7 – Wrap the cozy around the mast, with the darts towards the top. Secure with Velcro, and use the drawstring to gather it up tight.

Wheel Cover

This cover is a good-looking unobtrusive protective cover for the steering wheel. The cover simply drops down over the wheel and hangs there.

Step 1 – See Fig 4-38. Measure the diameter of the wheel (a). Add 1" to this measurement to allow the cover to fit comfortably loose. Decide how long you want the cover to hang below the wheel and take this measurement – from the top of the wheel to the hem (b). Measure the diameter of the hub (c).

Fig 4-36 Stitch the top and bottom hems.

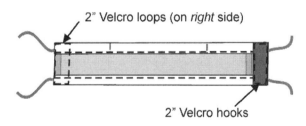

2" Velcro loops (on *right* side)

2" Velcro hooks

Fig 4-37 Stitch Velcro hooks along one end, and loops along the other end.

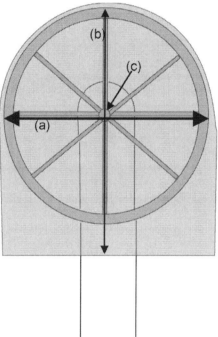

Fig 4-38 Measure the diameter of the wheel (a), the height the cover needs to be (b) and the diameter of the hub (c)

Step 2 – Mark out 2 pieces of fabric - Sunbrella or Stamoid are the best choices. First, mark out a circle (See Section 2 – Marking a Circle) based on the diameter (a) you measured in Step 1 above. Don't forget to add 1" to allow the fit to be comfortably loose. Mark another circle ½" outside this first circle for the seam allowance. (Fig 4-39)

Now mark two straight lines from the widest part of this circle, straight down to the hem as shown in Fig 4-40. Add 1" to the length, for a single hem.

In the center of <u>one</u> of the pieces of fabric, mark a circle equal to the hub's diameter (Fig 4-41). Then draw a line from the center of this circle, straight down to the hem. Mark two lines – one on each side – half the hub's diameter away from the center line.

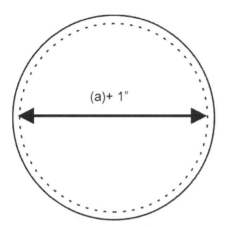

Fig 4-39 Mark a circle the diameter (a) plus 1". Mark another circle ½"outside of this for your seam allowance.

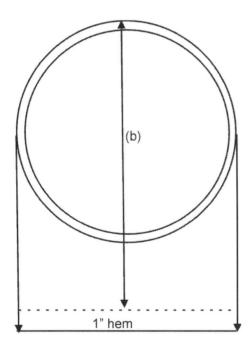

Fig 4-40 Draw lines straight down from the widest part of the circle to your desired length (b). Then add 1" for hem.

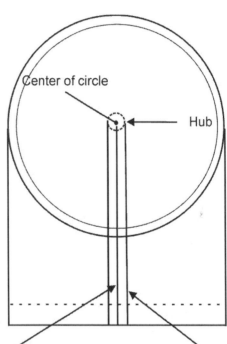

Fig 4-41
1. In the center, mark a circle the diameter of the hub.
2. Mark a line from the center of the circle straight down to the hem.
3. Then mark two lines, one on each side.

The two lines you just drew on each side of the center line will be the stitching line, so you need to mark another 2 lines ½" away, towards the center line, for a seam allowance. This last line will be the cutting line. See details in Fig 4-42.

Now you can cut out the 2 pieces of fabric.

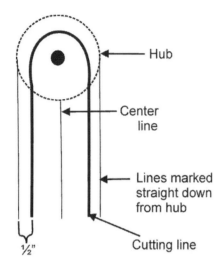

Fig 4-42 Draw the cutting line ½" inside of the marked lines

Step 3 – Reinforce the hub area as follows. Working with the piece of fabric that has the markings for the hub opening:

Apply ½" seamstick all along the edge of the opening. (See Fig 4-43) Turn it under ½", clipping the curve.

Stick a small u-shaped piece of vinyl to the *wrong* side to cover the clipped parts and to reinforce the hub area. (Fig 4-44) Cut the patch out a little big, you can trim it down later.
Stitch the 1/2" hem along the opening, catching in the u-shaped patch. (Fig 4-45)
Topstitch close to the fold.
Trim off any excess vinyl on the u-shaped patch if necessary.

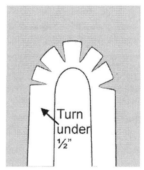

Fig 4-43 Apply seamstick along the raw edge of the opening. Clip the curve. Turn under ½".

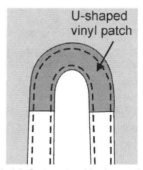

Fig 4-44 Cut out a U-shaped vinyl patch and stitch it over the clipped curve to hide the clipped raw edges.

Step 4 – With *right* sides together, staple the 2 panels together as shown in Fig 4-45. Make sure the staples are within the seam allowance so you won't have holes left in the fabric.

Stitch all around – except for the hem.
Remove all the staples.
Cut some notches in the seam allowances along the curve as shown in Fig 4-45, to remove the bulkiness when you go to turn the cover inside out.

Step 5 – Open up the cover along the hem as flat as possible and turn up a 1" single hem. If you are using Stamoid, seamstick the hem down, don't try to freehand it – it's too slippery.
Stitch the hem.

Step 6 – To keep the opening from flapping around, construct a short nylon webbing tab with a snap button as shown in Fig 4-46. Box-stitch this tab to the hem on the one side. Install a snap socket to the other side.

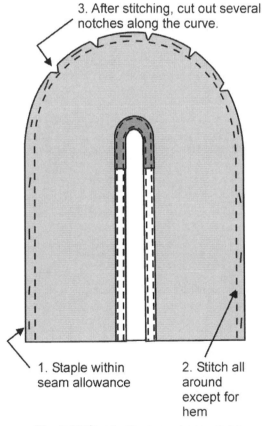

3. After stitching, cut out several notches along the curve.

1. Staple within seam allowance

2. Stitch all around except for hem

Fig 4-45 Staple the two pieces *right* sides together and stitch. Make notches along the curve.

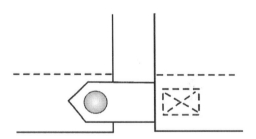

Fig 4-46 Construct a tab assembly from nylon webbing to close the lower edge.

Canvas for Cruisers

Equipment Covers and Bags

To cover all sorts of miscellaneous deck equipment – from jerry cans to jet skis, the principles are all the same.

The covers usually are required to protect the equipment from physical damage, salt spray, rain and sun. It is difficult to sew a cover that is totally waterproof. Even if it were, a vinyl cover will hold any moisture inside, and any metal or electronics inside will quickly dissolve into a pile of rust. Vinyl covers should somehow be vented to allow trapped water or moisture to escape. Vents can be mesh inserts, grommets or other openings.

Any topstitching on covers should be done so that the rain will drain off, and not drain into the inside (Fig 4-47)

Covers can be padded with foam to protect the boat from being scratched by heavy awkward and sharp things like dive tanks and drop boards. Or they can be lined with something fuzzy like Odyssey Soft Touch to protect finishes such as tables or furniture.

A cover can simply be a drawstring bag which drops over the equipment and tightens at the bottom, or it can be tailored to fit the equipment exactly. If the cover is to be used merely to protect the equipment during long-term storage (for example when the boat is on the hard), then simple drawstring bag covers are fine. But if the cover is to be used while people are on board, it is kind of nice to have the cover tailored and good looking.

The more tailored the fit of the cover, the more important it can be to make a plastic pattern first. Clear plastic is best for this – you can see through it to mark seams, protrusions and areas needing chafe protection.

If the equipment that is to be covered needs to be carried around, then you should consider a storage bag with handles. For more on storage bags, see the Section 7 - Interior Projects – Bags.

Described here are a couple of typical examples of items that get covered – a helm seat and a center console, but it can be adapted to any odd-shaped cover – maybe the helicopter on your mega yacht!

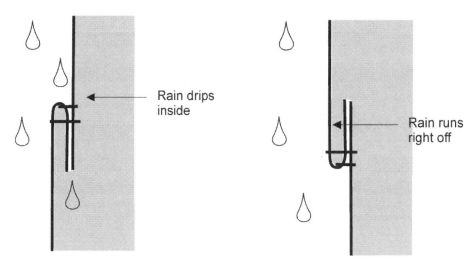

Rain drips inside

Rain runs right off

Fig 4-47 In this cross section you can see how you need to orient your seam allowance and topstitching so as to allow water to drain off instead of running inside.

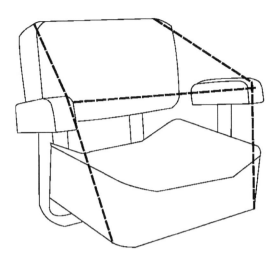

Fig 4-48a When patterning over gaps, stick tape between points for the pattern plastic to rest on.

Step 1 – If the equipment has large gaps, attach tape between the points as shown above. Apply seamstick to the upper surface of this tape, and to the edges of the equipment. If you are afraid that the seamstick will not come off, put painters tape on first.

Step 2 – Remove the seamstick paper. Drape the patterning plastic over the equipment and carefully smooth it on. The idea is to get it wrinkle-free..

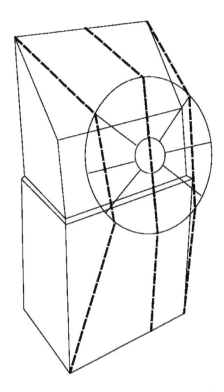

Fig 4-48b Imagine the irregular object more-or-less squared off when placing tape supports

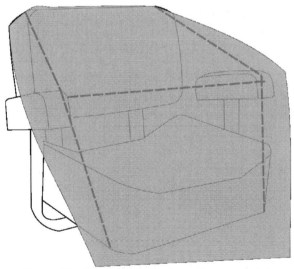

Fig 4-49a Drape the plastic pattern material over the chair and stick it down nice and smooth.

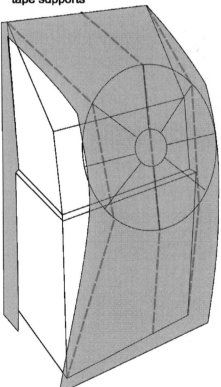

Fig 4-49b Plastic draped and stuck over front, top and back.

Canvas for Cruisers

With a permanent marker, make a series of dashed lines where the seam line will be. Mark some hatch marks to help you match the panels together. Cut off any large excess of plastic.

Now stick seamstick close to the line you made – if you stick right over the line, you might remove the marked line when you come to remove the seamstick!
Remove the seamstick paper and stick panels of plastic patterning material to the sides of the equipment..

Mark a series of dashed lines right over top of the previous marks you made.
Mark the same hatch marks as the previous layer.

Pinch in and mark darts if needed to take in the excess at curves or corners, and mark the location of any fasteners or zippers.
Mark the hem.

Mark Front, Back, Top, Bottom, inside, outside etc to help you orient things when you come to cut out and sew.

Step 3 – Clean up the pattern
Remove the plastic pattern material from the equipment. You can now lay out the pattern smooth and flat. S traighten the dashed lines you made for the seams.
Add at least 5/8" inch all seams – when you stitch using a ½" seam allowance this will give you a little extra room so the cover is not too tight.
Add the hem allowance, probably 2" for a 1" double hem, or 1" for a drawstring bottom.

Step 4 – Sew the panels together and make any attachments, zippers or holes according to the directions in this book.

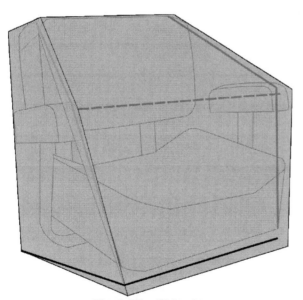

Fig 4-50a Side pieces on.

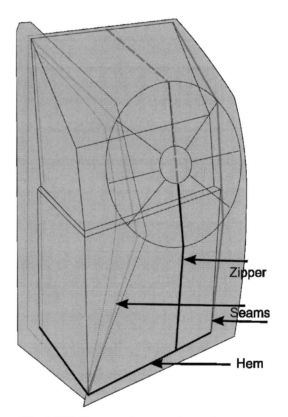

Fig 4-50b Seams, hem and opening marked..

128

BBQ Grill Cover

Drawstring Cover:

A perfectly functional bbq grill cover can simply be an acrylic canvas drawstring bag. It just drops over the grill and is kept from blowing off by a drawstring at the bottom.

This style is the best approach for a 'kettle' type grill. Measure as in Fig 4-53 and construct using the techniques shown in Section 3 – Drop Cover. And follow the instructions for the drawstring hem in Section 2 – Hems and Casings.

Tailored Grill Cover:

A tailored grill cover is fun to make and looks very nice. Whether you have a 'hard-chine' or a smooth cylinder for a grill, the steps are the same.

Step 1 – Cut a piece of acrylic canvas roughly to size, and drape it over the grill *right* side up as shown in Fig 4-54.

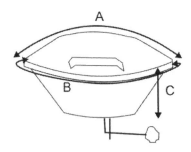

Fig 4-53 Measure the grill:
A = diameter of lid
B = circumference of lid
C = length of skirt

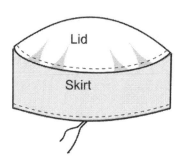

The grill cover is simply a loose-fitting drop cover with a drawstring bottom.

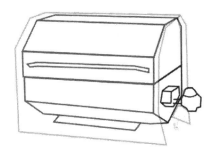

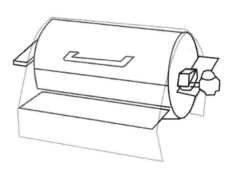

Fig 4-54 Drape an oversized piece of fabric over the grill.

Canvas for Cruisers

Step 2 – Starting with the easy side (that is, the side without the regulator sticking out of it), staple another oversized piece of fabric to the piece that is draped over (we'll call it the Top). (See Fig 4-55).

Place *wrong* sides together and staple the pieces together to achieve a nice fit but not too tight. Leave yourself at least a ½" seam allowance for when you go to sew it together.

If there is a handle at the front like in most grills, make a pleat in the front of the Top to allow for the handle. When making pleats, think about which way rain will fall on the cover – make the fold so that rain will run off, and not into the fold.

At the bottom, staple enough to get a nice fit but leave the bottom open so the cover can be put on and taken off easily.

Step 3 – Repeat the process for the other side of the grill. There are two ways of dealing with the regulator sticking out of the side. You can either drape a side piece over the whole protrusion and make a pleat to allow for it, or you can make a flat side piece and a separate little pocket for the regulator.

First way – make a pleat. See Fig 4-56.
With *wrong* sides together, staple an oversized piece of fabric to the Top, all around the outside. Let the fabric drape over the regulator area. Then take in a pleat or two below the regulator to take up the slack – but leave it loose enough so the cover can come off easily. Again, leave the bottom open, so the cover can be removed easily.
Continue to Step 4.

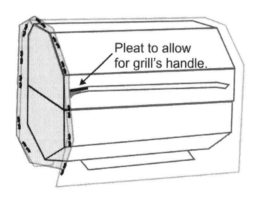

Fig 4-55 Starting with the flat side of the grill, staple an oversize piece of fabric to the Top piece all around, leaving the bottom open.

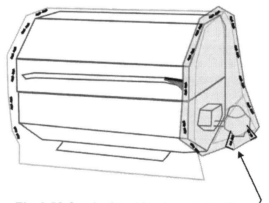

Fig 4-56 Staple the side piece to the Top loosely covering the regulator. Staple in a pleat or two to allow for the regulator.

Second way – make a pocket for the regulator. This is a bit trickier, so if you have limited fabric, you could either use plastic patterning material, or other scrap fabric to make a rough pattern.

Staple an oversized piece of fabric to the Top – just along the top and a couple of staples down along the sides just enough to hold it in place. See Fig 4-57.

The side piece will have to have a slit underneath the regulator and a hole around the regulator where it meets the grill, to allow the cover to come on and off. Holding the fabric side piece in place, cut a slit up from the bottom of the side piece. Then cut a small hole, enlarging the hole and adjusting its position until the side piece hangs smoothly along the side of the grill. If you are using your good fabric for this, just take it slow and make small cuts, adjusting the fit gradually. Make the hole just barely large enough to go around the regulator attachment point.

Now staple the rest of the side piece to the Top, down to the hem. Leave the bottom open to allow the cover to be taken on and off.

Continue to Step 4. The pocket part for the regulator will be explained later, in Step 10.

Step 4 – Now mark a nice level hemline all around the cover's bottom. You can either staple the hem up, or mark it with a chalk line.

Step 5 – Gently and carefully take the cover off the grill so you don't pull away the staples.

Step 6 – Because you stapled the cover together with *wrong* sides together, you need to make the seamline marks on the *wrong* side of the fabric also. To do this, gently spread the fabric at each place where a staple holds the fabric together. Make a small pencil mark on both pieces of fabric, where they are joined by the staple. It

helps to number a couple of the marks so you can match things up later. Now remove all the staples.

Fig 4-57

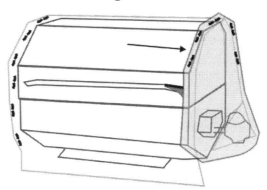

Staple an oversized piece of fabric to the top of the Top, and put a couple of staples along the side to hold in place.

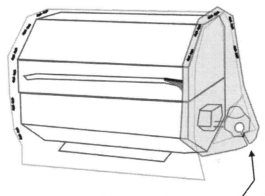

Cut a slit up from the bottom, and a small hole. Work the fabric around the regulator and enlarge and reposition the hole to fit around it.

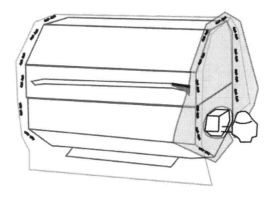

Flatten out the side panel around the regulator and staple the rest of the way, leaving the bottom open.

131

Step 7 – Lay the fabric pieces out flat. Mark a smooth stitching line along the dots you have made, adjusting a little if necessary.
Mark the hem fold line.
Mark where the pleats and darts are.
Add ½" seam allowance to all seams, and add 1" for a hem allowance and make a line. This is your cutting line.
Cut out the pieces along the cutting line.

Step 8 – Stitch any darts.
Now, with *right* sides together, staple the side pieces to the Top piece, matching up the marks you made. Stitch the side pieces to the Top piece.
Stitch a ½" double hem along the bottom.

Step 9 – See Fig 4-58.
Try on the cover *right* side out. Make two fabric-covered Velcro straps, about 5" long, with Velcro hooks – See Section 3 – Velcro Rollups.
Make two fabric covered straps, about 12" long, with Velcro loops.
Stitch these onto the hem at the front and back of the cover. These will go underneath the grill, to hold the cover on.

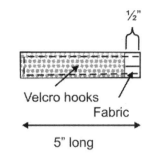

½"

Velcro hooks

Fabric

5" long

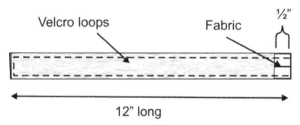

Velcro loops

Fabric

½"

12" long

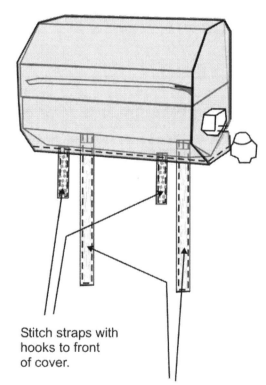

Stitch straps with hooks to front of cover.

Stitch straps with loops to back of cover.

Fig 4-58 Make fabric-covered Velcro straps to go under the grill and hold the cover on.

Step 10 – If you are making a grill cover with a separate pocket for the regulator, make a 'lid' (see Section 3 – Drop Cover) but leave the side seam open except for the first inch as follows:

Cut out a circular piece of fabric to the diameter of the regulator, and add 1" to the diameter for seam allowance.

Cut out a rectangular piece of fabric the same length as the lid's outside circumference, plus an inch or two. The width is the measurement from the outermost edge of the regulator to the side of the grill, plus 1" for seam allowances.

Make a fabric-covered Velcro strap about 10" long, with Velcro hooks on it. Fold one short edge of the fabric rectangle under by ½" (don't stitch yet)

and stitch the Velcro strap to the rectangle as shown in Fig 4-59-a (hook side up).
Stitch Velcro loops along the center of the rectangle and overlap onto the strap about an inch as shown in Fig 4-59-b.

Now stitch the circular lid to the side piece. Stitch the side seam only about 1" or so down the side, leaving the rest open. Stitch a single ½" hem along this side opening. See Fig 4-59-c.

Stitch the finished lid to the grill cover, with the opening of the lid towards the bottom of the grill. See Fig 4-59-d.

The Velcro strap wraps around the lid and the regulator to hold the cover on.

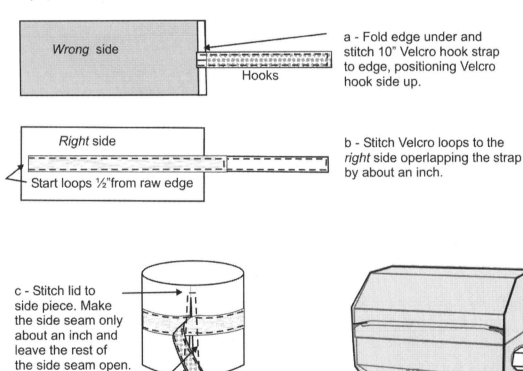

Wrong side

Hooks

a - Fold edge under and stitch 10" Velcro hook strap to edge, positioning Velcro hook side up.

Right side

Start loops ½"from raw edge

b - Stitch Velcro loops to the *right* side operlapping the strap by about an inch.

c - Stitch lid to side piece. Make the side seam only about an inch and leave the rest of the side seam open.

Turn the edge of the side seam under ½ and stitch a hem.

d - Stitch the little cover to the side, with the opening facing down.

Fig 4-59

133

Jerry Jug Covers

Plastic Jerry cans are expensive. If you have to store yours outside along the side decks, it doesn't take long for the hot sun to discolor them and damage the plastic. Then, not only do they look crappy, their life is shortened considerably. The answer…..covers of acrylic canvas.

You can choose a colour to match the sail cover or other canvas on the boat, or a neutral ivory or light grey which will make them less noticeable.

The cover can be a simple drop cover, or it can have an opening around the handle so you can move the jugs around with the covers on them. The opening also allows the jerries to be lashed securely in place with a line. A flap stitched to the cover and passing under the handle to the other side helps protect that part of the jerry from the sun, and helps keep the cover from flying off in the wind and sea.

Some covers are pretty fancy, with webbing loops and straps for affixing to lifelines, or some attempt to cover several jerries all together. It all depends on your boat, and your preference. The instructions that follow are for a single cover, with optional opening for the handle.

Fit – the cover must fit loosely, so that it can be used easily. It should drop easily over the jerry jug and not be a struggle, or you will hate using them. Plastic jerries expand a lot in the heat, so the best time to do a measuring and fitting is at high noon when the jerry is all puffed out. If this is not possible, make the measurement around the jug at least 3" too large, and make the side seam allowance 1" instead of ½". Then you can always let things out, but it's hard to make a cover bigger after the fact.

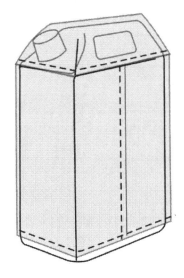 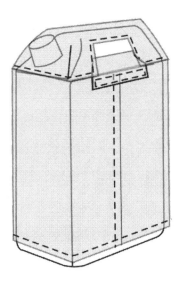

Fig 4-60 The jerry cover can be simply a loose drop cover, or an opening can be made so the jerry can be moved around easily with the cover on.

Step 1 – Wrap the jerry loosely in a piece of canvas (*wrong* side out) as shown in Fig 4-61. Staple in place, and mark the stitching line. Remember to keep the fit loose, and leave a fairly large seam allowance.

Step 2 – Stitch the side seam along the marked stitching line. Fold the seam allowance over to one side, and topstitch ½" away from the seam line.

Step 3 – Stitch a ½" double hem around the bottom.

Step 4 – Leave the cover *wrong* side out. Place it over the jerry again as shown in Fig 4-62.

Now take a rectangular piece of canvas and staple it along both long sides – *right* sides together. Staple the lid such that the hem of the jerry cover does NOT touch the ground. (This is so that water will not collect around the bottom of the cover and possibly blister or discolor the deck.)
When this is done, place a staple at the center point of the short sides.
Now, staple darts into the corners, to take up the excess. See Fig 4-63.

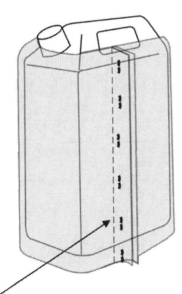

Fig 4-61 Wrap the jerry loosely with the canvas. Staple in place. Mark the stitching line.

Step 5 – Gently remove the cover. Stitch the darts and trim the excess seam allowance to ½". Stitch the lid onto the cover. Trim the seam allowance to ½". Turn the seam allowances up, and topstitch in place.

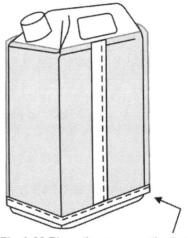

Fig 4-62 Place the cover on the jerry so that the hem does not touch the floor.

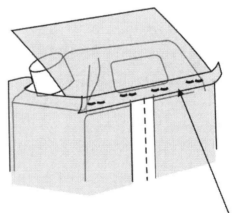

Fig 4-63 Staple a rectangular 'lid' to the top edge - along the long sides first. Then staple at the center point of the short sides. Staple in darts at the corners.

135

Step 6 – Turn the cover *right* side out. Put the cover back on the jerry. If you are not making an opening for the handle, you are done.

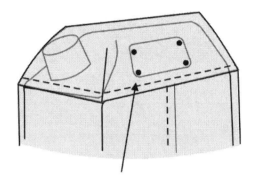

Mark corners of the opening.

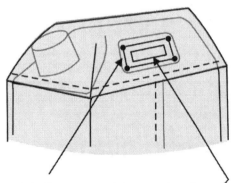

Join the corners into a rectangle. Mark another rectangle ½"inside the first one.

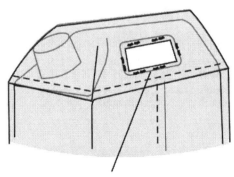

Clip the corners, and turn the edges under by ½". Staple in place for now.

Fig 4-64

Step 7 - To make an opening for the handle, mark the corners of both openings for the handles - See Fig 4-64.
Mark lightly – you are marking on the *right* side of the fabric. Remove the cover.

Flatten out the cover and mark the lines for the openings – lightly. This is the fold line. Mark another rectangle ½" to the inside of this one – this is the cutting line.
Cut out the rectangles along these cutting lines. Clip the corners, and turn the seam allowance to the inside. Staple in place for now.

Step 8 – Put the cover on the jerry and make any adjustments to the opening if necessary.
If you are adding a flap, measure:
The distance from one side of the opening, under the handle to the other side.
The width of the opening.

For the flap, cut a piece of canvas:
Width = the width of the opening plus 1" for seam allowances.
Length = twice the measurement you took from one side of the opening to the other, plus 2" for Velcro overlap, plus 1" for seam allowances.

Turn the long ends under ½". Fold the flap in half along its width, and staple in place. Cut a piece of Velcro loops and seamstick it along the folded end. Stitch the long sides close to the fold, and stitch on the Velcro. (See Fig 4-113 in the Dinghy Cover instructions.)

On one of the openings, place the raw edge of the flap under the lower edge, with the Velcro side facing down. Stitch in place, and stitch around the opening all in one step.
On the other opening, place Velcro hooks along the lower edge - on the *right* side of the fabric. Stitch the Velcro, and around the opening.

Drop the cover onto the jerry, thread the flap under the handle and secure it to the other side with the Velcro.

Wind Scoops

There are infinite designs for wind scoops – from a very simple flat panel, to big square-box structures designed to be rain and squall-proof. Much depends on whether you spend most time at anchor (when your bow will usually be facing into the wind), or at a dock where you can't control the direction of the wind
.

In its simplest form, a wind scoop is a flat panel of fabric which attaches behind the hatch. It is supported by lines tied to some available point like the forestay, lifelines or bow railing.

If the hatch opens toward the bow of the boat, you can easily open and close the hatch underneath this kind of flat wind scoop.
If the hatch opens toward the stern, it is more difficult – the wind scoop must be high enough to allow the hatch to be closed underneath it. Otherwise, you have to take the scoop down to close the hatch. This is inconvenient in the middle of the night!

A wind scoop can attach to the hatch on 3 sides, improving the rain-proofness and the ability of the scoop to catch wind from the sides and divert it into the boat.

It can be shaped like a big high box or a rounded dome. You will probably have to experiment with several designs before you find the perfect solution for your boat.

The wind scoop in the photo below features a batten along the top to hold it open, and is designed to be rain-proof as in Fig 4-67. Viewing windows allow you to see if any bad guys are sneaking up on you when the scoop is in the 'down' position.

Canvas for Cruisers

1. Simple Flat scoop

Here is a simple wind scoop that will keep out most rain:

This wind scoop is a flat piece of fabric – the width of the hatch at the back, and wider at the front edge. It should extend about 2 hatch openings forward, to keep out rain in moderate wind conditions.

Add 2" to the sides and to the aft end, for a 1" double hem. Add 2" at the front edge to hold a batten. The fabric piece should look something like Fig 4-65a.

On the front edge, reinforce the *wrong* side of the hem allowance by stitching on a small patch of vinyl where the ends of the batten will be. This will protect the fabric against chafe from the ends of the batten.

Stitch on a patch of vinyl on the forward corners – these corners take a lot of strain.
Stitch a 1" double hem on 3 sides – side edge, aft edge and other side edge.
Stitch a 1" double hem in the front edge for the batten.

In the forward corners, you can attach webbing loops, install grommets through the hem (also holds the batten in place) or sew rings to the corners. These are the strong points that will allow you to tie the corners to the attachment points on the boat.

To attach the scoop to the boat, two snaps behind the hatch will hold the scoop down in almost all wind conditions. Or you can use other types of fasteners such as twist lock.
For serious rainy conditions, you can install snaps further forward along the sides of the scoop so that you can snap it down along the sides of the hatch, and then tie the forward edge of the scoop very low to the deck. (Fig 4-65b)

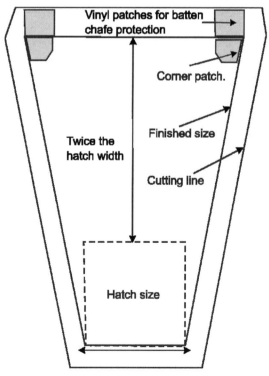

Fig 4-65a Mark the fabric based on the size of the hatch.

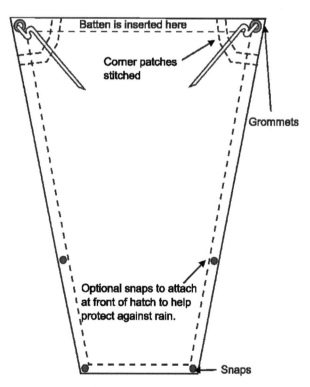

Fig 4-65b Stitch hems, reinforce corners and install snaps or other fasteners at hatch corners

138

2. Curved scoop

Another popular shape is a curved arrangement that can go around 3 sides of the hatch.

Measure the outside dimensions of the hatch - length (l) and width (w).
Mark out 2 pieces of fabric as in Fig 4-66. The foot measurement = length + half the width, all divided by 2 because there are 2 pieces.
Height is usually 5 - 6 feet or about 3 times your hatch length measurement.
Add ½" for seam allowance on the curved sides, and 1" on the straight sides.
Cut out.

Now just stitch the curved sides *right* sides together, Open it out, fold the seam allowance to one side and topstitch.
Make a 1" hem all around, reinforcing with webbing. Install snap fasteners or other type at the corner attachment points.

To hold the scoop up and forward, make an attachment point of a grommet or webbing loop at the top center, possibly reinforcing with a patch. This will have to be secured to some point on the boat to pull it up and forward.
To hold the scoop open you might also have to put attachment points somewhere along the side. Or a batten with pointy ends inserted into grommets. Try it on your boat to make adjustments.

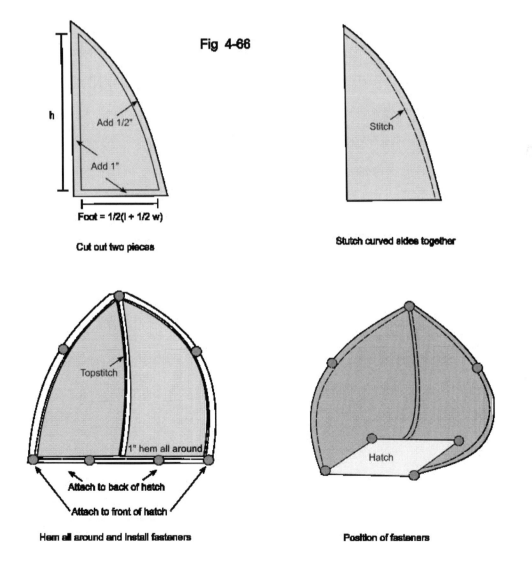

Fig 4-66

Add 1/2"

Add 1"

h

Foot = 1/2(l + 1/2 w)

Cut out two pieces

Stitch

Stutch curved sides together

Topstitch

1" hem all around

Attach to back of hatch

Attach to front of hatch

Hem all around and install fasteners

Hatch

Position of fasteners

Canvas for Cruisers

<u>To improve rain-proof-ness</u>:

To keep rain from blowing into the hatch, you can incorporate a flat rectangle of fabric or stiff vinyl like Strataglass, which sits straight up from the leading edge of the hatch like a fence to block the rain. But not so high as to block the air flow.

Side walls from the sides of the hatch to the 'roof' of the wind scoop helps keep out rain from the sides and gives you some place to stitch the 'fence'.

The roof of the wind scoop can come forward, and then slope down towards the deck so that the rain has trouble blowing up and over the inner 'fence' and into your bunk. See Fig 4-67. Sort of like a dorade.

To design such a scoop for your particular boat, you should make a pattern out of plastic, cardboard, or outline it with strings. Alternatively you can cut panels of fabric and staple them together to fit the boat.

Incorporating clear vinyl windows into the wind scoop can assist you in getting more light below, and allow you to stick your head up and see what is going on outside the boat!
Wind scoops can be fun to make, limited only by your imagination.

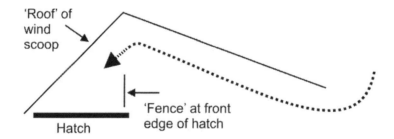

Fig 4-67 Side view of a rain-proof wind scoop. Note how the fence at the front of the hatch will block rain. The roof of the wind scoop slopes up and then slopes down to below the level of the fence. This way, rain has trouble blowing inside, up and over the fence.

Side Porthole Wind Scoop

Side portholes are usually very small, and therefore don't allow much air below when you are at anchor. A shaped scoop can be made to direct wind into the cabin.

Step 1 – Make a pattern out of brown paper, or thin cardboard as shown in Fig 4-68

Step 2 – Mark the pattern onto Sunbrella. Add 2" all around for a 1" double hem.

Step 3 – Turn a 1" double hem on all sides. Stitch and topstitch (Fig 4-69).

Step 4 – Install grommets at points b & c as shown. Install snap buttons in the other corners as shown. Install snap screw studs in matching places on the boat. Tie leech line to the grommets for attaching to the lifelines or stanchions.

If the hatch opens towards the outside, you will have to adjust the pattern to allow the hatch to open and remain in a horizontal position. See Fig 4-70 Stitch an insert to the aft end of the scoop so that the wind doesn't just blow right through.

As an alternative method of attachment, you can stitch in a boltrope to the top edge, and install a track to the boat; this will make the wind scoop more rainproof (Fig 4-71).

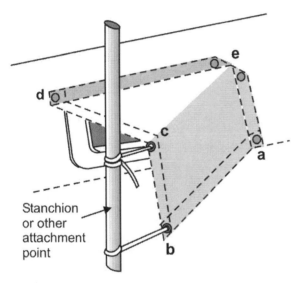

Stanchion or other attachment point

Fig 4-68 Make a pattern for the scoop

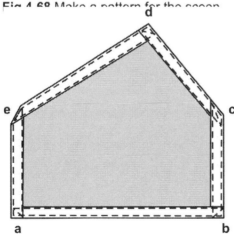

Fig 4-69 Make a 1" double hem on all sides and attach fasteners.

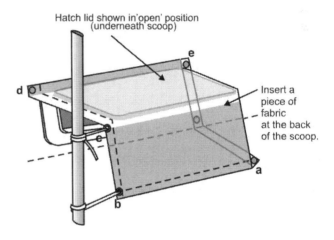

Hatch lid shown in 'open' position (underneath scoop)

Insert a piece of fabric at the back of the scoop.

Fig 4-70 If your hatch opens to the outside, you will have to place an insert at the aft end of the scoop to allow the hatch to open.

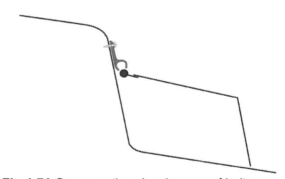

Fig 4-71 Cross section showing use of bolt-rope track attached to boat, and boltrope sewn onto top edge of windscoop

Wind Diverter

Once you get the air coming into the boat, you might want to direct it towards or away from certain areas. This can be made with just a very simple flat piece of fabric. It works best for a square hatch because the diverter can be turned any of 4 different directions. For a rectangular hatch, it can be turned only 2 directions. It can be made from canvas for privacy and shade, or out of clear vinyl if you want to let in light.

Step 1 – Measure the dimensions of the inside frame of the hatch (Fig 4-72).

Step 2 – Mark out a piece of fabric – one side will be the measured size of the hatch frame, and the opposite side could be up to a foot longer – depending on how far down you want the scoop to 'droop'. See Fig 4-73.
Add 2" all around for a 1" double hem. Cut out.

Step 3 – Turn a 1" double hem on all 4 sides. Stitch and topstitch. The hem might not be necessary if you are using clear vinyl.

Step 4 – Install snap buttons equal distances from each other along the 3 short sides. Install matching snap screw studs to the hatch opening.

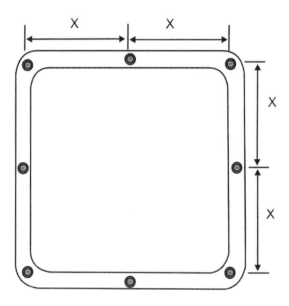

Fig 4-72 Mesure the size of the hatch frame. This drawing shows the evenly spaced placement of the snaps which will be used to attach the air diverter.

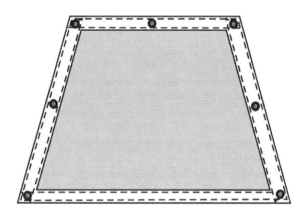

Fig 4-73 Note the wedge-shape of the diverter. Make a 1" double hem all around, install snaps.

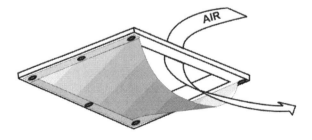

Fig 4-74 This shows the diverter installed, and how the air gets deflected.

Window Cover

Window covers are used in situations where there is a large window which lets in too much heat, or to protect the windows from crazing in the sun. They are usually made of vinyl mesh material, but you could use acrylic canvas, for total shade.

Window covers are simply flat pieces of fabric, hemmed and fastened to the outside of the boat, usually with snap fasteners. In the version I have described below, a vinyl frame is made for the inside of the hem – this makes a nicer, neater finish than simply turning the hems under 1".

If you want the window covers to look snazzier, you can make a frame all around on the *right* side of the window cover in a contrasting colour of vinyl, perhaps to match the sail cover. Rounded corners always look nicer than squared-off corners.

When making a set of window covers, cut all of them along the same grain of the fabric. Consider where the fastener studs will be placed – on the boat itself, or to the frame of the window. If there is no frame, or for some reason you can't attach the cover to the window's frame, you will need to add about 2" all around so that you can attach the cover to the boat itself (Fig 4-75).

If you don't have enough room around the window to put studs into the boat itself, you might have to use the adhesive snaps (SNAD's) to attach the cover to glass itself.

It is important to know that depending on what the window is made from (vinyl, acrylic, automotive glass), mesh materials could possibly transfer their grid marks to the window if the fabric is lying right up against the window. This is caused no so much by the fabric itself but rather the grit and dirt under the cover, combined with any flapping or motion of the cover combined with intense sun and heat. You can use lengths of piping made from yacht braid stitched along the inside of the cover, or little rubber 'feet' stuck to the fabric or the window itself. Anything to keep the mesh slightly off the window.

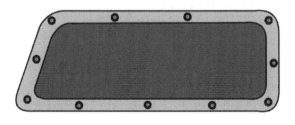
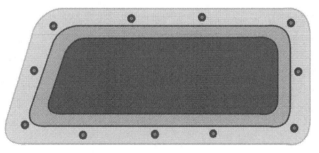

Fig 4-75 Your window cover will have to be larger if you are putting the fasteners on the boat itself, rather than on the frame of the window.

Canvas for Cruisers

Step 1 – If it is a smallish flat window, you can mark the shape directly on the fabric,
Measure the maximum height and width of the window.
Add a couple of inches to each dimension and cut out rough shapes of fabric.
Tape the fabric to the boat and mark the outlines of the outsides of the window onto the fabric.

If it is a complicated shape like a curved windshield make a plastic pattern for each window.
Run a line of painters tape all around the edge of the window, then place your seamstick on top of this tape. (Seamstick sticks VERY well to windows, so this will make it easy to remove after you are done patterning)
Remove the seamstick paper possibly a section at a time and place the patterning plastic onto the seamstick, nice and flat and wrinkle-free.
Mark the window outside edges and corners as a series of dashed lines, and any other references such as Top, Bottom, Outside etc.
Follow the instructions Making Patterns earlier in this book to mark out your fabric.

Step 2 – Cut out the fabric to size, adding a ½" seam allowance all around the outside (Fig 4-76).
(Don't add the ½" hem allowance if you are binding the edges)

Step 3 – See Fig 4-77. Cut out a frame of vinyl (Shelterite) to go all around the window. A 1" frame is usually OK, but it depends on the boat.

(Shelterite gives the window cover strength for attaching the snaps, and stiffness, but you can also use the same fabric as the window cover itself.)

Cut the pieces for the frame so that the frame is ½" smaller all around than the mesh which you have cut out. (See Fig 4-77).
If you prefer a neater look, you can cut a single piece of vinyl the same size and shape as the mesh fabric (but ½" smaller all around).
Lay the vinyl on top of the mesh, stitch around the inner edge and then trim away the inner portion to reveal the mesh window. (This wastes more fabric but is easier to sew)

Line up the outside raw edge of the vinyl frame to the stitching line on the mesh (the line ½" in from the raw edge) as shown in Fig 4-77. Staple in place. Don't use seamstick – it will eventually bleed through the mesh.

The window cover will look nicer if the frame is just very slightly tauter than the mesh fabric.

Stitch the inner seam.

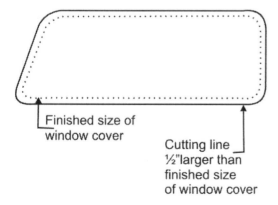

Finished size of window cover

Cutting line ½"larger than finished size of window cover

Fig 4-76 Cut out fabric allowing ½"seam allowance all around.

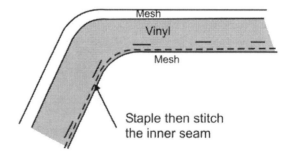

Mesh
Vinyl
Mesh

Staple then stitch the inner seam

Fig 4-77 Make a frame of vinyl and position it so it is ½"in from the raw edge of the mesh. Staple in place and stitch the inner seam.

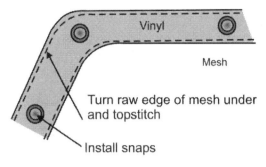

Turn raw edge of mesh under and topstitch

Install snaps

Fig 4-78

Step 4 – Now turn the raw edge of the mesh under ½" clipping curves as required. Staple in place. Stitch close to the edge (Fig 4-78).

Install snap screw studs to the boat, and then snap buttons in matching places to the window cover. (This a good use of the Quick Fit Snap tool you spent so much money on!)

Cubbyhole cover

Here's a good way to cover up those cubbyholes in a boat's cockpit, or open shelving inside the boat when you don't want the contents to spill out. It is just a flat rectangle, with a U-shaped zipper so that it can be opened and closed.

Step 1 – Cut out a rectangle of acrylic canvas, vinyl or other sturdy fabric roughly to size to cover the opening. Allow for a 1" double hem (i.e. cut at least 4" wider and longer than needed).

Tape the piece of fabric in place and mark out the position of the zipper so as to allow access to the cubbyhole.

Or
Make a plastic pattern.

Step 2 – Turn a 1" double hem all around the outside. Stitch and topstitch.

Step 3 – Install a #5 continuous zip or a coil-type zip, along the marked zipper line, stitching close to the tape's edge. (See Section 2 –Turned in zipper, and Zipper on a curve). Don't forget to put on the head.
Slit the opening with a sharp seam ripper. Turn the raw edges under and stitch close to the fold. You will have to notch the inner curve, and clip the outer curve to make the fabric fold under easily.

Step 4 – Install snaps (button side) to each corner of the cover, and maybe additional button snaps in the long edges if needed.
Screw matching studs into the boat.

If the cubbyhole cover is to be in the interior of the boat, you can install the zipper the opposite way – so that the flap falls down when open. This makes it easier to search around inside. The U-shaped installation makes the cover more waterproof.

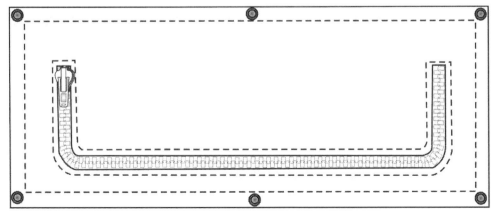

Fig 4-79 A cubbyhole cover allows access to the cubbyhole but allows it to be closed off.

Canvas for Cruisers

Hatch Covers

1. Opening Hatch Cover

This hatch cover is meant for opening aluminum hatches, where you don't want to drill holes into the frame for snap fasteners. It is designed to fit very tightly using a drawstring, and it can be left on all the time. You can open and close the hatch with the cover still on. Using light coloured Sunbrella lets some light in, but still protects the plastic window material.

The fit is critical. If you are making several of these hatch covers, it is best to make a pattern out of stiff clear plastic which you can use to mark the fabric accurately.
It helps to make a 'practice' cover of some scrap canvas so you can understand the proper fit for your particular hatch. Especially if you only have a limited amount of fabric to waste!

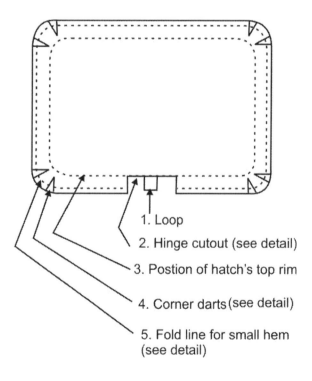

1. Loop
2. Hinge cutout (see detail)
3. Postion of hatch's top rim
4. Corner darts (see detail)
5. Fold line for small hem (see detail)

Fig 4-80 Basic features of the hatch cover. See text and other illustrations for details.

The cover must be sized so that the hem will barely overlap the lower lip of the hatch. If it overlaps too much, it will interfere with the gasket of the hatch and cause the hatch to leak.

There can be no allowance for turning raw hem edges under and under again, because it will create too much bulk. Therefore you must cut this cover out with a hot knife and make a ½" single hem.

The basic features are shown in Fig 4-80 – this is what the pattern will look like. Referring to the numbers in Fig 4-80:

1. This is the position for a small loop of flat binding which holds the cover taut across the hatch's center. Make the loop slightly too short of the hem fold line (about 1/8") for a tight fit.

2. This is the cut-out for the hinge. Cut the inner corners slightly rounded as opposed to square – it makes binding the edge easier. See Fig 4-81 for details.

3. Hatch's top rim. This is just a reference line on your pattern, but is important to mark so that you can measure accurately the distance down to the hem.

4. Corner darts. See Fig 4-82. Note how the hatch's top and bottom rims are marked onto the pattern, and how the point of the darts extend to just below the hatch's top rim. This is a small detail, but having the points of the darts end all at the same place really makes the hatch cover look perfect and professional. It helps to lightly mark the corners of the hatch's top rim onto the fabric, in order to position the points of the darts perfectly when you go to sew them.

5. A small ½" single hem. See Fig 4-83. This will contain a leech line. The hem fold containing the leech line must extend a scant ¼" inside the lower rim of the hatch. Enough to hold on to the hatch frame, but not enough to break the seal.

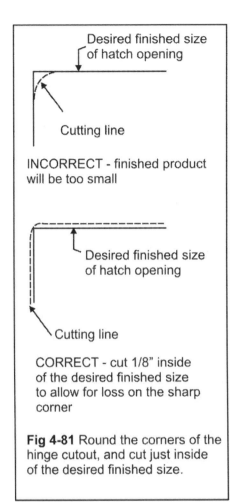

Desired finished size of hatch opening

Cutting line

INCORRECT - finished product will be too small

Desired finished size of hatch opening

Cutting line

CORRECT - cut 1/8" inside of the desired finished size to allow for loss on the sharp corner

Fig 4-81 Round the corners of the hinge cutout, and cut just inside of the desired finished size.

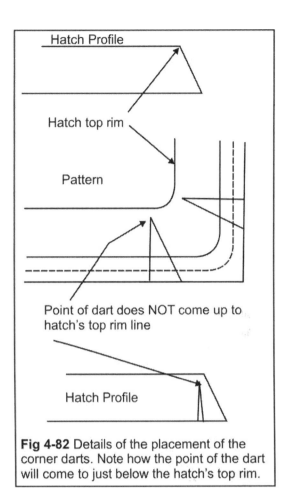

Hatch Profile

Hatch top rim

Pattern

Point of dart does NOT come up to hatch's top rim line

Hatch Profile

Fig 4-82 Details of the placement of the corner darts. Note how the point of the dart will come to just below the hatch's top rim.

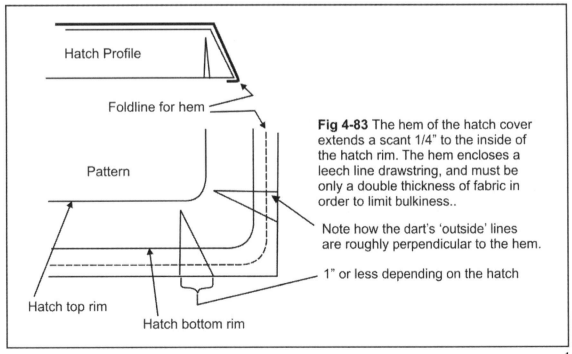

Hatch Profile

Foldline for hem

Pattern

Hatch top rim

Hatch bottom rim

Fig 4-83 The hem of the hatch cover extends a scant 1/4" to the inside of the hatch rim. The hem encloses a leech line drawstring, and must be only a double thickness of fabric in order to limit bulkiness..

Note how the dart's 'outside' lines are roughly perpendicular to the hem.

1" or less depending on the hatch

Canvas for Cruisers

To make the hatch cover:

Step 1 - Measure the length and width of the hatch's top rim. Add 2 ¼" all around for a standard Goiot™ hatch rim (but check the height of the hatch's rim). Mark the position of the hinge cutout. Make up a pattern as per Fig 4-80 through 4-83. Mark the cutting line and the darts.

Step 2 - Cut out the cover with a hot knife, leaving the outside corners square for the moment. (You will trim them into a nice curve after you have sewn the darts.)

Step 3 - Bind the edge of the hinge cutout with Sunbrella centerfold binding (Fig 4-84)

Step 4 - Stitch on the hinge loop (also Sunbrella centerfold) See Fig 4-85.

Step 5 - Make the darts. Keep in mind that the wide ends of the darts will be folded up into the hem. To take out any excess thickness and to make a tight fit, curve the stitching very slightly outside of the line at the hem. See Fig 4-86 for details.

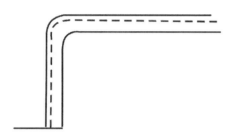

Fig 4-84 Bind the edge of the hinge cutout.

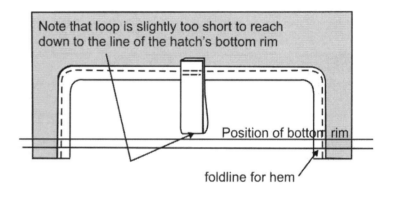

Fig 4-85 Stitch a loop of binding to the center of the hinge cutout, making the loop slightly too short as shown.

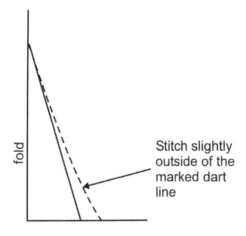

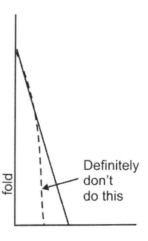

Fig 4-86 Solid line is the marked line for the dart. Dotted line is the stitching line.
Shown greatly exaggerated for clarity.

Step 6 - Trim corners into a nice rounded shape with a hot knife. (Fig 4-87)

Step 7 - Stitch a ½" single hem all around, placing a leech line inside. See Fig 4-88. At the corners, place the stitching line extra close to the leech line, making it hold tight there. This makes for a better fit. Tie a small loop in one end using a bowline.

To put the hatch cover on – position the cover over the hatch with the hinge loop over the hinge area. Push the hinge loop under the hinge to the inside of the hatch. Thread the loose end of the leech line under the hinge, through the hinge loop and through the small loop in the other end of the leech line. Reef the line down hard and force the corners of the cover around the corners of the hatch. Tie the leech line down to itself so it acts as a drawstring.

The cover should be very tight and a little difficult but not impossible to get on. Once in place, though, it is very secure and looks great.

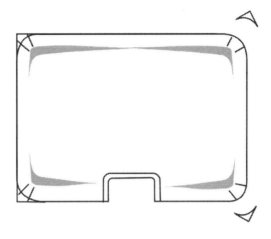

Fig **4-87** After stitching the darts, trim the corners with a hot knife to a nice rounded shape.

Fig **4-88** Stitch a small single hem, with the leech line encased inside.

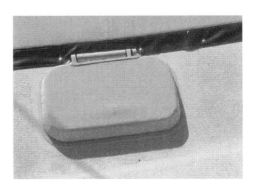

2. Simple Box Cover

This cover works well for wooden-framed hatches where you can screw snap-studs into the frame (Fig 4-89). The cover protects the wood from the sun. If you want to let some light into the boat, you can make an insert of clear vinyl as shown in Fig 4-90. See Section 5 – Bimini for how to make a vinyl insert.

This style can also be used on aluminum hatches if you don't mind putting fasteners into the hatch frame to hold down the cover.

If the cover is only to be used while the boat is laid up, then you can put fasteners into the deck. In this case, the cover will need a tab extension all around for the fasteners to attach to (Fig 4-91).

If you have leaky hatches, covers like this made out of vinyl can eliminate leakage while the boat is in storage (and to give you a chance to fix those hatches!).

The simplest covers are made out of one piece of fabric, covering the top and sides, with darts in the corners to square things off. Alternatively, there can be a piece for the top, and a separate band covering the sides. It depends on the shape of the hatch, and how perfect the fit is to be.

Simple darted cover:

Step 1 - Cut out a piece of fabric large enough to cover the top and 4 sides, plus hem. For the hem allow 1" if the height of the hatch allows it. If you are cutting out using scissors, allow 1 ½" so you can turn the raw edge under ½".

Step 2 - Lay out the piece of fabric over the hatch, pinch the corners in, and mark or staple. Stitch the darts, and trim the excess to ½" (Fig 4-92). If the hatch is beveled, the darts will be curved.

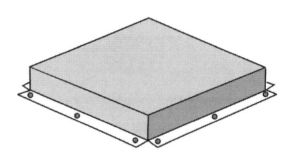

Fig 4-91 A hatch cover with a flange all around. Fastening onto the deck can solve the problem of leaky hatches.

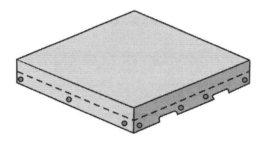

Fig 4-89 A simple box cover with snaps attaching the cover to the hatch frame.

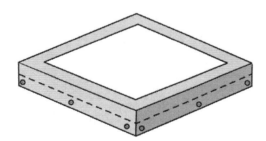

Fig 4-90 A clear vinyl or mesh insert lets in light.

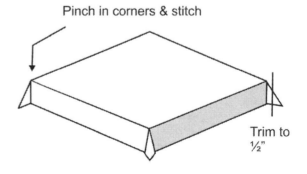

Pinch in corners & stitch

Trim to ½"

Fig 4-92 Lay a piece of fabric over the hatch, pinch in the corners and stitch.

Step 3 - Try on the cover and mark for the hem. Turn the hem under and stitch. If there are cutouts needed for hinges like in Fig 4-89, after hemming mark for these, cut out and bind the edges with centerfold binding

Install snap studs in the hatch frame, and snap buttons in the cover.

<u>Banded cover:</u>

Step 1 - Cut out a piece of fabric roughly to size, lay it out on top of the hatch and mark the outline of the hatch frame. Add ½" seam allowance all around. Or, make a plastic pattern.

Cut out a band for all around the outside, allowing for ½" seam allowance and 1" for the hem as above. (Fig 4-93).

If the hem needs to extend onto the deck for fastening tabs like Fig 4-91, make a banded cover with 4 separate bands – one for each side. Add another 2" to the height of the band to allow for the flange. See Fig 4-94

Step 2 - Staple the band to the top piece, and stitch ½" from raw edges If you are using a continuous band, at the corners, clip the seam allowance of the band down to just above the stitching line to help make the sewing easier.

Step 3 - Install stud fasteners in the hatch or deck, and then install the matching snap buttons in the cover.

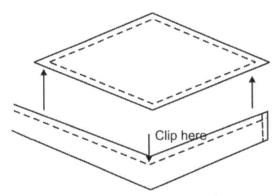

Fig 4-93 A banded hatch cover has one piece for the top of the hatch and a long band all around the outside.

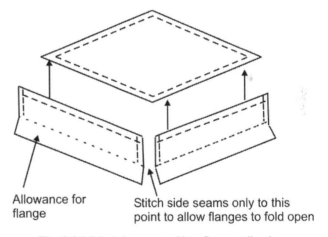

Allowance for flange

Stitch side seams only to this point to allow flanges to fold open

Fig 4-94 A hatch cover with a flange allowing the cover to be fastened to the deck.

3. Butterfly Hatch

Because a traditional Butterfly hatch is shaped, separate panels need to be made for each surface. Make a pattern out of plastic – mark the size and shape of the hatch, and then transfer the markings for the finished size to the fabric. Add ½" seam allowances to all the sides except the hem – for this, add the hem allowance as explained above, depending on whether the attachment point will be on the deck or to the hatch itself.

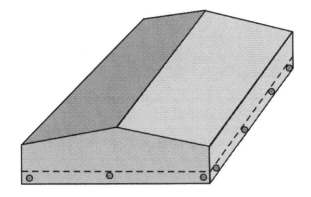

Fig 4-95 Cover for a Butterfly Hatch.

Handrail Cover

Fig 4-96a Simple handrail cover held on with snaps.

Fig 4-96b Attached using webbing tabs and snaps, close to ends

A cover for a handrail is usually done to protect a varnished teak handrail from the sun.

The first question to ask is whether the handrail will be covered only when the boat is in storage or at dock, or do the handrails need to be covered while the boat is sailing.

If a storage cover is all that is needed, then the cover can be a simple one, as in Fig 4-96. If the cover needs to be on while sailing, then provision will have to be made so that someone can get their hand under the cover to grab the rail, as in Fig 4-97.

Consider how the cover will attach to the handrail so it doesn't blow off. Snap fasteners as shown in Fig 4-96 are very secure but many people don't want their nice teak handrails to have holes drilled in them for the snaps.

The alternative is to use snaps, twist locks, ties or Velcro installed on the canvas itself, under each handrail opening, as shown in Fig 4-97.
The fasteners under the openings closest to the ends of the cover must be close to the ends, to prevent the cover from slipping back and forth.

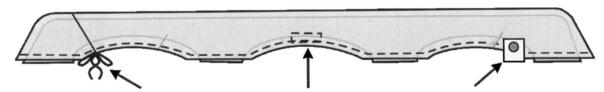

Fig 4-97 A handrail cover for use when sailing, so the handrailcan be gripped.

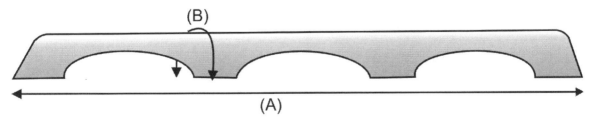

Fig 4-98 Measure up

153

Canvas for Cruisers

Simple Handrail Storage Cover:

Step 1 – Measure up – see Fig 4-98.
A - Measure the length of the handrail at its base. Add at least 4", even more if the rail is very long.

B - Measure the distance from the deck, up over the top of the handrail, and down to the other side. Add 1" if you are cutting out with a hot knife, otherwise add 2".

Step 2 – If you cut out with a hot knife, stitch a ½" single hem along <u>one</u> of the long edges. Otherwise stitch a ½" double hem.

Step 3 – Drape the cover over the handrail, *right* side down. Hold the hemmed edge just above the deck of the boat and mark the fold line for the hem for the other side. Just as in the jerry can cover, it is important for the cover to barely not touch the deck, especially if the deck is painted. The cover can trap water and blister the deck or cause dirt to accumulate and mold to grow.

While you have the cover in place, staple the curved ends to the shape of the handrail. See Fig 4-99.

Remove the cover and re-mark the stitching line for the curved ends. Also re-mark the hem line nice and straight. Trim away any excess fabric for the hem, and stitch the hem.

With *right* sides together, stitch the ends along where you stapled the ends. Trim seam allowances to ½".

Turn *right* side out. Attach snap fasteners to the cover and to the handrail. Or if you are not putting a snap stud in the handrail, install fasteners to go under the handrail at each end.

Handrail cover for use in sailing:

The only difference in this cover from the previous one is the addition of Velcro or snaps to hold the cover on below each opening of the handrail, and a slight adjustment in measuring:

Follow the previous Steps 1 through 3.
Use paper clips or small clamps to hold the fabric together under each of the handrail openings where the fastenings will be - to make sure you have enough slack in the fit of the cover.

Before removing the cover, mark the center position of these handrail openings and the position of any ties (See Fig 4-99). If the rail is big and thick, you will probably have to install snaps onto webbing tabs to reach under the rail

Step 4 – Remove the cover. Re-mark the stitching lines for the ends, and mark the fold line for the hem. Stitch the hem.

Step 5 – Stitch rectangles of Velcro to the areas you marked, or install snap fasteners into the hem. If you are using any ties for fastenings, stitch short pieces of leech line to these areas.

Step 6 – Fold the cover in half lengthwise *right* sides together, and stitch the ends.
Trim the excess seam allowances to ½".
Turn *right* side out.

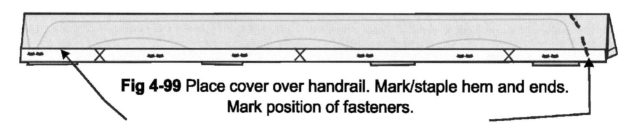

Fig 4-99 Place cover over handrail. Mark/staple hem and ends. Mark position of fasteners.

Cap Rail Cover

The only teak that is harder to keep looking nice than a handrail, is a cap rail. When the boat is not actively in use, you can cover these areas to make the varnish last longer.

Cap rail covers also work well to protect flat teak handrails such as on solid railings or stairways on a motor yacht.

The most durable fabric in the sun is acrylic canvas. Using Tenara thread will mean you won't have to restitch – ever.

The most difficult decision with cap rail covers is how to attach them. Usually there is a problem with attaching directly to the wood, as it spoils its looks. So have a look and see if you can attach to some point that can't be seen, such as underneath the rail or at its ends. Perhaps you can use snaps underneath the railing. Or you might be able to install grommets and lace the cover on underneath.

Short 1-2" of PVC pipe can be cut, slit and made into a "C" shape to hold the cover on kind of like a clamp.

What about Velcro attached to the underside of the rail, or Velcro tabs underneath the cover to attach to itself.

If the cap rail is curved enough, and it is an outside curve, you might even be able to put a drawstring in at the hem and draw it up tight underneath the cap rail (like a dinghy cover).

Using weights in the hem seldom works – the wind will always find a way to blow it off.

Once you have decided the attachment method, you might have to make a pattern. If the rail is straight, just measure the width and length. But many cap rails on boats are curved. A pattern made of thin cardboard (such as pieces of file folders taped together) works well. Just tape the cardboard to the top of the railing and mark the contour from underneath. (We'll call this piece the 'lid') See Fig 4-100.

Now decide how far the 'skirt' will have to hang on either side of the lid, and if it is the same length for the whole lid. See Fig 4-101.

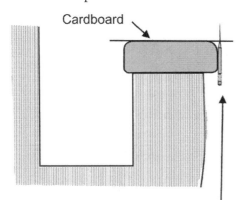

Fig 4-100 This is a cross section of a cap rail on the bulwark of a sailboat. Place a piece of cardboard on top of the cap rail, and mark from underneath, a line along the edge.

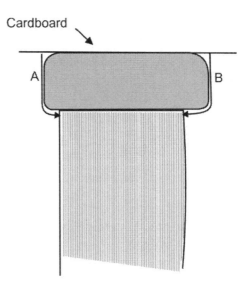

Fig 4-101 Measure down from the cardboard, to get the width of the 'skirt' sections A and B.

Mark the lid onto the fabric using the pattern or your measurements. Add ½" to each side for seam allowance. Cut out.

Cut out the skirt pieces:
Length = the length of the cap rail plus 1" for seam allowances.
Width = twice the measured height of the skirt, plus 1" for seam allowances.

Making a few hatch marks will help with this next step. See Fig 4-102.

Crease both skirt pieces in half along their length.

Stitch one skirt piece to the *right* side of each edge of the lid piece.(Fig 4-103)
If the lid is curved, clip the seams at the curved areas. Fold the seam towards the lid and topstitch.
(Fig 4-104)

Try on the cover. Mark the location of any fastenings. Remove the cover and install the fastenings to the cover and to the boat if necessary.

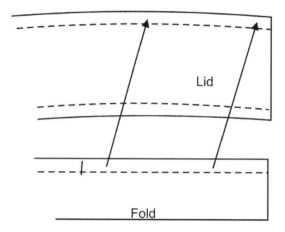

Fig 4-103 Fold skirt piece in half lengthwise, matching up the hatch marks.
Stitch to *right* side of lid.

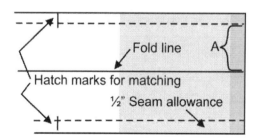

Fig 4-102 Skirt piece showing hatch marks to be used for matching up, and height of skirt (A)

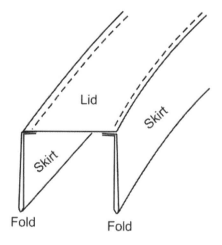

Fig 4-104 Skirt pieces stitched and topstitched to lid.

Dinghy Cover and Accessories

A dinghy cover is a pretty advanced project, but not out of range if you take your time. Study other dinghy covers before you decide on yours. There are a lot of imaginative ideas out there, but essentially, all share some basic elements.

First, a dinghy cover is meant to protect the dinghy from sun, dirt and chafe. Second, it can be made to look ugly so as to detract possible thieves, or it can be a real work of art and an expression of your skill and creativity.

The most important thing is the fit. To get a good fit, the easiest way is to make a plastic pattern. You can use newspaper or other paper too, but if clear plastic is available, it is nicer to work with. Some people stitch fabric panel 'blanks' together and then fit this to the dinghy, marking it up for the openings. This method has never worked for me.

To get the dinghy cover to hold tight to the dinghy is sometimes difficult. There are many ways of attachment. A lot depends on the design of the dinghy.

One method is to make a casing all around the outside of the cover, which holds a 1/8" leech line draw string. This is then tensioned drum-tight to hold the cover on. Ideally, the dinghy has a rub rail all around the outside so the leech line drawstring has something to grab onto.

No matter how tight you draw the leech line however, the long sections will tend to flap and can even scoop up water as you are riding along. Depending on your particular dinghy you might need additional attachment in these areas. You can install snap fastener studs onto hypalon or vinyl patches, and glue these to the dinghy using the proper recommended adhesive, then install snap sockets onto the cover. Or the new adhesive Snads. Could work both for the outside, and the inside hems.

Another popular method is to attach the cover to the dinghy with Velcro. You will never get Velcro itself to stick properly to an inflatable dinghy. So, instead, stitch Velcro hooks to a long strip of Hypalon or whatever the dinghy is made of. This is then glued, (using the type of glue recommended for the material the dinghy is made of), all around the dinghy's outside and inside rims. Velcro loops are then sewn to the dinghy cover.

There are other attachment methods including plastic hooks, buckles, bungee cord, fishing line drawstring and even drilling holes through the dinghy's rub rail.

Most dinghy covers are made of acrylic canvas, some of a good quality flexible vinyl like Stamoid. Vinyl can be slippery when wet. But it would make reinforcing holes easy, maybe even unnecessary.

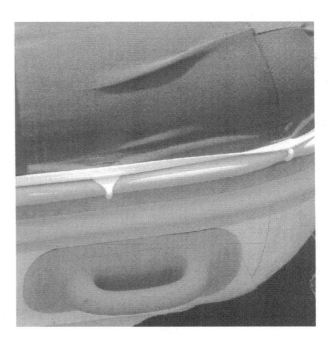

Canvas for Cruisers

Most covers need some kind of chafe patches sooner or later. You might as well put them on sooner – it's easier that way. The areas especially prone to chafe are along the rub rail and on the upper surfaces of the bow and stern ends where the dinghy can get trapped under docks. If you hoist the dinghy up on davits, check to see if there is any chafe – you will need to put patches there.

Where you sit can get chafe. Consider putting a layer of vinyl there if you use your dinghy a lot.

Check to see what people are doing at the aft end of their dinghies. Some dinghies have a problem while underway, with scooping water up underneath the cover and spewing water from the aft ends into the dinghy like Niagara Falls. In this case, you need to make an insert of mesh, or just an opening for the water to vent out the back instead of into the dinghy.

Once the cover is made, a tight fit can be achieved by deflating the dinghy a little, tightening the heck out of the drawstring, (or sticking the cover down with the Velcro) and then re-inflating. It is better to make the cover a tiny bit too snug rather than too loose.

For a drawstring cover, using 46" acrylic canvas is better than using 60" because the width is more convenient for making panels on most standard-size dinghies. For a Velcro'd cover, 60" is a convenient width.

When planning the cover, think about the position of the panel joins. Usually, there are either one or three panels for the bow, and then 2 or 3 panels along the sides. Maybe there's a way to arrange the panels so you don't have to have a seam where there is going to be an opening or hole in the cover.

This is one project where it is really worth the extra expense of using Tenara or Profilen thread. Dinghy covers are awful to restitch.

Drawstring Dinghy Cover

Step 1 – Make a pattern. Take the dinghy to the beach with some plastic pattern material, a big permanent marker, scissors and masking tape . Maybe a beer or two….. A calm day is best.

Make sure the dinghy is clean and dry enough so the tape will stick, and inflated to its normal state of turgidity.

Starting at the bow, tape pieces of plastic to the dinghy. You can use the seam lines of the dinghy itself to help you decide where your fabric pieces need to join together.
Cut out 'x's' in the plastic to allow the protrusions for oar locks and things to poke through. Smooth out the plastic and mark the opening. If you are having trouble making the plastic lay smooth, cut out the plastic hole to fit around the protrusion.

If you need to cut relief slits in the plastic where it needs to curve inward at the inside of the bow, make a little pie-shaped pattern to fill in the gap.

Take your time and work one piece at a time, trimming excess plastic off to keep things nice and neat.

Pinch in pleats (darts) where the fabric needs to curve to fit around the bow and stern.

Some people pattern the bow and only one side and then using the pattern as a flip-side mirror image for the other side of the dinghy. If you do that, flip the pattern piece over and try it on the dinghy to make sure it fits – some dinghies are not symmetrical..

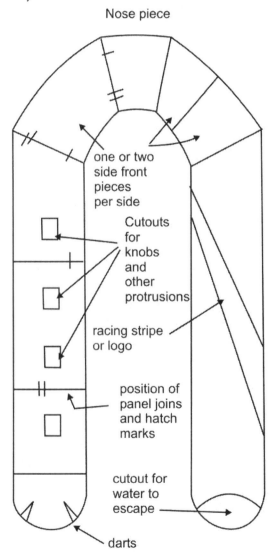

Fig 4-105 The basic elements of a dinghy cover.

Mark the following onto the plastic pattern:

The outside hem line - or the line where the cover will have to curve under the dinghy's rub rail.

The hem line on the inside and position of any snaps or Snads.

The outlines of all protrusions and openings.

The position of any grommets, buckles or hooks required to help hold the cover to the dinghy.

The size, shape and position of any chafe patches needed, including a possible chafe patch for your butt to sit on.

The seam lines where you will have to join panels – such as where the bow curves around, and where it meets the sides. Make hatch marks to help match up the panels later.

The size, position and shape of any darts – especially at the aft ends.

Speaking of the aft end – are you making openings to allow water to escape when you are zooming around? If so, mark the outline of these openings.

Mark the pattern pieces front and aft, 'outside' etc. so you can orient things when you get the pattern off the dinghy.

If possible, decide where you will make the side panel joins and mark these on the pattern.

If you are making racing stripes, letters, flags, logos or other artwork out of other colours of fabric, mark where these lines will be.

Sit and have a beer and look at your work. Have you marked everything? Considered everything? OK, now carefully peel off the pattern.

Canvas for Cruisers

Step 2 – Lay the plastic pattern face down onto the fabric. Use a dull pencil to trace a series of dashed lines on top of the marked magic marker lines. These marks will transfer to the canvas. If you are using dark canvas, you will have to reach under the edges of the plastic with a white pencil and mark a series of dashes where the lines are.

Mark the outlines for all the cutouts and any darts. Mark the panels #1,2,3 etc or however you want to keep then in order. Mark which way is forward to help you align things later. Don't forget the hatch marks, so that you can align the panels later.

Remove the plastic. Even out and straighten out the dashed lines with a pencil. Mark the seam allowances for where the panels join with another line 3/4" outside of that marked line. Mark the hem allowances with a line 2" outside of the lines marked for the rubrail, and the inside hem fold line marked from your pattern.

Cut out the fabric with a hot knife if you have one. Don't cut out the holes yet.

Step 3 - It is easier to do all the detail work on the separate panels before they are all sewn together into one big piece. So, for any openings which have to be finished, and for any chafe patches that have to be added, do these first, before sewing all the panels together.

If an opening or a chafe patch spans across any panel joins, well, then of course you will have to join the panels first.

The bow panel(s) - It might be just as easy to make the bow panel entirely out of vinyl – the bow area is subject to chafe everywhere. Otherwise, stitch on the chafe protection where required.

Step 4 – Finish the openings for all the protrusions. You can make the holes plain or fancy. In any case, squared-off holes are easier to stitch than round ones.

One way is to cut out the openings with a hot knife and bind the raw edge with centerfold or vinyl binding. This looks nice but is quite fiddly to do and extremely time-consuming to restitch if and when the time comes.

Another way is to make square, rectangular or octagonal patches of Vinyl or canvas.
See Fig 4-106.
Place the patch centered over the opening, *right* sides together.
Stitch around the hole, along the marked line. Then cut away the patch material and the dinghy cover material ½" inside of the stitched line.
Turn the patch to the inside.
Turn the raw edges (if any) under ½" and topstitch. (See Fig 4-106)

If you want to show off the holes with a contrasting colour of fabric, you can stitch the patch *wrong* sides together around the marked hole outline. Trim out the hole as above, and turn the patch to the *right* side.
Then topstitch the edge if it's a vinyl patch, or turn the raw edges of a canvas patch under ½" and topstitch

My favourite way of finishing the holes is using the method described in Section 2 – Patches and reinforcements – Reinforcing a hole.
Do all the construction, but DO NOT cut out the vinyl for the hole. When the cover is complete, try the cover on the dinghy and then gradually fit and cut out the holes. This allows the hole to be cut exactly in the right position, in case there are imperfections in the fit.

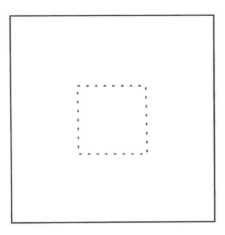

1.Position the patch over the marked opening on your dinghy cover.

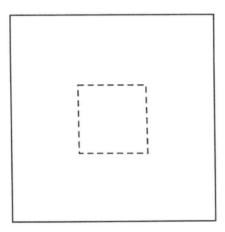

2. Stitch along the marked opening.

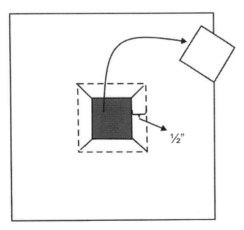

3. Clip out the center part, leaving ½" seam allowance. Cut slits into each corner.

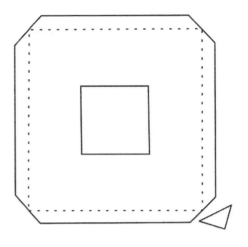

4. Push the patch through the center cut out, and smooth it out on the other side. Clip the outer corners as shown, and turn raw edges under ½"

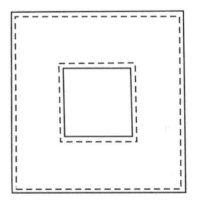

5. Topstitch along the outside and inside edges

Fig 4-106 How to make an opening.

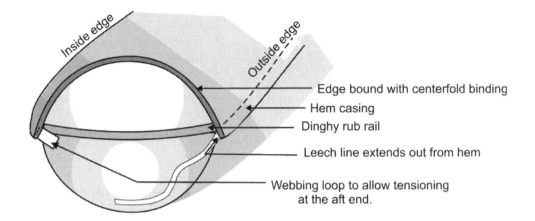

Fig 4-107 Aft End Openings of dinghy pontoon. Make a cutout so that the aft end remains uncovered, and bind this edge. Or make an insert of mesh fabric.

Step 5 - Aft End.

The dinghy cover will most likely have to go up and over the transom. Finish this area like an Inside Corner (Section 2 – Hems & Casings – Inside Corner).

For a plain opening, at the aft end of the pontoons, bind the raw edge with centerfold binding. (Fig 4-107)

If you are filling in this area with vinyl mesh, don't bind the edge. Instead, cut out the mesh using the plastic pattern – leave an allowance for the drawstring hem.
Make darts as marked in your pattern to conform to the shape of the dinghy's pontoons. Stitch it to the fabric panel, *right* sides together. Open it out flat and topstitch the mesh towards the fabric panel.

Step 6 – Join the panels

Stitch the panels together using a Topstitched Seam (see Section 2 - Seams).
Do one side, then the other, then the bow.

Your seam allowances were marked at ¾", so stitch ¾" from the raw edges. The extra seam allowance will enable you to make fine adjustments if you need to let things out a bit.

If there are any openings or chafe patches that cover more than one panel, stitch these now.

If you want, you can try the side panels on the dinghy, and the bow panel, to make sure they fit before you do the Topstitching.

Once you are happy with the fit of both sides and the bow, join them all together and topstitch.

Step 7 – Inside Hem

Hem the inside edge of the cover with a 1" double hem or whatever is required so that the hem fold line matches the pattern.

For a cover with Aft End Openings, stitch a loop <u>strongly</u> into the aft edge of the inside hem. (See Fig 4-107). This will be used to loop the leech line through to securely tension the aft end of the dinghy cover.

Step 8 – Outside edge.

This edge particularly is subject to a lot of chafe and needs to be covered with vinyl (e.g. Shelterite).

However, if you simply stitch a strip of vinyl to the raw edge and then turn up the hem, the vinyl will make it so thick that it will not gather nicely to a drawstring.

Mark a line 1 ½" up from the rubrail line. Mark another line ¾" below the rubrail line (this will be your hem fold line)

Cut out long strips of 2" wide Shelterite, and stitch the strips to the cover along the top line.

Place the drawstring along the hem fold. Turn up the hem with the drawstring inside and staple it in place. (it is hard and time-consuming to try to thread the line through the hem later.)

Stitch along the bottom edge of the Shelterite strip which will also enclose the drawstring.
This protects the edge from chafe but still allows for relatively easily gathering of the canvas underneath. See Cross-section Fig 4-108

Make a break in the hem and the drawstring at the bow. This is where you will do the tightening-up. Leave about 2 feet of leech line hanging free at all ends so you can really yank on it when you go to put the cover on.

If the dinghy cover has Aft End Openings, leave about a foot or so of leech line extending out the aft end as shown in Fig 4-107. This is used to tension the cover's aft end.

If there is not an Aft End Opening, or if the aft ends are mesh, extend the hem casing and leech line right around the aft end of the cover, over to the inside (where the webbing loop is shown on Fig 4-107). Double the leech line end back on itself and stitch it very securely down. It will be pulled on hard to tension the cover.

Step 9 – If your measurements and sewing have been accurate, the dinghy cover should fit tightly to the dinghy and not flap or fall off. But, if there is still a problem, don't despair. You might have to use grommets and tie-downs in strategic places, snaps or hooks which can hook under the rub rail.

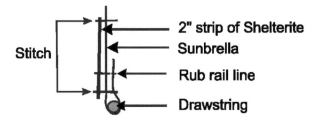

Fig 4-108 Cross section of hem showing how the vinyl strip covers the rub rail and drawstring extends below.

Canvas for Cruisers

Velcro'd Dinghy Cover

In some ways, a Velcro'd dinghy cover is easier to make. There is no drawstring. You don't need chafe protection at the rub rail. You do have to accept the fact that you have to glue some Velcro onto your (possibly) beautiful new dinghy. But I think the Velcro'd Dinghy cover is a little more tolerant to slight fitting and sewing inaccuracies.

Step 1 – Pick a nice day and take the dinghy to the beach, possibly accompanied by some cold beer. Bring plastic patterning material, seamstick and a magic marker.

Step 2 - Make a pattern.

Use the same method as described previously in the Drawstring Dinghy Cover with the plastic patterning material. If using seamstick, run a line of ¼" seamstick (the kind with the carrier strip) all around the dinghy where you figure the Velcro will go. This is usually all around the outside just above the rub rail, around the aft end of the pontoons above the rub rails, ending at the transom. On the inside of the dinghy, the Velcro usually runs under all the protrusions in a nice line

parallel to the outside line of Velcro, following the contour of the dinghy. Using plastic patterning material, place the plastic pieces over the dinghy pontoons, removing the seamstick paper a little at a time. Try to get the plastic on smoothly, with no wrinkles. Don't stretch it, just concentrate on getting it nice and even. When you come to the protrusions and handholds, just slit the plastic in an 'x' to go around these fittings.

At the aft ends of the pontoons, you will have to make pleats in the plastic patterning material – these will be darts in the fabric. Several small darts will give a more rounded result than a couple of large ones.

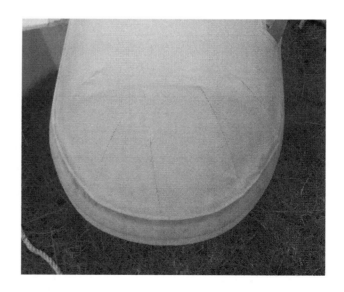

164

Mark the following onto the plastic pattern:

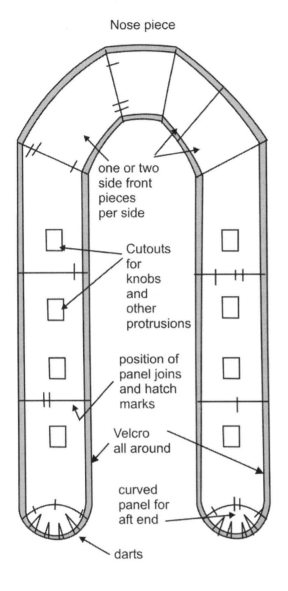

Nose piece

one or two side front pieces per side

Cutouts for knobs and other protrusions

position of panel joins and hatch marks

Velcro all around

curved panel for aft end

darts

Fig 4-109 Velcro'd Dinghy cover

The hem lines on the inside and outside based on the location of the Velcro.

The size, shape and position of any chafe patches needed.

The seam lines where you will have to join panels – such as where the bow curves around, and the sides – make hatch marks to help match up the panels later.

The finished size of the outlines of all protrusions and openings. If you are going to make flaps for underneath the handholds (see Step 5 below), mark how wide the flap should be – it should be narrow enough to fit comfortably underneath the handhold.

Mark the size, position and shape of any darts – especially at the aft ends of the pontoons. Speaking of the aft end – you can make a couple of separate fabric panels shaped like rounded arcs to curve around the stern ends instead of darts (see Fig 4-110).

Mark the front and aft, and 'outside' so you can orient things when you get the pattern off the dinghy.

Carefully peel off the pattern and remove the seamstick from the dinghy.

Step 3 – Lay the plastic pattern face down onto the *wrong* side of the fabric. Using a dull pencil, trace the outline, seam lines and cutouts as a series of dashed lines - as already explained in the Drawstring Dinghy Cover instructions.

If you are using 1" Velcro, add 1" all around for a 1" single hem. If you are using 1 ½" Velcro, then add 1 ½" all around.

Cut out the pieces of fabric.

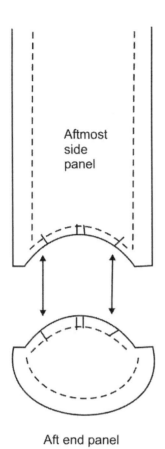

Aftmost
side
panel

Aft end panel

Fig 4-110 The aft end of the dinghy can be covered with a separate shaped panel.

Step 4 – Chafe patches - do all the detail work with chafe patches as explained in the Drawstring Dinghy Cover.

Step 5 – Openings for handholds - A nice look for an opening for a handhold can be achieved using vinyl patches on the inside of the cover, with a flap:

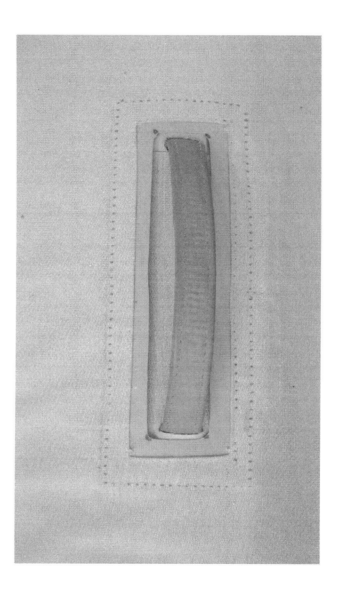

See Fig 4-111. Transfer the marks for the handhold opening to the *right* side of the fabric as follows - poke a pin through each corner, and

mark the corners on the *right* side. Then remove the pins and join the dots. (Use light marks, or a pencil that will erase or wash out. Remember, you are marking on the *right* side.) This is the fold line.

Still on the *right* side, mark another line ½" to the inside of the box you just made. This is the cutting line – but don't cut yet.

Cut out a piece of vinyl the size of the fold line, plus 1" all around. See Fig 4-112. Apply seamstick to the *right* side of the vinyl all around the very outside edge.

On the *wrong* side of the cover, center the patch over the marked hole, and stick it *right* side down onto the *wrong* side of the fabric.

Set aside the cover for now.

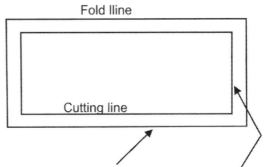

Fig 4-111 Transfer the markings for the handhold opening to the *right* side of the fabric. Mark another box ½"to the inside.

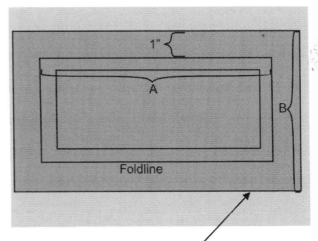

Fig 4-112 Cut out a patch of vinyl 1" larger than the marked foldline. Seamstick it to the *wrong* side of the fabric, centered over the marked foldline..

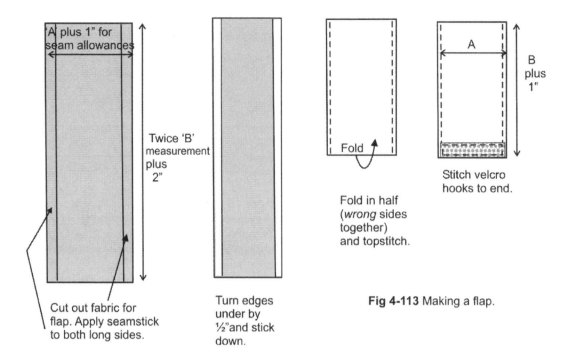

'A' plus 1" for seam allowances

Twice 'B' measurement plus 2"

Cut out fabric for flap. Apply seamstick to both long sides.

Turn edges under by ½"and stick down.

Fold

Fold in half (*wrong* sides together) and topstitch.

A

B plus 1"

Stitch velcro hooks to end.

Fig 4-113 Making a flap.

Make a flap of fabric as shown in Fig 4-113:

Finished width = the width of the flap, remembering that the flap has to fit comfortably under the handhold.

Finished length = the length of the vinyl patch plus 1" (shown as B in Fig 4-112).

Using seamstick, stick the flap onto the vinyl patch, Velcro side down. (Fig 4-114)

Stitch close to the edge of the vinyl, catching in the flap at the same time <u>at the top edge only.</u> Hold the flap out of the way when you get to the Velcro'd side of the flap, so as to NOT stitch it in with the vinyl flap. See Fig 4-115.

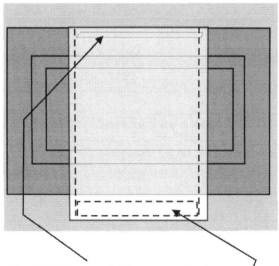

Fig 4-114 Seamstick flap onto vinyl patch, velcro side down, so that velcro extends off the end of the patch.

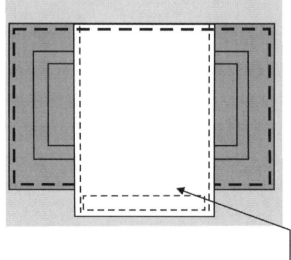

Fig 4-115 Stitch around the vinyl patch, close to the edges. DO NOT stitch the flap to the patch at the velcro end.

Stitch a length of Velcro to the *wrong* side of the cover, underneath the Velcro for the flap as shown in Fig 4-116.

Flip the cover over to the *right* side. It will look like Fig 4-117.

Carefully cut out the fabric along the cutting line, being careful not to cut the vinyl layer underneath (Fig 4-118).

Clip the corners and fold the raw edges under by ½". See Fig 4-119.

Stitch close to the fold – catch in the top edge of the flap underneath, but when you come to the bottom edge (with the Velcro) fold the flap away so you don't stitch through this end of the flap.

Leave the vinyl layer intact for now – you will cut it out when the cover gets put on the dinghy. The original cutting line is actually ½" to the inside of the foldline, but that's OK. This allows for the hole to be cut exactly where it should be, in case there are any imperfections in the fit of the cover.

(Once the opening is cut in the vinyl, the flap can be threaded through the handle of the dinghy, and will stick to the Velcro underneath. It makes for a nice look, helps the fit, and protects the little area of dinghy material underneath the handle.)

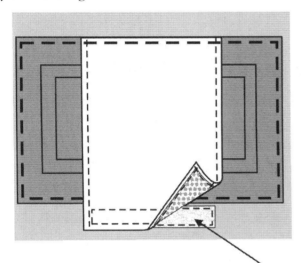

Fig 4-116 Stitch Velcro loops underneath flap's Velcro hooks.

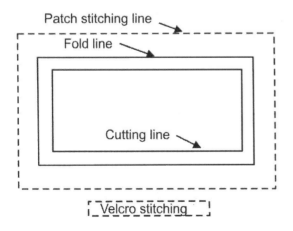

Fig 4-117 Seen from the *right* side, showing the stitching lines for the patch, the velcro, and the marked cutting line and fold line.

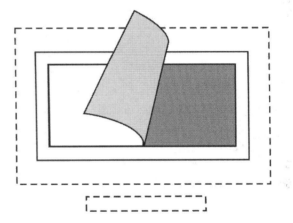

Fig 4-118 Carefully clip away the fabric along the cutting lines, being careful to NOT cut the vinyl underneath.

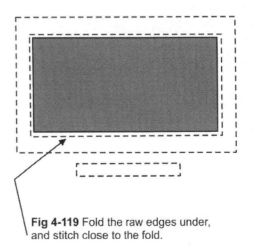

Fig 4-119 Fold the raw edges under, and stitch close to the fold.

Step 5 – Protrusions - Finish the openings for all the protrusions as described in the Drawstring Dinghy Cover, or use the same method just shown in Step 4 (without the flap).

Step 6 – Construct the aft end. Either make darts or use the curved pieces as shown in Fig 4-110.

Step 7 – Join the panels using a Topstitched seam (see Section 2 - Seams).

Step 8 – Fold the raw edges under by 1" (or 1 ½" depending on the width of the Velcro), along the marked hem line.

Stitch Velcro loops to the hem allowance on the *wrong* side of the cover. If you are using 1" Velcro hooks on the dinghy itself, try to get 1 ½" loops for the cover. This helps when it comes time to fit the cover on, to allow for any inaccuracies in the fit or changes in the dinghy's turgidity.

Depending on the type of dinghy, it often helps to leave an area of the cover 'Velcro-free' especially in difficult areas like the short, inside edge of the bow piece.

Fitting the inside edge, just behind the bow can be tricky. It can help to make a slit opening in the inside hem of the cover at that place, that will allow for adjustments in the fit.
If it happens that there is a fitting such as an oarlock or a handhold somewhere on the inside edge, you can leave this opening 'open' and use the slack to give the cover fitting some leeway.

Buy some Hypalon fabric or whatever the dinghy is made of, and cut it into strips equal to the width of the Velcro. This is critical – Velcro by itself, even the self-adhesive type will not stick to a dinghy for very long.

Butt the ends of the strips together and seamstick Velcro hooks to the material. Stitch the Velcro to the material close to the edges. Several shorter strips are better than one big long one.
Black is the best colour choice for the Velcro due to its extra UV durability. And polyester Velcro is better because it doesn't shrink as much as nylon and is more UV resistant.

Inflate the dinghy so it is quite firm but not hard as a rock. The idea is to try to have the Velcro strip the same tension as the dinghy itself. Glue the Velcro/vinyl strips to the dinghy with whatever adhesive is recommended to patch your dinghy. Let the glue cure well.. Leave a gap between the pieces of Velcro to allow for expansion and contraction of the dinghy.

To put on the cover drape the cover lightly on the dinghy. Starting at the bow – center the cover's bow piece and stick it down lightly. Then go to each aft pontoon edge and stretch the cover along the length of the pontoon – stick the aft edge down if possible. Working from the bow to the stern, fit the cover along the outside edges of the pontoons and smooth the cover over the top to the inside edge. Carefully clip out the holes in the vinyl patches as you go (if this was the type of openings you made). Once the cover is stuck 'loosely' down and fitted, then go around again and stick it down hard.

The Perfect Outboard Cover

An outboard cover can be a simple drawstring bag, and the outboard will be protected just fine. However, The Perfect Outboard Cover is beautiful and functional, and fits like a glove. It is padded with foam to protect the outboard cowling against bashing underneath docks and to protect the yacht's topsides when the dinghy is tethered alongside.

Step 1 – Make a plastic pattern as follows.

Stick ¼" seamstick all around the motor cover, just below the top edge. (Fig 4-120). Use the seamstick that has a plastic carrier strip and is not just pure goo. Don't leave the seamstick on the motor cover very long.

Peel off the seamstick paper.
Place a piece of patterning plastic over the top. (Fig 4-121). Without stretching the plastic, smooth it down all nice and even – no wrinkles. Even a little wrinkle in the plastic will be impossible to try to smooth out on the acrylic canvas.

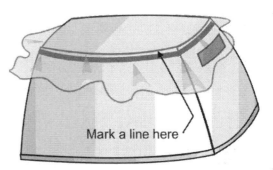

Fig 4-121 Smooth a piece of plastic over the top, and stick down.

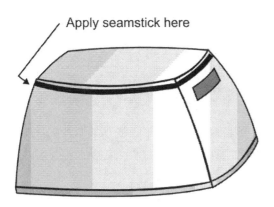

Fig 4-120 Stick seamstick all around the cover just below the top edge.

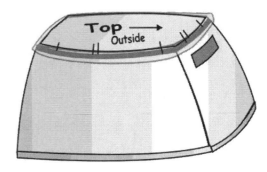

Fig 4-122 Pattern piece is labelled, top edge is marked and hatch marks are made. Excess plastic is trimmed off

Canvas for Cruisers

With a permanent marker, mark a line right along the top corner edge where the top meets the sides (Fig 4-121). Make a few hatch marks to help you match up the side pieces later. Mark any openings required for lights or any projections (Fig 4-122). Mark the piece 'Top' and 'Outside' and mark an arrow pointing to the front of the cover.

Trim off the excess plastic to within ½" or so of the marked line.

Apply seamstick to one of the sides of the outboard cover as shown in Fig 4-123. On the previously-made plastic pattern panel (in this case, the Top),stick the seamstick onto the plastic but NOT on top of the marked line, or when you remove the seamstick, you will remove the marked line with it! Continue the line of seamstick just inside the side edges and just above the ledge at the base of the cover.

Again, stick on a piece of plastic patterning material, nice and flat and even. Mark the edges as before, and make hatch marks (Fig 4-124). Label the piece, and mark which way is forward. Then trim off the excess plastic. (Fig 4-125).

Repeat the patterning process, applying seamstick and smoothing on the plastic for the front, back and sides.

Sometimes no matter how hard you try, you just can't work out the wrinkles – in this case make pleats in the plastic and mark for making darts in the fabric.

Mark hatch marks on each piece for matching up later, and mark the openings for the starter cord and air intake hole just barely to the inside of the actual holes.
Mark the lower edge where the hem will be – just above the outboard cover's lower rim.
Label each piece – top, front, back, left, right and which way is forward and outside so you can orient the pieces later.

Step 2 – Carefully remove the patterning plastic. Remove all the seamstick from the cover.

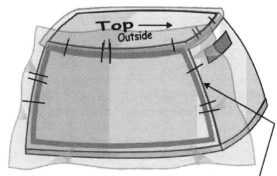

Fig 4-124 Smooth on the plastic. Draw a line all around the edge. Mark hatch marks in same place as the top piece of plastic, and mark new hatch marks on the sides.

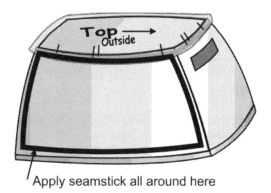

Apply seamstick all around here

Fig 4-123 Apply seamstick all around the outside of one side of the cover.

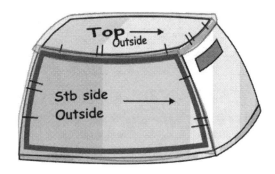

Fig 4-125 Trim off excess plastic. Label which side and 'Outside'

Step 3 – Mark out the fabric

Lay out the pattern pieces *wrong* side down onto the *right* side of acrylic canvas or other fabric. All the markings must be made on the *right* side of the fabric.

Pin the plastic out nice and flat with scratch awls on each corner. Remember that Sunbrella (especially dark colours) has a nap, so lay the pieces all the same direction on the fabric.

Reach under the plastic pattern and using a dashed line, mark the outlines, hatch marks and openings. (Fig 4-126).

Mark accurately – there is very little tolerance for error in this cover.
Use a white pencil or chalk because remember, you are marking on the *right* side of the fabric. So don't use a regular pencil or some other marker that will not come out.
Mark the hatch marks within the seam allowance, and mark the stitching lines reasonably faint so they are not so horrible to erase later.
Also mark the corners accurately with a dot.

Remove the plastic pattern pieces from the fabric.

The pieces need to be sewn oversized by about 1/8" to allow for the thickness of the foam you are going to use to line the cover. To help you do this, mark (except for the hem) the cutting line 5/8" to the outside of the marked dashed line you have drawn (Fig 4-127). This way, when you stitch using a ½" seam allowance, you will be making the cover 1/8" larger. Tricky!

To the side pieces, the front and the back, add 1" to the bottom for the hem allowance. If it is a big cover, add 1 ½" hem allowance instead.

For the openings, mark a box ½" to the inside of the original marks. This will be a fold line.

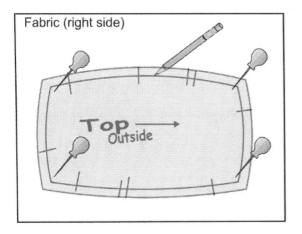

Fig 4-126 Reach underneath edges of the plastic and accurately mark stitching line, hatch marks and corners.

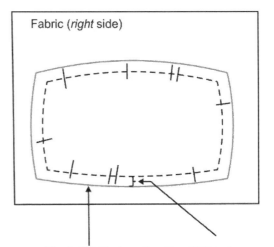

Fig 4-127 Mark cutting line 5/8" to the outside of the marked line.

Step 4 – Cut out the pieces

You can use scissors, no real need for the hot knife. Don't cut out the holes yet.

If you want to appliqué any kind of name, flag, logo, stripe, or other graphics, do so now on whatever panel you want.

If you had to make any darts, transfer the markings to the *wrong* side of the fabric and stitch the darts.

Step 5 – Foam Lining

Each panel will have a lining of ¼" thick foam. The foam has to be ever so slightly smaller than the fabric so you won't get wrinkles in the foam lining.

Here's one way to apply the foam to the fabric: Cut out pieces of foam roughly to the size of the panels. Lay out the fabric pieces *wrong* side down onto the foam.
For the side pieces and the front and back pieces, position the foam so that there is a straight edge, ½" above the fold line for the hem. (Fig 4-128).

Pin down one corner with a scratch awl. Stretch the foam slightly and stick a scratch awl in the next corner.

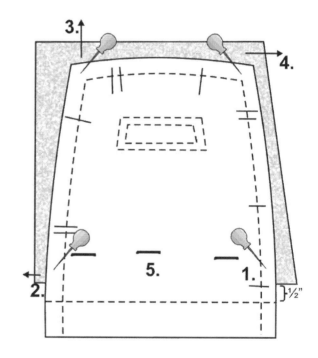

Fig 4-128
1. Position foam and stick in a scratch awl.
2. Stretch foam out this way. Stick in an awl.
3. Stretch foam out this way. Stick in an awl.
4. Stretch foam out this way. Stick in an awl.
5. Then put in the staples along the hem.

Work around all 4 corners, stretching the foam slightly and evenly so that it is slightly smaller than the Sunbrella. Not much, just a little. This will ensure you don't get any bumps or wrinkles underneath, in the foam.

Start stapling the foam to the Sunbrella, starting at the hem. Let the foam sit along a line ½" above the fold line for the hem. Staple about an inch above the raw edge of the foam.

While stretching the foam outwards all along the sides with one hand, use the other hand to staple the foam to the Sunbrella within the seam allowance. (Fig 4-129) Remove the scratch awls.

Here's another way, which I find easier:

Lay out the fabric pieces *wrong* side down onto the 'relaxed' foam.
Pin all 4 corners down with scratch awls.
Mark the outline onto the foam with a permanent marker.
Remove the scratch awls and cut out the foam along the marked line.
For the side and end pieces, cut 1 ½" off the bottom for the hem.

Position the foam underneath the fabric piece again so that the foam sticks out from underneath by about ½" or even less, at the side-hem corner. (See Fig 4-130).
Stick a scratch awl in this corner to hold it down.

Go over to the other side of the hem. Stretch the foam so that it sticks out underneath the fabric again, by about ½". Staple it. (Fig 4-130)
With the awl still holding down the one corner, pull on both the fabric and the foam so that the foam is flattened out underneath the fabric.

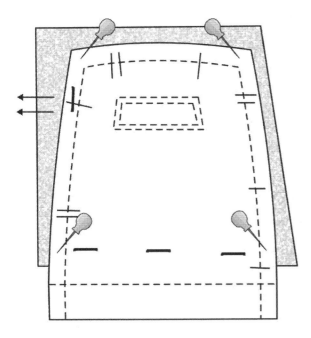

Fig 4-129 Stretch the foam out a little, and put in a staple. Repeat all around. Trim off excess foam

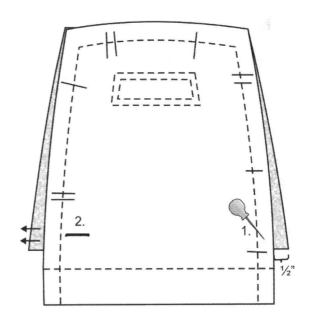

Fig 4-130
1. Position foam ½"above hem foldline and ½"outside of the Sunbrella. Stick in a scratch awl to hold in place.
2. On the other end, stretch out the foam by ½"Staple in place..

Canvas for Cruisers

Now staple your way back to the scratch awl, along the hem, stapling about an inch above the raw edge of the foam. (Fig 4-131)

Leave the scratch awl where it is.
Now, position the foam and staple the top corner so that again, the foam overhangs by about ½"or a little less.
Pull on the corner as before, with the scratch awl still holding down the other corner so the foam is nice and flat (Fig 4-132).

Working your way back towards the awl, pull the foam out from underneath the fabric by about ½" all along the side, and staple it in place evenly. (see Fig 4-133)

Staple the remaining corner, remembering to pull the foam out from underneath by about ½".
Stick in a scratch awl to hold it in place. Work your way along the top, and along the side as before, pulling the foam out from underneath by about ½" and stapling the foam evenly in place.
You now have a piece of foam that overhangs all the edges (except the hem) by about ½". When you remove the awls, the fabric pieces will be kind of puckery. But that's OK. When the cover goes on, the foam will stretch out nicely.

Stitch the foam to the fabric about ¼" from the raw edge of the fabric, (i.e. within the seam allowance). Don't stitch along the hem edges yet.
Remove all the staples except those at the hem edges. Leave these in for now.
Trim away the excess foam to be the same size as the fabric pieces.

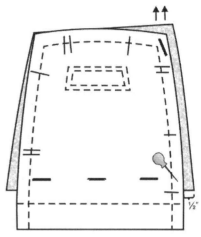

Fig 4-132 Go to the top corner, stretch out the foam ½"beyond the corner and staple.

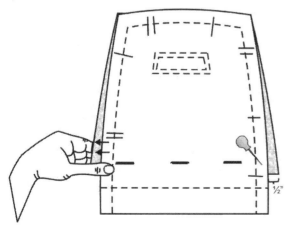

Fig 4-131 Stretch the fabric and foam out flat, and staple

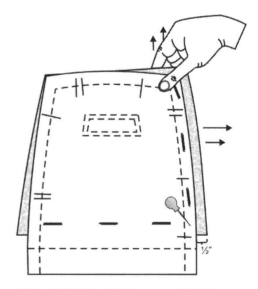

Fig 4-133 Stretch foam and fabric nice and flat.
Staple along the side, so that foam extends by ½"

Step 6 – Construct the cutouts.

Cut out a patch of vinyl (Shelterite) about 3" wider and longer than the size of the marked box. See Fig 4-134.

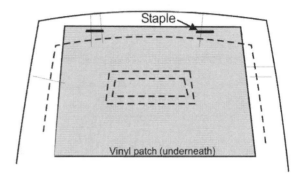

Fig 4-134 Center a patch of vinyl over the marked opening. Staple in place within the seam allowance.

Position the vinyl patch *right* side down, on the *wrong* side of the panel (that is, on the foamy side of the panel). The vinyl patch can extend into the seam allowances for now, but the stitching can NOT extend into the seam allowance at the top of the panel or the sides of the panel. If it does, make the finished size of the patch narrower here. The reason for this is because the vinyl will create too much thickness if it is included in the seam and it will go all wavy and not look nice.

Staple the patch in place within the top seam allowance.

Stitch the patch on with the *right* side of the fabric facing up, about 1" away from marked box. (See Fig 4-135).

Start and stop the stitching neatly and precisely at the center bottom. Make sure the stitching is parallel to the side seams, and an even distance away so it looks centered. Also stitch nice and straight and parallel to the top edge, OUTSIDE of and not within the seam allowance as shown.

Clip off the thread ends close to the fabric – you can singe them quickly with a lighter to remove them entirely. Or don't backstitch at all, pull the top thread through to the *wrong* side and tie off the ends. Remember, it's the details and workmanship that makes this cover so special.

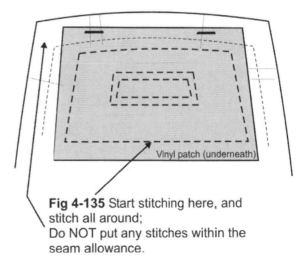

Fig 4-135 Start stitching here, and stitch all around; Do NOT put any stitches within the seam allowance.

Trim away the excess vinyl close to the stitching (See Fig 4-136).

c) Flip the panel over so the *right* side is up.

With scissors, cut about ½" inside of the fold line, through the Sunbrella only – NOT the vinyl. If you accidentally cut the foam, that's OK, you are going to remove it anyway. (See Fig 4-137)

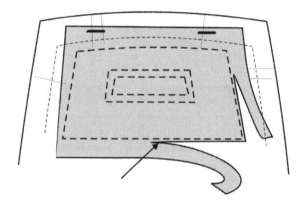

Fig 4-136 Trim off excess vinyl close to stitching

With a hot knife (if you have one), carefully notch the corners of the Sunbrella to the fold line (the line ½" in from the original marks). Don't burn the vinyl patch underneath. The use of the hot knife just makes the corners look nicer – no frayed edges.

Reach inside the hole you cut, and pull away the foam layer inside the stitching line of the hole. Use a pair of needle nosed pliers to get into the corners. You can just gently tear it away, no need to use scissors unless you have trouble.

Still working on the *right* side, tuck the Sunbrella under along the fold line. Again, starting and ending at the center bottom, topstitch all around close to the fold. (Fig 4-138)

To make it look really nice from the outside, don't use backstitching to secure your thread. Take the threads hanging on the outside and pull them to the *wrong* side. Tie a knot and clip off the ends. If the little ends try to show through the hole, just tape them out of the way with a little piece of seamstick (leave the paper on)

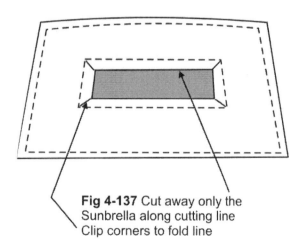

Fig 4-137 Cut away only the Sunbrella along cutting line Clip corners to fold line

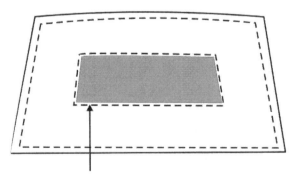

Fig 4-138 Turn under along fold line and topstitch close to fold line

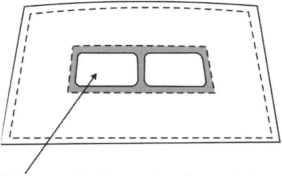

Fig 4-139 Cut a good looking opening with rounded corners, in the vinyl.
If the opening is large, leave a spine in the middle to prevent 'gaping'

Finally, trim away the vinyl to make the hole –
you can do this now, or wait until you start
sewing the panels together, to make sure you
have a good fit.

Cut the corners a little rounded so that they will
take any strain, and not the Sunbrella. For the
air intake hole, leave a 'spine' down the center,
so that the hole doesn't gape open (Fig 4-139).

Variation:
The air intake hole can be made out of vinyl mesh.
Follow the same process as described in this
'cutouts' section but make the patch out of mesh,
and don't, of course, cut an opening in it.

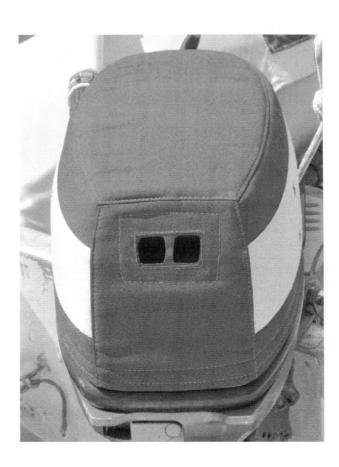

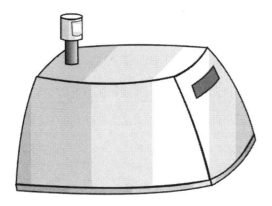

Fig 4-140 Some outboard covers have lights and other attachments.

Lights and other Attachments

Some outboard covers have places for attaching navigation lights and things (Fig 4-140). Usually the fitting can be screwed right through the Sunbrella. If this is the case, all you have to do is stitch all around the mark from the *right* side, and trim away the foam layer within the hole about ¼" away from the stitching. This makes it such that there is only a single layer of Sunbrella to screw through (Fig 4-141)

If the fitting needs an actual opening, follow the same procedure as above for the air intake opening described above (without the 'spine' of course).

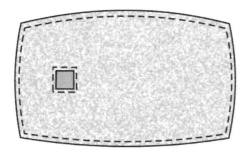

Fig 4-141 Stitch all around where the attachment is to go, and then cut away the foam, leaving a single layer of Sunbrella.

Step 7 – Stitch the Panels together

Now stitch all 5 pieces together as follows. Carefully match up the hatch marks and the corners.

This is one of the few times when I find that straight pins hold the pieces together accurately enough so you get a perfect match at the corners and along the desired seam lines. I place the pins in the same direction as the seam line and remove the pins as I approach them as I am sewing along. But staples can also be used. (Fig 4-142)

Fig 4-142 Place right sides together. Match corners and hatch marks. Stitch, starting ½"from the end, and using a ½"seam allowance to within ½"of the other end. Notice how the stitching line is1/8" outside of the original marked line.

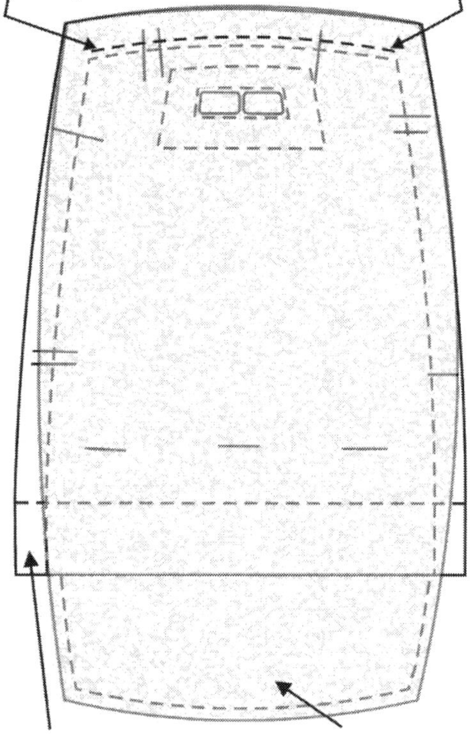

Back panel   Top panel

It is not important what order the pieces go together. I usually stitch in this order:

Stitch the Front to the Top, along the top seam, starting and stopping ½" in from the ends and using a ½" seam allowance.

Stitch the Back to the Top, ditto as above. If you want, you can try on the cover and see if your openings are going to fit right. If not you can make adjustments now in the two seams you just sewed.

Stitch the Sides to the Top, ditto as above. Again, you can do a trial fit for opening positioning.

Stitch the 4 side seams, starting ½" in from the top ends. Leave the top seam allowances free and stitch all the way down to the bottom of the hem.

The purpose for starting and stopping ½" in from the top corners is so that you won't get little folded over wrinkles at the corners.

Trim away a little of the seam allowance of the corners to reduce bulk.

Turn *right* side out and try on the cover. If you haven't cut out the openings in the vinyl for the holes, you should do this now.

Topstitch about ¼" from the seams. It looks nicest if you topstitch the top seam allowances towards the Top, and the seam allowances for the side seams towards the Sides. (Fig 4-143)

With scissors, trim off any raw edges of Sunbrella and foam close to the topstitching to reduce bulk.

Step 8 - Hem

Turn up the hem ¾" and staple close to the fold to hold it in place. (I know you made the hem mark 1", but if you only hem it ¾" it will leave a little hang over the outboard cover's lower ledge, and look nicer.) Staple so that the staple prongs are facing to the inside of the cover – easier to remove them later. The Sunbrella hem, when folded up, should cover the raw edge of the foam.

On the inside of the hem, stitch Velcro loops ¼" above the hem fold. The Velcro should cover up the hem's raw edge. If it doesn't, trim the hem a little bit. Stitch another row of stitching nice and straight and parallel, along the top edge of the Velcro. This row of stitching should catch in the foam, and hold it in place.

Stick a length of 1" sticky-back Velcro hooks all around on the outboard cowling, just above the ledge.

Put the cover on the outboard cowling. It won't be easy. The fit should be tight, smooth and no wrinkles. Perfect!

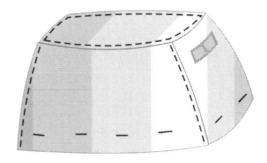

Fig 4-143 Topstitch

Canvas for Cruisers

Dinghy Anchor Kit

This isn't a cover, but seeing as how we're making things for the dinghy, it may as well go here.

Many people carry around in their dinghy, a little folding grapnel anchor and a few feet of small line to use as a stern anchor – to hold you off the dock, or as an anchor when snorkeling. Here's a great idea for a proper anchoring system in case the motor fails and you start drifting off to sea. It just might save you sometime!

The 'kit' consists of a foldable grapnel anchor, 250' of #8 cord, and the bag. Make the bag out of tough vinyl like Shelterite, and make the bottom of the bag from a scrap of medium-size trampoline mesh. If you can't find a little scrap of trampoline mesh, use 'regular' Textilene-type mesh, or use a piece of Shelterite and punch a bunch of holes in it with a grommet hole punch.

See Fig 4-144. The drawstring bag has a divider inside it. On one side goes the anchor and about 30 ft of line. This is for 'everyday' use.

On the other side goes the other 220' of emergency rode. The 250' of line is continuous, so you can feed out the whole length if you have to.
Don't use Polypro line – you need a line that sinks.

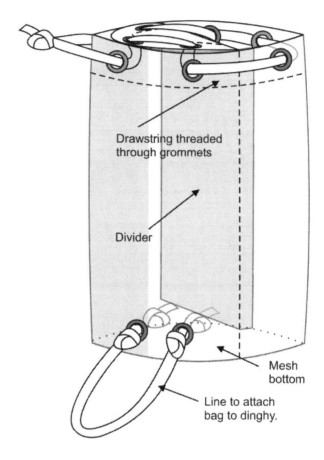

Drawstring threaded through grommets

Divider

Mesh bottom

Line to attach bag to dinghy.

Fig 4-144 The dinghy anchor bag is a drawstring bag with a partition, and a mesh bottom. It has a loop of line threaded through grommets for use in attaching the bag to the dinghy.

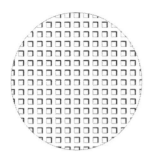

Fig 4-145 Cut out a circle of mesh about 9" diameter.

Step 1 – Cut a circle of trampoline mesh or other strong mesh about 9" in diameter (Fig 4-145).

Step 2 – Cut a rectangle of vinyl 30" by 'x', where 'x' is the height of your dinghy anchor plus 4". Add another inch for a single hem, and add another ½" at the bottom for a seam allowance. (Fig 4-146).

Step 3 – Mark out another rectangle about 9" wide and the same 'x' measurement plus 8" high. (Fig 4-147). Mark the top of the rectangle into an oblong semicircle as shown. This is the divider. Cut it out.

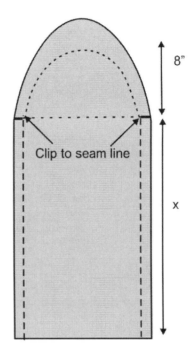

Fig 4-147 Cut out another piece of vinyl, the same height as 'x' plus a semicircle 8" high.

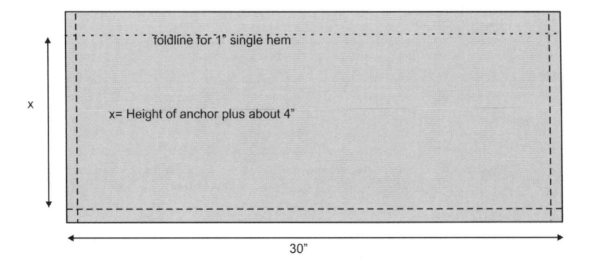

Fig 4-146 Cut out a rectangle of vinyl.

Fig 4-148 Stitch a 1" single hem along the top of the rectangular piece.

Step 4 – Turn a 1" single hem in the long side of the big rectangle (hereafter called the 'side'). See Fig 4-148

Turn a single hem along the curved side of the divider. Start with ½" at the sides, and taper to 1" in the center. Notch the curve to remove the excess and cut a slit ½" from each side to allow you to turn the hem as shown. It doesn't have to be pretty, just do the best you can.

Step 5 – With *wrong* sides together, stitch the divider to the side panel, about 8" in from the edges as shown. Stitch only to within 1" of the bottom (unhemmed edge). See Fig 4-150 and 4-151.

Step 6 – Bang in a couple of grommets about an inch and a half above the bottom edge of the side panel, about 1 ½" apart, somewhere in the 'loose' part of the side (which is still a flap at this point). See Fig 4-150.

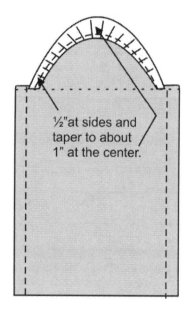

½"at sides and taper to about 1" at the center.

Fig 4-149 Turn a single hem along the top of the semicircle.

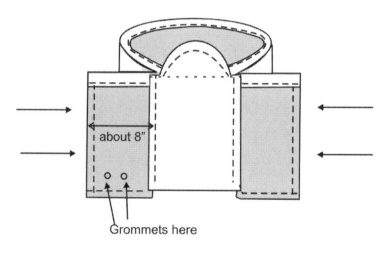

about 8"

Grommets here

Fig 4-150 Bring sides in towards each other and stitch divider to side panel about 8" in from each side..

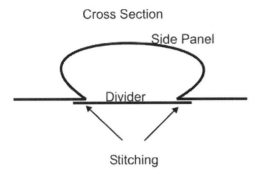

Cross Section

Side Panel

Divider

Stitching

Fig 4-151 Cross section, showing placement of divider.

Step 7 – Turn *wrong* side out. With *right* sides together, stitch the side panel to the mesh bottom, (see Section 3 – The Drop Cover). Do not catch in the bottom edge of the divider.

While stitching on the bottom, you can backstitch and break off the stitching in two places, and leave 2 openings through which you can thread a cable or chain. This may discourage some wanker from stealing your nice kit.

When you get close to finishing stitching the side to the bottom, stop. Stitch the side seam, trim it to ½" seam allowance and then finish stitching on the bottom of the bag, just like in The Drop Cover.
Turn *right* side out.

Step 8 – Install 6 grommets through the hem at the top, evenly spaced. Put 2 or 3 grommets into the curved hem of the divider, too.

Thread a piece of #6 cord through the holes for a drawstring, arranging things so that the curved part of the divider will fold over and act as a 'lid' for the compartment containing the 220' of emergency line.

Tie the ends of the drawstring together. Refer back to Fig 4-144.

Step 9 – Cut a piece of #8 cord 250 ft long.

Tie an overhand knot about 10" in from the end.

Push this end from the inside of the bag, through one of the grommets at the bottom of the bag, and pull until the knot comes up on the inside against the grommet.

Tie another overhand knot on the outside of the bag close to the grommet to keep the knot on the inside from moving around.

Still working with the same end of the line, tie another knot about 3" from the end of the line.

Insert the end through the other grommet at the bottom of the bag and tie another knot just inside of the grommet on the inside of the bag to keep that knot from moving around.

This should leave a loop about 5" long on the outside of the bag which you can use to tie off the bag to the dinghy. See Fig 4-144.

Starting from the knotted end of the line, flake 220' of the line into the compartment with the 'lid'.

Let the line trail over the divider into the other 'anchor' compartment. Flake the rest of the line into this compartment.

Tie the loose end onto the little anchor. Stick the anchor into the compartment and close the bag with the drawstring.

LifeSling Replacement Cover

The Lifesling cover, or storage bag is really just a box with a lid.

The front and back panels and sometimes the sides of the box are reinforced with plastic stiffeners and there is a pocket compartment inside to stow the polypro line. A flap on the back of the box is held in place with Velcro, and conceals the attachment points. The cover can be made of canvas (like Sunbrella), or vinyl. Its bottom and inside pocket can be mesh (like Phifertex Plus).

LifeSlings are mounted to the boat either on a vertical stanchion, horizontal railings or lifelines, or a combination of both See Fig 4-152. So there will be differences in construction details when we come to making attachment points and chafe protection. More

on this later, for now note how your LifeSling attaches to your boat when you are measuring up. The other important thing to take note of – what corner of the cover does the trailing rope come out of?

The old Lifesling cover is useful too because you can cut off the part which has the instructions and sew it onto the new cover. Having instructions on the cover may even be mandatory in certain countries in order to qualify as a safety device on your boat.

Use your old cover as a guide for making the new one.
Slit the tops of the front and back panels open and take out the stiffeners which you will use in the new cover.
If the old stiffeners are unusable, try to find some plastic at a hardware or craft store, failing this you could possibly use really heavy new Dacron sailcloth (like 10 oz) or even stiff clear vinyl window material

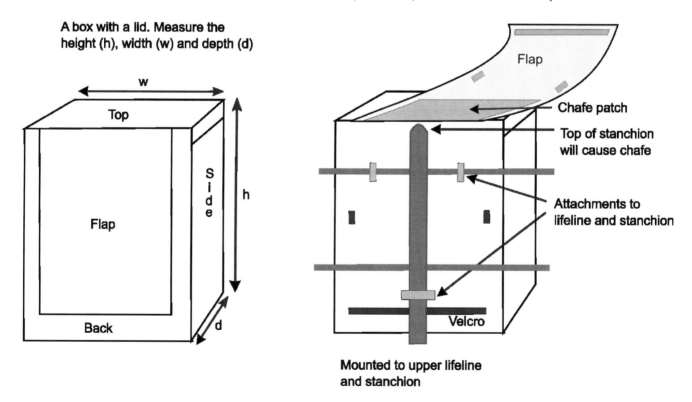

A box with a lid. Measure the height (h), width (w) and depth (d)

Top

w

Side

h

Flap

Back

d

Flap

Chafe patch

Top of stanchion will cause chafe

Attachments to lifeline and stanchion

Velcro

Mounted to upper lifeline and stanchion

Fig 4-152 The basics of how a LifeSling cover is constructed and mounted.

Step 1 – Measure and cut out panels

LifeSling Original Standard measures 22" h x 15" w x 6" d
LifeSling 2 measures 22" h x 12.5" w x 5" d

Measure yours to be sure See Fig 4-152 Measure h x w x d
½" seam allowances will be used, so cut out the fabric as follows:

Back	(h+1") by (w+1")
Back lining	(h+1") by (w+1")
Front	(h+1") by (w+1")
Front lining	(h+1") by (w+1")
Bottom	(d+1") by (w+1")

Side and Side Lining   (h+1") by (d+1")
* cut 2 if there is no stiffener, cut 4 if there are stiffeners

Lid   (w+5") by (d+3")
** Lid has a 2" rim and a ½" hem so this is included in the cut-out.

Lid Lining   (w+5") by (d+3")
*** Optional. If you are making the cover from Sunbrella, eventually the Sunbrella will lose its waterproof-ness. Then rain will enter the cover and no matter what kind of drainage you have the lines and float inside will stay damp and get moldy.
Lining the Lid with vinyl – say, 20 mil clear window material – will keep the rain out.

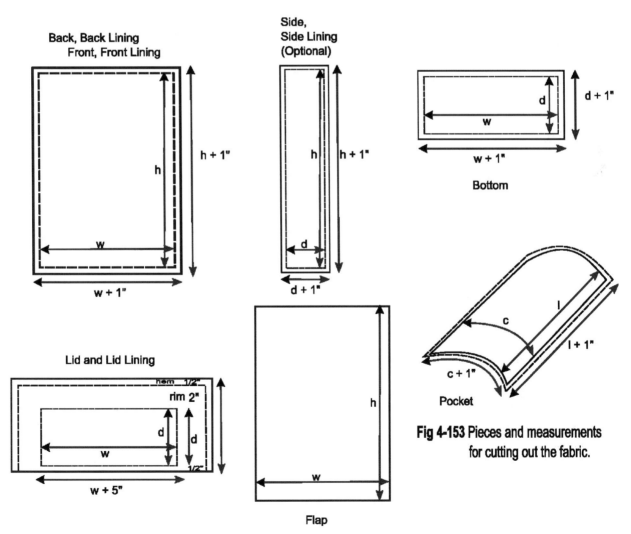

Fig 4-153 Pieces and measurements for cutting out the fabric.

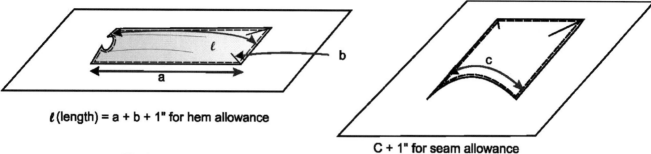

ℓ (length) = a + b + 1" for hem allowance

Fig 4-154 Measuring the Pocket

C + 1" for seam allowance

Pocket   (ℓ+1") by (C+1")
**** The Pocket can be tricky to measure because you have to measure the entire length from the top and around the curve to the bottom of the pocket. See Fig 4-154. The easiest way is to completely remove the pocket from the old cover, flatten it out and measure. If you don't want to do this follow Fig 4-154 to calculate it.

Flap   (w) by (h)
***** A hint on the Flap. It seems to me that LifeSling assumes you are attaching the kit to a very thin thing, like a wire lifeline, so that the Flap lays down nice and flat against the Back. If that is the case, use the cutting measurements above. But if your LifeSling is mounted to a railing or a stanchion as opposed to a skinny lifeline, you should increase the height or width measurement on the flap. To make up for the thickness of the railing or stanchion— the flap must go over that thick railing and need some room to reach the bottom or sides of the bag. You will probably be able to see this problem when you examine your old LifeSling in its position on your boat.

Cut out the Sunbrella pieces with a hot knife and label the *wrong* side of each panel so you don't get confused.

Chafe - If your LifeSling hangs over a stanchion it will be important to add chafe protection to the inside of the flap to keep the stanchion from poking through it. In this instance, cut a piece of vinyl like Shelterite the same size as the bag bottom.

Step 2 – Back panel details

Velcro - See Fig 4-155 Using your old cover, look at the Back and measure how far up from the bottom the Velcro strip is. Cut a piece of 1" Velcro loops the same length as this strip. Place the Velcro loops the same distance you measured, plus ½" (for seam allowance), up from the raw edge of your Back panel. Stitch.

Back
right side

Fig 4-155 Stitch Velcro loops in place using your old cover as a guide.

Stitch 2 more strips of 1" Velcro loops about 4" long, 1 ½" away from the side edges as shown.

Use your measurements from your old cover, or 7" down from the top edge of the Back panel is about right.

Attachments - See Fig 4-156 – these are pieces of webbing with some kind of fastener. Cam Buckle straps are very easy to make but a little fiddly to use. Velcro straps are more work to make but very easy to use. Both are adjustable for length.

You can use webbing straps with snaps or twist-lock fasteners. Since these will not be adjustable you will need to measure the exact length required for the webbing for your specific boat.

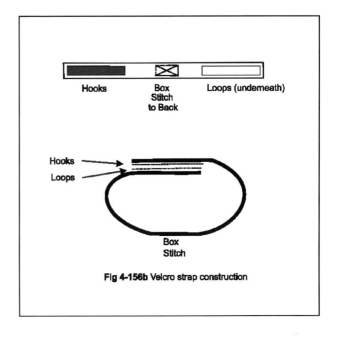

Fig 4-156b Velcro strap construction

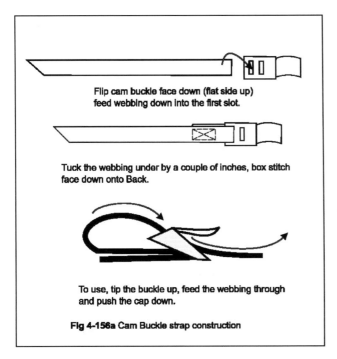

Flip cam buckle face down (flat side up) feed webbing down into the first slot.

Tuck the webbing under by a couple of inches, box stitch face down onto Back.

To use, tip the buckle up, feed the webbing through and push the cap down.

Fig 4-156a Cam Buckle strap construction

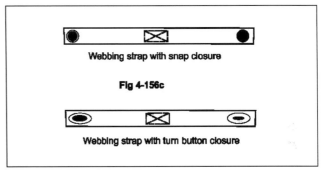

Webbing strap with snap closure

Fig 4-156c

Webbing strap with turn button closure

Reinforce the area where the straps will attach with a patch about 1" larger than the area. (See Section 2 – Patches and Reinforcements)

See Fig 4-157 Using a box stitch, stitch these attachment webbing pieces to the appropriate places on the Back according to your old cover.
If you don't like the way the old cover attached, you can take this piece to the boat and mark where the attachments need to be.

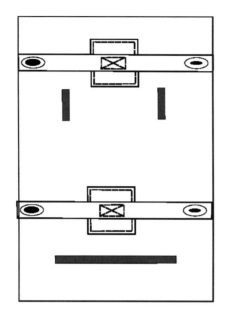

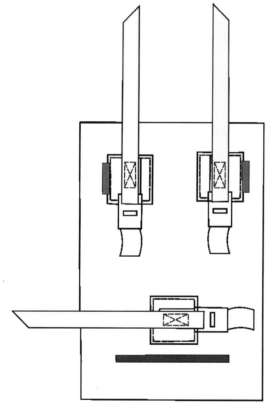

**Fig 4-157 Box stitch straps
to Back**

Step 3 – Inside pocket

Nip off the lower corners:
Take the bottom edge and fold it up and to the left, *right* sides together and matching up the raw edges as shown in Fig 4-158

Mark a 4 1/2" line and stitch. Trim off excess to ½"

Open up the piece, and now fold up the bottom edge the opposite way, up and to the right, matching up the raw edges. Again, mark a 4 1/2" line, stitch and trim off the excess leaving ½".

Open it up and turn it *right* side out so that the seams allowances are to the inside of the pocket. Turn the raw edges to the *wrong* side by ½" and stitch all the way around the pocket including the top edge. This might seem unnecessary considering it is vinyl mesh or hot-knifed Sunbrella, but it will add strength to the pocket when you go to stitch it to the bag panel.

Take the piece you marked Back Lining.
Using measurements from your old Lifesling cover, mark the pocket stitching line onto the Back lining *right* side. See Fig 4-159. Remember to add ½" to the measured distance from the sides for your seam allowance, and add ½" to the distance from the top.

Position the *wrong* side of the pocket onto the *right* side of the Back Lining.
Starting at the top edge of the Pocket, stitch the pocket to the Back Lining along the marked lines; when you get to the nipped-in corner seams, leave your needle in the down position and pick up the presser foot, pivot the project, adjust things and continue sewing.

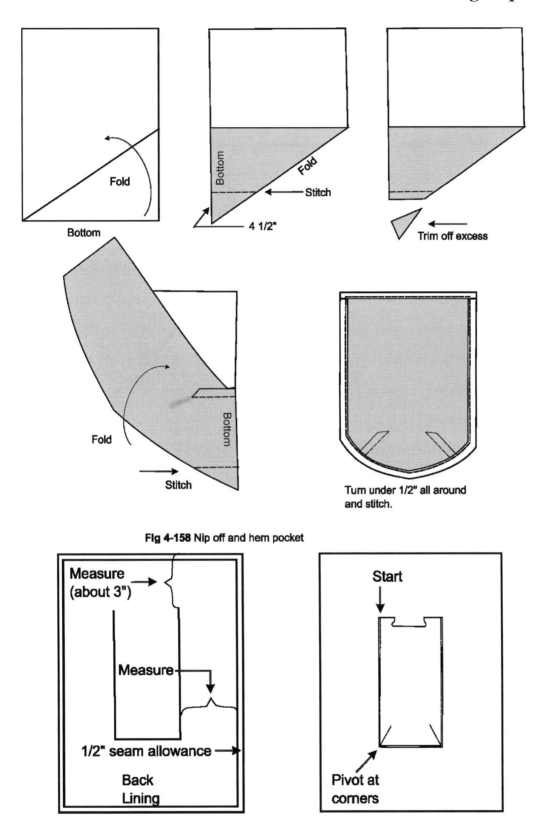

Fold

Bottom

Bottom

Fold

Stitch

4 1/2"

Fold

Trim off excess

Fold

Bottom

Stitch

Turn under 1/2" all around
and stitch.

Fig 4-158 Nip off and hem pocket

Measure
(about 3")

Measure

1/2" seam allowance

Back
Lining

Start

Pivot at
corners

Fig 4-159 Measure for position
of pocket, and stitch.

With *wrong* sides together, Stitch the back Lining to the Back along 3 sides, close to the raw edge.

Start stitching about 1" down from the top edge, go down that side, along the bottom and up the other side, stopping about 1" from the other side's top edge. Leave the top edges open so you can insert the stiffener later.
See Fig 4-160

Step 4 – Flap

See Fig 4-161
Turn in the sides towards the *wrong* side by 1" and crease down.
Turn the bottom up 1" and crease.
Seamstick 1" Velcro hooks to the *wrong* side of the flap about ¼" above the hem fold.

Optional - Chafe –If you are adding chafe protection for stanchion mounts – trim off 2" from the width of the chafe patch. Seamstick the vinyl chafe patch to the *wrong* side of the flap, ½" away from the top raw edge as shown. Tuck the side edges of the vinyl under the side hems so that you can stitch the sides of the chafe patch at the same time as you do the rest of the hem. It will look neater that way from the outside.

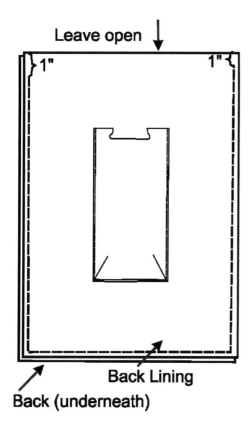

Fig 4-160 Stitch Back to Back Lining along 3 sides

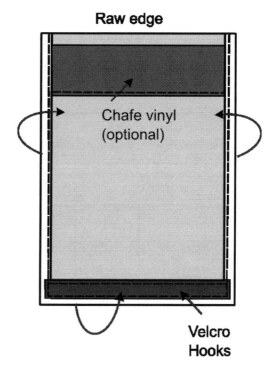

Fig 4-161 Turn sides in by 1", turn up bottom by 1" and stitch Velcro hooks along hem edge.

Stitch along 3 sides and stitch the Velcro and the vinyl as shown – nice and neat and straight as this stitching will be visible from the outside. The top edge will be dealt with later.

Lay the Flap *wrong* side down onto the *right* side of the Back so the long Velcro strip on the flap meets the Velcro on the Back.

Now mark the matching points onto the Flap where the short side pieces of Velcro need to be. See Fig 4-162
Remember to add some 'air space' if your flap has to stretch over a thick railing.

Remove the Flap from the Back and stitch the matching Velcro hooks onto the flap. – Hint – if you make the hook pieces a little longer than necessary, it can help later to adjust the Flap, especially if you are mounting on a rail as opposed to a lifeline.

Optional – Instructions See Fig 4-163 – if you chose to save the instructions from your old LifeSling cover, now is the time to stitch this onto the flap. Just cut out the instructions, place onto the *right* side of the flap (staple or seamstick in place) and stitch around the edge of the instruction panel.

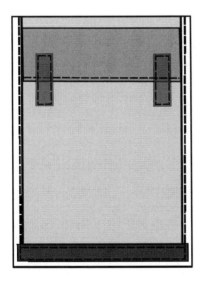

Fig 4-162 Mark location for hooks and stitch in place.

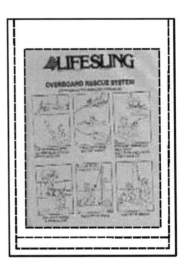

Fig 4-163 Cut out and stitch on Instructions

Place the finished Flap onto the Back with the Velcro all matched up. Match the top raw edge of the Flap to the top raw edge of the Back and Lining – trim off the Flap if necessary to fit. Staple the Flap to the Back along the top edge – don't staple to the Lining yet because you still have to insert the stiffener later - just staple the Flap to the Back for now.

Step 5 – Front panel

On the *right* side, position a length of 1" Velcro loops along the top as shown in Fig 164 . The Velcro should be 2" shorter than the width of the fabric, and place it 1 1/2" down from the top edge. Stitch.

Optional – if your LifeSling has instructions on its front panel and you want to use them, remove them from your old cover and stitch that panel onto your Front Panel.

Place the Front Lining onto the Front, *wrong* sides together.

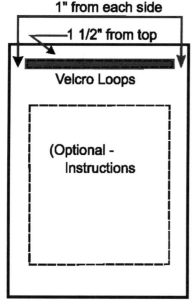

Fig 4-164 Stitch on Velcro loops and Instructions (optional) to *right* side of Front panel.

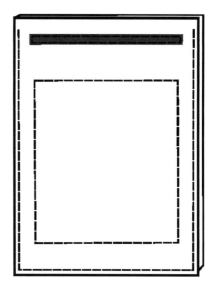

Fig 4-165 With *wrong* sides together stitch Front to Front Lining along 3 sides Start & Stop about 1" from the top.

Stitch close to the raw edges 3 sides only as shown in Fig 165 – start and stop your stitching 1" or a little less, down from the top edges, go around 3 sides.
Leave the top edge open so you can insert the stiffener later.

Step 6 – Prepare Sides

 See Fig 4-166
Cut 2 pieces of Velcro loops, 1 ½" long. Position them on the *right* sides, 1 1/2" down from the top edge and 1" in from the back edge as shown. Stitch.

Optional – if you are putting a stiffener in the Sides, place the Side and Lining *wrong* sides together and stitch 3 sides, close to the raw edge, just like you did the Front. Start and stop 1" or a little less from the top edges, and stitch 3 sides, leaving the top edge open so you can insert the stiffener later.

You can mark in the seam allowance 'back' as shown in Fig 4-166 so you will remember to orient things correctly when it comes time to assemble the cover.

Step 7 – Lid

With *right* sides together, stitch the Bottom to the Sides so it is all one long piece.

Optional – line the Lid with vinyl.
Place the vinyl lining on the *wrong* side of the Lid.
Stitch all around the outside, close to the raw edges to hold it in place.

With a hot knife clip ½" in from the back edge in the two places as shown in Fig 4-167
Nip in the forward corners just like you did for the pocket. Fold diagonally and stitch from point a to b as shown in Fig 4-167.

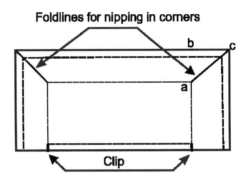

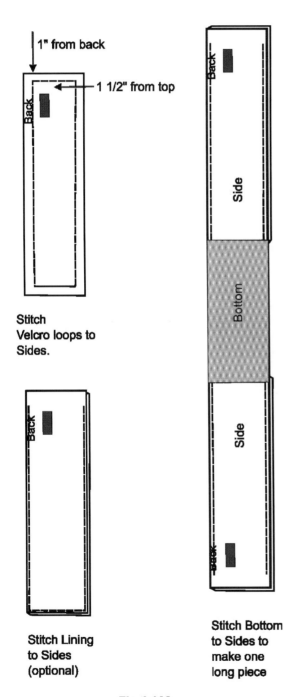

Fig 4-166

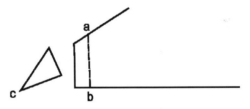

Fold corners diagonally. Stitch from point a straight down to point b, trim off corner

Fig 4-167 Clip lid and nip in corners

Canvas for Cruisers

Turn under and staple ½" along all edges except the area between where you made the ½" clips. Fig 4-168
Make sure you place the prongs of the staples on the *wrong* side, for easy removal later.

Cut pieces of 1" Velcro hooks – 2 pieces 1 ½" long and 1 piece the same length as the loops on the Front. Staple or stick in place on the *wrong* side of the Lid, about ¼" from the folded edge.

Stitch the Velcro and the hem all in one go, nice and neat and straight, as this stitching will be visible from the outside of the cover.

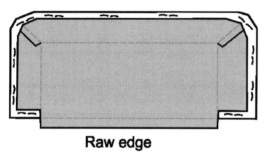

Raw edge

Fig 4-168 Turn edges under. Staple so prongs are facing the *wrong* side.

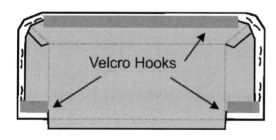

Velcro Hooks

Fig 4-169 Sew on Velcro Hooks

Step 8 – Assemble the Cover

See Fig 4-170
With *right* sides together, staple the Boxing strip to the Back Panel. It is easiest to staple the Bottom part of the Boxing to the Back first. Then work your way up the Sides. Clip the Bottom at the corners to make pivoting at the corners easier.
Stitch, starting and stopping 1" or a little less, away from the one top edge, and 2" away from the top edge where the trailing line will come out of the cover.

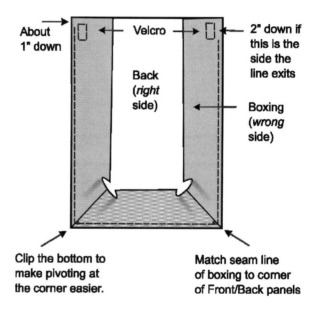

Fig 4-170 Stitch Boxing to Back and Front Panels

About 1" down

Velcro

2" down if this is the side the line exits

Back (*right* side)

Boxing (*wrong* side)

Clip the bottom to make pivoting at the corner easier.

Match seam line of boxing to corner of Front/Back panels

Now, staple the other side of the Boxing strip to the Front Panel. Stitch, starting and stopping about 1" down from the top edges.

Turn the cover *right* side out.
Insert the Back stiffener <u>only</u> for now. Smooth it out and staple the opening flat closed.

Attach lid – with *right* sides together stitch on Lid through Flap, Back and Back Lining through all thicknesses. See Fig 4-171

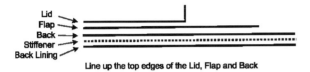

Line up the top edges of the Lid, Flap and Back

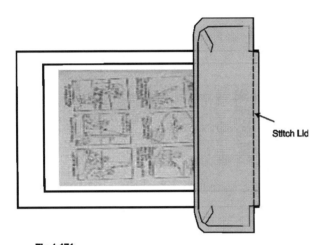

Fig 4-171

Insert the rest of the stiffener(s).

Finish the top edge. Fig 4-172

For the parts that have a stiffener (the Front and possibly the Sides), fold the top edge of the Lining towards the *wrong* side by ½" and crease down.

Now fold the top edge of the main cover panels up and over that folded edge to create a hem. Staple in place.

If there are no stiffeners, just turn the top edge down by ½" and staple in place.

Where the Lid joins the Back, fold the seam allowance towards the Back.

Start stitching at the corner where the trailing rope will come out. Stitch ½" hem all around the top of the cover – Side, Front, Side and topstitch the Lid to the Back. Stop there. This will leave an opening for the trailing rope to exit the cover.

Stuff the bag with the Lifesling. Let the attachment rope trail out the opening you left for it.

Flip lid up and over top of bag and secure with Velcro.

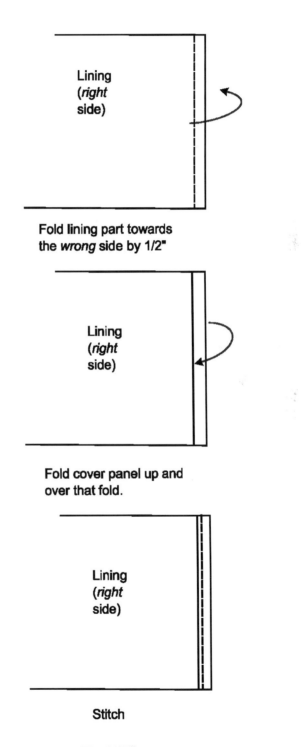

Fold lining part towards the *wrong* side by 1/2"

Fold cover panel up and over that fold.

Stitch

Fig 4-172

Canvas for Cruisers

198

Section 5

Exterior Projects

Canvas for Cruisers

Bimini, Dodgers & Centerpieces

Design considerations:

There are some important things to consider when designing cockpit canvas, whether you are making your own or getting it made by someone else.

1. On a monohull, don't use aluminum tubing for the frame. Aluminum is really too weak to take someone falling on it or grabbing it for support. Use good quality 7/8" or 1" 16 gauge stainless tubing.

Also, use stainless fittings and mounting hardware. Use #6 stainless screws for strength, and if the boat is thin fiberglass, put backing plates underneath.

People will grab the frame and fall against it, so it must be able to take it.

If you have a catamaran, then you will probably have to use aluminum due to weight restrictions. But get as heavy gauge tubing as practical, for maximum strength.

The dodger/bimini also should be higher than the tallest crewmember so they can stand upright under it – but this may not be possible. When the canvas is in place, the crew should be able, while standing, to look underneath the bimini without having to stoop.

2. If the boom is going to extend beyond the dodger's aft end, the height of the dodger & bimini needs to be a couple of inches lower (for safety clearance) than the boom. To measure for this, hoist the mainsail, center it and sheet it down so the boom is in the lowest position it will ever be under sail. Measure from the floor of the cockpit to the bottom of the boom, or to the bottom of any fittings hanging off it. Now you can put the main away.

3. Make the center of the frame's bows higher than the outside so that rain will run off and not pool on the canvas. If the bimini has a center bow, it looks more graceful to have the center bow higher than the others. See Fig 5-1

4. Consider whether you want to or need to fold up the bimini or dodger when not in use, or in case of stormy weather. The dodger should fold forward, but the bimini can fold forward or aft depending on where the sides mount to the coamings or the sides of the boat. If in practice, you never fold up the cockpit canvas then you can have rigid frames.

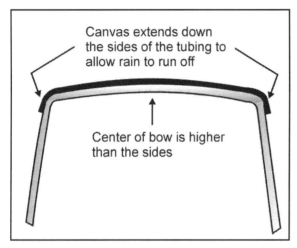

Cross Section - from Front

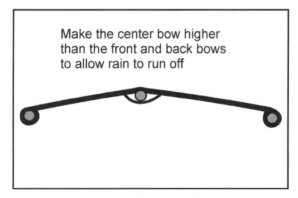

Cross Section - from Side

Fig 5-1 Design the frame so that rain will run off the sides, and not pool on the canvas.

5. Some boats have a mid-boom mainsheet which leads to a traveler in the cockpit, usually just aft of the companionway entrance..
If this is the case, there will have to be a split between the dodger and bimini. Build the bimini separate from the dodger, and leave a space between the two for the mainsheet to travel across. Then build a zip-in canvas or clear vinyl centerpiece to join the dodger and bimini for when you are at anchor.

If you are just going to have a simple 'at anchor' cockpit awning which zips to the aft edge of the dodger, all you will need to do is make an opening in the little awning to let the mainsheet through.

If your boat is a Ketch with the mizzen mast in the cockpit, you can adjust the center piece to allow it to fit around the mast, or eliminate the center piece altogether.

6. Consider how the canvas will affect the beauty and lines of the boat. It should not look like a box, and it should follow sleek lines if you have a sleek boat.
If there is a long distance between the bows of the frame, the canvas will have a tendency to sag and flap. It can help to hollow cut the sides, to prevent flapping. (See Fig 5-2)

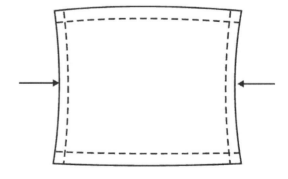

Fig 5-2 If the span between tubing is large, hollow cut the sides of the canvas to prevent flapping. (shown greatly exaggerated)

7. When considering what colour to use, remember that the dodger and bimini should not take away from the looks of the boat. Often, a colour matching the colour of the cabin top looks nice and unobtrusive. On the other hand, if you have a plain white boat, the colour of the canvas can jazz it up nicely. Most people make the dodger and bimini to match the colour of the sail cover. Many people think dark canvas is hotter to sit under, but then again, light canvas lets in more UV.

One more thing about colour and fabric. If you choose an exotic colour, or an obscure fabric, you will often have real trouble replacing parts of the canvas work as you travel the world. IF you are thinking of traveling the world, that is. Sunbrella is available worldwide, and the most common colours are:
Natural (white), Oyster, Linen, Toast
Navy, Captain Navy, Pacific Blue,
Mediterranean Blue
Forest Green
Silver Grey, Cadet Grey, Black

8. The canvas must be designed so that rain runs off outside of the cockpit, otherwise you and your cockpit will get drenched when it rains. It must be totally waterproof. Sunbrella, the most popular material is waterproof all right, but it loses its surface coating quickly if you wash it with detergent, or if you spray it periodically with bleach from underneath to kill mold growth. Re-waterproofing is necessary after such an aggressive cleaning.

Sea Mark is an example of an acrylic fabric with a heavy polyurethane lining bonded onto the fabric. This means no waterproofing required after cleaning, and you can wipe the underside for mold with a cloth instead of spraying. Much easier but mold can really grow fast on the underside in a damp environment.

Vinyl – like Stamoid or Weblon can be used and is seen more commonly on power boats.

If the frame cannot be designed to allow water to drain outside of the cockpit, you can make 'wings' extending off the sides and back of the bimini. They can be removable with zippers or ties, or could be permanently sewed on. They can be long, to the deck, to keep out sun and wind. Or they can be short and extend to the lifelines for partial shade and water drainage.

You can also add side curtains made of clear vinyl complete with zippers to totally enclose the cockpit. This gives superb protection from cold, rain and wind. In cold climates it can add living space in the form of a 'greenhouse' room.
In a bug-prone area, these side curtains can be made of mosquito screens.

9. The windows in the dodger should be clear. It sounds elementary, but many are very poor. Cloudy windows or vinyl that is all loose and wavy is terrible to see out of. Very thin Lexan is wonderfully clear, although you must be careful not to scratch it. However, it only lasts a couple of years and then gets yellow and very brittle.
Strataglass and O'Sea are excellent choices, with a life expectancy of 12 years. It is wonderfully clear and scratch resistant. But it is also very expensive so measure carefully.

40 mil is the best thickness to use on dodgers. 30 mil is much cheaper, so if you are on a budget, it will probably be just fine.
30 mil is flexible and easy to work with, and should last 3 years or so and then needs to be replaced. It is widely available all over the world, so it is easy to replace when the time comes.

10. If you are planning on making a full set – Bimini, Dodger, Centerpiece, Enclosure – it is best to do the Dodger and Bimini first (you can pattern both of these at the same time to save trips to the boat).
Then do the Centerpiece and finally the Enclosure (these can be planned out and patterned together).

Canvas for Cruisers

Bimini

There are several options for Biminis, depending on the boat.

Number of Bows - There could be 2, 3 or 4 bows. All biminis will have a fore and an aft pocket to attach to the frame. Boats with 3 bows will have a center pocket, and boats with 4 bows will have 2 center pockets.

Backstay - There might be a backstay which will have to poke through the Bimini.

Chafe - If people will be grabbing the Bimini at the front or back, you should put a chafe strip there.

Viewing Window - If you need to be able to look up to the top of the mast to see the Wind Indicator, there will need to be a Viewing Window.

Visors - A visor is a long strip of fabric which runs along the bow like an eyebrow or a ball cap visor. It will serve to shed rain and be an attachment point for a possible zipper if you are adding a sun shade, full enclosure or are making a California Dodger. Where pieces join together, the visor protects the zippers from the sun.

Side curtains hang from the side hems of the Bimini, Centerpiece and Dodger, so the sides don't need a visor.

Where the pieces zip together, there are visors, as well as visors for the Fore and Aft ends whether or not there are zippers there. The visors should be constructed differently depending on what angle they are meeting their attachment pieces.

Let's take a typical Bimini/Centerpiece/Dodger arrangement. Working from front to back:

Dodger – has a front visor straight down or at about 45 degree angle to the windshield. It has a back visor straight back or even slightly 'uphill' to the Centerpiece.

Centerpiece – has no visors. Its zippers hide under the visors of the Dodger and Bimini.

Bimini – has a front visor going straight forward to the Centerpiece or at about a 45 degree angle down. It has a back visor that could go back at about a 45 degree angle down, or go straight down, attaching to a back shade curtain or enclosure panel or nothing at all.

The Straight Down visor is cut out using the Bimini Top, very similar to the Pocket.

The 45 degree visor is just a rectangular piece of fabric the same length as the Bimini front or back edge.

And the Straight Forward or Straight Back visor is cut using the Bimini top, but mirror-image. All of these will be described in detail.

There is a fourth type of visor – a custom angle if you want to achieve the perfect fit. It uses the adjoining panel – Windshield, Centerpiece or Enclosure to cut out the visor, so requires patterning of these pieces at the same time you are doing your Bimini.

Usually most people make a plastic pattern. But if all you are doing is a bimini, you can make a 'blank' of fabric and use this, saving the patterning step.
If you are planning a Bimini, Dodger, Centerpiece and Enclosure, you definitely should make a plastic pattern.

Main Steps:

Here are the main steps for a Bimini project – each step will be explained in great detail below. Read and understand all of these instructions before you do anything.

Step 1 - Fabric method:
Cut out and join the large panels of fabric.
Take the fabric to the boat and fit it over the frame. Mark it up for size.
Take the fabric off the frame and even out the marks you made.

Step 1 – Pattern method:
Make a plastic pattern
Sew up the fabric panels
Transfer pattern to fabric.

Step 2 - Pockets
Mark and cut out the front and back pockets.
(A pocket is the sleeve that the tubing frame fits into).

Step 3 - Visors
Cut out front and back visors

Step 4 - Center Pocket
Cut out the center pocket.

Step 5 - Side Hems
Sew the side hems on the bimini and the pockets.

Step 6 - Construct the pockets.

Step 7 - Patches and reinforcements
Cut out, prepare and stitch to the bimini.

Step 8 – Chafe strip (Optional)
Cut out the leather or other chafe material for the forward edge

Step 9 - Finish the aft edge
Visor and Pocket.

Step 10. Finish the backstay area (Optional)

Step 11 - Finish the front edge
Visor and Pocket.

Step 12. Prepare and stitch on the center pocket(s).

Step 13 – Viewing Window (Optional)

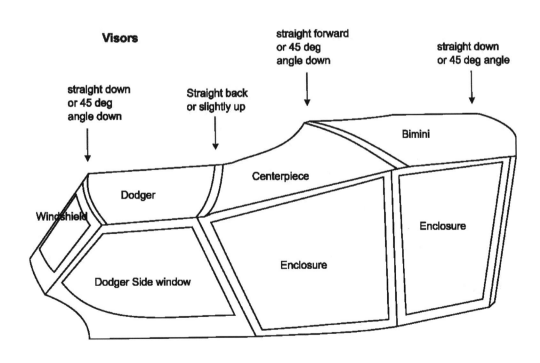

Canvas for Cruisers

The first thing to do is tie off the frame securely fore and aft with lines or webbing so that it does not budge at all
See Dodger – Fig 5-54 for tips on making straps. Or if you can get Strapping Tape, this works great too.

It helps to use a strap or line to pull the front and back bows towards each other at their center points – just a little, less than an inch – this way once you have made the bimini and installed it the frame will stretch out the fabric nice and taut.

When tying-off the frame, go under as opposed to over any center bows.

Tie off or tape off the Center Bow(s) securely in its existing location so it won't move when you take off the old Bimini. If there is no old Bimini, center these Bows within the area of the Bimini and make them nice and parallel to each other.

If you are replacing an old bimini, take note of anything you didn't like about it.

Then remove it..
Measure the frame's height at each side to see if it is still symmetrical. (Sometimes they get bent up). If it's bent, try to straighten it.
Usually it is necessary to join two pieces of Sunbrella to get a wide enough piece to cover the boat. This means there will be a seam lengthwise down the center. It may be possible for you to join the pieces along the steel bows, eliminating the center seam. It will depend on the particular boat and how best to utilize the fabric. See Fig 5-3.

If you do want to make the seam along a bow, it is best to make a plastic pattern.

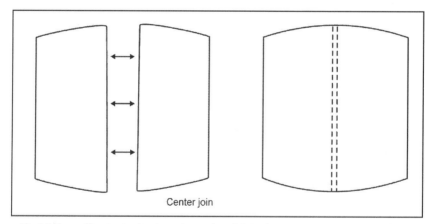

Center join

Fig 5-3 Depending on your boat, you can make a join in the center, or along the bimini frame

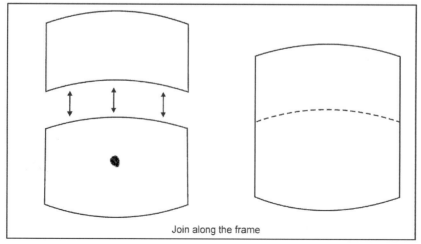

Join along the frame

Step 1 – Fabric Method

a) Measure up for the Fabric 'Blank'

Measure the distance between the fore and aft bows of the bimini frame. Add at least 16". This will give you the measurement for how long the fabric 'blank' needs to be.

Single backstay:

If the boat has a single backstay, tie a string from the center position of the aft bow to the center position of the forward bow. Measure the distance from where the backstay meets the string to the aft bow.(Fig 5-4 A) This will give you an idea of how long the backstay slit will need to be.

Double Backstay

Measure and note the locations of the backstay openings using Fig 5-4. To help you measure, tie a string from the center position of the aft bow to the center position of the fwd bow. Tie another string between the backstays.

The slits for the backstays do not have to go out to the sides. They can both go straight back like the Single backstay. It depends on your preference and what is most convenient for that particular boat.

If they go out to the sides, you will need to install webbing tabs and fasteners such as snaps or twist locks to take the strain off the opening at the hem edges

b) Make the Fabric 'Blank'

Cut 2 pieces of Sunbrella to length (Fore-Aft measurement plus 16") – use the 46" wide fabric or 60" depending on the size of the bimini.
Stretch it out on the floor and pin out one piece. See Fig 5-5.
Apply ½" or ¾" seamstick to one of the selvedge edges.

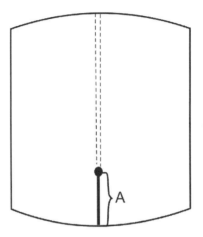

Single backstay opening

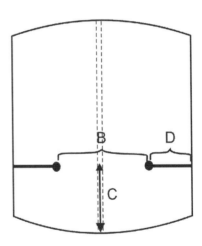

Double backstay openings

Fig 5-4 Seen from above shows the critical measurements for a single and double backstay arrangement.

Single Backstay:
Remember the measurement you made from the backstay opening to the aft bow? (The 'A' measurement in Fig 5-4). Measure from the aft edge of the fabric this distance, plus 8", and do not seamstick here. You will be leaving the end open so it can fit around the backstay.

Double backstay:
Seamstick the entire length along the selvedge.

Don't remove the seamstick paper yet. Overlap the two pieces by ¾" as shown in Fig 5-5. Pin it down securely at one end with a scratch awl, and then walk over to the other end. It is critical that you get the seam straight and the tension between the 2 pieces of fabric even.

It helps to fold the 2 edges in loosely. Squat at one end with the scratch-awl holding the other end. Take the corner of one of the panels of fabric in each hand; overlap ¾" and pull slightly to 'feel' the equal tension between the two panels. When you have an even tension, pin down this end.

Now, with both ends pinned, you can crawl over and pull off the seamstick paper, all at once. Make sure the edges are overlapped nice, straight and an even 3/4", and press the seam down with your fingers. Then roll the seam down hard.

Take the panels to the sewing machine, gently so as not to disturb the seamstick. If you're worried that the panels will fall apart, make light match-up marks so you can put things back together in the proper place.

Fig 5-5

Stretch out the fabric and apply seamstick all along one long edge.

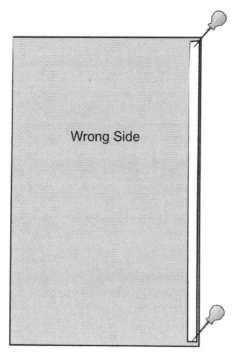

Wrong Side

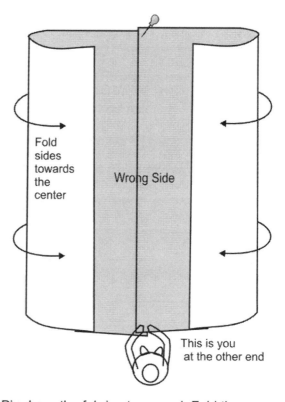

Fold sides towards the center

Wrong Side

This is you at the other end

Pin down the fabric at one end. Fold the sides toward the center. Go to the other end and stretch the fabric pieces so that the tension is equal between the two pieces.

Stitch two rows of stitches, one row close to each selvedge. Make the stitch length as long as possible to reduce puckering. Concentrate on sewing nice and straight. Fig 5-6.

If you want a more waterproof seam, you can use the topstitched or flat-felled seam – see Techniques.

c) Fit the Fabric Panel to the frame.

Lay the joined panel of fabric over the bimini frame – center the seam and let the excess fabric overhang the sides. Center the fabric front to back too - You should have at least 8" excess at the front and at the back.

Grab a big handful of clamps – you will need a lot of them. Wrap the fabric around the forward bow at the center of the bow and use a large clamp to hold it firmly in place. Go to the aft bow, stretch the fabric taut, and put a strong clamp at the center of the aft bow in the same place. See Fig 5-7.

Now, working along the fore and aft bows from the center to the outside, stretch out the fabric panel and clamp it to the bows. Keep the fabric tight and even, working out any wrinkles as you go. Clamp the frame only, otherwise you will get a 'dip' in the fabric and it won't fit right. Work one side at a time. Fig 5-7.

If there are no backstays, skip to e)

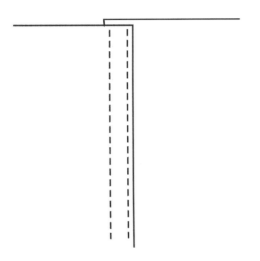

Fig 5-6 Stitch two rows of stitches, nice and straight.

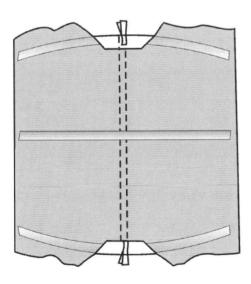

Seen from underneath - clamps are placed at the center fore and aft

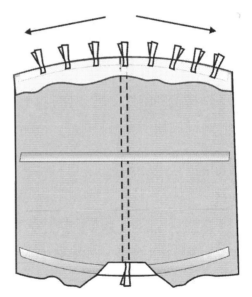

Then place clamps starting from the inside to the outside edges. Stretch the fabric nice and tight.

Fig 5-7 Drape the fabric over the frame and clamp it in place.

d) Double backstay: - do this only if using fabric panels

This is trickier but it can be done. Just take your time.

Tie two strings from the aft bow to the front bow so that the strings touch the backstays. Refer back to Fig 5-4 and measure the distance between the backstays at the point where the strings touch them (Fig 5-4 B). Also measure the distance from that point along the string to the aft bow. (Fig 5-4 C)

On the fabric 'blank', mark a chalk dot where you think the backstay openings should be, and make a chalk line from that point out to the outside edges (Fig 5-4 D). You should go perpendicular to the hem and along the straight grain of the fabric for ease of construction. Don't cut it yet.

Then take it to the boat and drape it over the frame. Clamp it down as best you can and make sure you are happy with the marked position of the holes and the slits.
Carefully cut the slits and fit the fabric panel to the frame.

Finish the backstay openings, (Skip to Steps 7 & 10 for how to do this) one at a time, trying on the fabric panel after the first slit is finished to make sure the second one still fits accurately

Once the backstay openings are complete, continue with the fitting:

Single Backstay - If the boat has a single backstay, DO NOT finish the opening yet.

e) Continuing with the clamping

When you get to the sharp bend at the outsides, you might have trouble working out the wrinkles and getting a nice fit. Keep clamping so that the panel extends down the sharp bend.
If you can't resolve the wrinkles, you will need to make darts at the center bow's curve to take in the excess (described later – in step f).

But first, measure and mark where the hem of the bimini will be along the sides. The hem should extend down the sides of the frame enough so that the bimini does not ride up, but not so much that you can't easily see under it. Try 4" down the sides of the legs from the point of the turn. See Fig 5-8.

Mark the hemline at the 4 corners of the bimini – at the front bow and the aft – on the *wrong* side of the fabric if you can. Then join the marks to make the hem nice and straight, and the same height on both sides. Put in a clamp if necessary, or have a partner measure the height of the hem. It can be a little higher in the front than the back to give the bimini a nice look, it can be higher at the center bow(s), but it depends on what looks right for each particular boat.

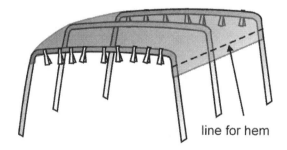

line for hem

Fig 5-8 The fabric is clamped in place and the hem line is marked.

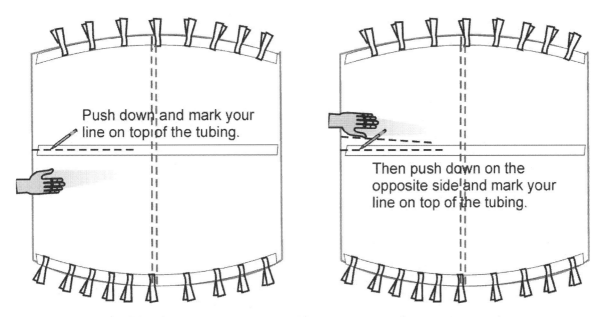

Fig 5-9 Marking a dart to work out the problem with wrinkling at the corners.

f) Now, if necessary, work out the problem with wrinkling: See Fig 5-9.

With both front and back bows all clamped down, take your hand and rest it aft of the center bow. Push down there to remove the wrinkle forward of the center bow. Mark a dashed line on the *right* side along the top of the center bow starting about a foot inside of where the bow starts to bend, and extend it to the hemline. If you are using fabric panels, make the marks faint – you are marking on the *right* side.

Let go.

Now take your hand and push down forward of the center bow, so that the wrinkle aft of the bow is removed. Make another pencil line along the top of the center bow to mark the other side of the dart.

If you were making a plastic pattern and you encountered bad wrinkling, instead of making a dart, it would be easy to make separate pieces for each section of the bimini – that is - from the Front bow to the Center, and from the Center to the Aft.

g) Mark the Bows

When getting ready to mark the bows, it helps to understand some anatomy of the Bimini Frame and how the pockets will attach and help support the frame.

If you have a 2-Bow Bimini, then it's easy – the forward and aft pockets support the Frame.

For a 3-Bow Bimini, the Center pocket supports the Frame but in a particular way. See Fig 5-10. The Support Bar for the center is on a hinge and wants to fall forward as shown by the arrow. So, the Center Pocket has to be sewn on so that the Pocket Fold supports this bar and keeps it from falling forward.. The curved arrows in the diagram show the pockets and how they wrap around the bars.

In a 4-Bow Bimini, there are 2 Center Pockets, each supporting the Support Bars in opposite directions.

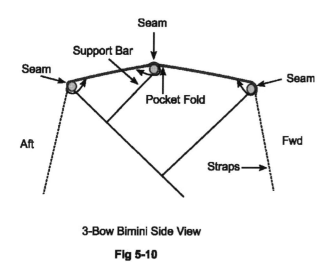

3-Bow Bimini Side View

Fig 5-10

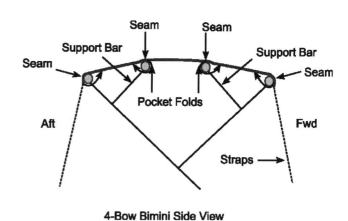

4-Bow Bimini Side View

OK, once you understand the physics, it helps you to figure out where to mark the bows.

Mark the Center Bow as shown in Fig 5-11.

On the *wrong* side of the fabric, make a pencil line along and directly above the forward edge of the center bow's tubing. (marked 'a' in the Fig).

This line will be used as a guide to fold the Center Pocket after it is sewn on – it is where the fabric will pull on the frame to hold it taut.

The line does not have to be marked all the way across – it can stop around 6" short of the bends of the bar.

On the *right* side, make a few light, unobtrusive marks along the center bow, directly over it. (marked 'b' in the Fig.) This line will be the seam line when you go to sew the Center Pocket piece to the bimini. It does not have to go all the way to the bends either.

-

Mark the forward and aft bows (see Fig 5-11). On the *right* side, make a faint pencil line (not too dark because you are marking the *right* side of the fabric here) along the front side of the tubing – The mark can be slightly high up – in other words, don't hold your pencil dead horizontal, hold it tilted a little upward and mark at about the 10-oclock position on the bar. The seam on the forward and aft bars wants to tilt upwards because of the stretch which will be applied to the finished Bimini, and also because of the visors.
Skip over where the clamps are and mark all the way down to the hem.

Make a mark (and label it) where your frame starts to bend downwards at each corner.

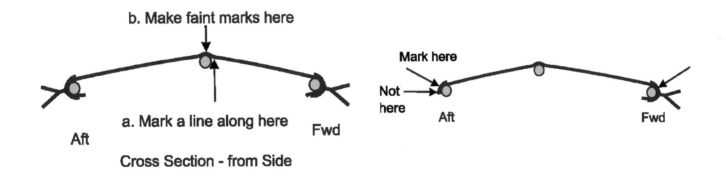

b. Make faint marks here

a. Mark a line along here

Aft Fwd

Cross Section - from Side

Fig 5-11 Mark Center Bow and Fwd/Aft Bows

Mark here

Not here

Aft Fwd

Canvas for Cruisers

h) Have a good look to see if there needs to be any attachment points for straps to support the frame. Usually there are 4 – one at each corner. Some biminis have eye-straps on the frame so you don't need to modify the Bimini for straps.

There may be another opening necessary for a backstay. Mark the position of the backstay.

i) If you will want a viewing window so you can look up to see the sail or wind indicator, mark out the size and position onto the fabric.

j) Take the fabric off the frame and even up the marks.

Transfer any marks you made on the *right* side onto the *wrong* side of the fabric. To do this, I usually poke pins through the marks on the fabric so I can see exactly where to make the mark on the other side.
The fabric panel should now look something like Fig 5-12
Working on the *wrong* side, use a straight edge to join the hem corner marks. Remember, if the bimini is large, hollow-cut these sides into a very slight curve.
Use a batten or other flexible stick, like a piece of plastic awning track, and mark smooth curves at the frame bows (marked 'a' in Fig 5-12)

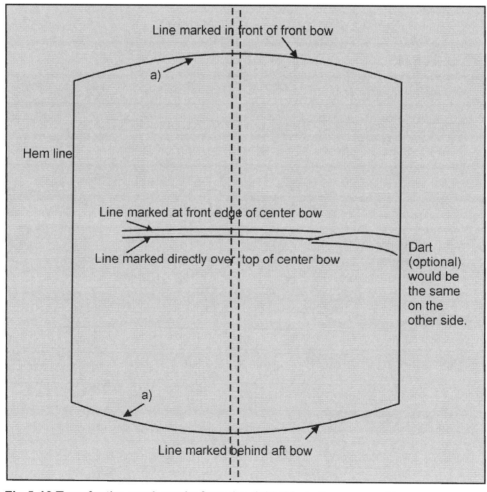

Fig 5-12 Transfer the rough marks from the *right* side to the *wrong* side. Even up the rough marks you made on the fabric.

214

Mark the cutting lines (labeled 'b' in Fig 5-13) as follows:

Mark the sides for a 2" double hem – that is, mark a line 2" from the hem fold line, and mark another line 2" further away for the cutting line.

Mark a curved line ½" outside of the front and aft lines for a seam allowance.

Refer now to Fig 5-14. "Miter" the fore and aft ends on all 4 corners, so that when you turn in the side hems, the edges will match.

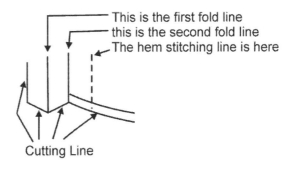

Fig 5-14 Detail of the corners, showing how the edge is cut to allow for folding up the hem

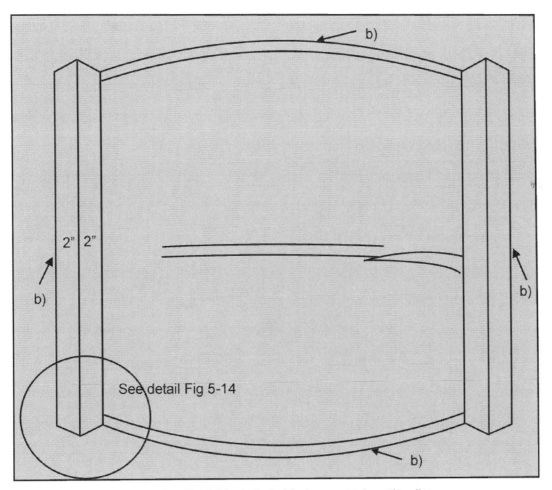

Fig 5-13 Mark the side hems and cutting lines.

k) Mark the position of the center-pocket patches as shown in Fig 5-15.

The center pocket is used to keep the bimini attached to the tubing frame, and the fabric gets quite a bit of stress on its ends. Therefore, this area needs to be reinforced or the bimini will rip.

The idea is that the patch should extend 2" beyond the 'stress' area on all 4 sides. The standard patch size for an average bimini is about 4" by 9". Position the patches parallel to the sides or parallel to the centerline of the bimini – whichever looks better. The patches also must be further aft rather than centered. Read ahead to Fig 5-40 and 5-41 to see why.

How far apart to put the patches? The center pocket does not need to extend all the way to

The side hems – it can stop about 6" short of the bend on each side. So, you can adjust the length of the pocket so that it is convenient to the length of a standard 'jacket' zip.

For example, if it looks like 49" would be a good distance apart, make it 48" because that is the standard length of a jacket zip. (Which come in 1 ft increments).

Continuing to mark up the *wrong* side of the fabric:

l) If you made a mark for a backstay opening, re-mark it nice and straight.

m) If you have to make darts, clean up the marked lines into smooth curves, and mark another curve ½" to the outside of these curves for seam allowances.

End of Step 1 – Fabric Method

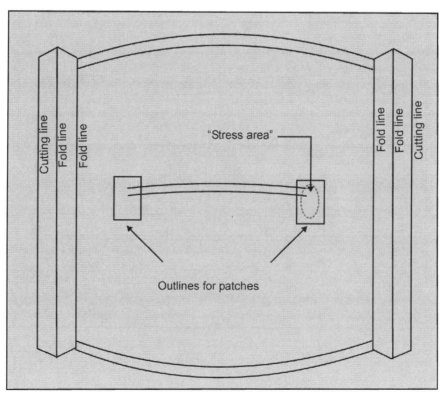

Fig 5-15 Mark the size and position of stress patches to be placed at the ends of the pocket.

Step 1 – Pattern Method

Apply removable tape to the frame – near the top-front of the Fwd Bow, near the top-back of the Aft Bow, and directly on top of the Center bow(s). (See Fig 5-11) Continue the line of tape along the bow curves past the hem line a little. With a permanent marker, mark where the seam lines will be - see notes with Fig 5-11. Measure and mark where the hem should fall. – see notes in the Fabric Blank method earlier

Apply seamstick directly over these lines.

Drape the plastic pattern material over the frame. Starting at the center of one of the bows, remove the seamstick a bit at a time, sticking the plastic down nice and smooth. Work out the wrinkles by pulling off the plastic and re-sticking as necessary. For more details see Patterning in the Dodger section further ahead in this Section.

Make a pattern for each section of the Bimini For a 3-Bow Bimini you will have 2 pieces – a Fwd and an Aft piece. And for a 4-Bow Bimini you will have a Fwd, Mid and Aft piece. Your pattern pieces will end up looking something like this:

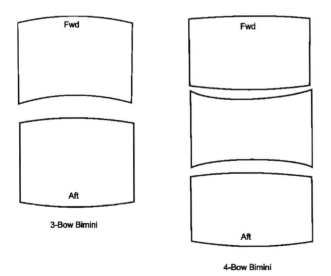

3-Bow Bimini

4-Bow Bimini

Where the panels will join, the seam line will be directly on top of the Bow.

Where the panel has a Pocket, the seamline will be slightly higher than the front or back edge of the Bow. Mark the center of the Bows, and the point where they start to curve downwards.

Where the panels will join there will be a Center Pocket. So from underneath the pattern, mark a line straight up from the Fwd or Aft edge of the Center Bow (depends on whether you are making a 2 or 4-Bow Bimini See Fig 5-10). This will be the fold line for the Center Pocket. While you're at it, measure for a convenient length for this Pocket – see if you can get it to be the standard length of a Jacket zipper like 36" or 48". The Center Pocket does not have to extend to the hems of the Bimini.

Mark the hem.

Patterning around backstays:
After draping your plastic on the bows, start to remove the seamstick a bit at a time. As you approach the backstays, make some scribbly hatch marks on the plastic in the area. Slit the plastic through them to make an opening so the pattern can go around the backstay. It doesn't have to be straight or accurate. Cut out a little hole there to go around the backstay, and then tape the plastic back together, matching up the hatch marks. Do the rest of the patterning and marking. Then mark a line from the backstay opening straight aft and perpendicular to the aft bow, or straight out to the hem if that is where you are going to make the opening
. Once you are all done, to remove the pattern, cut the plastic along this marked line.

Transfer the outline and marks to the Fabric.

Add 4" (2" + 2") hem allowances, and miter only the corners – Fwd and Aft, not the Center panel. Add ½" seam allowances at the front and back edges of each piece.

Canvas for Cruisers

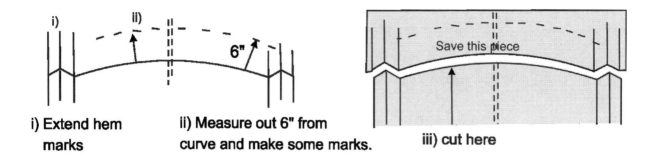

i) **Extend hem marks**

ii) **Measure out 6" from curve and make some marks.**

iii) **cut here**

Fig 5-16 Extend hem marks up 6" or so. Make some marks 6" out from the Fwd edge perpindicular to the edge.

Step 2 – Mark & cut out the front and back pockets.

OK, so far, you have not cut out anything. Working with the forward edge (See Fig 5-16)

You should have at least 6" of excess fabric fore and aft. (If you don't, don't despair – you can make the pocket pieces from separate pieces of fabric – skip to step i)

a) Take a ruler and make some marks 6" away from the leading edge. Hold the ruler perpendicular to the edge Fig 5-16

b) Cut along the original pencil line with a hot knife, separating the pocket piece from the large panel.

c) Place the large panel aside. Working with the scrappy looking end you just cut off, (we'll call it the 'pocket piece' from now on) join the marks you made into a smooth curve.

d) Remark the ends of the curve
Straighten out this curve by adding about ½" as shown in Fig 5-17, tapering the curve to the point you marked where your frame starts to bend. Mark the lines for the hem – the ½" will also need to be added to the hem marks

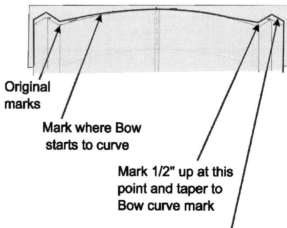

Original marks

Mark where Bow starts to curve

Mark 1/2" up at this point and taper to Bow curve mark

'Miter' the hem and add the 1/2"

Fig 5-17 Marking the curve for the pocket.

Remark the Pocket side hems –
The hem will need to be done differently depending on whether you are making an enclosure or not.

If you are not going to be adding an enclosure to this bimini, re-mark the hem fold lines and cutting lines – slightly 'inboard'. 1/8" of an inch is about right. This will make things easier to fit when you eventually attach the pocket piece to the bimini. See Fig 5-18a

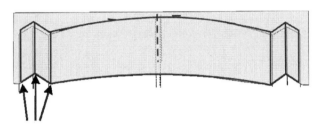

Fig 5-18a Re-mark hem lines slightly to the inside of the original lines.

If you are going to make an enclosure, the Pocket should not extend all the way to the side hems because the Pocket zipper will interfere with the Enclosure panel's zipper.
So, re-mark the hem fold line to be 1 ½" inboard of the original hem fold line. Then add a 2" single hem allowance.
See Fig 5-18b.

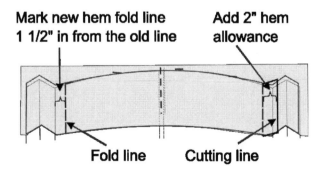

Mark new hem fold line 1 1/2" in from the old line   Add 2" hem allowance

Fold line   Cutting line

Fig 5-18b For a future enclosure, shorten the pocket by 1 1/2" on each end.

f) OK, now you can cut out the pocket piece with a hot knife. For the non-enclosure version, trim off half of the hem allowance as shown in Fig 5-19a.

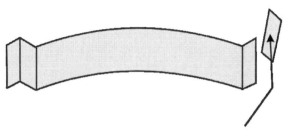

Fig 5-19a When cut out, the pocket piece will look something like this. Clip off the outer hem allowances because you will be making a single hem in the pocket piece.

g) Lay the pocket piece over the large panel and make some hatch marks so you can match things up later.
Fold and staple the pocket's hems under – you will actually be folding the hem to the *right* side of the Sunbrella but since the fabric is the same on both sides it won't matter. Trim with a hot knife, ½" off the tip of the curve as shown in Fig 5-19b to make zip installation easier later on.

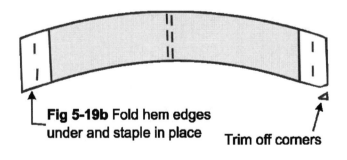

Fig 5-19b Fold hem edges under and staple in place   Trim off corners

h) <u>If you need to make openings in the bimini</u> for the attachment of straps to the metal tubing. Mark a u-shaped cutout on the pocket's outside curve. See Fig 5-19c

An easy way to do this is to use a roll of seamstick. Mark, using the roll's inner core, a curve using a little more than half its diameter. Then straighten out the ends so that it is u-shaped.
Cut out the opening with a hot knife. Use the little cutout piece as a template for the others.

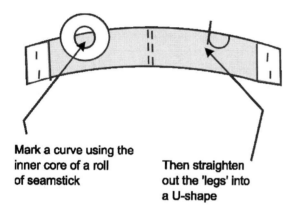

Mark a curve using the inner core of a roll of seamstick

Then straighten out the 'legs' into a U-shape

Fig 5-19c Marking openings for the attachment of straps to the bimini frame

i) <u>If you don't have enough fabric on the big panel</u> fore and aft to do all the above, just take a separate piece of fabric. Line it up with the same grain as the big panel – Sunbrella has a 'nap' and not only can appear different shades when viewed with or across the grain, it will also stretch differently and this could make your Bimini look funny.
Cut out the forward edge of the big panel, and then use this edge to mark the shape on the separate piece of fabric.
Follow all the rest of the steps above for marking and folding the hems and openings.

<u>Aft Pocket</u> - Repeat steps a) through i) for the aft edge.

<u>Step 3 – Visors</u>

Once you have decided what kind of visors you want for the front and the back of the Bimini – Straight Down, 45 degree, Straight Fwd/Back or Custom decide how wide they need to be.

A jacket zipper is 1 ½" wide, so if there is to be a zipper along the visor – for a Centerpiece or Extension, or for a removable Window panel - the visor should be 2" or -2 1/2" wide as its <u>finished size</u>. This will give it enough width for the zipper to be completely covered by the Visor. If there are no zippers then 1 ½" finished width is probably just fine.
Once you decide on the finished width of the Visors, make them all the same width for the exterior canvas on the boat or it will look funny.

Cut out the visor according to the instructions below.

<u>Straight Down Visor</u>
See Fig 5-20a
Tuck a piece of Sunbrella under the edge of the Bimini. Using the cut edge of the Bimini, mark a line – this is the cutting line.
Measure up ½" and mark another parallel line – this is the stitching line.
Measure up from the stitching line whatever the final width of your visor is going to be – 1 ½", 2" or 2 ½" and make another parallel line. If you are going to bind the raw edge you're done – this will be the cutting line.
If there is going to be no binding, measure up ½" and mark the final line for cutting..
Make some hatch marks at this final line so you can align things later when it comes to sewing.

Cut, then trim ends, leaving ½" for folding under. Flip the piece over and cut out another mirror image piece.

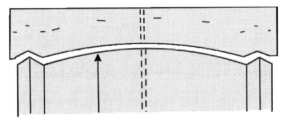

Use edge of Bimini to mark a line.
Move Bimini up 3 or 3 1/2" and mark again.

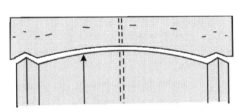

Fig 5-20a Use edge of Bimini to mark the curve of the visor, just like the Pocket.

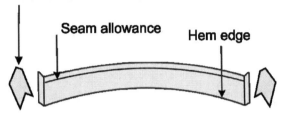

Use edge of Bimini to mark a line.
Move Bimini up 3 or 3 1/2" and mark again.

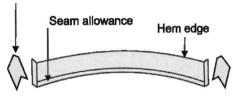

Fig 5-20b Use edge of Bimini to mark the curve, just like the Straight Down visor. The difference will be how you sew it to the Bimini

45 Degree Visor

Cut out a rectangular strip of fabric long enough for the edge - twice the finished size width (1 ½", 2" or 2 ½") plus 1" for seam allowances. If there is a backstay opening, of course, you will need to cut 2 separate pieces.
Add ½" seam allowance to each end.

Straight Fwd/Back Visor

See Fig 5-20b
Cut this visor out just like the Straight Down Visor. (Cut 2 mirror-image pieces). When you go to sew the visor to the Bimini you will have to make relief cuts into the seam allowance of the visor to make that inside curve stretch enough to fit the Bimini edge.
(Instructions later)

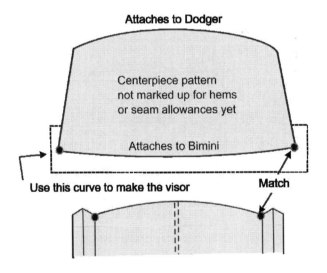

Fig 5-20c Custom visor uses the adjoining pattern to mark and cut out the visor.

Canvas for Cruisers

<u>Custom</u>
See Fig 5-20c
You can make the visor to the exact shape and angle as the adjoining piece by using the adjoining pattern piece to make the visor.

So let's say you have the Bimini going forward to a Centerpiece and you're really wanting an exact match along the visor so it is nice and flat.

Use the Centerpiece pattern for the visor.

Mark the edge, move up 3 or 3 ½" and mark again. Add the ½" allowance to the ends for folding over, same as the other visor instructions.
Cut 2 mirror-image pieces.

Prepare the Visors:

45-Degree

Fold each end to the *wrong* side by ½"
Fold in half *wrong* sides together, along the length.
Topstitch along the ends and folded edge.
Leave raw edges open for now.

All Others

If you are Binding the hem edge, fold each end to the *wrong* side by ½". Apply seamstick to the *wrong* side of one of the pieces and seamstick them together.
Bind the edge.

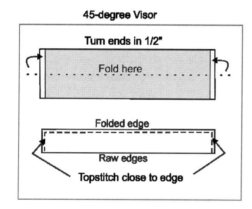

45-degree Visor

Turn ends in 1/2"

Fold here

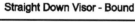

Folded edge

Raw edges

Topstitch close to edge

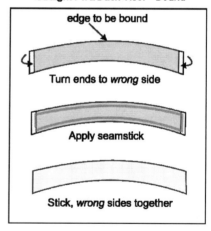

Straight Fwd/Back Visor - Bound

edge to be bound

Turn ends to *wrong* side

Apply seamstick

Stick, *wrong* sides together

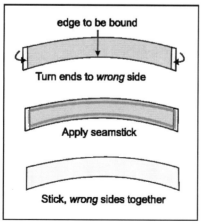

Straight Down Visor - Bound

edge to be bound

Turn ends to *wrong* side

Apply seamstick

Stick, *wrong* sides together

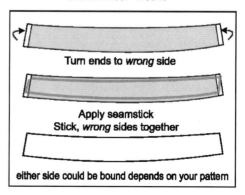

Custom Visor - Bound

Turn ends to *wrong* side

Apply seamstick
Stick, *wrong* sides together

either side could be bound depends on your pattern

If you are not Binding the hem edge, place pieces *right* sides together.

Stitch a ½" seam along the sides and hem edges.

Trim corners and clip curves.

Turn *right* side out and crease nice and flat.

Topstitch close to seam.

Straight Down Visor - no Binding

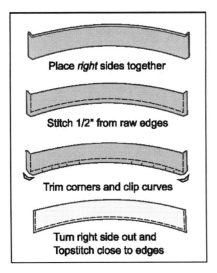

Place *right* sides together

Stitch 1/2" from raw edges

Trim corners and clip curves

Turn right side out and Topstitch close to edges

Straight Fwd/Back Visor - no Binding

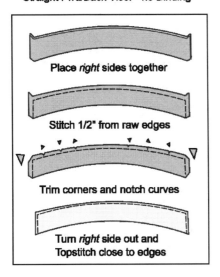

Place *right* sides together

Stitch 1/2" from raw edges

Trim corners and notch curves

Turn *right* side out and Topstitch close to edges

Custom Visor - no Binding

As above except either side could be stitched - depends on your pattern

Step 4 – Cut out the Center Pocket(s)

Make sure you cut the center pocket on the same grain as the panel. Sunbrella has different stretch characteristics depending on whether it is with the grain or across.

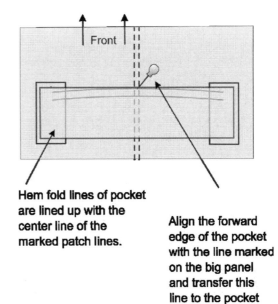

Hem fold lines of pocket are lined up with the center line of the marked patch lines.

Align the forward edge of the pocket with the line marked on the big panel and transfer this line to the pocket

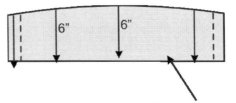

Measure straight down 6".
Usually you can make this edge straight, for easier zipper installation.

Fig 5-21 Cutting out the Center Pocket

Canvas for Cruisers

If you are using Fabric 'Blank':

a) Mark out a rectangle 8" wide, and long enough for a convenient length of the jacket zip you are going to use PLUS add 2" at each end for a 2" single hem.

Check this length against where you marked the patches on the panel. The fold lines of the pocket's hems should be at the center line of the patches.
Mark the fold lines for the hems onto the pocket piece. Cut out.

b) The large panel of fabric should still be on the floor, *wrong* side up.
Lay the pocket piece you just cut out *wrong* side down onto the large panel. (See Fig 5-21)
Position it so that its hem fold lines are at the center line of the patches and the forward edge of the pocket is at the line you marked for the center bow.
Pin the center down to hold it steady. Transfer the leading curve from the large panel onto the *wrong* side of the pocket piece. Reach under the edge of the pocket piece with your pencil and make the marks on the *wrong* side of the pocket piece.

c) Take the pocket piece off the panel, and cut along the curve you just marked.
Now measure 6" straight down (not perpendicular) from the curved edge, and mark another curve.
(Fig 5-21)
If the curve is not that great, usually you can make the aft edge straight, which is easier for zipper installation.

If you made a pattern, use the Bimini pieces to mark the curve: You can make the Pocket(s) a convenient length to match a Jacket zipper – say 36"

3-Bow Bimini – use the Forward edge of the Aft piece to mark the curve.
4-Bow Bimini – use the Forward edge of the Aft piece to mark the curve of the Aft Center pocket. Use the Aft edge of the Forward piece to mark the curve of the Fwd Center pocket.
Follow step c) above to finish cutting out the Pocket(s)

Step 5 – Stitch the side hems

Now you will finally feel that you are starting to make progress!

a) If the bimini has darts, stitch these:
Staple the fabric *right* sides together, matching up the inner point and the hem points. Stretch it to shape as needed and staple to keep it in place. Stitch along the marked pencil lines.
Fold the seam allowance aft and topstitch through all thicknesses.

b) Stitch the side hems of the large panel with a 2" double hem. See tips on hemming in Section 2 - Techniques. Topstitch close to the fold as shown in Fig 5-22.

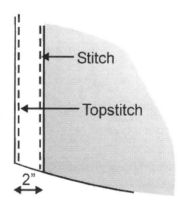

Fig 5-22 Stitch a 2" double hem along the sides.

c) Make 2" single hems in the center, fore and aft pocket pieces. Stitch and topstitch in one continuous line as shown in Fig 5-23 to save effort.

d) If there is to be a backstay opening, make a false hem on the pocket piece at the inner edges as follows: (see Fig 5-24)

First, trim off the inner ends at a bit of an angle. Cut out a little matching hem piece about 2" wide.

Topstitch the little hem pieces to the pocket pieces *wrong* sides together. (see Fig 5-25) Do not stitch the raw edges – these will be finished later with binding. You can staple the raw edges together to hold them in place if you want.

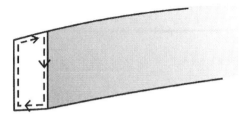

Fig 5-23 Turn a 2" single hem in the pocket pieces, stitching in one continuous 'go' to save stopping and starting.

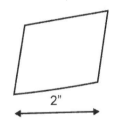

Trim off at an angle, and cut out a little piece of fabric for the hem.

Fig 5-24 If there is a backstay opening, make a little 'false hem' at the inner ends of the pocket pieces.

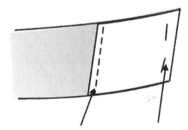

Topstitch and staple.

Fig 5-25 Place the hem piece on the pocket piece *wrong* sides together and topstitch.

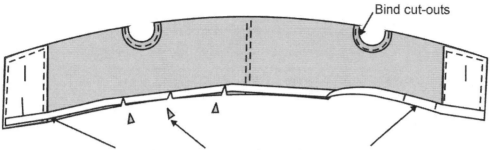

Apply seamstick, clip curves and turn edge under ½"Stick down.

Fig 5-26 Turn raw edge under and bind cutouts

Step 6 – Construct the pockets

a) Bind the raw edges of the cut-out curves in the pockets with double-fold Sunbrella binding (See Section 2 - Techniques) Because it is on a curve, you will have to stitch it on in 2 passes – unless you are really good and can catch in both edges in one go. (Fig 5-26)

b) Pin out the pockets nice & flat.
Apply ½" seamstick to the *wrong* side of the inner curves of the pockets.
Remove the seamstick paper.
Clip the curves.
Turn under ½" and roll down hard. (Fig 5-26)
Don't stitch it yet.

c) Flip the pocket pieces over.

d) Pick out enough jacket zips to do the job. You will probably need 5. Two for the forward pocket, 2 for the aft pocket and one for the center pocket.

When positioning the zippers, remember that the side of the zip with the head attached must always get sewn to the bimini itself and the other side of the zip goes on the pocket piece. The zip almost always closes so that the head ends up 'outboard'. Nobody wants an annoying zipper head hanging down in the center of the bimini and catching on their hair.

If by chance the zip heads would be in the way if they close so their heads are outboard, then position them so they close inboard at the center of the Bimini. If the heads are going to hang down and be annoying, just make a little patch of Sunbrella to cover them over, with a Velcro closure.

Always use a #10 size zip, and always a single head (i.e. one not 2 pull tabs on the head). Most people use 2 zippers, but there really is nothing wrong with having one long zip across the whole width of the bimini.

So, position the zip appropriately, and apply ¼" seamstick to the zip's tape which will be stitched to the pocket. Don't take off the paper yet.

Flip the zipper over and apply ¼" seamstick to the opposite side of the opposite tape as shown in Fig 5-27. If required, shorten the zip as shown in Section 2 - Techniques.

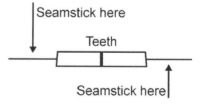

Cross section of zipper

Fig 5-27 Place seamstick on opposite sides of opposite zipper tapes.

e) Flip the zipper over again, remove the seamstick paper and stick this edge to the *wrong* side of the folded-over prepared edge of the pocket.

The teeth should show, and there should be a tiny gap (about 1/8") between the teeth and the pocket's folded edge, so that the zip head will slide along easily. (See Fig 5-28)

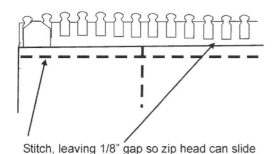

Stitch, leaving 1/8" gap so zip head can slide

Fig 5-28 Line up the zip along the edge of the pocket, with the teeth showing.

f) Stitch the zip to the pocket piece. Usually 1 row is enough, but if the zip will be subject to a lot of strain, stitch a second row.

g) Prepare all the pockets – fore, aft and center, like this and set these pockets aside for now.

Step 7 – Prepare reinforcing patches

Center Pocket Patches:

See Fig 2-76 and 2-77 in the Techniques section.

a) Cut out the patches from the same fabric as the bimini. Standard size is 4" x 9", so cut rectangles 5" x 10" to allow for turning the edges under by ½". It is important to cut the patches along the same grain as the bimini.

b) Stick ½" seamstick to the *wrong* side all around the edges of the patch. Remove the paper. Trim the corners off. Turn the edges of the patches under, as shown in Section 2 - Techniques, nice and straight and squared-off. Apply another line of seamstick all around the edges.

c) Stick the patches to the *wrong* side of the bimini in their marked positions. Roll down hard. Stitch close to the folded edges of the patches.

Backstay Reinforcing Patch:

a) If there is to be a backstay opening, you need to apply a reinforcing patch to this area.
The standard width is 7", and can be any length – cut it 8" wide and 3" longer than the length from the backstay to the aft edge of the bimini. It doesn't hurt to cut it a bit longer, and trim off the excess later.

b) Turn the edges under just like you did with the center pocket patches, except fold and stick down 3 sides only. Don't stitch these 3 sides yet, and leave the aft edge raw.

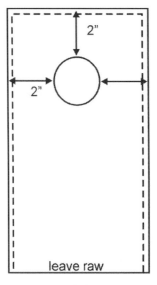

2"

2"

leave raw

Fig 5-29 The backstay patch marked up and with the edges stitched under on 3 sides. Don't cut out the hole yet.

c) Lay out the bimini on the floor *right* side down.

(For a Fabric 'Blank') - The aft end of the bimini's center seam should be unstitched, so overlap the aft edges so they are aligned like the rest of the center seam.

Position the patch over the aft end of the center seam, or centered along the aft edge.

The hole for the backstay should be positioned about 2" inside the folded sides all around, as shown in Fig 5-29 – but DO NOT cut out the hole in the patch yet. If the patch is too long, trim off the excess at the aft edge.

d) Stitch the patch to the bimini close to the folded edges of the patch, along 3 sides only as shown in Fig 5-29.

Step 8 – Cut out the chafe strip for the forward edge

You can use leather or vinyl to reinforce the forward edge of the bimini, where it will be subject to much chafe and touching of people's hands. Or you can use 2" nylon webbing but it won't last long in the tropics. If using leather or vinyl, follow the steps below to get the correct shape for the piece.

a) Lay out the leading edge of the forward pocket over the leather or vinyl and mark the curve.

Make sure you understand which is the *right* and *wrong* sides – the chafe strip will be stitched to the *right* side of the bimini.

b) Remove the pocket from the chafe material. Measure straight down (not perpendicular) 4" from the line you just drew on the material, and make a few marks. See Fig 5-30.

c) Lay out the leading edge of the pocket again, along the marks and mark another curve so that it is parallel to the first one.

d) Cut out the material and set aside for now. If you are using leather you will need big strong shears to cut it out. If you are using 2" webbing, just cut out a length of webbing with a hot knife and set aside.

Step 9 – Finish the aft edge

Stretch out the bimini piece on the floor *right* side up, and pin it down with scratch awls.

Place the visor piece along the aft edge, with raw edges even.

Arrange the visor so that, after you stitch it, the sides will line up to the side of the bimini as shown in Fig 5-31. Do not clip the curves of the visor unless you absolutely have to – this will most likely be necessary with a Custom visor.
Remove the topstitching and restitch the side seam of the visor if you have to, for an exact fit.
Staple the visor to the bimini with the staple prongs on the visor side (easier to remove later).

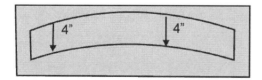

Fig 5-30 Mark out a piece of chafe material to match the shape of the forward edge of your bimini.

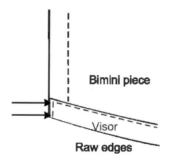

Bimini piece

Visor

Raw edges

Fig 5-31 Position the visor along the raw edge of the bimini piece with the ends meeting exactly

Place the pocket piece on top, *right* side down so that the *right* sides of the pocket and bimini are facing each other. (Fig 5-32). Line up the hatch marks and the raw edges and staple the 3 pieces together. Because you made the pocket piece just a little bit small, it should fit nicely.

Now stitch the seam ½" from the raw edge.

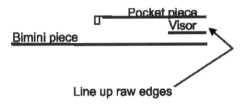

Fig 5-32 Cross section of assembly

Open out the Pocket and Visor so it looks like Fig 5-33. Crease the seam allowance toward the Bimini panel. Topstitch the pocket to the bimini close to the edge of the visor as shown..

Finish the backstay area if you need to, as outlined next in Step 10, then we will return to this aft edge and complete it.
If there is no backstay opening, flip ahead a couple of pages to "Step 9 – Continued".

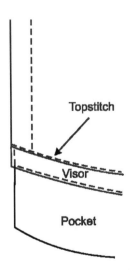

Fig 5-33 Open the Pocket out, fold seam allowances toward the bimini piece and Topstitch.

Step 10 – Finish the backstay area

There are several ways to finish off this area.

There will be a slit from the edge of the bimini to the backstay(s). The slit needs to be closed, and you can do this with a zipper or a simple Velcro flap. If you don't want leaks, a zipper closure will need a flap, which will also protect the zipper from sun damage.

The opening for the backstay itself should be reinforced so it doesn't chafe against the backstay. The opening around the backstay will need to be very tight or rain will drip down along the backstay into the cockpit. No matter how small you try to make the hole, rain will still run down the backstay. Furthermore, if you try to make the hole very small, movements of the mast caused by wind strength and point of sail can cause the backstay to shift – this could cause problems with wrinkling of your fabric or even ripping it. Not as much a problem on small boats but on big boats and especially catamarans this movement is more pronounced and the forces can be significant. If the opening is closed tightly with a zipper, this can damage the zipper.

So what to do.
A good compromise is to make the hole oversized to allow the backstay to shift a little, and add a cone around the opening to go a little ways up the backstay with a drawstring to keep it tightly closed.

Once you decide what to do, all these options are described here.

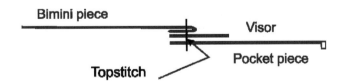

Fig 5-33 Cross Section

Canvas for Cruisers

OK, So far you have stitched the patch onto the backstay area back in Step 7.

<u>Oversized Hole:</u>

a) With a hot knife, make a slit through all layers from the aft edge of the bimini to the backstay hole. Cut out a small hole for the backstay to go through.

b) Bind the raw edge with a little strip of leather or vinyl at the backstay end, and Sunbrella centerfold along the rest. (Fig 5-34)

To close the slit, you can make a Velcro'd flap or a zippered opening.

.

Whether or not you install a zipper, it should be covered with a Velcro'd flap as follows:

<u>For a simple Velcro flap:</u> See Fig 5-35.

a) Cut a rectangle of Sunbrella about 1" shorter than required, and about 2 ½" wide.

b) Apply seamstick to all 4 edges. Trim the corners. Turn all edges under by ½" and stick down.

c) Stitch a piece of 1" Velcro loops to one long side of the flap.

d) On the *right* side of the bimini, position the flap along the backstay opening; so that it is tight to the backstay (helps prevent leaks). The aft edge of the flap should line up with the aft edge of the bimini.

e) Stitch the flap to the slit's edge.

f) Stitch Velcro hooks to the bimini so the flap can close over it.

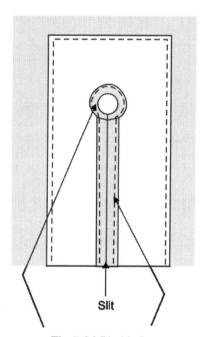

Slit

Fig 5-34 Bind hole with leather or vinyl and edges of slit with Sunbrella binding.

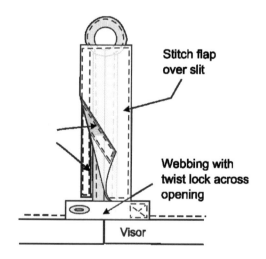

Stitch flap over slit

Webbing with twist lock across opening

Visor

Fig 5-35 A Velcro'd flap with a twist lock fastener across the opening for strength.

For additional strength at the aft edge, cut the flap about 2" shorter than required. Then you will have a space at the aft edge of the bimini where you can fashion a closure across the end. Make a little tab out of 1" nylon webbing, stitch it to the aft edge with a box stitch, and secure the other end across the opening with a snap or twist lock fastener.

This will definitely be necessary if your backstay slits go to the side hems of the Bimini.

As previously mentioned, a big problem with backstay openings is the fact that rain runs down the wire, and drips into the cockpit. If this is likely to be a problem for you, then fashion a cone of canvas, with a Velcro closure, and a drawstring. This wraps around the backstay and closes tight, to minimize leaking. The example shown below has the cone closing with Velcro. But you can extend a zipper from the edge of the Bimini right up the side of the cone to the top if you so desire.

For a Zippered opening:

After slitting the opening and binding it:

Line up the opening's edges. Position a jacket zip on the underside of the Bimini, from the backstay hole to the aft edge. Cover the teeth with the bound edges to help make it more waterproof.

If the hole for the backstay is large, you can position the zipper either way – in other words, when closed, the zip head can be either at the Backstay end or at the Bimini's aft edge. This is because the hole you are cutting is big enough so you can get the zipper started

However, if you are making a very small opening, the head would have to be next to the Backstay when the zipper is closed.

To take the strain off the zip end, you can make the little tab out of nylon webbing to close off the end.

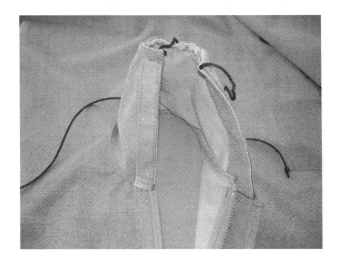 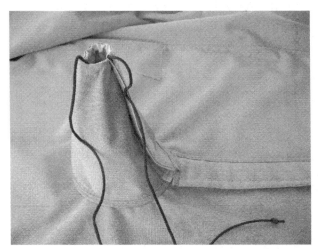

Canvas for Cruisers

For a very small opening:

This opening can be done two ways.
If you are confident of your measuring and patterning, install one zipper from backstay to hem edge, with the head next to the backstay when the zipper is closed.

If you want a bit of wiggle room, make the slit extra long. Then install a zipper with 2 heads. This will allow room for the backstay to move fore-and-aft but not side-to side.

Slit the opening. Stretch the 'legs' straight and bind the raw edge with Sunbrella binding.
Flatten the slit back into position. The backstay end will look a little fold-y but that's ok.
Install a #10 zipper onto the underside of the Bimini. Position the opening box of the zip at the Hem edge and adjust the zip to length at the Backstay end.
Put on the heads — one or two.
Add a webbing tab for strength at the hem edge.
Stitch on a Velcro'd flap on the upper side of the Bimini to protect the zipper and make it more waterproof.

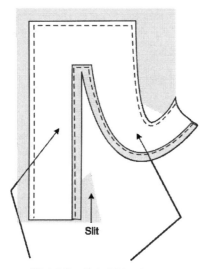

Stretch 'legs' straight out and bind raw edges.

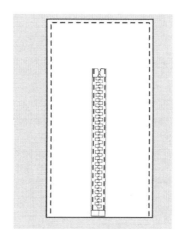

Stitch a Jacket zipper to the underside - shorten to required length.

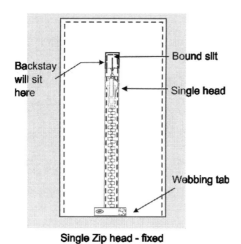

Single Zip head - fixed opening for Backstay

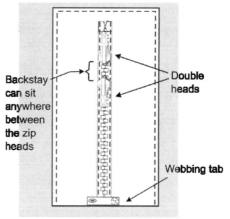

Double Zip heads - Backstay can move Fore and Aft

Fig 5-36

232

Step 9 Continued -

Flip the bimini over, *right* side down. Pin it out nice and flat.

Flatten the pocket piece onto the bimini *wrong* sides together. Remove the seamstick paper from the zipper tape. Starting at the center, and keeping the pocket and bimini nice and flat, stick the zipper on the pocket down. At the curves, the zipper will want to fold, so use your fingers to work in the pleats evenly. Roll down hard.
If you're afraid that the zipper will fall off before you can get it to the machine, just make some light pencil hatch marks between zipper tape and canvas, so you can line things up later at the sewing machine if this happens.

Stitch the zipper tape to the bimini. Usually one row of stitches is fine, unless it is subject to a lot of strain (then stitch 2 rows).

Step 11 – Finish the front edge

Follow the same procedure as Step 9 for the front edge – except, of course, you are working with one long visor and one long pocket this time.

a) Assemble the bimini/visor/pocket 'sandwich'.

b) Stitch the seam.

c) Open up the Pocket and Visor and flatten it out as in Fig 5-33.
If you are adding a chafe strip, DO NOT topstitch as in Step 9, otherwise Topstitch.

d) Chafe Strip – (Optional)

Apply ½" seamstick to the chafe strip you cut out in Step 8, or to the nylon webbing if that is what you are using.
Stick the chafe strip to the *right* side along the leading edge of the bimini.

Topstitch the chafe strip onto the bimini.
Stick down the pocket and stitch the zipper tape to the bimini the same way you did the aft pocket.

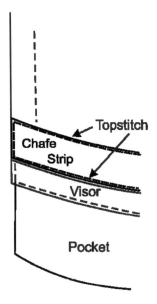

Place chafe strip on
***right* side of Bimini**
and stitch

Step 12 – Center Pocket

The fit is critical here. The center pocket should be marked on the bimini something like Fig 5-37:

The perfect curve:
Remember the line you marked along the top of the center bow? To get an even tension on the bimini, you will stitch carefully along this curved line. You can make the line a little straighter at the ends as shown in Fig 5-38, but don't make it any more curved or it will pull too hard at the ends and not at all in the center. Better to have less tension at the ends.

The Direction of 'pull':
The idea is that the 'pull' on the bimini should be in a horizontal direction, not vertical. See Fig 5-39.
In cross-section, you can see that the stitching line must be along the upper surface of the center of the tubing frame, not forward or aft of it.
If the stitching is too far forward, for example, you can see from the diagram that there will be a 'dent' in the bimini which will catch rain and dirt and look funny.

The stitching line should be along the top of the tubing, and then the fold of the pocket piece will be a little forward of this line, enclosing the tubing as shown.

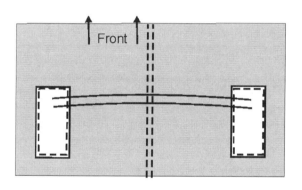

Fig 5-37 The center pocket will probably be marked out with slightly curved lines.

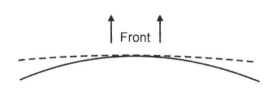

Fig 5-38 You can straighten out the curved line a bit (this is shown quite exaggerated),

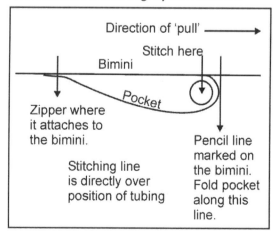

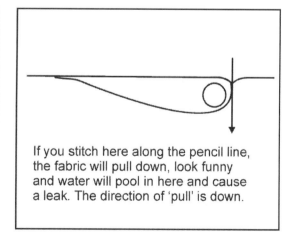

Fig 5-39 Looking at the cross-section of the pocket, the stitching where the pocket connects to the bimini must be directly over top of the tubing frame.

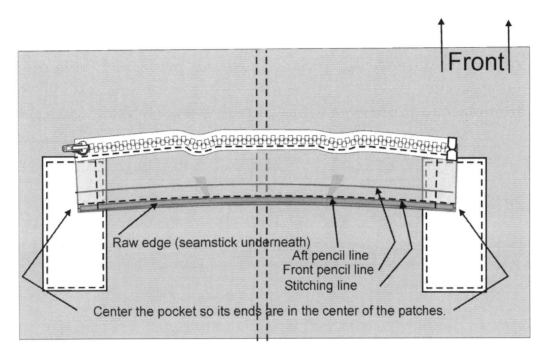

Fig 5-40 Place pocket right side down onto wrong side of bimini. Line up the raw edge of the pocket ½"to the aft of the aft-most pencil line.
In this illustration, it does not look centered on the patches, but don't forget you will be turning the flap down after stitching. Then it will be centered.
Stitch the pocket down allowing ½"seam allowance.

(These directions are for the Fabric Blank method. If you have made a pattern and your Bimini panels have seams at the bows, skip ahead to see how to sandwich the panels and pocket together. Stitch them together then follow these instructions starting with c) on the next page for completing the pocket installation.)

See Fig 5-40.

a) Apply ¼" seamstick to the *right* side of the pocket's leading edge (i.e. the edge that does not have the zip)

b) Place the pocket down onto the bimini with the *right* side of the pocket onto the *wrong* side of the bimini.

Line up the edge with the seamstick ½" to the aft of the aft most curved line that you have marked on the bimini. (You can mark a line ½" to the aft of the aft most line if you like, to help line up the raw edge of the pocket.)

This way you will be stitching directly over the aft pencil line (This was the line that is directly over top of the tubing frame).

Remove the seamstick paper and roll down hard. See Fig 5-40.

Stitch, ½" away from the pocket's raw edge, to make sure you cover up the seamstick. The idea is not to have any sticky stuff inside the pocket which will stick to the tubing and be a problem later.

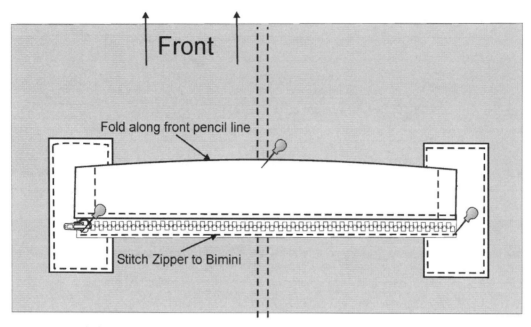

Fig 5-41 Fold the pocket so *wrong* sides are together. Pin it down and make it nice and flat.

c) Now fold the pocket over so that the *wrong* sides of the pocket & bimini are together. (See Fig 5-41) The pocket is now centered on the patch.

Crease the fold of the pocket along the forward-most curved line marked on the bimini. You can go very slightly forward of this line to cover up the mark.

Pin it all out nice and flat. Do not stitch this fold down.

d) Remove the paper from the zip's seamstick, and stick it down hard to the bimini. Stitch (usually 1 row). The center pocket is usually not subjected to a lot of strain.

If your Bimini is made of separate panels joined at the bows – layer the assembly as follows:

3-Bow Bimini
See Fig 5-42a
Lay the Aft panel *right* side up. Lay the Fwd panel on top, *right* side down matching the raw edges.

Center the Pocket *right* side down on top of these panels, matching the raw edges.
Stitch a ½" seam.
Open up flat, crease the seam allowance towards the Aft panel. Topstitch.
Proceed to c) on this page.

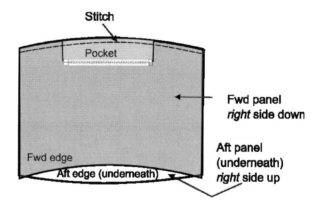

Fig 5-42 a   3-Bow Bimini

236

4-Bow Bimini

<u>Aft Center Pocket</u> – Lay the Aft panel *right* side up. Lay the Center panel on top, *right* side down, matching the raw edges. Because the curves are probably a little different, you will have to align these edges – use your pattern hatch marks and staple the panels together before sewing to do this.

Center the Aft Pocket *right* side down on top of these panels, matching the raw edges.

Stitch a ½" seam.

Open up flat, crease the seam allowance towards the Aft panel. Topstitch.

Proceed to c) on the previous page.

<u>Fwd Center Pocket</u> – Lay the Fwd panel *right* side up. Lay the Center panel (which is now attached to the Aft panel) on top, *right* side down, matching the raw edges. Staple in place. Center the Aft Pocket *right* side down on top of these panels, matching the raw edges

Stitch a ½" seam.

Open up flat, crease the seam allowance towards the Fwd panel. Topstitch.

Proceed to c) on the previous page.

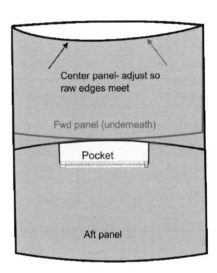

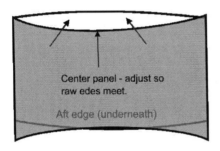

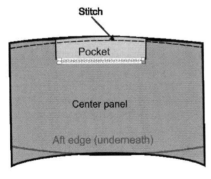

**Fig 42 b 4-Bow Bimini
Aft Center Pocket**

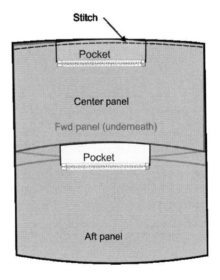

**Fig 42 c 4-Bow Bimini
Fwd Center Pocket**

Step 13 – Viewing window

a) Cut out a piece of clear vinyl 1" wider and longer than the desired finished size. Ordinary 30 mil window vinyl works OK, but Strataglass is preferable because it lasts in the sun.

b) Apply ½" seamstick all around the edges of the vinyl.

c) Stick the window in position, to the *wrong* side of the bimini.

d) Stitch all 4 sides, close to the edge of the vinyl. See Fig 5-42.

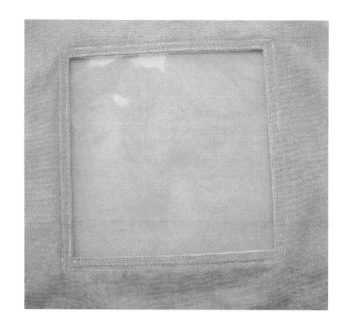

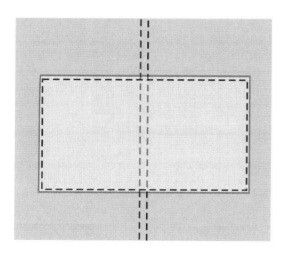

Fig 5-42 Position window on *wrong* side of bimini and stitch close to edges

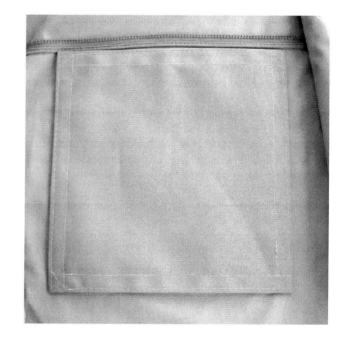

e) On the bimini fabric (*right* side), mark a line 1" inside the stitching line.
With scissors, carefully cut away the bimini fabric along this marked line.

Make a small cut diagonally into each corner, just to within ½" of the stitching line. See Fig 5-43.

Turn this raw edge under ½" and crease down the fold. The seamstick you already applied will help hold it down nice and flat.

f) On the *wrong* side, stick on a strip of Velcro loops all around the window. See Fig 5-44. Stitch the Velcro on, catching in the folded raw edge of the bimini fabric at the same time.

g) Cut a simple rectangle of fabric 1" wider and 1" longer than the size of window including its Velcro edges. Turn all 4 sides under ½" and stitch on Velcro hooks all around. This is used to cover the window up, when not in use, so the sun doesn't shine into the cockpit.

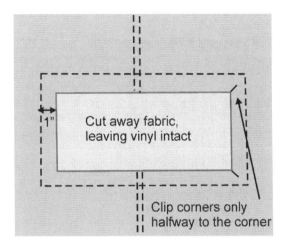

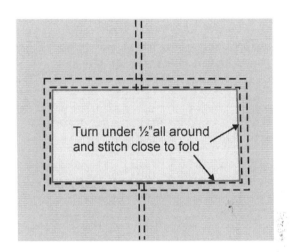

Fig 5-43 After stitching the vinyl on, cut away the bimini fabric and stitch the raw edges under.

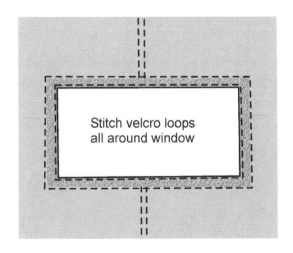

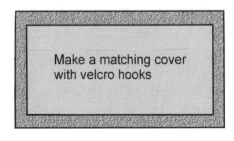

Fig 5-44 On the *wrong* side (underside) of the bimini, stitch on velcro loops and make a little rectangular piece to cover over the window from the sun.

Canvas for Cruisers

Side and Back Curtains

Removable side curtains are often attached to biminis for protection against sun and rain. Often, the material used is vinyl mesh which is available in an open-weave or a tighter weave for more shade.

When designing side curtains, think about the following:

- If you want shade protection, consider using tighter weave Awntex or Phifertex Plus or Sunbrella. More open weaves like Textilene or Phifertex provide less shade but let in more air.

Solid darker coloured side curtains can make the back of the boat look like a box! A light colour like white or off-white blends in with the deck.
Dark colour meshes are easier to see through than light colours - from the inside out. And it's harder for people to see into your cockpit from the outside. Dark also provides more shade. Look at other people's boats to help you decide.

- If the zippers on the dodger/bimini are black, put black zippers on the side curtains, even if they are white. It looks funny when black and white zip halves are zipped together.

- Zippers should close from the front to the back and from the outside to the inside (from toe rail to centerline of boat) for ease of putting them on.

- The half of the zipper with the head always goes on the side curtain part. This way, when the side curtains are removed, you don't have the zip heads hanging down all over the place.

A side curtain is quite straight and square, and has a zip at the top edge which closes front to back.

A stern curtain has a curved top edge to match the bimini. It can be split vertically and closed with a zipper to allow entry and exit from the transom of the boat.
They are great to have when anchoring in easterly trade wind areas because the sun will be shining right into your cockpit at the hottest part of the day.

In this example, we are making a vinyl mesh shade curtain for the stern of the boat, which is attached to a bimini with a zipper, and has a center zip opening.

Main steps:
Here are the main steps which will be described in detail further on:

1. Because you won't be sure of the exact size and shape, hem the bottom of the curtain only. You can also hem the sides, but do not hem the top.

2. Fit the curtain to the boat and mark the curve at the top.

3. Hem the sides (if you have not already done so), and finish the hem.

4. Attach zip(s) to the top edge.

5. Sew on the zip for the center opening, if any.

6. Install grommets or other attachments on the lower corners.

7. Install roll-ups if desired.

OK, here are the steps again, in detail:

Step 1 – Cut out the curtain roughly to size and stitch the hem.

On the boat, measure the height the panel needs to be at the center, and the width it needs to be.

Cut out a panel of fabric larger than you need it to be – that is, there needs to be an extra 4" at the bottom hem edge, about 1" at the top edge, and 4" at each side.

Stitch a 2"double hem. But stitch only the inner row of stitching and stitch only the hems you are sure of (the bottom edge and possibly each side). See Fig 5-45.

Step 2 – Fit the panel

*Note – if it has not already been done, remove the bimini from the boat and install one half of two #10 jacket zips to the inside edge of the aft visor of the bimini.
Make sure that the zipper head side is <u>not</u> the side you install, and make sure that the zips will close from outside toward the centerline of the boat.
Leave about an inch at the centerline between the two zips – they don't have to butt right up against each other.
Put the bimini back on the boat.

Zip up the other half of the zips onto the zips on the bimini - that is, the halves of the zips that you haven't sewn onto the shade yet.
If you will have to shorten this half, mark where this other half will end – to match the half that is already sewn onto the bimini.

Using small clamps, clamp the shade onto the zipper tapes so that the hem of the shade hangs nice and straight and at the level it needs to be.

Position the shade so that the side you see from sitting inside the boat is the hemmed side – in other words, the *wrong* side.

Cut away any excess material if it is in the way, and then you can do the final trimming later.

Once the panel is clamped in place and centered, mark on the panel a dotted line along the curve of the zipper teeth that is on the bimini. (Fig 5-46)
Also mark where the zips begin and end. Make some hatch marks on the zips and on the top edge of the panel to allow you to match up the pieces later.
If you have not already done so, mark the position of the side hems.
Take the panel and the other half of the zip off the boat.

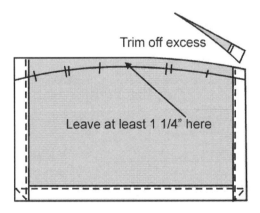

Fig 5-46 Hang the panel from the zips on the bimini.
Mark the curve of the top edge and make hatch marks on panel and zippers for matching up later.

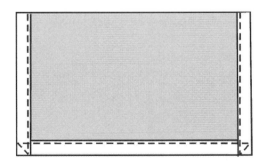

Fig 5-45 Hem the bottom and possibly the sides. Stitch only the first row, don't topstitch yet.

Canvas for Cruisers

Step 3 – Finish the hems

For the side hems, straighten out the marks you made on the boat.
Mark another line 4" outside of this line for a hem allowance. Cut along this outside line. Stitch a 2" double hem.

If you have already made a 2" double hem in the previous step, you will have to unpick some of the hem stitching so you can stitch around the corner where the bottom hem meets the sides.

Topstitch the three sides (see Section 2 - Techniques for how to do a double hem)

You now have a piece with finished and topstitched hems along 3 sides.

Step 4 – Install zip(s) along the top edge

a) Remark the dotted line you made on the boat into a nice even curve.

b) If you have not already done so, trim off enough excess material to allow easy zipper installation – leave about 1". You can do the final trimming later.

c) Shorten the zips to proper length (See Section 2 – Techniques – Zipper ends.)

d) You must stitch the zippers freehand i.e. you can't use seamstick or it will bleed through the mesh. That's why you made the hatch marks.

Working on the *wrong* side of the panel, align the hatch marks and stitch the zipper tape to the marked curve, *right* sides together, lining up the teeth to the marked line. See Fig 5-47.

e) Stitch very close to the edge of the zipper tape.

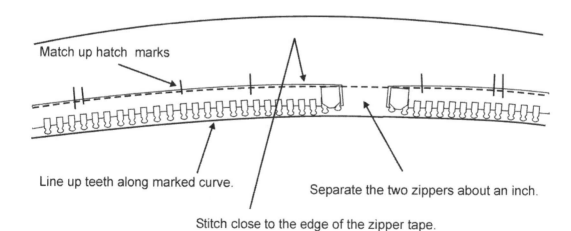

Match up hatch marks

Line up teeth along marked curve.

Separate the two zippers about an inch.

Stitch close to the edge of the zipper tape.

Fig 5-47 Detail of centerline area showing how to line up the teeth and where to stitch.

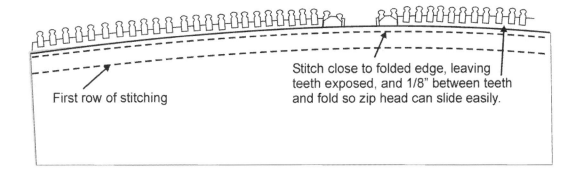

Fig 5-48 Turn the mesh under so that the zipper teeth are exposed. Stitch close to edge..

f) Fold the raw edge under to the *wrong* side, so that the zipper teeth flip upwards. Fold the mesh along the teeth so that they are exposed. Make the fold 1/8" from the teeth so that the zipper head can slide freely.

g) From the *right* side of the panel, stitch this fold down, close to the folded edge and about ¼" away from the first line of stitching. See Fig 5-48.

h) Trim away the excess mesh on the inside.

Step 5 – Install zip for center opening

a) Mark a vertical line down the center of the panel – from the center top between the two zippers, along the grain of the mesh, to the bottom of the hem as shown in Fig 5-49.

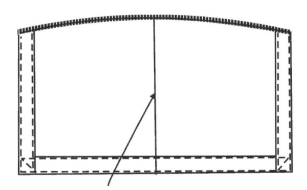

Fig 5-49 Draw a line dividing the panel in half

b) See Fig 5-50. Cut a piece of #10 continuous zipper a little bit too long for this opening. Split one end open a little and finish both sides of the tape ends. (see Section 2 - Techniques). Position the closed zipper so that the finished ends are at the hem line, and line up the teeth of the zip along the marked line. Leave the extra length hanging out the top for now.

Stitch the zipper onto the panel close to the edges of the zipper tape.

c) Split the zipper open along its teeth. Cut the mesh along the marked line, all the way to the top – you now have 2 separate pieces.

d) Bind the raw edges of the mesh's zipper openings with Stamoid double fold binding (see Section 2 - Techniques – Zipper edge finishes)

e) Put on the zipper head from the top of the panel. The panels are now joined together again.

f) Trim the excess zipper off at the top edge. Stitch a little 2-sided patch here to keep the zipper head from sliding off (see Section 2 – Techniques – Zipper Ends – Top Patch.)

Step 6 – Install #0 grommets at bottom corners

Bang in #0 grommets at the lower 'outboard' corners. You can attach lines here to tie down the shade. Fig 5-50.

Alternatively, you can use other fasteners like snaps or twist lock fasteners.

Step 7 – Install roll-ups if desired

Follow the instructions in Section 3 – Rollups.

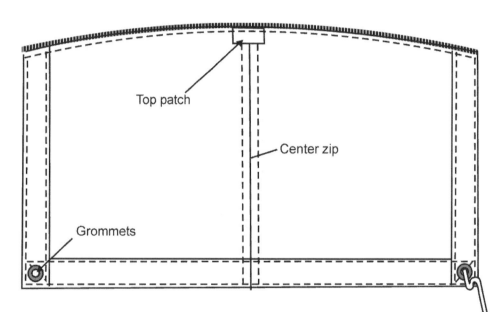

Fig 5-50 The zipper is installed down the center, with a top patch to keep the head on. Grommets are placed in the corners so they can be tied to prevent flapping. The center zipper opens from bottom to top.

Dodger

An ideal dodger protects the crew from wind and rain, is easy to see around, over and through, easy to move around it, and does not detract from the lines of the boat.

It may have zip-open windows to provide improved visibility and a breeze when desired. (Remember, though, when deciding to place these zips, to try NOT to place them over the companionway, in case the zip leaks!).

Some like the "West Coast" dodger – are made so that all the windows can zip out completely for maximum breeze action (this style is my personal favourite).

If you find that you don't want all the opening zips, you can make separate window covers to protect the cockpit from the 'greenhouse effect' while at anchor.

The dodger should be able to be folded forward and put away in case of really heavy weather. You can even make a sleeve to allow it to be folded up neatly inside. Boats that have this feature use the thinner 10 mil plastic for the windows though, not 20 or 30 mil like most dodgers. In reality, though, very few people ever fold up their dodgers because it is just too hard on the window vinyl.
Just about every dodger is different, so have a good look around other people's boats for ideas.

Read through all these instructions and understand everything before you start cutting out the fabric.

The way the dodger's forward windshield part attaches to the front of the boat is critical to pattern making and finishing. Many boats have a wedge-shaped piece of teak or plastic to which the windshield attaches. Others have a track and boltrope. Still others attach directly to the deck.

If this is the case, you will need to attach some kind of foam weather stripping to the forward edge of the windshield to prevent water from gushing up underneath the windshield. Even small breaks around obstructions such as fittings, openings for running lines, and handholds can let a lot of water pour in.

If you are starting from a frame, it helps to have a look at other people's dodgers for design ideas.

Frame:

A dodger is supported by a frame, which probably must be custom-fit to your boat. Go back and read the section on Bimini frames, but here are some additional considerations specific to dodgers.

1. The height of the boom, when the main is sheeted down hard will determine the maximum height of the dodger. But don't make the dodger high just because you can. It may end up looking like a box!

2. If you have a traveler in the cockpit, you need to separate the dodger part from the bimini part.

3. The width of the cabin top will determine the width of the dodger. The frame should fold forward around or on top of the cabin top.

4. You should be able to get in and out of the cockpit easily, and be able to move around the outside of the dodger to get to the foredeck easily and quickly. Consider adding grab rails to the dodger frame in strategic places.

5. Consider the position of the winches. You must be able to use the winch handle without banging your knuckles into the dodger frame, and the frame needs to clear the winches if you are going to fold it forwards.

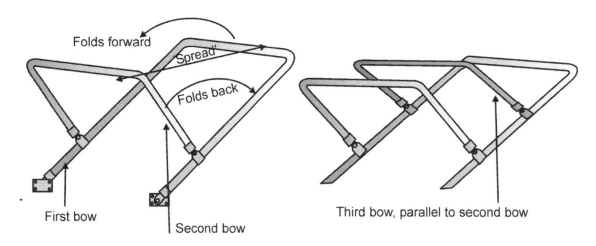

Fig 5-51 A two-bow and a three-bow frame.

6. The frame should be strong enough to withstand a person falling against it or a person grabbing it to save them from falling.

Most dodger frames consist of 2 bent pieces of tubing (called 'bows'). See Fig 5-51. If the 'spread' between the bows is greater than about 40", you should put in a third bow to give additional support. This 3rd bow is usually attached to the bow with the longest legs. Position this third bow so that it can fold up to the first (longest) bow, and is parallel to the 2nd bow.

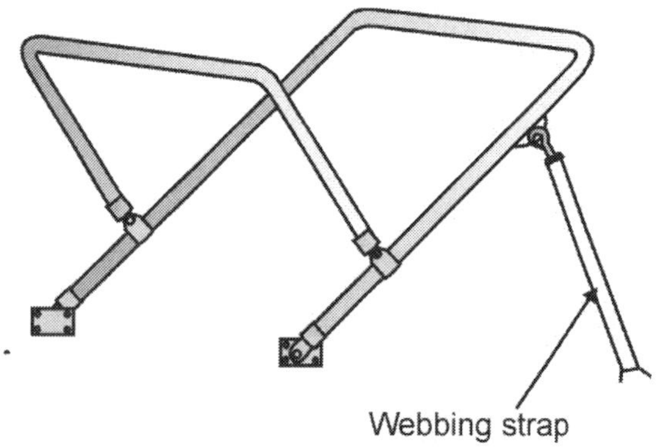

In a normal 2-bow dodger, the bow with the longer legs is attached to the boat's coamings (preferably to the outside to allow rain to drain off properly), and the other bow attaches to the first bow.

Most are designed to fold forwards, so the two bows should be the same shape. The one with the shorter legs may be a bit smaller to allow it to nest inside the other when folded forward. When the frame is folded forward, it must clear the companionway opening.

The tops of the bows should curve slightly downwards at the sides, to shed rain, and the front bow should be slightly lower than the aft bow to provide a nice, sleek look from the side, and to shed rain forward instead of into the cockpit!.

Usually the longest bow tilts aft, but this is not a hard and fast rule. The two bows usually are designed to sit at about a 90 degree angle to each other, and at about a 45 degree angle to the deck.

Webbing straps with snap hooks and buckles are used to tension the aft end of the frame, and the windshield windows serve to tension the forward end of the frame. See Fig 5-52.

Having made and installed the frame, you are now ready to make the dodger.

Fig 5-52 Often a webbing strap is used to tension the aft end.

Main steps:
1. Make the pattern.
2. Transfer the pattern to the fabric and cut out the pieces.
3. Dodger piece - Prepare and stitch on pockets and zips.
4. Dodger piece – Sew on chafe strip.
5. Dodger piece – hem the edges.
6. Windshield - Stitch reinforcing strip.
7. Windshield – Insert clear vinyl.
8. Join dodger piece to windshield piece.
9. Install fasteners

Step 1 - Make the pattern.

You can either make a plastic pattern or you can make up oversize panels of the fabric and then take these to the boat for fitting.
Never try to use the old dodger as a pattern – it is certainly all stretched out of shape and will not give a nice fit. However, do use the old dodger for ideas for changes you would like to make this time.

Read over all the basic notes on patterning in Section 2 - Techniques and then read on.

a) If replacing an old dodger, leave it on the boat and measure the distance between the front and aft bows of the frame at the 'roof'. Also measure the height off the deck at each corner. Make note of these measurements.

Mark where the existing dodger attaches to the boat and change it if you didn't like anything about it.

If there is no dodger and the frame is collapsible, push it forward into the 'down' position and mark a line on the boat where the frame meets it – the front of the windshield will attach to the boat at or in front of this line. Otherwise you won't be able to fold the dodger forward.

Have a look at the window material of the old dodger – sometimes they get heat-damaged from the hot frame next to it. If that's the case you'll need to address this in the new dodger

Measure the frame's height at each side, front and back. Is it even? Sometimes the frames get bent – if this is the case try to bend it back to shape. Measure the height of the side hem off the deck. If you want to adjust the height of the side hem, make note of this.

b) Use webbing straps or some kind of strong tape or string to hold the frame in its original position. See Fig 5-53. Don't use thick rope, or it will make a 'bump' in your pattern.

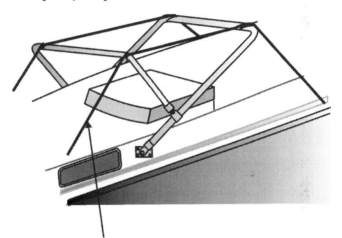

Fig 5-53 Tie off the frame securely so it sits in its normal position

Take the old dodger off the frame. Say goodbye to it.

Note: If you are making a lot of dodgers, make up webbing straps with loops and adjustable buckles to tension the frame strongly. (See Fig 5-54).

If the old dodger windshield was attached to the deck with a track and boltrope, you can make a special webbing strap with a little length of boltrope at one end instead of a loop (Fig 5-54).

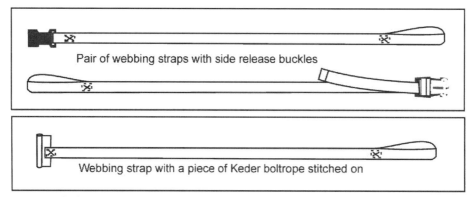

Pair of webbing straps with side release buckles

Webbing strap with a piece of Keder boltrope stitched on

Fig 5-54 Making up a set of webbing straps can help if you are making a lot of dodgers.

To use the straps, just loop one of the ends through themselves around the frame, and snap the side release buckle together, adjusting the length as needed.

If you are using fabric panels and not making a plastic pattern, follow the same directions below for fitting, but clamp the fabric to the frame similar to the instructions for the Bimini.

c) Making a plastic pattern:

To help the plastic stick to the frame, you can use ¼" seamstick. But be careful – make sure you have the kind of seamstick that has a 'carrier strip' of plastic, and is not just a line of gummy glue. Without the carrier strip, the seamstick will be impossible to get off the tubing and you will be very unhappy. In any case, leave the seamstick on the metal for as short a time as possible, and if you are working in the hot sun, stick masking tape down first and stick the seamstick to the tape.

Stick the ¼" seamstick to the frame – along the aft edge of the rear bow, along the front edge of the forward bow, and on the outside edge of the uprights. Also apply seamstick to the coaming area or side of the boat where the sides will attach to the boat.

d) Remove all the seamstick paper. Drape the plastic film over the bows. You will be making a

pattern for the 'roof' of the dodger first. Fig 5-55.

Standing off to the side, and working from inboard to outboard, stick the plastic down to the frame. Take one side of the plastic in one hand, and the other side in the other hand.

Work both bows together, tensioning the plastic both fore-and-aft and athwart ships so that there are no twists or wrinkles – same as described in the Bimini section.
The plastic should be snug, but not drum-tight.
If the wind is getting to be a problem, use clamps to help hold the plastic down.
Two pairs of hands sometimes helps, but if you are working with your spouse, it can be a test of the marriage!

Fig 5-55 "Roof" pattern is on, marked and excess is cut off.

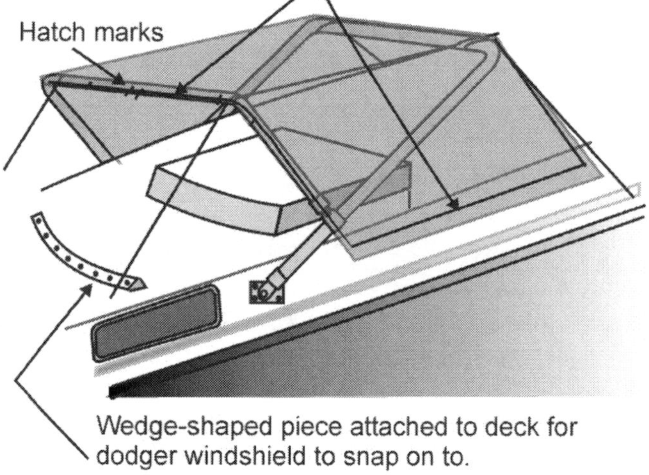

Hatch marks

Wedge-shaped piece attached to deck for dodger windshield to snap on to.

e) If there is any excess plastic getting in the way, trim it off roughly.

Using a wide permanent marker, mark a series of dashed lines along the bows – they don't have to be continuous and straight – you will even out the marks later.
Mark the aft edge of the aft bow. Mark the leading edge of the forward bow up higher than the horizontal – hold your marker up at a 45 degree angle. Mark the outside edges of the uprights.

Make several hatch marks, especially at corners and curves, so you can match the front and top panels when you go to sew them together.
The dodger will be held onto the frame by pockets just like the Bimini. Mark if there are any bars or straps which will limit the size and location of the Fwd and Aft pockets.

f) Now for the windshield.

If you are working with a brand new frame think about how the dodger windshield attaches to the front of the boat. One way of keeping the sea from squirting up and underneath the windshield is to affix a wedge of teak or plastic to the deck in a nice curve. The windshield then attaches to this wedge's front edge, usually with snaps. Lift-the-dots or twist lock fasteners can be used too.

Apply a line of ¼" seamstick to the front edge of the plastic pattern roof panel you just made. Don't put the seamstick right on top of the marked lines though, or when you remove the seamstick you will remove the marks too!
Apply ¼" seamstick to the front edge – the wedge or whatever surface the windshield will attach to the boat.

Remove all the seamstick paper.

g) Stick the plastic to the windshield area, standing off to the side and working center to

outside as before. Make sure the plastic is taut and has no twist or wrinkles. Cut away excess plastic if it is getting in the way.
Make notches in the plastic to allow it to go around the companionway hatch cover, cabin top fittings and any other fittings such as handrails or openings for lines.

If holding the pattern material down at the front edge at the deck is giving you trouble, you can help hold it down by installing (or using existing) snaps in their required positions. Screw the snap stud fitting right through the plastic pattern material. If you have a Quick-Fit snap Tool you can reinforce the plastic pattern material with duct tape and use the tool to hold the pattern material down.
If the leading edge of the windshield attaches to the horizontal surface of the cabin-top, you will need to allow for a flange so you can mount the fasteners – either a turn button or a lift-the-dot, not a snap.

h) With permanent marker, trace over the previous marks where the roof panel joins the windshield. Make matching hatch marks from the roof panel onto the windshield panel. Mark the outline where the windshield meets the deck. Again, just make accurate dashed lines – you will even up the marks later.

Mark the outline for the windows, the location of any zip-open sections, locations of fasteners, fittings, protrusions and any other special features. When marking the windows, try to keep them clear of the frame – it looks ugly and unplanned to have a frame sticking out in the middle of the window. Besides, the frame will heat up and cook the vinyl to a brownish colour. If this can't be avoided, mark where the frame is on the pattern, and plan on installing a strip of fabric to insulate the window from the metal tubing.

Mark on both the top panel and the windshield panel which side is the Outside, mark the starboard/port sides, and fore/aft so you will know how to cut it out and put it together.

Canvas for Cruisers

i) Dodgers have a top panel (roof) and can have sides (wings). The wings can be all one piece with the roof panel, but usually that will require a dart at the top bow where it attaches to the Top, because of the curvature of the frame. It can be easier to make a separate pattern and stitch the Top to the Wings at the Bow line.

The wings can be removable entirely (see California or West Coast Dodger for patterning and construction details), or you can make them so they fold forward out of the way of any winch handle action while sailing. Check to see if your winch handles are going to interfere with the wings

Apply seamstick to the outside of the aft bow (not directly over your markings) and to the outside of the boat's coamings.

Cut a piece of patterning plastic roughly to size and stick it to the frame. Mark the seam line if it will connect to the top panel, the hemline where it will attach to the boat's coamings, and the aft hem line running from the top panel down to the coaming. Make it a nice looking angle and consider the operation of the winch so the wing isn't in the way.

If you will be wanting a viewing window in the wing, mark this now. Keep in mind that if your wing is going to fold forward to stay out of the way of the winch handles, the window should be placed so that you are not folding the vinyl. Or you could make it a 2-piece window with a canvas divider in between.

j) Remove the pattern plastic from the frame and get that seamstick off the tubing right away.

Step 2 – Cut out the fabric.

The best way to arrange the pattern pieces is so that the side hems will lay parallel to the selvedges of the fabric. If the fabric is not wide enough, consider making a lapped seam down

the center. Sunbrella lays flatter and makes less wrinkles if cut out this way.

If you simply cannot do this due to fabric availability or cost, then lay out the pattern pieces so that the hem sides are perpendicular to the selvedges, but you might have problems with wrinkling in the fit.

In any case, lay out all the pattern pieces so they are on the same 'nap'. Sunbrella, particularly dark colours, look different shades depending on whether you are viewing it from the front or the side. And, if you lay out panels and pockets different ways, the fabric will have different stretch properties and may not fit perfectly flat.

Lay the plastic pattern with the marker-side down onto the fabric's *wrong* side. Pin it all out nice and flat with scratch-awls.

Using a dull pencil trace a series of dotted lines over the marked lines which will transfer the marked lines onto the fabric. (This works great for light-coloured fabric. If you are working with a dark fabric you will need to reach under the plastic and mark the fabric with a light coloured pencil). Mark the location of the windows and positions for the various fittings. Take the plastic off the fabric.

Even out the dashed lines on the fabric with a yardstick or flexible batten. Make another line ½" outside of the outside lines for seam allowance. Where there will be a hem, mark the fabric for a 2" double hem (that is, mark a 4" hem allowance).

Cut the windshield out of Sunbrella (or whatever fabric you are using for the dodger). A clear window will be inserted into it.

We will first do all the preparation on the 'dodger' piece (the roof and sides (wings) of the dodger) then we will do all the preparation on the windshield. Then the two pieces will be stitched together.

OK, ready?

250

Step 3 – Top Panel- Prepare pockets

For a 2-bow dodger, there will be 2 pockets – one fore and one aft.

Cut out the pockets as described in the Bimini section Steps 2, and 6.

For a 3-bow dodger there will be a Center Pocket too – again, use the instructions in the Bimini section Steps 2, 4, and 6 for cutting out and sewing.

Remember, unless there is a good reason why not, the zips should extend down the sides of the frame like a Bimini, and the zips close starting from the center toward the outsides. There can be a gap in the center if that makes it more convenient in terms of lengths of the zips. There can also just be one zipper – nobody says there has to be two. Install the zippers onto the pockets as described in the Bimini section Steps 2, 4 and 6.

If your dodger style does not include opening windows, you can get away with a short Fwd pocket because the windshield's attachment to the boat itself will serve to tension the Dodger's Top panel.

You can install visors on the dodger. These are necessary if you are making a 'West Coast" style dodger with completely removable windows because you use the visor to attach the zippers. A visor will be needed on the aft end of a dodger if you are making a centerpiece which attaches to a Bimini.

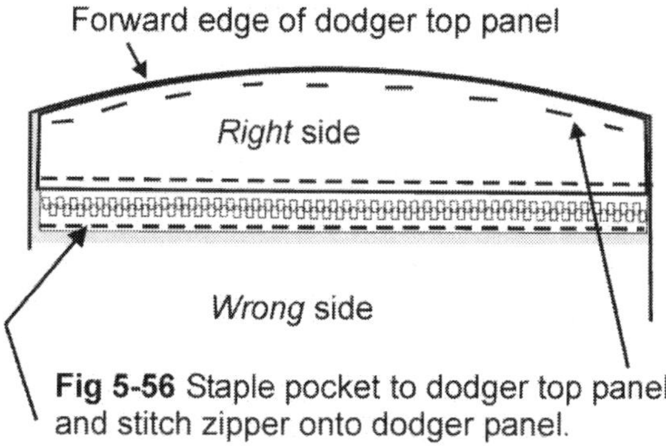

Forward Pocket – usually there is no visor.

You are going to put the front pocket on differently from the back pocket. See Fig 5-56.

Line up the forward pocket along the forward edge of the dodger top panel *wrong* sides together.

Staple the raw edges together for now.

Stretch out the work nice and flat and stick the free half of the zipper to the dodger's top panel. Stitch the zipper onto the dodger's top panel. (Note the zipper is straight in these illustrations but yours could just as well be curved).

Aft Pocket.

If you have a visor here, follow instructions in the Bimini section Step 3 for stitching and topstitching.

If there is no visor: - See Fig 5-57

With *right* sides together, stitch the aft pocket to the dodger top along the raw edge. Turn the pocket over to the *wrong* side and fold it down nice and flat along the stitching line.

Stick the zipper down onto the dodger's top panel and stitch.

If there is going to be a chafe strip here, skip to the next Step 4.

If there is to be no chafe strip here:

Unzip the Pocket. Open it out and crease the seam allowance toward the Top panel. Topstitch the seam allowance to the top panel.

Forward edge of dodger top panel

Right side

Wrong side

Fig 5-56 Staple pocket to dodger top panel and stitch zipper onto dodger panel.

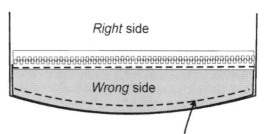

Right side

Wrong side

Fig 5-57 Aft edge. Stitch pocket to dodger top panel *right* sides together.

Step 4 - Dodger piece – Sew on Chafe strip.

You should reinforce any areas of the dodger's top panel which are exposed to possible chafe. If the sail happens to drop down and start rubbing back and forth along the frame, it won't take long for that Sunbrella to chafe right through.

Chafe strips are usually long strips sewn to the dodger where it meets forward and aft bows of the frame. You can use leather or 2" nylon webbing for chafe, or vinyl for both chafe and washability.

Either way, take the panel you have cut out for the dodger top. Lay it out on the leather or vinyl. Use the edge to mark a line along the curve for the edges you are going to reinforce – just like the instructions for the Bimini. Move the panel back 4" and mark a parallel curve.

* As a side note – if you have to piece the strip of vinyl, piece it at the center. See Fig 5-58. Stitch the strips *right* sides together. Open the seam allowance and, topstitch on a little strip to the *wrong* side to cover up the seam allowance as shown in the cross section. This adds strength.

If you are using 2" nylon webbing, of course all you have to do is hot-knife it to length.

If there are any other areas of chafe or strain on your particular dodger, prepare and stitch on patches as described in Section 2 – Techniques. Stitch on the chafe leather or vinyl to the front and/or aft edges of the dodger top panel, being careful not to catch in the pockets. (Fig 5-59)

Step 5 – Dodger piece – Hem and wings

If the Top panel includes the Wings as one piece, hem the lower and back edges of the panel.
Sew on a reinforcing strip to the bottom edges if necessary, to stiffen the hems and provide strength for fasteners. Sew a 2" double hem all along the edges.

If your wings are separate pieces of fabric, sew them to the Top panel with a ½" seam allowance. Topstitch.

Then hem the edges.

If your wings are detachable, reinforce the edges – see Windshield - Reinforcing strip next.
Install fasteners or zipper or whatever you are using between the Wings and the Top panel. You will install the fasteners where the Wings attach to the boat later, when you go to do the final fitting.

Now set this dodger piece aside until you are finished preparing the windshield.

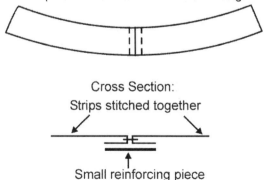

Fig 5-58 Chafe strip cut out and stitched together along the center. A small strip is topstitched to the back to add strength.

Cross Section:
Strips stitched together

Small reinforcing piece

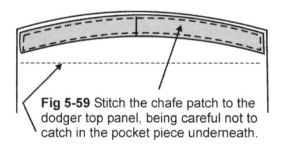

Fig 5-59 Stitch the chafe patch to the dodger top panel, being careful not to catch in the pocket piece underneath.

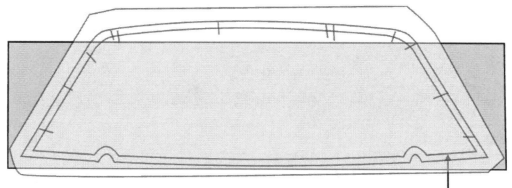

Fig 5-60 Lay the pattern onto the fabric and mark the leading edge cutting line
In this example there are 2 cutouts for eg. handrails.

Step 6 – Windshield - Stitch Reinforcing strip

a) At the leading edge of the windshield, where it meets the boat, there will need to be a reinforcing strip. This will strengthen the area where the snaps or other fasteners will be installed.

Lay out a piece of 7oz up to 10 oz Dacron long enough for the leading edge of the windshield and 3 or 4" wide.

Using the leading edge of the windshield pattern, mark the shape of the windshield where it will meet the deck onto the piece of Dacron sailcloth. Include any cutouts for deck hardware or other protrusions. See Fig 5-60.

Move the edge back 2 to 3" (depending on the size of the window and the height of the wedge or attachment point on the boat) and mark a parallel curve – smoothing out the lines for the protrusions if it makes sense. See Fig 5-61.

Using the Dacron strip as a pattern, mark out a strip of Sunbrella (or whatever fabric you are using). Add ½" to the top and to the bottom. This will be used to cover up the Dacron.

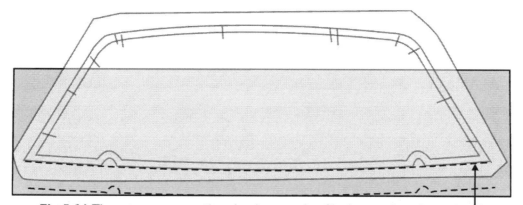

Fig 5-61 Then move your pattern back a couple of inches and mark another line along the leading edge. Note how the second line drawn is smooth ie. did not draw the cutouts for the handrails.

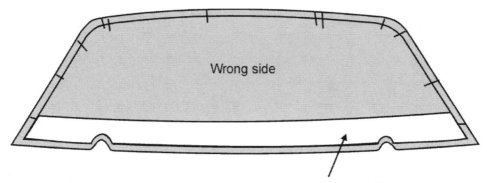

Fig 5-62 Seamstick dacron strip to wrong side of lower edge, ½"from the raw edge.

b) Seamstick the Dacron reinforcing strip to the *wrong* side of the windshield, ½" away from the raw edge (to reduce thickness) See Fig 5-62.

Apply ½" seamstick to the top edge of the Sunbrella strip, fold it under by ½" and roll it down hard. Stick another line of ½" seamstick to the folded edge. See Fig 5-63.

Staple the Sunbrella strip to the windshield, *right* sides together, lining up the raw edges.

Stitch ½" from raw edge. Fig 5-64.
Turn the reinforcing strip to the *wrong* side.
Remove the seamstick paper and stick down the Sunbrella strip, covering up the Dacron.
Stitch the Sunbrella strip on, close to the fold.
Topstitch, close to the stitched seam.

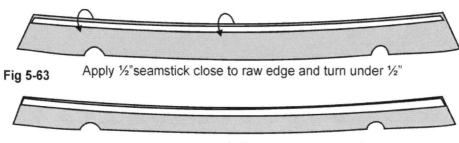

Fig 5-63   Apply ½"seamstick close to raw edge and turn under ½"

Then apply another row of ½"seamstick close to fold.
Don't take off the paper yet.

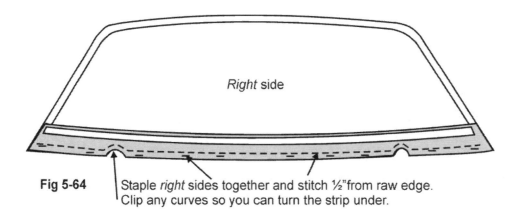

Right side

Fig 5-64   Staple *right* sides together and stitch ½"from raw edge.
Clip any curves so you can turn the strip under.

Note: IF the dodger has a windshield with a boltrope and track method of attachment, you can either:
- Insert a length of Keder boltrope in between the dodger piece and the reinforcing strip. (Fig 5-65)
- or you can make a folded-up hem of the Sunbrella, with a length of boltrope (a tube of plastic) in between the two layers of Sunbrella. Then topstitch close to the boltrope to hold it tight to the lower folded edge of the windshield. (Fig 5-66)

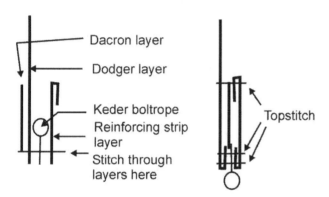

Fig 5-65 Stitch Keder boltrope into the reinforcing strip assembly.
Turn to the inside and topstitch.

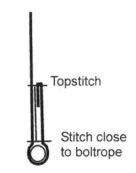

Fig 5-66 Enclose boltrope in hem and stitch

Step 7 - Insert clear vinyl into the windshield.

There are several styles of windows, limited almost only by your imagination. Described here are the most common types.

See Fig 5-68 on the next page.
The windows can be 'solid' or can open with zips. If they open, they can open in a curve like a smile, or an upside down smile - a frown. If they are to be curved, make the radius of the curve no less than 20" or you will have real trouble making a regular 'tooth' zipper curve enough. If you need a tighter curve, use a coil-type zipper. Either style, use size #10 for strength.

You can have straight vertical openings, too. If you use jacket zips, the windows can be totally removable. For removable windows, follow the principles of construction later in this section - see Framed Windows.

If you have opening windows, you will probably want to install rollups (see Assemblies section) Usually the windows roll up, but they can roll down too, and rest on the cabin top.

Here's how to install the window zippers. This example shows a curved application, but you can use this method to do straight zippers too.

One more important note when working with clear vinyl. Clear vinyl scratches very easily. Place a bed sheet or similar fabric on the cutting surface. After marking out the final shape of the window, cut out 2 pieces of paper about 1" smaller all around. Tape them with small pieces of masking tape to each side of the vinyl.

Clear vinyl is sticky – it tends to form a bubble in front of the needle because it resists going under the sewing machine's foot. This is much less problem with a walking foot machine but if you don't have one, try sewing with the clear vinyl on the underside.
Use a long stitch to limit perforations in the vinyl.

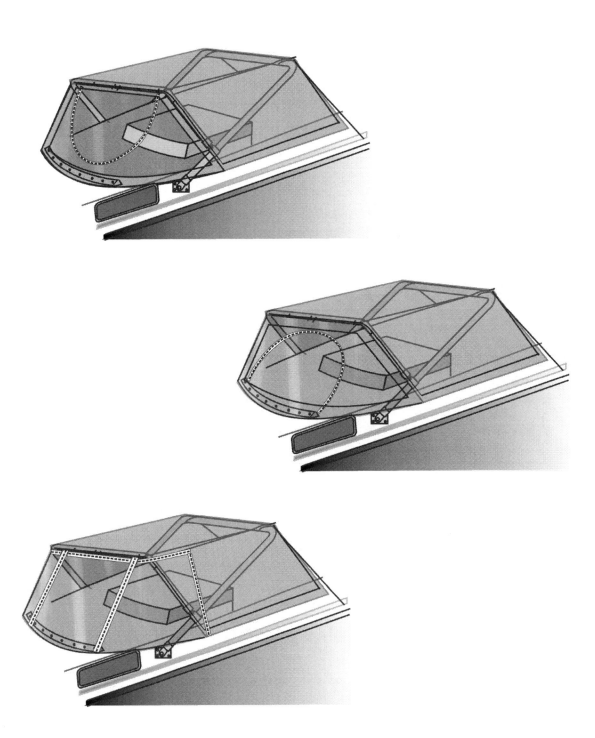

Fig 5-68 Three different dodger window styles. Top figure is the 'smile', center figure is the 'frown' and bottom figure is the 'West Coast style' with window sections that are totally removable.

a) Lay your window vinyl out nice and flat. Mark with a grease pencil the outline of the window from the canvas piece or the original pattern and mark the position of the zipper if you are putting one in.
(Fig 5-69).
<u>Be very careful if using the original pattern –</u>
<u>permanent marker will permanently mark the</u>
<u>clear window vinyl.</u> So place the pattern marker-side-down and place the vinyl window material on top of it. Use a grease pencil to mark the vinyl. Permanent marker can even transfer from the edge of your ruler to the vinyl so be careful.

Add 5/8" all around the outside for the cutting line. Cut out the clear vinyl nice and even.

b) On the outside (*right* side) of the vinyl, seamstick down 2 strips of double fold acrylic binding – one strip on each side of the marked zipper line, leaving a gap of about 1/8" between the 2 rows. See Fig 5-70. Don't fold the binding in half; just leave it flat just like it comes off the roll.

Stamoid double fold binding can also be used if you can find a suitable colour.

c) Stitch only the inner edges of the binding for now, as shown in Fig 5-70.
Flip the clear vinyl over so it is now *wrong* side up.

d) Apply ¼" seamstick to both tapes of a length of #10 zipper. On the inside (*wrong* side) of the window, stick down the zipper with the teeth along the marked line, covering up the binding strips on the other side. Gradually removing the seamstick paper a bit at a time, carefully stick down the outside curve first. Then gather (again removing the seamstick paper a little at a time) the inside curve with your fingers into a nice even gather to fit.
(Fig 5-71)

e) Stitch the zip down – usually with 4 rows – 2 rows on each side of the zipper tape.

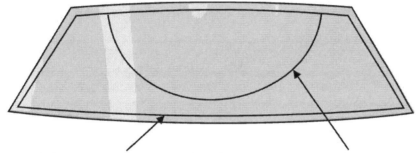

Fig 5-69 Mark the finished size of the window, and the line for the zip curve.
Mark 5/8" outside of the finished size for the cutting line.

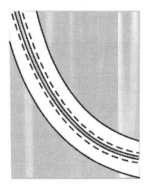

Fig 5-70 On the *right* side, stick down two rows of binding one on each side of the marked line. Stitch only the inner edges as shown.

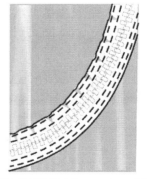

Fig 5-71 On the *wrong* side, stick down the zipper (face down), gathering the inner curve to fit. Stitch down with 2 rows of stitching.

f) Now, carefully slit the vinyl along the marked line, between the two rows of binding as follows: (Be careful not to cut the binding or damage the zipper teeth).

If you prefer to work from the outside (the side with the binding on it), use an exacto knife or a very sharp seam ripper - just make a little slit in the plastic, and then position the seam ripper so that the little knob is inside the slit.

If you prefer to work from the inside, (zipper side), separate the zipper by sliding your finger along inside it. Splay the zipper open and make a little slit with a seam ripper to get things started, then use scissors to cut a smooth line along the marked line.

Put on the zip head(s) Usually 1 maybe 2. And usually a single-pull to reduce bulkiness, unless you are going to want to open and close the window from inside and outside the dodger.

g) If the zipper does not extend all the way to the fabric 'frame' of the window, finish off the ends of the zipper with a little patch. Seamstick a patch of fabric about 2" square at the end of the zipper, covering the raw end. Stick a marching patch on the outside directly over top, covering the raw edge of the binding. Stitch.

Alternate method - Flap:
This type of zipper install can be prone to leaking through the crack between the two strips of binding, and then through the zipper teeth. For a more rain-proof install, don't use the 2 strips of binding and instead use one flap of fabric, shaped to fit the curve.

It should be at least 1 ½" wide to cover the zipper completely. Bind both of the curved long edges with doublefold bias binding.

For a 'smile' window:
On the inside of the window, stitch the zipper to the vinyl along the marked curved line.
On the outside of the window, stitch the flap to the inside curve of the zipper, along the same stitch line as the binding. It will hang down over the zipper and hide it.
(Note - when the window is rolled up, you will be able to see the zipper and seamstick of the one side of the zipper, from the outside of the dodger. If you don't like this idea, you can cover this edge with the doublefold binding laid flat to hide it – easiest to do this first before you sew on the flap.)

For a 'frown' window, stitch the flap to the outside curve so it hangs down over the zipper. Again, you can cover the other raw edge with flat binding.

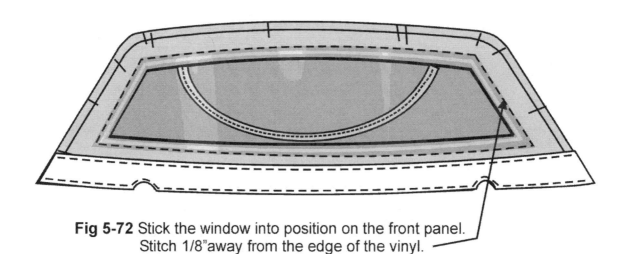

Fig 5-72 Stick the window into position on the front panel. Stitch 1/8"away from the edge of the vinyl.

Now install the prepared, clear window panel on the Sunbrella front windshield panel as follows. (This assumes that you have cut out the windshield panel out of solid Sunbrella).

You are going to sew the clear vinyl onto the Sunbrella, and then cut away the excess Sunbrella to expose the window. This can seem to be wasteful of Sunbrella but it makes the job much easier to do this way.

Apply ½" seamstick 1/8" away from the raw edge of the clear vinyl, all around the outside edge. Don't remove the paper yet.

Pin out the windshield panel fabric piece nice and flat with the *wrong* side up.

Position the window on the *wrong* side of the fabric with the window's *right* side down. The zipper side should be facing up.
Flatten everything out nice and stick the window in position, gradually peeling a little of the seamstick paper off at a time.

Stitch, 1/8" from the raw edge of the vinyl – you should actually be stitching through the very edge of the seamstick glue. Stitching through the glue helps make the window more waterproof, but can gum up the needle, so you might have to wipe it clean periodically.

Flip the panel over, so the vinyl side is down.

On the fabric, mark a line 1" to the inside of the line you just stitched.

Carefully, so as not to scratch the vinyl, trim away the fabric on this line with scissors, exposing the window.
Clip any curves or corners VERY carefully with a hot knife to reduce fraying. (placing the corner of a wooden ruler under the fabric keeps the vinyl safe underneath). Clip these curves only to within ½" of the stitching line – this is important – don't clip all the way to the stitching line. See Fig 5-73.

Still working on the outside, turn the raw edge of the fabric under ½". Use the seamstick that's already on the vinyl to hold the folded edge down nice and neat and flat. Stitch close to the fold as shown in Fig 5-73

Usually, the inside of these windows are left alone because this makes it easier to replace the windows in the future when they get all cloudy and scratched. But if you want, you can 'dress' the inside with doublefold bias binding laid out flat.

If you are going to have roll-up straps, make and stitch these in place. (see Section 3 – Rollups) The rollups will be stronger and tend to distort the windshield less when the window is rolled up if they are attached at the Fabric-to-frame join rather than directly on the clear vinyl.

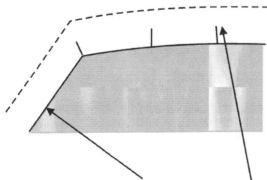

Fig 5-73 Trim away fabric to within 1" of stitched line, exposing the window. Clip curves and corners to within ½" of stitched line.

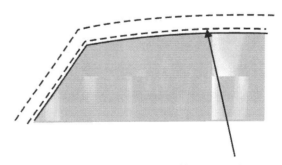

Fold under ½" and stitch close to fold.

Step 8 - Join the Top Panel to the windshield piece.

Staple the windshield to the top, *right* sides together, matching up the hatch marks. Stitch using a ½" seam allowance. Open up flat, zip open the pocket and push it towards the windshield. Crease the seam allowance toward the Top panel and topstitch.

Step 9 - Install fasteners.

Try on the dodger.

Mark the positions of the snaps or other fasteners and install accordingly. If you are using snaps, use the short screw studs if the boat is fiberglass, and drill the pilot holes big enough or you will get cracks in the fiberglass. Use the longer screw studs for wood.
If you are fortunate enough to have a QuickFit Snap tool kit, it can help a lot.

Lift-the-dot or one-way snap fasteners are good especially for corners, because they will only release if pulled up from one direction

California or West Coast Dodger

A California Dodger is usually designed with a more squar-ish look rather than rounded. This gives more headroom under the dodger.
This Dodger also has large windows which can be totally removable. This gives you great visibility and ventilation.
So really, the California Dodger is just a Bimini with Enclosure panels.

Many of the heavy detailed instructions are covered in the previous Bimini and Dodger sections. Here are some additional notes and detailed instructions for making enclosure panels.

There are many, many options for a California Dodger so it's important to consider these before you start to pattern and sew.
Here are the main ones, but have a good look around any marina and you will probably see more.

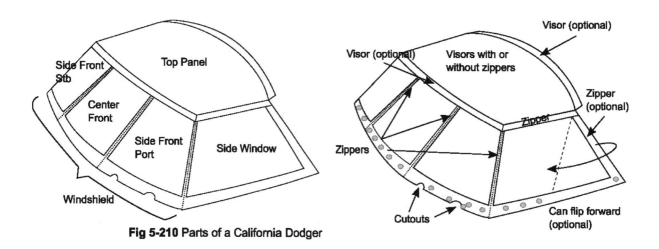

Fig 5-210 Parts of a California Dodger

Decide if you want all of the window panels – windshield and side panels - to be individually removable. Especially the windshield – this area usually is in three sections. Depending on this attachment, patterning and construction are different.

This windshield is almost all clear vinyl with minimal fabric frames, for maximum visibility. There are two straight vertical zippers, not a 'smile' or 'frown'.

Windshield Variations:

1) No Zipper: (Fig 5-211)
You can have the Windshield assembly stitched to the Top Panel without a zipper just like a 'regular' Dodger.
In this case the Dodger needs no front Visor. (But actually, if you really want a visor, go ahead, after all, it is your boat.)
The Center Front unsnaps and rolls up from the outside of the Dodger.

2) One Long Zipper: (Fig 212)
The entire 3 sections of the Windshield can be zipped to the Top Panel's Visor with one long zipper. The Center Front unsnaps and rolls up from the outside of the Dodger.

3) Three Short Zippers: (See Fig 5-213 next page)
You can have each individual Windshield panel removable so you would have 3 smaller zippers attached to the Top Panel's Visor instead of one long one.
The Center Front can either roll up from the outside, or from the inside.
From the inside, it can unzip at the top and roll or flop down onto the boat top. I prefer this because I think it's a pain in the butt to have to go outside and unsnap the Window, or to go outside and snap it back up when it starts to rain.
The Side-Front windshield panels have their own zippers connected to the Top Panel. These

top zippers can be partially opened and let that window flop down a little, for more air flow.

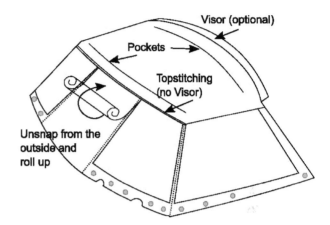

Fig 5-211 No Zipper

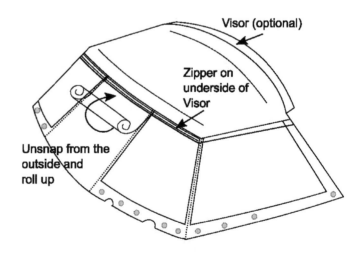

Fig 5-212 One Long Zipper

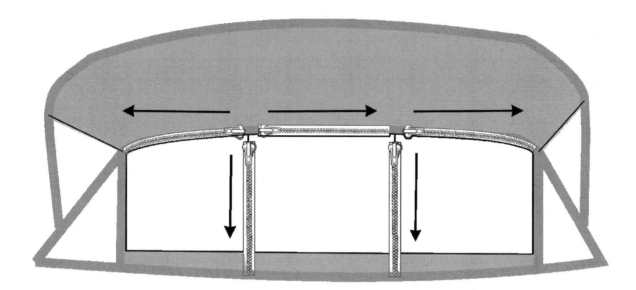

Fig 5-213 Three Short Zippers - seen from inside the Dodger
and showing the direction they open.

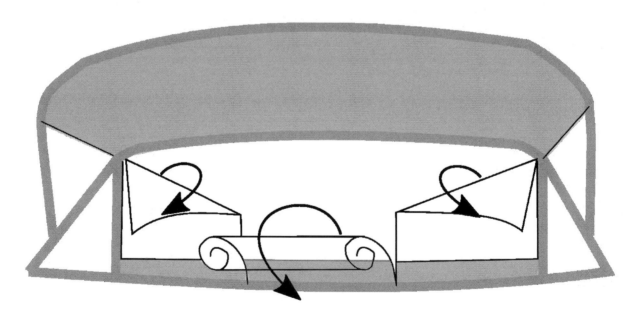

Unzip from the inside of the Dodger

No matter what your Windshield Variation is, the Side Windows can be completely removed using jacket zippers. These instructions assume you will be removing these Side Windows entirely when you are sailing, in order for the winch handles to have room to operate.

If you do not want to remove these while sailing, then when patterning, just mark a line where you would like the wing to fold forward out of the way.(See Fig 5-210) (Don't forget to figure your knuckles into this measurement).

When you are constructing the Side Windows, the folding part will be made of fabric so you're not creasing up the window vinyl

OK.

Once you have understood all that and decided what you want, here's some instructions for patterning:

Patterning is the same for all Windshield Variations except markings along the top of the Windshield. So read ahead to if you are putting One Long Zipper to pg 273 or if you are doing Three Small Zippers, read ahead to pg 276 for special notes.

When patterning, do the Windshield first. The method is the same as patterning for a Dodger Windshield.

See Fig 5-214.

Work your way around the windshield and make the cutouts for any deck lines or other equipment. Mark the Forward Bow at a 45 degree angle up from the horizontal – this is where the seam line will be for joining the windshield to the Top Panel. Make some match-up marks on this seam line.

Then, leaving the Windshield pattern in place, trim off the excess plastic and stick a line of seamstick on the plastic – don't stick directly on top of your marks or the seamstick might pull the marks off the plastic when you go to remove it. (Fig 5-215)

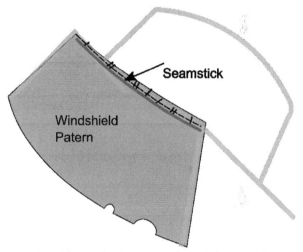

Fig 5-215 Apply a new line of Seamstick

Pattern the Top panel just like it was a Bimini.(See Bimini section)

If the frame is square enough, you can probably get the plastic to lay smooth right down to the coamings on the sides of the boat. If not, trim the excess pattern material off the Top panel and pattern the sides separately.

Mark right over top of the line you previously drew where the Windshield joins the Top panel, and mark the match-up marks too.

Mark where the side hems of the Top Panel will be – it should be similar to the Bimini – the hem extending about 4" down from the curved part of the frame. Go stand at the helm and check to see if

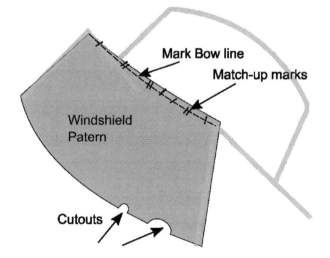

Fig 5-214 Pattern the Windshield

263

Canvas for Cruisers

it is going to give you good visibility so you won't have to duck to see under it.

There will be a zipper along the hem of the Top panel, to hold the Side Windows. Fig 5-216 c) So, on both the Top pattern, and the Side Window pattern - mark the line of the Top panel's hem edge, and mark where the zipper should start and stop..
If your Side Window is going to fold forward, mark where this line should be. (Fig 5-210)

Back to the Windshield and Side Windows: Mark where the Window Panel joins will be – most have 5 window panels – 2 sides, and 3 front pieces. Make match-up marks along these lines so you can align them.

Mark if there are any bars of the frame touching the window – these areas need either a strip of canvas to protect the window vinyl from cooking from the hot metal. Or you can wrap the bar itself in a piece of fabric with Velcro closure to insulate it from the clear window vinyl.

Mark a dashed line along the bottom of the Windshield where the Fabric border will join the clear vinyl –you can even out the marks later but have a look at it and see what will look right – not too much fabric but enough to look right and reinforce the fastener area.

Your finished pattern should look something like Fig 5-216.

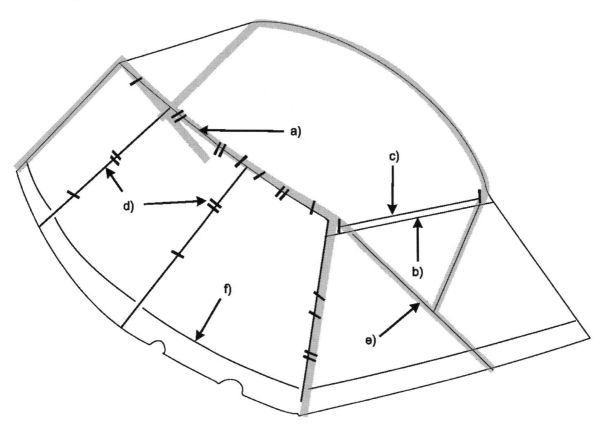

Fig 5-216

a) Windshield/Top Panel join and match-up marks
b) Side hem
c) Side Window zipper
d) Window panel joins and match-up marks
e) Bars
f) Fabric edge

Variation 1 - No Top Zipper:

Step 1 - Remove the Pattern. Even out your marks and transfer the Top Panel pattern to the Fabric. Add ½" seam allowances at the Front and Aft ends, and add 4" for a 2" double hem along the sides. (See Bimini instructions)

Step 2 - Make the Top just like a Bimini. There will be no Front Visor (unless you really want one) but you need to have an Aft Visor if you are adding a Centerpiece or Extension panel.

The Pockets will not extend all the way to the side hems. They will stop short of the hem edges by 1 ½" so that the pocket zippers don't interfere with the Window panel zippers.

Construct and stitch on the Aft pocket.

For this variation, prepare the forward pocket – hem and zippers - but DO NOT stitch it on to the Top panel yet – this will be done after you've finished preparing the Windshield..

After hemming the sides of the Top panel, stitch on a #10 Jacket Zipper to each hem where you marked the zipper to start and stop. The head should be towards the front of the boat when the zipper is closed. Adjust it for length and line up the closed zipper so its bottom tape is along the folded hem edge – that way it is completely hidden from the sun. Stitch with 2 rows of stitching, only the top tape of the zipper for now. Separate the other side of the zipper and place it aside – (label it so you won't get the 2 sides Port and Starboard - mixed up.)
See Fig 5-217

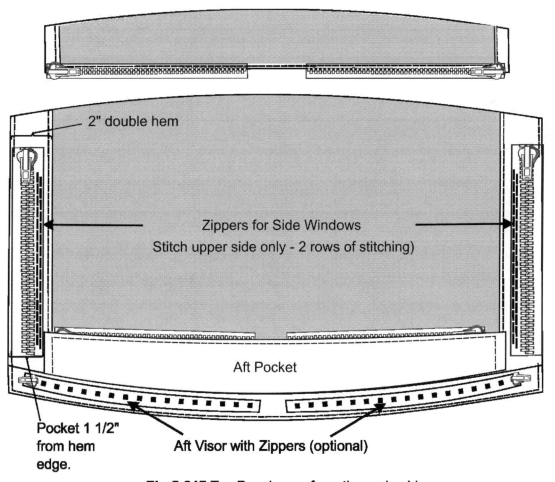

Fig 5-217 Top Panel seen from the underside

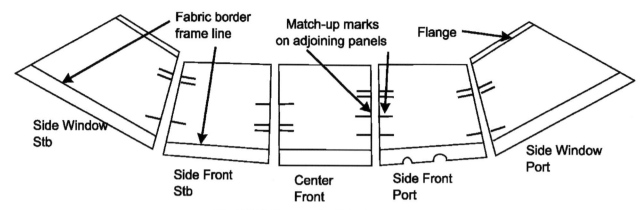

Fig 5-218 Cut out the Window pieces

Step 3 - Cut out the clear vinyl.

Cover your work area with bed sheets or something to protect the clear vinyl from scratches.

When marking, be very careful of permanent marker. Don't lay the pattern marker-side-down onto the clear vinyl as the ink can transfer to the vinyl. Instead, lay the pattern ink-side-down and place the vinyl on top. Use a grease pencil only.

Carefully mark the match up marks for adjoining panels. See Fig 5-218

Mark the frame line where the fabric border will go along the bottom edges.

See Fig 5-219. It is important to remember that the Side Windows will need to be cut so that there is a 3/4" 'flange' along the tops that will hide under the Top panel's hem. This is to

protect the zipper from the sun. So have a look at the diagram and think about where your pattern is marked – if the hem fold line is marked on your Side Window pattern, add 3/4" to the top edge of the vinyl.

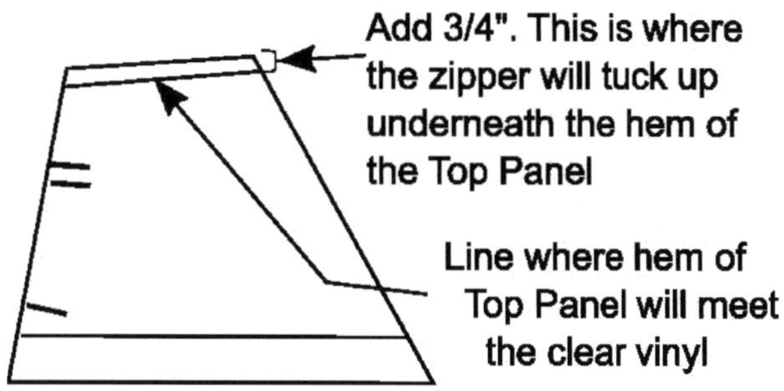

To really protect the clear vinyl from scratches, cut pieces of paper about an inch smaller than where the fabric frame will be. Tape it to both sides with little pieces of masking tape to protect the plastic from scratches while you are working with it.

Mark each window panel Center, right, left, side etc so you won't get them mixed up. Mark inside and outside, top and bottom so you orient them correctly.

Hint: While finishing off the windows, keep your pattern handy and check to make sure your work is matching up to the pattern as you go along.

Add 3/4". This is where the zipper will tuck up underneath the hem of the Top Panel

Line where hem of Top Panel will meet the clear vinyl

Fig 5-219 Adding to the top of the Side Windows

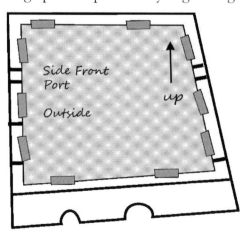

Fig 5-220 Tape paper to both sides. Label.

Step 4 - Finish the bottom edge of all of the window panels:

Note – if you need to add a protective strip to prevent the window from being cooked by the frame, do this first. Cut 2 strips of fabric (for inside and outside), turn the long ends under and seamstick according to your pattern marks.

Now for the facings:

Fig 5-221 Cut out and add 1/2" to top for seam allowance.

Mark out a piece of Sunbrella with the same contour as the lower edge of the pattern. Use the pattern to mark the straight line for where the top edge of the fabric frame will be. Add ½" seam allowance to this top edge. (Fig 5-221) Flip the piece over and use as a pattern to cut out a mirror image.

Fig 5-222 Stick a line of seamstick along edge.

Stick a line of seamstick to the *wrong* side along the top edge. (Fig 5-222)

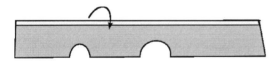

Fig 5-223 Fold edge over and stick down

Turn the edge towards the *wrong* side. Crease down, remove the seamstick paper and stick down. (Fig 5-223)

Fig 5-224 Apply seamstick to folded edge

Apply a row of seamstick to the folded seam allowance.(Fig 5-224)

Also put some seamstick along the lower edge. Lay the *wrong* side of the facing onto the *right* side of the vinyl, matching the lower edge. Remove the seamstick paper and stick down to the clear vinyl.

Flip the piece over. You can leave the vinyl – no need to trim it as it provides a pretty good reinforcing layer for fasteners. If you decide to trim the lower part of the vinyl to within ¾" of the stitching then you will need to add in a reinforcing strip under the facing, for the fastener attachments.

Stick the other piece of facing down right over top of the facing on the other side.

Stitch close to the fold. Stitch very close to the raw edges to hold them together. See Fig 5-225.

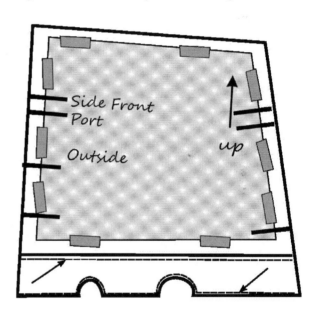

Fig 5-225 Stick facings to each side of window. Stitch close to fold and raw edge.

Optional – do this now or later - Bind the lower edge with ¾" bias binding. The reason I say optional is that you can wait to do this until you go to fit the window panels onto the boat. Just in case there are any alterations needed to that bottom edge.

Step 5 - Finish the top edge of the Front Windshield panels:

Mark out a piece of Sunbrella the same contour as the top edge of the window panel. Mark another line 1 ½" down. Add ½" seam allowances to both sides (So your strip is 2 1/2" wide). Flip it over and use it as a pattern to cut out another mirror image. (Fig 5-226)

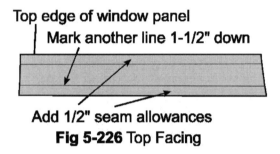

Fig 5-226 Top Facing

Stick a line of seamstick to the *wrong* side along the bottom edge. Turn the edge towards the *wrong* side. Crease down, remove the seamstick paper and stick down. Apply a row of seamstick to the folded seam allowance. (Fig 5-227)

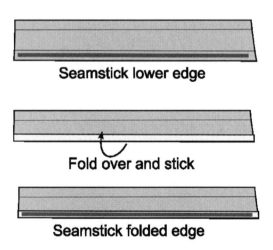

Fig 5-227 Turn lower edge in by 1/2"

Lay the *wrong* side of the facing onto the *right* side of the vinyl, with the raw edge of the Sunbrella sticking out ½" above the vinyl edge. See Fig 5-228. (This is the seam allowance for attaching the window to the Top panel.) Remove the seamstick paper and stick down to the clear vinyl.

Flip the piece over. (You can trim a little off the edge of the clear vinyl if you're worried that it will get in the way of your seam line)

Stick the other piece of facing down right over top of the one on the other side so that you are sandwiching the clear vinyl in between the Sunbrella. Stitch close to the fold and close to the raw edges to hold the 2 Sunbrella raw edges together.

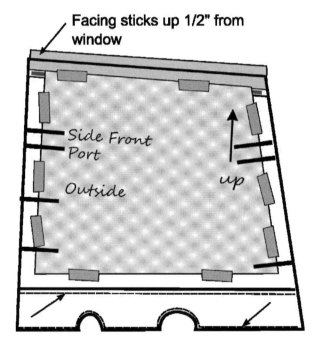

Fig 5-228 Stick facings to each side of window. Stitch close to fold and raw edge.

Step 6 – Finish the Top edges of the 2 Side Windows

Since this edge is straight, all it needs is a folded-over bound edge as follows:

(See Fig 5-229) Cut pieces of Sunbrella 4" wide and long enough for the top edges of the Side Windows.

Turn the long edges under ½" with seamstick, and re-apply seamstick to the seam allowances just like you did with the other facings.

Crease the binding piece down the middle, *wrong* sides together.
Position the binding so the edge of the window vinyl is in the crease. Check the size against your pattern and adjust the position of the fabric binding if necessary to match the pattern. Stick down the binding. Stitch close to the folded edge.

Stitch on the other half of the zipper to the top edge, in the starting and stopping positions you have marked on the pattern. The teeth should be exposed. (Refer back to Section 2 – Zippers – Fig 2-22)

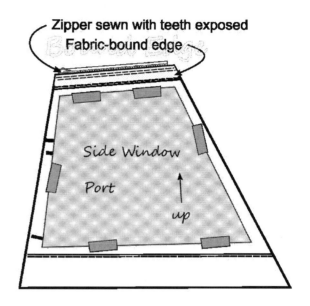

Fig 5-230 Side Window with top binding done

Step 7 - Finish the Vertical edges:
Now we are going to bind the edges and install the zippers on all the windows that adjoin each other.

Lay out all your window panels next to each other so you are looking at the Inside of the windows. (See Fig 231. Not all panels are shown, for the sake of space)

Extend the match up marks so that they are about an inch long - you need to still be able to see them once the edge is bound.

(Read ahead to pg 272 - Notes for the Side Windows to decide how you're going to finish the aft edge of the Side Windows)

Cut strips of fabric 3" wide. And long enough to go the entire length of your windows.

Turn the long edges under ½" with seamstick and crease the fabric in half along its length – nice and neat. Apply another row of seamstick to the folded seam allowances. Similar to Fig 5-229.

Cut 4" wide. Seamstick edges.

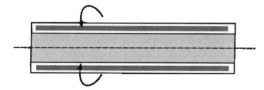

Fig 5-229 Turn under 1/2".
Seamstick folded edge.
Crease in half.

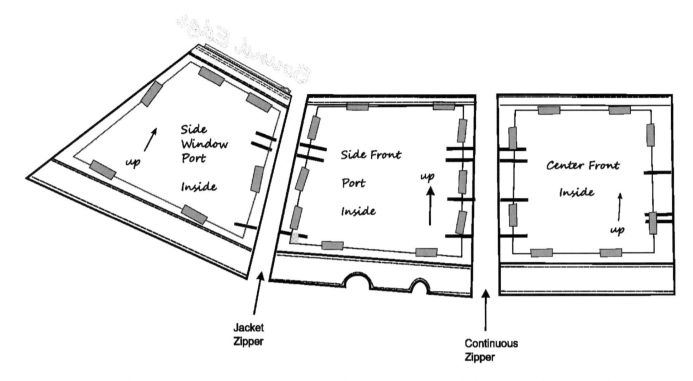

Fig 5-231. Lay out the windows next to each other. Bottoms have facings and binding (optional). Tops have facings. Side Window top has zipper. Match-up marks lined up.

Verify your window panel to the pattern and stick the fabric binding to the window, placing the edge of the vinyl in the folded crease. Don't stitch yet – get your zippers and everything all stuck down then stitch all in one go, to avoid multiple rows of stitching.

The 2 zippers on the Center Front Windshield should be #10 continuous (if you don't have any Continuous zipper, just cut the starter box and post off a Jacket zipper.)
The zippers between the Side Fronts and the Sides need to be #10 jacket zips. Start the zips 1 ½" down from the top. Arrange things so the heads will be at the bottom when closed.

I use single pull sliders because I don't usually fool around with the zippers from the outside of the Dodger. But you can use double sliders – they are just bulkier that's all. If your center window rolls up from the outside of the Dodger then make sure to have the zipper pull on the correct side.

Stick ¼" seamstick to both zipper tapes on the side of the zipper that will be stuck onto the Window. With the windows butted and aligned next to its neighbour, stick the zipper down with the teeth lined up along the join. Stick down hard and make some light hash marks in case things fall apart.

(For the two zippers on the Center window, you will have to make a little top patch of vinyl to finish off the top end of the zipper – but wait until all the zippers are installed to do this.)

Cut the bottoms of the zipper to length (should end just above the lower edge) and finish the raw ends. (See zipper section)
Some people don't like the look of the zippers from the inside of the Dodger. They get grubby looking, especially if they're white. So you can hide the tape and still leave the teeth exposed as follows.

270

After the binding and the zippers are stuck down, seamstick on ¾" binding in a matching colour to the canvas to cover up the exposed zipper tape on the inside. Keep it about 1/8" from the zipper teeth though, so it doesn't interfere with the operation of the zipper. Baste everything together with seamstick – facing, zipper and ¾" binding (if you are using it), then stitch all at once to avoid multiple rows of stitching.

Carefully unzip the zippers and separate the panels.

Carry the windows one at a time gently to the sewing machine. Stitch on the zippers.

Once all the zippers are installed, zip the Center Window to the Side Fronts and make a Top Patch for each zipper (See Section 2 – Zippers – Top Patch Fig 2-17) to keep the heads from coming off the ends.

Now the Windshield is one big piece.

I have never noticed my zippers getting sun damaged or windows leaking, when they are made butted-up to each other like this. But, if you are afraid of that happening, you can make vertical flaps which close with Velcro to cover up the zipper join from the outside of the windshield.

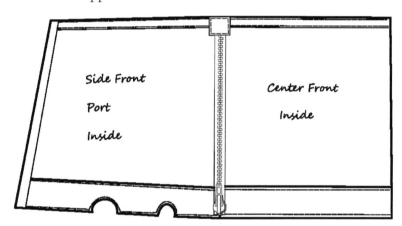

Fig 5-232 Showing Center Front joined to Side Front. Top Patch to keep head in place. Zip head at the bottom when closed.

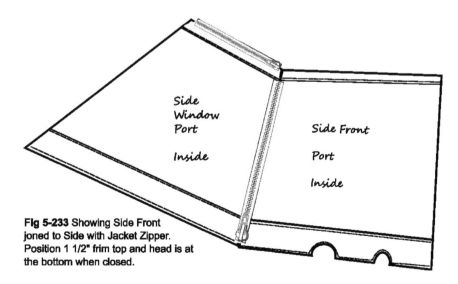

Fig 5-233 Showing Side Front joned to Side with Jacket Zipper. Position 1 1/2" frim top and head is at the bottom when closed.

Canvas for Cruisers

Notes for the Side Windows:

If you are making an enclosure, you will need zippers at the aft edges of the Side Windows.

If your side window is going to fold forward out of the way while sailing, you can cut the vinyl in 2 pieces to allow folding, or make part of the window out of clear vinyl, and part out of canvas. See diagrams.

Step 8 – Stitch the Windshield to the Top Panel and the Fwd Pocket just like a 'regular' Dodger. (See Step 8 in the Dodger section)

Step 9- Try on the Dodger. Zip in the Side Windows.
Install fasteners at the lower edge.

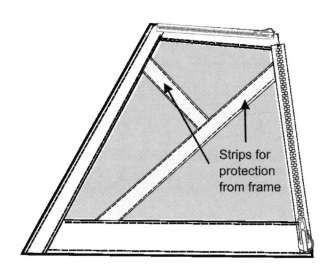

Strips for protection from frame

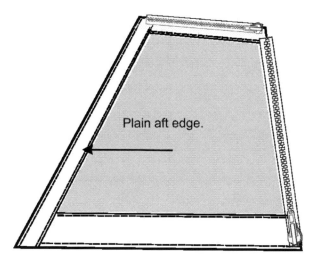

Plain aft edge.

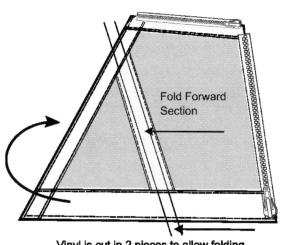

Fold Forward Section

Vinyl is cut in 2 pieces to allow folding

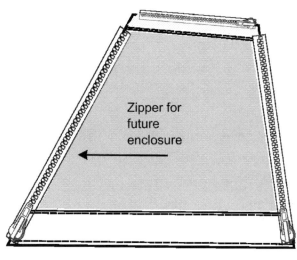

Zipper for future enclosure

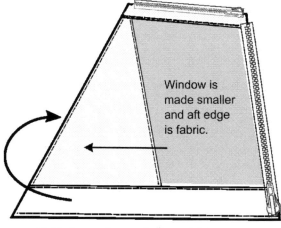

Window is made smaller and aft edge is fabric.

Folds forward towards the outside while sailing.

Variation 2 - One Long Zipper

This style of Windshield attachment requires a front Visor on the Top Panel.

Step 1 – Make a Pattern.
Follow all the same steps as "No Top Zipper" above.

One extra mark to make is the starting and stopping position of the One Long Zipper. The teeth of the zipper will lie 1" below the join line between the Top Panel and the Windshield.

Mark this line onto the Windshield, and mark where the zipper will start and stop – about 3" in from the sides of the Windshield.

Once you have done your patterning, you should have pieces something like this:

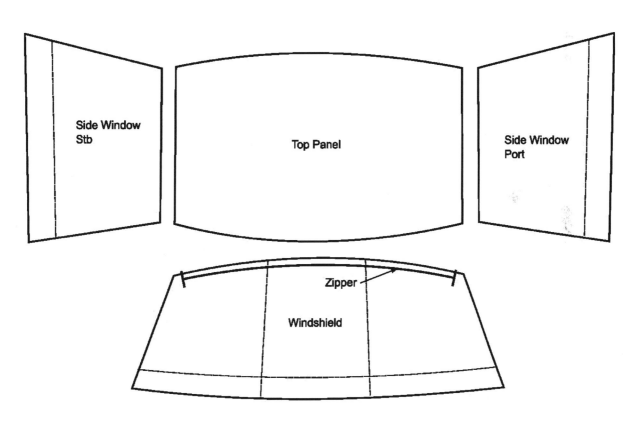

Fig 5-234 After patterning (match up marks not shown) with extra line showing position of One Long Zipper

Canvas for Cruisers

Step 2 - A very difficult little corner to figure out is the corner right where the Top Panel joins the Windshield and Side Window.
It is an area where zippers meet and is prone to gaps and therefore water leakage. So we need to reposition the pattern and decide where the join between the Windshield and the Side window really needs to be and where that join meets the Top panel.

Tape the pattern back together along the Side Window – Top Panel join. (if it's all one piece well then you're ok). Tape the Windshield Side Front to the Side Window so things meet at the critical corner.
See Fig 5-235

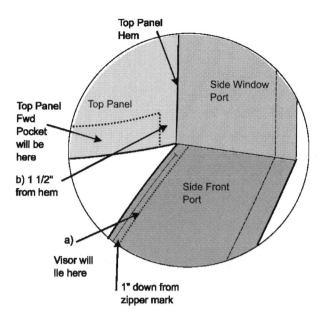

Fig 5-236 Close up of the corner, panels shown in different shades for clarity. Mark Visor line a) and Pocket Line b)

(See Fig 5-237)
Extend the lines of the Visor and the hem to represent where the zippers will go. Take some zippers and lay them along the pattern to help you visualize.
Where those 2 zipper lines meet will determine where the critical corner needs to be.

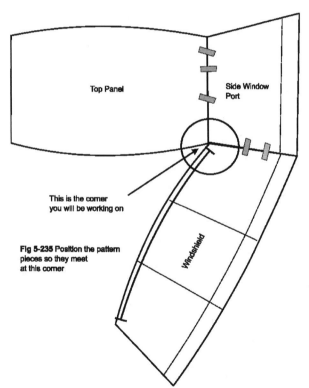

Fig 5-235 Position the pattern pieces so they meet at this corner

On the Windshield, mark a line where the lower edge of your visor will lie – that is 1" down from the marked zipper line on the pattern. (Fig 5-236 – a)

On the Top Panel, mark where the forward Pocket will be – 1 ½" from the hem edge. (Fig 5-236 –b)

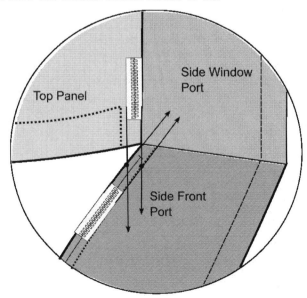

Fig 5-237 If you lay some short zippers along where they will be sewn, and extend the lines, you can see where they intersect (shown as black dots)

274

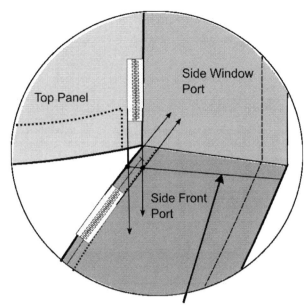

Fig 5-238 This is the new line for the Side Front - to - Side Window join.

Mark a line through the intersection points, and continue down to the bottom of your Side Front pattern to make a new line for the join. Make hatch marks so you can match the Side Front to the Side Window.

Phew.

Now you can untape your pieces – leave the Windshield/Side window taped together and cut a new line along the revised Side Front / Side Window join.

Step 3 - Make up the Top Panel just like a Bimini. Note the following:

Even out your marks and transfer the Top Panel pattern to the Fabric. Add ½" seam allowances at the Front and Aft ends, and add 4" for 2" double hem along the sides.

There will be a Front Visor. And there will be an Aft Visor if you are going to attach a Centerpiece or Extension to the Aft end of the Dodger. Review the Visor information in the Bimini section. The Front Visor needs to be 2" wide so a #10 jacket zipper can fit underneath and be covered by the Visor.

Start the Front and Aft Pockets 1 ½" up from the side hems so as not to interfere with the side window zippers.

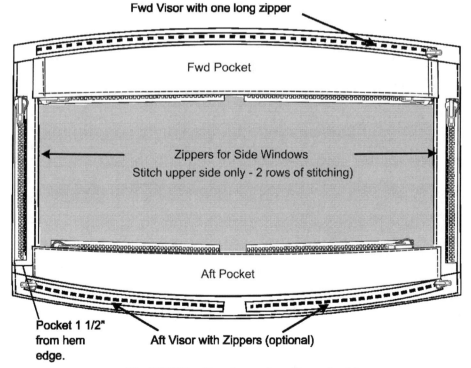

Fig 5-239 Top Panel seen from the underside

Canvas for Cruisers

Install one jacket zipper on the underside of the visor, starting and stopping about 3" short – that is 3" up from the ends of the visor as marked on your pattern - to allow room for the Windshield/Side window join.

Install a zipper to each of the Top Panel side hems – matching the location from your pattern. Position things so that the side of the zipper with the head will be stitched onto the window panel – that way you won't have a zipper head hanging down when the window is removed. Set the starting post just onto the visor as this will give the side window more support strength.

Step 4 – Cut out the clear vinyl

For the front windshield pieces, <u>cut the top along the line you marked on your pattern where the zipper teeth will lie.</u>

The Side Window will be the same as the No Zipper variation – that is:
Cut so that there is a 3/4" 'flange' that will hide under the Top panel's hem. So add ¾" to the top line on your side window pattern since that is the line where the Top Panel's hem fold is.

Step 5 - Finish the Bottom, Top and Vertical edges of all the window panels as described previously.

Step 6 – Zip the 3 Windshield pieces all together into one big panel.
Sew the matching zipper half from the Front Visor onto the top of the Windshield panel, so the teeth are exposed. Start and stop the zipper as marked in your pattern.

Step 7 – Attach the Top Panel to the Boat. Zip in the Windshield. Zip in the Side Windows. Install the bottom fasteners.

Variation 3 - Three Front Zippers

Step 1 – Make a Pattern following all the same steps as "No Top Zipper" above.
Mark the divisions for the Windshield pieces.
The teeth of the top zippers will lie 1" below the join line between the Top Panel and the Windshield. Mark this line onto the Windshield, and mark where the 3 zippers will start and stop. The zippers for the Stb and Port Side Fronts will start about 3" in from the sides of the Windshield.

Step 2 – Take the pattern off the boat and even out the marks.
Mark the Critical Corner (see Step 2 in the One Long Zipper variation) and re-mark the line where the Windshield joins the Side Window.

Step 3 – Make the Top Panel just like a Bimini and the same notes as in Step 3 previous.
Instead of installing one jacket zipper on the underside of the visor, install 3 jacket zippers according to your marks on your pattern. On the Side Front windows, arrange the heads so that when the zipper is closed, the heads are inboard. The Center window usually shouldn't matter.

Step 4 – Cut out the Clear Vinyl
Same as Step 4 previous.

Step 5 – Finish the bottom edges of all the window panels as described previously.

Step 6 – Finish the Tops of all the window panels using the Side Window instructions.
Install all the matching zippers from the Visor and Hems to the 3 windshield panels and Side Windows. All windows have teeth exposed.

Step 7 – Finish the vertical edges and install all the zippers. The zippers on the Center Front will be jacket zippers not continuous.

Step 8 - Put the Top panel on the boat. Zip in all the windows and install the fasteners.

Centerpiece or Extension Panel

A centerpiece on a boat is a piece of canvas which zips onto the aft end of a Dodger and joins to a Bimini.

If there is no Bimini, it could just be an extension off the back of the Dodger, tied off or with a batten in the aft end.

Depending on the boat, it can be a near-vertical piece possibly made of clear vinyl, or more usually, it is a sloping piece up to about 5 feet wide or so joining the 2 structures.

The centerpiece can be kept in place while sailing, or it could be removable in the case where the mainsheet goes to the traveler in the cockpit – then the centerpiece must be removed when you are sailing.

The hardest thing about centerpieces is getting the fabric to sit nicely with a minimum of wrinkles. The centerpiece typically is not flat – it curves at one radius for the dodger bow and then usually curves at a different radius for the bimini bow.

When making a pattern for a centerpiece, it is very important to mark the hatch marks between the pattern and the adjoining structure, so you can get as close a match as possible – this helps smooth things out and reduce wrinkles. But you can never get it perfect, really.

The centerpiece is usually constructed in conjunction with the dodger and bimini. The dodger's aft edge and the bimini's forward edge need to have visors to receive zippers.

If you are planning on an enclosure, the side hems of the Centerpiece need to extend down to match the hems of the Dodger and the Bimini. The side hems of the Centerpiece can be curved upwards to make it easier to see under, or to make a nice looking line from the dodger to the Bimini.

If there is not to be an enclosure, the Centerpiece can be narrower than the Dodger and Bimini so it does not necessarily need to extend all the way down to the hems. This makes it easier to pattern because it's not so curvy. But, think about rain and how it will run off the Centerpiece – maybe right into the cockpit!

Patterning is different depending on whether you are retrofitting a Centerpiece onto an existing Dodger/Bimini, or if this is part of a 'new' set where the patterns for the Dodger/Centerpiece/Bimini are all done at once.

Patterning of the Centerpiece as part of a new Bimini-Centerpiece-Dodger Set:

Step 1 - Pattern the Dodger Top panel, then the Bimini Top panel.

(You should have the Bows marked and the match-up marks made) Trim the excess plastic off and re-apply seamstick to the plastic pattern material along the bows (not directly over your marks).

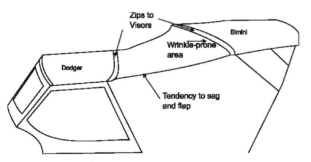

Fig 5-240 Centerpiece between Dodger and Bimini

Canvas for Cruisers

Pattern the Centerpiece.

Most Centerpieces are pretty flat, but if you are having trouble resolving the wrinkles and don't like the look of things make the pattern in 2 halves like this:

See Fig 5-241. Run a line of tape (like masking tape) right down the center between Dodger and Bimini. Cover up the other side of the tape too, with tape so it doesn't get stuck in your hair when you're moving around the boat.

Stick a line of seamstick to the upper side of the tape, leave the paper on. You should already have seamstick on the bows of the Bimini and Dodger.

If the Centerpiece is long, it can help to run strings or tape at the hem and maybe even in between center and hem, to help take out the sag in the pattern plastic.

Stick on one half of the pattern — starting at the longest span between Bimini and Dodger which is probably the hemline. Stick the plastic nice and square between Dodger and Bimini working your way to the center. It might get floppy here if your Centerpiece is curvy. Remove the seamstick paper on the center tape and make pleats where required to make the pattern fit as smoothly as possible.

If your Centerpiece is flattish, this will be easy, you will need pleats if your Centerpiece is curvy. Several small pleats are better than one or 2 large ones.

Pinch the pleats in, mark where they meet and match-up marks. Don't worry about marking all the way to the ends but make a dot if you can, where the pleat ends.

Trim off the excess plastic at the centerline. Run a line of seamstick along the centerline on the plastic pattern. Work the other side of the pattern the same way.

Mark the Bows, and match-up marks for where the Centerpiece joins the Dodger and Bimini.

Mark the side hem lines, the centerline, and where the zippers start and stop.

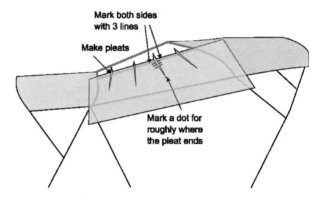

Fig 5-242 Typical pattern but yours could be different. Stick plastic down and take in darts to take up the excess. Mark sides and end of each pleat as shown.

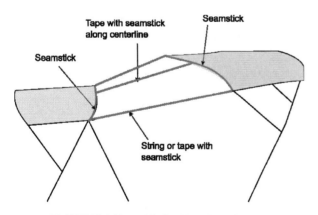

Fig 5-241 Bimini top and Dodger top patterns done. Reapply seamstick to bows.
Tape and seamstick supports center. String or tape and seamstick can be used to support hems.

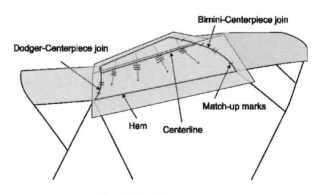

Fig 5-243 Mark the pattern.

Step 2 - Remove the pattern from the boat.

If the Centerpiece is flat, all you need to do is trim the pattern:
The front and back edges of the Centerpiece will need to be cut back by 1". This is because the zippers installed on the Bimini and Dodger Visors will stick out 1" from them.
Then you will need to add back in, a ½" seam allowance on the front and back edges.
So, this means that you will actually need to cut off just ½" from the front and back edges of the pattern.

If the Centerpiece is curvy and you had to make the more complicated pattern with pleats:
Trim off the front and back edges by ½" as above.
Cut the pattern in two along the centerline. It might look something like this: (one half shown for the sake of space)

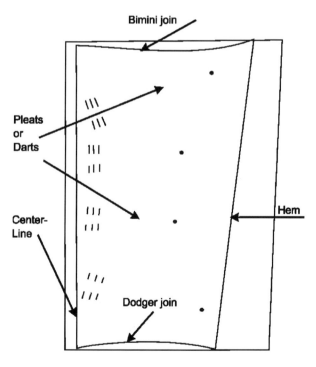

Fig 5-244 Raw pattern.

Mark up the outline:

Add 2" or 4" for a 1" or a 2" double hem.
Trim ½" off the ends.
Add ½" or ¾" to the centerline for a lapped seam.
Trim the pattern to these lines.

Fig 5-245

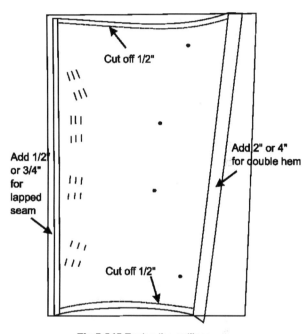

Fig 5-245 Revise the outlines.

Using the 3-lines you made for the pleats, mark a straight line at their edge, through the dot and right out to the edge of the pattern. (See Fig 5-246)

Cut along one of these lines.

Overlap the pattern so the 3 lines meet on the other side of the pleat. Tape it down nice and flat.
The pattern will take on a curved shape:
See Fig 5-246

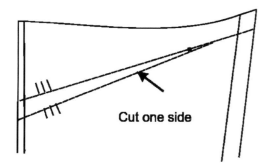

Cut one side

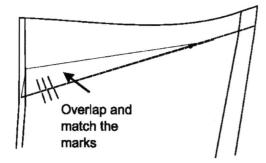

Overlap and
match the
marks

Fig 5-246 Make darts.

Patterning for Retrofitting a Centerpiece on an
already existing Bimini and Dodger

Step 1 – Install zippers onto Dodger and Bimini

Note: If the Dodger has no visor you will need
to install one. (See Dodger section)

Install jacket zippers onto the underside of the
Visor ¼" from the seam line where the visor
attaches to the Dodger or Bimini.
Place the zippers so that when the zipper is
closed the heads are outboard. If you have to
shorten the zippers, shorten both sides of the
zipper to the same length.

Step 2 – Prepare for patterning
Pin the Dodger or Bimini out nice and flat and
make a plastic pattern of the curved shape of
the visor edges you just worked on.

Mark a line for the zipper teeth and where the
zippers start and stop.

Step 3 - Put the Bimini and Dodger back on the
boat.

Measure the distance from the Dodger to the
Bimini along the longest span (usually the hem line)
Measure where the Centerpiece will be the widest
(usually at the Bimini join)
Cut out a 'blank' of plastic pattern material about 6"
longer and wider than the measurements you made.

If the Centerpiece is flat and if you're lucky, you
might be able to get a decent pattern by clamping
the pattern somehow to the visors good enough for
you to create a fit.
If not, or if the centerpiece is curvy, here's another
way:

Step 4 – Prepare the pattern
You will need to make 2 'blanks' – one for each
half, and pattern just as described previously with
making the pleats.
Using the patterns you made from the Dodger and
Bimini edges, mark the contours of the front and aft
edges of the Centerpiece.
Install the other half of the zippers from the
Dodger/Bimini visors to the pattern blank.
(Reinforce the plastic if necessary with duct tape or
similar.)
This will allow you to attach the pattern securely to
the Bimini and Dodger.

Step 5 – Make the pattern just as described above.
Remove it from the boat. Remove the zippers and
mark the pattern up as previously described.

Construction:

Mark out the fabric using the pattern.

If you made the pattern in 2 halves, join the panels
with a lapped seam.

If the sides are very curvy, you won't be able to
make a hem. So just add ½" for seam allowance and
make a facing instead like you will be doing to the
front and back edges as described below.

If the sides are straight, cut a reinforcing strip of Dacron or Shelterite 1" or 2" wide. Tuck it inside the hem to give it support, and stitch and topstitch a double hem.

Make front and back facings as follows:
On a piece of Dacron or Shelterite, use the fabric panel to mark a line matching the contour of the edge. Mark another line 1" down. Cut out.

Mark another identical piece from fabric. Add ½" seam allowances to each long edge.

Seamstick the reinforcing to the *wrong* side of the facing within the seam lines.
Stitch the facing to the Centerpiece edge *right* sides together with a ½" seam allowance. Turn to the *wrong* side.
Turn the raw edge of the facing under and staple in place. Stitch.

Install the matching sides of the zippers to the *wrong* sides of the Centerpiece so the teeth are exposed.

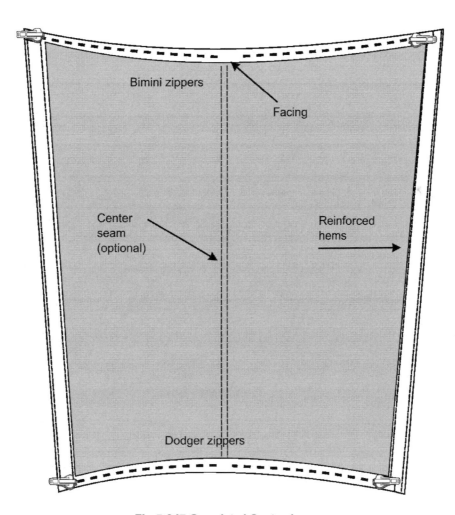

Fig 5-247 Completed Centerpiece.
Could have zippers along side hems
for possible enclosure

Centerpiece Wings

One final note on Centerpieces.
Depending on the design of your cockpit, and the frame for the Dodger and Bimini, some canvas just has the obnoxious habit of dumping rain right into the cockpit.

If you don't want or need a full enclosure, this problem can be mostly solved with the addition of a couple of canvas wings.

These tuck up underneath the side hems of the Centerpiece and the Bimini – that way rain sheds off the canvas top and then down the wing and clear of the cockpit.

The wings are attached to the Bimini and Centerpiece hems with Jacket zippers.

The hem of the wings will need some type of attachments to the boat – possibly grommets with string or bungee which can attach to lifelines or other attachment points. This will keep the wing out to the side to shed rain and provide more shade in the cockpit.

Make sure there is no gap where the forward corner of the wing attaches to the Dodger top. A gap here can dump a lot of water. This corner needs to be tucked up under the Dodger hem or visor – secure it in place with a snap, twist fastener or hook. You can try Velcro but it is usually not strong enough.

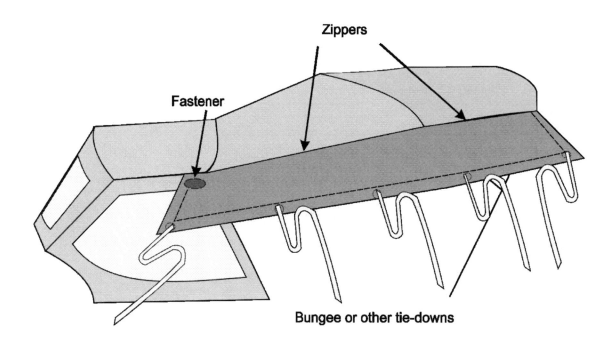

Fig 5-248 Side Wings for rain and sun.

Full Enclosure

A full enclosure of clear vinyl extends your living space by enabling you to sit outside in the rain or cold, and protects you from the elements while sailing. Before designing yours, have a look around the marina or the anchorage and see what other enclosures look like.

An enclosure is not difficult to make but you must carefully make a pattern taking into consideration the various shapes of your cockpit and its protrusions, and ensure the zippers meet the neighboring pieces of the enclosure exactly.

Each piece zips onto the bimini along the top, and to its neighbors at the sides, and fastens onto the deck or coaming using snaps, twist lock or lift the dot fasteners.

The panels can have rollups so that the entire panel can roll up out of the way when you don't need them, or you can put curved 'smile' zippers in with rollups.

It is usually not possible to pattern and sew up an entire enclosure in one Go. After making the first panel, you can hang each successive panel and mark the exact position of the zipper and ensure the panel hangs nice and square.

To add an enclosure to existing canvas, you will need to have jacket zippers on the Bimini's side hems and aft Visor.
With the Bimini on the boat, mark where the zippers need to start and stop – an inch or so from the frame so you can get your fingers in there and start the zipper.
Install jacket zippers along the inside of the Bimini's side hems so that the zipper tape is covered completely. Position them so when closed the heads are towards the back of the boat.

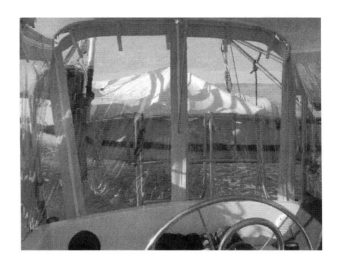

Install 2 jacket zippers on the underside of the aft Visor so that when closed the heads are outboard. Stick a line of seamstick to the other side of the zipper tape, leave the paper on for now.
Put the Bimini back on the boat.

Now you're ready to make the pattern:

To help support the patterning plastic, it can help to run a vertical line of tape along where you think panel breaks will be. Stick a line of seamstick to this tape.
Run a line of seamstick along where the bottom hem will be.

Now cut a piece of patterning plastic roughly to size. Drape it on the outside of the frame. From inside the cockpit, remove the seamstick paper from the zipper and hang the plastic squarely from the side hem's zipper.
If it's too windy, the seamstick might not be strong enough so you might have to use clamps, or sew the zipper to the plastic.
Once you have the top edge smoothed out and stuck, go outside and work on smoothing down the sides and hem, working out the wrinkles.

Once you have everything stuck down nice and smooth, mark:
- the outline for the sides and hem.
- where the zipper(s) starts and stops, and make some marks along the zipper teeth.
- from the outside, make a few marks along where the hem of the Bimini meets the pattern plastic. Label everything.

Remove the pattern by unzipping the zipper carefully – if it falls off, well you have the marks you made, right?

Note: Usually construction is done so you can see the zippers from inside the enclosure. There is a way to hide the zippers completely – read on before cutting out the clear vinyl.

Lay the pattern out, even out your marks and mark the zipper teeth line. Remove the zipper from the pattern. Re-mark the line ½" down – this is the cutting line for the clear vinyl. Cut out the clear vinyl.

Make facings and hems as described in the previous projects Bimini & Dodger

Zippers get grubby after awhile, especially white ones. If you don't want to see the zipper at all from inside:

For the horizontal zippers:
Cut out the clear vinyl using the pattern – use the zipper teeth line for the cutting line. Cut a 4" strip of fabric. Turn the long edges under by ½" using seamstick. Crease in half lengthwise. Run another line of seamstick on the folded edge. So far it's just a normal binding. However, don't position the edge of the vinyl at the crease. Position it ¾" from the crease.

Stick the zipper to the outside of the enclosure panel – the edge of the zipper tape should lie right along the edge of the binding, and the teeth along where the edge of the clear vinyl is (which you will be able to feel inside the binding)
Stitch the zipper
Now when you go to put the enclosure panel on the Bimini, that ¾" flap will cover the zipper on the Bimini, and because the zipper is on the outside of the enclosure panel, you can't see it from the inside.

If you want, you can use this method to install the vertical zippers too – but be aware that if you are going to roll them up, the cover flap can get in the way if it's stuck underneath its neighbour.

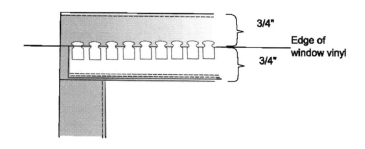

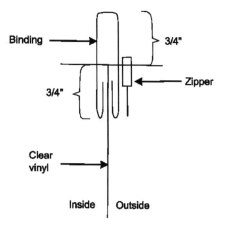

Fig 5-249 Showing crease of binding ¾" up from edge of window vinyl. Zipper is on the outside of the window.

Enclosures can get pretty hot sometimes. If you want ventilation options, you can put in a 'smile' window (see Dodger section).

If you want a screen option, you can make interchangeable enclosure panels using mesh fabric or no-see-um screening. But this makes for a lot of storage.

If you want both options and no storage consider making a permanently stitched in insert in your clear window panel.

1. Mark the smile window – the line will be where the zipper teeth will go. (cut a little slit in the line to make slitting the window later a little easier.)

2. Use this shape to cut a piece of mesh ¾" larger.

3. Stick ¾" bias binding to the edge of the mesh. Stitch only the inner edge of the binding. Set aside for now.

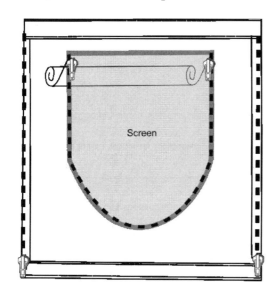

Fig 5-250 Enclosure panel has screen insert. Smile window rolls up - zipper is stitched to screen's frame.

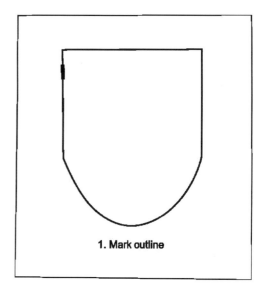

1. Mark outline

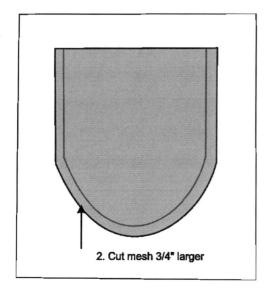

2. Cut mesh 3/4" larger

3. Stick and stitch 3/4" binding to edge

4. Stick a #10 coil zipper to the inside of the vinyl window panel with teeth along the marked line. Make it extra long about an inch so that later you can get the heads on easier. Stitch the inner edge.

5. Flip the window over to the outside. Apply a line of ¼" seamstick all around the edge of the mesh and stick down, covering the zipper. Stitch the outside edge, catching in the zipper.

6. Flip the window over mesh side down. Separate the zipper teeth. Carefully slit the vinyl along the line being careful not to cut the mesh. Put on the zipper head(s). Trim off the excess zipper if you made it extra long.

7. To finish the top edge, stick ¾" binding along the top right over top of the one on the other side. Make top patches so the window looks good from both the inside and the outside. Make rollups.

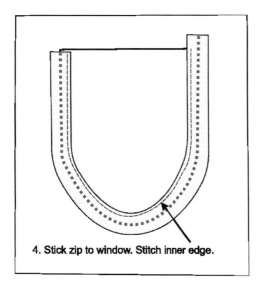

4. Stick zip to window. Stitch inner edge.

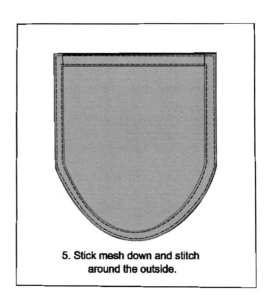

5. Stick mesh down and stitch around the outside.

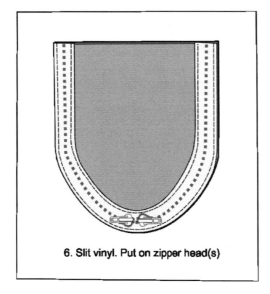

6. Slit vinyl. Put on zipper head(s)

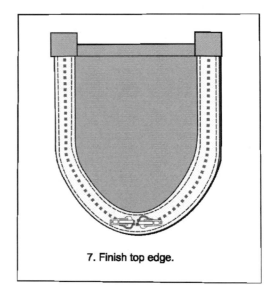

7. Finish top edge.

Mainsail Cover

Design considerations:

The basic cover consists of two matching sides, sewn together along the 'spine'. It is hemmed at the bottom with a fastening system of some sort and the mast end wraps around the mast with a fastening system.

The cover should be loose enough at the hem so that the sail can 'breathe' underneath, but not so loose that the cover is flappy.
It should be reinforced in certain areas, and there might need to be cutouts for winches, lazy jacks or other hardware.

Fastening systems at the mast vary, but most common are a zipper, twist lock fasteners or hooks.

The hem is secured at the bottom using side-release buckles, twist lock fasteners, or hooks and shock cord.

Check out other boat's sail covers before deciding on a final design – some are very imaginative and innovative.

The instructions that follow are for a 'conventional' sail cover – the type you remove and put away while sailing. For the on-boom type, which stays in place while sailing, read on to the next project.

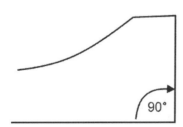 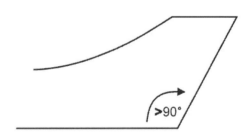

Fig 5-79 To create a 'belly' for fullness, cut the angle at the gooseneck to be slightly greater than 90° (shown greatly exaggerated here)

The size and shape of the sail can affect the design of the sail cover. If the mainsail is very full or highly roached, the sail cover might need a 'belly'. This can be achieved by cutting the 'mast' end of the sail cover at a slightly greater angle than 90 degrees, so that when straightened up, a little fullness is created (Fig 5-79)

Or you can add a 'teardrop' shape (Fig 5-80) to the mast end to create fullness (See On-Boom Sail Cover later in this section for instructions on how to measure and stitch this)

On large boats, the sail will tend to hang down under the boom at the aft end because of the size of the flakes, and lay on top of the boom at the mast end. (Fig 5-81)

It is important to remember this so that you end up with a nice horizontal hem that covers everything.

The aft end should be tapered to prevent flapping (Fig 5-82)

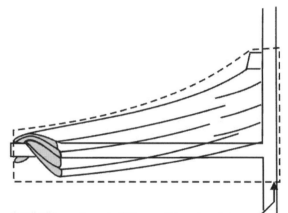

Fig 5-81 If the aft end of the sail hangs down below the boom, make the front end of the cover below the boom too, for a nice horizontal hem.

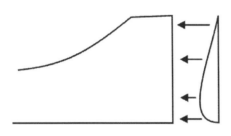

Fig 5-80 A separate piece cut like a teardrop can add fullness to the front of the sail cover.

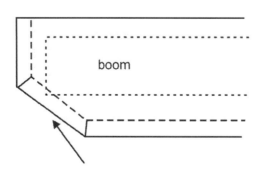

Fig 5-82 Taper the aft end to prevent flapping

Most boats have the sail cover wrapping right around the mast, held shut with a collar at the top and some kind of closure like a zipper along the mast.

However, if you don't want the mast covered due to interfering hardware or whatever, you can secure the cover directly to the sail.
Cut the top of the sail cover the size and shape of the sail's headboard (don't forget to add seam allowances). Line this end with vinyl. Where the pocket part is, stitch the 2 sides of the sail cover *right* sides together, and turn inside out.

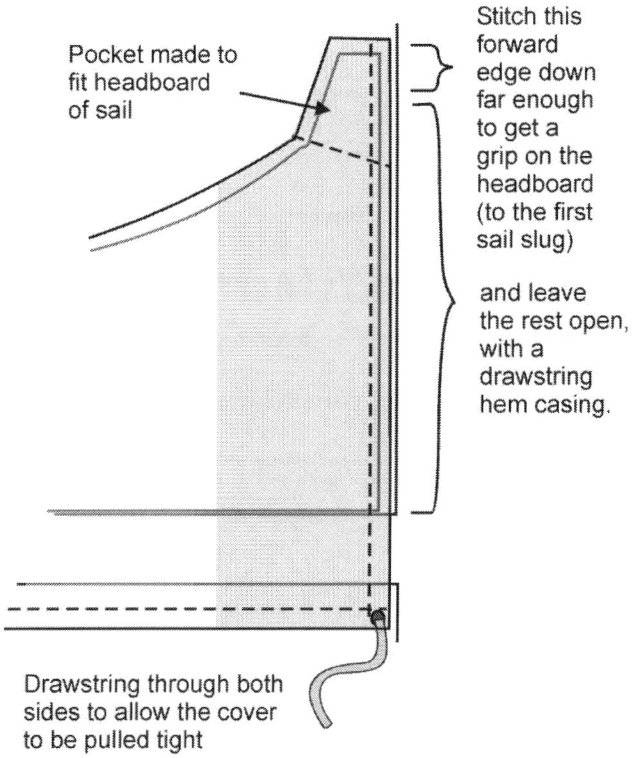

Fit it over the headboard and pull down hard underneath the boom. Secure the cover underneath the gooseneck with grommets and cord or some other strong fastening system (Fig 5-83).

Most sail covers are made of Sunbrella. It is water resistant which keeps the sail nice and dry, and breathes, so that condensation does not build up on the sail. Sunbrella comes in lots of colours – so it is ideal for sail covers. However, it cannot tolerate chafe, so you will have to reinforce these areas. The best reinforcing materials are Dacron sailcloth for larger areas, and leather or some kind of vinyl like Shelterite for smaller patches or heavy chafe areas.

If you are using an old sail cover for a pattern, take a close look at it to see where the chafe areas are – then reinforce these areas in the new cover.

There might be some hardware on the mast which will interfere with the sail cover. In these cases, create cutouts in the cover, or just allow enough material to cover them right over. In the case of winches on the mast, sometimes it is easier and more attractive to just have the fabric cover right over the winch, rather than trying to position correctly and construct a cylinder of fabric to cover the winch.

Pocket made to
fit headboard
of sail

Stitch this
forward
edge down
far enough
to get a
grip on the
headboard
(to the first
sail slug)

and leave
the rest open,
with a
drawstring
hem casing.

Drawstring through both
sides to allow the cover
to be pulled tight

Fig 5-83 This cover has a pocket to contain the sail's headboard. The front vertical edge of the cover contains drawstrings. This allows the cover to be pulled down tight and tied underneath the gooseneck for a tight fit around the sail.

Canvas for Cruisers

Main Steps:

1. Measure up – or use the old cover as a pattern.
2. Line the fore and aft ends with Dacron.
3. Reinforce the headboard area for chafe.
4. Stitch the hem and 'mast' edge. Add hem closures.
5. Stitch the 'spine'
6. Finish the aft end.
7. Sew zipper or other closure to the mast end.
8. Make the closure for the top of the mast end.
Optional:
9. Make cutouts for winches or other hardware.

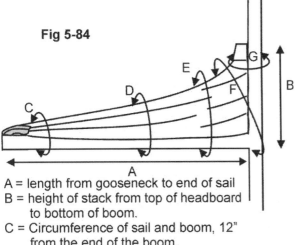

Fig 5-84

A = length from gooseneck to end of sail
B = height of stack from top of headboard
    to bottom of boom.
C = Circumference of sail and boom, 12"
    from the end of the boom.
D = Circumference halfway along the boom.
E = Circumference 1/4 of the way along
    the boom.
F = Diagonal circumference
G = Circumference of headboard and mast.

10. Make lazy jack slits.

Step 1 - Measure up – or use the old cover as a pattern.
If you are making a sail cover right from scratch flake the mainsail down onto the boom in its normal position. Put on the sail ties if you use them. Measure as shown in Fig 5-84.

If you are using an old cover as a pattern, lay out the new fabric flat on the floor.

Place the old cover onto the fabric with the bottom of the cover 2" away from the selvedge.. (This allows for a 1" double hem). If the boat is big – say, over 60', place the bottom of the cover 4" away from the selvedge to allow a 2" double hem.

With scratch awls, pin down the old cover on the fabric as nice and flat as you can get it.

With the old sail cover lying on top of the new fabric, mark its outline. Don't agonize about making the line straight and true yet – just mark the outline with a series of dashed lines.
Take away the old cover.

Even out the curve of the spine using a batten, length of awning track or some other long flexible object. If you are working alone, make use of scratch-awls to help hold the batten in position while you true-up the curve.

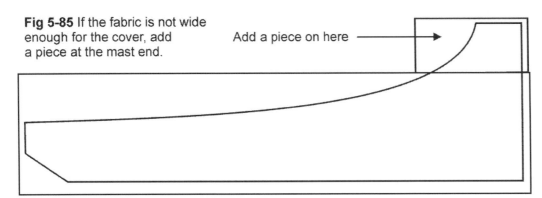

Fig 5-85 If the fabric is not wide enough for the cover, add a piece at the mast end.

Add a piece on here ⟶

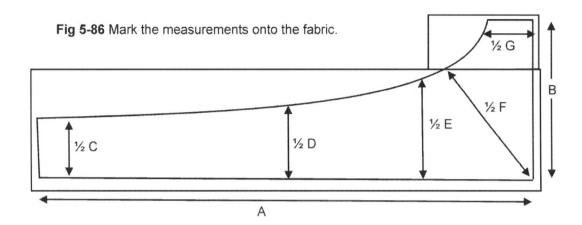

Fig 5-86 Mark the measurements onto the fabric.

If the sail cover is too wide for the fabric, join a short panel to the front end as shown in Fig 5-85. Use a lapped seam (Section 2 – Seams).

Remember, Sunbrella has a 'nap', especially the dark colours - appearing different colours depending on whether you view it from lengthwise or widthwise – so join the panels along the same grain.

If you are making the cover from scratch (in other words, you don't have an old cover to copy), mark out the fabric according to the measurements you have made (See Fig 5-84 and 5-86

First, measure along the selvedge of the fabric, the length 'A'.

Make another line the same length, parallel and 2" away (assuming a 1" double hem). You now have one line on the fabric, length 'A', 2" away from the selvedge.

At the mast end, mark a line straight up from the first line, length 'B'

Divide the measurements 'C', 'D', 'E', 'F' and 'G' in half and make a mark at the appropriate positions as shown.
Join these points with a smooth curve using a batten or other flexible object.

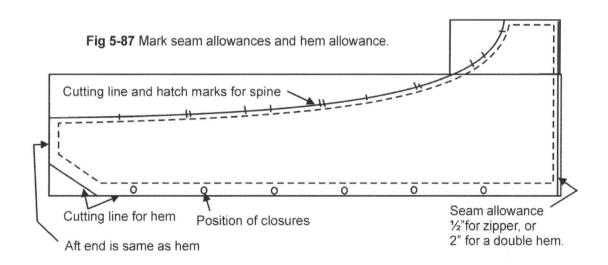

Fig 5-87 Mark seam allowances and hem allowance.

Cutting line and hatch marks for spine

Cutting line for hem   Position of closures

Aft end is same as hem

Seam allowance ½"for zipper, or 2" for a double hem.

Canvas for Cruisers

Now follow the rest of these instructions, whether you are making the cover from scratch, or using an old cover as a pattern:

Mark the hem and seam allowances as follows (See Fig 5-87):

<u>Hem</u> – Taper the aft end as shown, to prevent flapping. Start the taper 6" to 12" from the aft end, depending on what looks right to you. Mark the positions of the closures, inside the hem line so you don't cover up the marks when the hem is folded up. Somewhere between 24-36" apart, depending on what looks right. If you are going to make slits for lazy jacks, however, don't mark the positions of the closures yet.

<u>Spine</u> -
Mark a line ½" away from the curved line you marked for the spine. This is the cutting line. Make hatch marks along the spine – to help match the two panels once you are ready to join them.

<u>Mast end</u> – If there is going to be a zipper here, add ½" seam allowance. If using hooks or other closure, add a hem allowance by drawing a line 2" from and parallel to the marked line. This will give you a 1" double hem.

<u>Aft end</u> – Mark the same as the hem – i.e. draw the cutting line 2" from the hem line or 4"

depending on whether you are making a 1" or a 2" double hem.

Cut out the fabric panel – best done with a hot knife if you are using Sunbrella.

Now use this panel to mark and cut another identical, mirror image panel. Place the cut-out panel *right* side down onto the fabric and mark the outline. Mark the matching hatch marks along the spine. Remove the panel and mark up the mirror image panel with the same marks as the original. Cut out the second panel.

Optional – If you are going to appliqué on the boat's name or whatever, do this now. See Section 3 – Lettering.

<u>**Step 2** - Line the fore and aft ends with Dacron.</u>
(For all these steps, prepare both sides of the sail cover the same way.)
The front and back ends of the sail cover are subject to chafe, so you should line them. Sailcloth is a good choice because it does not add a lot of weight or bulk.

Cut a piece of 4 oz, 5 oz or 6 oz Dacron sailcloth 1 hem-allowance-width shorter than the hemmed bottom (in this case, 2" shorter), and extending right out to the raw edges of the non-hemmed sides. See Fig 5-88

For the mast end, it will be easier if you just leave the Dacron piece as a rectangle, then trim off the curved edge after it is sewn on.

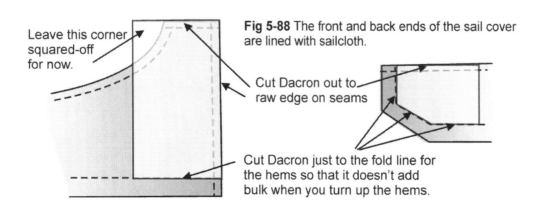

Leave this corner squared-off for now.

Fig 5-88 The front and back ends of the sail cover are lined with sailcloth.

Cut Dacron out to raw edge on seams

Cut Dacron just to the fold line for the hems so that it doesn't add bulk when you turn up the hems.

Stick ½" seamstick onto the Dacron all around the outside, and in rows about every 6" or so as shown in Fig 5-89.

Remove the seamstick. Position the Dacron piece over the mast end of the cover on the *wrong* side. Stick it down hard.

Stitch the Dacron to the cover, close to the raw edges. Don't stitch along the hem edges – these will be caught in when you do the hem. (Fig 5-90)

Step 3 - Reinforce the headboard area for chafe.

Usually, the headboard area needs an extra layer of reinforcing because it is so subject to chafe.

Cut out a suitable shape of vinyl or leather, stick it to the *wrong* side of the sail cover and stitch all around its edges as shown in Fig 5-91.

Reinforce any additional problem areas with vinyl patches – usually on the *wrong* side of the cover. For example where winches or mast steps might rub. If you have an old sail cover that you are replacing, have a look at the old cover for clues as to where there tends to be chafe.

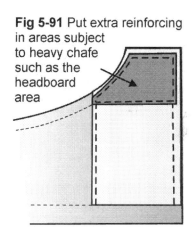

Fig 5-91 Put extra reinforcing in areas subject to heavy chafe such as the headboard area

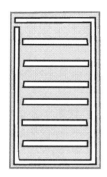

Fig 5-89 Place rows of seamstick on the Dacron to hold it in place.

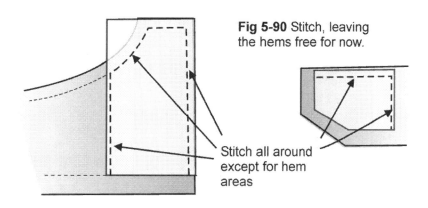

Fig 5-90 Stitch, leaving the hems free for now.

Stitch all around except for hem areas

293

Step 4 - <u>Stitch the hem and 'mast' edge. Add hem closures.</u>

Note: It is easier to hem the sail cover before it is stitched along the spine – this allows you to work with smaller pieces.

But, if you are unsure as to whether the hem will lie level to the boat, then save the hemming for last. This way, you can try on the cover and straighten the hem if necessary.

If you are going to use side-release buckles as the closures, prepare them now as follows:

See Fig 5-92. For each 'female' buckle end, cut with a hot knife a piece of nylon webbing 3" long.
Thread the webbing through the buckle loop and set aside for now.

For each 'male' end cut a piece of webbing about 7" long.
Turn one end under ½" and under again ½".
Stitch in place.
Thread the opposite end through the male end.
(See Section 3 – Buckle Strap).
Set these aside for now.
Go back to the cover.

Crease up the first fold of the bottom hem, and crease up the first fold of the aft end.

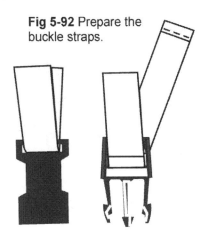

Fig 5-92 Prepare the buckle straps.

If there is <u>not</u> going to be a zipper at the mast end, crease this first hem fold up too.

The first crease is 1" if you are making a 1" double hem.
Use a tool with an edge like a staple remover, metal ruler or dull knife.

Turn up the hem again (don't need to crease) and freehand stitch the hem and aft end (and the mast end too if you are not putting in a zipper).

If you don't trust yourself to sew the hem without creating a 'roped' appearance, staple the hem first. Certainly, staple the Dacron areas because they are slippery, being careful not to stitch the staples inside the hem – they will rust in there and look horrible!

If you are putting a drawstring in the aft end, insert a piece of cord into the hem before stitching. Leave an opening for the line to exit both at the top (spine) and bottom. The cord at the spine end will be stitched together when you go to stitch the spine.

As you are stitching up the hem, stitch on the buckle closures (if you are using these).
If you are going to put in slits for lazy jacks, however, don't stitch on these buckles yet.
Stitch all the 'females' along one side, and all the 'males' along the other side. For the 'female' part, with the webbing folded in half, let the buckle hang about ½" below the hem fold and attach it with a neat box stitch through both layers of webbing. See Fig 5-93.

On the other panel, attach the male ends. The end of the webbing for the males extends about an inch into the hem area, and ends up being a fairly short little adjustable strap. Make a neat box stitch for these webbing pieces to secure them.

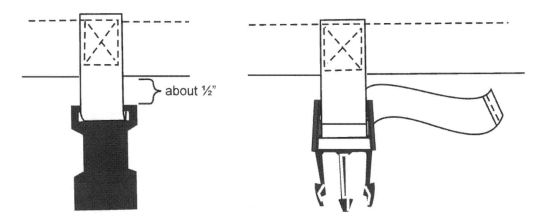

{ about ½"

Fig 5-93 While you are stitching the hem, stitch on the buckles so they hang down below the hem.

Make nice neat corners (see Section 2 - Hems) and topstitch. (See Fig 5-94)

Other closure systems (Fig 5-95):

If using plastic sail hooks, stitch these on separate to stitching the hem. These hooks tend to break and you will have to replace them periodically.

Twist lock fasteners, or wire hooks with grommets/bungee can also be used.

When considering whether to use bungee, remember that you will have to eventually replace the bungee, especially in the tropics. Using short lengths is more cost-effective, and easier to replace than a long continuous bungee threaded through the hem.

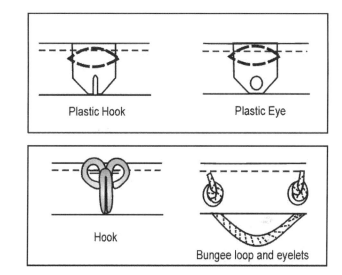

Plastic Hook   Plastic Eye

Hook

Bungee loop and eyelets

Fig 5-95 Other types of closures

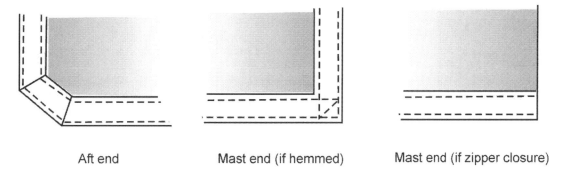

Aft end   Mast end (if hemmed)   Mast end (if zipper closure)

Fig 5-94 Make the corners nice and neat.

295

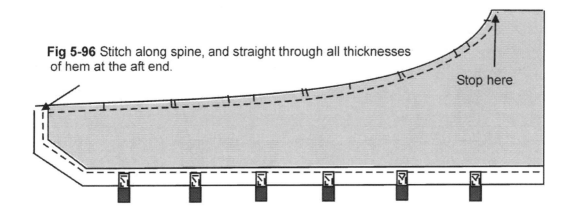

Fig 5-96 Stitch along spine, and straight through all thicknesses of hem at the aft end.

Stop here

Step 5 - Stitch the 'spine'

Lining up the hatch marks, staple the two panels of the sail cover together, *right* sides together. See Fig 5-96

Stitch the spine. Sew right over the hem at the aft end – don't try to make a nice continuous hem.

Open out the cover, and with the seam allowance creased over to one side, make 2 rows of topstitching as shown in Fig 5-97.

Step 6 - Finish the aft end.

To allow the cover to be stretched along its spine back to the topping lift, make a loop of webbing and a triangle ring assembly as shown in Fig 5-98)

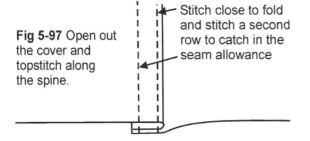

Fig 5-97 Open out the cover and topstitch along the spine.

Stitch close to fold and stitch a second row to catch in the seam allowance

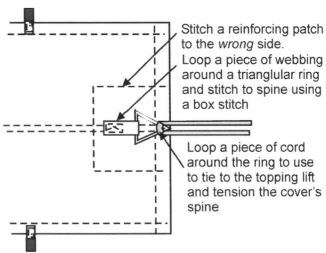

Stitch a reinforcing patch to the *wrong* side.
Loop a piece of webbing around a trianglular ring and stitch to spine using a box stitch

Loop a piece of cord around the ring to use to tie to the topping lift and tension the cover's spine

Fig 5-98 Looking down at the aft end of the sail cover. A reinforcing patch is sewn to the center spine area. A triangular ring is sewn to the spine using a piece of webbing, and a loop of cord is threaded through the ring.

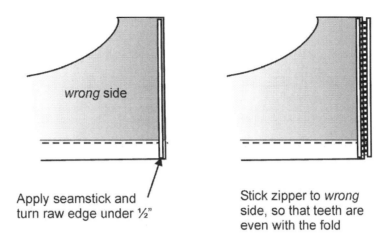

wrong side

Apply seamstick and
turn raw edge under ½"

Stick zipper to *wrong*
side, so that teeth are
even with the fold

Fig 5-99 Turn the raw edge under and stick and stitch
the zipper to the forward edge of the cover.

a) Stitch a reinforcing patch of vinyl, 2" larger all around than the dimensions of the webbing, to the *wrong* side of the cover. Cut a piece of 1" or 2" webbing, thread it through the triangle ring and then stitch the assembly to the *right* side of the cover, centered over the reinforcing patch.

b) Tie a piece of line to the triangle and it can then be tied to the topping lift to tension the cover's spine and make it look nice.

Step 7 - Sew zipper or other closure to mast end.

See also Section 2 - Zippers.

To the sail cover, apply ½" seamstick to the *wrong* side of the mast edges. Turn the raw edges under ½" and roll down hard.

Shorten the zipper if required (see Section 2 - Zippers). Don't forget to put on the head. Apply ¼" seamstick to a #10 jacket zipper, to both of the zipper tapes. Separate the 2 halves of the zipper.

Stretch out the mast end of the cover *wrong* side down and pin it out with scratch awls. Position the zipper under the folded edge so that it will close from bottom to top. Cover the zipper teeth with the folded edge.
Stitch this side on with 2 rows of stitching.

Stretch out the other side of the cover with scratch awls. Stick the other half of the zipper down in the same position as the opposite side and stitch two rows.

To take the strain off the zipper at the lower end, make a tab assembly across the end with a short piece of nylon webbing and a snap or twist lock fastener (See Fig 4-46 Wheel Cover).

a) Stitch across ends. Clip corners

b) Turn right side out and topstitch

Fig 5-100 Constructing the collar.

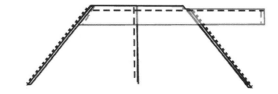

c) Stitch to top edge of cover

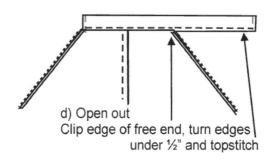

d) Open out
Clip edge of free end, turn edges
under ½" and topstitch

Step 8 - Make the closure for the top at the mast end.

Option 1 – Collar

See Fig 5-100
Cut out a strip of fabric 4-6" wide and long enough to go around the mast 1 ½ times.

a) With *right* sides together, fold the strip in half lengthwise. Stitch ½" from short ends.

b) Clip off corners. Turn *right* side out and topstitch the ends.

c) With *right* sides together, sew both the raw edges of the collar to the top of the sail cover.

d) Open out flat, turn the raw edges of the flap under by ½"and topstitch.

Option 2: Collarless closure (Fig 5-101)

Cut out two pieces of fabric shaped like the tab in Fig 5-101. Make sure to add ½" seam allowances on all sides.
With *right* sides together, stitch all around all the sides except the short side (which will be stitched to the cover), ½" from the raw edges.
Clip corners and turn *right* side out.
Stitch this tab to the top edge of the sail cover as shown.

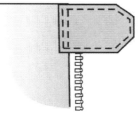

Fig 5-101 For a collarless closure, construct and stitch a double-layer tab to the top edge of the sail cover

To fasten the top flap, you can use Velcro, hook and bungee, or simply a piece of line sewn to the free edge of the collar which is wrapped around the mast and tied tight. See Fig 5-102.

Velcro:
On the inside of the tab or collar extension, stitch a strip of 1" Velcro hooks.
On the opposite side of the sail cover, stitch matching Velcro loops.

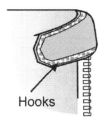
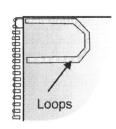

Hooks

Loops

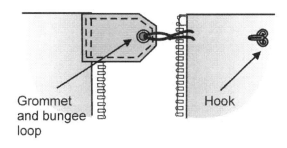

Grommet and bungee loop

Hook

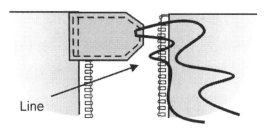

Line

Fig 5-102 The tab can be fastened with velcro, a hook and line, or a long line tied all the way around the mast.

Hook & Bungee:
Stitch on a sail hook to one side. On the other side install a grommet and insert a bungee loop. The bungee loop can be pulled over the hook.

Line
Stitch a length of line to the tab or collar extension long enough to wrap around the mast and tie up the collar end tight.

Step 9 - Optional - Make cutouts for winches or other hardware.

Try on the sail cover. Mark the positions for any cutouts required.

If making an opening for a winch, mark out the hole, a generous size, but cut it out 1" less in diameter to allow for the ½" seam allowance all around. (See Fig 5-103)
Make a simple cylinder (See Section 3 – Drop Cover).
Stitch this cylinder with its side seam facing down, to the hole you cut in the sail cover.

Other openings may require leather or webbing binding applied to the edges for chafe and strength.

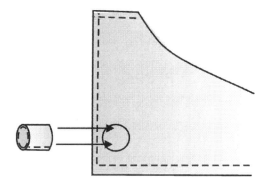

Fig 5-103 Making an opening for a mast winch.

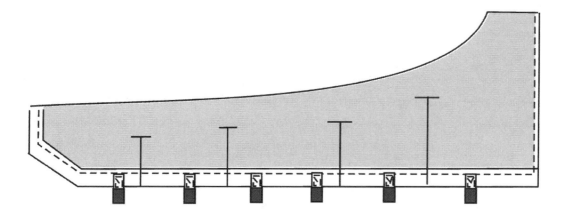

Fig 5-104 Mark position of lazy jack slits

<u>**Step 10** - Optional - Make lazy jack slits.</u>

a) Try on the sail cover. Mark where the lines for the lazy jacks must go through the cover. Make the marks light, because you are marking on the *right* side of the cover. The openings for the lazy jacks will probably be about 2/3 of the way up the sides of the cover.
Take the cover off.

b) Transfer the marks to the *wrong* side. From the point where the lazy jack exits the cover, mark a line straight down and perpendicular to the hem. (Fig 5-105 A)

Make another mark at the top of the slit, 2" wide and parallel to the hem so it looks like a "T" See Fig 5-105B. Also mark a fold line from the ends of the "T" down to the hem. (Fig 5-105 C)
Cut these "T" slits with a hot knife. (Lines A and B in Fig 5-105)
The slits can be closed with short jacket zips, but this is pretty expensive to build, and fiddly to use. Instead, close off the slits with flaps of fabric and closures as follows:

c) Apply seamstick to the *wrong* side along the both edges of the slit. Do not remove the paper yet. Cut out a rectangle of Dacron – 6 or 8 oz – about 9" wide and 3" longer than the slit. (Fig 5-106)

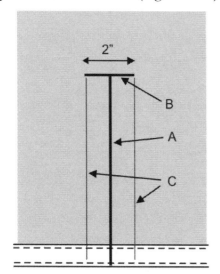

Fig 5-105 Mark the "T" shaped lines for the lazy jack slits (A and B), and the fold lines (C).

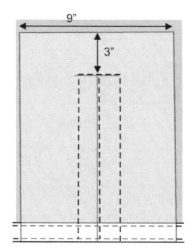

Fig 5-106 Cut out a piece of Dacron 9" wide and 3" longer than the slit.

Cut a "T" slit in the Dacron the same size as on the sail cover, and trim away 1" on each side. (Fig 5-107)

Apply Seamstick all around the outside edge of the Dacron, and center it over the slit. Remove the seamstick paper and stick it down. (Fig 5-108)

Fold the edges of the slit opening to the inside, over the Dacron. Remove the seamstick paper and stick them down as shown in Fig 5-109.

Cut a piece of 1" or 2" wide nylon webbing 4" long. Stick this down to the *wrong* side, along the top edge of the "T" slit as shown in Fig 5-109.

Now stitch around the edge of the Dacron, the hem edge of the slit, and topstitch close to the fold, catching in the webbing piece (Fig 4-110).

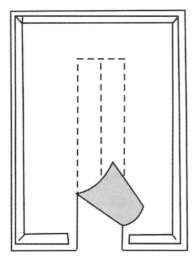

Fig 5-107 Cut out the center area of the Dacron patch and apply seamstick all around the outside edges.

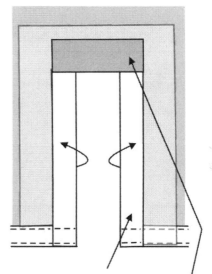

Fig 5-109 Turn the edges to the inside and stick down.
Stick down a piece of webbing along the top of the slit.

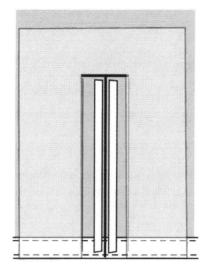

Fig 5-108 Center the Dacron face down over the slit and stick down.

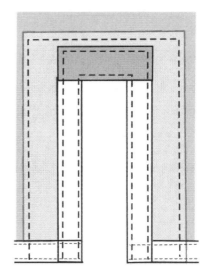

Fig 5-110 Stitch

d) Cut out rectangles of fabric about 5" wide, and the length of the slits plus 1". Cut one rectangle for each slit.
Make a 1" single hem along one long side and both short sides. See Fig 5-111.

e) Install 3 twist lock eyelets in the hems of the long sides as shown in Fig 5-111 – one at the top corner, one at the bottom corner and one in the center.

f) With *right* sides together, seamstick the flaps to the cover. Line up the bottom hem of the flap to the bottom hem of the cover, and position the flap so that when folded over, it will cover the slit as shown in Fig 5-112.
Also position the flap so that the side you are going to stitch is towards the mast. (This way, rain won't be able to blow in through the flap).

Stitch the raw edge of the flap to the cover, with ½" seam allowance.

Flip the flap over into the 'closed' position, and topstitch the long side that you just finished stitching to hold it down.

g) Install the fasteners.

Install twist lock studs on the sail cover, underneath the positions of the eyelets on the flap, so that the flap is held closed.

At the bottom edge of the sail cover, next to each corner of the lazy jack flaps, install the hem closures, whether it is buckles, hooks or whatever.

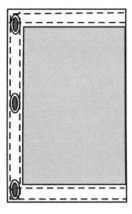

Fig 5-111 Make flaps with a 1" double hem around three sides. Install 3 common-sense eyelets along the edge.

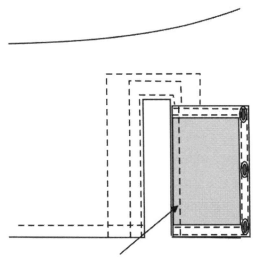

Fig 5-112 With *right* sides together, stitch the flap to the sail cover

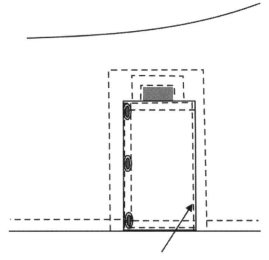

Fold the flap over the slit and topstitch.

On-Boom Sail Cover

This is a sail cover that stays on the boom when the main is hoisted. The cover is zipped open along its spine and the sail is raised and dropped down into the cover.
It consists of two mirror-image halves of fabric, one on each side of the boom.

These covers are used in combination with lazy jacks – which serve to hold the cover up and control the sail as it is dropped into it.

Most have battens along the length of the cover to hold it upright, make a nice straight appearance and as an attachment point for the lazy jacks.

To attach the cover to the <u>boom</u> you can:

a) If there is a track on the boom, and the sail is loose-footed, the track can be used to attach the bottom hem of the cover to the boom, using slides and short pieces of webbing. This is the method shown here.

b) If the boom has a track and the sail is not loose footed, the slides can be removed from the sail and used on the cover, making the sail loose footed but still contained within the cover.

c) If you don't want to take the slides off the sail, the cover can be attached together at the hem with short pieces of webbing (with or without fasteners) so that the webbing pieces will go in between the slides on the sail.

d) Still others use awning track riveted to each side of the boom, and boltrope or slugs stitched onto the cover's hems.

This is quite a big project and each boat is different in its requirements. Read through these entire instructions before starting. It also helps to look at other people's boats for ideas.

This is one project which you should think about spending the money to use Tenara or Profilen brand thread. These threads last forever in the UV. Believe me, once you finally get this cover put on the boat, you will never want to take it off to restitch!!

The zipper is on the top of the cover and so is really prone to degradation from the sun. Plan on making a generous flap to cover the entire zipper, possibly even secured shut with Velcro.

To attach the cover at the <u>mast</u> you can:

a) Tension the cover along the mast using webbing along the cover's 'mast' edge, and a couple of small pad eyes screwed into the mast. (This is the method shown here).

b) You can use boltrope and track up the mast as an attachment. This method also helps keep water out of the cover and keeps it from flapping in the wind.

c) A separate little rectangular cover can be made to wrap around the mast. This secures the front of the cover, and keeps out rain. It attaches with jacket zips to the mast end of the cover, and is usually removed when the main is raised.

Think about how you will reef the main with this cover on. There needs to be some way of the reefing lines to exit the cover – usually with a reinforced slit in the bottom hem of the cover.

If you have Main Steps:

1. Measure up.
2. Mark up and cut out the fabric.
3. Do all the reinforcing patches.
4. Prepare the pocket for the batten.
5. Make the Teardrop.
6. Install the Zipper.
7. Cut openings for lazy jacks.
8. Sew the Hem and put on the slides
9. Finish the forward end.

Step 1 - Measure

See Fig 5-113.
Take a pad of paper to the boat for making notes and a diagram. With the sail resting on the boom in a 'normal' flaked position measure:

(a) = Total length along the boom from the front edge (aft of the mast) to the aft end of the sail.

(b) = Circumference of the sail (not including the boom) about 1-2 feet from the aft end – the distance from the aft end should be about where the flakes kind of start, so that the aft end of the sail cover won't taper down to be too skinny. Make this measurement comfortably

loose but not sloppy. In your notes, mark down how far forward you made this measurement.(Let's call this measurement the Aft Offset)

(c) = Height of the 'stack' of the sail at the mast end – this is the height of the stacked sail straight up the mast from the bottom of the sail to the top of the headboard.

(d) = Circumference of the sail (not including the boom) at the forward end. Again, comfortably loose.

(e) = Width of the headboard, if any.

(f) If your sail has slugs sitting in a track, run a tape measure from the gooseneck back to the end of the boom. Mark on your notes the inch marks where each slug sits.

Note where your reefing lines are and make some diagram notes.
And finally note the number of cutouts required for lazy jacks (usually 4 on each side).

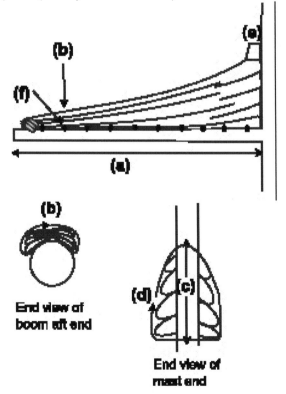

End view of boom aft end

End view of mast end

Fig 5-113 Measure up for the cover.

304

Step 2 - Mark out the fabric

Refer to Fig 5-114 on the next page.

Find a big clean area and lay the fabric out flat.

a) The bottom hem is straight, so start there. Mark the total length along the selvedge of the fabric.
This length will be:
(measurement (a) x 1.0125)
PLUS 4" for the aft hem
PLUS + ½" seam allowance for the front.
You multiply your measurement (a) by 1.0125 to allow for shrinkage – when sewing long seams the thread tends to pucker up the fabric and your project gets shorter. Better to cut a little longer and you can trim off later if needed.

b) From the aft end mark a line perpendicular to the selvedge about 11" or so.
Now measure towards the front end of the cover the length of your Aft Offset. From this point measure up perpendicular to the selvedge:

½ of the aft end's measured circumference (b),
PLUS 4" (for hem)
PLUS 6" for the batten pocket
PLUS , plus ½" (seam allowance).
Make a <u>dot</u> here.

c) While you are at the aft end, mark for the 2" double hem:
4" forward of the aft line, make another line the same length. See detail in Fig 5-114.

d) Now go over to the front end. Mark straight up perpendicular from the selvedge, the height of the stack (c) plus 4" (for hem), plus ½" for seam allowance, plus 6" (for the batten pocket). Mark another line 1/2" forward of this for the cutting line. See details in Fig 5-114.

e) Still at the front end, at the top of the line you just drew, mark a line parallel to the hem whatever the width of the headboard is, plus 1" for seam allowances. If there is no headboard, make this line 3-4".

f) Now, make a smooth curve from the aft end of this headboard line through the dot you made at (b) extending to the aft end of the sail cover, using a long flexible batten or other object. If the sail has a huge roach in it, make the line less curved or even straight.

g) Mark a line 4" inside of the lower selvedge edge for a 2" double hem

h) Mark a long straight line for the batten – whatever looks right for the cover but here are some guidelines.

The centerline should be about 10-12" down from the TOP at the aft end, and 14-16"" down from the TOP at the forward end.

The higher you place the batten, the harder it will be to do up the zipper. Remember that above the batten line, that part of the fabric is actually the sail cover's 'top'. The narrower this is, the more you will have to pull the battens toward each other in order to close the zipper. So don't put the batten up too high, or there will be a lot of strain on the zipper.

Also, the line should tilt 'uphill' as shown in Fig 5-114. The steeper the 'uphill', the better water will run off the groove created by the batten pocket.

(i) Mark 2 more lines 3" away – one above and one below.

j) Mark where the cutouts will need to be for the lazy jacks. See details in Fig 5-115. Space them as follows: E.g. If there are to be 4 openings, make the first one 1/8 of the total length from the aft end, the last one 1/8 of the total length from the front end, and space the rest ¼ of the total length apart.

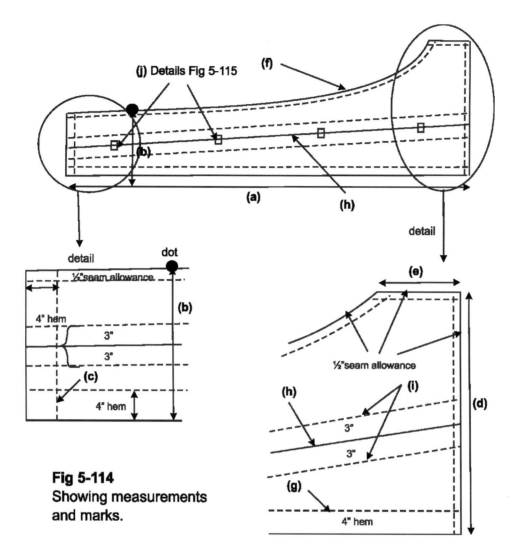

Fig 5-114
Showing measurements
and marks.

Mark them 4" high by 2" wide, centered over the batten pocket fold line, then mark another line ½" outside of this as shown. They look best if they are placed square and parallel to the hem.

Place a 5/8" round batten along the marked center line for the batten pocket.

Mark where the end of the batten will be at each end of the batten pocket foldline. The batten should extend from the aft end hem foldline to within about 4" of the forward end. Cut the batten to length.

Use this piece to mark and cut out another identical <u>mirror-image</u> panel.

Note: The zipper along the spine needs to be covered with a flap to protect it from the sun. If your cover is not that curvy at the spine <u>on one of the panels</u>, add 1 or 2" along the top so you can make a flap before you stitch on the zipper. If the cover is too curvy you won't really be able to fold the flap down very well, so you'll need to make a separate flap.

Cut out the piece of fabric with a hot knife. Cut out the holes for the lazy jacks with a hot knife and clip the corners of the lazy jack holes out to the stitching lines with a hot knife.

Transfer the long lines marking the batten pockets <u>only</u>, to the *right* side of the fabric, using a white pencil, chalk or very light pencil marks.

Step 3 - Stitch all the reinforcing patches:

Note: you are making two identical mirror-image panels. Whatever construction you do to one panel must be repeated for the other panel.

a) Head Patch
Refer to Fig 5-116.

Cut a piece of vinyl (Shelterite) about 4" by 8". Apply seamstick around the outside edge of the patch. Stick the patch to the *wrong* side of the sail cover - centered over the place where the batten ends. Place the patch so that the short sides of the patch extend beyond the batten pocket stitching lines by about an inch as shown.

Stitch along the long sides of the patch - the short sides will be caught in when you stitch the batten pocket.

If your sail has a headboard:
Make a large vinyl patch an inch or so in from the front, and down to the hem fold line.
Stick this over the first patch.
Stitch 3 sides close to the edge of the vinyl, leaving the lower hem side free – it will be caught in with the hem.

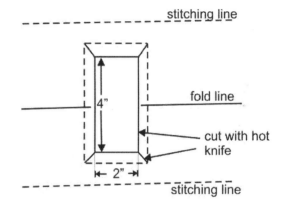

Fig 5-115 Openings for lazy jacks.

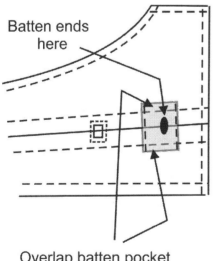

Batten ends here

Overlap batten pocket stitching lines by about 1"

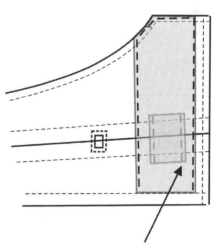

Stitch a large patch over the smaller one to reinforce the headboard area.

Fig 5-116 The area where the batten ends needs very strong reinforcement. Place a patch over the area and then reinforce the whole front area as shown.

Canvas for Cruisers

b) Reinforce all the Cutouts

Apply ½" seamstick to the *wrong* side of the raw edges of the cutout opening (Fig 5-117). Leave the paper on for now.

Cut out vinyl patches 6" wide and long enough to extend ½" above the top batten stitching line and all the way down to the hem fold line as shown in Fig 5-118.

On the *right* side, apply seamstick all around the edges of the vinyl patch.
Center the patch *right* side down onto the *wrong* side of the fabric over the cutout and stick it down.

Stitch 3 sides, leaving the hem side free for now. Do all the remaining cutouts the same way.

Flip the sail cover over to the *right* side. Remove the seamstick and turn the edges of the cutout under by ½". Topstitch down. Fig 5-119.

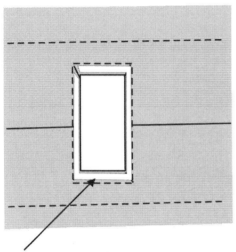

Fig 5-117 Apply seamstick all around the cutout opening

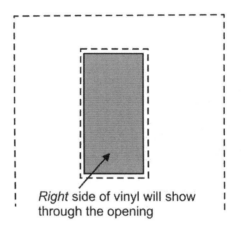

Right side of vinyl will show through the opening

Fig 5-119 Turn raw edges under and topstitch

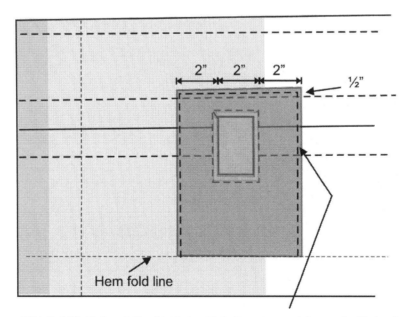

Fig 5-118 Cut out vinyl patch, stick to *wrong* side, and stitch along 3 sides.

c) Reinforce the Aft end with a Dacron patch

Cut a piece of 5 oz or 6 oz Dacron 12" wide, and long enough to go from the top raw edge to the fold line of the hem.

Seamstick the Dacron to the *wrong* side as shown in Fig 5-120.
Staple the other 3 sides in place to hold them securely for now.
Stitch only the forward edge – the rest will be caught in with hems and seams.

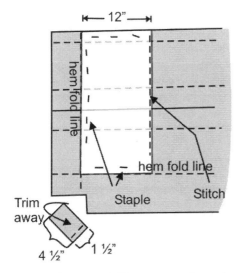

Fig 5-120 Place a patch on the aft end, stitch and staple in place.

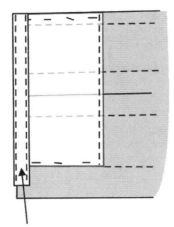

Fig 5-121 Stitch a 2" double hem at the aft edge

Trim away the corner as shown in Fig 5-120.
Make a 2" double hem in the aft end (see Section 2 – Hems and Fig 5-121).
Topstitch close to the fold.

To close off the batten pocket construct a buckle assembly as follows:

Cut a piece of 1" nylon webbing about 5" long. Insert the webbing through the center crossbar of a Ladderlock buckle. Position the webbing so that the ends match. Position the buckle face up (that is, the little dent on the buckle's end is facing down towards the fabric). Set the end of the buckle right at the hem fold. (See Fig 5-122). It also needs to be at the uppermost side of the batten pocket, closer to the fold line, on the *right* side of the fabric. Stitch it to the cover using a box stitch.

Cut another piece of webbing about 8-10" long (you can shorten it later if you need to), making an angled cut at one end. Stitch the square end to the end of the cover with a box stitch as shown in Fig 5-122.

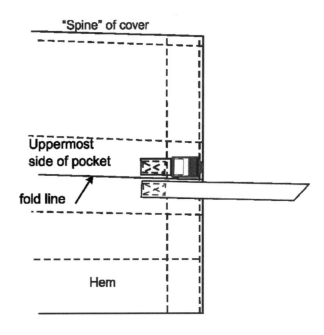

Fig 5-122 Stitch a buckle and webbing to the aft end to contain the batten.

Optional:
One more area that might need addressing is the issue of water drainage. A conventional sail cover is open at the bottom, so any rain that comes in after the Sunbrella loses its waterproofness, just runs out under the boom. But on this sail cover, the water will tend to pool up inside, which is never a good thing. If the attachments at the bottom are webbing straps connecting the two sides together, this helps with drainage because the bottom is more open. But you might need more.

So, you can make some long skinny mesh drainage 'windows' above the stitching line of the hem (See Fig 5-129) The construction is the same as the Viewing Window in the Bimini section.

Step 4 – Stitch the batten pocket With *wrong* sides together, fold along the centerline of the lines marked for the batten.
Staple in place Stitch along the stitching lines, forming a long pocket for the batten to go into.

Fig 5-123 After stitching the batten pocket, reinforce the forward end with 6 rows of stitching, then fold the pocket upwards and topstitch as shown

See Fig 5-123. At the mast end of the cover, at about the center of the small reinforcing patch you made for the batten end, make 6 rows of stitches close together. Stitch through the pocket layers only – NOT right through the cover and everything. This closes off the end of the pocket for the batten.

From the *right* side, fold the pocket upwards, and topstitch the batten pocket close to the stitching line, so that the batten pocket will want to face upwards.

Step 5 - The Teardrop

The teardrop insert at the mast end of the cover allows for the thickness of the flaked sail and relieves any strain on the cover when the boom is moved from side to side.

If you are making a separate little cover to go around the front of the mast, you won't need the teardrop. Instead, turn the mast edge of the sail cover under ½" and stitch half of a jacket zip (the side <u>without</u> the head) on each side. (The side of the zip with the head goes on the little cover).

Cut a piece of the fabric the shape of a half-teardrop as shown in Fig 5-124.

The 'fatness' of the teardrop is not an exact science – it depends on how full and bulky the flaked main is at the front. But do make the curve of the teardrop the same length as the forward edge of the cover.

Taper the lower edge of the curve into a flat straight line 2" from the hem fold line, and add a 4" allowance for a 2" double hem at the forward edge. Add ½" seam allowance along the curve as shown in Fig 5-124. Cut out with a hot knife.

Use this piece to cut another teardrop - mirror image.

Line the teardrop with 5 or 6 oz Dacron for chafe protection, and to maintain a better shape.

Extend the Dacron to the raw edge of the curved side of the teardrop, but only out to the fold of the forward hemline to reduce bulk. See Fig 5-125.

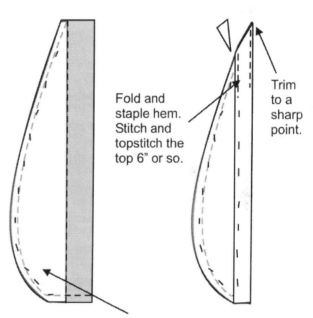

Fig 5-125 Staple Dacron lining to the *wrong* side. Turn a double hem along the straight edge. Stitch only the top 6" leaving the rest stapled for now.

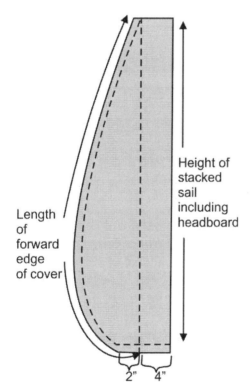

Fig 5-124 Cut out a piece of fabric shaped as above.

Turn a 2" double hem along the straight edge as shown in Fig 5-125, but stitch and topstitch only the top 6" or so (you will do the rest later when you do the hem of the cover). Trim the top edge to a sharp point.

At the front of the sail cover, staple up the first 6" or so of the bottom hem (2" double hem). With *right* sides together, line up the curved edge of the teardrop to the forward raw edge of the cover.

The pointed tip of the teardrop should end up about 1" below the top edge of the cover, to allow for the zipper to be installed later. (Fig 5-126).
The bottom of the teardrop lines up with the fold line of the cover's hem.

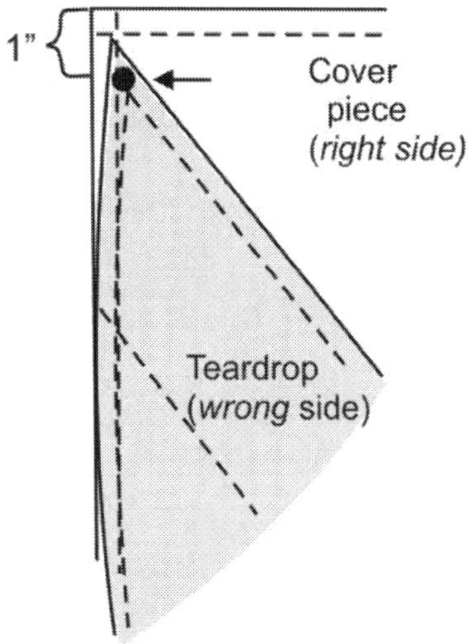

See Fig 5-127. Staple the teardrop to the cover, working out the curve into the straight edge of the cover, and stitch. Fold the seam over toward the cover and topstitch.

Turn up the 2" double hem along the length of the cover's bottom. Stitch and topstitch the hem of the cover and the teardrop.

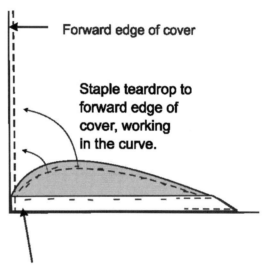

Fig 5-127 Staple up the first few inches of the cover's hem. Then match the hem fold of the teardrop to the hem fold of the cover.

Fig 5-126 Position teardrop on the cover's forward edge. The tip of the teardrop is about 1" below the top of the cover.

Step 6 - Zipper

The zipper really needs to be of the 'jacket' type - that is, a separating zipper. Usually you can't get one that long, but you can make a pseudo-separating zipper out of a continuous one.

The instructions here are for the zipper to be sewn on so that the teeth are exposed. But you can position the zipper so the teeth are just inside the fold. This will help. But a better way is to have a flap completely covering the entire zipper – including both sides of the long tail sticking out the back. I even added a line of Velcro to mine so the wind won't blow it open.

a) Apply ½" seamstick to the *wrong* side of the top raw edge of the cover. Remove the paper, turn the raw edge under by ½" and stick it down.

b) Cut a length of continuous #10 zipper. The length should be the length of the cover's spine PLUS about 10".

Stretch out the zipper and pin it down. Apply ¼" seamstick to the zipper tape as shown in Fig 5-128.

Open up one end of the zipper a little and stick on the little vinyl patch stop ends. (see Section 2 – Zippers)

c) Lay one side of the cover *wrong* side down on the floor. See Fig 5-129 on the next page.

With a scratch awl, pin the closed zipper down with the finished end (the end with the little vinyl stop patches) at the 'mast' end. Stretch it out to the other end, leaving the 10" extending out the aft end.

Now take the aft end of the canvas in one hand and the zipper in the other. Pull the zipper and the canvas to make the tension between the zipper and the canvas even so that neither one is stretched more than the other. It takes a bit of practice. Pin this aft end down. There will be about 10" of the zipper hanging off the aft end.

Position the zipper along the folded edge of the cover so that the teeth are exposed. The fold should be about 1/8" away from the teeth to allow the head to slide freely. Remove the seamstick paper and stick the zipper down.

Stitch the one half on with 2 rows of stitching.

d) So far the zipper is still zipped up in one piece. Make a pencil mark on the opposite zipper tape (the one that you have not stitched yet) at the aft end of the cover where the zipper ends at the canvas. See Fig 5-129.

Now separate the 2 zipper halves.

e) Stick the other half of the zipper down onto the other side of the cover. As before, pin it down at the mast end, and stretch it out to the aft edge, lining up the pencil mark you made on the zipper tape to the aft edge of the canvas. Again, let the 10" extra trail off the end for now. Stitch to the cover using 2 rows of stitching.

(If you cut one side larger for a flap, fold the flap to the inside then place the zip so the tape edge is along the raw edge of the flap.)

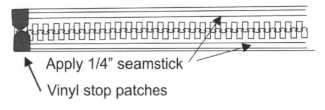

Apply 1/4" seamstick

Vinyl stop patches

Fig 5-128 Apply seamstick to the zipper tape and finish the ends with stop patches.

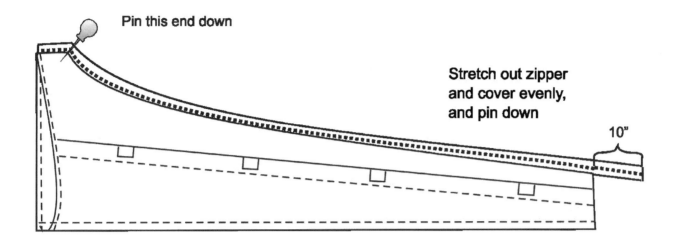

Pin this end down

Stretch out zipper
and cover evenly,
and pin down

10"

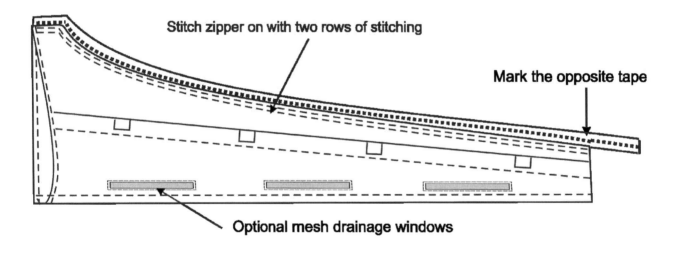

Stitch zipper on with two rows of stitching

Mark the opposite tape

Optional mesh drainage windows

Fig 5-129 Position the zipper along the spine of the cover, leaving about 10" or so sticking out the end. Stick it down and stitch. Mark the opposite tape where it meets the aft end of the cover.

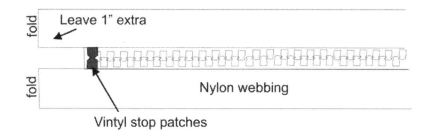

Fig 5-130 Encase the zipper tape in nylon webbing, leaving the teeth exposed.

f) Finish the long ends trailing off the back:

Singe the raw end of the zip's tape with a hot knife to keep it from fraying.
Put on the zipper head so it zips the sail cover closed when it is moved towards the mast.
Stick the small vinyl patches at the ends of the zip to keep the head from coming off.
(Fig 5-130)

Stick seamstick to some 1" webbing and bind each zip's tape with the webbing, leaving the teeth exposed. Fold the webbing over at the aft end to make a double layer of webbing, and leave an inch of extra length as shown in Fig 5-130. Extend the webbing about 4" or so onto the cover itself. Don't stitch it yet.

Insert a short piece of nylon webbing about 2 ½" long into one side of the webbing tail so as to cover the little vinyl patches on the zipper.
(See Fig 5-131). (This will have a snap put in it so as to take the strain off the end of the zipper).
Stitch along the outside edges of the webbing tail as shown in Fig 5-132. Leave the little flap free – this is where you will put the snap.

g) Put in 2 #0 grommets in each nylon 'tail' near the attachment point of the cover as shown in Fig 5-132. These are used with lines to stretch the cover out along the boom.
Install a snap button onto the little flap, and a snap socket into the tail.

If you have not done so already, add a flap to cover the zipper including the tail.

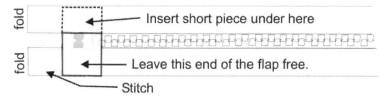

Fig 5-131 Insert a short piece of webbing into the folded-over webbing

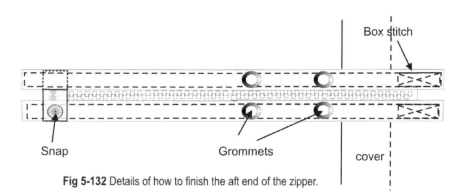

Fig 5-132 Details of how to finish the aft end of the zipper.

Canvas for Cruisers

Step 7 - Cut openings for lazy jacks

Cut out triangular-shaped openings for the lazy jacks as follows. See Fig 5-133.

Position the batten pocket so it lies flat on a solid surface. Use a grommet punch tool to punch out 3 holes, right through both layers of vinyl and down ½" or so from the fold as shown.

DO NOT punch through the entire sail cover – only the batten pocket vinyl layers.

Then use scissors to cut between the holes to make a rounded triangle as shown in Fig 5-134.

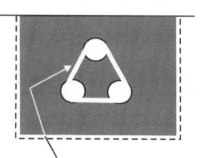

Fig 5-134 Cut between the holes and discard the little cutout piece.

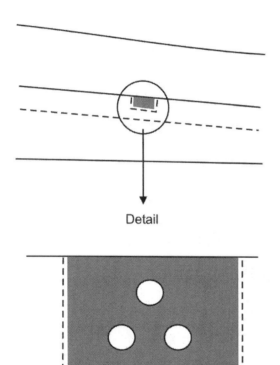

Detail

Fig 5-133 Punch out 3 holes in each of the batten pocket cutouts.

Step 8 - Hem slides

The way the mainsail attaches to the boom will give you different options for connecting the cover together at the bottom and attaching the cover to the boom.

If the main is loose-footed and there is a sail track on the boom, it can be used to attach the cover to the boom as follows. See Fig 5-135.

Cut pieces of 1" webbing 4-5" long.
Box-stitch one end to the hem of one side of the cover.
Thread the end through a sail slide and box-stitch the other end of the webbing to the other side of the cover, thus joining the 2 panels.

There should be a slide about every foot or so along the length of the cover.
Start about 4-6" from the gooseneck and from the clew to stay away from any hardware (check your boat to make sure)

If the main has slugs that fit into a track instead of stitching both ends of the webbing strap to the sail cover, stitch one end only. Install a common sense fastener eyelet to the other end of the webbing. Install a commonsense stud to the opposite side of the sail cover (See Fig 5-136),
Check the diagram you made so your webbing straps won't interfere with the existing slugs on the sail.

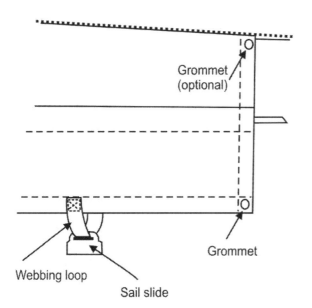

Fig 5-135 Stitch webbing with sail slides along the bottom edge of the hem.

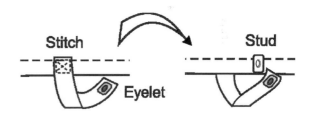

Fig 5-136. Stitch one side of the webbing to one side of the cover. Install a common sensi eyelet to the webbing. Install a common sense stud to the sail cover on the other side.

If the main has a boltrope fitting into a track –
this is a hard one.

You can burn slits with a hot knife into the foot
of your sail to thread the webbing straps
through.

You can try making the webbing straps out of
thin Dacron and slide them into the track along
with the sail's foot and hope they don't chafe
through.

You could even stitch the hem of the sail cover
all along the sail just above the boltrope.

Or maybe extend the cover right around the
boom and have fastenings underneath. (Fig 5-
138)

The best option would probably be to install
two tracks – one on each side of the boom –
and sew a Keder boltrope to the hem of the sail
cover.(Fig 5-137)

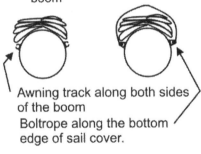

Fig 5-137 End view of
boom

Awning track along both sides
of the boom
Boltrope along the bottom
edge of sail cover.

Fig 5-138 Awning track and boltrope
can be used to hold the cover onto
the boom.
Or the cover can completely cover
the boom, and attach underneath it.

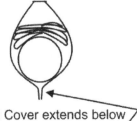

Sail Cover extends below
the boom and attaches
underneath.

Put a #0 grommet in the hem at each aft corner.
This will allow the cover to be tied closed and
stretched back along the boom to tension it
properly.

Step 9 - Finish the forward end

The forward end of the cover must be stretched
vertically in order to look good. And the cover must
be stretched fore and aft along the boom for the
same reason.

The details for each particular boat may vary, but
here's one method: (Do the same procedure to both
cover panels.) See Fig 5-139.

a) Cut a piece of 1" nylon webbing 7-8" long. Fold
it in half to make a loop.

On the *right* side, box-stitch the loop to the lower
edge with the loop facing forward as shown.

Tie a 24" length of leech line to this loop. Do the
same on the other side of the cover.

b) Cut a piece of 1" nylon webbing long enough to
go along the front edge of the cover..

Make a small loop at the bottom, and loop the other
end through a Ladderlock buckle which is
positioned about 4" from the top edge.

Cut another piece of 1" nylon webbing about 18"
long.

Assemble the 2 pieces of webbing so that the 18"
length goes underneath the section with the
Ladderlock

Stick and stitch, using box stitches at the Ladderlock
end and the lower loop end.

Tie a 24" length of leech line to the lower loop.

Do the same to the other side of the cover.

The lines at the bottom are used to attach the cover
tightly at the gooseneck.

Put the sail cover on the boat as follows:

If the sail is loose footed, detach the clew. Push the sail off to one side and feed the sail cover slugs into the track.

If the foot has slugs, detach the clew and pull the sail off the track. Then feed the sail back onto the track, interspersing its slugs with the slugs or loops on the sail cover.

Pile the sail up in between the 2 halves of the cover. Hoist the sail and flake it back into the cover.

Insert the battens – they should pull the cover taut along its length but they don't have to be super-tensioned in there.

Attach the lazy jacks – push the lazy jack line through the triangular hole, underneath the batten and secure the line to itself. This way the batten carries the weight and not the canvas.

Secure the mast edge with the webbing loops and leech lines – Tie off the cover at the gooseneck. Loop the webbing at the top through some attachment point on the side of the mast – (you might possibly have to install small pad eyes on each side of the mast). Thread the webbing through the Ladderlock buckle to tension the cover vertically at the mast.

Tension the cover along its length - at the aft end tie lines into the grommets you installed in the reinforced zipper tape and tighten it to the topping lift or other convenient point.

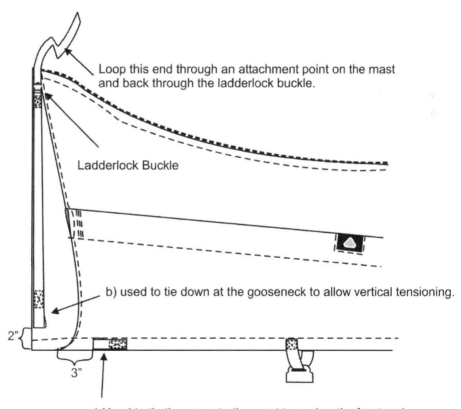

Loop this end through an attachment point on the mast and back through the ladderlock buckle.

Ladderlock Buckle

b) used to tie down at the gooseneck to allow vertical tensioning.

2"

3"

a) Used to tie the cover to the mast to anchor the front end.

Fig 5-139 Webbing loops are stitched to the forward end of the cover to allow tensioning and attachment to the mast.

The little cover

If you are going to have a separate cover going around the front of the mast, it can be a simple rectangle, hemmed at the top and bottom and the matching zippers from the big cover sewn onto the sides.

If the front of your sail cover is shapely, then a flat rectangle will be tight at the belly and loose and floppy at the top and bottom. If that's not OK with you then make a pattern for a shaped cover.

Line the little cover with Dacron to protect it against chafe.

Sailing with the Cover

A cover of this type is excellent for daysailing and short passagemaking, maybe even long passages in easy weather.

When you start to sail with this cover, you might find that the cover gapes open and flops around- this could be a serious issue in big winds on long passages or storm conditions. The cover could catch water and it could start to chafe your sail or itself. In a sudden squall the sail cover can interfere with doing a fast reef. On really long passages, you might find that the lazy jacks chafe the mainsail.

Most of these issues can be solved - retractable lazy jacks that loosen and tie up against the mast; a fitted little cover at the forward end to keep windage out of the cover; an easily removable cover (using the little webbing straps with commonsense fasteners) for long passages or racing; or an option is to make the cover so it can furl – roll up the cover around the battens on each side and tie with sail ties or buckle straps.

Furling Sail Sacrificial Cover

Most furling headsails have a strip of fabric stitched along the leech edge to protect the sail from the sun. If yours doesn't, or needs replacing, here's how.

If you are replacing the sacrificial and the Dacron of the sail itself is still in good shape, then you can stitch on a replacement strip. The replacement should be at least 1" wider than the original, so that you are not re-stitching along the same seam lines.

If the Dacron is old and weak, (you can tell by trying gently to rip the fabric or running your fingernail along the grain of the cloth) adding a row of stitching will definitely weaken the sailcloth further and it will likely rip along the seam. It might be time for a new sail.

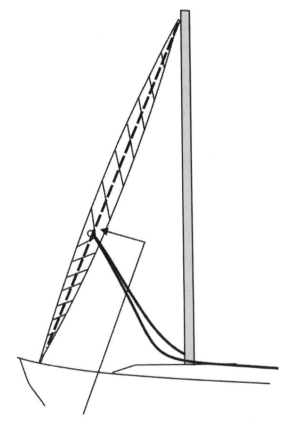

Fig 5-140 Chalk line marked roughly in line with where the clew meets the rolled-up sail.

The most common fabric to use is acrylic canvas, or you can use special UV-protected sailcloth.

If you are simply replacing the sacrificial, measuring is easy, just remember to make the new panels of fabric at least 1" wider than the old. But putting sacrificial on a sail that never has had any requires some measuring. Sometimes a sail will have definite dirty or worn marks indicating where it has been exposed to the sun. In this case, you can use this as a guideline as to where to place the sacrificial.

Otherwise, while the sail is rolled up on its furler, you will need to send someone up the mast. Start at the top and slide down along the forestay, marking a chalkline, in line where the clew meets the rolled up sail, from the top to the bottom. (See Fig 5-140).

Now take the sail off the boat. Spread it out flat and measure the length of the leech and the foot.

The width of the panels is equal to the widest area to be covered, plus at least 4". This allows for a couple of inches overlap in case of inaccurate furling, a ½" hem on the one side and 1 ½" to wrap around the sail's edge.

Usually the panels along the foot are narrower than the leech. And usually all the panels along the leech are the same width, as are the panels along the foot. But you can taper them if you want to.

Cut panels of fabric, preferably with a hot knife. Using seamstick, turn one of the long edges of each panel under by ½". Then place a row of seamstick all around on the *wrong* side of each panel. (Fig 5-142). Use the special super-sticky seamstick if you can.

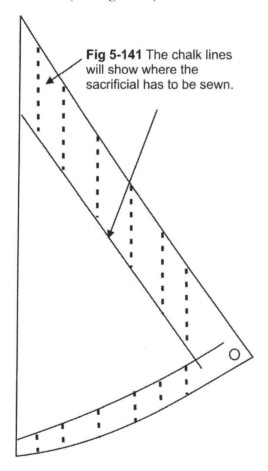

Fig 5-141 The chalk lines will show where the sacrificial has to be sewn.

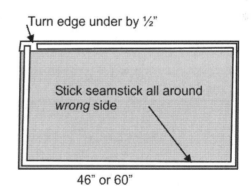

Turn edge under by ½"

Stick seamstick all around *wrong* side

46" or 60"

Fig 5-142 Cut and prepare panels of fabric.

Canvas for Cruisers

See Fig 5-143. Start sticking the panels along the sail's edge (make sure you are sticking it to the correct side of the sail!). Place the edge with the ½" fold to the inside, and let the raw edge trail over the edge of the sail by 1 ½". Fold the raw edge over the sail's edge and stick it down. You will probably also need to use staples or pins or even spray adhesive to hold things in place.

At the tack and clew rings and at any leech line cleats, neatly trim off the fabric around the hardware, turning the raw edge under ½". With a chalk, mark the diagonal pattern for the stitching.(Fig 5-144)

If you can, place all the panels on the sail and then carefully move the sail to the machine to stitch. Or stitch it in sections.

Stitch all along the outside edge first – be careful not to catch in any leech or foot lines in the hem. Then stitch along the inside edge of the panels. Stitch about ¼" from the edge of each panel join, being careful not to catch in the leech line. Finally, make a diagonal pattern of stitching to secure the fabric to the sail.

At the clew, and the tack, where the sail is very thick, you might have to hand stitch.

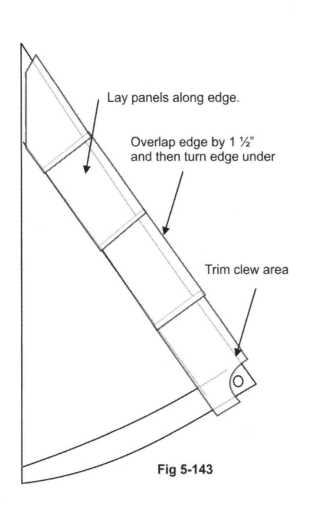

Lay panels along edge.

Overlap edge by 1 ½" and then turn edge under

Trim clew area

Fig 5-143

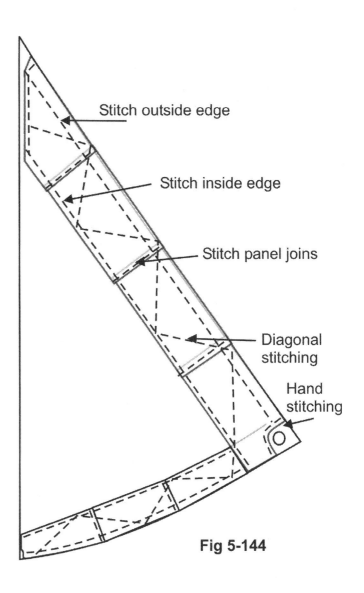

Stitch outside edge

Stitch inside edge

Stitch panel joins

Diagonal stitching

Hand stitching

Fig 5-144

Foredeck Sail Bag

This is a canvas bag used to store a hank-on headsail outside, on the deck, so that valuable interior space is not taken up storing a sail. If the sail will be stored permanently outside, consideration should be made to make the sail bag as waterproof as possible, and have good drainage should any water get inside. Any rain or seawater getting inside the bag will create a mold problem for the sail. For long term storage, such as when the boat is laid-up, the sail should definitely be brought indoors.

The bag is basically a flat piece of (usually) acrylic canvas, with closures along the forestay and along the bag's top. The closure can be Velcro and/or twist fasteners, or zippers. The addition of a strong webbing loop or stainless steel ring at the aft end will allow the bagged sail to be lifted off the deck. And the addition of some carrying handles will help when it comes time to stow the sail below.

The first thing to decide is whether the sail will be stored flaked and rolled up into a ball, or will it just be flaked and stored as a long sausage. The sail should be left hanked onto the forestay, and flaked or rolled as it would normally be stored.
Also, will the jib sheets be coiled and stowed inside the bag, or left hanging out? If they are left hanging out, there needs to be an opening for the lines to exit the bag.

Here are instructions for three possible styles of foredeck bag.

Sail Sausage:

The sail sausage (Fig 5-145) – is just a long bag to enclose the sail. It is suitable for a large sail, flaked and maybe semi-rolled so it is not so long. Lift it off the deck using ties to available stanchions or possibly rig a lifting harness attached to the jib halyard.

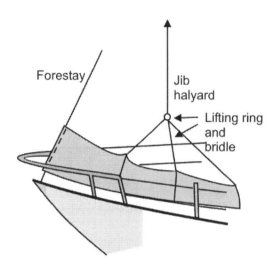

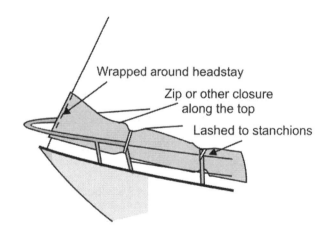

Fig 5-145 Sausage Bag. The bag is long, and can be lifted off the deck using the jib halyard, or can be tied along the rail, stanchions or lifelines.

Canvas for Cruisers

Step 1 - Measure up.

Let the sail down to the deck, and flake it as you normally would. If it is a big genoa and you don't want the sailbag to be that long, you can try rolling and bundling up the clew end into a neater package.

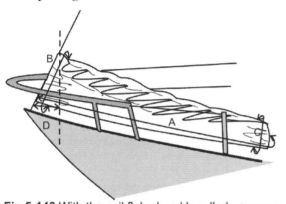

Fig 5-146 With the sail flaked and bundled, measure:
A - length of sail from forestay to the center of the aft end.
B - Circumference of sail at forestay
C - Circumference of sail at aft end
D - Distance from forestay to an imaginary line straight down from the forestay.

See Fig 5-146. Measure the length from the forestay to the center of the aft end of the sail bundle (A). Measure loosely the circumference of the sail at the forestay (B), and at the aft end of the bundle(C). Imagine a line from the forestay where it meets the head of the sail, straight down to the deck. Measure the distance along the deck from this imaginary line to the tack of the sail at the forestay (D).

Step 2 – Mark the measurements you made onto a piece of fabric –usually acrylic canvas is used. See Fig 5-147.

Add at least 2" to the aft edge for a 1" double hem. Add 2" to the forward edge, and mark for a 4" flap as shown in the diagram.

If you are closing the long edge with a zipper, add ½" seam allowance. If using common sense fasteners or Velcro, add 2" to both long sides for a 1" double hem.

Cut out the fabric.

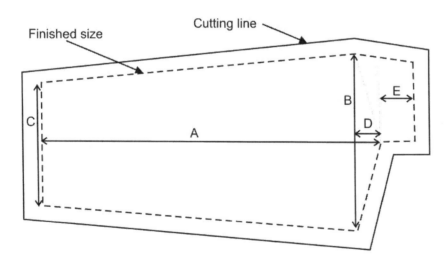

Fig 5-147 Mark out the finished size of the bag. Then add seam allowances and/or hem allowances.
A - length from forestay to aft end of sail.
B - Circumference of flaked sail at forestay
C - Circumference of sail at aft end of bundle.
D - Forestay to tack measurement
E - Add about 4" here for a flap.

Step 3 – Finish the edges.

Hem the forward and aft edges. Refer back to Section 2 – Hems and Casings, for working and reinforcing an inside corner.

Along the long edges, install a jacket zipper – see Section 2 – Zippers, or install Velcro or other fastenings if you are not using a zipper.

Step 4 – optional.

It is a good idea to place drainage places in the bag in case water gets inside. Either install grommets along the bottom of the bag (don't forget to reinforce these areas with patches of fabric), or stitch in mesh inserts. (Make these the same way as the Viewing Window – See Section 5 – Bimini – only use mesh instead of clear vinyl.)

Step 5 - Stitch lifting straps or handles in place as required.

Step 6 - Install closures at the aft edge – this could be commonsense fasteners, and at the front edge of the flap.

Your particular style may be different, but an example of a finished bag is shown in Fig 5-148.

To use the bag, open it up and lay it flat on the side deck. Let the sail down onto the bag, flake and bundle the sail into the bag. Fasten the aft end and the long edge. Hoist the bundle up off the deck. Then wrap the flap around the head stay to enclose the forward edge of the sail.

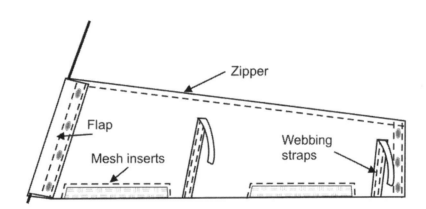

Fig 5-148 In this example, the sausage bag has a zipper closure along the top, two drainage mesh inserts, and commonsense fasteners at the aft end, and the wrap-around forestay flap. Webbing straps are stitched to the bag for use in tying the bag to the lifelines.

Canvas for Cruisers

Foredeck Bag:

This Foredeck bag – for a medium sized jib or staysail, has the sail flaked and rolled as much as possible, and can be lifted off the deck with the jib halyard attached to a webbing loop or stainless steel ring. It can have optional handles so it can be used as a 'regular' sailbag when it is time to bring the sail indoors for storage. The sheets can either be coiled and stored inside the bag, or left hanging out. The top closure could be a zipper

along the spine, or it could be offset to one side so that the bag is more waterproof. Drainage areas can be installed in the bag's bottom. This example has a zipper installed along the front edge of the bag to close it at the forestay.

Step 1 - Measure up.
The measurements are done exactly the same as the

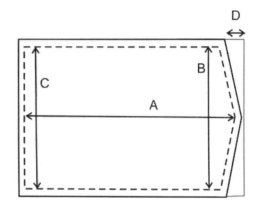

Fig 5-150 Mark measurements onto fabric.
A - Length of sail bundle
B - Circumference at forestay
C - Circumference at aft end
D - Forestay to tack measurement.
Add ½"all around for seam allowance.

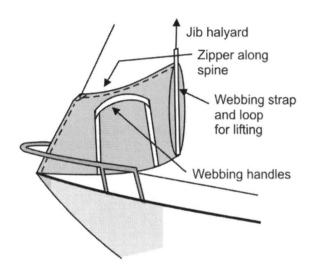

Fig 5-149 The foredeck bag encloses a flaked and rolled sail in a compact bundle. It can be lifted off the deck using the jib halyard

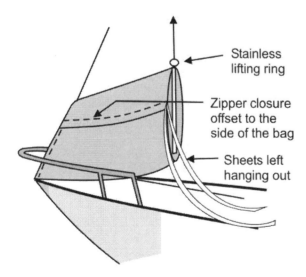

If the zipper closure along the spine is to be offset to the side, then add enough for a flap and hem allowance. One side of the zipper will be stitched an equal distance in from this edge, and the other side of the zipper will be stitched to the edge of the flap.

326

Sausage bag (Fig 5-146). The shape of the sail bundle will probably be more rectangular due to the fact that the sail is flaked and bundled into a roll.

Step 2 – Mark the measurements onto a piece of acrylic canvas – see Fig 5-150.
Add ½" seam allowances all around.
Cut out the fabric.

Because this bag is more of a cylinder than the sausage bag, it will require a circle of fabric at the aft end of the bag. (See Section 3 – Drop Cover).
Cut out a circle of fabric to fit the end.
Calculate the radius of the circle, and draw the circle – using the instructions in Section 2 – Drawing a Circle. Make sure to leave ½" seam allowance all around.

Step 3 – Install drainage areas if desired – grommets or mesh inserts (See – Sausage bag).
Fig 5-151

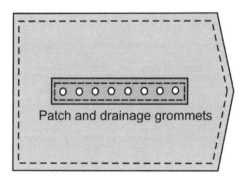

Fig 5-151

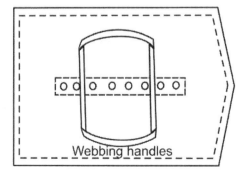

Fig 5-152

Step 4 – Stitch on lifting handles (optional). See Section 7 – Shopping bags. See Fig 5-152.

Step 5 – Install jacket zippers - one in the spine, and one at the forestay opening. Reinforce the area where the two zippers meet with a vinyl patch to protect against chafe. Fig 5-153.

Step 6 – Stitch webbing onto the circle of fabric, with or without a stainless steel ring (Fig 5-154). Stitch the 'lid' onto the prepared bag.

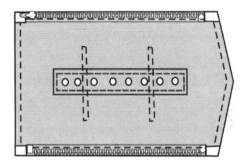

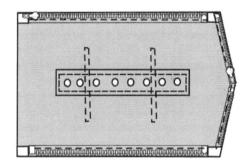

Fig 5-153 Install zippers along spine and along front edge.

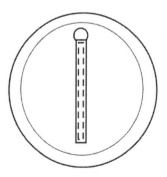

Fig 5-154 Webbing and stainless ring for hoisting.

Canvas for Cruisers

Triangle bag:

This Triangle bag is a simple flat piece of canvas, not particularly watertight, but suitable for smaller sails.

Step 1 - Measure up.
Bundle up the sail, holding it in shape with lines as necessary. See Fig 5-156.
Measure the size of the sail bundle – at the base, and along the forestay.

Step 2 - Mark out acrylic canvas fabric in the shape shown in Fig 5-157. The angle of the straight sides should not be too much, to allow for fullness in the bag.

Add 2" to one straight side for a flap overlap for the forestay, and then add 2" for hem allowance all around. See Fig 5-158.

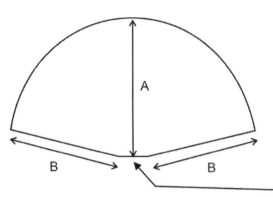

Fig 5-157 Mark the fabric according to your measurements. Leave a 'flat spot here to wrap around the forestay at the tack.

Fig 5-155 A simple triangle, wrapped around the forestay and the sail. Sheets hang out the end.

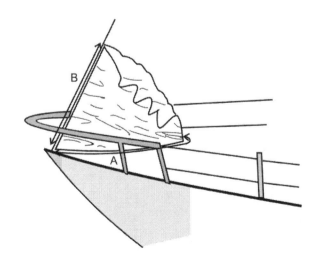

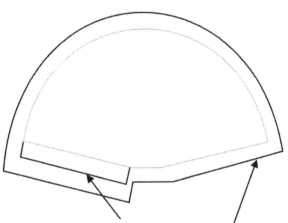

Fig 5-158 Mark for a 2" flap and then add 2" hem allowance all around.

Fig 5-156 Bundle up the sail and measure
A - the length of the sail's base
B - the length at the forestay.

Step 3 – Stitch a 2" hem all around. Notch the curves and the corners. See Section 2 – Hems & Casings.
Stitch vinyl reinforcing patches at the head stay area, and at the inside corner. Fig 5-159

Step 4 – Stitch lifting handles with reinforcing patches as shown in Fig 5-160. Refer to Section 2 – Patches and Reinforcements.

Step 5 – Try on the bag. Mark the positions to install common sense fasteners along the curved back, and along the forestay edge, leaving openings for the sheets, tack and hoist at the forestay. Remove the bag and install the fasteners.

To use the bag, open it out flat. Lay it on the deck with the curved side to the back. Let the sail down onto the bag, bundle it up and then close the bag using the fasteners along the back. Hoist the bundle and use the fasteners along the forestay to help lift the sail off the deck. The lifting handles can also be used, and are useful when removing the sail entirely to stow it below.

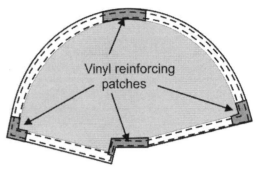

Fig 5-159 Stitch and topstitch the hem.

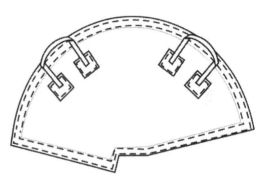

Fig 5-160 Lifting handles stitched on.

Canvas for Cruisers

Awning

Design considerations:

A well-designed and strongly constructed awning will keep the boat cool and shaded from the sun, keep things dry in the rain, may even be used to collect rain water, and should last many years.

It should not detract from the appearance of the boat, and not flap in the wind. The awning should be able to withstand average trade winds of 20 knots or so. If it gets windier, it is just not sensible to leave it up – it creates windage on the boat and repairs for you later.

The biggest challenge with awnings is getting the right shape and configuration for a particular boat. Spend some time looking at other people's boats if you can, and get some ideas.

Consider how to attach the awning to the boat. For a sloop, the awning usually runs from aft of the mast over the boom to the backstay.

A slit can be fashioned to let the awning pass beyond the topping lift and/or backstay.
But if you already have a Bimini, especially if it has Wings, your awning probably only needs to go back to the Topping Lift.

For a ketch, the awning runs between the main and mizzen masts. (Fig 5-161)

Additional slits may be necessary if the awning needs to extend past any shrouds.

For a 'shaped' aft end (Fig 5-162), a plastic pattern should be made first to get the right shape.

The front corners of a main awning are usually secured to the shrouds. There may or may not be a cut-out to accommodate the mast. The front of foredeck awnings are secured to the bow rail where the lifelines are attached.

The aft end can be stretched across a stiff batten to keep it taut, curved around a flexible batten, or attached to some other strong attachment points such as davits or boom gallows. Running backstays can be used for attachment points as long as they are tensioned well.

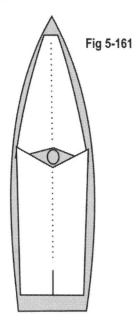
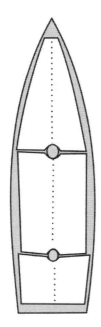

Fig 5-161

Sloop - shown is a foredeck awning and a main awning with overlap. Slit at the aft end to go around a backstay.

Ketch - shown is a foredeck awning and a main awning with no overlap, and an aft awning. Cutouts are made around the mast.

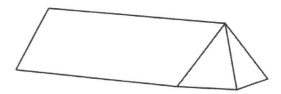

Fig 5-162 Awning with triangular insert at aft end for additional sun shade.

The awning must not rest on the boom, or else both the awning and the sail cover will chafe. The easiest way to prevent this is to use a halyard to suspend the awning along its spine; stitching stainless steel rings in the spine for this purpose. (Fig 5-163).

In addition to a main awning, a separate foredeck awning can be made to shade the front end of the boat. It can be low and close to the deck, providing less windage, or it can be high enough to walk under. If you make it low to the deck, be sure you can walk around it easily in case you have to get at the anchor in a hurry. Also, design it so that the forward edge is low to the deck and at least a foot forward of the forward hatch, to reduce the amount of rain that can get below.

The main and foredeck awnings can be designed so that they overlap each other and provide full coverage against rain and sun.

Shown in the photo below is a main awning with side curtains that extends back to the Topping Lift – the Bimini (when its wings are in place), takes care of shade in the cockpit. The Foredeck awning is low and small enough to step around in order to go forward.

You will probably never see a professionally made awning that uses ropes along the spine and along sides for attachment. This is because you can never really get the awning pulled tight using ropes. Sure, the ropes are very taut, but the awning fabric itself, since it is not sewn to the rope, will always be puckered and therefore flap and look sloppy. Use nylon webbing and stainless steel rings instead as shown below.

Side curtains can be attached along the sides of the awning to help reduce heat when the sun is low. Adding ties or rollups allows the side curtains to be rolled up when they are not needed

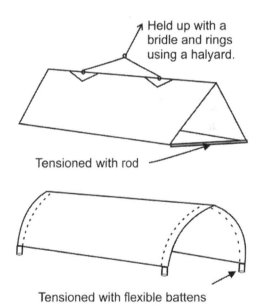

Held up with a bridle and rings using a halyard.

Tensioned with rod

Tensioned with flexible battens

Fig 5-163 Using battens to support the awning.

Canvas for Cruisers

Materials:

Sunbrella is the most commonly used fabric for sailboat awnings. Stamoid is also another choice if you want a totally waterproof awning. Keep in mind that Sunbrella won't tolerate chafe, and Stamoid won't tolerate flapping.

Using old sails is really a false economy – Dacron is not good in the sun anyway (that's why we make sail covers), and it flaps noisily in the wind.

V92 thread is the minimum thickness to use, and if the awning is going to get a lot of use in the hot sun, consider using Tenara or Profilen thread – it is expensive and not every machine works well with it, but will last forever.

You will also need a lot of 1" tubular webbing, 1" stainless steel rings, and some vinyl for chafe patches.

Measuring Up:

Get out a bunch of lines – you will use these to make an 'outline' of the awning.

Start by tying a line taut from the mainmast to the mizzen or backstay. The line should be parallel to the water, and the height you want the peak of the awning to be.

Tie two more lines - from the first line at the mainmast point, to the outermost shrouds on each side. Slope them with a downhill pitch at whatever height off the deck you want them to be. This represents the 'roof' of the awning.

Now tie a long line from the same point on the shrouds to the aft attachment point, again, parallel to the water. The aft attachment point could be a temporary 'batten' like a boathook lashed to the backstay.

Finish outlining the awning by tying a line from the aft attachment points to the aft end of the centerline.

Now step back or get into the dinghy and look at the lines from a distance. Is it parallel to the water? Does the pitch look OK? Try to imagine it with the fabric in place – does it detract from the boat's appearance? If the boat is very curved such as a canoe stern, it might look better if the sides of the awning are curved too.
Go back to the boat now and make any adjustments. Get ready to take some measurements.

Measure:

1. The centerline or 'spine'. The finished awning should be 6"-8" shorter than this length so that it can be stretched really taut.

2. From the centerline to the side lines – at the mainmast, and the aft end.
If the awning sides need to be curved, measure 4 or 5 additional points and make a diagram.

3. If there are going to be side curtains and/or a stern curtain, take several measurements from the side lines down to the lifelines, and make a diagram.

The side curtains may be different lengths depending on the taper of the boat. It is best to make them about 3" or so too short, so that when stretched out and attached to the lifelines, they will be taut.

If any part of the awning is going to be 'shaped' as described above, now is the time to make a plastic pattern.

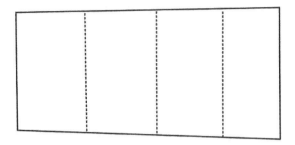

Fig 5-164 Fabric panels for the awning - run the seams athwartships.

The fabric panels will probably be positioned athwart ships (See Fig 5-164). Calculate fabric yardage requirements based on the width of the fabric being used. Sunbrella comes 46" or 60" wide and Stamoid is 59" or 80" wide.

Allow 1" for seam allowance between panels, and 4" hem allowance on the sides and each end.

A 'basic' awning consists of joined panels of fabric. There are 2 or more center patches with rings for hoisting. At the corners and at the ends are patches with rings, and there is webbing all around the outside and along the spine.

Its overall shape could be a rectangle, tapered, or pointed at one or both ends.

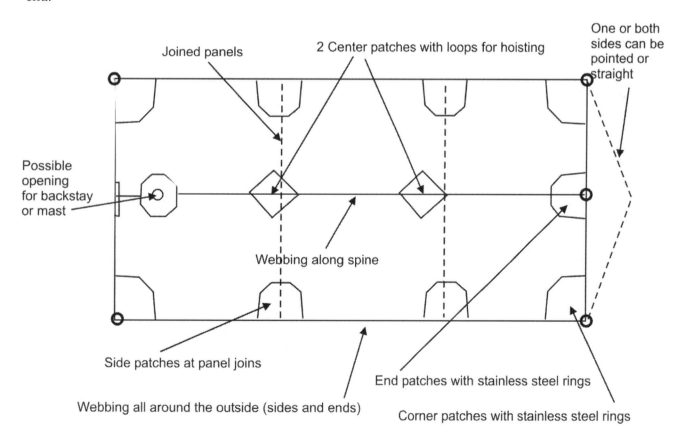

Fig 5-165 Basic features of an awning.

Canvas for Cruisers

Main Steps:

1. Cut and join the panels.

2. Trim to size.

3. Stitch on patches.

4. Construct center spine and possibly backstay/topping lift opening.

5. Make side curtains and roll-ups (optional)

6. Stitch on webbing at sides and ends.

Step 1 - Cut and join the panels.

Cut out the fabric panels to length according to your diagram and the measurements you have made. Make the panels a couple of inches too long rather than too short. You can trim any excess later, but it's difficult to add on!

Join as many panels as needed to cover the boat. A flat-felled or Topstitched seam is best. (See Section 2 - Seams)

Spread the joined panels out on a large surface and transfer all the measurements and marks from your diagram, onto the fabric.

Make note of:

1. Basic outline. Mark the finished shape of the awning. Remark the outline into a slightly concave curve to reduce flapping. How much curve? Take 2% of the length of the side. At the center of the side measure in to this number, and use a batten or flexible rod to mark a smooth curve as shown in Fig 5-166. Add seam allowances and hem allowances where required.

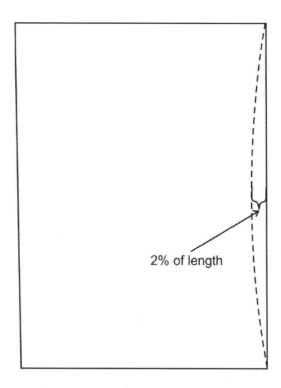

2% of length

Fig 5-166 Hollow-cut the sides to prevent flapping.

Then make another line ½" outside of this as the cutting line.

Also mark:

1. Centerline (The spine).

2. Location of center patches for hoisting with a halyard.

3. Location of backstay/topping life slit, and slits for shrouds, if any.

4. Outline of mast cut-out if any. Add ½" for seam allowance.

5. Location of side patches (usually at the panel joins and used to tie the awning to an attachment point such as a lifeline)

6. Location of side curtain panels (usually between the main panel joins).

Step 2 - Trim to size.

Using a hot knife (for Sunbrella), cut out along the cutting lines.

Step 3 - Stitch on all the patches.

The strain on the awning will be considerable, so it is important to make very large and strong patches at all attachment points. (See Section 2 – the Multi-layer patch)

Hexagonal shapes with straight sides are easier to sew neatly than curved ones.
Make the patches at least 6" wide to spread the load; otherwise the stitching will pull out.

Fig 5-167 (next page) shows the various styles of patches you will need to use.

Construct all the patches (See Section 2 - Patches and Reinforcements).

Position all the patches on the *wrong* side of the awning, except for the lifting patches – stitch these to the awning's *right* side along the spine.

Line up the raw edges of the patches with the fold line (not the raw edge) of the awning edge. Stitch close to the folded edges of the patch, and again ½" away.

If there is going to be a batten at the aft end of the awning, incorporate a multilayered, strong pocket to receive the batten end. A double layer of 2" webbing can serve as a pocket in this case.
If it will not weaken the batten, you can screw in an eye-bolt on each end of the batten to use to tie to whatever attachment points you are using.

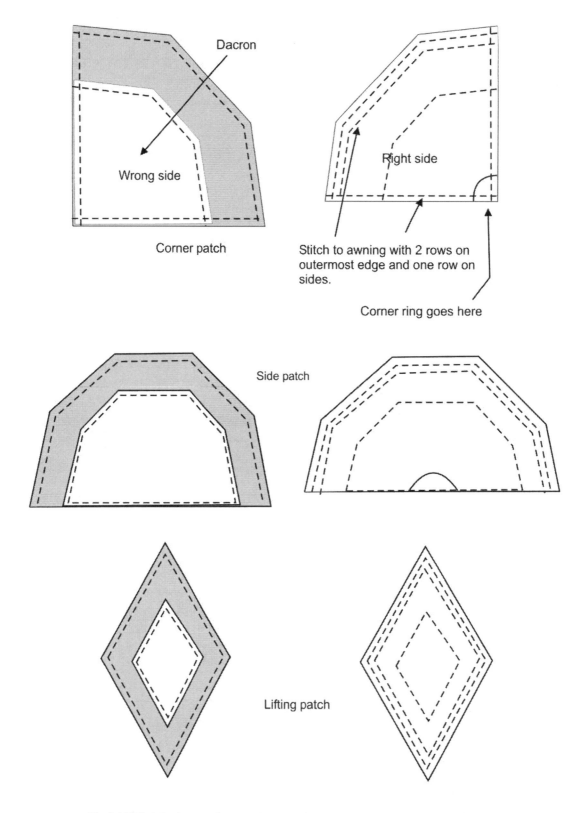

Dacron

Wrong side

Corner patch

Right side

Stitch to awning with 2 rows on outermost edge and one row on sides.

Corner ring goes here

Side patch

Lifting patch

Fig 5-167 Reinforcing patches consisting of a layer of Dacron and a layer of fabric.

Step 4. Construct the center spine and possibly a backstay or topping lift opening.

Stretch out the awning on the floor *right* side down – so you're looking at the underside of the awning.
Stretch out a length of 1" tubular webbing and apply ½" seamstick.
On the *wrong* side of the awning, stick the webbing along the spine, careful not to stretch the webbing. See Fig 5-168.

Over time, the webbing shrinks and will cause the awning to pucker if you stretch it when applying it.

At each end where there is a patch, loop the webbing around a stainless steel ring and overlap the webbing about 6" (see detail in Fig 5-168).

Stitch all around along the edge of the webbing from one end to the other.

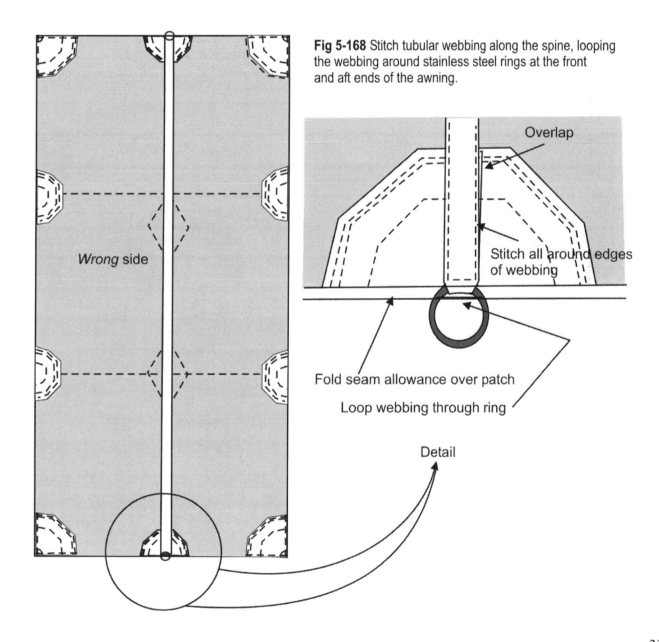

Fig 5-168 Stitch tubular webbing along the spine, looping the webbing around stainless steel rings at the front and aft ends of the awning.

Wrong side

Overlap

Stitch all around edges of webbing

Fold seam allowance over patch

Loop webbing through ring

Detail

Canvas for Cruisers

Backstay or Topping Lift slit:

If the awning is to have a slit, fashion an opening with a webbing tab closure for strength. See Fig 5-169.

The slit can have a zipper closure, or Velcro. See full details in the Bimini section.

Be sure to tension the tab closure so that the tab takes the strain, not the opening.

A reinforcing patch will need to be fitted around the backstay opening, so that the ring is forward of the backstay (to allow tensioning along the spine).

If your awning is going to have to pass by a Topping Lift AND a Backstay, then you will need to make a buckle attachment aft of the Topping Lift to hold the awning strongly together at the spine, and possibly a zipper to close the spine between the Topping Lift and the Backstay.

If the awning has a cutout for the mast, reinforce this area with a shaped, strong patch and possibly a closure of some sort – maybe a webbing strap with buckle to go around the mast.

Hoisting Patches

On the *right* side, or top side of the awning, insert a piece of tubular webbing into a ring and stitch one in the center of each of the hoisting patches, along the same line as the spine.
Use the box-stitch and extra rows – this area takes a lot of strain. See Fig 5-170.

Some boats with in-mast or boom furling use the boom as a center support for the awning. The awning will chafe the paint on the boom, so line the underside of the awning in this area with Odyssey soft-touch with the fluffy side outside – so that the fluffy side will touch the boom. A 9" wide strip should be wide enough.

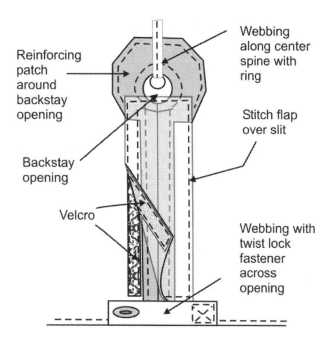

Fig 5-169 Reinforce the backstay opening

Reinforcing patch around backstay opening

Webbing along center spine with ring

Stitch flap over slit

Backstay opening

Velcro

Webbing with twist lock fastener across opening

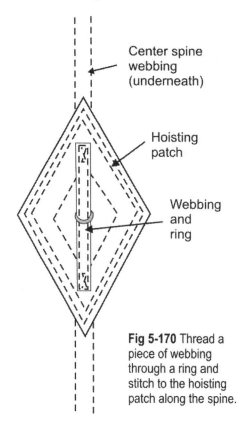

Center spine webbing (underneath)

Hoisting patch

Webbing and ring

Fig 5-170 Thread a piece of webbing through a ring and stitch to the hoisting patch along the spine.

Step 5 - Make side curtains and tie-ups (optional)

If there are to be side curtains, now is the time to attach them, before you finish the sides with webbing.

a) Mark out the side curtains per the diagram you have made. Add 2" to sides and one end for a 1" double hem.
Stitch a 1" double hem on 3 sides, leaving the top edge raw. Fig 5-171.

Using 60" wide Sunbrella and cutting the fabric in half to make panels 30" wide usually works pretty well.

If you don't trust yourself, you can leave the bottom hem of the side curtains till last – in order to get a nice level hem. Just hem the 2 sides only, stitch the side curtains to the awning and do all the finishing. Then try on the awning and mark the lower hems.

Optionally, you can make the side curtains as all one big panel, for rain protection or whatever, and some kind of zipper opening for people to get on and off the boat. One big long side curtain, though, will be almost impossible to roll up.

In the lower corners of the side curtains, install webbing loops and line, grommets and line, grommets and bungees and hooks, or whatever you are using for attachment points to secure the lower edge of each side curtain to the lifelines. Fig 5-172.

This can be left until later when the awning gets fitted to the boat, if you need to space the tie-downs to fit available attachment points.

b) Make enough rollups (see Section 3 - Rollups) for the side curtains. Alternatively, you can insert a piece of line between the side curtain and the awning and just tie up the side curtains.

The rollups or tie-ups should be placed 4-6" from each end of each side curtain..

Raw Edge

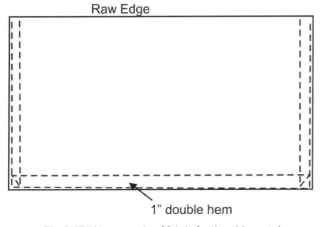

1" double hem

Fig 5-171 Hem panels of fabric for the side curtains.

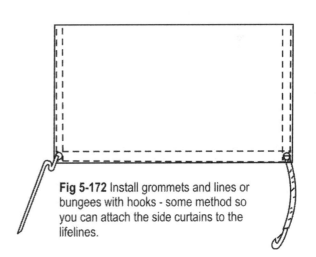

Fig 5-172 Install grommets and lines or bungees with hooks - some method so you can attach the side curtains to the lifelines.

Overlap the edge of the side curtain over the edge of the awning, by ½" just like you were doing a simple lapped seam (Fig 5-173).

Insert the rollups. (This is assuming simple ladderlock rollups – see Section3 – Rollups)) Consider the direction the curtains will be rolled up, and position the buckles accordingly. It is best to try to keep the buckles to the inside of the awning when the curtains are hanging down, to keep the buckles out of the sun. See Fig 5-173.

Stitch the side curtains to the awning.

If there are no side curtains, crease the raw edge of the awning under ½" all around the sides and ends.

Stick ½" seamstick to a long length of tubular webbing, stretching out the webbing with scratch awls before applying the seamstick.
Stick the webbing to the *wrong* side of the awning, all around the outside edges. See Fig 5-174 on the next page.

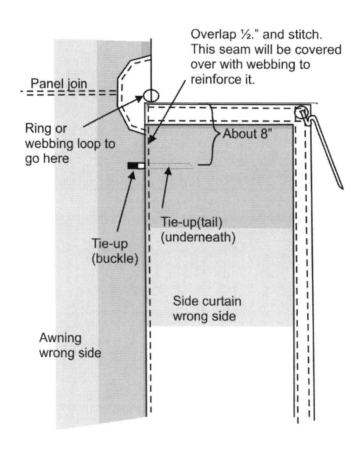

Panel join

Overlap ½." and stitch.
This seam will be covered over with webbing to reinforce it.

Ring or webbing loop to go here

About 8"

Tie-up (buckle)

Tie-up(tail) (underneath)

Side curtain wrong side

Awning wrong side

Fig 5-173 Position the side curtains between the awning's panel joins, leaving space for the ring or loop tie down point. Insert the tie-ups so the buckle is to the *wrong* side of the awning.
Stitch the side curtain assembly to the awning.

When you come to a patch, loop the webbing through a stainless steel ring, and double it back at an angle, to spread the load and reduce thickness. See Fig 5-174 details.

Position the rings so that the folds of the webbing are near the edges of the fabric. The ring should stick out. If the rings are too far inside the edge of

the awning, when you tension the awning, there will be a funny looking fold at the corner.

Cut the webbing off short of the Dacron layer of the reinforcing patch. This is important. All the stress is at the end of the webbing. If it extends into an area that is weak, it will rip the fabric.

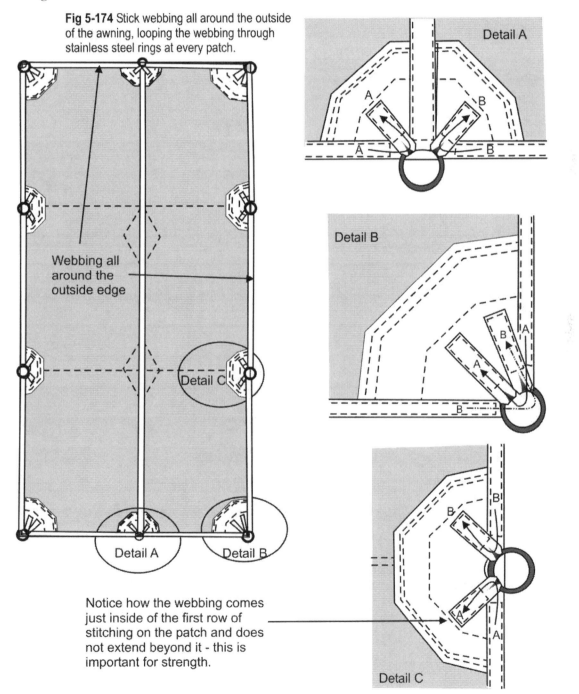

Fig 5-174 Stick webbing all around the outside of the awning, looping the webbing through stainless steel rings at every patch.

Webbing all around the outside edge

Notice how the webbing comes just inside of the first row of stitching on the patch and does not extend beyond it - this is important for strength.

Detail A

Detail B

Detail C

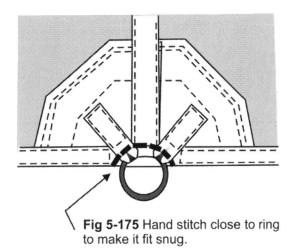

Fig 5-175 Hand stitch close to ring to make it fit snug.

After the webbing is all sewn on, hand stitch close to the ring (see Fig 5-175).

If you are intending to put a curved batten at the aft edge as shown in Fig 5-142, make a long batten pocket for it (see Assemblies). Note however that you don't really see many awnings of this type – they are complicated to hoist and even more difficult to douse quickly in a sudden squall. , but might be just fine at a dock (Fig 5-176).

Catching rain:

If you want the awning to be able to catch rain, you should set up the awning and live with it for awhile to see where the most logical place would be to set up a drain spout. It is important that the awning does not flap, or all the rain water will flap away!

The drain spout should be at a point where the rain naturally drains, and close to the deck fills. Mark this position, and reinforce the area with a 6" patch. Install a 1" plastic through hull fitting. Attach a hose, and run it to the tanks or a bucket. A piece of light line can pull the area down if needed to create a low spot. Voila!

Rigging the awning

It is essential that the spine and sides of the awning be as tight as possible to reduce flapping. Flapping will shorten the life of the awning considerably. Use the rings and line to really stretch the awning tight. Fashion a bridle to hoist the awning a few inches off the boom with the main halyard.

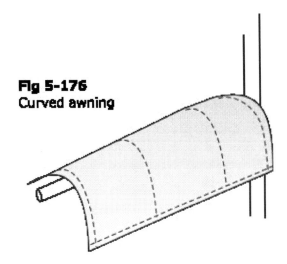

**Fig 5-176
Curved awning**

Boat Storage Cover

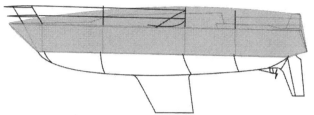

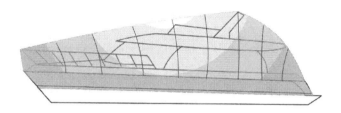

Fig 5-177 A boat cover can go inside of the stanchions as shown above, or it can cover the entire boat as shown on the right.

Depending on the size of the boat, a custom cover can be a very big project. But, if you love your boat, store it a lot and want to keep it clean, dry and undamaged from the elements, a full boat cover is the way to go.

Design:
There are many things to think about before you start this kind of a project:

Does the cover need to just cover the deck, or does it need to go all the way down to the waterline?
If the boat is painted a dark colour, there is a lot to be said for having the cover go all the way to the waterline and protect the paint from fading. A cover can, however, chafe the paint if it starts to flap in the wind. So it needs to fit tight and possibly be lined with a fuzzy fabric such as Evolution.

Will there be snow? If so you will need to design the cover so that there are no flat or concave areas where snow can build up. If there is a lot of snow, the center spine should be high so there is steep run-off.

Will there be a lot of rain? If so then you need to have the cover really waterproof or make very sure that the water runs off and doesn't pool on the cover. To compound the problem, the boat needs ventilation too, or mold will build up underneath it. A vinyl cover will have to be vented to prevent this.

If the rain is dirty, the cover will get dirty too, so you might as well pick a brownish or grayish colour for the fabric.

For a sailboat – will the mast be up or down?
If the mast is up, openings will have to be made for the mast, stays and the shrouds.

The boom can be used as part of the support spine for the cover but the cover can chafe the boom's paint job. Preventing flapping and reinforcing this area with Evolution helps.

If the mast is down but stored on top of the boat, then openings will need to be made to allow the mast to stick out each end.

Will the cover enclose the stanchions, or will it go inside of them, leaving the stanchions sticking out?

Canvas for Cruisers

Having the cover over top of the stanchions will give you more room inside if you are planning on doing work in there. It will necessitate adding reinforcing against the chafe the stanchions will cause when they try to poke through the cover.

Horizontal support might be needed if the lifelines are too loose and wobbly to support the cover solidly. But a cover going right over the stanchions and lifelines can be simpler to make.

If the cover goes inside of the stanchions, then the surface of the Top can be steeper, smaller and tighter, which may allow rain and snow to run off better. It will be more complicated to make because openings will have to be made for each stanchion base, and possibly mast, stays and shrouds.

Is there a bowsprit? This should be covered too, and since it extends forward of the forestay, there will need to be a slit for the forestay or it might have to be a separate zip-in section.

If the boat is large – 40' or so, you can make the cover in 2,3 or even 4 sections which zip together, with zips covered by generous flaps.

For visiting the boat while it is covered, or to work on it, you can install 2 vertical zippers about 3 feet apart so you can have a roll-up panel to be used as a doorway.

Will the cover be used in trailering? If so, it has to fit very tight and there must be absolutely no flapping of the fabric.

Do you want to be able to walk underneath the cover, and possibly work on the deck within it? Then it needs to have headroom and a zippered door opening. The higher it is though, the more windage it will have.

Chafe areas – If the cover flaps in the wind at all, there will be chafe and undue strain on the fabric. Depending on what the fabric is chafing against, either the fabric, or the surface of the boat will be damaged. Usually it is the fabric, but remember, fabric can actually chafe paint and varnish. If the toe rail is nice varnished teak, you will need to line this area with Odyssey soft touch.

Strain areas – any place on the cover that is subject to strain – such as the tops of the stanchions, corners and areas where there will be tie ropes – must be reinforced or the fabric will tear.

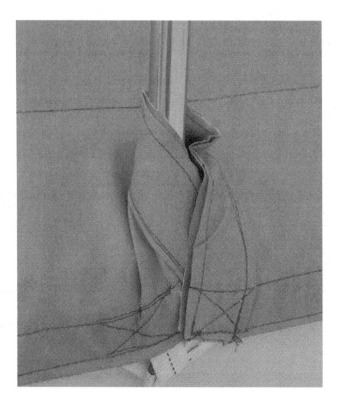

Materials:

Acrylic canvas is a good choice for all kinds of covers, and a full boat cover is no exception. But for a large boat it can be very heavy. So a material like Sunbrella SurLast or WeatherMax80 can work – it is lighter in weight but still has the same characteristics as Sunbrella.

TopGun is a popular choice but also heavy, and it has a reputation for being abrasive to the hull.

A vinyl such as Stamoid can be used and is waterproof – but it cannot tolerate flapping and you will have to install vents in the cover to prevent condensation inside.

A lighter colour such as tan or grey will deflect heat and make the boat cooler underneath.

Cover Patterning and Construction:

Every boat storage cover will be unique and different. It is impossible to describe all the variations in making a custom cover. So the basic techniques described here will have to be modified to suit the particular boat.

The cover described here is for a sailboat, with the mast off. Refer to Fig 5-178.
This cover is divided into two sections connected with a zipper to make it smaller and easier to handle.

The Top is made of panels of fabric stitched together. The Top extends from a support along the center spine of the boat, down to the toe rail. The Top passes to the inside of the stanchions – that is, the stanchions stick out of the cover, the bow pulpit is exposed, but the stern rail is covered.

The Skirt on this cover consists of a series of fitted flaps, broken at each stanchion base because of the fact that the stanchions are sticking out of the cover. The Skirt flaps are connected together by Velcro. They curve and fit tight to the shape of the hull. Velcro is not always a good choice because it deteriorates over time – you could use zippers with generous flaps.

If you are not going to cover the entire hull down to the waterline, you won't need a separate skirt. Just extend the cover down past the toe rail about 6-12" so that rain and snow can run off.

At the bow, the sides of this cover are connected together with Velcro. Many covers use grommets and lacing, or you can stitch webbing loops instead of the grommets so the grommets won't scratch the boat. A product called E-Z Lace can also be used.

At the stern, the Skirt is fitted to the shape of the transom.

There is an opening in the cover – a zippered 'door' in the side. If the boat has a rear transom scoop or a swim platform, the door opening could be at the stern.

Main Steps:

1. Design and construct the support frame.
2. Measure up and make a diagram
3. Make a plastic pattern
     - or –
   Make a fabric 'Blank'
4. Construction:
     - Cutouts
     - Zippers
     - Reinforcing patches
     - Chafe protection
5. Trial fit and mark hem
6. Optional Skirt
7. Straps and Sandbags

345

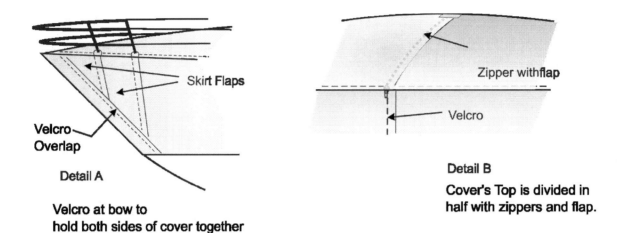

Skirt Flaps

Velcro Overlap

Detail A

Velcro at bow to
hold both sides of cover together

Zipper withflap

Velcro

Detail B
Cover's Top is divided in
half with zippers and flap.

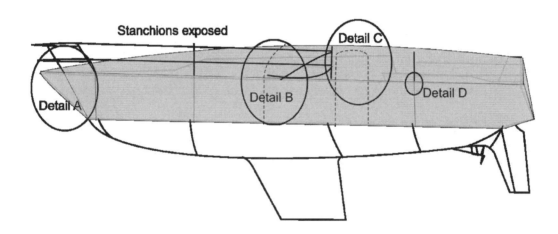

Stanchions exposed

Detail C

Detail A

Detail B

Detail D

Fig 5-178 Details of the features of this storage cover.

Detail C
Zippered door opening

Detail D
Opening to go around Stanchion base.
(Collar to keep out rain not shown)

Step 1 – Design and construct the support Frame

The boat should be put away just as if it is in storage. That is, mast up or down as the case may be, solar panels off, exterior canvas off, etc.

If the mast is up, the boom can be used to support the back end of the cover. Then construct a spine support from the mast to the bow. It could be a simple wooden board and support or you could have a custom aluminum or PVC one made.

If the mast is down and on top of the boat, use it for a center spine.

If not, or for a powerboat, a full length center spine is needed. A length of PVC pipe can be used - securely attached, from the center of the transom (say, the center of the aft pulpit) to the point of the bow at deck level. This will create a smooth curve to allow rain and possibly snow to run off.

The next steps depend on your circumstances, and the size of the boat.

Basically, you can either fit the fabric panels onto the boat, or you can first make a plastic pattern.
Fitting the fabric panels directly onto the boat will involve several trips out to the boat. So if the boat is far away, then you will probably want to make a pattern. If the boat is large, this can add quite a bit of cost of materials to the project, but overall maybe less hassle and transportation cost to and from the boat. Besides, the plastic patterning material can be reused.
If the boat is smaller, like a jet-ski, a pontoon boat or an open boat like a canoe or skiff, then a plastic pattern makes a lot of sense.
If the boat is some distance away but still convenient, you can use a diagram to help design and construct the cover, fitting the fabric

panels out in stages as you make visits to the marina.
In the ideal situation, the boat is in your backyard, and you can make several trips out to it.

Step 2 – Measure up and make a diagram

To estimate how much fabric you will need, make a diagram:

For the Top
Measure the total length of the center spine.

Now you are going to design where the panels of fabric will be. If the mast will be up and your cover will be in zippered sections, it makes sense to have a zipper join at the mast. So start your diagram for panels here and work forward and aft from there.

Measure perpendicular to the spine down to the toe rail or the rub rail (for the Long Skirt version) or to the bottom of a short skirt if that is what you are doing. If the spine is pretty much horizontal, you can measure straight between the spine and the toe rail. But the more the spine is tilted, the more important it is to measure perpendicular to the spine – imagine how the panels will be tilted.

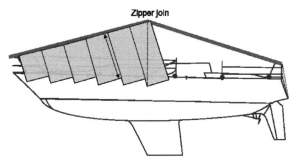

If the frame has a high pitch, then the panels will lie tilted. So measure from the spine, perpindicular to the toe rail.

Do this measurement at intervals of whatever is the width your fabric, minus 1" (which will be seam allowances for the panels) Make a diagram.
It might look something like Fig 5-179a

Canvas for Cruisers

For the Transom – Measure the width and length of the fabric panel that will be required to cover the transom and extend down to the hemline.

For the Skirt – If you're not using the waterline, snap a chalkline onto the boat if necessary, to mark a smooth straight line for the hem.
Measure from the base of the bow pulpit stanchions straight down to the hem.

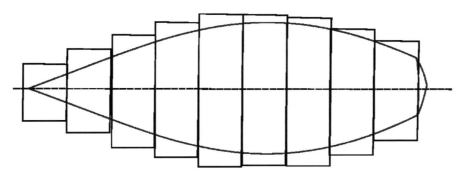

Fig 5-179a Measure from spine to toe rail at intervals
of the fabric width (less 1")

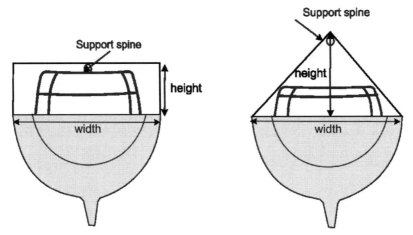

Transom panel can be rectangular or more triangular
depending on boat and support frame.

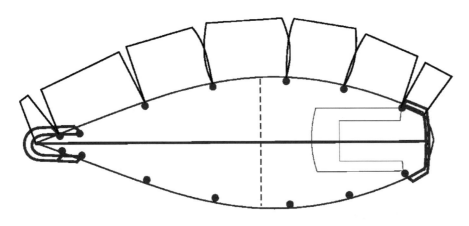

Skirt panel diagram might look something like this.

Most boats bulge out at their midships, and then taper in at the bow. The stern may bulge out or taper in. This will affect the shape of the skirt panels – in other words, the skirt panels won't be nice straight rectangles. So drop a line down from each pair of stanchions, tape the line to the boat at the waterline. Measure the distance between these lines at the stanchion bases, the fattest part of the boat and at the waterline. Make a diagram

Using your diagrams, add up yardage required. Add about 1 foot to each Top panel – better to cut them oversize than have them too short. And it doesn't hurt to add 15% for reinforcing, openings and other unexpected things. Be prepared to faint when you see how much fabric it's going to take.

If you are making a door, measure where it should be and include it on the diagram. If the door is on the side, one side of its zip opening should be at a stanchion base.

If you are putting in a zip so as to make the cover into two or more sections, mark where this will be on the diagram.

Step 3 – Make a Plastic Pattern, or Make a Fabric 'Blank'

Plastic Pattern
Set up the tape – See Fig 5-179b:
Run a line of tape all around the boat at the toe rail (A) – you should use tape such as packing tape or painting masking tape. Test it first to make sure it comes off cleanly, and does not damage your varnish or paint.

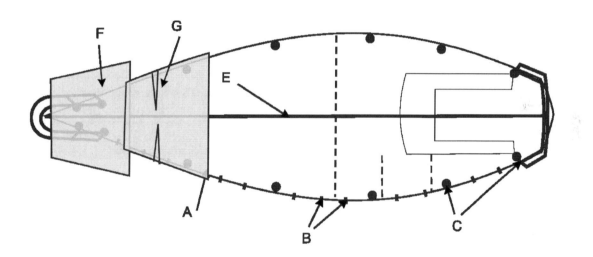

Fig 5-179b
A) Run tape and mark a line all around the edge of the boat where the Top will meet the Skirt
B) Make match-up marks about every 2 feet
C) Mark locations of stanchion bases.
D) Cover marked line with double-sided tape.
E) Run tape and mark a line along the spine. Cover with double-sided tape.
F) Lay plastic patterning material across the top, stick to the spine and along the outer edge.
G) Make darts to take in the excess. Continue patterning the stern.

On the tape, mark a straight line with permanent marker. This will be the seam line between the Top and the Skirt. Do the same with the stern rail, where the Top will meet the back piece for the transom.

Make match-up marks about every 2 feet (B). Now cover over the marked line with clear double-sided tape – super sticky seamstick might be needed to hold the large plastic panels in place. Leave the paper on for now.

Run tape along the spine (E). From your diagram, mark where the fabric panel joins will be. Stick on double-sided tape to help hold the plastic in place.

It helps to run strapping tape from toe rail, over the spine to the opposite toe rail at intervals to support the plastic.

See Fig 5-179b.

Pattern the Top.

Start placing panels of plastic over the spine and extending a little past the toe rail or rub rail (F). It is best to pick a calm day, and work with a partner that you get along with. Bring along clamps to help hold things in place, your notebook and a big permanent marker . Depending on the size of the boat and the width of the patterning material, you can lay panels along the entire length of the boat, or you might have to lay panels of plastic athwartships.

You might have to make markings as you go – depends on whether you have to stand on the deck, or whether you are working from a dock, ladder or scaffolding on the hard, or from a dinghy in the water.

If the mast is up, you will need to slit the plastic to go around the mast and shrouds, cut out a hole to accommodate them, and then re-tape the plastic back together. Then you will need to

mark a line for an opening so you can get the cover on and off (like the backstay slit in the bimini). Keep in mind that this opening will have to extend right down to the bottom of the Skirt, so try to position the opening line to meet the toe rail at an existing opening at a stanchion base. It can get pretty complicated if your boat is a ketch.

Because the Top will be curvy, pinch the plastic into darts where required, and mark these for a shaped, tight fit (G). Making these darts at the seams between fabric panels – which you marked along the spine - or along any openings in the Top will reduce the number of seams (and possible leakage) in the Top.

Mark:
  - Location of zippers – for panel joins and door opening
  - Match up marks between panels
  - Location of any chafe patches required
  - Mark a line along the spine
  - Mark on the pattern an accurate line directly over top of the line you made on the rub rail or toe rail tape. Include the match up marks, and location of the stanchion openings if any.
  - The seam and match-up marks where the Top will meet the back piece at the stern rail
  - Match-up marks between Top and Skirt panels
  - Label each panel and make a diagram in your notebook

Have a good look at the pattern. If you think the cover might sag, such as on long expanses of fabric, it might help to modify the frame or make batten sleeves, or a line of webbing with rings and lines to lift it and stretch it out, or lifting patches with lines which can be tied to, say, the lifelines or other attachment points. Mark the pattern with these details.

Pattern the Transom area.
Drape a piece of patterning plastic over the transom area, smoothing out the wrinkles and making darts

where required. Mark the seam line using the taped lines – at the top edge of the stern rail where it meets the Top, and along both sides of the stern rail where it meets the Skirt. Mark the seam lines and the match-up marks.

Now remove the plastic pattern for the Top. This allows you to work on the deck and pattern the Skirt with a helper on the dock, on a ladder or in the dinghy.

Pattern the Skirt.

If the double-sided tape is still OK, use it to stick plastic panels along the rail for the Skirt. Otherwise just stick on another layer of double-faced tape.

Refer to Fig 5-180.
Drape panels of plastic patterning material along the rail, over the double-faced tape. Mark a line directly over top of the original line on the rail (D). Include the match up marks (C). At the stanchion bases, pinch in darts straight down to the hem (A), to achieve a tight fit along the hull's curve. Mark the darts and tape in place.

Tape along where the rear edge of the Skirt will meet the Transom piece. Mark a line on the tape and match-up marks. Then run a line of seamstick on this line. Now position the last Skirt panel piece and trace this seamline onto the skirt pattern.

After all the Skirt pieces are taped in place, mark a nice straight level line for the hem (E). Label all the panels and make a diagram in your notebook.

Label everything – mark the panels A, B, C etc, fore/aft, port/stb and inside/outside or some way, according to your diagram so that you can match things up later.

Remove the pattern from the boat and start marking out your fabric - remember to add match-up marks, seam allowances, hem allowances (use a 2" double hem on the Skirt), and overlap (at least 1") for the Velcro'd panels.

Cut out the fabric – all at once or a bit at a time, and construct the cover. Use the instructions below, starting with Step 2.
Just omit all the parts about fitting the fabric to the boat

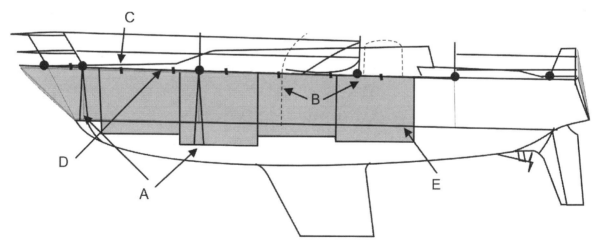

Fig 5-180 Drape panels of plastic patterning material along the rail.
A - Darts at stanchions to make cover curve around the hull
B - Mark location of zippers
C - Mark match up marks
D - Mark line along the Top-Hem join
E - Mark hemline.

Canvas for Cruisers

<u>Fabric 'Blank'</u>

<u>Work on the Top first.</u>

Cut out the panels according to your diagram – cut them oversize a little so you can trim them back later. You don't want them too short!

Stitch the panels together. (If your cover is in two or more sections, keep the sections separate.) Use a Topstitched seam. Consider water and how it runs off the tilted spine (Fig 2-10) – it should run off and not into the seam.

Prepare the boat with tape and super sticky seamstick just like you would if making a plastic pattern – this has already been described.

Go to the boat and drape the Top over the spine of the frame (*wrong* side down). Arm yourself with a bunch of clamps, scissors, maybe a stapler and marking pencils. With clamps and possibly a partner to help hold things in place, begin fitting the cover.

There will be several places where you will have to make a slit in the fabric to make it fit around stanchions, stays and other hardware.

To do this, start at one end. Smooth the fabric down and find the place where it meets the stanchion or shroud. Make a dot here. Now mark from the dot straight down and vertical to the toe rail. This will be where the slit will be – just like a backstay in a Bimini.
With scissors, cut a slit in the fabric. If needed make little cuts to accommodate the shroud, or rail or stanchion so that the fabric can lay smooth around the object.
Once you cut the slit, you might find that the cover will fit better if you overlap the fabric slit back together, or maybe there will be a gap. Just mark this on the fabric and/or make notes so you can adjust the sewing of the slit later.

Work your way forward or aft, one side of the boat at a time. Stick or clamp the cover down to the toe rail as you go along. This will take quite awhile, so just take you time.

Mark any chafe patches and any darts required to achieve a tight fit. Mark where the door opening is (if you are installing one). You will be marking on the *right* side, so use pencil that can be erased or washes off.

Use the tape on the boat with the line marking the join between the Top and the Skirt to mark this seam on the fabric. If the fabric is light coloured, you can just use a dull object to rub the fabric and allow the mark to be transferred to the underside of the fabric in a series of dashed lines.
It is just like making a plastic pattern only you are using the fabric itself.

Take the cover off and lay it out flat. Re-mark the seam line where the Top joins the Skirt into a nice smooth line. Add ½" for seam allowance, and cut along this line.

Do all the construction for the Top – which is described in the nest steps. Once it is done, take it to the boat and try it on – cut out the Skirt panels oversize and bring them along.

If everything is OK with the Top, you can start stapling on the Skirt panels and fitting out the Skirt.

Step 4 – Construction

Stitch the door opening.(Optional)

Use a length of continuous zipper chain – no need for a separating jacket-type zipper.
Give careful consideration to how rain-proof the zipper opening will be. It could let in a lot of water if the teeth are exposed, and the door is not quite vertical. The teeth should be covered with a generous flap.

Add a Top Patch at the top and orient the zipper so that the head is at the bottom when the zipper is closed.
The zipper can extend all the way to the bottom of the Skirt, or you can use an overlapping flap with Velcro to join the skirt panels together below the toe rail.

See Fig 5-181, and also refer to Section 2 – Zippers for stitching instructions.

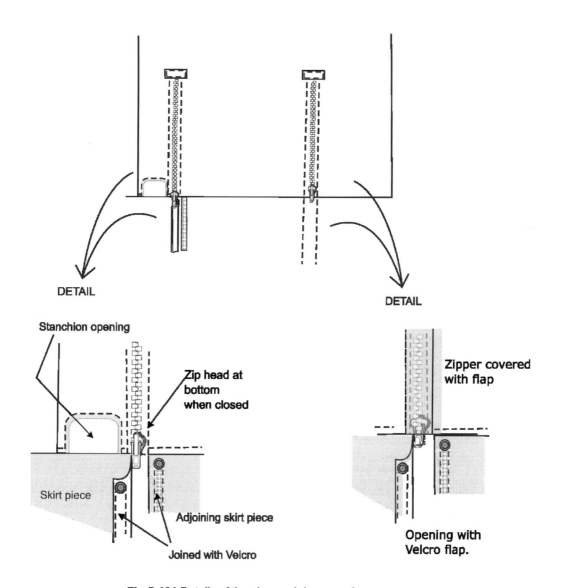

Fig 5-181 Details of the zippered door opening

Canvas for Cruisers

<u>Finish the openings for the stanchions and shrouds</u>

There are several ways to finish these openings. See Fig 5-182 for ideas.

If the opening is right at the toe rail and there is going to be Skirt, you could finish the openings as 5-182a. Also refer to Section 2 – Reinforcing a hole. At the toe rail end of the slit, the Skirt will have to have a break in it.

Once the Skirt is sewn on, then you can install a collar and fastening to keep out the rain.

You could make a simple 2-layer vinyl patch – one on the inside and one on the outside, slit open and install a zipper. Like 5-182b.

Or you can bind the slit edges and install the zipper. See Bimini section Fig 5-34.

All openings will need a collar with closure to keep out rain. Like 5-182c.

All ends will also need to have a little piece of webbing with a commonsense fastener, snap or other fastener to take the strain off the slit – especially if the slit is closed with a zipper.

Fig 5-182

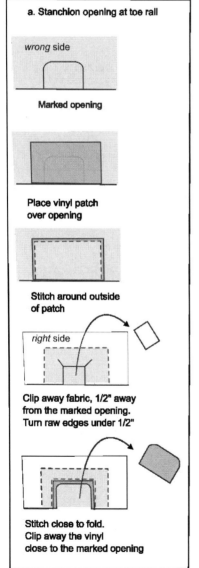

a. Stanchion opening at toe rail

wrong side

Marked opening

Place vinyl patch over opening

Stitch around outside of patch

right side

Clip away fabric, 1/2" away from the marked opening. Turn raw edges under 1/2"

Stitch close to fold. Clip away the vinyl close to the marked opening

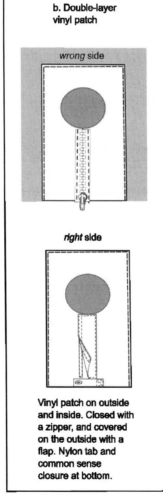

b. Double-layer vinyl patch

wrong side

right side

Vinyl patch on outside and inside. Closed with a zipper, and covered on the outside with a flap. Nylon tab and common sense closure at bottom.

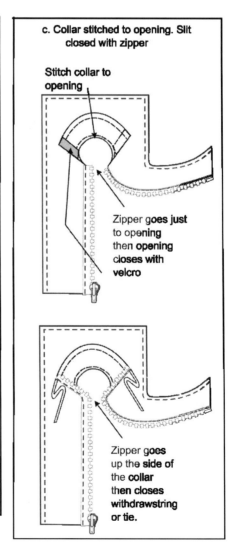

c. Collar stitched to opening. Slit closed with zipper

Stitch collar to opening

Zipper goes just to opening then opening closes with velcro

Zipper goes up the side of the collar then closes withdrawstring or tie.

Finish the openings for the Forestay and
Backstay.

These slits are constructed just like the Backstay
slit for the Bimini. The slit runs along the spine
and should be closed with a zipper covered with
a flap. The ends of the zipper should have a
little webbing tab with closures like
commonsense fasteners, or snaps, to take the
strain off the zipper.

You can try to make the opening really small to
limit rain coming in, but it will be easier to cut
the hole oversize. Then construct a rectangular
or cone-shaped collar with a Velcro closure or
drawstring, to keep out water.

Stitch the connecting zipper.

If you are breaking your large cover into two
halves with a connecting zipper, stitch one or
two jacket zips to join the two panels together.
Position the zippers so when closed, the heads
are at the toe rail. Cover the zippers with a
generous flap with Velcro to hold the flap down
to help keep the water out.
Also make a generous flap to cover the opening
where the two zippers meet at the spine, again
to keep water out.

If the cover is large or you expect to stretch out
the Top very tight, then you should reinforce
this connection as follows:
Stitch webbing loops with side release buckles
across the zipper – at both ends and perhaps
somewhere in between. . Position the strap so
that the buckle takes the strain, and not the
zipper.

If the mast is going to be up, you will need to
install 2 jacket zips, and construct a collar.
The collar will be in 2 halves – half on the Front
cover, and half on the Aft cover. The zippers
can come all the way up the side of the collar
and then secure the collar tight to the mast with
Velcro or a drawstring.

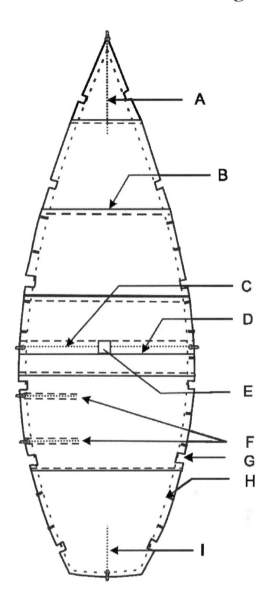

Fig 5-183 The Finished Top
A. Forestay slit (if mast is up)
B. Joined panels of fabric.
C. Zippers joining 2 separate
pieces to make the cover
more manageable.
D. Velcro'd flap to protect zipper.
E. Flap to keep out water - or
collar (if mast is up).
F. Zippered door opening
G. Stanchion base opening.
H. Seam where Skirt joins Top.
I. Backstay slit (if mast is up)

Canvas for Cruisers

Chafe Patches and Reinforcing

Where required, add chafe patches to the inside of the cover (See Section 2 – Patches and Reinforcements).

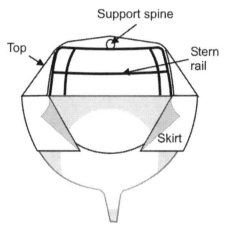

Fig 5-186 Transom - Top and Skirt are constructed and transom is still open.

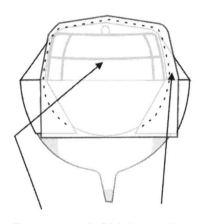

Drape a panel of fabric over the transom. Clamp or staple in place, fitting to the transom area. Mark the seam.

Step 5 – Trial Fit and mark Hem

Construct the Transom piece

The stern piece will need to be fitted around the stern rail and the shape of the transom. If you are using a Fabric Blank, then you should take the Top panel(s) to the boat and do a trial fit.

Use clamps or staples to hold the stern Blank to the Top panel.

Mark any slits and openings required for hardware and stanchions. Mark the seamline between transom piece and Top panel.

Remove the cover, re-fair the marks you made into nice smooth curves. Construct the cutouts just like you did the Top panel.
Stitch the transom piece to the Top panel.

Hem

If you are making a Skirt – the Transom area can be fitted out in one piece and constructed after the Skirt is done as shown in Fig 5-186.

If you are making a 'Shortie' cover – i.e. not going all the way to the waterline – mark a straight and level line for the hem. Mark the location for any tie down straps.

Reinforce the hem with Shelterite or webbing Construct webbing loops, or install grommets for tie-downs.
Some people make sandbags to weigh down the hem.

356

<u>Step 6 – Skirt</u>

<u>Cut out the Skirt panels</u>.
Using the diagram and the measurements you took or the pattern you made, mark out the skirt panels onto the fabric. Depending on how far apart the stanchions are, you will have to piece together panels of fabric.

For each panel, first measure and mark the length. Add ½" for seam allowance at the Top, and add 4" at the bottom for a 2" double hem. From your measurements, mark out on the fabric the width at the Top, the width at the middle and at the hem. Mark these side seams into a smooth curve. And mark a cutting line 1" outside of this line.

Cut out the Skirt panels – you can leave the forward edge uncut for now, to allow for fitting on the boat. Cut the aft edge, however. Turn this aft edge under and stitch Velcro loops to the *wrong* side.
Work from bow to stern. (If your cover is in 2 sections, work the Aft section from the stern towards midships.)

With *wrong* sides together, staple the first 2 Skirt panels to the Top (port & stb) along the stitching line. Position the panels so the Velcro'd edge is aft of the Stanchion opening.

Mark a line on the Skirt panels where the 2 sides meet at the centerline at the bow of the boat. Cut away the excess fabric to 4" and staple together at the bow. Depending on whether you are using grommets and lacing, or webbing loops and lacing, or Velcro, mark these details on the fabric.
(See Fig 5-184).

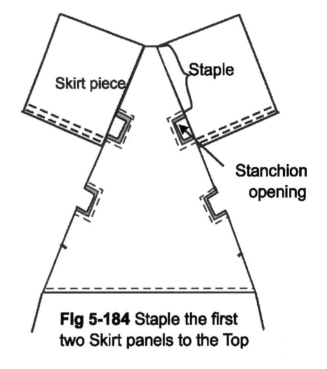

Fig 5-184 Staple the first two Skirt panels to the Top

Staple the next pair of panels on. Where the second pair of Skirt panels meets the first, mark a line. Velcro hooks will be stitched here, underneath the Velcro loops of the first pair of panels.
(Fig 5-185)

Proceed to fit the Skirt panels in this way, a pair at a time or several pairs at a time depending on how many trips you want to make to the boat. The cover will get bigger and bigger, so it might help to stitch temporary webbing loops to the hem area to keep things under control.

Step 7 – Fastenings and Sandbags

Take off the cover.
Finish the bow edge with Velcro, or if using grommets or webbing loops, make a 1" double hem and install the grommets or webbing loops.

On the forward edges of the panels, mark a line 2" parallel to the line you made and cut. Turn the forward edge of the panels under 1". Stitch Velcro hooks along the *right* side of this edge.

The hem can be stitched as you go or better to leave it until all the panels are stitched on. That way you can mark a smooth straight line along all panels.

Stitch webbing loops or install grommets in the hems – at the corners of the panels.

Fold the seam allowances toward the Top and topstitch the Top-Skirt seam.

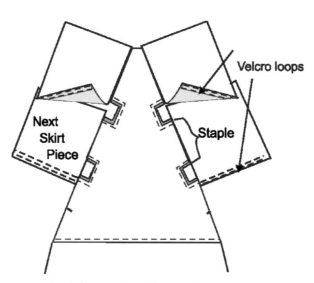

Fig 5-185 Position the next pair of Skirt panels under the first pair, and staple in place.

Weather Cloths

Weather cloths are useful for protection against wind and waves while sailing, and for privacy while at anchor.

In their simplest form, they are just a rectangle of cloth, hemmed on all 4 sides. Grommets are placed all around the outside, and laced to the lifelines, stanchions and toe rail. If the boat does not have a toe rail with holes in it, you might need to install some kind of attachment pad eyes to the deck for the weather cloths to attach to.

Some boats need shaped weather cloths depending on the shape of the cockpit. Usually weather cloths are installed along the sides of the boat from the halfway point to the aft end, and the stern is left without weather cloths.

When designing weather cloths, leave a couple of inches of space between the bottom of the weather cloth and the deck. This is because when it comes to getting hit by a big wave, the fabric will never be strong enough to withstand this force unless there is a place for the water to drain. The fabric will lose every time. You will end up with bent stanchions and ripped weather cloths.

Also, consider whether you can see over the top of the weather cloth while you are sitting in the cockpit. If they are too high, you will have to stand up to look around and this can get tiresome.
If you really do want very high weather cloths, you could make the top few inches of the weather cloth (or even the whole weather cloth) out of clear vinyl. (Reinforce the grommet areas with Shelterite vinyl or nylon webbing).

Normally, weather cloths are attached using grommets and lacing cord. This is also the method that takes the longest time to attach and take down. You can attach them with any other kind of fastener you desire if you want to be able to put them up and take them down quickly.
Most cruisers find once they have weather cloths, they keep them up permanently because they provide nice privacy in the cockpit.

To construct weather cloths:

a) Measure out the length and height at various places and make a diagram.
b) Note any cutouts you might need for deck hardware like blocks, fairleads and cleats.
c) Mark out the fabric per the measurements and add 2" all around for a 1" double hem.
d) Cut out the fabric.
e) Turn a 1" double hem all around.
f) Insert grommets at each corner and evenly spaced all around about 8" apart.

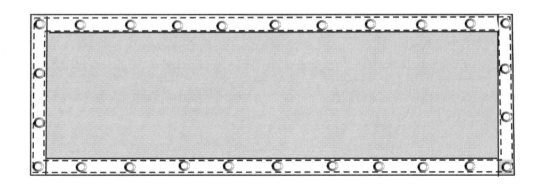

Fig 5-187 A simple weather cloth. A rectangle of fabric is hemmed all around and grommets inserted so it can be laced to the boat.

Sail Ties and Tie-Downs

Tie-Downs can be simply a length of nylon webbing with a loop sewn in one end as shown in Fig 5-188.

Wrap the sail tie around the sail, pull the end of the strap through the loop, tighten the strap around the sail and secure the end with an overhand knot. These are usually used to tie down the mainsail after you have flaked it onto the boom.

Tie-downs can also be made with Velcro as shown in Fig 5-189.

1) Cut a length of 1" nylon webbing – tubular or regular, depending on strength required. Tubular is stronger.

2) Seamstick Velcro hooks to one side, stopping short by about the circumference of the object to be wrapped (in this case, the flaked sail on the boom).

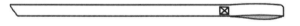

Fig 5-188 A simple tie-down is just a piece of webbing with a loop sewn into one end.

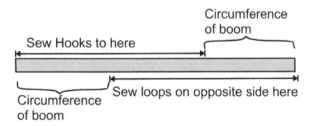

Fig 5-189 A fancier tie-down of webbing and velcro.

3) Seamstick Velcro loops to the other side and the opposite end of the webbing, again stopping short by the circumference of the object.

4) Stitch all around the outside of the Velcro, close to the edges.
The 'blank' area on each end of the webbing provides a place where the Velcro will not be exposed to the sun.

Jacklines and Hoists

Jacklines (or lifelines, as they are called in many countries) and hoists must be constructed to be very strong – especially jacklines since this is your last defense against going overboard!

Use the strong blue heavy nylon webbing 6000 lbs breaking strength and nothing else. It is expensive, but if you take care of them – i.e. rinse them in a bucket of freshwater, and stow them inside when not in use, they should last a lifetime.

Some people use rope or wire – these are strong but roll underfoot and can cause you to slip and fall.

The best attachment method is the webbing itself. At one end, a loop can be stitched and then it can be looped around some strong attachment point like a through-bolted cleat with backing plate. Then the free end can be wrapped around a cleat at the other end of the boat just like you were cleating off a docking line, pulling the webbing taut.

A strong ring or shackle can be stitched into the loops – but make sure they are strong. Try imagining the weight of a 200+ lb man being dragged along overboard in gale conditions and plan for the worst.

To stitch a loop:

Cut a length of strong webbing the required length, plus 7" of overlap for each loop you plan to have. If you don't have a hot knife, singe the ends to prevent unraveling.

Overlap at least 7" for jacklines, and 6" for dinghy hoists. See Fig 5-190. Stick down with seamstick to hold in place.

1) Starting at one end as shown, stitch along the length to the opposite end.

2) Leaving the needle down, raise the foot of the machine and turn the strap 90 degrees. Stitch one single stitch.

3) Again, leaving the needle down, raise the foot and turn 90 degrees.

4) Stitch back along the length to the opposite end.

5) Repeat – there should be at least 10 rows of stitches.

You can also stitch across the ends 3 or 4 rows for good measure.

Make sure the sewing machine is producing perfect tension on the stitches. The stitches along the length should sink in to the webbing and become almost invisible – this helps protect the stitches from the sun.

Fig 5-190 Cross-section of jackline.

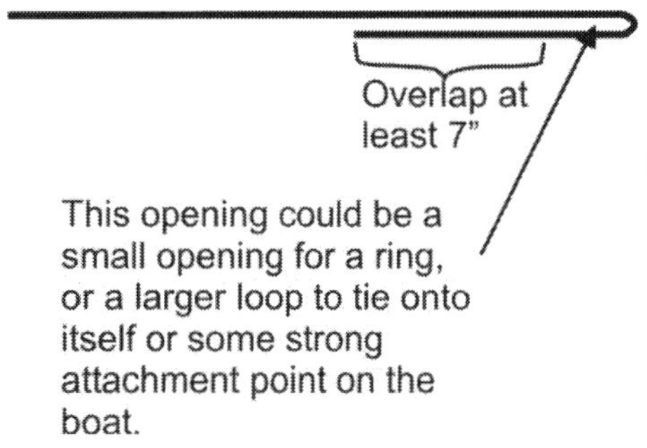

Overlap at least 7"

This opening could be a small opening for a ring, or a larger loop to tie onto itself or some strong attachment point on the boat.

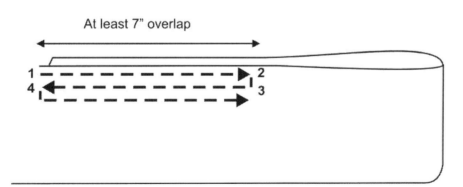

At least 7" overlap

Fig 5-191 Details of how to stitch the loop.
1. Start stitching (don't forget to backstitch)
2. Turn 90 degrees and take one stitch.
3. Turn 90 degrees and stitch to other end.
4. Turn 90 degrees and take one stitch.
   Repeat for at least 10 rows.

Catamaran Trampoline

Design and Purpose:

A catamaran trampoline serves a number of purposes:
It extends the available deck area without adding much weight or water resistance.

It must be
comfortable,
weather resistant,
allow water to penetrate it without tearing it apart.

Materials

The first consideration in choosing the material for a trampoline is the degree of openness required. The more tightly woven the mesh, the more difficult it is for water and air to pass through it; this can affect the seaworthiness of the boat. So, for an offshore boat, open mesh is better. Also, the larger the trampoline, the larger should be the openings in the mesh, so that it presents less resistance to wind and waves.

Trampolines can be made from 3 basic styles of materials – Mesh, Webbing or Netting.

<u>Mesh</u> is more 'solid' and therefore more comfortable to sit and walk on. It does not stretch much, so any 'give' must be taken by the attachment method. Its strength and openness depends on the weave.

Large cats usually use the heavy square hole vinyl coated woven polyester.

Small to medium size nets can be made from Polyester or Dacron knit mesh. It is a moderately open, knitted mesh, but it is not as strong as the square hole mesh. It is also not as UV resistant.

Small catamarans use a tightly woven mesh made of polypropylene treated for UV resistance. It does not let much water through it. It comes in black. Textilene can also work for smaller areas such as on beach cats.

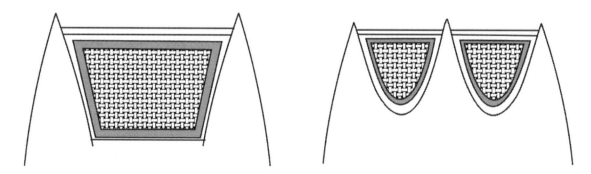

Fig 5-192 Catamaran trampolines can be in one piece or two.
They could have straight sides, or be form-fitted.

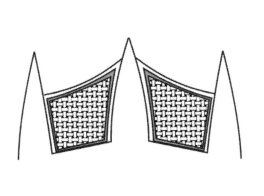 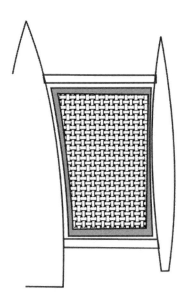

Fig 5-193 In these Trimaran examples you can see the need for some support at the forward edge of the bow trampoline (such as a cable), and the large area of the wing trampoline connecting the main hull to the ama.

<u>Webbing</u> nets are made by basket-weaving 1" or 2" polyester webbing. They are very strong, don't stretch much, and depending on the weave can be more or less resistant to wind and waves. Again, depending on the material used, they can be heavy, and they are not as comfortable as mesh.

Webbing nets can be made by weaving one continuous piece of webbing in a diagonal pattern, resulting in loops all around the edges. The webbing is then stitched at each junction so that it does not shift around. This makes for a very strong trampoline because there is less reliance on stitching. The loops all around the perimeter are attached to the boat by attaching each loop to some attachment point, or by running a rod or batten through the loops and then attaching the batten to the attachment point. This makes for less chafe on the webbing loops.

The webbing net can also be made by basket weaving pieces of webbing, cutting the finished woven product to size, and then reinforcing and finishing the border with vinyl and some attachment method. This is not as strong as the

continuous woven style.

Designing and making a webbing net from scratch is beyond the scope of this book. Because of availability of materials, and specialized coating processes it is probably best left to the professionals. But, if your boat has an existing webbing net and you just want to replace it, then by all means use the existing design. The materials to use are critical - polyester is better in sun than nylon, and definitely use Tenara thread or be prepared for a lot of restitching!

<u>Netting</u> which looks like fishnet, provides far less resistance to water. They are usually pretty stretchy, and not so comfortable, but are very light and depending on the material, can be very strong. An open net trampoline can be difficult for the do-it-yourselfer, however because it will need to be stretched to shape to accommodate the border. That is assuming you can procure the netting material. Also, the professionals often add special vinyl coatings to the product which improves its UV resistance.

Canvas for Cruisers

Attachment methods:

Trampolines can be attached to the boat by a number of different methods, but they all have one thing in common – they must be absolutely strong.

Heavy wall aluminum tracks can be attached to the boat either along a cross beam, or along the deck edge – similar to a mast or boom track. The trampoline will need boltrope or sail slugs sewn in to the border to fit into the track. The sail slugs should be metal – plastic slugs are weaker, and break.

Stainless Steel eye bolts, pad eyes or special lacing knobs can be strongly attached to the hull with backing plates to create a fixed lacing point. In this case, the trampoline will have to be made so the locations of the lacing points match the locations on the boat.

Still other boats rely on cables for otherwise unsupported sides, or integral tracks molded right into the boat.

Whatever the attachment method, consider how the hardware will chafe on the trampoline and plan reinforcing accordingly. Each boat is different in its strong areas, and each boat owner is different in their requirements for comfort and sailing style, whether it is fair weather day sails, offshore cruising, or racing.

<u>Tension and Gap</u> – The trampoline must be tensioned properly in order for it to be safe and comfortable to walk on. The most common method is to use a lacing system, which allows the trampoline to be pulled tight across the expanse that it covers. The problem with lacing is that it creates a gap between the boat and the trampoline. This gap should be 2" – 6" - not so big that your foot goes through it, but a gap is also quite helpful when the waves want to come through.

A solid attachment such as a boltrope eliminates the gap entirely. But it then creates more resistance to the waves coming up from underneath. Wrapping the mesh entirely around a beam, batten or cable also eliminates the gap.

At least one edge of the trampoline needs to have a 'tensioning' method of attachment – this means lacing.

<u>Making a Mesh net:</u>

Mesh nets are definitely within the scope of the home sewer. Large cruising catamarans often use square hole mesh with a reinforced border of fabric (vinyl or acrylic). They are attached to the boat using grommets, line, straps, bolt rope or slides. The attachments can be all around the perimeter, or one of the edges can be left open, perhaps supported by a wire cable and strong pad eyes. Using mesh makes it is easy to cut the trampoline into any custom shape.

You should definitely use Tenara thread for this project. Regular thread, even if sold as 'UV' thread breaks down far too quickly, and the safety of the trampoline will quickly degrade.

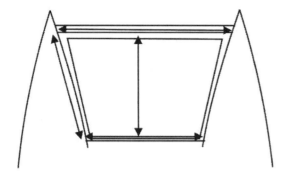

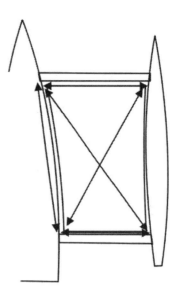

Fig 5-194 By taking several measurements and making up a diagram, the shape of some trampolines can be marked directly onto the mesh. As long as the shape is simple.

Step 1 – Measure up.

If you are fortunate to have an existing trampoline which you are replacing, then use it as a pattern, modifying it as you see fit. Otherwise, you will need to take a few measurements, or make a pattern.

Trampolines must not only fit the area you are covering, they must also take into consideration where the attachment points are, and where the stresses are likely to be. Again, if you have an existing trampoline, have a look at it to see where the wear points were, and plan on reinforcing accordingly.

Decide how big the gap between the boat and the trampoline is going to be.

Measure and make a diagram if the trampoline is a simple shape, otherwise, make a plastic pattern. If the attachment points on the boat are fixed, then note these locations on the pattern or in your measurements so that you can make matching attachment points in the trampoline.

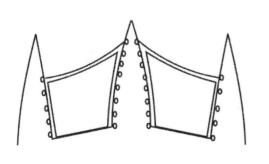

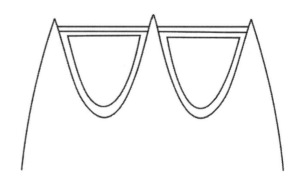

Fig 5-195 But if the design is complicated and curvy, or if there are fixed attachment points, a plastic pattern will be necessary.

365

Canvas for Cruisers

Step 2 – Cut out the mesh.

Join two pieces if necessary. If there is a join, it must be very strong. A good method is to overlap the two edges 3 or 4 holes. Weave a leech line through the holes. Cover the join with a strip of UV resistant vinyl like Stamoid, stitching with at least 4 rows. (See Fig 5-196).

Remember, there is no such thing as too strong when it comes to trampolines.

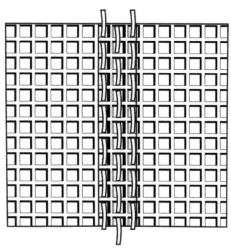

Fig 5-196 Joining trampoline mesh
Match up the mesh's holes
and weave a leech line through
3 or 4 rows. Then stitch a strip of vinyl
to both sides of the trampoline, to
protect the leech line from chafe and sun

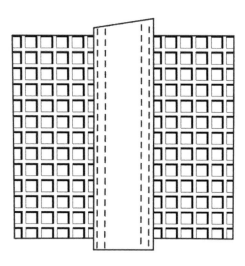

Step 3 – Construct the border.

These instructions are for a grommet or boltrope border. Read on for instructions for a batten or cable border.

For a grommet border, I like to seamstick a row of rope line, or webbing all around the outside edge of the trampoline mesh first. (Fig 5-197)

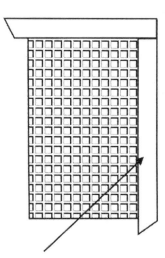

Fig 5-197 Seamstick
½"nylon webbing to the
edge of the mesh.

Cut a strip of strong vinyl such as Shelterite about 4-6" wide (depending on the size of the trampoline). Apply seamstick all around the outside of the strip. Fold it in half lengthwise. Stick it to the trampoline's border. (Fig 5-198)

If the border is curved, you will have to clip the curves to fit, or if it is very curved, cut out two separate pieces of vinyl – one for the top and one for the bottom.

Stitch the border to the trampoline with at least 5 rows of stitching. You can use the heaviest and strongest thread your machine can handle – even if it is not so UV resistant.

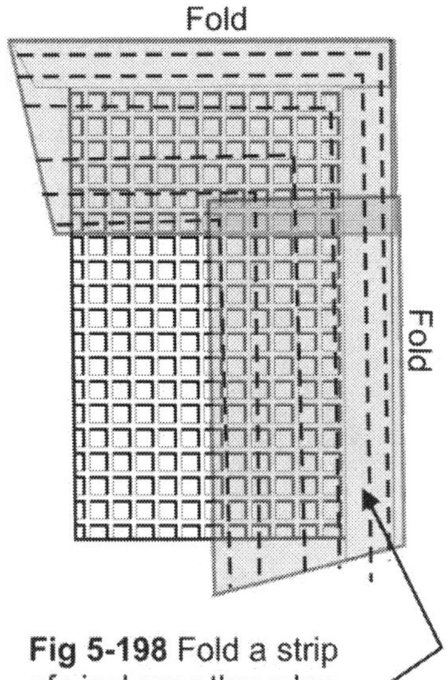

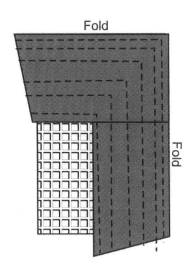

Fig 5-198 Fold a strip of vinyl over the edge to cover the webbing. Stitch at least 5 rows.

Now cut another strip of vinyl 1" wider than the first one. This is the covering for the construction you just did, to strengthen the border and to protect the stitching underneath from the sun. Apply seamstick, fold the strip in half lengthwise as before. Stitch at least 5 rows using Tenara thread if possible. (See Fig 5-199)

Grommets (preferably stainless spur grommets) inserted into a reinforced border are a good choice if the trampoline is curved or other unusual shape. The grommets should be no more than 6" apart to spread the load. Placing the grommets just to the inside of the webbing allows the webbing to take the strain as opposed to the fabric, and supports the lacing line in case the grommet fails. (See Fig 5-200)

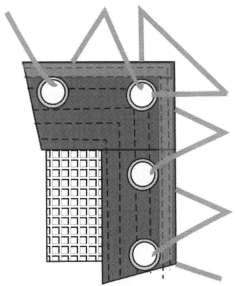

Fig 5-200 Once the grommets are installed, the webbing inside will provide reinforcement to the edge of the trampoline.

If you want to eliminate the gap between the trampoline and the boat, you can install grommets along one reinforced edge as above. Then wrap the mesh around a beam on the boat, and to create tension, lace this edge under the trampoline to a second row of grommets installed in a reinforced row on the underside of the trampoline. (This will only work for a straight side.)

Fig 5-199 Stitch another layer of vinyl over the first layer.

367

Canvas for Cruisers

Boltrope – (Fig 5-201) can be stitched into one or more sides of the trampoline. It is not as strong as lacing, but eliminates the gap between the trampoline and the boat. Make sure the boltrope is big enough for the track, otherwise it can pull out under load. On the side which is to have the boltrope, don't reinforce with webbing or line. Stitch the boltrope to the border with several rows of stitching and backstitch well at the ends.

Battens and Cutouts – (Fig 5-202) Round battens, heavy wall ½" PVC, stainless steel rod or aluminum tubing can be used to stiffen and strengthen a straight border. Make a sleeve to accept the rod, and cutouts exposing the rod. The lacing goes around the rod through the cutouts. This places all of the load onto the stitching, so the stitching has to be very strong.

Cable - Similarly, cable can be sewn or inserted into a hem if there is no other good attachment method. It is rough on fabrics, so the cable should be the vinyl coated type, or run it through a pvc pipe to protect the fabric from chafe.

Webbing loops (Fig 5-203) can also be used. Sew V-shaped loops to the underside of the trampoline so that the webbing is protected from the UV as much as possible. It is a last resort method of attachment and needs to be checked often for UV degradation and chafe.

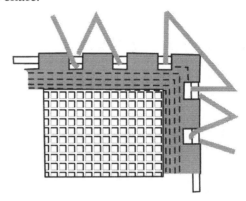

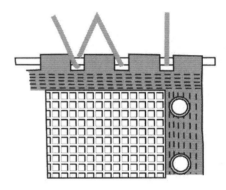

Fig 5-202 A rod inserted along one or more sides of the trampoline, with cutouts to accommodate the lacing lines.

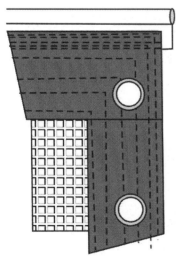

Fig 5-201 Keder or boltrope stitched along one side of the trampoline for an attachment without a gap.

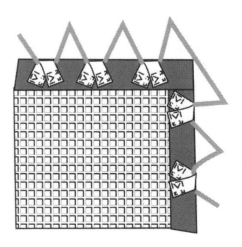

Fig 5-203 Webbing loops sewn onto the underside of the trampoline's border.

Step 4 – Installation - lacing patterns

Installing the trampoline onto the boat with lacing involves the use of a continuous length of line. This should be ¼" braided polyester line with a core with a breaking strength of at least 1000 lbs. Tie off the ends with half hitches so that you can adjust the tension if necessary. Inspect the rope regularly for chafe and weathering.

There are 4 basic styles of lacing:

Perpendicular lacing – Placing the line at a 90 degree angle to the boat reduces chafe, and provides strong tensioning. It is a good method to use for a batten-border trampoline. The lacing points should be less than about 10" apart and the attachment points need to allow the line to pass through twice. Secure the line at each end so it doesn't slide, and you can also knot the line at one or two midpoints along the sides of the trampoline – just in case a line chafes through, the whole side won't unravel.

Zigzag – This is easy to do and easy to tension the trampoline. The line will move a little, and therefore chafe, so you need to inspect the line regularly. At each end, make a perpendicular lacing to prevent movement. The lacing points should be 6" or less apart.

Double lacing – A combination of the above 2 methods, this uses the most line but works if the attachment points on the boat are greater than 10" apart. The grommets can be placed ½ of this distance apart (to distribute the load on the trampoline), and still be supported by the boat's attachment points.

Individual lacings – If the attachment points on the boat are greater than about 10" then you will need to make individual lashings using two or three wraps of line.

Fig 5-204

Slugs

Rod

Perpendicular lines, running from a batten-cutout border to slugs in a track on the boat.

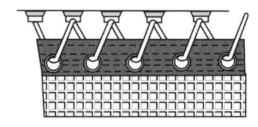

ZigZag lacing on a grommet border onto slugs on the boat.

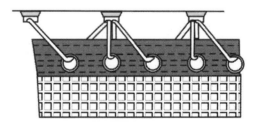

Double lacing, which requires half the number of attachment points on the boat than the number of grommets.

Canvas for Cruisers

Section 6
Cushions

Canvas for Cruisers

Interior vs. exterior cushions

If a boat is reasonably dry inside, there is no reason why regular interior upholstery fabrics, materials and techniques cannot be used to make interior cushions. Interior cushions can be simple or fancy, but above all they should be soft and comfortable.

Because exterior cushions are exposed to the elements – salt water, sun & rain - and are often stepped on, and spilled on, the materials really need to be very durable and cleanable. But they also need to be comfortable – you will know on your first long passage whether you have a winning combination of fabric and foam!

The mattress on your bed is a special case – most important, it needs to be comfortable. If you can afford it and spend enough time on your boat, consider getting a custom made sprung or good quality foam mattress – your back will not hurt anymore and you will get much better sleep. If you're really good, you might even try modifying an existing sprung mattress to fit your V-Berth!

If you are in the habit of coming below all salty from swimming in the ocean, and plop down on the cushions or mattress, it will very quickly get a clammy, continually damp feel. That is because the salt grinds into the fabric, and then absorbs moisture from the air. It will never dry out completely, and will start to go moldy and stink. Rinse yourself off with fresh water and your upholstery job will last much longer.

Design considerations

Size & Shape – Start by considering the space available. Many boats have poor little platforms that you can hardly get your butt on, never mind being able to relax and slouch around in the narrow shelf allocated to seating. If there is a way to make it wider - even an inch makes a difference sometimes – do it. Maybe you can make the backrests out of a little thinner foam and then the seats will seem wider.

Take some measurements of a really comfortable sofa you have sat on. What makes it so comfortable? Probably because it is big and soft but with enough support that you can get in and out of it easily. The backrest is probably high enough that you can rest your head on it while say, watching TV.

How about lying down on the settee? Is it wide enough so that you would be able to sleep there? A curved settee looks really great, but do you need this space for sleeping either at anchor or underway? If so, it needs to be long enough, wide enough and straight.

Some boats have knee-rolls – these are built up areas at the front edge of the seat. They look nice and are comfortable to sit on. But if you are sleeping here, if the knee roll is too high or hard, it will be uncomfortable. And the crack in the seat can hold dirt.

Is there a place on the boat where you can lay athwart ships? This is nice for those medium-to-rolly passages and rolly anchorages. Otherwise you are stuck in a lee cloth, and personally, I hate them.

Speaking of lying down – how about the bunks? If you can design something that can use standard size bed sheets, this will save you work customizing or tucking things in. Of course, the V-Berth cannot be standard, but maybe its width at the wide end can be designed to match king or queen sheets.

Consider where the cushions will be divided. Large cushions for settees look nice, may be nicer to sleep on, and are less work to make. But it gets old very quickly when you have to dive under a large cushion all the time to retrieve things stored below. Maybe you can break them up to match the lockers below.

If you have storage under a bunk or V-Berth, this cushion or mattress might need to be divided too – usually along the centerline, so that nobody has to sleep on the crack.

Canvas for Cruisers

Pattern & Colour

Prints are one way of adding colour and style to a boat's interior. Large prints will make a small space look smaller, and will require extra material for matching the pattern up. Just like wallpapering, the fabric should be cut out so that the pattern is nicely in line for all the cushions.

Small prints suit a small space better and probably won't need to be matched up. Plain colours, of course, are the easiest because they don't require matching – colour and interest can be added with contrasting piping, or a few throw cushions.

Some busy, wavy or striped appear to 'move'! Stand back from it and if it makes you even slightly seasick, choose another pattern.

As far as colour goes, you probably already know that light colours will show dirt quicker than dark and dark colours can make an already dark wood-varnished interior look like Aladdin's cave. It depends on the boat, and your lifestyle.

Cushion styles

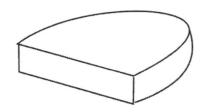

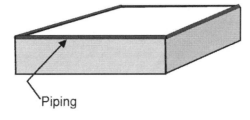

Fig 6-1 Box cushions

Box Cushions are the simplest type to make. They are rectangular like, well, like a box, circular like a cheesecake, or some other kind of combination. See Fig 6-1.

But they all have the same feature – a top, a bottom, and a side band (also called 'boxing') going all around. They can close with a zipper inserted in the side band, or in the cushion's bottom.

Piped Cushions are cushions with a line of piping inserted in the seams. This serves to make the seams stronger by protecting the stitching, and makes it nicer looking. (Fig 6-2).

Bull Nose Cushions have side bands on 3 sides, leaving the front rounded. They have a nice soft look, but may not sit behind the fiddle as nicely as the box cushion.(See Fig 6-3)

Fig 6-2 A box cushion with piping.

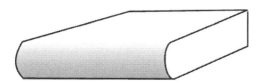

Piping

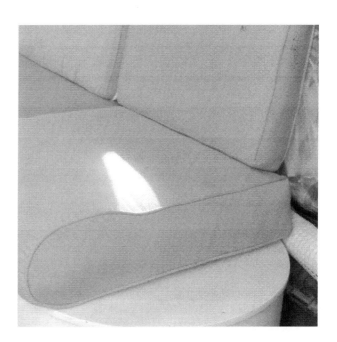

Fig 6-3 A bull nose cushion has a rounded front edge.

You can add additional padding at the front of the seat to make a knee bolster, or at the top edge of the seat back to make a headrest. A seat cushion with a knee bolster may be more difficult to sleep on.

Overstuffed Cushions can be made by piping along the centerline of the cushion's side bands (Fig 6-5), making pleats in the corners or by quilting the surface (or using quilted material). Or you can achieve a soft look by making the cushion covers loose fitting, wrapping the foam in quilting batting and strategically placing buttons in the cushion.

Knee Bolsters & Headrests constructed separately from the cushion itself are more complicated to make but look really professional. Before thinking about doing bolstered cushions, think about whether you will need to sleep on them – they're not all that comfortable.

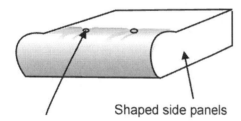

Optional - Buttons to create shape

Fig 6-4 A bull nose cushion can be built up at the front to make a knee bolster and can have buttons to give it additional shape.

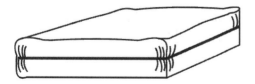

Fig 6-5 Gather the corners into a center band for an overstuffed look

Materials:

Foam
See also Section 1 – Materials.

Interior cushions - Don't use cheap foam. It is a waste of money and will really make you unhappy with your upholstery efforts. 4" thick firm foam is usually used for seats. Foam density is measured in pounds – the lower the number, the softer the foam. Firmer foam will not bottom out when you sit on it and the more expensive foams will last a long time. Wrapping the foam in polyester batting (quilt batting) will add roundness, softness and fill up the corners.

If you are thinking about recovering old foam, check its condition. If it is moldy, it will get your brand new fabric all moldy very quickly.
And if it is worn out unevenly i.e. thinner in places, you will have trouble getting a new cushion cover to fit it properly.
If you are trying to use the old foam as a pattern, consider that it may have shrunk and changed shape. If the fit of the foam is critical to the space it is going into, such as a settee, it is better to make a pattern of the space instead.

Exterior cushions - Closed cell foam is often recommended for exterior cushions. It floats, and does not absorb water. However, after 2 days of sitting on it during a passage, your butt will hurt so much you will be crying.
To soften closed cell foam, you can glue on a 1" layer of ordinary foam over top. The upholstery fabric should then be vinyl to keep the water out of the ordinary foam.
Closed cell foam shrinks – quite a lot. When I buy brand new closed cell foam, I put it in a hot place for as long as I can to force it to shrink before doing the upholstering. You can bake it in the sun but cover it up from the UV. And, make sure you keep the foam nice and flat. If stored curled up or twisted, it will permanently take on that shape.

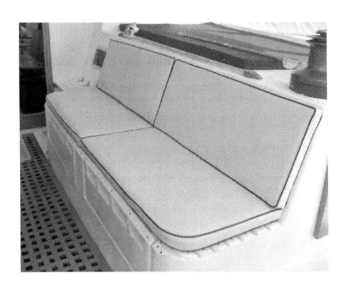

There is another type of foam called open-cell foam. This foam is soft and comfortable, and has a 'crunchy' sound when you sit on it. The water runs right through it so it is great for exteriors. It is also very expensive, and it sinks immediately if it blows overboard. If you want the cushion to float, and to prevent 'bottoming out', glue a layer of ½" closed cell foam under the open cell foam using spray adhesive. Punch holes in the closed cell foam before gluing to the open cell foam so that it can drain.

<u>Fabric</u>
Exterior cushions get wet. The best fabric for exterior cushions is vinyl because it repels water and cleans easily. Sunbrella is also a popular choice but it is harder to keep clean. Many people like vinyl mesh fabrics for cushions but I think it is like sitting on a screen door. For cushion bottoms vinyl mesh works well because it will allow the foam to drain.

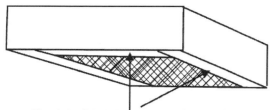

Fig 6-6 Stitch bands onto the cushion's mesh bottom to hide the mesh from view.

If you are using mesh for the bottoms of the cushions, stitch 2" wide borders of the upholstery fabric along the bottom edges that might be seen (See Fig 6-6). This way, in case the sides shift or don't fit perfectly, you won't see the mesh bottom.

Choice of fabric will depend on the look you want to achieve. For a sharp tailored look, a box cushion with or without piping, made with a smooth fabric like acrylic canvas or vinyl looks nice.
Overstuffed, softer cushions for interiors can be made with softer materials such as any upholstery fabric that could be used in a house.

For the long-lasting properties that is desirable on a boat, fabric containing nylon adds strength, acrylics are easy to care for and durable. Cottons and polyesters are not so durable.

For mattresses, if the bed is always made up, think about upholstering the mattress out of some other material than the settees – especially if the upholstery fabric is very expensive.

Trim & Notions

For thread, you can use V92 or V69.

Zippers

Usually, #5 zippers are strong enough. Anything smaller is not really strong enough. Use the continuous style – it comes by the yard, and can be cut to the required length, adding the sliders when the zipper is stitched into the cushion.

If you are cruising on salt water, always use plastic zip heads, even on interior cushions. Metal heads will corrode in a salt environment.
'Locking' zipper heads have a little metal tooth inside that makes it lock. This little tooth can cause problems when it corrodes. I use non-locking on my cushions for this reason.

The zipper can be stitched into one hidden side of a box cushion, or it can be stitched onto the underside surface of the cushion. Both techniques are described here.

If the zipper is being placed in the cushion's bottom, decide first if there will be snaps or other attachments. Position the zipper so it does not interfere with the attachments. See Fig 6-7.

The zipper should go along the length of the cushion bottom, and for easiest stuffing of the foam, right down the center, and as long as possible. The zipper can go on a diagonal grain if the bottom is made of fabric or a tight weave mesh. But not regular mesh – the mesh will stretch out of shape too much.

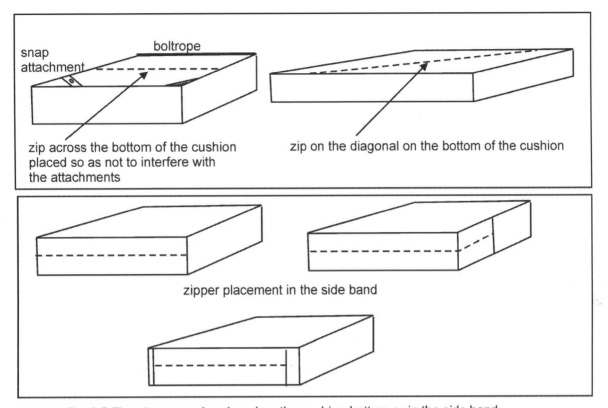

Fig 6-7 The zipper can be placed on the cushion bottom or in the side band.

If the zipper is to be placed in the side band, the ends of the zipper can be stitched right into the seam of the side band. Or it can continue around the corners to make stuffing the cushion easier. It can also be cut off short of the seam as shown in Fig 6-7.

Zippers are the most common, but not the only way to close a cushion. Another possible method of closure is Velcro. It is easy to stitch, and there is no worry about zippers breaking or corroding. Just remember to leave enough fabric in the side band or bottom for overlapping the Velcro.

Piping

If you are making piping, try to get the proper welt cord to put inside it. It is made from hard foam and is great because it does not stretch and holds its shape nicely around corners. A substitute is 1/8" nylon or polyester cord. See Section 2 - Techniques for how to make piping.

Buttons

Buttons are used to give the cushions shape and interest, and are definitely recommended for around an inside curve.

The best and easiest way to make covered buttons is to take a scrap of fabric to an upholstery shop or loft and have them make the buttons up, using their special tooling. Make sure the metal is aluminum and not steel or they will rust and stain the fabric.

Making them yourself is possible but often the home-button covering kits are too weak and the buttons tend to pull apart.

To sew the buttons on to the cushions, place all the completed cushions in position on the boat. Pin a string from one end of the set of cushions to the other so the string is level and looks about the right height. Mark the positions of each of the buttons with a large headed straight pin along the level of the string. Try to place the buttons evenly spaced as much as the cushions allow it.

Cut a long piece of strong waxed twine. Thread it double through a very long needle. Thread it through a backing button, and then pierce through the cushion from directly in back of the marked position to the front, coming out where you made the mark for the button.
Pull the needle through the cushion then thread the needle through the covered button.

Now pierce back through the cushion to near the same place you started.
Thread the needle through the backing button again. Pull the thread so that the foam is compressed to the desired look.
Tie off the thread under the backing button with a secure square knot.

The buttons will have to be removed to wash the cushion covers.

Fastening Methods

How will the cushions stay in place? In most boat interiors, there are fiddles to keep the seat cushions from falling off. In cockpits, there are usually no fiddles, so the cushions will either have to be stowed below if they slide around too much while underway, or they will have to be secured in place.

If the cushions are made of open cell foam, they should be attached securely to the boat. Open cell foam is light, and if the cushion blows overboard it will sink instantly!

Boltrope

One good way to secure seat cushions is using a boltrope on the cushion and a track screwed into the boat. (See Fig 6-8) It makes a very secure attachment but the cushion is not as easily or quickly removed as some of the other methods.

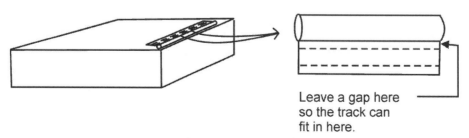

Leave a gap here
so the track can
fit in here.

Fig 6-8 Stitch a length of boltrope to the cushion bottom and attach awning track to the boat for a very secure attachment.

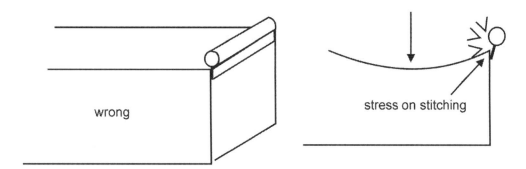

Fig 6-9 Stitching the boltrope to the cushion's top edge will make it prone to ripping when people step or sit on the cushion.

The boltrope can be stitched into the cushion's bottom edge or anywhere in its middle depending on the boat. Unless the cushion foam is very firm, do not stitch the boltrope into the top edge as shown in Fig 6-9. When you step on the cushion, a lot of stress will be on the boltrope and it will rip eventually.

Snaps & Tabs

A reasonably secure attachment is to place snaps on finger-tabs into the cushion's bottom corners or accessible sides. (See Fig 6-10)

These need to be positioned so that when the cushion is lying in place, a person can get their fingers underneath to snap the cushion onto a snap stud screwed into the boat.

One problem with snaps is that when the cushion is not in place, you have a snap stud sticking up out of the seating area. So try to place the snap studs where people won't hurt their feet by stepping on them.

To make a snap attachment:

After the cushion bottom is cut out, decide where the snap attachments will be.

For a corner attachment, install a snap on a piece of webbing. (Or you can install the snap later, if you have a suitable tool, and then you can fit it to the boat).

Place the webbing across the corner (Fig 6-10), with the snap's button side to the inside, and staple it in place. When you assemble the cushion bottom to the side piece, the webbing will be stitched into the seam.

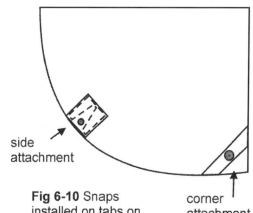

Fig 6-10 Snaps installed on tabs on the cushion's bottom allow you to snap the cushion to the boat.

side attachment

corner attachment

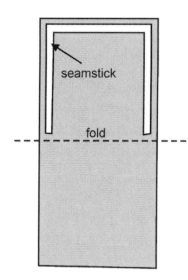

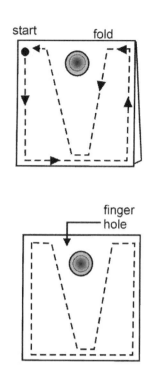

Fig 6-11 To make a fingerhole, cut out a rectangle of vinyl, fold in half and install a snap button. Stitch to the cushion's bottom leaving an opening for your finger.

For an attachment elsewhere along the side, make a folded patch of vinyl as follows, and place it so that the finger hole is accessible.

Cut out the vinyl about 2" x 6" (See Fig 6-11).
Apply seamstick to the *wrong* side.
Fold it over, *wrong* sides together.
Install a snap button at the fold.
Stitch as shown in Fig 6-11 to the cushion's Bottom.

In some instances, vertical tabs on the front of the cushion such as shown in Fig 6-12 can work. But these always seem to come off at the worst times. Turn buttons or lift-the-dots can work, but they stick out and might get in the way.

For vertical tabs, a good secure arrangement is to sew a length of webbing into the cushion's bottom seam as shown in Fig 6-13 and use a cam buckle instead of the snap.

Velcro is a great way to attach cushions and is seen the most for interior cushions. Sew Velcro loops to the backs of the cushion seat backs and stick matching hooks to the bulkhead. This allows fast access to any lockers behind the cushion. Self adhesive Velcro hooks can work, but if they don't stick properly to the surface, or tend to come off with repeated use, try to find VelStick™ brand hooks that are molded onto a stiff plastic backing strip. Screw these into the bulkhead for a good, secure attachment.

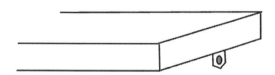

Fig 6-12 A tab sewn to the front of the cushion with a snap to attach to the boat.

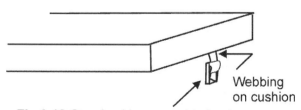

Fig 6-13 Cam buckle secured to boat

Pattern Making

The best choice for pattern making is patterning plastic and a magic marker. You can then transfer the marks directly to the fabric – just as described in the Dodger section.
Brown paper or newspaper is second and third choice.
Be very careful with permanent markers and vinyl – the marker can easily rub off from the plastic pattern onto the *right* side of the vinyl and it will never come off!

If the cushions have vertical sides, patterning consists of placing the pattern material down on the surface and marking the outline of the finished size of the cushion.

Mark where the zipper will go, and the position of snaps, Velcro or other attachments, if any. Also mark front/back, which cushion it is e.g. port seat back, and which side is up.

If the cushion has beveled sides, such as when a cushion is angled up the side of the hull, you will need to make note of this. (See Fig 6-14) The easiest way is to take an L-square sit it flat onto the seat. Measure the distance (at the height of the thickness of the foam) to the hull (shown as (b) in Fig 6-14).

Measure like this every foot or so and mark these measurements on the pattern. This is how much larger you will have to make the cushion's top than the cushion's bottom.

Remember that the backrests will not be the exact height of the settee area's back – you have to subtract the thickness of the seat cushions from the height of the backrest (see Fig 6-15).

Make the pattern for all the cushions all at once, so that you can match the divides in the backrests to match the divides in the seat cushions. That is of course, if you plan to have them match!
If you have storage lockers under the cushions, divide up the cushion pieces so that it will be convenient to get at the locker below.

If the fabric needs to be matched, mark a line across all adjoining cushions. For example, if it is a horizontal stripe or a large print, run a horizontal line across all the cushion backs and the seats. If you are using a vertical stripe, mark a vertical line through the cushion back through to its matching seat. This can help with lining up prints and stripes when you come to cutting out the fabric.

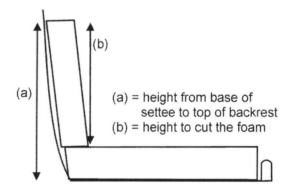

(a) = height from base of settee to top of backrest
(b) = height to cut the foam

Fig 6-15 Cross-section of settee area showing how you need to make the backrest shorter in height to allow for the thickness of the seat foam.

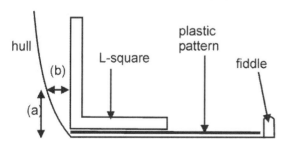

Fig 6-14 Cross-section of settee area showing how you need to take into account the fact that the cushion is beveled.

(a) = thickness of foam
(b) = measurement to mark on your plastic pattern

Cutting the Fabric

Lay out the pieces so that there will be a long thin strip left over for the side pieces and piping. See Fig 6-17.

Sunbrella has a 'nap' – especially on dark colours. It can look different shades depending on whether you are looking at it lengthwise or across the grain. Lay out the cushion tops considering which way they will be seen from. (Fig 6-18)

If using acrylic canvas, cut piping along the length of the fabric, not across its width. It is easier then to bend it around corners. Ideally, piping should be cut along the bias, but this can waste a lot of material, and you may not want to do that.

Vinyl stretches more in one direction than the other. (lengthwise vs. across its width). So consider this when laying out the pieces. Place adjacent seams next to each other across the same grain.

If you are using stripes or have a pattern that needs matching up, use the lines you made on the pattern to help with lining up the adjoining pieces.

If you are using the foam to mark out the fabric Tops and Bottoms, seam allowances are not normally added. This causes the foam to compress inside and fills out the cushion. If you're working with dense closed-cell foam however, you will need to add seam allowances.

If you are using a pattern, mark out the tops & bottoms onto the fabric according to the pattern. Add seam allowances and cut out the pieces. Use the pieces to cut out the foam

eg. A u=shaped settee

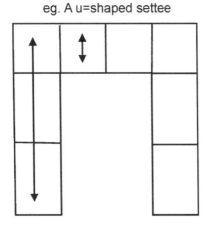

Fig 6-18 Lay out the fabric so that the nap goes in one direction

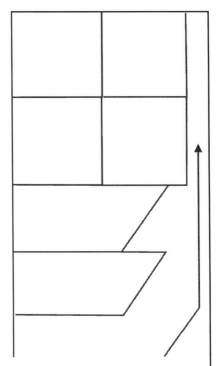

Fig 6-17 When planning the layout of the fabric, leave a long area along the side of the fabric for the side bands

Cutting the Side Bands (Boxing)

Cut the sideband pieces the same width as the thickness of the foam plus ½". When sewn, the boxing will end up being ½" too narrow, creating a nice 'muffin top' look.

If you are putting zippers in one of the side bands, add another 1" to the width of that side piece. This allows you to turn the raw edges under at the zipper teeth.

If you have a beveled side on a 45 degree angle, such as two backrests going into a corner, you can calculate the width of the boxing as follows: (See Fig 6-16).

$a^2+b^2= c^2$
'a' is the thickness of the foam.
'b' is the measurement of the bevel you made when you were doing the pattern.
Remember, if the beveled side is the side to which you will be attaching the zipper, add 1" to its width.

If the angle of the bevel is not 45 degrees, use the foam piece to mark out the boxing.
Either make a paper or plastic pattern of the foam edge, or just stand the foam up on its beveled edge onto the fabric and mark the outline. It's a bit awkward, but it can work.

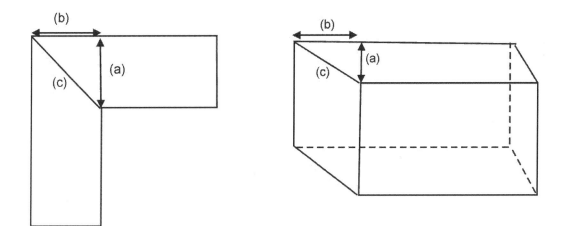

Fig 6-16 Looking at the backrests from above, how do you calculate how wide to make the side panel (c)?

Canvas for Cruisers

Cutting the Foam

Use the fabric pieces to mark the cutting lines for the foam with permanent marker.
This will mean that the foam will be 1" too wide and 1" too long for the fabric (the width of the seam allowances) and will ensure a nice snug fit. Do not do this for closed cell foam, however. It does not compress nearly as much as regular or open cell foam. Cut it only slightly oversize.

For a bull nose cushion or a nipped in cushion, use the original plastic or paper pattern, add ½" all around, and cut out the foam to this size.

When recovering existing foam, use the foam to mark out the fabric. This line dawn on the fabric will be the cutting line, and the stitching line will be ½" to the inside of this line.

To cut the foam, there are special electric foam-cutting tools available which will get a perfect 90 degree angle on the cut.
A substitute is an electric knife, a serrated bread knife or a long-blade razor knife.

If cutting manually, use lots of sawing action and little pressure to get a less wavy edge. It takes concentration and practice to get a nice 90 degree angle.
It helps to mark both sides of the foam. Lay the foam alongside the edge of a table lining up the mark on the underside. Then you can run your knife through the mark on top of the foam and use the table edge to guide the knife from underneath. Place the 'good' foam piece you are cutting on the table and let the scrap hang off the table. Support the scrap end so it's more or less level and not hanging down. If the knife starts to bind and gets hard to cut, it helps to splay out the foam as you're cutting, to take the pressure off the knife.

For beveled sides, use the Top and Bottom fabric pieces to mark the foam. To cut the

beveled side, lay the piece of foam upside down along the edge of a table or other similar surface. Place the line marking the upper surface along the table's edge. Cut along the line from the lower surface, using the table's edge to guide the knife along the line on the upper surface.
This beveled edge on the foam can now be used to measure or pattern the boxing.

Construction

Piped Box Cushion

Step 1 – Cut out the Top Panel sometimes called a top plate – to a measured size, or to the size of the foam or to a pattern. Refer to the above information on cutting the foam and cutting the fabric.

If using a plastic pattern, lay the pattern face down on the *wrong* side of the fabric.
Use a dull pencil to trace dashed lines along the pattern's lines – because you have laid the plastic face down, the magic marker from the plastic will transfer onto the fabric. (See Fig 6-19).

If the fabric is dark, cut off the excess plastic around the pattern close to the pattern marks. Use a white pencil to reach under the plastic and make the marks on the fabric.

This dashed line will be the stitching line. Remove the plastic.

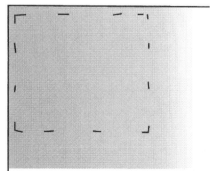

Fig 6-19 Lay the pattern face down on the *wrong* side of the fabric and mark the outline as a series of dashes

If there is a bevel on the cushion as described in Fig 6-14, adjust the outline marks according to the measurements you made and marked on the pattern.

Join the dashed lines and even them out with a yardstick (or flexible batten if the line is curved). (Fig 6-20)

Mark another line ½" outside of this line – this will be the cutting line. (Fig 6-21)
Cut out.

Lay the Top *right* side down, onto the fabric you are using for the Bottoms.
Mark the outline around the outside of the Top. (Fig 6-22)
Make matching hatch marks all around on the Top and Bottom to allow for matching when you go to sew the side pieces on. This way the cushion cover won't 'twist'.

If the cushion has a bevel, then just use the pattern as the Bottom without adjusting the measurement.

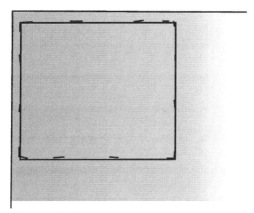

Fig 6-20 Even out the marks using a straight edge and mark - this is the stitching line.

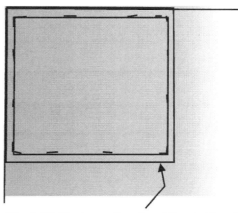

Fig 6-21 Mark another line ½" outside of the line you just made - this is the cutting line.

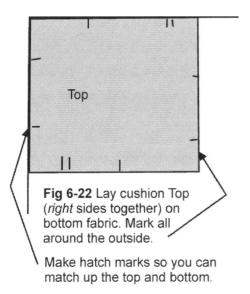

Fig 6-22 Lay cushion Top (*right* sides together) on bottom fabric. Mark all around the outside.

Make hatch marks so you can match up the top and bottom.

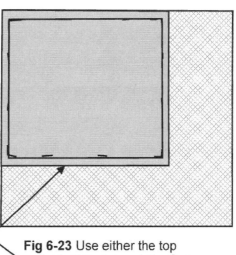

Fig 6-23 Use either the top or the bottom to mark the foam.

387

Step 3 – Use the Top or Bottom fabric piece to mark the foam, and cut it out. (Fig 6-23)

Step 4 – Cut out the side bands.

Cut out the side bands ½" wider than the thickness of the foam. Eg. For 3" thick foam, cut the side bands 3 ½" wide. This will make them a little too small, and will compress the foam, making a nicer, tight fit.

If the cushion has a beveled side, cut that band ½" wider than the actual measurement of the foam on that beveled side. (See notes above for measuring for beveled sides)

If you are putting a zipper in one of the side bands, cut this band 1" wider than the others. And cut it whatever the finished length is, multiplied by 1.0125. This is because the side band shrinks in length when the zipper is sewn in. It won't make much difference in a small cushion, but can matter in a large one. Then cut this band in half along its length.

Fig 6-24 Staple piping to *right* side with raw edges even.

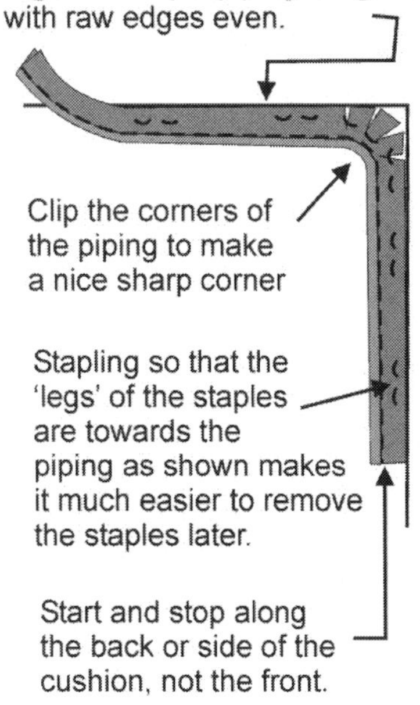

Clip the corners of the piping to make a nice sharp corner

Stapling so that the 'legs' of the staples are towards the piping as shown makes it much easier to remove the staples later.

Start and stop along the back or side of the cushion, not the front.

Step 5 – Cut out the fabric strips and assemble the piping (see Section 2 – Piping).

If the cushion is to have two rows of piping – on the Top and on the Bottom – it is often easier to assemble the side bands – i.e. zipper and stitching into one long length - and then staple and stitch the piping to the cushion's side band. Section 2 – Piping – parallel rows and read ahead to zipper installation.

Others prefer to stitch the piping to the Top and to the Bottom first, and then attach the side band.

Staple the piping to the *right* side of the tops, with the piping to the inside of the cushion, and the raw edges even. (See Fig 6-24)

Start and stop at the back or side of the cushion, not the front and try to arrange things so that any piping join is not going to be visible.

Optional – stitch the piping to the top piece. Then when you go to sew on the side band, you will be able to see your first row of stitching and can stitch just slightly inside of this stitching line. This will ensure the piping is stitched nice and tight into the seam and you won't see two rows of stitches.

Set aside the Top for now.

Step 6 – Do the construction on the cushion bottom – zippers, if this is where you are putting them. See Section 2 – Zippers.

Construct the snaps or tabs (see Cushion Attachments earlier in this section), or boltropes

Step 7 – If the zipper is to be placed in the cushion's side band, do this now.

Consider whether you want the zipper to disappear into the corner of the cushion, make the zipper extend around the corners, or make the zipper a little too short, so that the side band curves around the corner to meet the zipper band (Refer back to Fig 6-7)

Either way is fine, but the zipper disappearing into the cushion's corner makes things unnecessarily complicated.

Extending the zipper around the corners makes it much easier to stuff the cushion and should be used if you are making a very large cushion.

Cut a length of continuous #5 zipper a couple of inches longer than required.

There are a couple of ways to install a zipper into a cushion's side band. Here's one way:

Zipper with Hidden Teeth:

Stitch the 2 halves of the side band *right* sides together, ½" from the raw edge (Fig 6-29).

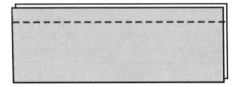

Fig 6-29 Stitch right sides together

Open out the band, and open out the seam allowance as shown in Fig 6-30.

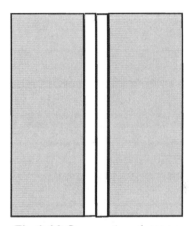

Fig 6-30 Open out and press seam allowance flat

Place the closed zipper on the seam allowance, lining up the teeth along the stitched fold as shown in Fig 6-31.

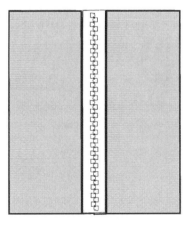

Fig 6-31 Lay zip along seam line

Stitch the zipper tape down along both sides (Fig 6-32).

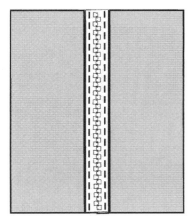

Fig 6-32 Stitch

Using a seam ripper, carefully open up the seam that joins the 2 halves of the band, exposing the zipper teeth

Put on the zipper head. Position it halfway along the zipper, leaving the zipper teeth closed both in front and behind the head.

Another way to install the zipper:

<u>Zipper with Teeth Exposed:</u>

Apply seamstick to the *wrong* side of the raw edges where the zipper is to go. (See Fig 6-33)

Turn the raw edges of the band under ½" and stick down. (See Fig 6-34).

Apply ¼" seamstick to both tapes of the zipper.

Stick and stitch the zipper to the folded edge of the fabric (Fig 6-35), leaving the teeth exposed. (see also Section 2 - Zippers)

Fig 6-33 Apply seamstick to the raw edges

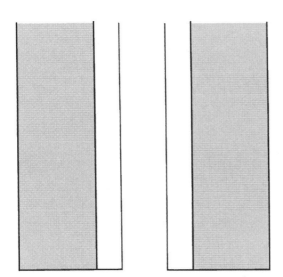

Fig 6-34 Turn the raw edges under ½"

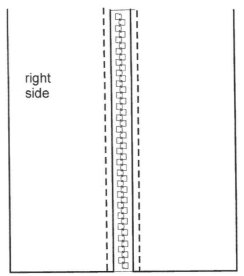

right side

Fig 6-35 Stick the folded edges to the zipper tape, leaving the teeth exposed.

Step 8 – Stitch the side band to the Top.

Stitch the side band to the Top freehand (no staples or pins) if possible, holding the side band on the bottom. Holding the fabric this way as you sew makes the Top tend to 'pop out' nicely because the side panel will get stretched slightly by the feed dogs on the sewing machine. Around the corners, the side piece should be a little loose.

Use staples to help hold the pieces together if you need to but this means the sewing machine's feed dogs cannot help you with the tensioning as above.

Just like in the Drop Cover, as you get close to stitching the band on, it will become apparent where the side seam needs to be. Stop stitching the band to the Top, stitch and topstitch the side seam of the band and then finish stitching the band to the Top.

Put the joins for the side bands on an unseen side as shown in Fig 6-36. Topstitch the join.

Step 9 – Transfer the hatch marks from the Top to the adjacent side, then directly across to the opposite side of the side band. (See Fig 6-37).

Step 10 – Place the Bottom onto the side band, *right* sides together. Match up the Bottom's hatch marks to the side band's hatch marks.

Staple the Bottom to the side band. At the corners, try to duplicate the radius of the curve so that it is the same as the Top. Otherwise, the Top's corners will be rounded due to the piping and the Bottom's corners will be sharp and square if it has no piping.

Stitch.

Step 11 – Turn the cushion cover *right* side out.

Stuff the foam into the cushion cover. Position both the top and bottom seam allowances so that they go toward the side band (if using Sunbrella or other fabric), or allow the seam allowance to go its own preferred way (if using vinyl)

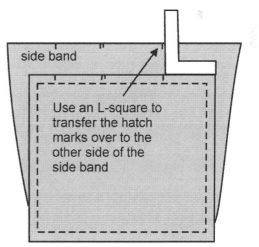

Fig 6-37 Transfer the hatch marks over to the other side of the cushion band.

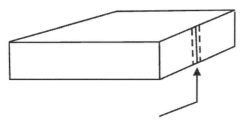

Fig 6-36 Join on backside of cuhion

Bull Nose Cushion

Cut out the foam 1" wider and longer than needed to fill the space. Usually the foam is soft enough so that you don't need to carve off the sharp forward edges – especially if you are wrapping the foam in batting. But if you think the edges might show, then shave off the forward edges.

Mark the outline of the cushion onto the fabric according to the pattern.

If you are using different fabric for the bottoms – measure the length of the foam, plus the front edge the thickness of the foam plus at least 2" so the fabric can disappear under the cushion. Fig 6-38 measure A to B.
Add 1/2" for seam allowance.

If you are not using different material for the bottoms, just cut one piece of fabric long enough to go along the Top, over the Front and along the Bottom (see Fig 6-38 measure A to C.

Cut out the back band. Depending on whether you are putting the zipper in the back band or in the bottom, you will cut out the back band in one piece or split it into two halves. See instructions above in the Piped Box Cushion.

Measure for the side bands – length and thickness of foam. Add 1/2" to these measurements. (Once sewn using a ½" seam allowance, this will make the side bands end up ½" too small, ensuring a tight fit). Cut out the side bands, and round the forward edges.

If you are using some other fabric for the bottoms, stitch the top piece to the bottom piece, *right* sides together.
Fold the seam allowance over toward the 'good' fabric side and topstitch.
If the zipper is going in the cushion's bottom, the attachment seam "B" as shown in Fig 6-38 is a good place to insert the zipper.

You will need hatch marks like in the box cushion, so that when you sew on the sides, the cushion won't 'twist'. So, after cutting out the main cushion piece, fold it in half, putting the crease along the front of the bull-nose, and match up the backs. See Fig 6-39. Mark some hatch marks.

Using the instructions already described above:

Cut out and prepare piping if you are using it.

Staple the piping to the side bands. Depending on the boat and your preference, the piping can go all the way around the side band, or just along the top edge which can be seen ("A" to "B" in Fig 6-38).

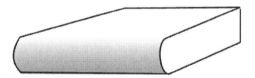

Fig 6-38 Special considerations for the bull nose cushion.

Cross section of bullnose cushion foam. The front edge will compress into a rounded shape because of the way you make the side band.

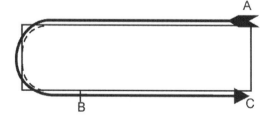

If you are making the bottoms of the cushion out of some less expensive fabric, measure your 'good' fabric from "A" to "B", and your bottom fabric from "B" to "C".
If you are making the cushion out of all one fabric, measure from "A" to "C". Don't forget to add seam allowances.

Install the zipper in the back band, or insert the zipper into the cushion's bottom.

Stitch the back band to the cushion piece at the top and bottom, *right* sides together (Fig 6-40).

Staple the side bands to the cushion piece, starting at the Top. When you have stapled the Top side to the side piece, transfer the hatch marks from the top side to the side band, and over to the opposite side of the side band, so that you can match up to the hatch marks on the cushion bottom (Fig 6-41).
Staple the band along the Bottom of the cushion, matching up the hatch marks.

Now staple around the rounded nose careful not to make any pleats, and along the back.

Stitch.

Turn the cushion *right* side out and stuff in the foam.

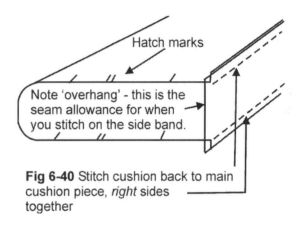

Fig 6-40 Stitch cushion back to main cushion piece, *right* sides together

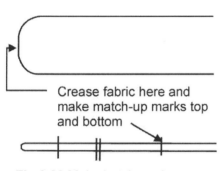

Fig 6-39 Make hatch marks so you can match up the side bands to the top/bottom.

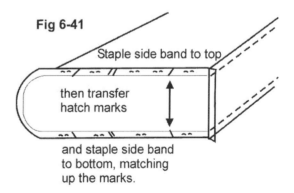

Fig 6-41

393

Canvas for Cruisers

Built-up Cushion

A bolstered cushion can be accomplished by taking the bull nose cushion above, and building up the seat at the area under your knees, (or the headrest area in the case of a seat back).

Use an extra piece of foam 1-2" thick and 4-6" wide, glued onto the main piece (See Fig 6-42). The sharp edges can be carved off with knife or scissors if your foam is dense and you think the sharp edge will show through the fabric. Wrapping the cushion in batting can help hide these edges.

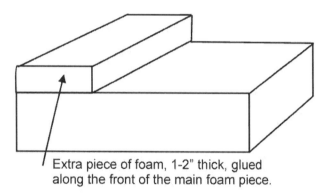

Extra piece of foam, 1-2" thick, glued along the front of the main foam piece.

Fig 6-42 To make a cushion with a built-up front edge, glue on an extra piece of foam.

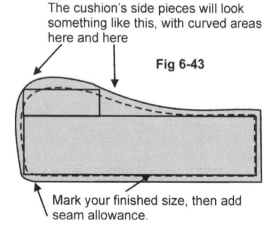

The cushion's side pieces will look something like this, with curved areas here and here

Fig 6-43

Mark your finished size, then add seam allowance.

Make a pattern for the side bands. The easiest way is to stand the cushion up on its side on a piece of plastic pattern material and trace around the side contour. Add ¼" along the long sides, and along the top and bottom edges. (Once you have stitched with a ½" seam allowance, this will ensure a tight fit at the corners.) Round the corners. Cut out the side pieces. (See Fig 6-43).

After the side pieces are cut out, glue on some polyester batting to the foam to make the cushion look softer and more rounded.
Because the top of the cushion has a bolster, some length will have to be added to the cushion's main piece so that it can curve around the headrest or knee bolster (See Fig 6-44).

The construction is the same as the bull-nose cushion.

Buttons can be sewn to the cushion just behind the edge of the bolster to add shape and make the fabric curve nicely around the bolster.

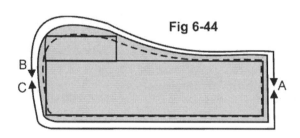

Fig 6-44

The top of the cushion (A to B) is longer than the bottom (A to C) because it has to curve around the bolster.

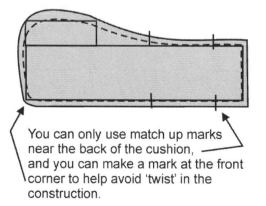

You can only use match up marks near the back of the cushion, and you can make a mark at the front corner to help avoid 'twist' in the construction.

Bolstered Cushion:

Cushions with separate bolsters consists of two separate compartments for 2 separate pieces of foam. It differs from the built-up cushion in that there is a distinct 'crack' between the two pieces of cushion foam – this crack gives the cushion a distinct look and the cover fits nice and tight. But the crack holds dirt, and often the tension is so great where the divider piece pulls on the crack that the fabric actually rips and comes undone there. Stitching this crack with the longest possible stitch can help since there are less perforations to weaken the fabric. The cover cannot be taken off for laundering, so these covers are almost always made from vinyl.

The pieces can be mounted on a piece of board, or with no base. It looks very professional.

Some boat seats have very imaginative designs with curvy bolsters, multicolours and piping. If you are recovering one of these, take the cushion cover off and have a good look at how it was constructed.

If the foam is in bad shape and needs to be replaced, cut the foam so that hangs over all edges of the backer board by ½". If the board is not already marked, mark a line where the two pieces of foam meet.

These instructions for a simple straight-line bolster. If the cushion you are doing is imaginative and complicated place the foam (new foam probably) and make a plastic pattern, Remember that because the foam is cut ½" too big you don't need to add seam allowances to the fabric <u>except</u> for the seam where the two thicknesses of foam join together. Label all the pieces and make match-up marks.

<u>If there is a backer board:</u>

Step 1 – Cut out the fabric for the main piece. The fabric will have to wrap around underneath the backer board, so add a couple of inches at each end. (See Fig 6-46).

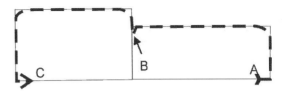

Fig 6-46 Measure the main piece from point 'A' underneath where it wraps around the backer board, to 'B' where the seam will be for the bolster (allowing 1" for seam allowance) then around to point 'C' where it wraps around the backer board.

Add 1" at the spot marked (B) for a seam allowance. See Fig 6-47 for the way the piece of fabric should look.

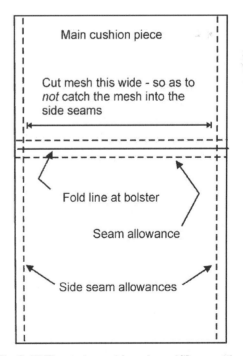

Fig 6-47 The main cushion piece. When cutting out the mesh divider, cut it only as wide as this piece minus the seam allowances.

Use the foam pieces to mark out the side bands. Round the corners where the corners of the foam will be.

Sometimes, depending on how hard you reef down on the mesh when stuffing the cushion, a wrinkle can form in the side band. Normally this wouldn't be a problem since the adjoining cushions usually cover this. But if yours doesn't adjoin or of you don't want any kind of wrinkle, you can cut a little dent right where the crack will be. Not much – ½" or less – in a smooth curve.

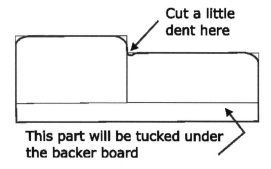

Step 2 – Cut out a piece of mesh vinyl fabric for the divider.

The width of the vinyl mesh is the width of the cushion's top piece <u>minus</u> seam allowances.

The depth of the vinyl mesh is the depth of the thinner foam piece plus about 2".

On the mesh piece, mark a line the depth of the thinner foam plus 1".

Eg if your thinner seat foam is 4", mark a line 5" away from the raw edge.

(This line will be used to tension the mesh evenly onto the backer board.)

Step 3 – Fold the main piece of fabric *right* sides together, along the line of the bolster (B). Stitch the mesh to the *wrong* side of the shorter section of the folded fabric as shown in Fig 6-48.

Some people like to see piping in the crack. If this is the case then cut the fabric instead of folding and stitch in the piping.

(There now will be twice as much space for dirt to collect)

And, of course if you are using different colours of fabric then you need to cut this panel in two sections.

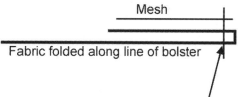

Fig 6-48 Fold the fabric *right* sides together along the bolster line, and stitch mesh to fabric allowing ½" seam allowance

Open out the fabric. Install piping onto each side of the panel if you are using it.

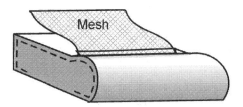

Fig 6-49 Stitch side bands on

Step 4 – Stitch on the side panels being careful not to catch in the mesh piece (See Fig 6-49). Match where the crack meets the little dent.

Turn the work *right* side out.

Step 5 – Place the thinner foam on the backboard. Place the fabric cover on top. Put in a couple of staples at the back corners and a couple in between just to hold things in place for now.

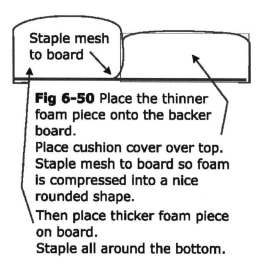

Fig 6-50 Place the thinner foam piece onto the backer board.
Place cushion cover over top.
Staple mesh to board so foam is compressed into a nice rounded shape.
Then place thicker foam piece on board.
Staple all around the bottom.

Staple the mesh to the backer board along the line marked on the backer board. Match the line you made on the mesh piece which will compress the foam by about ½". Strive for even tension and a nice rounded shape (See Fig 6-50).

Now place the thicker piece of the foam down on the backer board, stuff it into the fabric cover.

Flip the piece over and staple the cover down all around onto the backer board so it makes the cushion into a nice shape.
Make sure the corners are at the corners of the backer board and put 3 or 4 staples, starting at the center - in each side – first do the front, then the back. Then one side and the other. Flip it over and see if you're happy with how it looks as you go – especially where the crack meets the side panel.

Then do the corners – folding over and cutting off excess where necessary. When you're happy with the tension, install all staples about an inch apart, evenly and in a straight row, about an inch or whatever makes sense inside of the edge of the backer board. Cut off the excess fabric if you like, to neaten things up.

If the bolstered cushion is to have no wooden base, the construction is basically the same. See Fig 6-51.

Measure and cut out the main piece like Fig 6-46, except just add ½" seam allowance at each end instead of the 2" wrap-around allowance.

Cut out and construct the mesh insert.

Cut out a separate piece of cushion bottom material to take the place of the backer board – add ½" seam allowances.

In this bottom piece, put in 2 zippers to receive the 2 foam pieces.
Instead of stapling the mesh partition to the backer board, stitch the partition to the cushion's bottom panel.

The cushion will become a 2-part cushion with a zipper in each section to stuff in the foam.

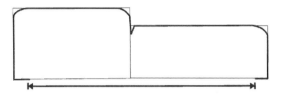

Fig 6-51 A bolstered cushion with no backer board will need a piece of bottom fabric cut to the length shown above.

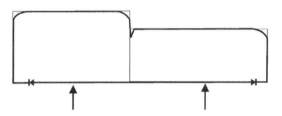

Insert a zipper the width of the cushion bottom - one for each compartment.

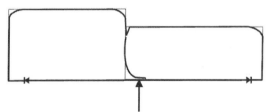

Stitch the partition to the cushion bottom

Canvas for Cruisers

'Nipped In' Cushion

This makes a nice throw cushion. It is basically just 2 squares of fabric, joined together by a piped seam (Fig 6-52).

For the following instructions, assume the foam to be 2" thick.

Step1 – Cut out 2 squares of fabric, the finished size of the cushion, plus 1 ½" all around as shown in Fig 6-53.

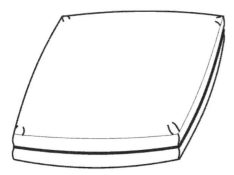

Fig 6-52 A Nipped-In cushion has folded in corners and a piped seam

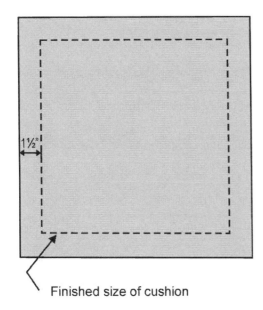

Fig 6-53 Cut out two pieces of fabric the desired size of the cushion plus 1 ½"all around.

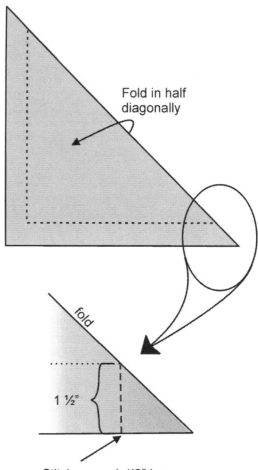

Fold in half diagonally

Stitch seam 1 1'2" long

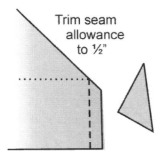

Trim seam allowance to ½"

Fig 6-54 Nipping In the corners.

Step 2 – With *right* sides together, fold each corner along a 45 degree angle, matching the raw edges. See Fig 6-54. At each corner, stitch a seam 1 1/2" long, perpendicular to the raw edges.

Trim off the corner to a ½" seam allowance. Open it out flat, fold it diagonal the other way and do the other 2 corners the same way. Prepare the second fabric square the same way.

Step 3- Measure and make enough piping (contrasting colour looks nice) to go around the perimeter. Staple the piping all around one of the cushion pieces. (see Section 2 – Piping for how to do this, and how to make joins)

Step 4 – Install a length of zipper in one side as follows:

Cut a length of #5 continuous zipper a couple of inches shorter than the length of a finished side.

Stitch one side of the zipper tape to one cushion side, and the other to the cushion piece with the piping – so that the teeth are hidden (see Section 2 - Zippers). See Fig 6-55.

Put on the head, and zip up the zipper, leaving it open a couple of inches.

Step 5 – With *right* sides together, stitch around the other 3 sides and around all 4 corners.

Step 6 – Unzip the zipper all the way. Turn the cushion *right* side out and stuff in the foam.

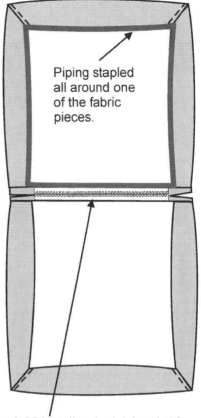

Piping stapled all around one of the fabric pieces.

Fig 6-55 Install a zip, joining the 2 panels along one side. The zipper teeth should be hidden in the seam.

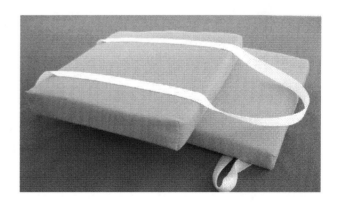

Canvas for Cruisers

Cushion Covers

Often called 'crew covers', these are used to protect and keep the nice mega yacht cushion fabric clean from the partying and debauchery of the crew. When the owners of the yacht arrive, the crew covers come off.

They work equally well for the cruising boat. But be warned – crew covers take longer to whip off the cushions when company arrives unexpectedly than the old towel you usually use!

You can use any durable, absorbent, cleanable or comfortable fabric – even vinyl can be used.

Basic rectangular cushion cover:

This cover consists of 3 pieces – 2 side pieces and one piece running along the back, top, and front. See Fig 6-56.

Step 1 – Cut 2 side panels – allow at least ½" seam allowance and an extra 3" or so to tuck underneath the cushion. (Fig 6-57)

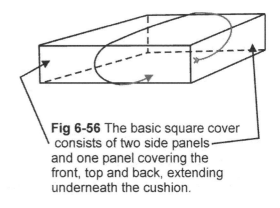

Fig 6-56 The basic square cover consists of two side panels and one panel covering the front, top and back, extending underneath the cushion.

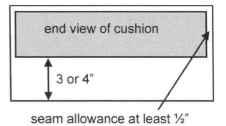

end view of cushion

3 or 4"

seam allowance at least ½"

Fig 6-57 The side piece is cut the size of the side panel of the cushion. Add ½"seam allowance and 3 or 4" to the bottom to allow it to be tucked under the cushion.

Step 2 – Cut one panel to cover the top, front and back, and add enough to tuck 3" or so underneath the cushion. See Fig 6-58.

Step 3 – Drape the large fabric piece over the cushion. Place it *right* side down and center it so there is an equal amount on each side. (Fig 6-59)

Place one side panel onto the side of the cushion *right* sides together. See Fig 6-59.

Holding the fabric pieces in place, start stapling the side piece to the main piece all along the top and all around the sides of the side panel. It will look all lumpy, but just get it as close a fit as you can for now.

At the corners, make little gathers and let the side panel's corners go a little rounded (See Fig 6-60).

Staple on the other side panel the same way.

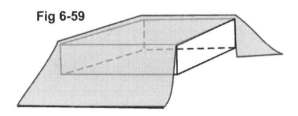

Fig 6-59

Drape the main piece over the cushion

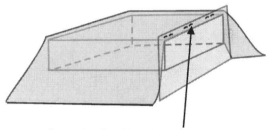

Start stapling the side piece along the top, *right* sides together, and continue along the front and back, but not underneath.

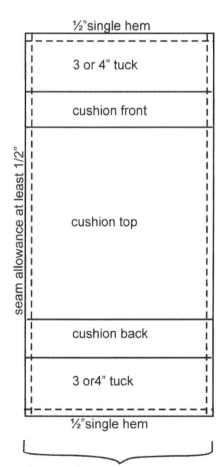

Fig 6-58 Cut out the main piece a little wider than necessary to allow for trimming and fitting.

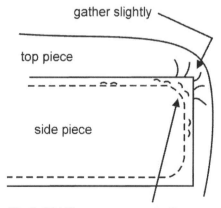

Fig 6-60 When you come to the corners gather the top piece into the corner if necessary. Allow the corner to go a bit rounded - no need to keep it perfectly square.

401

Canvas for Cruisers

On the underside of the cushion, miter the forward-facing corners as shown in Fig 6-61 and staple in place. Mitering the corners just means you make a seam at a 45 degree angle. (Fig 6-61)
It also helps to mark where the exact corner is with a pencil, so you can match it up when you go to sew.

Step 4 – Take off the stapled cover (gently!). Even out the stapling by removing and re-stapling where necessary, and straighten up the stitching lines.

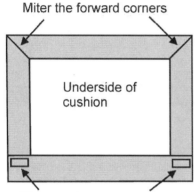

Fig 6-61
Miter the forward corners

Underside of cushion

Velcro to be sewn here on the rear flap.

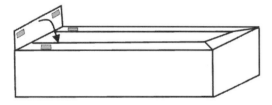

Fib 6-62 Flap with velcro closures

Step 5 – Stitch.

Stitch along where you have stapled.
Remove the staples.
Trim seam allowance to ½". If the raw edges are not hot-knifed, finish the raw edges by zig-zagging or serging.
Fold the seam allowance over to one side and topstitch.

Step 6 – Turn all the raw hem edges (which are on the underside of the cushion) under ½" and ½" again if the fabric will fray.

Step 7 – Leave the back end as a 'flap' and close it with Velcro. See Fig 6-62.

The cushion's front slips in under the miters then you can close it snug with the Velcro flap.

<u>Free-form sides:</u>

Some cushions have side panels that are 'raised' at the forward edge for a bolster effect. Cover these the same way as the basic rectangle.
Cut the side panel in a rectangular shape wide enough to cover the widest part of the side panel. Staple the side panel to the large top panel all around following the free-form shape (Fig 6-63).

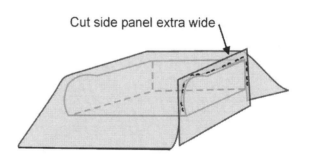

Cut side panel extra wide

Fig 6-63 Staple the side panel to the top panel following the free-form shape.

Alternate way:

Sit the cushion's side down onto the fabric and trace all round the contour of the side panel onto the fabric. (Fig 6-64).

Remove the cushion from the cover fabric. Add ½" seam allowance and 3" or so wrap-around for underneath the cushion. This can make the stapling part much easier.

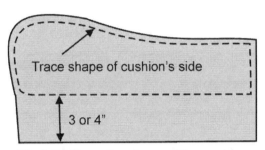

Fig 6-64 Trace the shape of the cushion onto the fabric. Add seam allowances and allowance for tucking in underneath.

Seat cushion – free form asymmetrical shape:

Sometimes cushions have curved sides that don't really work very well with the method described above.

In this case, extend one of the side panels right around the corner to where the cushion starts to curve. See Fig 6-65.

Because the cushion is not symmetrical, you will have to staple the fabric *wrong* sides together.

With *wrong* side down, drape the main piece of fabric over the cushion.
Staple the side pieces on, *wrong* sides together.
Cut off the excess fabric if necessary, on the curve.
Then spread apart the stapled seams and put lots of pencil hatch marks on the inside (*wrong* side) of the fabric – especially at the curve.
It may help to number a couple of the hatch marks to help in matching them up later.
Also make some marks to guide you where the seam line is to be.
Miter the corners where possible, and decide where the closing flap is going to be as shown in Fig 6-66.

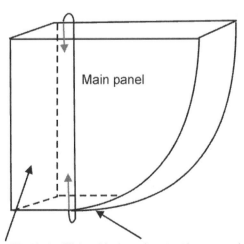

Fig 6-65 This side band extends around the corner to the point where the curve of the cushion starts.

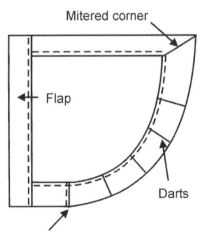

Fig 6-66 Details of cushion bottom

Take the stapled cover off the cushion. Remove all the staples.

Reassemble the pieces *right* sides together, lining up the hatch marks and marked seam line, and re-staple the pieces together.

Stitch.

Try on the cover and make any adjustments. Trim off seam allowances to ½". Finish the raw edges if necessary.
Topstitch.

Finish the raw edge at the bottom by turning under ½". Make darts or stitch in shock cord at the curve to keep it a tight fit. Stitch Velcro on to close the flap.

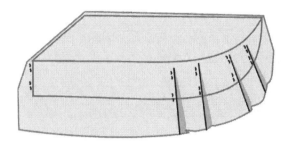

Fig 6-67 Drape fabric over cushion, *wrong* side down. Staple in the corners, and the pleats on the curve.

Alternate way:

This style is just like having a fitted sheet on a bed.

Simply cut the fabric roughly to size – large enough to cover the top, sides and 3 or 4" under the cushion.

Drape the fabric over the cushion *wrong* side down.

Staple in the corners, and staple pleats in at the curved side.

Remove the fabric, even out the stapled seams and mark the seam lines and pleats.

Remove all the staples, and re-staple *right* sides together.

Stitch, trim the seam allowance to ½" and finish the raw edges if necessary.
On the bottom edge, make a casing by turning the raw edge under and insert a shock cord or leech line all around. If using a leech line, add a barrel lock to allow you to tension the line.

Seat Back

A cover for a seat back is done basically the same way as a seat cover, except that the way the cover is attached might have to be changed slightly to make it more secure.

If the seat's back is wood, you can Velcro the cover directly to the seat's wooden back as shown in Fig 6-68.

Or an overlapping strip of Velcro can be installed across the back to hold it securely on (Fig 6-69).

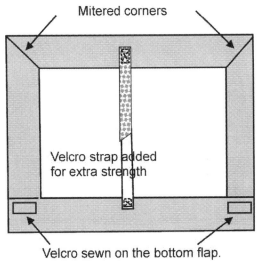

Mitered corners

Velcro strap added
for extra strength

Velcro sewn on the bottom flap.

Fig 6-69 A velcro strap across the back holds the cover on more securely.

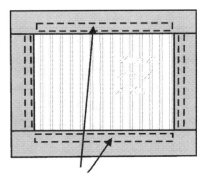

Fig 6-68 Velcro cover
to wooden backer board

Canvas for Cruisers

Instead of mitering the corners, the corner seams can be stitched to whatever thickness the seat back is, leaving the ends open (see Fig 6-70.)

Sew on small squares of 1" Velcro on the corners.
This will allow the sides to be folded in, then the top and bottom to be folded over and held closed with the Velcro.

Seat Back – Inside curve

This cover is made using the same idea as the Basic Rectangular Cushion Cover above – 2 side panels and a wrap-around main piece.
But it is a little trickier, because you have to take out the excess fabric out of the concave surface (See Fig 6-71).

To construct this cover, cut out the 2 end panels as shown in Fig 6-72.

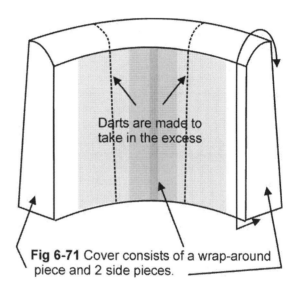

Darts are made to take in the excess

Fig 6-71 Cover consists of a wrap-around piece and 2 side pieces.

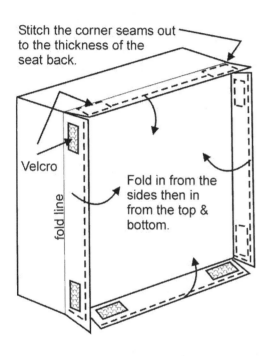

Stitch the corner seams out to the thickness of the seat back.

Velcro

fold line

Fold in from the sides then in from the top & bottom.

Fig 6-70 Instead of mitering the corners, the cover can be closed with small squares of Velcro.

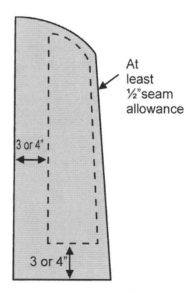

At least ½"seam allowance

3 or 4"

3 or 4"

Fig 6-72 Cut out the side panels to the shape of the cushion. Add 3-4" along the back and along the bottom.

Cut out the main panel – the width of the cushion's back side (plus seam allowance) by its height (plus enough to go behind the cushion at both the top and bottom, plus hem). See Fig 6-73.

Drape the fabric *right* side down onto the cushion if it is symmetrical, or *wrong* side down onto the cushion if it is asymmetrical.

If you need help holding the fabric in place, try push pins or large headed straight pins. Just push them straight in like a big pin cushion. You would of course NOT do this to leather, vinyl or any fabric that would show pin holes!

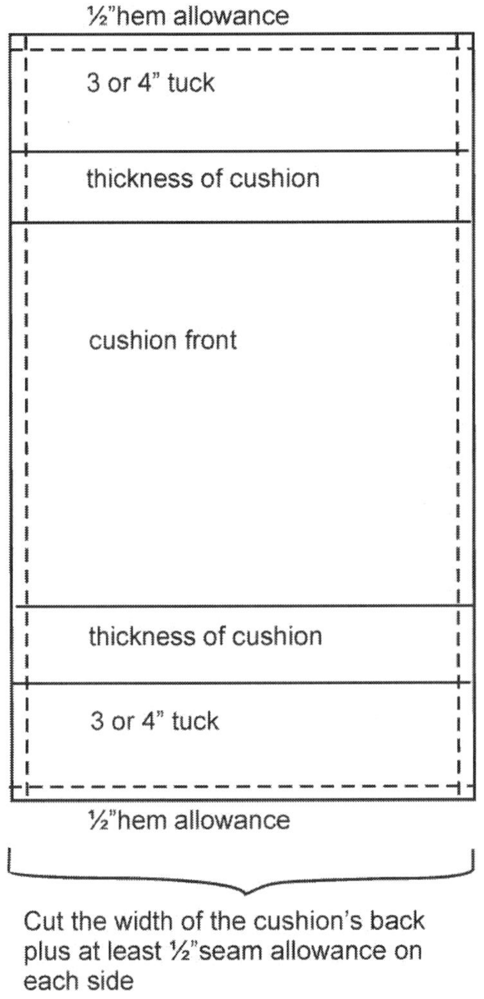

Staple the side panels to the main panel. Don't worry about the excess fabric on the main piece yet. Stitch the side pieces to the front piece.

Sometimes it helps to stitch on the Velcro tabs at this point, in order to hold the cover securely onto the cushion.

Drape the cushion cover onto the cushion again, and tighten it up using the Velcro or push pins. If the cushion is symmetrical, try on the cover *wrong* side out, otherwise, try it on *right* side out.

Now staple the front panel into darts to take in the excess fabric. See Fig 6-74.

Staple darts or pleats to take in any excess fabric underneath the cushion's bottom or over its top. Keep the fit a little loose.

If you had to work with the fabric *right* side out, when you remove the cover for final sewing, you will have to transfer the stapled seam line to the *wrong* side of the fabric for final stitching.

Hem the raw edges and add Velcro loops to the cover, and staple-gun Velcro hooks to the cushion's backboard if there is one.

½"hem allowance

| 3 or 4" tuck |
| thickness of cushion |
| cushion front |
| thickness of cushion |
| 3 or 4" tuck |

½"hem allowance

Cut the width of the cushion's back plus at least ½"seam allowance on each side

Fig 6-73

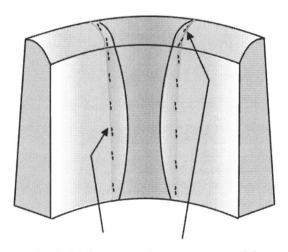

Fig 6-74 Gather up the excess material into darts and staple

Canvas for Cruisers

Alternate way:

Make a top panel, side panels and a bottom panel.

Use these to shape the fit of the inside curve – thus avoiding the darts. See Fig 6-75.

Either sit the cushion down onto the fabric and trace the top/bottom/side contours, or make a plastic pattern.

Use push-pins to attach the plastic to the cushion (if the cushion is woven fabric), or you can try ¼" seamstick if the cushion is leather or vinyl (try on a non-visible area first to make sure it does not leave a sticky residue!).

If the face of the cushion is not a rectangle (e.g. the cushion is wider at the top than the bottom), the easiest way is to make a plastic pattern first. (See Fig 6-76)

Again, use push-pins or seamstick to hold down the plastic while you mark the outlines.

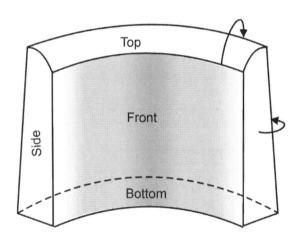

Fig 6-75 Make separate pieces - front, sides. top and bottom. Note that the top, bottom and side pieces will have to extend around to the back.

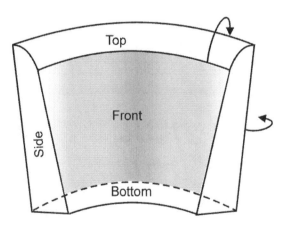

Fig 6-76 A concave cushion with the top wider than the bottom.

Quickie Cushion Covers

Crew covers for several identical cushion backs or seats can be made all at the same time. Described here is a set of covers for seat backs, fit loosely with a zipper in the back.

Step 1 – Measure the circumference (c) and the width (w) of each cushion. (Fig 6-77). The fit should be a bit loose, so measure accordingly.

To each (w) measurement, add the cushion's depth (d), plus 1" for seam allowances.

To the (c) circumference, add 1" seam allowance.

Step 2 – Cut a piece of fabric the '(c)' measurement by the total length of all the '(w)' measurements.

Mark a pencil line every '(w)' measurement as shown in Fig 6-78.

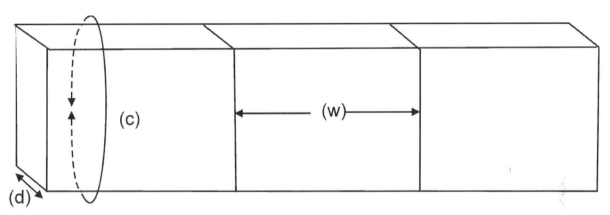

Fig 6-77 Measuring up for several identical cushions

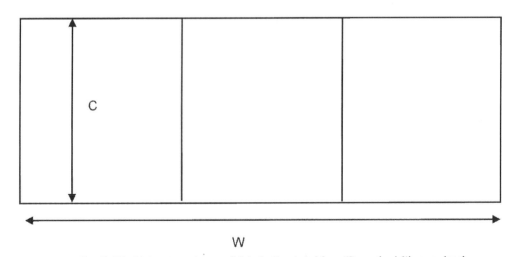

Fig 6-78 Cut out a piece of fabric the total length and width required.

Step 3 – Turn the long edges under ½".

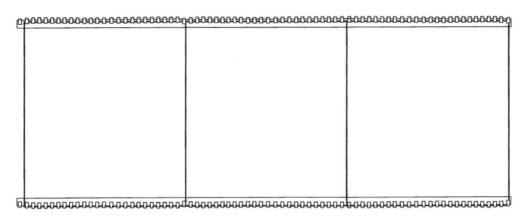

Fig 6-79 Stitch continuous zip along each long edge

Cut a length of #5 continuous zip the total length of the W measurements.
Separate the 2 halves.
Stitch one half to one long side, and the other half to the other side as shown in Fig 6-79.
Put on one zip head for each cushion, and position one head on each section. Zip up the 'tube' so that the right sides are together.

Step 4 – Fold the 'tube' (*right* sides together) along the zip as shown in Fig 6-80.
Hot knife or cut along the pencil lines through all thicknesses.
Still with *right* sides together, stitch a seam ½" away from the raw edges. (Fig 6-81).

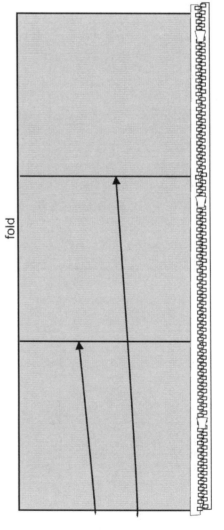

Fig 6-80 Cut sections apart at marked lines.

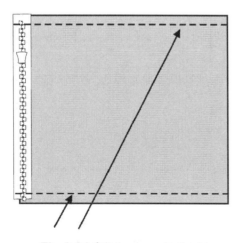

Fig 6-81 Stitch along both sides

Step 5 – 'Nip' in the corners to the depth measurement of the cushion. See Fig 6-82 and see further details under 'Drop Cover'.
Trim off the corners as shown in Fig 6-83.

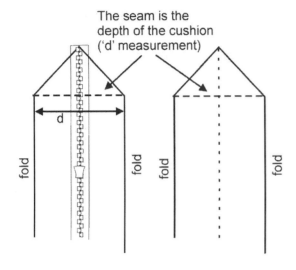

Fig **6-82** Re-fold so that the zip (on one side) or the fold (on the other side) is to the center, and stitch across the end - this 'nips in' the corner

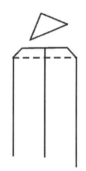

Fig **6-83** Trim off the corner to ½" seam allowance

<u>Vinyl covers</u>
If you are making a vinyl cover to protect an exterior cushion from rain, try to make as few seams as possible, to limit water leaks. Keep in mind, though that even the best vinyl cover will leak eventually and hold moisture inside of it.
Put in a drainage vent somewhere in the cover, in a place where the water is most likely to drain should it get inside as follows.

Cut out a rectangle of vinyl mesh. Stitch it to the *wrong* side of the vinyl ½" away from the raw edges of the mesh. (See Fig 6-84).

Flip the piece over. On the *right* side of the vinyl, trim away a neat rectangle, close to the stitching line. (Fig 6-85). This will make a 'window' of mesh.

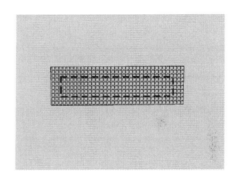

Fig **6-84** Stitch a piece of mesh to the *wrong* side, and trim off the excess mesh to ½"of the stitching line

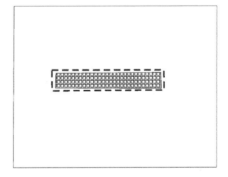

Fig **6-85** On the *right* side, trim away the vinyl to expose the mesh window.

Canvas for Cruisers

Section 7
Interior Projects

Canvas for Cruisers

414

Open Bags:

Shopping Bag

(Fig 7-1) This is a great bag to replace all those environmentally unfriendly plastic grocery bags that can quickly take over the boat!

Any kind of sturdy fabric or vinyl can be used and this is a good way to use up that excess fabric you don't need. It is also a great way to use up the good parts from an old sail. A bag made from vinyl mesh makes a decent storage bag for rope.

Step 1 – Cut out a piece of fabric. The width is the finished width of the bag, plus 1" for seam allowances plus about 4".
The length is double the desired length of the bag, plus about 6".

So, if you want the finished bag to be 16" wide by 18" high by 4" deep, cut the fabric 21" x 42".

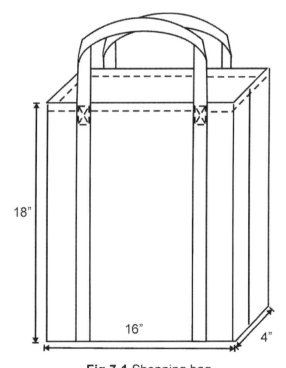

Fig 7-1 Shopping bag

Step 2 - Webbing can be used for the handles as shown in Fig 7-2.

Or you can make handles from the leftover long pieces of scrap. Cut out long strips about 3" or 4" wide. (You can even stitch short strips together to make a long length for the handles.).
Turn the long ends of the strips under ½" and then fold the strip in half lengthwise, matching up the ½" folded sides.
Stitch close to the ½" folded side.
A strap 106-108" long works pretty well on a bag 16x18x4 as shown here.

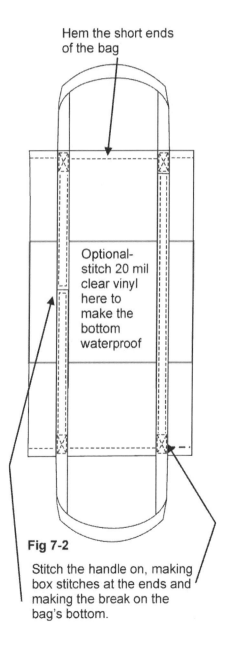

Hem the short ends of the bag

Optional- stitch 20 mil clear vinyl here to make the bottom waterproof

Fig 7-2

Stitch the handle on, making box stitches at the ends and making the break on the bag's bottom.

415

Canvas for Cruisers

Step 3 - Stitch a hem into the short ends of the bag by turning under ½" and under again.

Optional – stitch a scrap of 20 mil vinyl to the bottom area of the bag. This really helps keep the bread dry when transporting groceries in a wet dinghy!

Step 4 – Stitch on the handle to the *right* side of the bag as shown in Fig 7-2 so that the two handles are the same length.

Because the handle extends all the way around the bottom of the bag, it makes for a stronger bag. Use a box stitch on the handles at the hem edges for extra strength.

Additional tips on applying handles can be found further along in this Section – see Zippered Bag – Tote Bag.

Step 4 – Now fold the assembly *right* sides together and stitch the side seams. (Fig 7-3)

Step 5 – Refold the bag so the side seam is to the center, and 'nip in' the bottom, making about a 3 or 4" seam.
This forms the squared-off shape for the bottom of the bag. (Fig 7-4)

Decorate it with the boat name using fabric paint and you will have yourself a great reusable shopping bag!

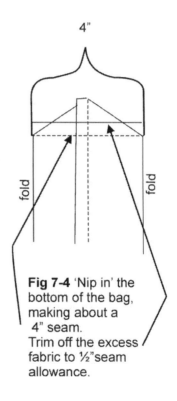

4"

fold

fold

Fig 7-4 'Nip in' the bottom of the bag, making about a 4" seam.
Trim off the excess fabric to ½"seam allowance.

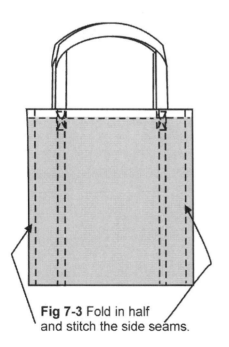

Fig 7-3 Fold in half and stitch the side seams.

Canvas Bucket

A canvas bucket is nothing more than an upside down drop cover with handles (see Drop Cover in Section 3).

Depending on the purpose for the bucket, it can have a square bottom or a round bottom, and it can have special-purpose pockets of various sizes and shapes, with or without flaps inside or outside the bucket.

Canvas buckets can be used for many purposes – here's some:
a carry-all for your 'going sailing' gear (GPS, winch handles, binoculars etc)
a 'going up the mast' bucket (tools, parts)
a beach picnic bucket
a snorkeling gear bucket
a 'cleaning the bottom' bucket
a tool bucket
You get the idea.

So all that is required is to figure out what kind of 'stuff' you will be putting in the bucket, and plan what size and shape it needs to be, and how many pockets it needs.

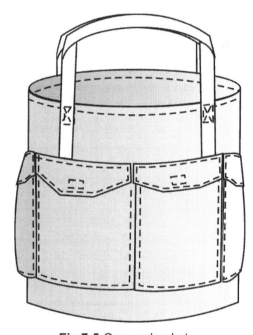

Fig 7-5 Canvas bucket

Canvas for Cruisers

A basic round-bottom bucket with pockets is constructed as follows:

Step 1 - Cut out a circle of fabric for the bottom, remembering to add ½" seam allowance all around. (Fig 7-6)

Cut out a rectangle the desired height of the bucket (plus ½" seam allowance at the bottom, plus 2" for a hem at the top), by the circumference of the bottom at the raw edge (plus 1" for seam allowances). (Fig 7-6)

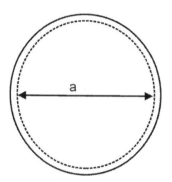

Fig 7-6 'a' is the finished size of the bucket bottom

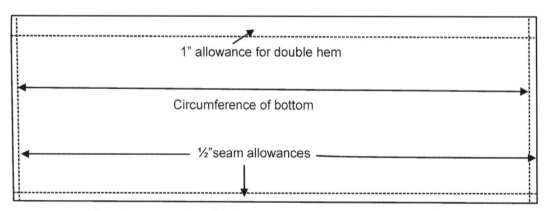

1" allowance for double hem

Circumference of bottom

½"seam allowances

Cut out the side piece using the circumference measurement of the bottom, and add seam and hem allowances.

Step 2 - If the bucket is likely to get water inside and you want it to drain, reinforce a little area in the bottom by stitching a patch of fabric on, and install a couple of grommets for drainage. Or make a little mesh window in the bottom for drainage.

Step 3

Working with the rectangular side piece, stitch a 1" double hem in the top edge (turn under 1" and 1" again, and stitch). If you need the bucket to be held open with a ring or a stiffener, don't hem the top yet. If you want the top edge to be stiff, insert a 1" strip of 10 oz Dacron, 30 mil window vinyl or other really stiff material into the hem before you fold it under.

Step 4 - Stitch on patch pockets to the inside or outside of the rectangular piece depending on your design as follows:

Cut out a rectangle for the pocket. See Fig 7-7.

With *wrong* sides together, turn the top edge under ½" and stitch. See Fig 7-8.

Now with *right* sides together, turn this stitched top edge down 1". Stitch the sides as shown. Trim the top corners as shown in Fig 7-9, and turn the hem *right* side out. Topstitch the hem down.

Trim off the bottom corners and turn all the outside edges under ½". If there is going to be a flap covering the pocket, you can stitch on a little square of Velcro hooks as shown to keep the flap closed. (Fig 7-10)

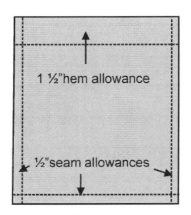

Fig 7-7 Cut out a rectangle of fabric for the pocket to the desired size plus seam and hem allowance.

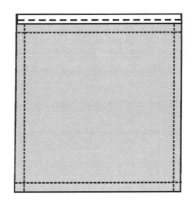

Fig 7-8 Turn the top edge under by ½"and stitch.

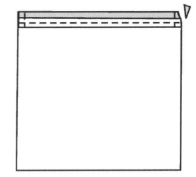

Fig 7-9 Turn top edge under 1". Stitch sides, trim off corners.

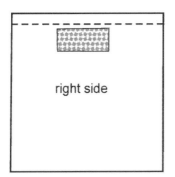

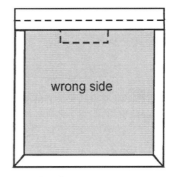

Fig 7-10 Turn the edges under and (optional) stitch on a piece of Velcro.

419

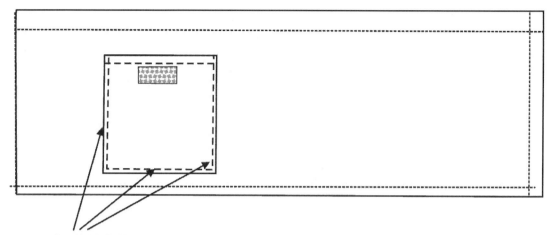

Fig 7-11 Stitch pocket to bucket's side panel.
To make several pockets, simply make a long rectangular
pocket, and separate it by stitching.

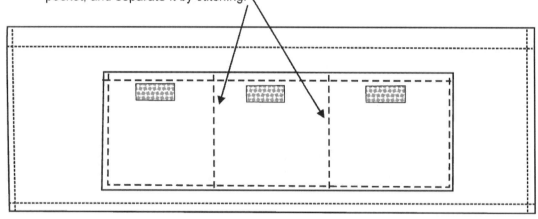

Stitch the pocket onto the rectangular side piece
of the bucket (Fig 7-11).

If there are several pockets you can make a
larger rectangular pocket, and divide it by
making rows of stitching as shown in Fig 7-11.

Construct the flaps by cutting out 2 pieces of
fabric for each flap as shown in Fig 7-12,
leaving ½" seam allowance all around.

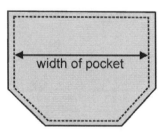

width of pocket

Fig 7-12 Cut out pieces for
pocket flaps the width of the
pocket, plus seam allowances.

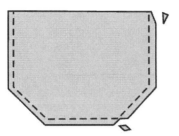

Fig 7-13 Stitch along 3 sides, and trim all corners

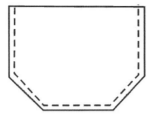

Fig 7-14 Turn inside out and topstitch

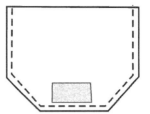

Fig 7-15 Stitch velcro loops to the underside of the flap.

Stitch *right* sides together along 3 sides as shown in Fig 7-13, trim the corners and turn inside out.

Topstitch (Fig 7-14)

Stitch on a small square of Velcro loops if desired to keep the pocket closed (Fig 7-15)

Stitch the flap over the pocket (Fig 7-16).

Step 5 – After all the pocket construction is complete, stitch the rectangular side piece to the bucket's bottom. (See Section 3 - Drop Cover for diagrams and more details).

With *right* sides together, start stitching the side to the bottom.
Start and stop a couple of inches from the corners of the rectangle. When you are almost finished stitching on the side to the bottom, stop.
Stitch the side seam.
Now finish stitching the side to the bottom

If the bag needs to stay open, you can stitch some boltrope all around the top edge, or hem in a wooden or stainless ring.

For handles, you can use nylon webbing, stitching on securely with a box stitch.

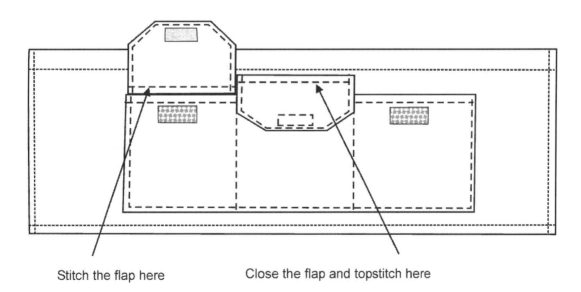

Stitch the flap here   Close the flap and topstitch here

Fig 7-16 Stitch the flap over the pocket.

Canvas for Cruisers

World's Best Tool Bag

This is a great bag for organizing and storing tools and equipment. It has different sized pockets all around the outside for various tools, and a strong handle reinforced with rope. Make several. They make terrific gifts!

Use any strong canvas or vinyl material –For this design, all you will need is about 3/4 yd of 60" wide material, 28" of scrap old rope, and 74" of 1" webbing.

Step 1 – Cut out the fabric pieces according to the diagram below.

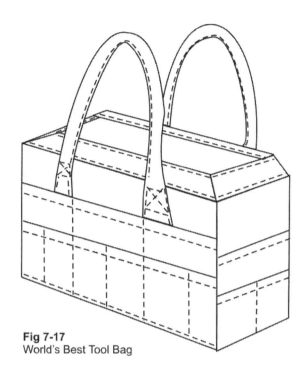

Fig 7-17
World's Best Tool Bag

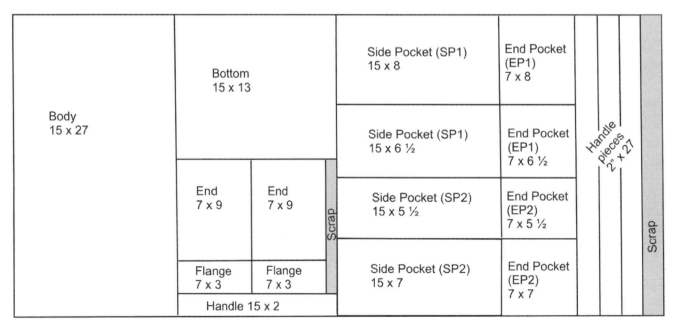

Fig 7-18 Cutting layout

Step 2 – Hem the top edges of all the pocket pieces. (SP1's, SP2's, EP1's and EP2's). Stitch a ½" single hem if the material doesn't fray (or if you used a hot knife to cut out the fabric), If the fabric is likely to fray, make a ½" double hem, or bind the raw edges. Fig 7-19.

Step 3 – Prepare the pocket sections.
Keeping the *right* sides up, place the smaller EP1 on top of the larger EP1, matching the lower edges and the sides. (Fig 7-20)

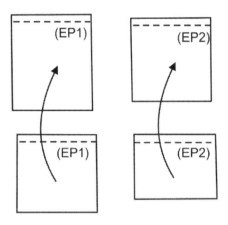

Fig 7-20 Place smaller end pieces on top of larger ones.

Staple along the edges to hold in place.

Stitch down the center to partition it into two pockets. (Fig 7-21)

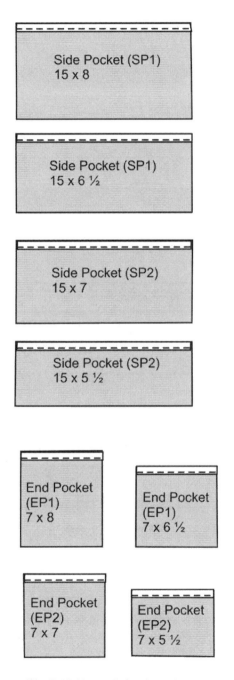

Fig 7-19 Hem all the top edges of all the pocket pieces.

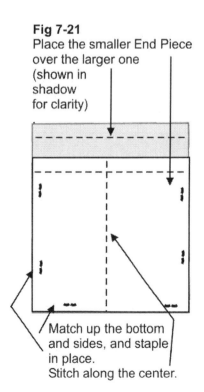

Fig 7-21
Place the smaller End Piece over the larger one (shown in shadow for clarity)

Match up the bottom and sides, and staple in place.
Stitch along the center.

423

Now staple the *wrong* side of this assembly to the *right* side of the End piece, matching the lower edges and sides. Stitch ¼" from raw edges. Remove the stapes.

Do the same with the EP2 pieces.

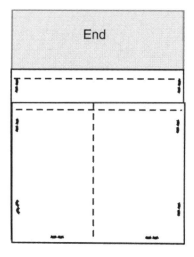

Fig 7-22
Now place this on top of the End piece. Staple to hold in place.

In a similar fashion, place the smaller SP1 piece on top of the larger SP1, again matching the bottom and side edges. Stitch down the center, and 2 ¾" in from each edge to form the pocket partitions. See Fig 7-23. Stitch ¼" away from the raw edges to hold the pieces together, and remove the staples.
Do the same with the SP2 pieces.

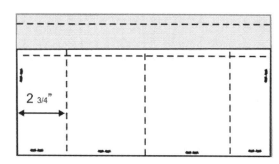

Fig 7-23 Place smaller Side Piece on top of larger one, matching up the bottom and side edges. Stitch down the center, and 2 3/4" in from each side.

Step 4 – Prepare the Body
Center a piece of 13" long webbing over each short end of the Body piece as shown in Fig 7-24.
Overlap the webbing ½" over the raw edge of the Body.
Stitch close to the edge of the webbing to hold it in place.
Fold the webbing in towards the *wrong* side, and fold in again, to encase the webbing in the fabric. Stitch close to each edge of the webbing, catching the webbing in with the fabric.

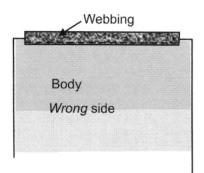

Fig 7-24 Center webbing over the raw edge.

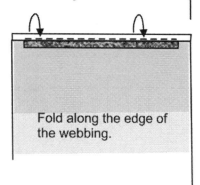

Fold along the edge of the webbing.

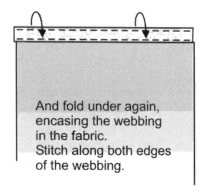

And fold under again, encasing the webbing in the fabric. Stitch along both edges of the webbing.

424

Step 5 – Make the handles

a) Using the same method as described in
Section 2 – Making Piping (see Fig 2-
34), stitch the handle pieces together
into one long piece.
Use the order as shown in Fig 7-25.
Trim seams and staple the seam
allowances open.

b) Seamstick webbing to the *wrong* side of
the handle according to the
measurements shown in Fig 7-25. Place
two lengths of old rope along the
handle part, centered over the webbing
pieces.

c) Stitch the webbing ends and the rope
ends as shown in Fig 7-26 to hold them
in place. If your sewing machine can't
handle stitching through the rope, then
hand stitch that section to hold the ends
of the rope in place.

d) Now fold the strap lengthwise, *wrong*
sides together along the rope and stitch
1/2" from the raw edges so the rope is
encased. Stitch only where the rope is,
leave the rest of the handle 'flat'.
If the raw edge is likely to fray, finish it
with zigzag stitch, or bind this edge.

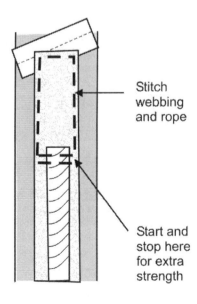

Stitch
webbing
and rope

Start and
stop here
for extra
strength

Fig 7-26 Stitch the ends
of the webbing and
rope to secure the ends.

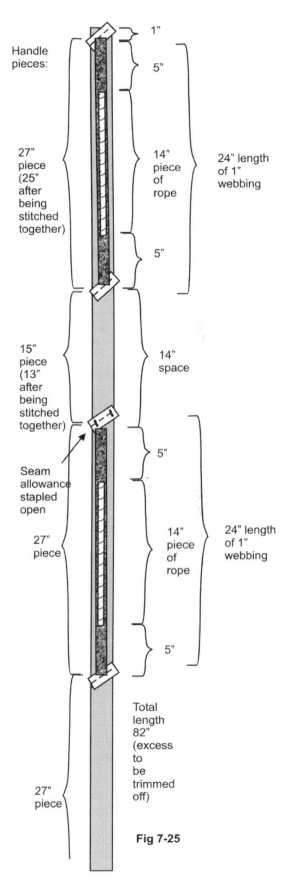

Handle
pieces:

27"
piece
(25"
after
being
stitched
together)

1"

5"

14"
piece
of
rope

24" length
of 1"
webbing

5"

15"
piece
(13"
after
being
stitched
together)

14"
space

Seam
allowance
stapled
open

27"
piece

5"

14"
piece
of
rope

24" length
of 1"
webbing

5"

27"
piece

Total
length
82"
(excess
to
be
trimmed
off)

Fig 7-25

425

Step 6 – Stitch Handle to Body

Take the Body piece and mark some chalk lines on its *right* side using Fig 7-27. (make light lines or use washable pencil)

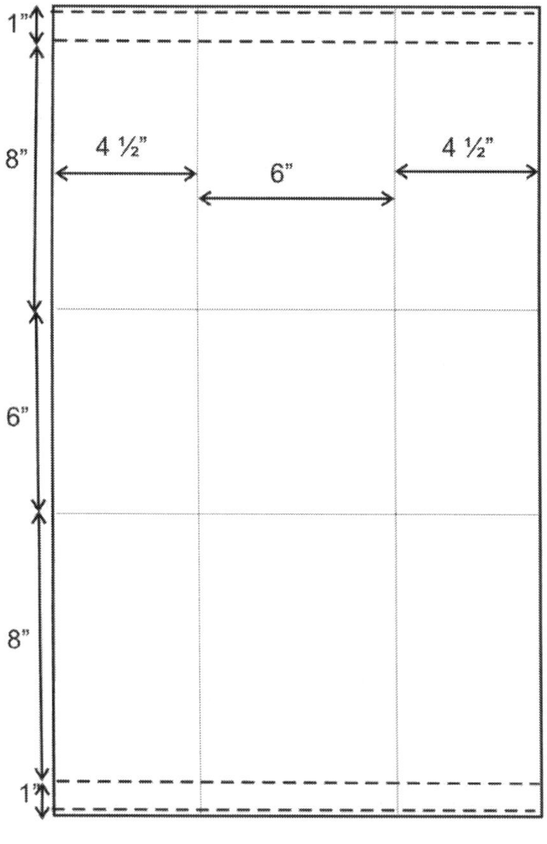

Lay the handle along the marked lines as shown in Fig 7-28.

Mark the point where the final join needs to be in order to make the handle into a loop, and stitch the last join seam.

Position the handle again, and secure in place with staples, or seamstick. Stitch in place as shown, making strong box stitching at each corner.

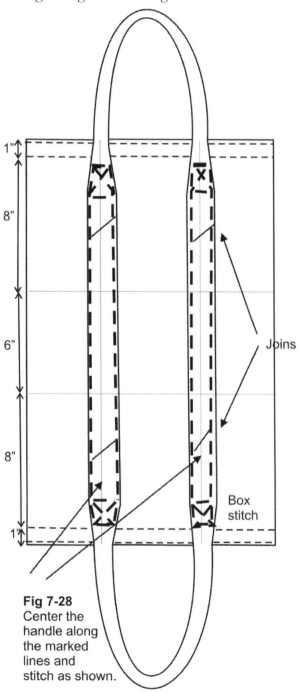

Fig 7-27 Mark lines on the Body piece.

Joins

Box stitch

Fig 7-28 Center the handle along the marked lines and stitch as shown.

Step 7 – Stitch Side Pockets to Body
Place side pockets onto Body, *right* sides together so that the seam line on the Side Pocket aligns with the fold line on the Body (see Fig 7-29). Stitch along the fold line.

Now fold the side pocket back so that the *wrong* side of the pocket is on the *right* side of the Body. Topstitch the side edges and the bottom. Also make two vertical lines of stitching through all layers as shown, to further partition the side pockets.

Fig 7-29

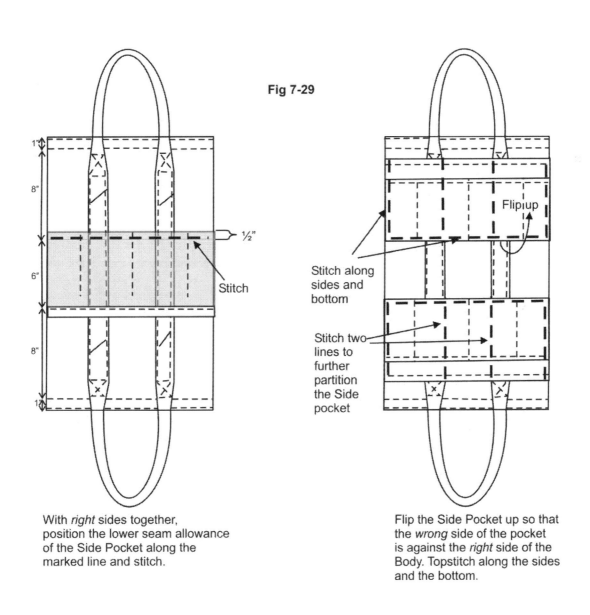

With *right* sides together, position the lower seam allowance of the Side Pocket along the marked line and stitch.

Flip the Side Pocket up so that the *wrong* side of the pocket is against the *right* side of the Body. Topstitch along the sides and the bottom.

Step 8 – Make end Flanges and stitch to Body: See Fig 7-30.

With *wrong* sides together, fold each Flange in half along its length. Center a 6" length of 1" webbing inside the flange, along the fold. Stitch along the fold to hold the webbing in place.

Finish the short raw ends of the flange if necessary to prevent them from fraying.

Now working with the Body, overlap the flanges by ½" to the underside of the Body and stitch in place. See Fig 7-31.

Take the other end of the Flange to the other side of the body and stitch in place the same way. Now the bag now is starting to look like a bag, with open ends.

Fig 7-30

With *wrong* sides together, fold flange in half along its length.

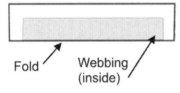

Fold   Webbing (inside)

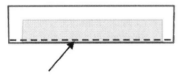

Stitch here to hold webbing in place

Finish the ends if necessary to prevent fraying.

Fig 7-31

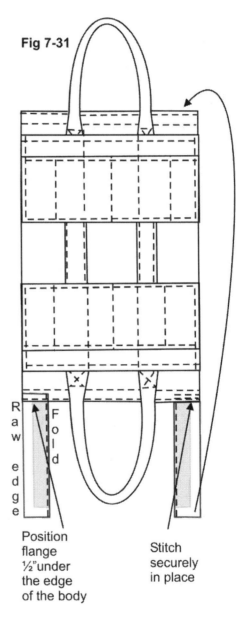

Position flange ½"under the edge of the body

Stitch securely in place

Then fold the bag around so you can position the opposite ends of the flanges to the other side of the bag. Stitch the opposite ends of the flanges in place.

Step 9 - Stitch End pieces to Body.

With *right* sides together, staple the prepared Ends to the Body, matching up the bottom, sides and corners as shown in Fig 7-32.

Stitch all around the End.

Turn the bag right side out.

Step 10 – Make and insert a bottom stiffener.

With *right* sides together, fold the bottom piece in half along its length. Stitch two sides as shown in Fig 7-33, trim the corners and turn inside out.

Stuff in a stiffener (old thin-ish plastic cutting boards work great). Turn the raw edges under and stitch.

Sit the stiffener in the bottom of the bag.

Fig 7-33

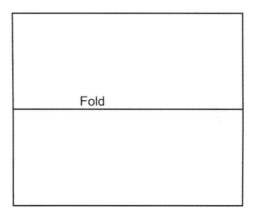

Fold Bottom piece in half, *right* sides together.

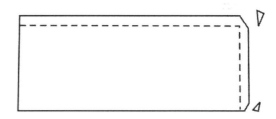

Stitch two sides, ½"from raw edge. Trim corners.

Turn inside out.
Insert stiffener.
Turn the remaining raw edges to the inside, and stitch the opening,

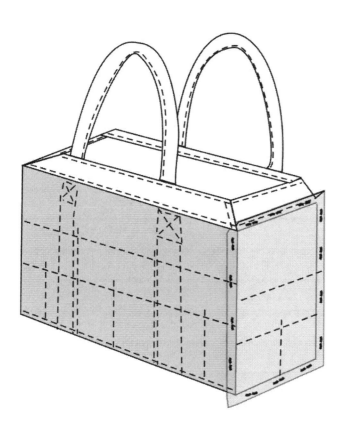

Fig 7-32 With *right* sides together, staple the End Piece to the Body, matching up the corners and sides. Stitch all around, ½"from raw edges.

Canvas for Cruisers

Wine Storage bags

A very simple and practical way to store glass bottles, this idea uses up any scrap upholstery fabric or Sunbrella you might have on hand.

The bags store very compact when empty and don't add much to the storage space when filled. They keep the bottles from clinking and breaking underway and work great.

Simply cut pieces of fabric 13" wide x 15" long. Or if you have long scraps to use up, you can cut
them 7" by 30". This will give you a bag of finished size 6 X 14.

Stitch a ½" single hem in the top edge. If you didn't cut out the fabric with a hot knife, make a ½" double hem.

Fold the piece in half vertically (horizontally if you are using long strips of fabric) *right* sides together.

Stitch along the long seam and along the bottom. If you used a hot knife, you don't even have to finish the seams!
Turn inside out and you're done!

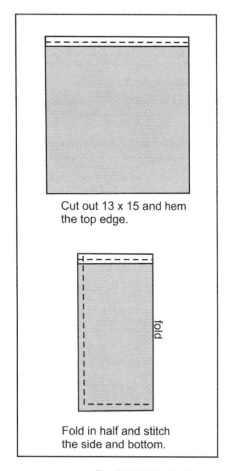

Cut out 13 x 15 and hem the top edge.

Fold in half and stitch the side and bottom.

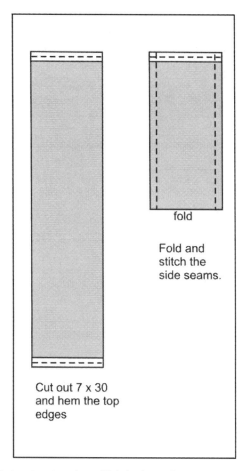

fold

Fold and stitch the side seams.

Cut out 7 x 30 and hem the top edges

Fig 7-34 Wine bottle storage bags. Cut out rectangles of fabric, hem the top and stitch *right* sides together.

Drawstring Bags

Simple 1-piece Drawstring Bag

This is a simple drawstring bag, made of one piece of fabric. It has a casing at the top holding a drawstring, and the bottom is 'nipped in' to form a squared-off bottom.

It can be made of canvas, mesh, nylon or any other material, really, depending on what you are using it for.

Step 1 – Decide on the finished size of the bag. Width x Height x Depth. See Fig 7-35.

In this example the bag is 12" wide x 18" high x 6" deep

Cut the fabric as follows:

H = desired height + ½ of Depth + ½" seam allowance + hem allowance (usually 1").

In this example, H = 18 + 3 + ½ + 1 = 22 ½"

L = 2 x desired width + 2 x desired depth + 1" seam allowance

In this example, L = 24 + 12 + 1 = 37"

Step 2 – Finish the top edge as follows.

Turn the corners of the top edge under as shown in Fig 7-36 and stitch.

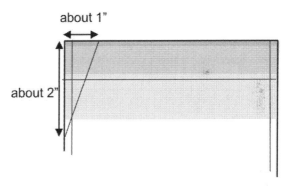

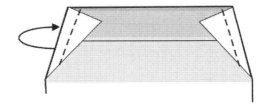

Fig 7-36 Turn the top corners under as shown and stitch ½" from fold

Fig 7-35 One-piece drawstring bag.

Canvas for Cruisers

On the *wrong* side, lay out a length of cord along the top edge. Turn the edge over the cord by about 1" or whatever feels right, leaving the cord along the fold. Stitch down the hem with the cord inside. (Fig 7-37).

If you are going to need to label the bag with its contents, it is easiest to do this now before the bag is all sewn up. Use fabric paint or permanent marker.

Step 3 – Fold the fabric in half vertically, *right* sides together.
Stitch along the side and bottom of the bag as shown in Fig 7-38.

Step 4 – Nip in the bottom of the bag.
Fold the bag so that the seam is in the center, forming two triangular 'ears'. Measure so that the seam you will stitch is equal to the desired depth of the bag. See Fig 7-39.

Stitch across these triangular ears, and trim the seam to ½"

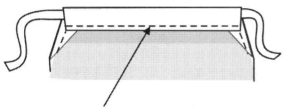

Fig 7-37 Lay the drawstring along the fold line, fold the hem over and stitch the cord into the fold.

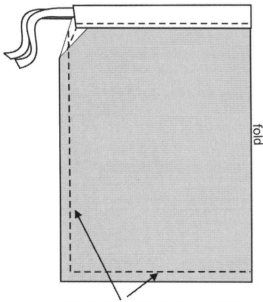

Fig 7-38 Fold in half and stitch along side and across bottom.

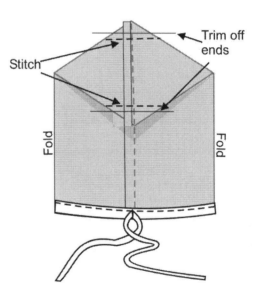

Fig 7-39 'Nip In' the corners. The length of the stitched line is equal to the desired depth of your bag.

Round-Bottom Duffle Bag

This bag has a drawstring at the top, and a
separate round piece for the bottom. It is
suitable for larger articles.(Fig 7-40)

The method of construction is identical to the
Canvas Bucket above. Before attaching the side
piece to the bottom, stitch in a hem and
drawstring identical to instructions in the
Drawstring Bag above.

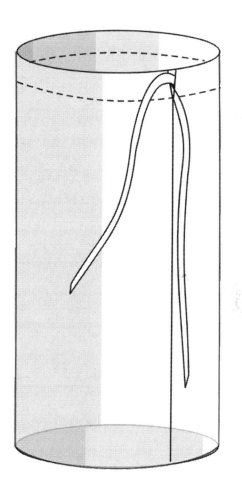

Fig 7-40 A round-bottom duffel bag
is just a canvas bucket with a
drawstring in the top.

Canvas for Cruisers

Plastic Bag Bag

This is a terrific little bag to keep control of all those plastic grocery bags you seem to end up with. It is a simple sausage bag – you stuff the bags in one end, and take them out of the other end. You can jam a lot of plastic bags into this little compact bag!

All you need is:
A scrap of soft fabric 13" x 19"
Elastic – about 6"
Leech line – about 18"
A barrel lock.

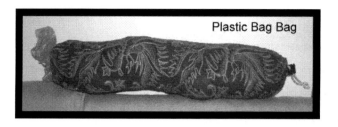

Plastic Bag Bag

Step 1 – Turn the raw edges of the short sides (which will be the top and bottom of the bag) under by ¼" and stitch. See Fig 7-41.

Step 2 – With *right* sides together, stitch the side seam and finish the raw edges if required. (Fig 7-41)

Step 3 – Turn the bag *right* side out.

Step 4 – See Fig 7-42. Turn one end under ½", inserting the leech line inside. Stitch close to the folded edge. Leave a section of hem unstitched (about ½" or so) so the leech line can come through.

Fig 7-41

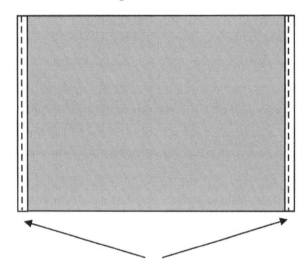

Turn the raw edges under by 1/4" and stitch

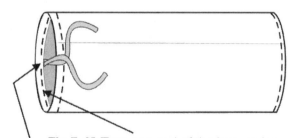

Fig 7-42 Turn one end of the bag under by ½"inserting the leech line into the fold before stitching. Leave about ½"or so unstitched, so the leech line can stick out. ,

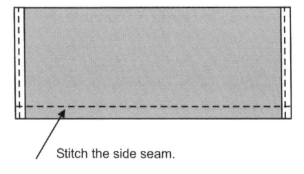

Stitch the side seam.

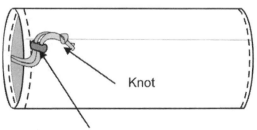

Knot

Attach a barrel lock to the leech lines and tie off the ends.

Step 5 – Attach the barrel lock to the leech line. Knot the ends of the leech line.

Step 6 – Turn the other end under by ½", again leaving an opening of about ½".

Step 7 – Thread elastic through this casing with a safety pin. Remove the pin and knot the ends of the elastic – adjusting the length of the elastic so the bag end gets held shut comfortably. See Fig 7-43

Now load up the bag! Stuff your plastic grocery bags into the end with the leech line, using the leech line and barrel lock to close the end of the bag. Remove the plastic bags from the elastic end.

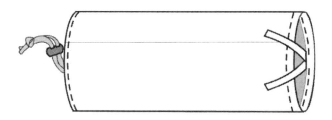

Fig 7-43 Make a ½"casing in the other end. Thread a piece of elastic through the casing, pull it comfortably tight and knot the elastic. Trim off any excess ends of elastic.

Zippered Bags:

Tote Bag

This style of bag can be used to contain and carry anything from clothing, dive equipment, laundry, sailboards, food and emergency gear (the dreaded 'ditch' bag).

The bag can have 1 or 2 handles, and 1 or 2 zip heads, depending on the length of the bag.
A #10 zip is the best to use – stronger than a #5.

The bag can have separate circular panels of fabric for its ends, or the ends can simply be 'nipped in'. (Fig 7-39 above)

The bag can be made to open out flat, and if it is meant to carry something heavy, it should have extra strong handles. This is all shown below.

The basic bag described here has a zippered opening, with handles going all the way around the bag for strength. See Fig 7-44.

Step 1 – Decide on the size of the bag.
Mark and cut out the fabric in any of the styles shown in Fig 7-45.

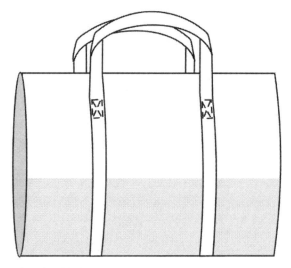

Fig 7-44 This tote bag has circular ends and a zipper closing. The handles extend all the way around for extra strength.

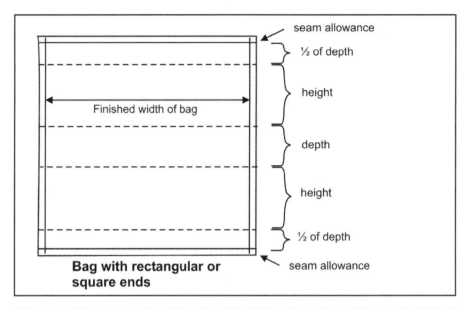

Bag with rectangular or square ends

seam allowance
½ of depth
height
depth
height
½ of depth
seam allowance

Finished width of bag

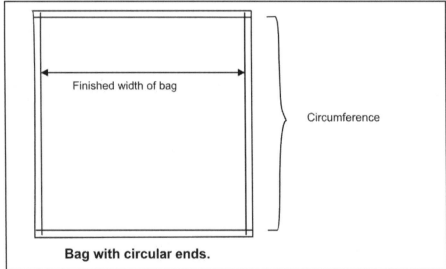

Bag with circular ends.

Finished width of bag

Circumference

Fig 7-45

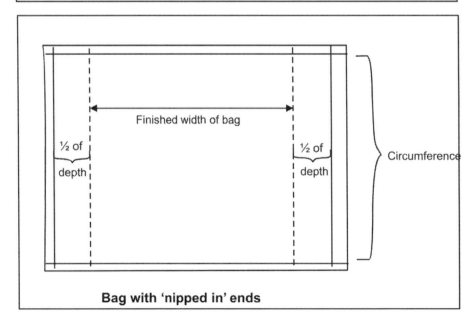

Bag with 'nipped in' ends

Finished width of bag

½ of depth

½ of depth

Circumference

Step 2 - Cut a length of #10 continuous zip to the finished width of the bag plus seam allowances.

Step 3 – Apply ½" seamstick to the *wrong* side of the bag's ends where the zip is to go (Fig 7-46).

Turn these ends under ½" and stick down as shown in Fig 7-47.

With zip closed, apply ¼" seamstick to both tapes of the zip. Separate the zip. Stick and stitch one side of the zip to one side of the bag. (Fig 7-48). The teeth can be exposed or you can line up the teeth along the folded edge so the teeth will be covered when the bag is closed.

Step 5 – Stick the other zipper tape to the other side of the bag, stretching out the zip and the fabric so that the zip matches at each end to get the tension even.

Step 6 – Attach the handles. If you just need average strength and the bag is not to be exposed to sunlight a lot, you can use 1" polypro webbing.

Apply ½" seamstick to the webbing except for the part of the webbing which will be the handles. Pin out the webbing and really stretch it. Then apply the seamstick (Fig 7-49).

Stick the webbing to the *right* side of the bag. See Fig 7-50. Place the join at the bag's bottom so that it will not be so visible when the bag is finished. Remember that webbing shrinks more than the fabric, so do not stretch the webbing at all when sticking it on. In fact, try to put a slight 'gather' in the webbing so that the webbing can shrink over time and not distort the bag.

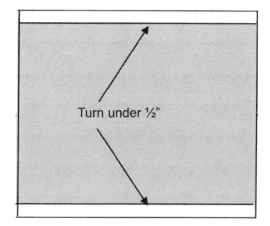

Fig 7-47 Turn under ½"and stick down.

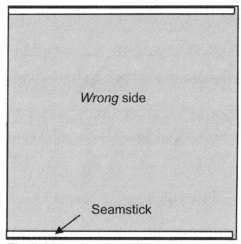

Fig 7-46 Apply seamstick to the raw edges where the zip is to go.

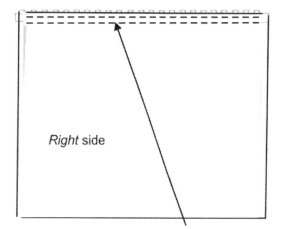

Fig 7-48 Stitch zip to one side, with teeth covered by fold

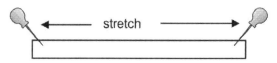

Fig 7-49 Apply seamstick to the webbing.

If there will be heavy stress at the handle, a reinforcing patch should be placed where each side of each handle ends.(see Section 2 – Patches)

Stitch the handle to the bag along the edges of the webbing. To make the handle attachment point very strong, make a box stitch where the handle attaches to the bag - at a point just below the side of the bag as shown in Fig 7-50.

Step 7 – Put on the zip head(s).

Step 8 – Finish the ends of the bag. You can make simple 'nipped in' ends, or stitch on circles or squares of fabric at each end.(see Section 3 – Drop Cover)

To make the bag with 'nipped in' ends - fold the bag in half *right* sides together and stitch the side seams of the bag. Then fold it so the bottom centerline lines up with the zipper, and stitch the seam across the end, clipping off the triangular pieces left. (see Fig 7-39 above) Nip in the bottom of the bag the same way.

Tote Bag Variations:

<u>To Open Flat:</u>

A bag which can open out flat is especially useful for heavy pieces of equipment. The heavy object can be placed onto the opened out flat surface of the bag, and then the bag can be zipped up around the object.

In this case, the zip goes around 3 sides, plus about 3" in at the bottom of each side. This allows the bag to open out flat.(Fig 7-51)

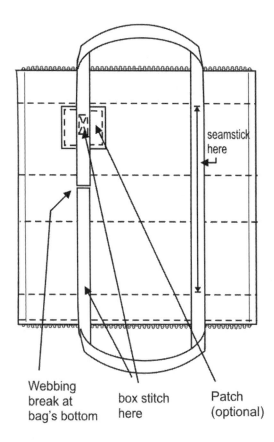

Webbing break at bag's bottom box stitch here Patch (optional)

Fig 7-50 This figure shows how to position the webbing handle on the fabric, and the position of a stress patch, if any.

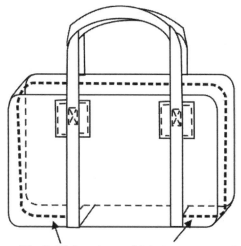

Fig 7-51 In a bag which can open out flat, the zip extends partially around the bottom of the bag.

To make it, the steps are actually quite similar to a basic box cushion:

Step 1 – Cut out the front and back to the desired size, adding ½" all around for seam allowances.

Make hatch marks just like in the box cushion, to allow you to match up the side piece.

Cut out two long bands to go on the sides. For the length - Plan how big the bottom piece will be (the piece without the zip), then cut the band so it's a couple of inches too long. Don't forget to add seam allowances where the bottom piece joins the long piece.

For the width - The long band will have to be split in half to receive the zip, so cut it an extra 2" wide to allow for the seam allowances.

E.g. If the bag is to be 4" deep, cut the band that will have the zip (4" + 2") = 6" wide.

The other shorter band for the bottom will not have a split in it, but you will need to add 1" to the width for seam allowance.

E.g. if the bag is to be 4" deep, cut the bottom band (4" + 1") = 5" wide.

Cut out a length of continuous #10 zip, a couple of inches longer than needed.

Step 2 – Working with the long band of fabric, cut it in half along its length if you have not already done so.

Apply seamstick as shown in Fig 7-52 and turn one long edge of each band under ½" (Fig 7-53).

Apply ¼" seamstick to both of the zip tapes

Stretch out the zip and one of the bands, and stick down one side of the zip (Fig 7-54). The teeth can be showing, or not, your choice.
Stitch the zip with one or two rows of stitching.

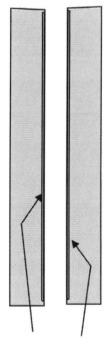

Fig 7-52 Apply seamstick to long edges

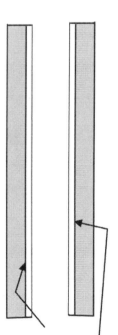

Fig 7-53 Turn long edges under ½" and stick down

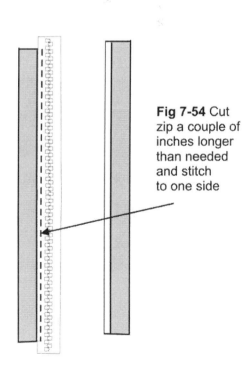

Fig 7-54 Cut zip a couple of inches longer than needed and stitch to one side

439

Trim off the zip so it is the same length as the tape.
Separate the two halves of the zip.

Stitch the other half of the zip onto the other half of the band, matching the ends so the tension is even. (Fig 7-55)

Apply a zip head and zip the 2 halves back together.

Step 3 – With *right* sides together, stitch one of the ends of the long band (the one with the zip) to one end of the bottom band. (Fig 7-56)

Fold the seam allowance away from the zip and topstitch it down. Careful not to break the needle when stitching over the zipper teeth.

Step 4 – Now the rest of the steps are just like making a box cushion. Start sewing the band to either the front or back piece of the bag. Start with the bottom (short) band - center it to the bag's bottom.
It is faster and easier to stitch without staples or pins. Just hold the two pieces together and freehand stitch.

Step 5 – When you get a few inches from the end, stop. Trim the long band to size.
Sew the long band to the bottom band as before, (add another head if desired first), and topstitch.

Continue sewing the band to the front or back piece until you have sewn it all around.

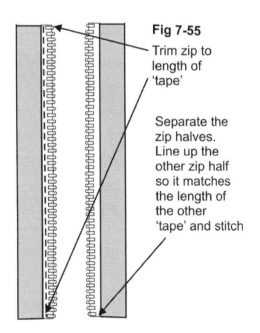

Fig 7-55

Trim zip to length of 'tape'

Separate the zip halves. Line up the other zip half so it matches the length of the other 'tape' and stitch

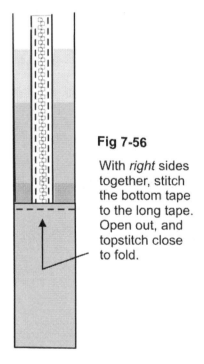

Fig 7-56

With *right* sides together, stitch the bottom tape to the long tape. Open out, and topstitch close to fold.

Step 6 – Transfer the hatch marks from the front or back piece to attached band, and across to the other side of the band.

Use the hatch marks to line up the other side of the band, and stitch the band all around to the other side of the bag.

Step 7 – Topstitch all around. Fold the seam allowances towards the band and place the stitches close to the fold on the band, not on the front or back piece (easier)

Step 8 – Stitch on the handles. (see above)

Strong Handles

For a very strong handle, as in the case of a 'ditch bag', use 2" nylon webbing for the handles. (See Fig 7-57).

Make stress patches, 2" larger all around than the 'box stitch' areas (e.g. if using 2" webbing for the handles, make the patch 6" square). Stitch the patch onto the inside of the tote bag.

Then, put two rows of ½" seamstick very loosely onto the webbing. In other words, stretch out the webbing with scratch awls, and try to pucker the seamstick as you apply it. You don't want the seamstick to make the webbing shrink in as it ages.

Pin out the bag, placing the scratch awls at its stress patches or at the zip seams.

Apply the nylon webbing to the bag really loosely – push on the webbing so that it is almost 'gathered' onto the bag. This is because the nylon webbing will really shrink over time and distort the bag.

Speaking of ditch bags – If you want the bag to float (and who doesn't??) you can build inserts into the bag to hold closed-cell foam, or stitch a strong webbing loop so it can be clipped with a

shackle to say, a fender, to make it float. Check it when the bag is loaded up to make sure there is enough floatation!

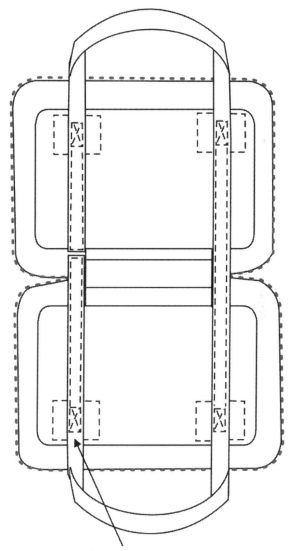

Fig 7-57 *Right* side of opened-out bag. The handles are 2" webbing and are reinforced with 6" square patches at all 4 corners.

When sewing on the patches, start and stop here, so that your backstitches are hidden under the webbing.

Canvas for Cruisers

Goin' to Town Bag

Here's a great little bag to keep your 'stuff' together and relatively dry in the dinghy, when you don't want to lug the backpack around. The size and design is variable, with optional interior or exterior pockets.
It is also a way to use up scraps of fabric!

Step 1 – See Fig 7-58. Cut out a piece of any kind of sturdy fabric – upholstery vinyl, Shelterite, even Sunbrella if you don't care about water-proof-ness - about 15" x 30".

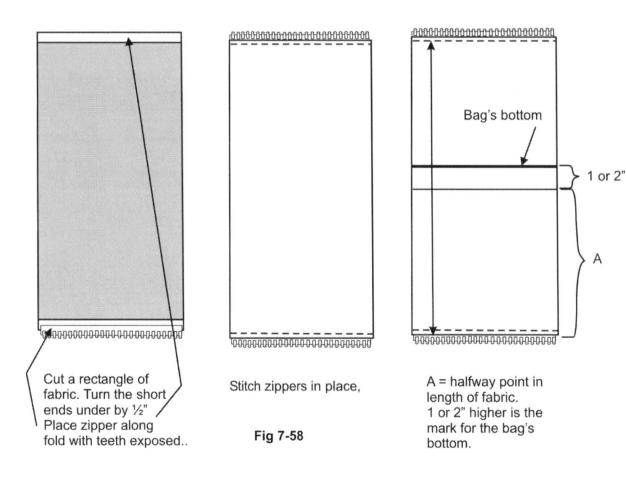

Cut a rectangle of fabric. Turn the short ends under by ½" Place zipper along fold with teeth exposed..

Stitch zippers in place,

Fig 7-58

A = halfway point in length of fabric.
1 or 2" higher is the mark for the bag's bottom.

Bag's bottom

1 or 2"

A

Step 2 – Turn the raw edges of each end under by ½". Cut a piece of continuous zipper the same length as the end. (#5 is good, but you can use any size). Place the zipper's tape under the folded edge so that the teeth are exposed. Stitch.

Step 3 – Make a mark on the fabric to show where the bag's bottom is. The mark will be offset from the fabric's halfway point by 1 to 2" as shown in Fig 7-58.

Step 4 – (Optional) Exterior pocket.
See Fig 7-59. Cut out a rectangle of fabric the same width as the bag, and whatever height you want the pocket to be – add ½" for seam allowance and ½" for hem to the height measurement.

Make a ½" single hem in the top edge.
Turn the bottom edge under by ½".
Place the pocket piece on the bag's *right* side, aligning the pocket's folded lower edge to the line marked on the bag for the bag's bottom. Line up the side raw edges. Stitch close to the sides and bottom to hold the pocket in place.

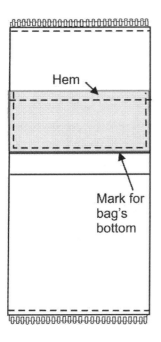

Fig 7-59 Exterior pocket

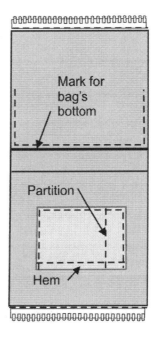

Fig 7-60 Interior pocket

443

Step 5 – (Optional) Interior pockets- stitch on the *wrong* side. It could be any size or shape. One idea is shown in Fig 7-60. Cut out a piece of fabric, turn all the raw edges under by ½". Stitch a hem in the top edge, then stitch the pocket to the *wrong* side of the bag. Just remember to position the hem (or 'open' side of the pocket) facing the opposite end of the bag from the exterior pocket - so that when the bag is folded in half, both interior and exterior pockets face the right way.

Step 6 – Fold the piece along the mark for the bag's bottom. Note how there will be have to be another fold at the bag's top now, which will make the zipper offset, so that it is at the front of the bag and not on its end. See Fig 7-61.

Put on the zipper head. Zip up the zipper but leave the zipper open about 3" so that you will be able to get your fingers in to open the zip later to turn the bag inside out.

Stitch the side seams. Trim the corners.

Step 6 – Unzip the zipper and turn the bag inside out. Done!

Fig 7-61 Fold the bag in half along the mark for the bag's bottom.

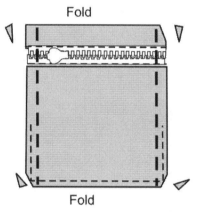

Fig 7-62 Stitch along sides. Trim corners. Open zipper and turn inside out.

Sheet Bag

This is a mesh bag, held closed by PVC pipe and shock cord, with handles to hang it from a winch or other place. See Fig 7-63.

The sides can be curved, or angled. The idea is that the bag can be hung up and filled using just one hand and the bungee makes it snap closed by itself.

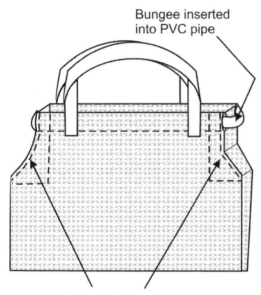

Fig 7-63 Mesh sheet bag with top stiffened with PVC pipe.
Sides can be curved or angled

Step 1 – Pile up the sheet line and try to figure out what size of bag will hold it.

Cut 2 pieces of vinyl mesh the required size.

E.g. for a 'volume' of 12" high x 15" wide x 5" deep (as shown in Fig 7-39), cut 2 pieces as follows:

Height = 12" + ½" (bottom seam allowance) + about 4" (casing) = 16 ½"

Width = 15" + 2 ½" + 2 ½" (to allow for the depth) + ½" + ½" (seam allowances) = 21"

Step 2 - Finish the ends of the top edges of both pieces as follows. See Fig 7-64.

Mark the desired shape for the side openings (curved or angled).
The distance in from the sides is ½ of the 'depth' (in this case, 2 ½").
You will be turning the top edge down in order to make a casing, so make sure you allow for this by making the cut-out area high enough.

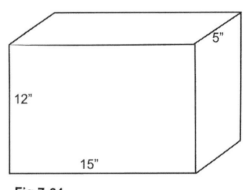

Fig 7-64

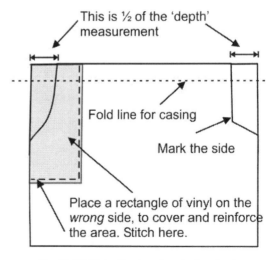

Fig 7-65 This figure shows the features of the sheet bag and measurements.

445

Canvas for Cruisers

Cut a piece of vinyl in a rectangle, to cover and reinforce this area. Place the vinyl on the *wrong* side of the mesh and stitch as shown in Fig 7-65.

Trim away the mesh, ½" from the marked side line leaving a ½" seam allowance. (Fig 7-66) Clip the corner.

Turn the raw edge of the mesh under ½" and stitch the mesh to the vinyl, close to the fold as shown in Fig 7-67.

Trim away the excess vinyl close to the folded edge of the mesh as shown in Fig 7-68. If the side is angled rather than curved, make the inside corner round, not sharp. This way, the vinyl will take any strain on the corner, not the mesh.

Step 3 – Stitch the casing for the PVC pipe. With *wrong* sides together, fold the top edge towards the *wrong* side the required width for the casing.

Stitch it down with 2 or 3 rows of stitching as shown in Fig 7-69. It must be strong.

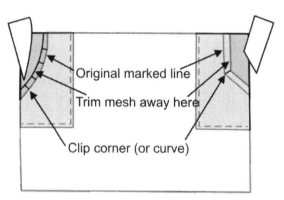

Fig 7-66 After stitching on the vinyl patches, trim away the excess mesh fabric ½"away from the seam.

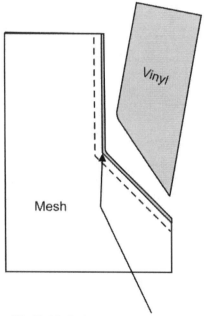

Fig 7-68 Cut away excess vinyl. Cut this corner rounded, not sharp.

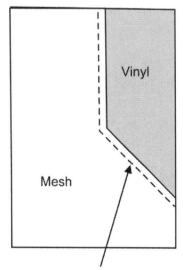

Fig 7-67 Turn mesh under ½"and stitch close to fold

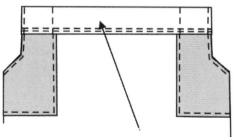

Fig 7-69 Turn casing down to the *wrong* side and stitch

Step 4 – With *right* sides together, stitch the 2 pieces together all around 3 sides (Fig 7-70). Make 2 rows of stitching for strength.
Stitch extra rows at the top corners as shown to make it really strong there.

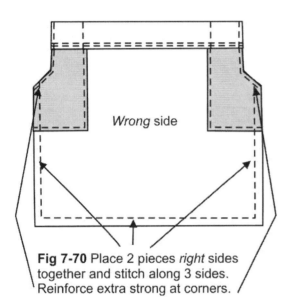

Fig 7-70 Place 2 pieces *right* sides together and stitch along 3 sides. Reinforce extra strong at corners.

Step 5 – Make cutouts for the handles as shown in Fig 7-71.
Use a grommet punch and make 3 holes for each of the 4 handle attachment points, right through the folded casing.
Clip in between the holes with scissors, to make triangular shaped cutouts.

Step 6 – Cut 1" PVC pipe to the exact length of the casing in the top of the bag. Insert the pipe into the casing.

Push shock cord through one pipe and then the other, joining the pipes together with the shock cord.

Join the shock cord so that it keeps the pipes together, but not so tight you can't get your hand in the bag.

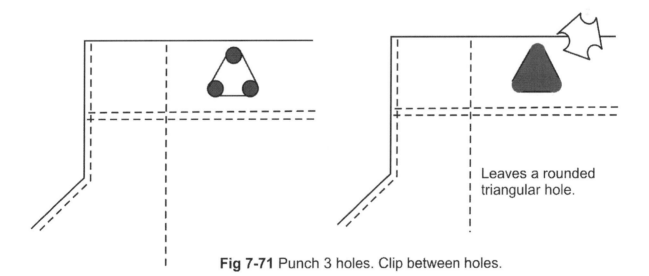

Leaves a rounded triangular hole.

Fig 7-71 Punch 3 holes. Clip between holes.

Step 7 – For handles, cut two pieces of 1" nylon webbing with a hot knife.
Loop the webbing into the hole cutout, under the pipe and through the hole cutout on the other side of the pipe. Sew the webbing in place with a box stitch (See Fig 7-72).

Sheet Bag – Bulkhead Mounted

Step 1 – Cut a piece of vinyl mesh the desired width, plus seam allowances, and twice the desired height plus hem allowances as shown in Fig 7-73.

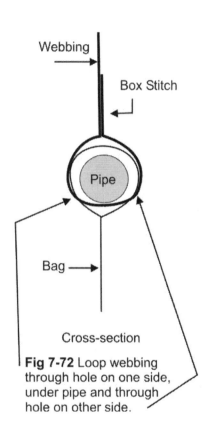

Fig 7-72 Loop webbing through hole on one side, under pipe and through hole on other side.

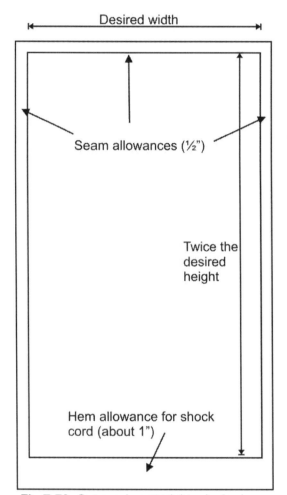

Fig 7-73 Cut mesh material to desired size plus seam and hem allowances.

Step 2 – Hem a piece of shock cord into one end of the mesh.

The ends of the shock cord should be well inside the seam allowance on the sides of the bag (See Fig 7-74).

Tension the shock cord, which will cause the mesh to pucker, and stitch the ends of the shock cord well to hold them in place.

Step 3 – Fold the end of the mesh without the shock cord under by ½", *right* sides together.

Now fold the mesh (*right* sides together) such that the back is larger than the front by 1 or 2",. Use Fig 7-74 for reference for the fold lines.

Stitch side seams (Fig 7-75).

Turn the bag *right* side out.

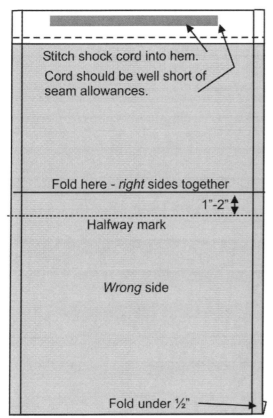

Stitch shock cord into hem.
Cord should be well short of seam allowances.

Fold here - *right* sides together

1"-2"

Halfway mark

Wrong side

Fold under ½"

Fig 7-74 Stitch shock cord into a hem on one end. Also shown in this diagram are the fold lines for the next step.

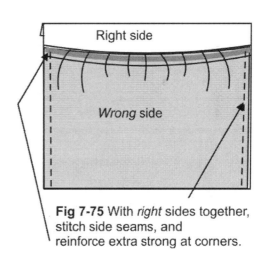

Right side

Wrong side

Fig 7-75 With *right* sides together, stitch side seams, and reinforce extra strong at corners.

Step 4 – Stitch a length of boltrope to the top (Fig 7-76) so you can attach the bag to a bulkhead with a track.

Grommets, snaps, turn buttons or other attachment method can also be used.
If using boltrope, reinforce the ends with 2 vertical rows of topstitch – this area takes the most strain.

Also, if using boltrope, always make the boltrope a little too long – ½" or ¾" – otherwise, the fabric will rip at the edges (see Fig 7-77).

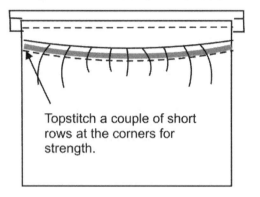

Fig 7-76 Stitch boltrope across top

Topstitch a couple of short rows at the corners for strength.

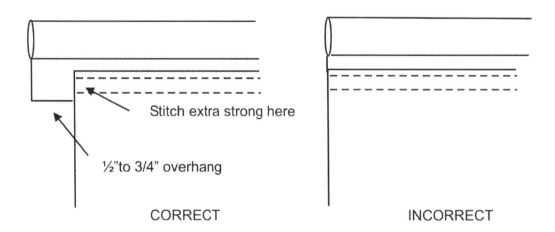

Stitch extra strong here

½"to 3/4" overhang

CORRECT   INCORRECT

Fig 7-77 Boltrope should always be a bit too long for the object it is supporting.

Pockets

Storage Pockets

A set of storage pockets is simply a flat backing piece of canvas or Dacron, with various sizes and shapes of pockets sewn on. These storage pockets can be used inside or out, in any area of the boat.

For example, a storage unit can be made for the nav table's instruments, galley cooking tools, the engine room most-used tools, in the cabins for reading glasses, alarm clock etc, in the closets for shoes and clothing, all the little off-cuts from your sewing projects, and even in the head for cosmetics and supplies. Anywhere there is a blank wall is an invitation for storage pockets!

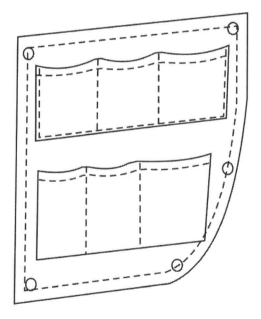

Fig 7-78 Pocket back is custom-shaped to fit the available space, and the pockets are custom designed to store the things you need to store.

The pocket backing can be free-form shaped to fit the available space.

The storage pocket unit can be attached to the surface with snaps, Velcro, screws or other fastenings.

Step 1 – Decide on the items you are going to store in the storage unit. Arrange them out on a table and determine the most efficient layout, based on the space available. Heaviest and largest items are best placed at the bottom.

Step 2 – Decide what material to use.
For a strong backing, use heavy 9 oz Dacron to line the back.
If you need to see inside the pockets, consider using clear vinyl for the pockets.
If you need ventilation or drainage for water, make the pockets out of mesh fabric.

Step 3 – Mark out the backing piece onto the fabric, adding 2" all around for a 1" double hem.
If there is to be a Dacron lining, cut this out too, with no hem allowance. Place this Dacron piece onto the *wrong* side of the backing piece.

Make a 1" double hem all around the backing piece. If there is a Dacron lining, catch in the Dacron with the hem.

Mark out where the attachment points will be so that the pockets don't interfere with it.

Step 4 – Measure the sizes of pockets required based on the stuff you are storing.

Unless the item to be stored is very flat, cut out the pockets to the desired height and width - in a 'wedge-shape', or make pleats in the bottoms of square pockets (Fig 7-79), so that the tops of the pockets can 'puff out' and can hold what you need them to hold.

Add seam allowances on three sides and a hem allowance on the top sides of the pocket pieces. Cut out the pockets and hem the tops with a double hem.

If drainage is needed for whatever reason, install grommets near the bottom of the pockets, or make them out of mesh.

Step 5 – Mark up the backing piece where the pockets are to be placed.

Turn the raw edges of the remaining 3 sides of the pocket under by ½".

Staple, seamstick or pin the pockets in place. Stitch along the three sides of the pocket, leaving the top open.

Step 6 – Install attachment fasteners at the corners.

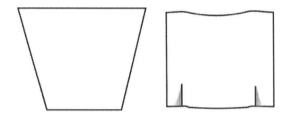

Fig 7-79 Cut pocket pieces as a 'wedge' shape or make pleats in a square pocket to create room inside the pocket.

Envelopes

<u>Tool envelope</u>

This is a portable 'kit' to organize and store tools, supplies or other items all together in one convenient place.

All you need are scraps of Sunbrella, Dacron and clear vinyl, and maybe some bits of centerfold binding.

The envelope opens out flat like a book to display the items inside. The items are stored in clear vinyl pockets so it is easy to see what's inside.
There is a seam down the center 'spine' to separate the two sides of the pockets. Flaps of Sunbrella fold in toward themselves, then the whole kit is folded along the spine and closed with snaps or Velcro.

Step 1 – Cut a piece of Sunbrella the desired size of the tool pouch. See Fig 7-80 for the pieces to cut out.

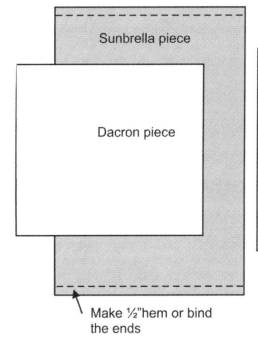

Make ½"hem or bind the ends

Sunbrella piece

Dacron piece

Clear vinyl piece (2" longer than the dacron, and the same width)

foldline for hem

Fig 7-80 The three components of a tool envelope - the backing piece of acrylic canvas, the dacron piece and the vinyl piece.

Make a ½" hem or bind the ends of the Sunbrella
piece. (Fig 7-81)

Step 2 – Cut a piece of Dacron to act as a
'background' for the storage pockets. The
Dacron piece is the same width as the Sunbrella
piece, and not as long. This is because one of
the Sunbrella 'overhangs' will become a flap
when the envelope is folded up onto itself, and
the other flap will cover over the pockets.

Apply seamstick all around the outside edges of
the Dacron.
Place the Dacron on the Sunbrella piece as
shown in Fig 7-81. Stitch it to the Sunbrella at
the top and bottom edges.

*Note – this pouch is meant to close with
snaps. See Fig 7-82. If you want to use Velcro
instead, then mark out where the divisions are
to go (if any) for the pockets.

For pockets where the Velcro loops are directly
underneath the hooks, stitch small pieces of Velcro
onto the Dacron to hold the pocket closed – before
you stitch on the clear vinyl.
And stitch Velcro loops to the Sunbrella side so the
large flap can hold the kit closed when it is folded
up.

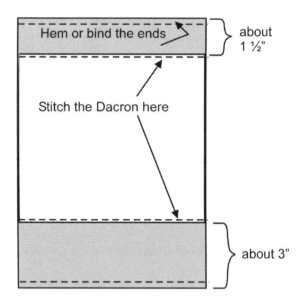

Fig 7-81 Place the dacron on
the canvas and stitch.

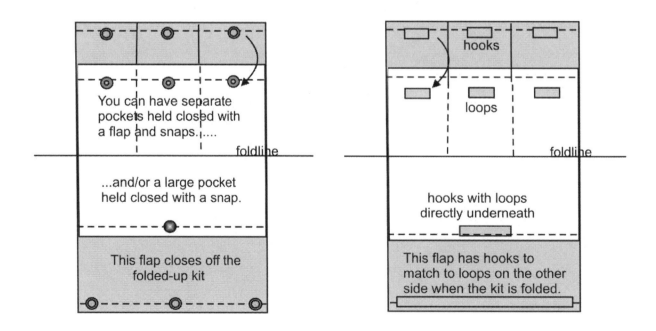

Fig 7-82 The whole kit folds in half and is held closed with snaps, velcro or even ties.

Step 3 – Cut out a piece of clear vinyl the same width as the Dacron but 2" longer. Fold a 1" single hem at each end so that it is the same size as the Dacron piece. Stitch & topstitch.

Again, if you are using Velcro, mark the positions required, and stitch on Velcro hooks to the clear vinyl. (Fig 7-83).

Step 4 – Apply ¼" seamstick to the very edges of the Dacron, and stick down the vinyl *wrong* side down on top of the Dacron (Fig 7-84).

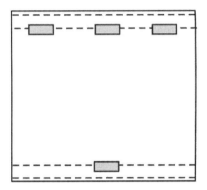

Fig 7-83 Cut out a piece of clear vinyl to width, but 2" longer. Make a 1" single hem in each end. Stitch on velcro if that is the fastening you are using.

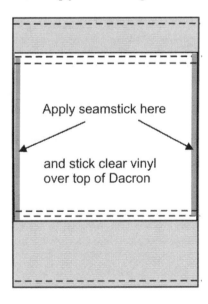

Apply seamstick here

and stick clear vinyl over top of Dacron

Fig 7-84 Apply seamstick to the very edges, and stick clear vinyl over top of the Dacron

Stitch close to the raw edges to hold the three layers – (Sunbrella, Dacron and clear vinyl) together (Fig 7-85).

Stitch binding to both side edges to finish them off (Fig 7-86). If you don't happen to have any centerfold binding, you can use flat binding or 1" webbing.

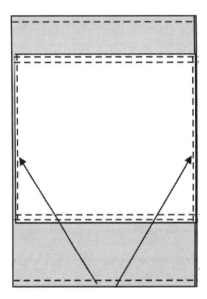

Fig 7-85 Stitch close to edges

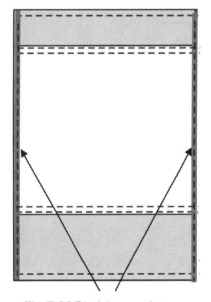

Fig 7-86 Bind these edges

455

Step 5 – Stitch the assembly down the middle through all thicknesses – this is the fold-in-half-line. (Fig 7-87)

If you want pocket divisions, mark these on the vinyl with grease pencil and stitch through all thicknesses. (Fig 7-87)

With a hot knife, slit the Sunbrella pocket flaps just down to the vinyl, along the pocket lines if desired. This will enable you to open one little pocket and still keep the others closed.

Step 6 – Install snaps to hold the pockets closed. (Fig 7-88). Close the pockets. Fold the kit along its centerline and fold the other flap over it to keep it closed. Install snaps.

The tool envelope idea can be modified any way you want to accommodate any custom storage requirements.

For example, you can have a storage envelope arrangement which folds in thirds. Or you can make a storage roll, as I did to store all the fid tools for splicing lines – the little skinny pockets fit all the various fids, and I roll it all up and tie it closed with leech lines.

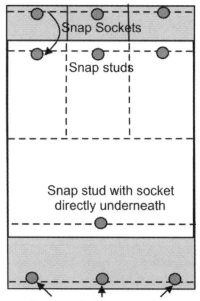

Fig 7-88 Install snaps to close partitions and flaps.

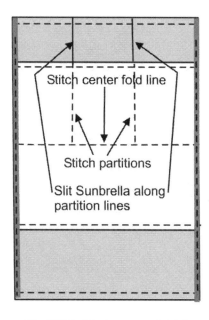

Fig 7-87 Stitch center fold line and partitions. Slit Sunbrella flaps if desired.

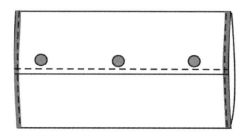

Fig 7-89 The storage envelope all closed up.

Dacron envelope

To make a good-looking envelope that can hold any flat objects such as ships papers:

Step 1 – Using a hot knife, cut a piece of 9 oz Dacron the desired finished size of the envelope, plus ½" seam allowance all around.(Fig 7-90).

Step 2 – Cut another piece of 9 oz Dacron the same size and shape, but add on for the flap at the top as shown in Fig 7-91.

Step 3 – Bind the top edge of the rectangular piece with centerfold binding (a contrasting colour looks nice). See Fig 7-92.
If the envelope is going to close with snaps or Velcro, install this closure now.

Step 4 – Staple the rectangular piece over the flap piece, *wrong* sides together.
Stitch close to the raw edges down one side, across the bottom and up the other side.
Remove staples. (Fig 7-93)

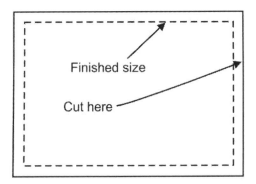

Fig 7-90 Cut a piece of Dacron the desired finished size of the envelope plus ½"all around for seam allowances eg for a 9x12 envelope, cut 10 x 13

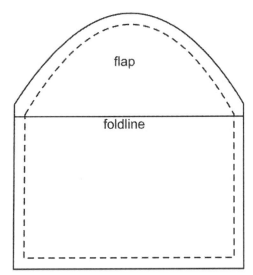

Fig 7-91 Cut out another piece of Dacron, but add the flap on the top.

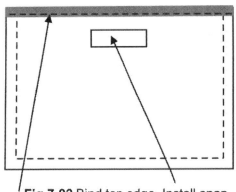

Fig 7-92 Bind top edge. Install snap, velcro or buckle closure

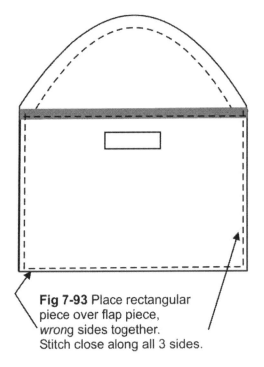

Fig 7-93 Place rectangular piece over flap piece, *wrong* sides together. Stitch close along all 3 sides.

457

Step 5 – Bind all remaining edges (sides, bottom and top flap) with centerfold binding.

Use one piece at the bottom edge, and then a separate piece for the sides and flap (easier to sew this way). See Fig 7-94.

Step 6 – Crease the flap down and install the matching fastener to the flap part.

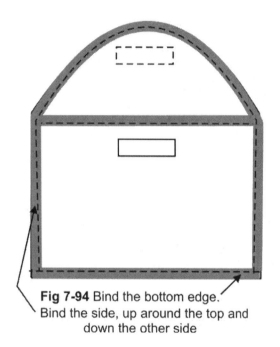

Fig 7-94 Bind the bottom edge.
Bind the side, up around the top and down the other side

Drop board Bag

A bag to store the companionway boards is basically an envelope – a piece of fabric (usually acrylic canvas), folded along the bottom.
It has a flange along both sides, meant to have snaps installed so that the envelope can be attached to a bulkhead. (See Fig 7-95)

Alternatively, the envelope can hang in place with a rope or webbing handle, or grommets or hooks along its top edge.

In fact, you can adapt this idea into a carry-bag. Simply add a couple of handles and a Velcro closure and you have a little bag to carry any flat objects like ships papers, laptop or books.

Step 1 – Measure the size and depth the envelope will have to be to hold the drop boards. The fit should be loose so you don't have to struggle to insert the boards, and to allow for their thickness.

Allow an inch at each side for the fastenings, and an inch or so at the top if you want a Velcro closure. If each drop board is to have its own partition so it doesn't touch the others, then cut out partitions

Fig 7-95 Drop Board bag

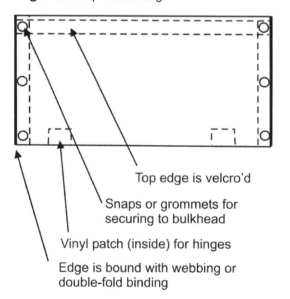

Top edge is velcro'd

Snaps or grommets for securing to bulkhead

Vinyl patch (inside) for hinges

Edge is bound with webbing or double-fold binding

for these, the same width, and allow for a little hem at the top and bottom of the partition.

Step 2 – If there are any hinges or sharp edges on the drop boards, note the position of these on the fabric. Reinforce these areas with vinyl patches – on the *wrong* side of the fabric (see Fig 7-96).

If the drop boards are scratch-prone plastic or finely finished wood boards, you can line the fabric with fuzzy-back Odyssey Soft Touch or other soft fabric to protect the finish.

Step 3 – Turn the hem under at the top edges.

Stitch on Velcro or other closure system as shown in Fig 7-97.

Step 4 – Fold the fabric in half, *wrong* sides together. See Fig 7-98.
Insert the partition(s) if you made any.

Stitch the sides together through all thicknesses, very close to the raw edges.
Then bind this edge with centerfold binding.

Topstitch again about an inch inside this edge – make sure the boards will fit – don't stitch in too far! This will make a nice flat area for the fasteners.

Step 5 – Install snaps, grommets or other fasteners along the sides of the envelope, and matching studs or hooks into the bulkhead or wherever you will be storing the drop boards.

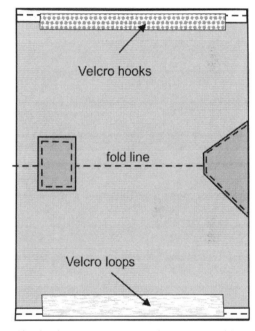

Fig 7-97 Velcro sewn to the *wrong* side for a closure

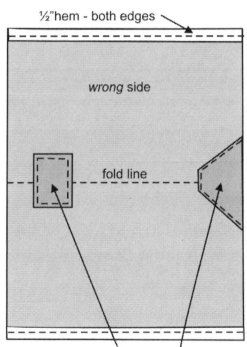

Fig **7-96** Stitch vinyl patches to any areas which might touch sharp edges and turn a ½"hem in the ends.

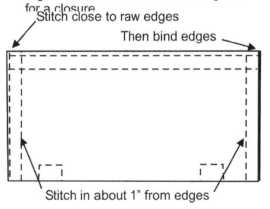

Fig 7-98 Stitch the sides and bind the edges.

Canvas for Cruisers

Floor Covers

A floor cover is a piece of fabric, usually Sunbrella, made to fit a specific floor area. It is intended to save and protect the wood or carpeted flooring underneath.

Make a pattern out of plastic for the area to be covered. It should be a tiny bit smaller than the area to be covered, to allow it to lie nice and flat. (Fig 7-99).

Transfer the pattern onto the Sunbrella. Add a hem allowance. If the piece is large, add 4" all around, which will enable you to sew a 2" double hem. If the piece is small, add 2" all around so you can make a 1" double hem.

Consider if and how the floor cover will be attached to the floor.

Normally, the floor cover can just lay there on the floor and needs no attachments. This is because they are usually used at anchor or at the dock while the crew or workmen are aboard the yacht. When the owners arrive, the floor covers are rolled up and stowed away.

However, if you are planning to sail with the floor covers on, you might need to attach them somehow to the floor so you don't fall and kill yourself!

Attachment Methods:

1) Rubber Backing
You can sew that non-skid waffle-weave looking rubber matting that you see in all the chandleries onto the underside. 'Quilt' it to the underside before doing the hems as shown in Fig 7-100.
Note, however, it will definitely stick to and destroy varnished floors so beware! It is probably better to use proper rubber backing specially designed for rugs, but again, you should definitely test it on a varnished area first.

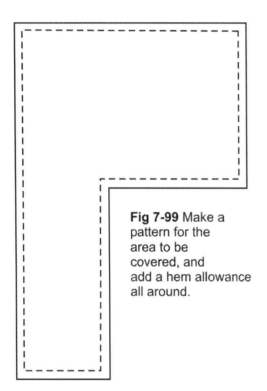

Fig 7-99 Make a pattern for the area to be covered, and add a hem allowance all around.

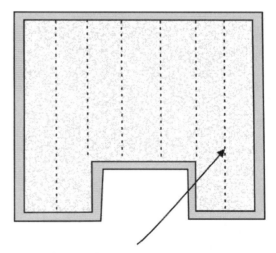

Fig 7-100 Run lines of stitching through all thicknesses to 'quilt' the rubber backing material to the fabric

2) Velcro

Sew 2" Velcro hooks all around the cover, and then it will stick to most carpets. Be careful, though, the hooks can make the carpet go all fuzzy and ugly – test it first.

Maybe you can just get away with sticking the Velcro on in small areas that can't be seen.

If you are going to use Velcro, for the cover to look good, stitch it on with as few rows of stitches as possible. Here's how (See Fig 7-101):

Mark out the outline of the floor cover. Add ¾" all around for the hem allowance instead of the 2" or 4" stated above.

Apply seamstick to one edge of 2" wide Velcro hooks (i.e. not down the middle of the Velcro), and stick the Velcro hooks to the *wrong* side of the floor cover, aligning the edge without the seamstick to the marked line.

Stitch the edge of the Velcro that is furthest away from the raw edge first.

If the sewing machine is having trouble – breaking threads and skipping stitches – try stitching with the Velcro side down. In this case it is important to apply the Velcro in a nice even line from the raw edge of the fabric.

Now fold the raw edge of the floor cover under the Velcro and stitch close to the fold (Fig 7-102).

3) Snaps

Floor covers can also be held down by snaps – this is a more secure attachment method and works well for stairs. Attach the snap stud to the floor (screw-type) and the snap socket to the fabric.

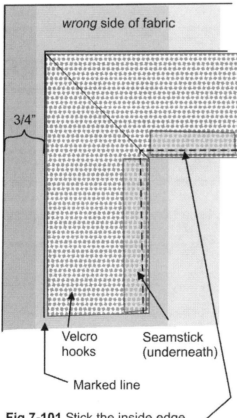

wrong side of fabric

3/4"

Velcro hooks   Seamstick (underneath)

Marked line

Fig 7-101 Stick the inside edge of the Velcro down, and stitch close to the edge.

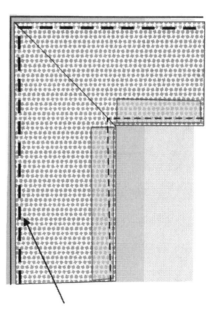

Fig 7-102 Fold the 3/4" edge under the Velcro and stitch close to the fold

Fig 7-103 For a stair runner, cut a long length of fabric. Hem both sides and one end. Then take it to the boat for a fitting.

To cover stairs, measure the width and make one long runner first.
Hem both long sides and one end (Fig 7-103).
Install a snap socket in each hemmed corner.

Take it to the boat. See Fig 7-104. For a set of straight stairs, install studs at the backs of the steps to match the sockets you installed in the floor cloth. Stretch the floor cloth taut up to the back of the next step, and mark positions for snaps. Then install the snaps and studs.
Continue on up the stairs and mark for the hem at the end. Take the floor cover off and sew up the hem, and install the last two snaps.

It gets more complicated if you have to fit odd-shaped areas such as spiral stairs or landings and turns, but the principle is the same. Cut the runner up as required, and staple the pieces together to the proper size and shape.

You might have to make other widths and shapes for these types of stairs.

Carefully remove the stapled and marked up runner from the boat.

Lay it out and even up the staples and marks, then stitch *right* sides together.
Trim off the seam allowances and topstitch along the stair edges and risers as shown in Fig 7-104.

Install snap buttons to the hem of the floor cover just below the crease of the riser parts, and then take the cover to the boat again.

Install the snap stud screws to the back of the stair steps, starting from one end of the cover, making the cover fit nice and tight.

Lee Cloths

This design is very strong without being bulky. It can be removed easily when not needed, or to clean it.

Step 1 – Using 46" Sunbrella, cut it in half to create 2 – 23" wide pieces. (Usually you are making 2 lee cloths – one for each settee).

The length can be variable, but 4 feet is about normal.

There should be a space of at least a foot at the person's head and at their feet, for ventilation.

Fig 7-104 Side view showing placement of snaps.

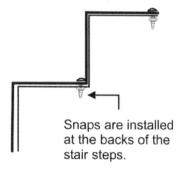

Snaps are installed at the backs of the stair steps.

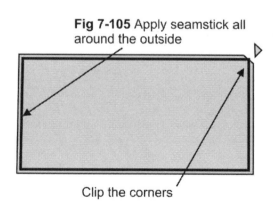

Fig 7-105 Apply seamstick all around the outside

Clip the corners

Step 2 – Apply ½" seamstick to the *wrong* side of all 4 sides close to the raw edges. (Fig 7-105) Clip the corners in to the ½" line. Turn these raw edges under ½" and stick down hard.

Step 3 – On the *wrong* side, apply another line of ½" seamstick onto the seam allowance, all around the short sides and one long edge again, close to the fold (Fig 7-106).

Step 4 – Remove the seamstick paper and stick 1" nylon webbing along the long edge. Tuck the ends of the webbing under 4-6", making a loop large enough to pass a line through. (This line will be used to tie the lee cloth to a bulkhead to hold it up.) See Fig 7-107. Don't stitch it yet.

Step 5 – Now stick 1" nylon webbing to the *wrong* side of both short sides.
Start at the lower edge, run the webbing up to the top, over top of the horizontal webbing at the top, and then under the horizontal webbing (for extra strength) and tuck it under by 4-6". See Fig 7-108.

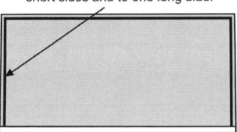

Fig 7-106 Apply seamstick to short sides and to one long side.

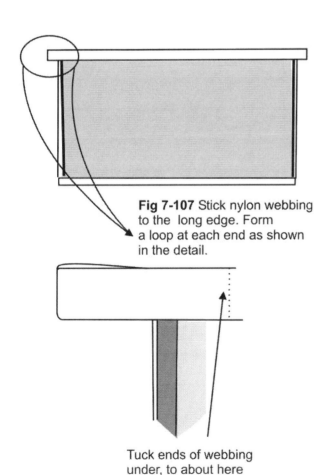

Fig 7-107 Stick nylon webbing to the long edge. Form a loop at each end as shown in the detail.

Tuck ends of webbing under, to about here

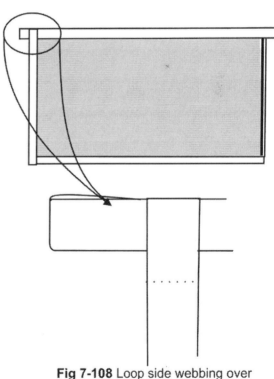

Fig 7-108 Loop side webbing over the horizontal section of webbing

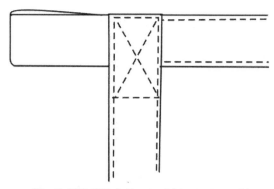

Fig 7-109 Stitch the webbing on, making a box stitch at the corners.

Step 6 – Stitch along both edges of the webbing. (Fig 7-109).
Make a box stitch at the corners.

Step 7 – Sew a length of boltrope to the lower edge. Make the boltrope a little too long – i.e. let a little - ¾" or so – hang out of both ends. This will make it easier to insert into the track. Make two rows of stitches and stitch extra strong at the ends.

Step 8 – Install some track to the settee or base of the bunk. If there is a fiddle, you may need to install the track about 4" in from the fiddle to prevent the fiddles from digging into your back with each roll of the boat. Try it and see with your particular boat.

Alternative method:

If you want the lee cloths permanently attached and stowed under the bunk, then make the Lee Cloth the same way as described above, except for the bottom edge.

For the bottom edge, simply make a 1" single hem perhaps reinforcing it with a strip of Dacron to add strength without bulk.

Then cut a strip of wood or a batten the length of the lee cloth.
Place the lower edge of the lee cloth on the settee or bunk base as shown in Fig 7-110, and place the batten over top.

Drill through the batten and lee cloth, through to the base every 4-6" and install short screws to hold the batten and cloth down.

The lee cloth can be stowed under the cushion or mattress when not in use.

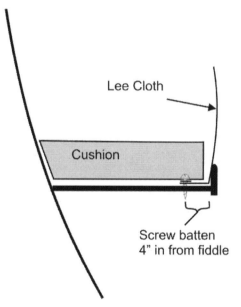

Fig 7-110 The lee cloth can be permanently attached to the base of the bunk using screws and a batten.

Fitted Sheets and Bedspreads

One thing is for sure – beds on most boats are a real problem both for making up day to day and for fitting sheets and bedspreads.

If you are lucky, the boat will have an ordinary rectangular mattress that you can get at from 3 sides like a bed in a house.

But probably you will be struggling to make up an awkwardly-shaped V-Berth or a berth that is alongside a bulkhead and you have to physically crawl all over the bed to make it up.

In this case, you need a system that is as easy as possible to make up and looks good even if it's a bit rumpled from you having to climb all over it.

Bedspreads

I have found that a quilted coverlet looks nice – using a low-loft quilting batting makes it practical for the tropics.

For colder climates, a ready-made big thick comforter or a nice down-filled duvet can be altered to fit a boat mattress.

To alter a down-filled duvet:

Take the store-bought duvet and lay it out flat somewhere in the open, like on a clean dock.

Take the V-Berth or mattress cushions out of the boat and lay them out face down on top of the duvet.

Mark a chalk outline of the cushion onto the duvet about 2" larger all around than the mattress. (See Fig 7-111)

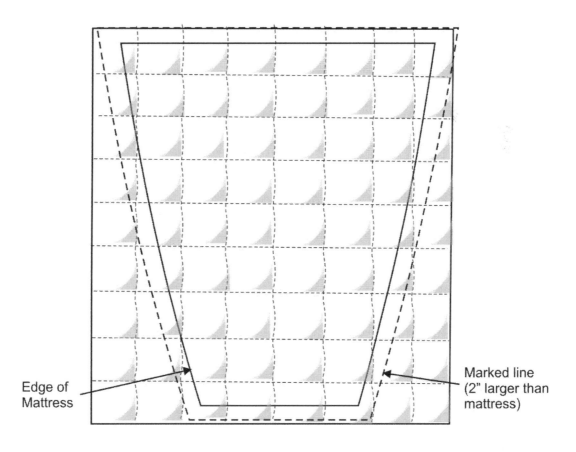

Edge of Mattress

Marked line (2" larger than mattress)

Fig 7-111 Marking out a down filled duvet to suit a V-Berth.

If you are going to make a duvet cover, you should mark out your fabric while you have the cushions out of the boat. Skip ahead to the next page to see how.
Put the cushions back on the boat.

OK, back to the duvet:

Place a line of straight pins along the marked line as shown in Fig 7-112.

Stitch 2 rows of stitching – one row on each side of the pins. Remove the pins.

Cut between the stitching rows along the original marked line.

Bind the raw edge with ribbon or bias binding as shown in Fig 7-113.

<u>To alter a synthetic-filled comforter</u> – follow the same steps above for measuring.

Stitch just one single row of stitching along the marked line.

Trim outside of, and close to the stitching. Bind the raw edge with a matching bias binding or use scraps from the fabric you have cut away.

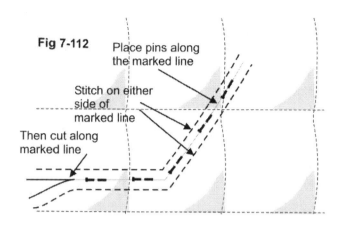

Fig 7-112
Place pins along the marked line
Stitch on either side of marked line
Then cut along marked line

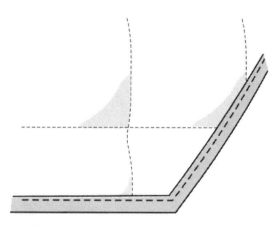

Fig 7-113 Bind raw edges

Duvet Cover

Now that you have a nice fitted duvet, you can make a duvet cover. This cover is simply an envelope of fabric with a long zipper down one side so you can stuff the duvet in.

These long zippers are smaller than the 'normal' #5 canvas zips – they are lighter 'dressmaker' weight and are available by the yard in fabric stores.

If altering a store-bought duvet cover, re-use the long zipper that comes with the duvet cover.

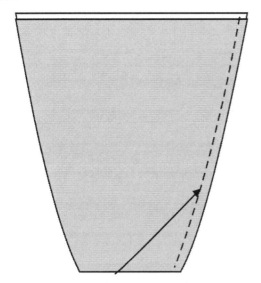

Fig 7-114 Baste top to bottom *right* sides together

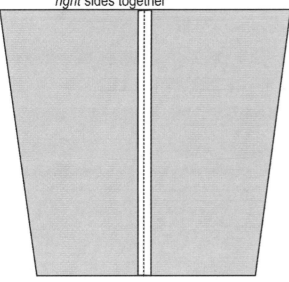

Fig 7-115 Press seam open

If the V-Berth or bunk is symmetrical, you can make a reversible cover with different colour or pattern on each side.

To mark the shape, use the same method as described with the duvet – lay the mattress face down onto the fabric. Mark the line as you did the duvet – but about 2 ½" larger all around than the size of the mattress (the extra ½" is for the seam allowance).

Insert a long zipper along one side. To do this: Using a long stitch, baste the top and bottom pieces together along one side only, *right* sides together.(Fig 7-114).Press the seam open (Fig 7-115).

Place the long zipper along the seam line, lining up the teeth to the center line.
Stitch the zipper on about 3/8" away from the zipper teeth as shown in Fig 7-116.

Remove the basting stitches holding the 2 pieces together. Don't forget to put on the zipper head! Open up the zipper a bit so you can get your hand in there later to turn the cover inside out.

Now stitch the front to the back, *right* sides together as shown in Fig 7-117.

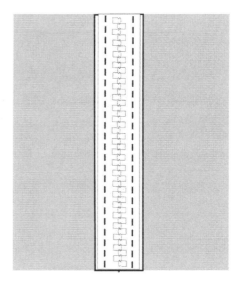

Fig 7-116 Align zipper teeth along the seam and stitch both sides of the zipper.

467

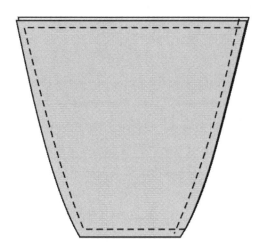

Fig 7-117 Stitch the remaining seams *right* sides together.

Finish the seams with zigzag or serging, to keep the raw edges from fraying.

Turn *right* side out and stuff the duvet into the cover.

Low-loft bedspread

A compromise between a thick comforter and a flat, tight fitting tailored bedspread (which is hard to keep nice and neat on a boat) a low-loft quilt. It works great for the tropics.

Quilt batting which is very thin is available. Check around – some can even be ironed on! It is a pretty simple process to make a top out of whatever bedspread fabric you like, and make a lining for underneath (or reversible). Light quilting cotton works well - it is cool, colourful and washable.

The fabric pieces and the quilt batting should be about 2-3" longer and wider than the actual measurement of the mattress. This is because the project 'shrinks' when you do the quilting.

Once the Top and Bottom fabric pieces are cut out, lay the quilt batting down on a large flat surface. Lay the bottom layer on top of the quilt

batting, *wrong* side down as shown in Fig 7-118. Pin out the corners and sides. If using iron-on batting, iron the bottom layer onto the quilt batting. Now lay the top layer on top of that - *right* sides together. Pin the three layers together all around the outside as shown in Fig 7-119. Trim off the excess batting.

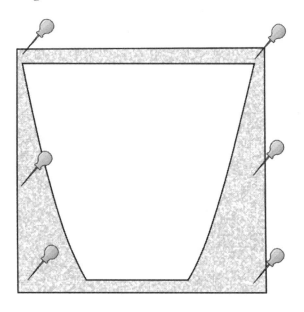

Fig 7-118 Lay quilt cover on top of quilt batting, *wrong* side down.

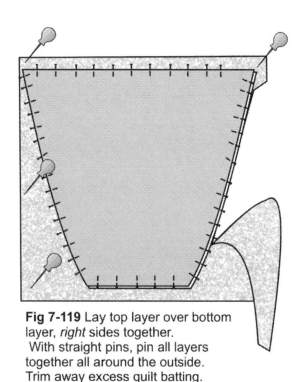

Fig 7-119 Lay top layer over bottom layer, *right* sides together.
With straight pins, pin all layers together all around the outside.
Trim away excess quilt batting.

Stitch all around the outside, ½" from the raw edges. Leave an opening 18" – 24" long to turn it inside out.
Turn inside out.
Turn the raw edges of the opening under by ½" and stitch closed, close to the fold.

Lay the quilt out flat. Pin out the corners and sides again. Iron the whole thing together. Using a piece of string, start to mark a quilting pattern by pinning along the quilt lines –

every 4-6" is normal. See Fig 7-120 and Fig 7-121. Don't try to pin the whole quilt at once.

Pin all one direction (Fig 7-122) then take it to the sewing machine and quilt it by stitching straight along the pinned lines.

Lay out the quilt again and pin in the other direction (See Fig 7-123). Take it to the machine and quilt it.

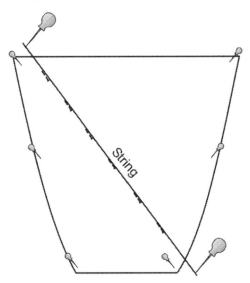

Fig 7-120 Lay out the first string.
Pin along the string through all layers.

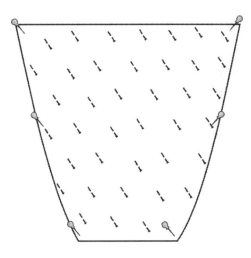

Fig 7-122 Continue moving the string along and pin along the string lines.

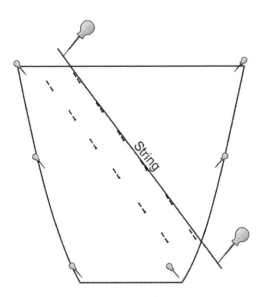

Fig 7-121 Move the string along
4 to 6" and pin along the string again.

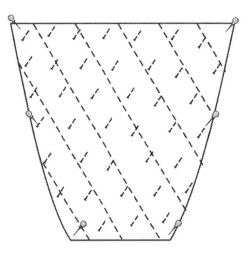

Fig 7-123 Now pin the other direction
using the same method with the string.

Canvas for Cruisers

If you don't want the quilt to just lay there on the bed, in other words if you need the quilt to be 'anchored' down at the foot end of the bed, or along the sides, add a section of plain, unquilted fabric to the ends or sides, and a casing for elastic, snaps, buttons or other attachment.

Fitted sheets:

Altering store-bought sheets to a boat's mattress is not difficult. Buy sheets based on the widest part of the mattress (e.g. buy King size if the V-Berth is king-wide at the top).

Usually one corner of the sheet can be aligned to one corner of the mattress and that way you won't have to adjust that particular corner.
It might be easier to fit if the existing elastic is removed or cut off from the fitted sheet.

Lay the sheet, *right* side up, on top of the mattress (Fig 7-124). Mark the corner(s).

Take the sheet off the bed. For the corners that are a 'normal' 90 degree corner (as in the upper corners of a V-Berth or a cabin bunk), make a dart as shown in Fig 7-125 and 7-126. Trim away the excess sheet material and finish the cut edge so it doesn't fray (Fig 7-127).

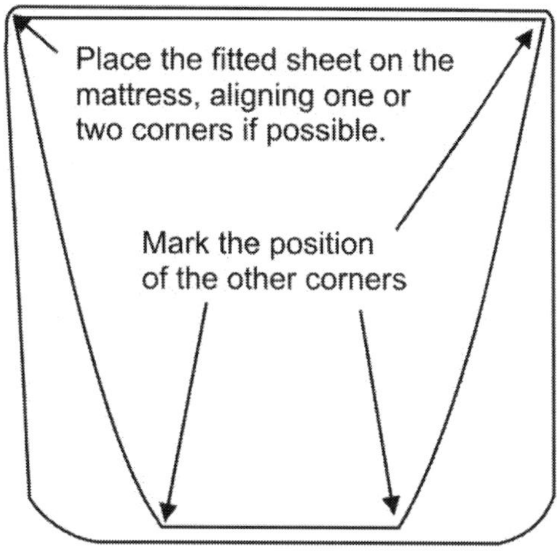

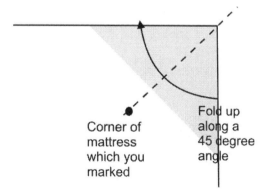

Place the fitted sheet on the mattress, aligning one or two corners if possible.

Mark the position of the other corners

Fig 7-124

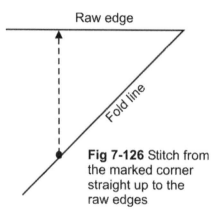

Raw edge

Fold line

Fig 7-126 Stitch from the marked corner straight up to the raw edges

Corner of mattress which you marked

Fold up along a 45 degree angle

Fig 7-125 Fold the corner into a diagonal from the corner of the sheet to the mark you made for the corner of the mattress.

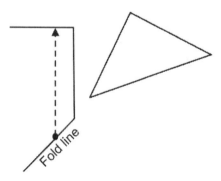

Fold line

Fig 7-127 Trim away the excess and finish the raw edge.

470

For a curve:

If it is an outside curve, mark the curve of the upper edge of the mattress onto the bed sheet. Add the depth of the mattress plus 2".
(See Fig 7-128)

If it is an inside corner or curve, stitch in an insert of extra fabric here - See Fig 7-129.

To elasticize the corners, cut lengths of elastic. The length will depend on how 'strong' the elastic is. There are two ways of attaching the elastic. Make a casing and insert the elastic, adjusting the tension to make the sheet fit snug.

Or stitch the elastic directly to the hemmed sheet, stretching the elastic as you sew so that when released it gathers the fabric.

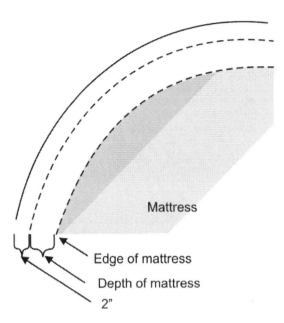

Fig 7-128 Outside curve - measure out from the edge of the mattress by the depth of the mattress plus 2"

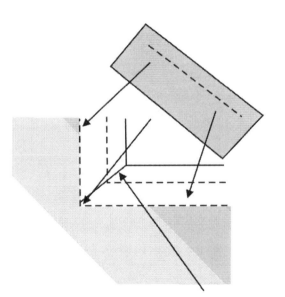

For an inside corner, clip the fabric from corner to edge of fabric. Then sew in a rectangular insert

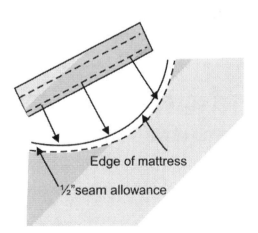

For an inside curve, stitch on a rectangle of fabric.

Fig 7-129 To finish inside corners or curves, a piece of fabric must be added to the edge as shown above.

471

Canvas for Cruisers

Top sheets:

I think the easiest way to make up the bed is to have the top sheet fitted and elasticized at the bottom or foot end just like a fitted sheet. Otherwise you are breaking your back trying to pry up a mattress and tuck a flat sheet neatly underneath.

Make the top sheet at least 10" wider at each side than the mattress so you can roll around in bed under it and not lose the sheet.

To fit the sheet – lay the top sheet on the mattress, aligning the top hemmed edge of the sheet to the top of the mattress as you desire.

Mark on the sheet where the corners are at the foot of the bed.
Make darts in the foot and insert elastic around the corners. Hem the sides.

Another way to attach bed sheets is, believe it or not, buttons. I finally sewed several large buttons to the surface of my sprung mattress in the V-Berth, and put matching reinforced buttonholes in the edges of the sheets. No more back breaking trying to tuck in sheets under a heavy mattress!

Pillowcases and bolsters:

Pillow shams and cylindrical bolsters can be made to stow bedding, extra blankets and pillows when not in use.

A pillow sham can be as simple as 2 rectangles of fabric stitched together and held together with Velcro, snaps or a zipper as shown in Fig 7-130.

Or it can be an envelope with an open back as shown in Fig 7-131.

A cylindrical bolster can be made to fit a rolled up spare blanket (Fig 7-132).

Fig 7-130 A simple pillow sham - 2 rectangles of fabric with zipper or other closure at the end.

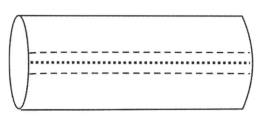

Fig 7-132 A cylinder with a zipper closure can be used to stow a spare blanket.

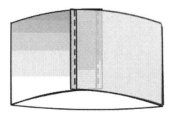

An open folded-over pillow sham. Hem the short ends of a long piece of fabric and overlap the ends as shown.

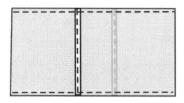

Stitch the long sides together.

Fig 7-131

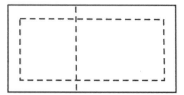

Turn inside out. You can topstitch an inch or so in from the edges to give the sham a border.
Stuff the pillow in the opening.

Curtains

Curtains on boats tend to get damp and so it is important for them to be easily removed and made of washable fabric.
Curtains can be used for privacy, to keep out sun or to divide areas within the boat.
A weighted curtain made out of mosquito netting makes a great mozzie screen for the large entrance doors on a catamaran.

Because a boat moves, it is usually necessary to anchor the curtains somehow so that they don't sway or blow around. A casing at both the top and bottom can do the trick, or tiebacks can be installed to prevent them from swaying around.

If the fabric is lightweight and the curtains are not attached at the bottom by a casing, then weighting the hems helps to keep the curtains from blowing around.

Curtains on windows will be exposed to UV, so cotton is not a good choice unless you want to line them.

There are many systems out there for fastening the curtains to the boat. It can be simple like a rod (or even a string!) and a casing. There are tracks and tabs – either overhead or wall mounted, pleater tape and hooks, snap tape and others. Decide how you are going to attach the curtains before going ahead and measuring up.

Styles:

Curtain with Top Casing

These are the easiest to make. For a plain hanging curtain:

Measure the width and height of the area you want to curtain (see Fig 7-134.)

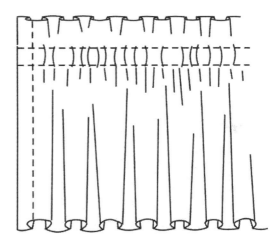

Fig 7-133 A casing curtain is just a panel of fabric, hemmed at top, bottom and sides, with an opening for a rod at the top and possibly the bottom too.

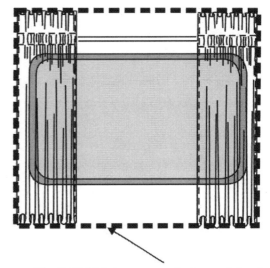

Fig 7-134 Measure area to be curtained

Canvas for Cruisers

To the height, add 2 to 4 inches for a bottom hem (whatever looks right for the scale of the curtain), add the required allowance for the rod casing (and ruffle if desired), and add another 1" for a top hem allowance.

The finished width of the curtain should be at least half as wide again as the area you want to curtain, then add a total of 3" for the side hems.

If it is to be split down the middle as shown in Fig 7-134, then obviously you have to divide this total width in half to make 2 panels.

Cut out the fabric and piece it together if necessary to make the long panel(s).

Hem the ends – turn the raw edge under ½" and then under again 1". Stitch close to fold.

Turn the top edge under ½" and turn under again enough to contain the curtain rod. For a ruffle above the rod as shown here, allow for this by turning the top edge under by the size of the ruffle and the curtain rod.
Stitch in the casing by stitching 2 rows and leave the ends open to allow you to insert the rod.

Hem the lower edge.

Curtain with Top and Bottom Casings –

If you are putting a casing rod in the bottom too, then repeat the above steps for the bottom.

Position the rod casing so that the fit is tight enough to make the curtain folds look slightly taut and not sag.

Lining:

To line the curtain, cut a piece of lining fabric the same size as the curtain.

Place the lining and the fabric *right* sides together and stitch as shown in Fig 7-135.

Turn inside out and make the hems and casings.

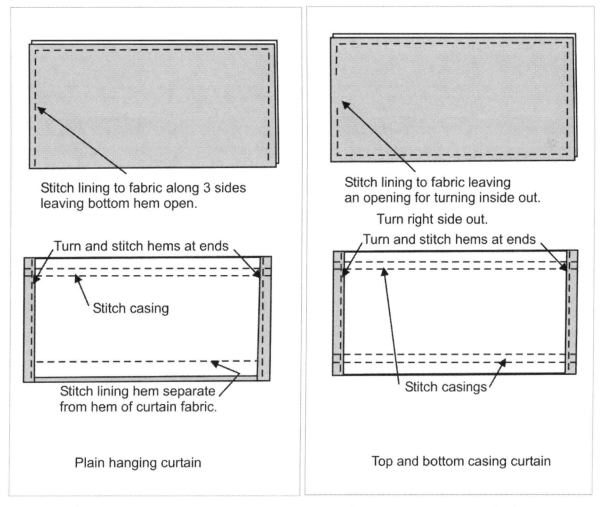

Fig 7-135 Curtains with linings are constructed differently depending on whether they are just plain hems, or have a casing at both the top and the bottoms.

Pleated Curtain -

Pleated curtains are usually made 2-3 times wider than the area to be curtained.

The pleats are held in place by a special very stiff piece of fabric designed especially for this purpose. This header tape is readily available at most fabric stores.

Measure the area as in the casing curtain instructions above. Allow for the lower hem as above, but because the top hem will encase the header stiffener tape, allow about an extra 4" for this.

Cut a piece of header tape equal to the curtain's width, minus the width of the side hem.

Starting in from the end by the width of the side hem, overlap the edge of the header tape onto the *wrong* side of the curtain fabric by ½" as shown in Fig 7-136. Stitch.

Turn the tape under towards the *wrong* side so that the stiffener is now encased by the fabric as shown in Fig 7-137. Don't stitch it down, just press it.

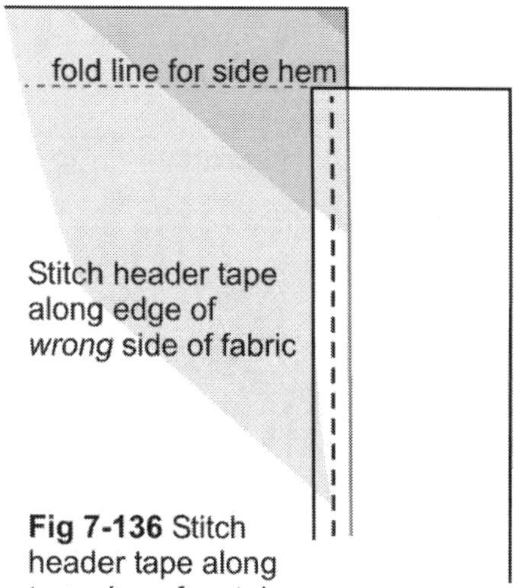

Hem the bottom and sides of the curtain. The hem of the curtain and the lining should be separate, but the sides are stitched together.

If the curtain is to have a lining, cut out a piece of fabric for the lining and hem the bottom. Lay the lining and the curtain *wrong* sides together.

Tuck the top edge of the lining under the fold of the stiffener so that the hem of the lining hangs about ¼" shorter than the curtain fabric. See Fig 7-138.

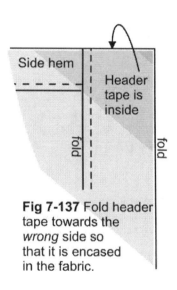

Fig 7-137 Fold header tape towards the *wrong* side so that it is encased in the fabric.

fold line for side hem

Stitch header tape along edge of *wrong* side of fabric

Fig 7-136 Stitch header tape along top edge of curtain.

Fig 7-138

Stitch the lining to the stiffener

Then tuck the ends of the lining under the side hems and stitch through all thicknesses.

The hem of the lining is about 1/4" or so above the hem of the curtain.

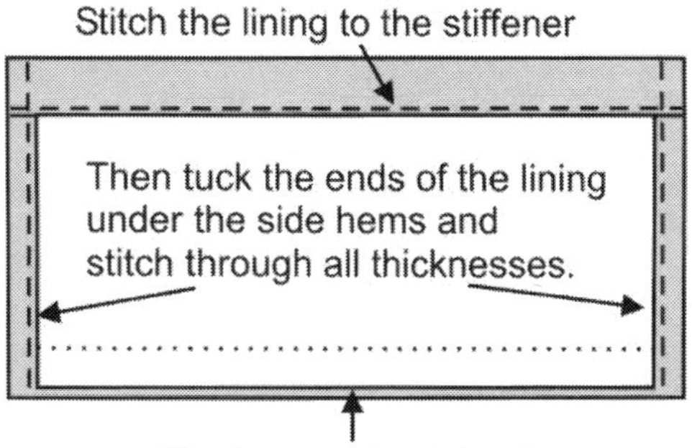

Pin the lining into place, catching in only the fabric-encased stiffener. You don't want to see the stitching through to the *right* side of the curtain. Open it out and stitch.

Now lay the curtain out again as shown above in Fig 7-138.

Turn in the hems on the sides, so that the lining is tucked underneath the curtain fabric. Stitch.

To figure out how many pleats are needed to take up the extra material make a diagram as shown in Fig 7-139

Subtract the finished desired width of the curtain from the fabric piece you have made. Whatever the difference is will be what you need to take up with pleats. Divide this difference by 3 to 5" depending on how big the pleats are going to be.

E.g. If the piece you have sewn is 45 inches long and you want it to end up with 15 inches.

45 – 15 = 30.
30" of fabric will have to be 'used up' in the pleats.

If each pleat is 5", then you will have to make 6 pleats (30 / 5 = 6).

OK, so if you have 6 pleats, which will take up 30", the other 15" must be divided up evenly.

For 6 pleats, there will be 7 spaces.
15 divided by 7 = about 2".

Space the pleats 2" apart and take any remaining difference out of the ends.

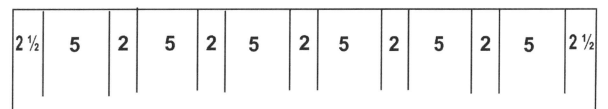

In this case, for a 45" piece of fabric, you have six 5" pleats = 30"
Plus five 2" spaces = 10"
Plus two 2 ½"ends = 5"
Total 45"

Fig 7-139 In order to figure out the size to cut the fabric, make a diagram of the curtain showing the size and placement of the pleats.

Canvas for Cruisers

To make the pleats:

Fold the curtain panel *right* sides together along the pleat lines as shown in Fig 7-140.

Make a row of stitching about ½" longer than the length of the stiffener.

To make a pinch pleat, fold the pleat allowance in thirds and hand tack the pleat together.(Fig 7-141)

To make a box pleat, simply fold the pleat down flat as shown and hand tack the sides.

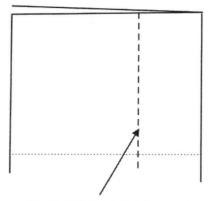

Fig 7-140 Fold curtain panel *wrong* sides together and stitch ½" past the line of the stiffener.

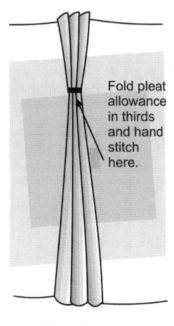

Fold pleat allowance in thirds and hand stitch here.

Pinch Pleat

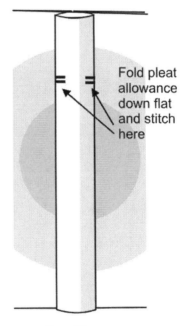

Fold pleat allowance down flat and stitch here

Box Pleat

Fig 7-141 Making pinch pleats and box pleats.

Mosquito screens

Every boat is unique and different in its requirements for screens and there are as many different types and designs as there are cruisers.

In most areas of the world, mosquitoes are simply a nuisance, but in some tropical areas malaria and dengue are real concerns, so it becomes really important to have good screens.

Here are some ideas to get you started:

Screening material:

Stay away from any screen made of metal. It will very quickly turn to rust.

The very fine no-see-um screening works great to keep away the tiny no-see-um bugs, but they do limit the amount of air that comes below.

Some screening material is soft and drape-able, and others are stiffer – the type you choose depends on how you intend to fasten it to the boat.

Attachment methods:

Velcro is a convenient way to attach screens. Sew the Velcro loops to the screen itself, and attach the hooks to the hatch or other opening.

One big problem with Velcro is getting it to really stick to the hatch opening. After repeated attachment and removal of the screens and the occasional dunking of rain, quite often the Velcro comes off in places and leaves a dirty gluey residue on the hatch frames.

There are 2 ways of solving this. A product called VelStick is available which is 4 ft lengths of semi-rigid plastic with Velcro permanently attached to it. The VelStick is screwed onto the opening.

If you cannot get this, I have had success at epoxying the Velcro hooks to thin wood strips (or even directly to the hatch frame), and then screwing the strip assembly to the surface. Use a two part fiberglass epoxy or polyester resin – the Velcro will stick to the wood like dynamite and never come off.

Instead of Velcro, you can try to sew rubber gasketing or Velcro loops all around the hem, and add snaps to attach the screens tightly to the boat. Gasketing can be made from a thin strip of closed-cell foam encased in a strip of fabric. The gasketing will form a seal to reduce the number of bugs getting into the boat.

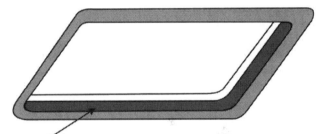

Fig 7-142 Vel-Stick hooks are screwed into the inner hatch frame area.

Make a simple flat screen and stitch Velcro loops all around the outside.

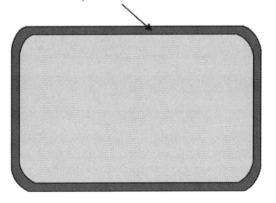

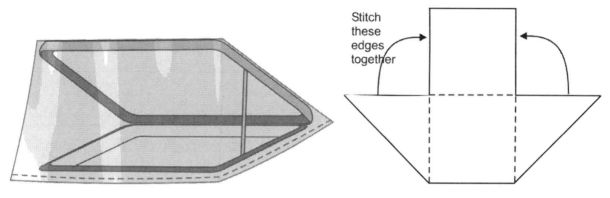

Fig 7-143 Tent-shaped netting with weights or chain sewn into the hem drapes over the hatch.

Stitch these edges together

Cut one piece of screening this shape, or sew pieces together.

Some people don't like to drill holes in their boats or glue on Velcro, especially if the hatches have beautiful wood frames. In this case, use lead weights or lightweight non rusting chain. Some drapery shops sell lead shot tape by the yard – it is a small fabric tube which contains oval pieces of lead and is used to weight down sheer draperies. Sew the weights into the hem of the screens to hold the screens down onto the deck.

One style is shaped like a tent as in Fig 7-143. It can be shaped to fit the open hatch, or it can simply be a large square of soft netting with weights all around the hem. It just drapes over the hatch and is held in place with weights around the hem. With this type of screen you can open and close the hatch from the inside of the boat, but you need to go outside to put it up or take it off.

Another style is a flat screen made oversize to the size of the hatch opening like in Fig 7-144.

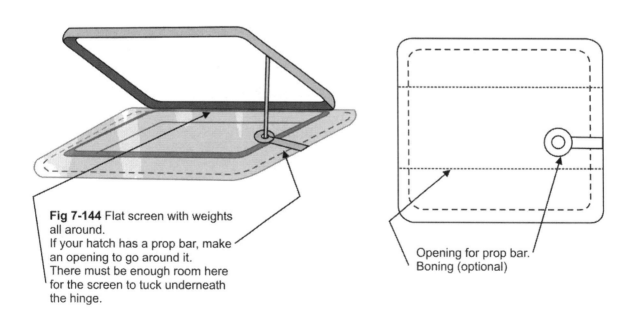

Fig 7-144 Flat screen with weights all around.
If your hatch has a prop bar, make an opening to go around it.
There must be enough room here for the screen to tuck underneath the hinge.

Opening for prop bar.
Boning (optional)

If the hatches have locking bars to prop up the hatch, then you will have to make a little casing with Velcro closure to go around the bar.

There must be enough space at the hinge of the hatch to allow the screen to be draped in there.

This type of screen can be put on and off from inside the boat, but you have to pull it off to close the hatch when it rains.

If you put enough weights around the hem, the screen can take a lot of wind without blowing off. Three rows of ¼" lead shot tape can take over 30 knots of wind and the screen will not blow off.

If the hatch is large, and the netting is very soft, stiffeners will be needed to keep the net from sagging down through the hatch. Boning - used in strapless dresses and available in fabric shops - works great.

Companionway screens are necessary so that people can come in and out of the boat and not let in all kinds of bugs. These screens need to be easily opened and closed.

One way is to use soft netting with the lead weights sewn all around 3 sides of the screen as shown in Fig 7-145.

Attach it with snaps along the top of the companionway and let the weighted screen drape over the opening to rest on the seating area or combing. Simply pull the screen aside to get in and out.

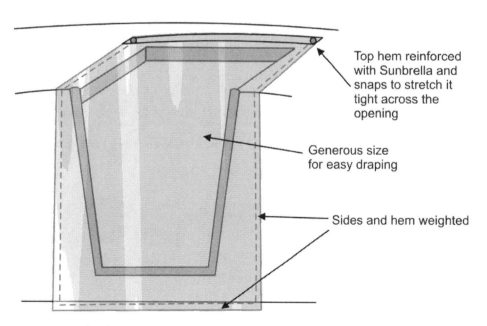

Top hem reinforced with Sunbrella and snaps to stretch it tight across the opening

Generous size for easy draping

Sides and hem weighted

Fig 7-145 Companionway screen

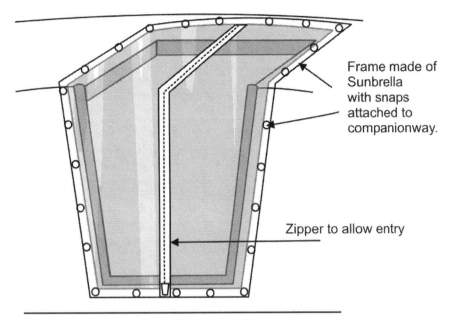

Frame made of Sunbrella with snaps attached to companionway.

Zipper to allow entry

Fig 7-146 This companionway screen is attached to the boat with snaps and has a zipper to allow entry.

More rigid screening can also be used. Attach it to the companionway with snaps or other attachment, and make a zipper opening as shown in Fig 7-146.

Or make rigid frames the same shape as the drop boards and attach the screen to them. (Fig 7-147).

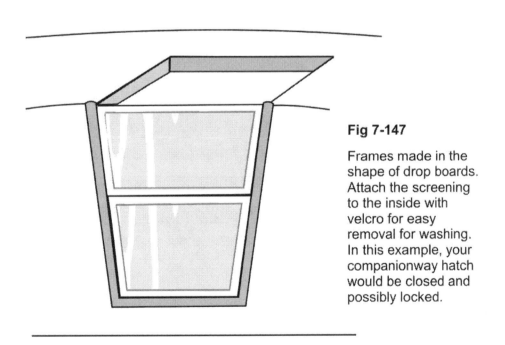

Fig 7-147

Frames made in the shape of drop boards. Attach the screening to the inside with velcro for easy removal for washing. In this example, your companionway hatch would be closed and possibly locked.

Canvas for Cruisers

484

Section 8

Repairs

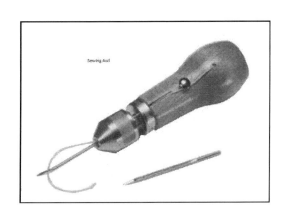

Canvas for Cruisers

General Restitching:

Every couple of years, check the stitching in all exterior canvas, especially where the thread has been exposed to the sun. Using a scratch awl or a seam ripper's dull edge (the back side), push it under a stitch. Try to break the stitch – gently! If it breaks easily, then a restitch is needed.

Another way to test for thread strength is to scratch at it with your fingernail. If the thread disintegrates, you need to restitch for sure.

If the thread used to be dark, and is now white, this is a sign that the thread is starting to degrade.

When testing a seam or a zipper for whether it needs to be restitched, don't just grab it and recklessly rip it! You can use the previous stitching, however flimsy, to hold the fabric in place while you stitch it again. If you have gone and ripped it all apart, then you have to seamstick it and start all over again!

Restitch right over the previous stitching in all areas where the thread is suspect. Stitch from the outside where possible, so that you can go over the previous rows accurately. Try to add as few additional perforations as possible as this weakens the fabric.

Where there are 2 rows of stitching, such as where panels are joined, stitch 1 row only, between the existing rows.

Zippers are usually restitched with 1 row only, in between the existing rows.

If there is already a hand-stitch repair, leave it in if it has been neatly done. Otherwise, leave the hand stitching in until just before you get to it with the machine. Then remove it. This way, the hand stitching will help hold the fabric in place until you can get to it with the machine.

Exposed zippers generally last 2-4 years in the tropics. Black lasts longer than white. To test whether a zipper needs to be replaced, scratch the teeth with your fingernail. If powdery dust comes off then it is soon time to replace the zipper. And, obviously if the teeth break when you scratch at them, it's definitely time to replace.

Remember, the best repairs are the repairs that don't look like repairs. In other words, it looks like this was meant for it to be in the first place.

Never try to cheat, and repair anything with just insignia sticky-back cloth. It is only thin spinnaker cloth, and is really very weak. Just use it to hold the rip in place while you patch it properly.

Other than replacing windows in dodgers, the most common repairs are caused by chafe, and stress rips. Try to figure out what caused the rip or chafe and correct the problem, and add chafe protection and stress patches.

Canvas for Cruisers

Chafe

Adding Chafe Protection to Dodger or Bimini leading edge:

(The quick and dirty method)

Cut out a piece of vinyl roughly to size. Spread out the dodger or bimini nice and flat. Apply ½" seamstick to the leading edge of the dodger on the *right* side of the fabric as shown in Fig 8-1.

Stick the *wrong* side of the vinyl to the *right* side of the fabric.

If the vinyl needs to be pieced because it is too short, piece it at the center or symmetrically on each side, so it doesn't look funny on the boat. Stitch the vinyl to the fabric, with the vinyl on the bottom. This way you can stitch closer to the leading edge of the fabric.

Trim off the excess vinyl at the leading edge, close to the stitching line. A sharp seam ripper works well for this.

Flip the piece over, vinyl side up.

Measure and mark straight down about 4" from the leading edge as shown in Fig 8-2. Cut the vinyl to shape.

Apply ½" seamstick to the *wrong* side of the vinyl and stick down the vinyl. Stitch the remaining edges.

Stress Rips

Try to figure out why it ripped in the first place and then engineer a patch or repair so it doesn't happen again.

A common rip is found in boltropes – at the ends as shown in Fig 8-4 in this example of a sheet bag. This can be prevented by cutting the boltrope a little bit too long, so that it protrudes from either end as shown in Fig 8-5.

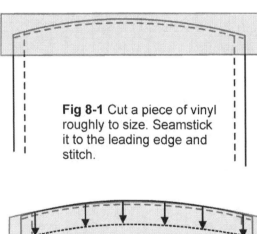

Fig 8-1 Cut a piece of vinyl roughly to size. Seamstick it to the leading edge and stitch.

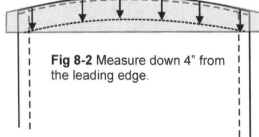

Fig 8-2 Measure down 4" from the leading edge.

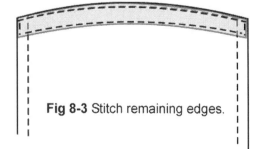

Fig 8-3 Stitch remaining edges.

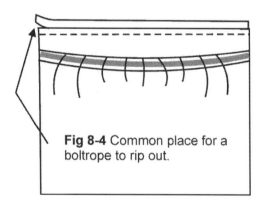

Fig 8-4 Common place for a boltrope to rip out.

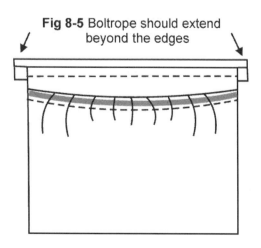

Fig 8-5 Boltrope should extend beyond the edges

Replacing Dodger Windows:

This is not as hard as you think, although you really need a nice big flat surface to do it properly.

The method described below will result in the replacement window being ½" larger, all around, than the old one. This allows for the old ugly and dirty window material to be completely removed.

But, what if you don't have the space around the old window to allow the new one to be ½" bigger? In this case you will have to make the new window the exact same size, and stitch it directly over the old one – when you remove the old window, you will have a 'frame' of the old window material underneath in the seam allowance. It is not as good looking, certainly. But maybe you can compromise. Maybe there are only certain sections where you can't make the window bigger, and other sections where you can make it bigger so you can remove the old stuff completely. It all depends on the piece you are working with.

Step 1 – Measure the size of the window roughly and cut a piece of 30 or 40 mil clear vinyl about 2" oversized all around.

Step 2 – Repair any breaks or tears on the old window with sticky tape 'band-aids'. (Insignia cloth works well but any kind of sticky tape will work). Don't tape over any seams or you will have trouble removing the tape later.
If the old window has any decorative trim or binding around its edge, you will probably need to remove this.

Step 3 – Lay the old dodger out *right* side down, nice and flat. This is so you are working on the inside surface of the dodger. Make sure it is 'relaxed' – that is, there are no diagonal twists or wrinkles. If necessary, lay the piece flat overnight on a flat surface to let it flatten out.

Lay the new vinyl window material over the old one. DO NOT remove the old window.
Trace the new window it ½" oversized with a white grease pencil. See Fig 8-6. If you don't have room to make the window ½" bigger, then you will have to trace the new window to be the same size as the old one.

Cut out the window material neatly along the grease pencil line. Carefully set the new piece of window aside for now.

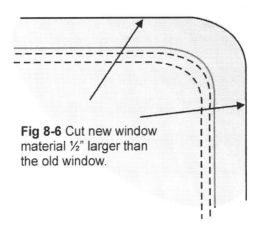

Fig 8-6 Cut new window material ½" larger than the old window.

Step 4 – Carefully cut the stitching of the old window, by laying the razor blade of new, non rusty, sharp exacto knife flat between the old window and the dodger fabric frame. Keep it flat, and let the old window stay in its original position.

It does not matter which side you cut from, but you will probably see that it is logical to lay the dodger *right*-side down and cut the stitches on the *wrong* side. Just cut the stitches. DO NOT REMOVE THE WINDOW.

Step 5 – Apply ½" seamstick to the *right* side of the new window material close to the raw edge.

Leave the seamstick paper on and lay the new window material *right* side down (that is, seamstick side down) over the *wrong* side of the old window.

Removing a little of the seamstick paper at a time, stick the new window right over top of the old window. See Fig 8-7.

You will see that because you cut the new window ½" oversize that the seamstick will be stuck to dodger material and not onto the old window.
If necessary, peel up the old dodger window if this is not the case so that the new vinyl sticks down onto fabric and not to the old window.
Staple the vinyl down if necessary – that is, if you can - to help hold it securely in place. Don't remove the window yet.

Fig 8-7

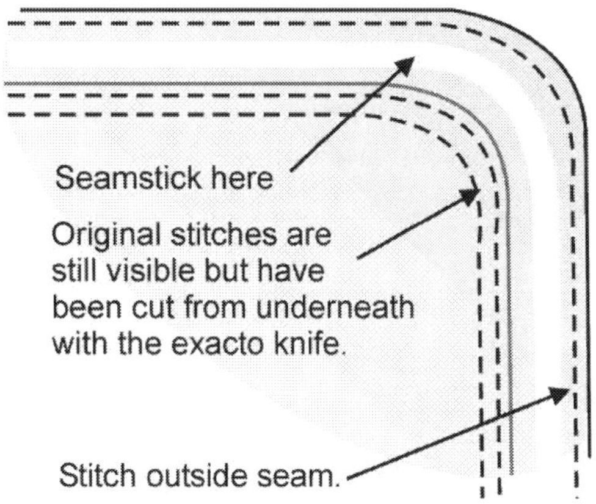

Seamstick here

Original stitches are still visible but have been cut from underneath with the exacto knife.

Stitch outside seam.

Step 6 – Carefully move the dodger to the sewing machine and stitch the outside seam. Depending on the dodger and how much room you have to work in, you could stitch the sides separately to avoid twisting and possibly stretching the dodger out of shape as you try to turn corners. In other words, stitch the top edge, then the bottom edge in two separate 'goes'. Then turn the dodger and stitch the vertical edges in two separate 'goes'.

Step 7 – Pull out the old threads. This will be easy because they are all cut. Now you can remove the old window.
If you had to stitch directly on top of the old window material, then you will have to carefully cut the old window out leaving the old window material embedded underneath the new material.

Step 8 – Stitch the inside seam of the new window as shown in Fig 8-8. Because the new window is ½" larger all around than the old one, the fabric overlap will be bigger. So, you may choose to make a third row of stitching on this inner edge to hold it better and make it look right.

Alternatively, you can turn the raw edge of the fabric under *before* you stitch it. It depends on the dodger. If you think you need to, you can use seamstick to hold this inner edge down, or just stitch it freehand.

You might end up with some ugly looking frame areas if you had to keep any of the old window material. I am not in favour of 'dressing' up the frame areas because it adds a lot of stitching and therefore perforation holes in the fabric and vinyl. But if you want, you can stitch doublefold binding to cover the frame in order to clean things up.

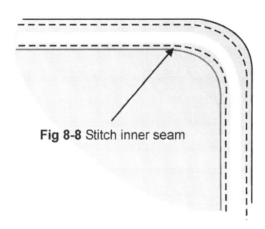

Fig 8-8 Stitch inner seam

Canvas for Cruisers

Sail Repair

There are a couple of very good, very detailed books out there covering sail theory, design and repair. If you have a special interest in sail construction and repair, you should refer to the real experts. Here, I will cover the things you need to know to do your own maintenance and repair, and hopefully reduce your time and money spent at the sail loft!

Sail Repair Kit

Here is a start to setting up a basic sail repair kit to keep on board. It should be tailored to suit your needs:

Tools:
Sewing Palm
Hand sewing needles, assorted sizes
Sewing Awl
Thread – V92 or larger
Waxed twine
8" Bent scissors
Seam rippers
Yardstick
Webbing 1" - tubular is best
Hot knife (nice to have)

Materials:
½"Seamstick
Adhesive Dacron tape assortment
    - 2", 3" 6" wide
Sticky back insignia material
    (nice to have but difficult to store)
Dacron cloth, various weights
Shelterite vinyl, or leather for chafe patches
Leech line
Any hardware specific to your sails – eg.
Slugs, grommets, hanks, leechline cleats
Batten pocket elastic

Preventative Maintenance:

It is much easier to maintain your sails than it is to repair them. Here are the most important things to remember to extend the life of your sails:

Cover them from the sun when not in use. I know after a long and rough passage you are tired, but force yourself to cover those sails.

Don't let your sails flog in the wind. Get them under control as soon as possible.

Check them over periodically. Take the sail down and spread it out flat. Check the following:

Check the stitching by using a sewing awl, or the dull side of a seam ripper to push gently underneath a few stitches and see how easy the stitching 'pops'.
 Or, if you can scratch out the stitching with your fingernail, it's definitely time for a restitch.

Check for Chafe - Look for dirty parts on the sail that could be a sign that it is exposed to the sun in that section. Look for chafe especially where the sail could chafe against the spreaders, and along the leech where the topping lift or shrouds could be rubbing against it. In these areas the cloth or the stitching could be dirty or fuzzy-looking, indicating chafe.

Look at all the fittings to make sure they are still strong and the stitching is good. (Maybe a good time to remind yourself to get some spare fittings in case any do fail.)

Types of Sail Repairs

Restitching:

This is the simplest repair. Well, relatively simple. If you find that the stitching scratches away or 'pops' easily under the pressure from a scratch awl, restitch these seams before they fall apart totally.

If the sail is triple-stitched, just stitch along the center of the seam, using as long a stitch as possible. (See Fig 8-9). If you can, re-use the original stitch holes to reduce the number of perforations in the cloth.

Use the guidelines 'General Restitching' at the beginning of this section.

Push the needle through, and pull it out the other side with a set of pliers but be careful not to wiggle the needle too much or it will break. I think an old-fashioned sewing awl is a great tool for hand stitching. Get one, and follow the instructions that come with it.

If you are hand sewing seams use a zig-zag method so that the stitch line can stretch along with the cloth. Stitch a row as shown in Fig 8-10, then go back in the opposite direction, using the same stitch holes. Making marks at regular intervals, say, ¼" or 3/8" will help you make even stitches.

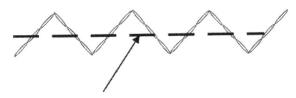

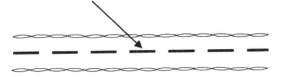

Fig 8-9 Stitch down the center of triple-stitch, or down the center of a double row of stitching.

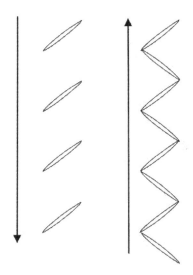

Fig 8-10 Starting at one end, make a row of diagonal stitches. Then go back the other way and use the same holes to make a zig zag.

Hand Sewing

When you get to the parts of the sail that have many layers, it can get to be tough going. You might have to break out the sewing palm and hand needle.

When using a needle and palm, it can help to force a hole in the cloth first with an awl. I have even resorted to putting a triangular hand sewing needle into an electric drill and drilled a hole through the really thick parts!

Canvas for Cruisers

Repairing Seams:

If the seam has let go completely, here is how to put it back together.
Clean off the old thread pieces. Make sure the cloth is clean and dry.

Have a look at the edges of the cloth. If the cloth itself is frayed or damaged, stick some sticky-back insignia or Dacron tape over it to reinforce the area.

Pin out the sail on a flat area using scratch awls.
Stick a line of seamstick to the seam allowance of the bottom layer.

Lay the top layer of cloth in place, using needle holes, wear marks etc to re-establish the original shape of the seam. Really long seams such as luff-to-leech have a curve built into them to create the sail shape.

When you have the two layers lined up, with even tension on both pieces, start pulling off the paper backing and stick the two pieces of cloth together. Press firmly.

Make a few match-up hatch marks across the seam with a pencil, just in case the seamstick falls apart while you have the sail under the machine.

Stitch the seam with zig zag or two rows of straight stitch.

If you think the stitching will be subject to chafe, cover the stitching with a strip of sticky-back tape to help protect it.

Patching Holes and Rips:

The first question to ask yourself is – why did the rip or hole happen in the first place? If it was chafe or improper reinforcement, do some reinforcing on the sail. If something on the boat punctured or ripped the sail, you need to eliminate that problem or it will happen again.

In any case, there are two ways of patching a sail. The Quick and Dirty Method, or the Proper Job.

Quick And Dirty – this will work for small holes and rips (4" – 6" max) and will also work for larger repairs until you can get the time to do a Proper Job.

Small holes & rips – if the rip is in an unstressed area of the sail, cut two adhesive sticky-back patches about 2" – 3" larger all around than the damaged area.

Flatten out the area. Peel off a corner or a little of the side of the paper backing. Lay the patch over the area, stick the corner down and make sure the patch is in position. Then gradually unpeel the paper and stick down the patch. Turn the sail over and apply the other sticky-back patch in the same area on the other side.

Proper Job – Cutaway Patch

In this method, a new piece of Dacron is stitched neatly over the hole, then the old cloth is cut away, leaving a ½" overlapping 'frame'. It is the only method to use for a large hole or tear – don't try the Quick and Dirty method.

The weight and type of patch cloth should be as close to the original sail as possible. If it is too light, the cloth might rip, if it is too heavy, the sail will get distorted.

Also, when cutting out and lining up the patch, it is important to line up the patch cloth's weave to the sail's weave. If you don't do this, the patch will distort under wind load and act funny.

The first thing to do is lay out the sail flat and clean up the mess.

Line up the cloth and the seams in their original positions. Tape the edges together as best you can with masking tape or other sticky tape. Just enough to hold it together while you are stitching on the patch. Fig 8-11.

Try to make the area as flat as possible. Pin it down securely with scratch awls so it doesn't move at all.

Mark the outline for the patch on the sail. It should be 3" larger all around than the damaged area. The marked lines should be in line with the cloth's weave as much as possible. See Fig 8-12

Stick a line of seamstick all around the marked area. Don't remove the paper backing yet.

Using a hot knife, carefully cut out the bad area to the inside of the seamstick.
 See Fig 8-13.

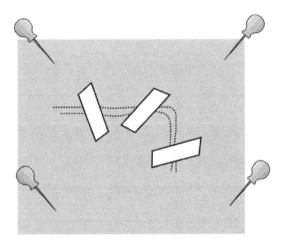

Fig 8-11 Flatten out the damaged area and patch it together with tape. Use scratch awls to hold it in place.

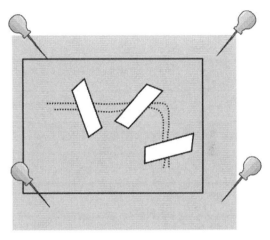

Fig 8-12 Mark the size and shape of the patch. It should be 3" or so larger than the damaged area.

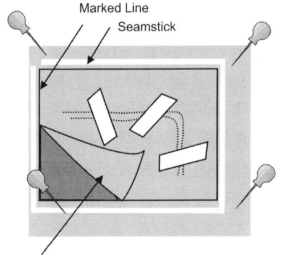

Marked Line
Seamstick

Fig 8-13 Cut away the old damaged cloth along the marked line.

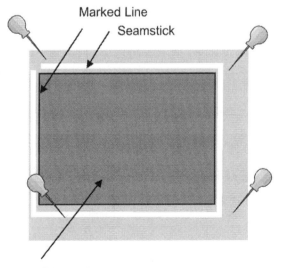

Marked Line
Seamstick

Old cloth removed

Canvas for Cruisers

See Fig 8-14. Cut out a piece of sailcloth to cover the area. Lay the patch over the damaged area, and mark about 1/8" to the outside edge of the seamstick.
Cut out the new sailcloth patch with a hot knife.

Fig 8-14

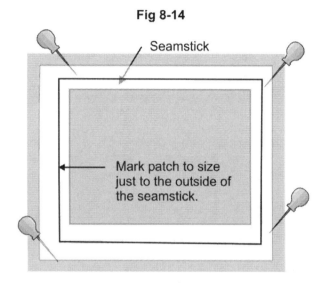

With a hot knife, cut out a new patch of sailcloth to cover the area.

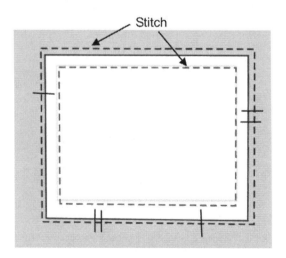

Make match-up marks in case the seamstick comes unstuck, then stitch the patch on close to the raw edges.

Lay the patch over the area, covering the seamstick. Line it up carefully.

Start at one end of the seamstick and gradually remove the paper backing, sticking the patch down well.

Make some match-up marks in case the seamstick lets go when you get the sail under the machine.

Stitch the patch onto the sail using a zigzag, or two rows of straight stitch.

Hardware and High-Stress Areas

Batten Pockets – When batten pockets tear, it is usually because the batten doesn't fit snugly, and/or the sail has been allowed to flog excessively.

First, check the batten itself and if there are any rough ends, sand them and/or or cover them with end protectors or tape.

Check that the pocket ends match the length of the batten. If necessary, take the batten pocket apart and check that the pocket ends are reinforced on the inside with leather or vinyl.

Often too, the batten pocket elastic on the inside of the pocket is all worn out or torn and that is why the batten can no longer be properly tensioned. Replace the elastic and reinforce the inside of the pocket if necessary.

Clew – The clew of a sail is subject to tremendous chafe, strain and flogging, and often the stitching is constantly exposed to the sun – such as on some roller furling headsails. It is a difficult area to repair if you don't have a huge sail repair machine, as it involves hand stitching.

If the webbing holding a clew's big pressed ring or D-ring is falling off, it will need to be re-stitched in place.

If the pressed ring has partially ripped out of the sail, the webbing will need to be replaced and restitched.

If the clew's ring has totally pulled out of the sail, clean up the corner by hot-knifing a curve to match the ring. Cut lengths of webbing straps, thread them through the ring and tension the webbing so that the ring is tight against the sail.
 The webbing will stretch under load so the ring must be in there tight.
Sew through the webbing and sail layers using a needle and palm, or a sewing awl, and a zig zag stitch (Fig 8-10).
Get comfortable, you will be at it for awhile.
Maybe a nice cold beer would help…..

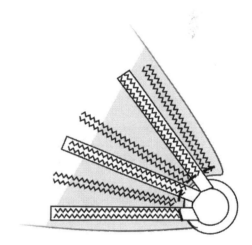

Fig 8-15 To repair a clew, insert lengths of webbing through the ring and stitch with zig zag. The webbing straps can be overlapped as shown on the top diagram, or they can be offset - this make more stitching but the material is not so thick. Oh the agony.

Canvas for Cruisers

Appendix i

Fabric requirements for making bias binding.

e.g. For a piece of binding 1" wide and 50" long, cut out a square of fabric 8" wide.

This is the size of the strip of fabric itself, so if you are making doublefold binding, make sure to consider the ¼" that you turn each edge under.

For a 1" wide strip: Length (")	Fabric req'd
50	8" square
72	9
98	10.5
128	12
162	13.5
200	15
242	16.5
288	17.5
338	19
392	20.5
450	22
512	23.5

For a 1 ½" wide strip: Length (")	Fabric req'd
75	11.5" square
108	13.5
147	15.5
192	17.5
243	20
300	22
363	24
432	26
507	28.5
588	30.5

For a 1 ¼" wide strip: Length (")	Fabric req'd
62	9.5 " square
90	11.5
122	13
160	15
202	16.5
250	18.5
302	20
360	22
422	23.5
490	25.5
562	27

For a 1 ¾" wide strip: Length (")	Fabric req'd
87	13" square
126	15.5
171	18
224	20.5
283	23
350	25.5
423	28
504	30.5
591	33

Canvas for Cruisers

For a 2" wide strip: Length (")	Fabric req'd
64"	12" square
100	15
144	17.5
196	20.5
256	23.5
324	26
400	29
484	32
576	34.5

For a 2 ¾" wide strip: Length (")	Fabric req'd
88	16.5" square
137	20
198	24
269	28
352	32
445	35.5
550	39.5

For a 2 ¼" wide strip: Length (")	Fabric req'd
72	13.5" square
112	16.5
162	20
220	23
288	26
364	29.5
450	32.5
544	35.5

For a 3" wide strip: Length (")	Fabric req'd
72	17.5" square
150	22
216	26
294	30.5
384	34.5
486	39

For a 2 ½" wide strip: Length (")	Fabric req'd
80	15" square
125	18.5
180	22
245	25.5
320	29
405	32.5
500	36

For a 3 ¼" wide strip: Length (")	Fabric req'd
58	14.5" square
104	19
162	23.5
234	28.5
318	33
416	37.5
526	42

For a 3 ½" wide strip: Length (")	Fabric req'd
63	15.5" square
112	20.5
175	25.5
252	30.5
348	35.5
448	40.5

For a 5" wide strip: Length (")	Fabric req'd
90	22" square
160	29
250	35
360	43

For a 4" wide strip: Length (")	Fabric req'd
81	17.5" square
128	23.5
200	29
288	34.5
392	40.5

For a 6" wide strip: Length (")	Fabric req'd
52	19" square
108	26
192	34.5
300	43

For a 7" wide strip: Length (")	Fabric req'd
56	20.5" square
126	30.5
224	40.5

Index